Harvard Business School
Research Colloquium

Contributors

Carliss Y. Baldwin
Christopher A. Bartlett
Richard E. Caves
Alfred D. Chandler, Jr.
Dong Sung Cho
Marquise R. Cvar
Yves L. Doz
Dennis J. Encarnation
M. Therese Flaherty
Mark B. Fuller
Pankaj Ghemawat
Donald R. Lessard
Amir Mahini
Sanjeev K. Mehra
Michael E. Porter
Richard A. Rawlinson
A. Michael Spence
Hirotaka Takeuchi
Louis T. Wells, Jr.
M. Y. Yoshino

COMPETITION
in Global Industries

Edited by
MICHAEL E. PORTER

Harvard Business School Press
BOSTON, MASSACHUSETTS

Harvard Business School Press, Boston 02163
94   93   9 8

Library of Congress Cataloging-in-Publication Data

Competition in global industries.

(Research colloquium / Harvard Business School)

Includes index.
1. Competition, International. 2. International
business enterprises. I. Porter, Michael E., 1947–
II. Series: Research colloquium (Harvard University.
Graduate School of Business Administration)
HF1414.C66   1986   338.8'8   86-18377
ISBN 0-87584-140-6

Contents

III. ORGANIZATIONAL FORMS AND CHALLENGES

IV. EMPIRICAL EVIDENCE OF GLOBAL COMPETITION

Foreword

Founded in 1908, the Harvard University Graduate School of Business Administration celebrated its seventy-fifth anniversary in the academic year 1983–84. We chose to take this opportunity to involve our faculty in thinking seriously about the challenges and opportunities ahead in important fields of management research and teaching.

Field-based empirical research, within and across organizations, has always been fundamental to Harvard Business School's ability to meet its objectives of educating business managers and helping to improve the practice of management. In some respects, we are creating a distinctive model of research. We have often broken through the bounds of traditional disciplines and methodologies to borrow whatever tools and concepts were needed for a particular inquiry. In addition, we have been less concerned with testing existing theory than with generating new insights. And while we often find ourselves drawn to problems that are broad in scope, we strive for results that are operationally significant to managers.

Because Harvard Business School faculty members are committed to pursuing research on the way business actually *does* function, as well as theoretical explorations of how it perhaps *should* function, they can give students and practitioners a vital perspective on the real world of professional practice. Their continuing close contact with operating businesses keeps Harvard Business School faculty at the frontiers of management practice. Research conducted by the faculty often yields insights that are of considerable practical benefit to managers in both day-to-day operations and longer-range planning.

In sponsoring the colloquium series of 1983–84, we hoped to set the course for research development over the next decade, and in particular to encourage greater emphasis on multiperson, multiyear studies of major issues. The complexity of many issues confronting business today almost requires that academicians find more effective forms of collaboration in doing our research. The problems we study are often beyond the capacity of any individual researcher.

In addition to encouraging a reshaping of researchers' work habits, the conferences promised to help strengthen the ties between Harvard Business School and the outside academic and business leadership communities. The series comprised sixteen conferences held at the Harvard Business School campus, each lasting two to five days. Papers were presented by eighty members of the HBS faculty and an approximately equal number of practitioners and academics from other institutions. Altogether, some 450 academics and practitioners were involved as discussants and participants.

Some of these colloquia focused on current research topics, such as U.S. competitiveness in the world economy, productivity and technology, global competition, and world food policy. Others concentrated on establishing agendas for the coming decade's research and course development in a particular field. Clearly, these were not tasks to be attempted in isolation. Rather we wanted to work jointly with others in business, government, and the academic world who could contribute and would themselves gain from the undertaking. The papers presented in this volume have all benefited from the thoughtful discussion they received at the colloquium and have been re-worked since then.

Beyond exploring research findings in particular areas, we hoped that these colloquia would sustain and enliven the continuing dialogue between students and practitioners of management. From that melding of perspectives, we have found, insights emerge that can revitalize the education of future managers and refine current professional practice. In that spirit of cooperative endeavor, I am proud to introduce this collection of essays.

JOHN H. MCARTHUR
Dean of the Faculty
Harvard Business School

Preface

This book, about strategy for competing internationally, was itself the result of a global strategy. It grew out of a research program involving scholars located all over the world, and I hope it illustrates that global coordination in research is both possible and productive. It was also refined and sharpened by a group of senior business executives and academics drawn, in approximately equal proportions from Europe, Asia, and North America, who came to Harvard to share their experiences. The exchange of views among this truly global group was a unique opportunity for all of us involved.

The Harvard Business School provided a unique setting and sponsorship for a project of this scope and magnitude. On behalf of my colleagues, I would like to thank Dean John McArthur and many others at the School for their encouragement, administrative help, financial support, and hospitality. I would also like to thank the business executives who gave so generously of their time in coming to Harvard to discuss this research. They were: Andre Benard, Royal Dutch Shell; William W. Boeschenstein, Owens Corning Fiberglas; M. J. Chung, Hyundai Heavy Industries; Matthew O. Diggs, Jr., Copeland; Jack Garonzik, Mars; Raymond Gilmartin, Becton Dickinson; David Gordon, *The Economist;* John Hanson, Caterpillar; Edwin P. Hoffman, Citibank; Takashi Kiuchi, Mitsubishi Electric; Jan Leschly, E. R. Squibb; T. S. Lin, Tatung Company; W. S. Lin, Tatung Company; Victor E. Millar, Arthur Andersen; Joseph Y. Pillay, Singapore Airlines; Mario Schimberni, Montedison; Shozo Shimuzu, NEC Corporation; C. Sun, Tatung Company; Donald Taylor, Rexnord; Koichi Tsundoa, Sony. Our thanks go as well to the scholars from around the world who so stimulated our thinking through formal participation as discussants.

They were: Joseph Bower, Dong Sung Cho, Robert Kaplan, Theodore Levitt, Richard Meyer, Robert Stobaugh, Pierre Wack—all of the Harvard Graduate School of Business Administration; Herman Daems, European Institute for Advanced Studies in Management; Lawrence Franko, Fletcher School of Law and Diplomacy; John McGee and John Stopford, London Graduate School of Business Studies; C. K. Prahalad, University of Michigan Graduate School of Business Administration; Donald Sexton, Columbia University Graduate School of Business; Raymond Vernon, Harvard University; and Steven C. Wheelwright, Graduate School of Business, Stanford University.

Finally, no editor can accomplish a task such as this book without a great deal of help and support. My colleagues who contributed to the book were unusually patient and always dedicated. Kathleen Svensson who administered the Colloquium did a marvelous job of bringing off a complex event. Lyn Pohl, who coordinated the assembly and production of the book, was not only superb at it but was a calming influence on all of us. Finally, my wife Deborah not only made it possible for me to live through the experience, but gave me intellectual and moral support in countless ways.

January 1986   Michael E. Porter
Boston, Massachusetts

Introduction and Summary

International competition has become one of the most important issues facing firms and governments today. It is not a new subject: nations have been trading for hundreds of years and multinational companies have been an important feature on the business landscape since the turn of this century. As a result, international trade is among the oldest subjects in economics, and every self-respecting business school has had courses on international business for decades. Yet today the interest in international competition has arguably never been greater, not only among managers but among researchers as well.

Why the new interest? The reasons appear starkly in the data on international trade and investment for just about any country in the world. Trade has exploded since the 1950s, while foreign investment has been significant and growing rapidly since the 1960s. Countries are now inextricably tied to each other through the thread of international competition. Competing internationally is a necessity rather than a matter of discretion for many firms. Policies toward industry and international economic relations are at the forefront of the policy agendas for governments.

While much is known about international competition, much more is unknown. Research in international competition has concentrated on the problems of doing business in a foreign country as well as on the unique problems of the multinational as compared to the domestic firm. Indeed, these problems represented the first and most pressing issues facing the growing number of firms learning to compete internationally. Today, however, many firms have overcome these problems and confront new and more complex ones. Firms can no longer view the domestic and foreign spheres as separate and different but must see the whole—how to conceive and implement overall strategies for competing globally. At the same time, much of what firms have learned about international competition must be relearned because of a rapidly changing environment. Old ways of competing internationally have become obsolete, and new concepts have elevated new players, such as the Japanese firms, to prominence.

If the old agenda for international firms was how to deal with foreign market circumstances, then the pressing new agenda is both broader and different. It is how to manage established networks of far-flung overseas activities as a single, effective unit. Firms are searching for ways to convert worldwide production, marketing, research and development, and financial presence into a competitive advantage. They face both pressures and offers of support from home and host governments and must decide when and how to respond. Firms are confronting also a bewildering array of coalitions among international competitors, as well as pressing management problems of implementing their own interfirm agreements. Finally, they struggle continually, against vexing organizational barriers, to coordinate units located around the globe to work together. Easy organizational solutions, such as establishing international divisions or global product organizations, have not proven entirely satisfactory.

THE CHANGING CURRENTS OF INTERNATIONAL COMPETITION

Firms confront today's agenda of international competition amid currents and cross currents of change. Particularly since World War II, a number of broad forces have led to growing international competition and widespread globalization of industry scope. Some of these forces are continuations of well-established trends, while others have emerged more recently. They are:

Growing similarity of countries. The growing similarity in available infrastructure, distribution channels, and marketing approaches—a long-term trend—is continuing. More and more products and brands are available everywhere, manifesting similar buyer needs in different countries. Large retail chains, television advertising, and credit cards are just a few examples of once-isolated phenomena that are rapidly becoming universal.

Fluid global capital markets. National capital markets are merging into a global capital market, characterized by large flows of funds between countries. Freer and more global capital markets have amplified the short-run variability of exchange rates as well as forces that are equalizing the cost of capital among countries.

Falling tariff barriers. Successive rounds of bilateral and multilateral agreements have lowered tariff levels markedly since World

War II. At the same time, regional economic pacts such as the European Community (EC) have been formed to facilitate trade and other relations among countries.

Technological restructuring. Industry after industry has been significantly affected by some technological revolutions that are reshaping competition—microelectronics, information systems, and advanced new materials. These developments are significant enough to shake up industry structures and create unprecedented opportunities for shifts in international industry leadership.

Integrating role of technology. Technology is not only reshaping industries but contributing to bringing countries together. Electronics and new materials are working singly and together to yield more compact, lighter products that are less costly to ship. Transportation costs themselves have fallen. Increasing ease of communication and data transfer are creating opportunities to link operations in different countries. Firms are able to integrate and coordinate far-flung activities in more and more complex ways, aided by the permeation of information technology into manufacturing, logistics, R & D, and other firm activities. Finally, information is flowing more freely to buyers located everywhere, and buyers are increasingly aware of and demanding products of world class.

New global competitors. All these forces have triggered shifts, sometimes dramatic ones, in international competitive position. New players, principally from East Asia, have become full-fledged international competitors in the space of a decade. They have exploited the new international competitive conditions as well as the cross-cutting technological changes to leapfrog well-established rivals. The intensity of competition has also risen markedly, elevating the standard for international competitive success.

CROSS CURRENTS

While the currents of change just discussed have led to growing international competition, some important cross currents have made the patterns of international competition different and more complex since the 1960s and early 1970s:

Slowing rates of economic growth. While the 1960s and early 1970s were prosperous times in which an expanding pie provided room for many nations to partake, the last decade has been marked by slow and fitful world economic growth. Beginning notably with the first oil crisis, firms in many industries have been faced with slow and even negative growth and intense competitive rivalry. Less opportunity at home has made succeeding in international competition particularly important for firms, and the absence of buoyant growth has reshaped the attitudes of governments toward foreign penetration at home and the success of local companies abroad.

Eroding types of comparative advantage. Traditional sources of comparative advantage, such as labor costs, natural resources, and technology access, are receding in importance. New technologies are making direct labor costs a smaller and smaller fraction of the total costs, and many nations with low labor costs have gained the ability to produce advanced goods. The technological lead of developed versus developing countries is often fleeting, as technology diffuses rapidly among countries through licenses, engineering companies, the scientific community, and multinational companies themselves. Markets for natural resources and components have become increasingly global, largely eliminating access to them as a sustainable edge. All these changes have upset traditional competitive balances among nations.

New forms of protectionism. While the post-war trend toward free trade has brought tariffs down and spawned regional trade pacts, the pressures and upheavals of the new international competition have taken their toll in a new wave of protectionism. Protectionism is not only on the rise but is taking more and more subtle forms, with requirements for local content and local ownership prominent among them.

New types of government inducement. Another manifestation of the rising intensity of international competition is the growing rivalry among governments to attract foreign investments. Prospective foreign investors are greeted by dozens of bidders offering enticing packages that can strongly affect the economic attractiveness of locational choices. Governments are also increasingly aggressive in assisting their local firms to compete overseas.

Proliferating coalitions among firms from different countries. The increasing globalization of industry combined with the upheaval of competitive positions have spawned a proliferation of coalitions among firms from different countries. Firms are seeking to combine strengths and overcome weaknesses through collaboration that is broader and deeper than the marketing joint ventures and technology licenses of the past. Governments often force or encourage such collaboration in preference to merger or to allowing foreign firms to prevail in their country.

Growing ability to tailor to local conditions. As pressures for globalization are both increasing and changing, technology is complicating the choice of global strategies at the same time as it makes them more necessary. While the new technologies support globalization, they also have the important attribute of allowing customized or tailored product offerings reflecting local conditions at much lower cost. Computer-aided design and manufacturing offer new levels of flexibility, as do automated order processing and other activities controlled by computer-based information systems. Segmentation, whether based on country differences or otherwise, is more feasible. The need to standardize products worldwide is diminishing.

THEMES

As a group, these currents and cross currents in international competition are making more and more industries global in competitive scope, but in increasingly complex ways. They require that firms adopt a global approach to strategy and to managing every functional area, be it production, marketing, finance, or R & D. Yet this global approach must increasingly involve multiple production and R & D sites, as well as the need to respond simultaneously to country needs while reaping the benefits of global presence. The new conditions also require that firms find ways of actually getting far-flung, worldwide units to cooperate.

A number of themes have emerged in international competition that are richly illustrated in the chapters of this book:

1. *There is no one pattern of international competition nor one type of global strategy.* The chapters in this book show the wide variations in international competition across industries. Sometimes an international industry is nothing more than a collection of largely separate domestic industries. In other industries, competition is global, though in many different ways. Similarly, there is no archetypal global strategy, but numerous ways of competing globally that reflect different mechanisms through which a firm's international presence yields competitive advantage.

2. *The globalization of competition has become the rule rather than the exception by 1986.* Because of shifts in buyer needs, technology, government regulation, and other causes, many industries have today become global in their competitive scope. Even sectors such as consumer package goods, telecommunications, and services that were once largely separate domestic industries in each country have begun the process of globalization. The particular forces driving globalization as well as the resulting patterns of competition vary widely from industry to industry. However, firms in many if not most industries today must confront the need to set strategy with a global perspective.

3. *The nature of international competition has changed markedly in the last two decades.* The currents and cross currents of change described earlier have made the imperatives of international competition look different today than they did when international activity took off in the 1950s and 1960s. The result is that neither simple export-oriented international strategies nor decentralized country-focused

strategies are or will be appropriate in most industries. Strategies such as Toyota's historical approach, with most activities concentrated in Japan, are giving way to strategies involving more complex but highly coordinated global networks. A model is IBM's approach of performing R & D, manufacturing, and marketing in many countries, but reaping economies of scale through operating large facilities in a number of countries while balancing imports and exports in each country. The changes in international competition have affected every functional area; and historical ways of doing things, as well as research based on earlier periods, are no longer sufficient to guide today's strategic choices. Many firms are prisoners of their history, however, which makes new lessons difficult to learn.

4. *Coordination among increasingly complex networks of activities dispersed worldwide is becoming a prime source of competitive advantage.* In each functional area of a firm, whether it be finance, marketing, production, or R & D, the need to coordinate activities in different countries has become an imperative. The chapters in this book chronicle the dispersion around the world of production sites, R & D laboratories, service organizations, and procurement groups. Different activities within the firm are being located in different countries, raising the complexity of the coordination task. The most advanced market for many products is no longer the United States so firms must have the ability to scan markets around the world and transfer knowledge among units in different countries. Those firms that exploit their international network through coordinating across countries are turning out to be the winners.

5. *Governments are increasingly both promoting and protecting against global competition, requiring new approaches to government relations.* While governments are usually portrayed as getting in the way of global strategies, the chapters in this book suggest a more subtle role. While governments are intervening in global competition in new ways, they are also aggressively seeking to help firms based within their borders to become more successful global competitors. In the process, governments are also competing among themselves to attract foreign firms. Governments can no longer be viewed as just a problem to circumvent carrying out international strategies but also as a source of opportunity. Firms must discover ways of responding to governments' concerns without compromising their global strategies and recognize the interdependence of the relations with government in different countries.

6. *Global strategies frequently involve coordination with coalition partners as well as among a firm's own subsidiaries.* Firms that have entered broader coalition agreements with foreign firms have often found them difficult to reconcile with the need for global coordination. The history of such agreements is a checkered one, and many fail to

achieve the desired benefits or, worse still, undermine firms' international competitive positions. The firms who can make international coalitions work will have an important edge in international competition.

7. *Implementing a global approach to strategy requires a difficult organizational reorientation for many firms.* In each functional area of the firm, there are formidable barriers to implementing a global strategy. Country parochialism, cultural and language differences, and the sheer complexity of the task undermine the ability of managers to take a global perspective and lead to seemingly never-ending reorganizations in many international companies. Those firms that can overcome the organizational impediments to a global strategy will be rewarded handsomely. The solutions arise as much from attitudinal changes, education, and organizational processes as they do from formal reporting relationships.

COMPETITION IN GLOBAL INDUSTRIES

These seven themes in today's international competition represent the agenda for this book. Its central focus is on the problems of international competition in industries and on the ways a firm can configure and coordinate its international activities in order to gain a competitive advantage over domestic and foreign rivals. Through adopting the perspective of a firm's overall international strategy in an industry, the book aims to provide new insights into international competition as well as to integrate and put in context the extensive previous literature. Adopting the perspective of overall strategy casts doubt on the validity of some findings that make sense only if a particular country, foreign market entry, or interfirm agreement is viewed in isolation. Actions taken in one country can often undermine a firm's position in other countries or in its global network as a whole.

This book grows out of the Colloquium on Competition in Global Industries held at the Harvard Business School in April 1984, as part of the celebration of the school's seventy-fifth anniversary. A series of studies was commissioned for the colloquium that were tightly integrated around the theme of competing in global industries. Growing out of the conceptual framework presented in the first chapter, chapters 2 through 9 examine the implications of global competition for overall strategy as well as for each important functional area of a firm, including production, technology development, marketing, finance, and government relations. Chapters 10 through 13 examine the problems of organizing to compete globally and explore the role of coalition agreements among firms in international strategy. Chapters 14 through 17 explore global competition empirically, employing careful historical analysis, in-depth case studies, and cross-sectional econometric techniques.

The chapters in this book aim to achieve three objectives. First, each chapter briefly surveys the state of knowledge about its subject area so that this book can serve as a reference. Second, each chapter presents a new conceptual framework and/or empirical findings that seek to advance our knowledge about international competition. Third, each chapter attempts to delineate some of the most important implications for practice, so that the business reader will benefit as well as the business scholar.

The book is divided into four parts. Part I, **Conceptual Foundations,** presents a conceptual framework for analyzing international competition and the choice of international strategy. Chapter 1, "Competition in Global Industries: A Conceptual Framework," sets forth an approach to framing international competition and its strategic implications for firms. It shows how international strategy revolves around the way a firm configures its activities worldwide and how it coordinates among geographically dispersed activities. The chapter shows how configuration and coordination affect competitive advantage and illustrates the broad strategic options available in a global industry. The framework presented is then employed to examine the changing patterns of international competition since the turn of the century.

Chapter 2, "Modeling Global Competition," abstracts from the richness of global strategic choices to develop a microeconomic model of global competition. It focuses on the tradeoffs between responding to local conditions and standardizing to reap global economies, and illustrates the parameters that have the most influence in determining market outcomes. The role of government policy is investigated as is the way in which different industry structures affect economic welfare. The chapter illustrates the power of rigorous economic modeling to yield insights that inform and sharpen more comprehensive frameworks.

Part II, **The Functional Agenda,** explores the implications of global competition for each functional area of the firm. Chapter 3, "Coordinating International Manufacturing and Technology," considers the effects of global competition in two important areas. It illustrates the ways in which manufacturing networks can be coordinated globally and presents evidence about actual practice drawn from indepth studies of a group of U.S. firms. The chapter also explores the organizational mechanisms that facilitate international manufacturing coordination as well as the sequence of steps through which firms can best proceed to capture the benefits of coordination.

Chapter 4, "Three Roles of International Marketing in Global Strategy," identifies the roles of marketing in global strategy: configurating the marketing function internationally, coordinating among marketing units located in different countries, and the role of marketing in unlocking possibilities for global approaches in manufacturing and technology development. The chapter explores each role in detail and illustrates their importance through a survey of marketing practices in a sample of Japanese multinationals.

Chapter 5, "Finance and Global Competition: Exploiting Financial Scope and Coping with Volatile Exchange Rates," treats the role of finance in global strategy. It shows how finance is affected by global competition, both in how firms approach financing as well as in the way financial performance is measured. The chapter presents guidelines for how to measure performance in a world of rapidly fluctuating currency values.

Chapter 6, "The Capital Factor: Competing for Capital in a Global Environment," builds on the previous chapter to examine cost of capital differences among countries and the resulting role of financing in creating a competitive advantage for the global firm. The chapter shows not only how differences in the market cost of capital among countries are eroding, but also how government tax concessions and other forms of incentives can have an important and lasting impact on a firm's effective cost of capital. The chapter presents approaches to evaluating various types of government incentives.

Chapter 7, "Government Policies and Global Industries," turns attention to the broader role of government in global competition. It describes why governments are concerned about global competitors, and how these concerns are not the same for different types of global industries. The chapter develops some guidelines for dealing with governments, while at the same time preserving the benefits of a global strategy.

Chapter 8, "Competitive Strategies in Global Industries: A View from Host Governments," moves to the role of government in promoting global competition by attracting foreign investments. It illustrates the increasingly intense competition among countries for investments and the strategies employed by different countries to succeed in attracting them. The chapter illustrates how a rich knowledge of a government's goals in seeking foreign investment and its organizational arrangements for managing it can enhance a firm's ability to deal with foreign governments.

Chapter 9, "Government Relations in the Global Firm," continues the discussion of the previous two chapters by exploring the internal arrangements used by multinational firms to manage government relations. It identifies a number of broad approaches to managing government relations in a sample of large multinationals and illustrates the conditions under which each is appropriate. The chapter shows how a country-by-country approach to dealing with governments is increasingly inappropriate in today's global industries.

Part III, **Organizational Forms and Challenges,** describes the role of alliances with other firms and organizational structure in implementing global strategies. Chapter 10, "Coalitions and Global Strategy," examines international coalitions among firms, an organizational form prominently chosen in the past decade. The chapter explores the strategic motivations for coalitions of various types as well as their risks. It highlights the instability of coalition agreements as well as the way in which the nature of each partner's contribution to a coalition affects its ultimate success.

Chapter 11, "Patterns of International Coalition Activity," draws on the concepts in chapter 10 to explore the incidence of coalitions involving U.S. firms. Employing a large sample of coalitions formed since 1970, the chapter seeks to describe and explain in what industries coalitions have been formed, between what types of firms, and covering what activities. The data base also provides evidence about the countries of origin of firms with which U.S. companies have been allying.

Chapter 12, "Building and Managing the Transnational: The New Organizational Challenge," concludes Part III by examining the problems of organizing firms to implement a global strategy. It shows how the organizational challenge has grown in response to the new patterns of international competition, and how firms can cope with it. The chapter stresses the role of management processes and culture in implementing global strategies, in contrast to previous literature that has focused on organizational structure alone.

Part IV, **Empirical Evidence of Global Competition,** takes a variety of approaches to examining the globalization of competition over time and in particular industries. Chapter 13, "The Evolution of Modern Global Competition," charts the rise of the modern multinational corporation by employing careful historical analysis. It describes the rise of the large multinational in the United States, Great Britain, Germany, and Japan, and explores the industries in which each nation's multinationals appeared. The chapter also presents evidence on the differing approaches to managing international activities that have characterized firms in each nation.

Chapter 14, "Entry of Foreign Multinationals into U.S. Manufacturing Industries," examines statistically an important decision of the global competitor, the decision to invest abroad. It explores the patterns of foreign investment in the U.S. market between 1975 and 1981, seeking to explain the forces that have caused it to grow markedly but at different rates across industries. The chapter also addresses the approach to foreign entry into the United States, embodied in the choice between acquisition and establishing a de novo foreign subsidiary. The chapter provides evidence of the role of global strategy in guiding such choices.

Chapter 15, "Case Studies in Global Competition: Patterns of Success and Failure," describes the history of global competition in four industries. It charts the evolution of each industry to a global pattern of competition and the factors underlying the success of a global competitor in the industry. The chapter provides rich insight into the process of globalization, as well as an illustration of how many of the ideas described earlier in the book have affected competitive success in particular industries.

Chapter 16, "Global Competition in a Salient Industry: The Case of Civil Aircraft" and chapter 17, "Changing Global Industry Leadership: The Case of Shipbuilding," conclude the book by examining global competition in depth for particular industries. Chapter 16 takes a close look at global competition in commercial aircraft. The case of commercial aircraft is important because the industry combines compelling economic motivations for a global strategy with a high level of salience to national governments. The chapter describes why commercial aircraft became an increasingly global industry, why Boeing ascended to world leadership, and how the changes in global competition described earlier in the book have affected competition in aircraft. This case illustrates the complexity of today's global competition in a world where governments are intruding in subtle ways. Chapter 17 describes how world leadership in the shipbuilding industry has shifted three times since 1850. The reasons why are a microcosm of many of the important changes in the pattern of international competition. The chapter also raises some important issues for the future of global competition in examining the potential role of China and other developing nations in shipbuilding.

Global competition is no longer a trend but a reality. Today, global competition can rarely be dealt with simply through exports or with free-standing foreign subsidiaries. It must be met through coordinated global networks of activities. Understanding global competition will be the difference between success and failure for many firms and some governments. This book will meet its objectives if it sheds some light on this vital task.

I

CONCEPTUAL FOUNDATIONS

1

Competition in Global Industries: A Conceptual Framework*

Michael E. Porter

International competition ranks high on the list of issues confronting firms today. The growing importance of international competition is well recognized both in the business and academic communities, for reasons that are clear when one examines just about any data set that exists on international trade or investment. Figure 1.1, for example, compares world trade and world GNP. Something interesting started happening around the mid-1950s, when the growth in world trade began to exceed significantly the growth in world GNP.[1] A few years later, by 1963, foreign direct investment by firms in developing countries began to grow rapidly.[2] The 1950s marked the beginning of a fundamental change in the international competitive environment. The change has been accelerated by the emergence across a wide range of industries of potent new international competitors, from countries such as Japan, Korea, and Taiwan, calling into question theories of international competition that placed advanced nations in the driver's seat. It is a trend that continues to cause sleepless nights for many business managers.

The subject of international competition is far from new. A large body of literature rooted in the principle of comparative advantage has investigated the many implications of the various theoretical models of international trade.[3] Considerable research on the multinational firm exists, reflecting the growing importance of the multinational since the turn of the century. I think it is fair to characterize this work as resting heavily on the multinational's ability to exploit know-how

*This chapter has benefited from comments by Richard A. Rawlinson, M. Therese Flaherty, and Louis T. Wells, Jr.

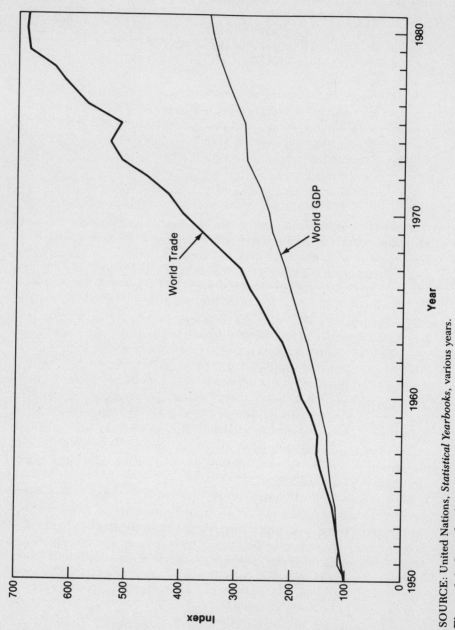

SOURCE: United Nations, *Statistical Yearbooks*, various years.

Figure 1.1 Growth of World Trade

and expertise gained in one country's market in other countries at low costs, thereby offsetting the unavoidable extra costs of doing business in a foreign country.[4] A related body of knowledge also exists in companies and in writing on the problems of entry into foreign markets and the life cycle of how a firm should compete abroad, beginning with export or licensing and ultimately moving to the establishment of foreign subsidiaries.[5] Finally, many of the functional fields in management have their branch of thinking about international issues, for example, international marketing, international finance. Most attention is concentrated, by and large, on the problems of doing business in a foreign country.

As rich as it is, however, our knowledge of international competition does not address some pressing questions facing today's international firms. Though research and practice have provided some guidance for considering incremental investment decisions to enter new countries, at best we have an incomplete view of how to conceive of a firm's overall international strategy and how such a strategy should be selected. Put another way, we know more about the problems of becoming a multinational than about strategies for managing an established multinational.[6]

This chapter and those that follow seek to explore the implications of international competition for competitive strategy. In particular, what are the distinctive questions for competitive strategy that are raised by international, as opposed to domestic, competition? Many of the strategy issues for a company competing internationally are very much the same as for one competing domestically: a firm must still analyze its industry structure and competitors, understand its buyer and the sources of buyer value, diagnose its relative cost position, and seek to establish a sustainable competitive advantage within some competitive scope, whether it be across the board or in an industry segment. These are subjects I have written about extensively.[7] But there are some questions for strategy that are peculiar to international competition, and that add to rather than replace those examined by other authors. These questions all revolve, in one way or another, around how what a firm does in one country affects or is affected by what is going on in other countries—the degree of connection among country competition. It is this connection that is the focus of this book.

PATTERNS OF INTERNATIONAL COMPETITION

The appropriate unit of analysis in setting international strategy is the industry, because the industry is the arena in which competitive advantage is won or lost. The pattern of international competition differs markedly from industry to industry. Industries vary along a spectrum from *multidomestic* to *global* in their competitive scope.

In multidomestic industries, competition in each country (or small group of countries) is essentially independent of competition in other countries. A multidomestic industry is one that is present in many countries (e.g., there is a consumer banking industry in Sri Lanka, one in France, and one in the United States), but one in which competition occurs on a country-by-country basis. In a multidomestic industry, a multinational firm may enjoy a competitive advantage from the one-time transfer of know-how from its home base to foreign countries. However, the firm modifies and adapts its intangible assets in order to employ them in each country, and the competitive outcome over time is then determined by conditions in each country. The competitive advantages of the firm, then, are largely specific to the country. The international industry becomes a collection of essentially domestic industries—hence the term multidomestic. Industries where competition has traditionally exhibited this pattern include retailing, consumer packaged goods, distribution, insurance, consumer finance, and caustic chemicals.

At the other end of the spectrum are what I term global industries. The term global—like the word "strategy"—has become overused and perhaps misunderstood. The definition of a global industry employed here is an industry in which a firm's competitive position in one country is significantly affected by its position in other countries or vice versa.[8] Therefore, the international industry is not merely a collection of domestic industries but a series of linked domestic industries in which the rivals compete against each other on a truly worldwide basis. Industries exhibiting or evolving toward the global pattern today include commercial aircraft, TV sets, semiconductors, copiers, automobiles, and watches.

The implications for international strategy of this distinction between multidomestic and global are quite profound. In a multidomestic industry, a firm can and should manage its international activities like a portfolio. Its subsidiaries or other operations around the world should each control all the important activities necessary to do business in the industry and should enjoy a high degree of autonomy. The firm's strategy in a country should be determined largely by the competitive conditions in that country; the firm's international strategy should be what I term a country-centered strategy.

In a multidomestic industry, competing internationally is discretionary. A firm can choose to remain domestic or can expand internationally, if it has some advantage that allows it to overcome the extra costs of entering and competing in foreign markets. The important competitors in multidomestic industries will either be domestic companies or multinationals with stand-alone operations abroad. Such is the situation in each of the multidomestic industries listed earlier. In a multidomestic industry, then, international strategy collapses to a series of domestic strategies. The issues that are uniquely international revolve around how to do business abroad, how to select good countries in which to compete (or assess country risk), and how to achieve the one-time transfer of know-how or expertise. These are questions that are relatively well developed in the literature.

In a global industry, managing international activities like a portfolio will undermine the possibility of achieving competitive advantage. In a global industry, a firm must in some way integrate its activities on a worldwide basis to capture the linkages among countries. This integration will require more than transferring intangible assets among countries, though it will include such transfer. A firm may choose to compete with a country-centered strategy, focusing on specific market segments or countries where it can carve out a niche by responding to whatever local country differences are present. However, it does so at some considerable peril from competitors with global strategies. All the important competitors in the global industries listed above compete worldwide with increasingly coordinated strategies.

In international competition, a firm has to perform some functions in each of the countries in which it competes. Even though a global competitor must view its international activities as an overall system, it still has to maintain some country perspective. It is the balancing of these two perspectives that becomes one of the essential questions in global strategy.[9]

CAUSES OF GLOBALIZATION

If we accept the distinction between multidomestic and global industries as an important taxonomy of patterns of international competition, a number of questions arise. When does an industry globalize? What exactly do we mean by a global strategy, and is there more than one kind? What determines the type of international strategy best suited to a particular industry?

An industry can be defined as global if there is some competitive advantage to integrating activities on a worldwide basis. To make this statement operational, however, we must be very precise about what we mean by activities and also what we mean by integrating. To diagnose the sources of competitive advantage in any context, whether it be domestic or international, it is necessary to adopt a disaggregated view of the firm, which I call the value chain.[10] Every firm is a collection of discrete activities performed to do business in its industry—I call them value activities. The activities performed by a firm include such things as salespeople selling the product, service technicians performing repairs, scientists in the laboratory designing products or processes, and accountants keeping the books. Such activities are technologically and, in most cases, physically distinct. It is only at the level of these discrete activities, rather than the firm as a whole, that competitive advantage can be truly understood.

A firm may possess two types of competitive advantage: (1) *low cost*, or (2) *differentiation*. These grow out of the firm's ability to perform the activities in the value chain either more cheaply or in a unique way relative to its competitors. The ultimate value a firm creates is what buyers are willing to pay for what the firm provides, which includes its physical product in addition to any ancillary services or benefits, such as design assistance, repair or more timely delivery than competitors. Profit results if the value created through performing the required activities exceeds the collective cost of performing them. Competitive advantage is a function of either providing comparable buyer value more efficiently than competitors (low cost), or performing activities at comparable cost but in unique ways that create more buyer value than competitors and, hence, command a premium price (differentiation).

The value chain, shown in Figure 1.2, provides a systematic means of displaying and categorizing activities. The activities performed by a firm in any industry can be grouped into the nine generic categories shown. The labels may differ based on industry convention, but every firm performs these basic categories of activities in some way or another. Within each category, a firm typically performs a number of discrete activities that are particular to the industry and to the firm's strategy. In service, for example, firms typically perform such discrete activities as installation, repair, parts distribution, and upgrading.

The generic categories of activities can be grouped into two broad types. Along the bottom are what I call *primary* activities, which are those involved in the physical creation of the product or service, its delivery and marketing to the buyer, and its support after sale. Across the top are what I call *support* activities, which provide inputs or infrastructure that allow the primary activities to take place on an ongoing basis.

Procurement is the obtaining of purchased inputs, such as raw materials, purchased services, machinery, and so on. Procurement stretches across the entire value chain because it supports every activity, that is, every activity uses purchased inputs of some kind. There are typically many different discrete procurement activities within a firm, often performed by different people. Technology development encompasses the activities involved in designing the product as well as in creating and improving the way the various activities in the value chain are performed. We tend to think of technology in terms of the product or manufacturing process. In fact, every activity involves a technology or technologies, which may be simple or sophisticated, and a firm has a stock of know-how about how to perform each activity. Technology development typically involves a variety of different discrete activities, some performed outside the R & D department.

Human resource management is the recruiting, training, and de-

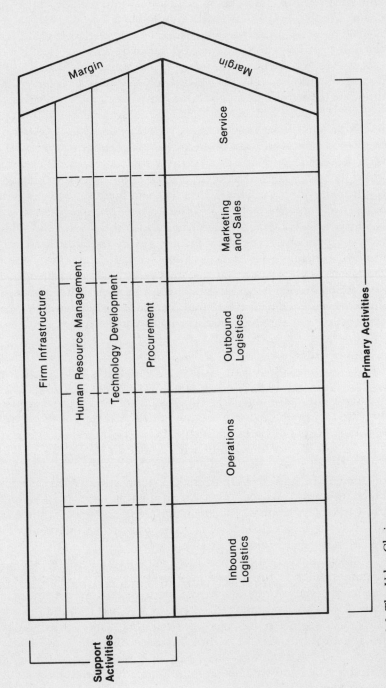

Figure 1.2 The Value Chain

velopment of personnel. Every activity involves human resources, and thus human resource management activities span the entire chain. Finally, firm infrastructure includes activities such as general management, accounting, legal, finance, strategic planning, and all the other activities outside of specific primary or support activities but essential to enable the entire chain's operation. Each category of activities is of differing relative importance to competitive advantage in different industries, although they are present in all industries.

Activities in a firm's value chain are not independent, but are connected through what I call linkages. The way one activity is performed frequently affects the cost or effectiveness of other activities. If more is spent on the purchase of a raw material, for example, a firm may lower its cost of fabrication or assembly. There are many linkages that connect activities, not only within the firm but also with the activities of its suppliers, channels, and ultimately its buyers. The firm's value chain resides in a larger stream of activities that I term the value system. Suppliers have value chains that provide the purchased inputs to the firm's chain; channels have value chains through which the firm's product or service passes; buyers have value chains in which the firm's product or service is employed. The connections among activities in this system also become essential to competitive advantage. For example, the way suppliers perform particular activities can affect the cost or effectiveness of activities within the firm.

A final important building block in value chain theory, necessary for our purposes here, is the notion of *competitive scope*. Competitive scope is the breadth of activities the firm performs in competing in an industry. There are four basic dimensions of competitive scope: segment scope, or the range of segments the firm serves (e.g., product varieties, customer types); industry scope, or the range of related industries the firm competes in with a coordinated strategy; vertical scope, or what activities are performed by the firm versus suppliers and channels; and geographic scope, or the geographic regions in which the firm operates with a coordinated strategy. Competitive scope is vital to competitive advantage because it shapes the configuration of the value chain, how activities are performed and whether activities are shared among units.

International strategy is an issue of geographic scope. Its analysis is quite similar to that of whether and how a firm should compete locally, regionally, or nationally within a country. In the international context, government tends to have a greater involvement in competition and there are more significant variations among geographic regions in buyer needs. Nevertheless, these differences are matters of degree and the framework here can be readily applied to the choice of strategy by firms who compete in large countries consisting of several regions or cities.

International Configuration and Coordination of Activities

A firm that competes internationally must decide how to spread the activities in the value chain among countries. A distinction immediately arises between the activities labeled downstream on Figure 1.3, and those labeled upstream activities and support activities. The location of downstream activities, those more related to the buyer, is usually tied to where the buyer is located. If a firm is going to sell in Japan, for example, it usually must provide service in Japan and it must have salespeople stationed in Japan. In some industries it is possible to have a single sales force that travels to the buyer's country and back again; some other specific downstream activities such as the production of advertising copy can sometimes also be performed centrally. More typically, however, the firm must locate the capability to perform downstream activities in each of the countries in which it operates. (Chapter 4 describes the configuration of international marketing and sales activities in more detail, as well as marketing's broader role in global strategy.) Upstream activities and support activities, conversely, could conceptually be decoupled from where the buyer is located in most industries.

This distinction carries some interesting implications. First, downstream activities create competitive advantages that are largely country specific: a firm's reputation, brand name, and service network in a country grow largely out of a firm's activities in that country and create entry/mobility barriers largely in that country alone. Competitive advantage in upstream and support activities often grows more out of the entire system of countries in which a firm competes than from its position in any one country.

Second, in industries where downstream activities or other buyer-tied activities are vital to competitive advantage, there tends to be a more multidomestic pattern of international competition. In many service industries, for example, not only downstream activities but frequently upstream activities are tied to buyer location, and global strategies are comparatively less common.[11] In industries where upstream and support activities such as technology development and operations are crucial to competitive advantage, global competition is more common. In global competition, the location and scale of these potentially footloose activities is optimized from a worldwide perspective.[12]

The distinctive issues in international, as contrasted to domestic, strategy can be summarized in two key dimensions of how a firm competes internationally. The first I call the *configuration* of a firm's activities worldwide, or the location in the world where each activity in the value chain is performed, including in how many places. The second dimension I call *coordination*, which refers to how like or linked activ-

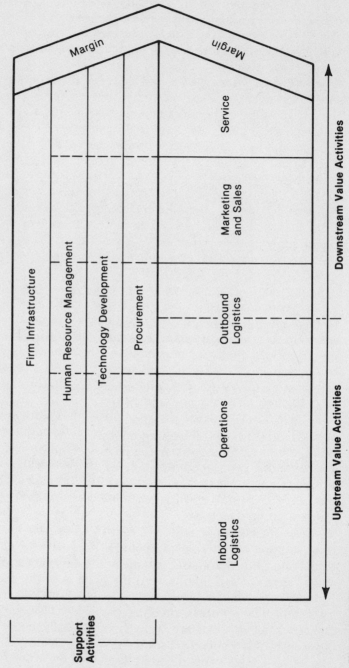

Figure 1.3 Upstream and Downstream Activities

Table 1.1 Illustrative Configuration of Activities Globally for a U.S. Company

Activities	U.S.	Canada	U.K.	France	Germany	Japan
Inbound logistics	X		X		X	X
Operations						
Components	X		X			
Assembly	X				X	X
Testing	X				X	X
Outbound logistics						
Order processing	X					
Physical distribution	X	X	X	X	X	X
Marketing and sales						
Advertising	X	X	X	X	X	X
Sales force	X	X	X	X	X	X
Promotional materials	X					
Service	X	X	X	X	X	X
Procurement	X					X
Technology development	X					X
Human resource management	X	X	X	X	X	X
Firm infrastructure	X					

ities performed in different countries are coordinated with each other. If, for example, there are three plants—one in Germany, one in Japan, and one in the United States—how do the activities in those plants relate to each other?

A firm faces an array of options in both configuration and coordination for each activity in the value chain. Configuration options range from *concentrated*—performing an activity in one location and serving the world from it, for example, one R & D lab, one large plant—to *dispersed*, that is, performing the activity in every country. In the extreme case, each country would have a complete value chain. Table 1.1 illustrates an example of configuration of worldwide activities in an industry.[13] A firm need not concentrate all its activities in the same country. Today, in fact, it has become common to concentrate activities in diferent countries.

Coordination options range from none to many. For example, a firm producing in three plants could at one extreme allow each plant to operate with full autonomy, including different production steps and/or different part numbers. At the other extreme, the plants could be tightly coordinated by employing the same information system, the same production process, the same parts, specifications, and so forth. Options for coordination in an activity are typically more numerous than the configuration options, because there are many possible types of coordination and many different facets of an activity on which to coordinate.

Table 1.2, lists some of the configuration issues and coordination issues for several categories of value activities. In technology devel-

Table 1.2 Configuration and Coordination Issues by Category of Activity

Value Activity	Configuration Issues	Coordination Issues
Operations	Location of production facilities for components and end products	Allocation of production tasks among dispersed facilities Networking of international plants Transferring process technology and production know-how among plants
Marketing and Sales	Product line selection Country (market) selection Location of preparation of advertising and promotional materials	Commonality of brand name worldwide Coordination of sales to multinational accounts Similarity of channels and product positioning worldwide Coordination of pricing in different countries
Service	Location of the service organization	Similarity of service standards and procedures worldwide
Technology Development	Number and location of R & D centers	Allocation of research tasks among dispersed R & D centers Interchange among R & D centers Developing products responsive to market needs in many countries Sequence of product introductions around the world
Procurement	Location of the purchasing function	Locating and managing suppliers in different countries Transferring knowledge about input markets Coordinating purchases of common items

opment, for example, the configuration issue is where R & D is performed: at one location or two or more locations and in what countries? The coordination issues have to do with such things as the allocation of tasks among R & D centers, the extent of interchange among them, and the location and sequence of product introduction around the world. There are configuration issues and coordination issues for every activity.[14]

Figure 1.4 is a way of summarizing these basic choices in inter-

Figure 1.4 The Dimensions of International Strategy

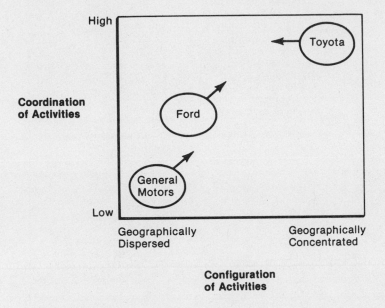

Coordination
of Activities

High

Low

Geographically
Dispersed

Geographically
Concentrated

Configuration
of Activities

national strategy geographically on a single diagram, with coordination of activities on the vertical axis and configuration of activities on the horizontal axis. The firm has to make a set of choices for each activity. If a firm employs a very dispersed configuration, placing an entire value chain in every country (or small group of contiguous countries) in which it operates and coordinating little or not at all among them, then the firm is competing with a country-centered strategy.[15] The domestic firm, operating in only one country, is the extreme case of a firm with a country-centered strategy. As we move from the lower left-hand corner of the diagram up or to the right, we have strategies that are increasingly global. Figure 1.4 can be employed to map strategic groups in an international industry because its axes capture the most important sources of competitive advantage from an international strategy.[16]

Figure 1.5 illustrates some of the possible variations in international strategy. The simplest global strategy is to concentrate as many activities as possible in one country, serve the world from this home base, and tightly coordinate through standarization those activities that must inherently be performed near the buyer. This is the pattern adopted by many Japanese firms in the 1960s and 1970s, such as Toyota. The position of Toyota is plotted on Figure 1.4 along with key competitors. However, the options apparent in Figures 1.5 and 1.6 make it clear that there is no such thing as one global strategy.

There are many different kinds of global strategies, depending on

Figure 1.5 Types of International Strategy

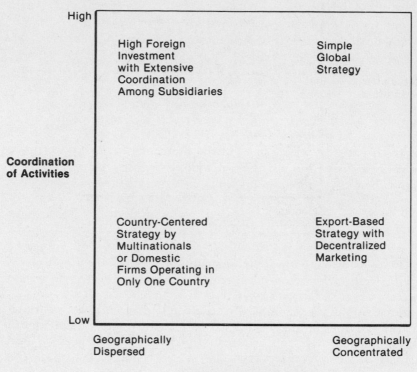

Coordination of Activities

High

High Foreign
Investment
with Extensive
Coordination
Among Subsidiaries

Simple
Global
Strategy

Country-Centered
Strategy by
Multinationals
or Domestic
Firms Operating in
Only One Country

Export-Based
Strategy with
Decentralized
Marketing

Low

Geographically
Dispersed

Geographically
Concentrated

Configuration of Activities

a firm's choices about configuration and coordination throughout the value chain. In copiers, for example, Xerox has until recently concentrated R & D in the United States, but dispersed other activities, in some cases using joint-venture partners to perform them. On dispersed activities, however, coordination has been quite high. The Xerox brand, marketing approach, and servicing procedures have been quite standardized worldwide. Canon, on the other hand, has had a much more concentrated configuration of activities through somewhat less coordination of the dispersed activities. The vast majority of Canon's support activities plus most manufacturing have been performed in Japan. Aside from the requirement to use the Canon brand, however, local marketing subsidiaries have been given quite a bit of latitude in each region of the world.

Competitors with country-centered and global strategies can co-exist in an industry, but global strategies by some competitors frequently force other firms to follow suit. In automobiles, for example, Toyota has employed a relatively simple global strategy to achieve the position of low-cost producer. General Motors has historically competed with a country-centered international strategy, with separate manufacturing facilities and even separate brand names in different regions, while Ford has practiced only regional coordination. As the arrows indicate, all three companies are modifying their international strategies today—the U.S. firms toward more global strategies and Toyota toward becoming more dispersed as its international position grows.

A global strategy can now be defined more precisely as one in which a firm seeks to *gain competitive advantage from its international presence through either a concentrated configuration, coordinating among dispersed activities, or both*. The one-time transfer of intangible assets, emphasized in the literature, is just one of many ways. Measuring the presence of a global industry empirically must reflect both dimensions and not just one. Market presence of firms in many countries and some export and import of components and end products are characteristic of most global industries. Hence, intra-industry trade is a good sign of the presence of global competition, and its growth is one indication that the incidence of global industries has increased. High levels of foreign investment or the mere presence of multinational firms are not reliable measures, however, because firms may be managing foreign units like a portfolio.

Configuration/Coordination and Competitive Advantage

Understanding the competitive advantages of a global strategy and, in turn, the causes of industry globalization, requires that we specify the conditions under which concentrating activities globally and/or coordinating dispersed activities leads to either lower cost or differentiation. In each case, there are structural characteristics of an industry that work for and against globalization.

The factors that favor concentrating an activity in one or a few locations to serve the world are as follows:

- economies of scale in the activity;
- a proprietary learning curve in the activity;
- comparative advantage of one or a few locations for performing the activity;
- coordination advantages of co-locating linked activities such as R & D and production.

The first two factors relate to *how many* sites an activity is performed at, while the last two relate to *where* these sites are. Comparative advantage can apply to any activity, not just production. There may be some locations in the world that are better places than others to perform other activities such as research or creation of advertising materials. India has become a center for software writing, for example. Government can promote the concentration of activities by providing subsidies or other incentives to employ a particular country as an export base—in effect altering comparative advantage—a role many governments are attempting to play today.

There are also structural characteristics that favor dispersion of an activity to many countries, because they create concentration costs. Local product needs may differ, nullifying the advantages of scale or learning from one-site operation of an activity. Dispersing a range of activities in a country may facilitate marketing in that country by signaling commitment to local buyers and/or providing greater local responsiveness. Dispersing an activity may facilitate learning or gaining know-how in the activity, as a number of sites increases information flow and managers get closer to more markets. Transport, communication, and storage costs can make it inefficient to concentrate the activity in one location.

Government is also frequently a powerful force for dispersing activities, through tariffs, nontariff barriers, and nationalistic purchasing (nationalistic purchasing can exist without a direct government role as well). Governments typically want firms to locate the entire value chain in their country, because this creates benefits and spillovers to the country that often go beyond local content.[17] Dispersing some activities may sometimes allow the concentration of others, through placating governments or through linkages among activities that will be described below. Dispersion is also encouraged by the risks of performing an activity at one place: exchange rate risk, political risk, risk of interruption, and so on. The balance between the advantages of concentrating and dispersing an activity normally differ for each activity (and industry). The best configuration for R & D is different from that for component fabrication, and this is different from that for assembly, installation, advertising, and procurement.[18]

The desirability of coordinating like or linked activities that are dispersed involves a similar balance of structural factors. Coordination potentially allows the sharing and accumulation of know-how and expertise among dispersed activities. If a firm learns how to operate the production process better in Germany, transferring that learning may make the process run better in U.S. and Japanese plants. Differing countries, with their inevitably differing conditions, provide a fertile basis for comparison as well as opportunities for arbitrating knowledge, obtained in different places about different aspects of the business. Knowledge may accumulate not only in product or process technology but also about buyer needs and marketing techniques. A firm coordinating internationally may also receive early warning of industry changes by spotting them in one or two leading countries before they become broadly apparent and transferring the knowledge to guide other activities elsewhere. The initial transfer of knowledge in establishing a foreign subsidiary is recognizable as one case of coordination among dispersed activities. However, it is clear that knowledge is continually created and can flow among all subsidiaries. The ability to accumulate and transfer this knowledge among units is a potent advantage of the global competitor over domestic or country-centered competitors.[19]

Coordination among dispersed activities also potentially improves the ability to reap economies of scale in activities if subtasks are allocated among locations to allow some specialization, for example, each R & D center has a different area of focus. This illustrates how the way a network of foreign locations is managed can have a great influence on the ability to reap the benefits of any given configuration of activities. Viewed another way, close coordination is frequently a partial offset to dispersing an activity.

Closely related to this is the relationship between international coordination in one activity and the configuration of another. For example, coordination in the marketing activity involving information exchange about buyer needs in many countries may allow a central R & D facility to design a standard or easy-to-modify product for sale worldwide, unlocking the scale economies of a concentrated configuration in R & D and production. Such a linkage among separate activities has been exploited by Canon in the design of its personal copier, described in chapter 4. Similarly, dispersing procurement may allow concentrating manufacturing, since sourcing from many countries can open up the opportunity to export to them.

Coordination may also allow a firm to respond to *shifting* comparative advantage, where movements in exchange rates and factor costs are significant and hard to forecast. For example, incrementally increasing production at the location currently enjoying favorable exchange rates can lower costs. Coordination can also reinforce a firm's brand reputation with buyers through ensuring a consistent image and approach to doing business on a worldwide basis. This is particularly valuable if buyers are mobile or information about the industry flows freely around the world. Coordination may also differentiate the firm with multinational buyers if it allows the firm to serve them anywhere and in a consistent way. Coordination (and a global approach to configuration) enhances leverage with local governments if the firm is able to grow or shrink activities in one country at the expense of others. Finally, coordination yields flexibility in responding to competitors, by allowing the firm to respond to them differently in different countries and to retaliate in one country to a challenge in another. A firm may choose, for example, to compete aggressively in the country from which a challenger draws its most important volume or cash flow in order to reduce the competitors' strength in other countries. IBM and Caterpillar have practiced this sort of defensive behavior in their Japanese operations.

Coordination of dispersed activities usually involves costs that differ by form of coordination and by industry. Local conditions in countries may vary in ways that may make a common approach across

countries suboptimal. For example, if every plant in the world is required to use the same raw material, the firm pays a penalty in countries where that raw material is expensive relative to satisfactory substitutes. Business practices, marketing systems, raw material sources,
local infrastructures, and a variety of other factors may differ across
countries as well, in ways that may mitigate the advantages of a common approach or of the sharing of learning. Governments may restrain
the flow of information required for coordination, or impose other barriers to it. Transaction costs of coordination among countries can also
be high. International coordination involves long distances, language
problems, and cultural barriers to communication. Such problems
may mean in some industries that coordination is not optimal. They
also suggest that forms of coordination that involve relatively infrequent decisions, such as adopting common service standards or employing the same raw materials, will enjoy advantages over forms of
coordination involving ongoing interchange such as transshipping
components and end products among facilities.

There are also substantial organizational challenges involved in
achieving cooperation among subsidiaries, because of difficulties in
aligning subsidiary managers' interests with those of the firm as a
whole. The German branch does not necessarily want to tell the U.S.
branch about their latest breakthroughs on the production line because it may make it harder for them to outdo the Americans in the
annual comparison of operating efficiency among plants. These vexing
organizational problems mean that country subsidiaries often view
each other more as competitors than collaborators.[20] As with configuration, a firm must make an activity-by-activity choice about where
there is net competitive advantage to coordinating in various ways.

Some factors favoring dispersion of activities also impede coordination, while others do not. Transport costs raise few barriers to coordination, for example, while product heterogeneity creates substantial ones. Product heterogeneity and the actions of government often
have the special characteristics of impeding *both* concentration and
coordination, giving them a particularly strategic role in affecting the
pattern of international competition.

Coordination in some activities may be necessary to reap the advantages of configuration in others as noted earlier. The use of common raw materials in each plant, for example, allows worldwide
purchasing. Moreover, tailoring some activities to countries (not
coordinating) may allow concentration and standardization of others.
For example, tailored marketing in each country may allow the same
product to be positioned differently and hence sold successfully in
many countries, unlocking possibilities for reaping economies of scale
in production and R & D. These possibilities are discussed in chapter
4 of this book. Thus, coordination and configuration interact.

Diversification into related industries can also shape the best
global configuration/coordination in a single industry. For example, a

diversified firm may be able to produce a number of related products in dispersed plants, instead of concentrating production of one product in a single plant, and still achieve economies of scale. This reflects the fact that sharing activities among units competing in related industries may serve the same strategic purpose as sharing them in competing in many countries—namely, scale or learning economies.[21]

Diversification can also create new options for bargaining with governments. For example, exports in one business unit can be traded for the ability to import in another. IBM follows this approach, seeking a balance of trade in each country in which it operates. Diversification in a variety of industries may also facilitate bartering. Conversely, diversification may raise a firm's overall commitment to a country, increasing the host government's leverage. For all these reasons, the extent of a firm's diversification should be a consideration in its choice of international strategy.

Configuration/Coordination and the Pattern of International Competition

Industries globalize when the benefits of configuring and/or coordinating globally exceed the costs of doing so. The way in which an industry globalizes reflects the specific benefits and costs of global configuration and/or coordination of each value activity. The activities in which global competitors gain competitive advantage will differ correspondingly. Configuration/coordination determines the ongoing competitive advantages of a global strategy, growing out of a firm's overall international position. These are additive to competitive advantages a firm derives/possesses from its domestic market positions. An initial transfer of knowledge from the home base to subsidiaries, is thus one, but by no means the most important, advantage of a global competitor.[22]

In some industries, the competitive advantage from a global strategy comes in technology development, and firms gain little advantage from concentrating primary activities which means that they are dispersed around the world. A good example is the manufacture of glass and plastic containers, where transport cost leads to a dispersion of plants but opportunities to perform R & D centrally and to transfer production know-how among plants yield significant advantages to global firms. In other industries, such as cameras or videocassette recorders, firms gain advantages from concentrating production to achieve economies of scale and learning, but give subsidiaries much local autonomy in sales and marketing. Finally, in some industries there is no net advantage to a global strategy and country-centered strategies dominate; the industry is multidomestic.

An industry such as commercial aircraft represents an extreme case of a global industry (e.g., placement in the upper right-hand corner of Figure 1.4). Three competitors, Boeing, McDonnell Douglas, and Airbus, all have global strategies. In value activities important to cost and differentiation in the industry, there are compelling net advantages to concentrating most activities to serve worldwide markets and coordinating the dispersed activities extensively. For a detailed description of the industry, see chapter 16. Yet, host governments have a particular interest in the commercial aircraft industry because of its large trade potential, defense implications, and R & D spillovers. The competitive advantages of a global strategy are so great that all the successful aircraft producers have sought to achieve and preserve them. In addition, the power of government to intervene has been mitigated by the paucity of viable worldwide competitors and the enormous barriers to entry created, in part, by the advantages of a global strategy. The result has been that firms have been able to assuage government through procurement. Boeing, for example, is very careful about where it buys components. Boeing seeks to develop suppliers in countries that are large potential customers. This requires a great deal of extra effort by Boeing to transfer technology and to work with suppliers to ensure that they meet its standards. Boeing realizes that this is preferable to compromising the competitive advantage of its strongly integrated worldwide strategy. It is willing to employ one value activity (procurement), where the advantages of concentration are modest, to help preserve the benefits of concentration in other activities. Recently, commercial aircraft competitors have entered into joint ventures and other coalition arrangements with foreign suppliers to achieve the same affect, as well as to spread the risk of huge development costs.

Segments and vertical stages of an industry frequently vary in their pattern of globalization. In aluminum, the upstream (alumina and ingot) stages are global industries. The downstream stage, semifabrication, is a group of multidomestic businesses, because product needs vary by country, transport costs are high, and intensive local customer service is required. Scale economies in the value chain are modest. In lubricants, automotive motor oil tends to be a multidomestic industry, while marine engine lubricants is a global industry. In automotive oil, countries have varying driving standards, weather conditions, and local laws. Production involves blending various kinds of base oils and additives, and is subject to few economies of scale but high shipping costs. Distribution channels are important to competitive success and vary markedly from country to country. Country-centered competitors, such as Castrol and Quaker State, are leaders in most countries. In the marine segment, conversely, ships move freely around the world and require the same oil everywhere. Successful competitors are global. A third and different industry is lodging, where most segments are multidomestic because the majority of activities in the value chain are tied to buyer location and country differences lead to few benefits from coordination. In high-priced business-oriented hotels, however, competition is more global. Global competitors such as Hilton, Marriott, and Sheraton have dispersed value chains, but employ common brand names, common service standards, and worldwide reservation systems to gain advantages in serving highly mobile business travelers.[23]

Just as the pattern of globalization may differ by segment or industry stage, so may the pattern differ by groups of countries. There are often *subsystems* of countries within which the advantages of configuration/coordination are greater than with other countries. For example, configuration/coordination possibilities may be high in competing in countries with similar climatic conditions (such as the Nordic countries) because they have similar product needs. Subsystems can be based on geographic regions, climatic conditions, language, state of economic development, extent of government intervention in competition, and historical or current political ties. In the record industry, for example, possibilities for coordination are great among the Spanish-speaking countries and countries with a large Spanish-speaking population such as the United States. Where there is extreme government intervention, geographic isolation, or very unusual product needs, countries can be effectively outside the global system or any subsystem.

International strategy has often been characterized as a choice between worldwide standardization and local tailoring, or as the tension between the economic imperative (large-scale efficient facilities) and the political imperative (local content, local production). It should be clear from the discussion so far that neither characterization captures the complexity of a firm's international strategy choices. A firm's choice of international strategy involves the search for competitive advantage from global configuration/coordination throughout the value chain. A firm may standardize (concentrate) some activities and tailor (disperse) others. It may also be able to standardize and tailor at the same time through the coordination of dispersed activities, or use local tailoring of some activities (e.g., different product positioning in each country) to allow standardization of others (e.g., production). Similarly, the economic imperative is not always for a global strategy—in some industries a country-centered strategy is the economic imperative. Conversely, the political imperative in some industries may be to concentrate activities where governments provide strong export incentives and locational subsidies.

The essence of international strategy is not to resolve tradeoffs between concentration and dispersion, but to eliminate or mitigate them. This implies concentrating and dispersing different value activities depending on industry structure, dispersing some activities to allow concentration of others, and minimizing the tradeoff between concentration and dispersion by coordinating dispersed activities.[24]

The Process of Industry Globalization

Industries globalize because the net competitive advantage of a global approach to configuration/coordination becomes significant. Sometimes this is due to exogenous environmental changes, such as shifts in technology, buyer needs, government policy, or country infrastructure. In automotive supply, for example, the industry is globalizing as buyers (the auto producers) become increasingly global competitors. In other industries, strategic innovations by a competitor can unlock the potential for globalization. For example, a firm may perceive a means of providing local content without dispersing scale-sensitive value activities, such as local installation and testing. Other tools to unlock globalization include: reducing the cost of modifying a centrally designed and produced product to meet local needs, such as modularizing the power supply in an otherwise standard product; increasing product homogeneity by designing a product that incorporates the features demanded by every significant country; or homogenizing worldwide demand through product repositioning. In electronic products such as communications switching equipment, for example, Northern Telecom, NEC Corporation, and Ericsson have benefited from product architectures which permit modularization of software and relatively low-cost modification to fit different country needs. Environmental changes and strategic insights frequently go hand in hand in changing the pattern of international competition.

There may be problems in the transition from multidomestic to global competition in industries where domestic or country-centered competitors have already established entry or mobility barriers that are market-specific. The possession by country-centered or domestic competitors of strong brand names, strong distribution channel relationships, or long-standing buyer relationships, will retard the penetration of global firms. Firms also face difficulties in shifting from country-centered to global strategies if they have a legacy of dispersed worldwide activities and organizational norms that place great authority at the country level. Domestic firms can sometimes be more successful than established multinationals in becoming global competitors, because they start with a cleaner slate than do firms who must rationalize and reorient their international activities.

The ultimate leaders in global industries are often first movers: the first firms to perceive the possibilities for a global strategy and move to implement one. For example, Boeing was the first global competitor in aircraft, as was Honda in motorcycles, IBM in computers, Kodak in film, and Becton Dickinson in disposable syringes. First movers gain scale and learning advantages that make competing with them difficult. First-mover effects are particularly important in global industries, because of the association between globalization and economies of scale, learning, and flexibility achieved through worldwide configuration/coordination. Global leadership can shift if industry structural change provides the opportunity for leapfrogging to new products or new technologies that nullify past leaders' scale and learning; again, the first mover to the new generation/technology often wins.

Global leaders often begin with some advantage at home, whether it be low labor cost or a product design or marketing advantage. They use this as a lever to enter foreign markets. Once there, however, the global competitor converts the initial home advantage into competitive advantages that grow out of its overall worldwide system, such as production scale economies or the ability to amortize R & D costs. While the initial advantage may have been hard to sustain, the global strategy creates *new* advantages that can be much more durable.

A good example is automobiles, where Toyota and Nissan initially competed in simple, small cars on the basis of low labor costs. As these companies achieved worldwide penetration, however, they gained economies of scale and accelerated down the learning curve. World scale allowed aggressive investments in new equipment and R & D. Today, the Korean competitor Hyundai competes in small, simple cars based on low labor costs. Toyota and Nissan have long since graduated to broad lines of increasingly differentiated cars, drawing on the advantages of their worldwide positions.

Global Strategy and Comparative Advantage

It is useful to pause and reflect on the relationship between the framework I have presented and the notion of comparative advantage. Is there a difference? The traditional concept of comparative advantage is that factor-cost or factor-quality differences among countries lead to production in countries with advantages in a particular industry which export the product elsewhere in the world. Competitive advantage, in this view, grows out of *where* firms perform activities.

The location of activities is clearly one source of potential advantage in a global firm. The global competitor can locate activities wherever comparative advantage lies, decoupling comparative advantage from the firm's home base or country of ownership. Indeed, the framework presented here suggests that the comparative advantage story is richer than typically told, because it not only involves production activities (the usual focus of discussions) but also applies to other activities in the value chain, such as R & D, processing orders, or designing advertisements. Comparative advantage is specific to the *activity* and not the location of the value chain as a whole.[25] One of the potent advantages of the global firm is that it can spread activities to reflect different preferred locations, something a domestic or country-centered competitor does not do. Thus, components can be made in Taiwan, software written in India, and basic R & D performed in Silicon Valley, for example. This international specialization and arbitrage of activities within the firm is made possible by the growing ability to coordinate and configure globally, and can be difficult to accomplish through arm's-length or quasi-arm's-length transactions because of risks of contracting with independent parties as well as high transaction costs.

While my framework suggests a more complex view of comparative advantage, it also suggests, however, that many forms of competitive advantage for the global firm derive less from *where* it performs activities than from *how* it performs them on a worldwide basis; economies of scale, proprietary learning, and differentiation with multinational buyers are not tied to countries but to the configuration and coordination of the firm's worldwide system. While these advantages are frequently quite sustainable, traditional sources of comparative advantage can be very elusive sources of competitive advantage for an international competitor today, because comparative advantage frequently shifts. A country with the lowest labor cost is overtaken within a few years by some other country; as has happened repeatedly in shipbuilding as Japan has replaced Europe only to be replaced by Korea (see chapter 17). Moreover, falling direct labor cost as a percentage of total costs, increasingly global markets for raw materials and other inputs, and freer flowing technology have diminished the role of traditional sources of comparative advantage.

My research on a broad cross-section of industries suggests that the achievement of sustainable world leadership follows a more complex pattern than the exploitation of comparative advantage per se. A competitor may start with a comparative-advantage-related edge that provides the basis for penetrating foreign markets, but this edge is rapidly translated into a broader array of advantages that arise from the global approach to configuration and coordination described earlier. Japanese firms, for example, have done a masterful job in many industries of converting fleeting labor-cost advantages into durable systemwide advantages because of scale and proprietary know-how. Over time, these systemwide advantages are further reinforced with country-specific advantages such as brand identity in many countries as well as distribution channel access.

Many Japanese firms were fortunate enough to make their transitions from country-based comparative advantage to global competitive advantage in a buoyant world economy while nobody paid much attention to them. European and U.S. competitors were willing to cede market share in "less desirable" segments such as the low end of the product line, or so they thought. The Japanese translated these beachheads into world leadership by broadening their lines and reaping advantages in scale and proprietary learning. The Koreans and Taiwanese, the latest entrants in consumer electronics and other industries with low-price strategies, may have a hard time replicating Japan's success. Products have standardized and growth is slow, while Japanese and U.S. competitors are alert to the threat. Japanese firms enjoyed first-mover advantages in pursuing their strategies that the Koreans and Taiwanese do not.

Global Platforms

The interaction of the home country conditions and competitive advantages from a global strategy that transcend the country suggest a more complex role of the country in firm success than implied by the theory of comparative advantage. To understand this more complex role of the country, I define the concept of a "global platform." A country is a desirable global platform in an industry if it provides an environment yielding firms domiciled in that country an advantage in competing globally in that particular industry. The firm need not necessarily be owned by investors in the country, but the country is its home base for competing in a particular industry. An essential element of this definition is that it hinges on success *outside* the country, and not merely country conditions that allow firms to successfully master domestic competition. In global competition, a country must be viewed as a platform and not as the place where all a firm's activities are performed.

There are two broad determinants of a good global platform in an industry, which I have explored in more detail elsewhere.[26] The first is comparative advantage, or the factor endowment of the country as a site to perform particular important activities in the industry. Today, *simple factors* such as low-cost unskilled labor and natural resources are increasingly less important to global competition than *complex factors* such as skilled scientific and technical personnel as well as advanced infrastructure. Direct labor is a minor proportion of cost in many manufactured goods and automation of nonproduction activities is shrinking it further, while markets for resources are increasingly global and technology has widened the number of sources of many resources. A country's factor endowment is partly exogenous but partly endogenous, the result of attention and investment in the country.

The second determinant of the attractiveness of a country as a global platform in an industry are the characteristics of a country's demand and local operating environment. A country's demand conditions include the size and timing of its demand in an industry, factors recognized as important by authors such as Linder and Vernon.[27] They also include, however, the sophistication and power of local buyers and channels, and the particular product features and attributes demanded. These latter factors are frequently more important today than size and timing of demand, because income differences among many developed countries are relatively small and industries develop simultaneously in many countries. Local operating conditions relevant to investment success include the customs and conditions for doing business in a particular industry as well as the intensity of local competition. Strong local competition frequently benefits a country's success in international competition rather than impedes it, a view sometimes used to advocate the creation of "national champions." Japanese machine tool and electronic firms, Italian ski boot manufacturers, German high performance automakers, and American minicomputer companies all illustrate the spur of local competition to success abroad.

Local demand and operating conditions provide a number of potentially powerful sources of competitive advantage to a global competitor based in that country. The first is first-mover advantages in perceiving and implementing the appropriate global strategy. Pressing local needs, particularly peculiar ones, lead firms to embark early to solve local problems and gain proprietary know-how. This is then translated into scale and learning advantages as firms move early to compete globally. The second benefit is motivation. Sophisticated, powerful customers, tough operating problems, and a formidable local rival or two promote rapid progress down the learning curve and conceiving of new ways of competing. The final potential benefit of local demand conditions is a baseload of demand for product varieties that will be sought after in international markets. The role of the country in the success of a firm internationally, then, is in the interaction between conditions of local supply, the composition and timing of country demand, and the nature of the local operating environment with economies of scale and learning.

The two determinants of country competitiveness in an industry interact in important and sometimes counterintuitive ways. Local demand and needs frequently influence private and social investment in endogenous factors of production. A nation with oceans as borders and dependence on sea trade, for example, is more prone to have universities and scientific centers dedicated to oceanographic education and research. Similarly, factor endowment seems to influence local demand. The per capita consumption of wine is highest in wine-growing regions, for example.

"Comparative disadvantage" in some factors of production can be an advantage in global competition when combined with pressing local demand. Poor growing conditions have led Israeli farmers to innovate in irrigation and cultivation techniques, for example. The shrinking role of simple factors of production relative to complex factors such as technical personnel seem to be enhancing the frequency and importance of such circumstances. What is important today in international success is unleashing innovation in the proper direction, instead of passive exploitation of a country's static cost advantages, which shift rapidly and can be overcome. International success today is a dynamic process resulting from continued development of products and processes. The forces that guide firms to undertake such activity are central to the success of a country's firms in international competition.

A good example of the interplay among these factors is the television set industry. In the United States, early demand was in large screen console sets because TV sets were initially luxury items kept in the living room. As buyers began to purchase second and third sets, sets became smaller and more portable. They were used increasingly in the bedroom, the kitchen, the car, and elsewhere. As the TV set industry matured, table model and portable sets became the universal product variety. Japanese firms, because of the small size of Japanese homes, gained early experience in small sets. They dedicated most of their R & D to developing small picture tubes and compact sets. The Japanese also faced a compelling need to reduce power consumption of sets because of the existing energy crisis, which led them to rapid introduction of solid-state technology. This, in turn, facilitated reducing the number of components and automating manufacturing. The whole process was accelerated by the more rapid saturation of the Japanese home market than the American market and a large number of Japanese competitors who were competing fiercely for the same pie.

In the process of naturally serving the needs of their home market and dealing with local problems, then, Japanese firms gained early experience and scale in segments of the industry that came to dominate world demand. U.S. firms, conversely, pioneered large-screen console sets with fine furniture cabinets. As the industry matured, the experience base of U.S. firms centered on a segment that was small and isolated to a few countries, notably the United States. Aided by intense competitive pressure, Japanese firms were able to penetrate world markets in a segment that was not only uninteresting to foreign firms but also one in which the Japanese had initial-scale learning- and labor-cost advantages. Ultimately the low-cost advantage disappeared as production was automated, but global scale and learning economies rapidly took over as the Japanese advanced product and process technology at a rapid pace. This example illustrates how early demand for TV sets in the United States proved to be a disadvantage rather than the advantage that some views of international competition paint it to be. Moreover, Japan's comparative disadvantage in energy proved to be an advantage in TV sets (and a number of other industries).

The two broad determinants of a good global platform rest on the interaction between country characteristics and firms' strategies. The literature on comparative advantage, through focusing on country factor endowments, minimizing the demand side, and suppressing the individual firm, is most appropriate in industries where there are few economies of scale, little proprietary technology or technological change, or few possibilities for product differentiation.[28] While these industry characteristics are those of many traditionally traded goods, they describe few of today's important global industries.

THE HISTORICAL EVOLUTION OF INTERNATIONAL COMPETITION

Having established a framework for understanding the globalization of industries, I am now in a position to view the phenomenon in historical perspective. While this discussion anticipates some of the material covered in chapter 13, it provides a way of validating the framework and isolating important issues for global competitors today. If one goes back far enough, relatively few industries were global. Around 1880, most industries were local or regional in scope. The reasons are rather self-evident in the context of my framework. There were few economies of scale in production until fuel-powered machines and assembly-line techniques emerged. There were heterogeneous product needs among regions within countries, much less among countries. There were few if any national media; the *Saturday Evening Post* was the first important national magazine in the United States and developed in the teens and twenties. Communication between regions was difficult before the telegraph, telephone, and railroad systems became well developed.

These structural conditions created little impetus for the widespread globalization of industry. Those industries that were global reflected classic comparative-advantage considerations. Goods were simply unavailable in some countries who imported them from others, or differences in the availability of land, resources, or skilled labor made some countries desirable suppliers to others. Export of goods produced locally was the predominant form of global strategy adapted. There was little need for widespread government barriers to international trade during this period, although trade barriers were quite high in some countries for some commodities.

Developments around the 1880s, however, marked the beginnings of what today has blossomed into the globalization of many industries. The first wave of modern global competitors grew up in the late 1800s and early 1900s. Many industries went from local (or regional) to national in scope, and some began globalizing. Firms such as Ford, Singer, Gillette, National Cash Register, Otis, and Western Electric had commanding world market shares by the teens, and operated with integrated worldwide strategies. Early global competitors were principally U.S. and European companies.

Driving this first wave of modern globalization were rising production scale economies, because of the advancements in technology that outpaced the growth of the world economy. Product needs also became more homogenized in different countries as knowledge and industrialization diffused. Transport improved, first through the railroad and steamships and later in trucking. Communication became more efficient with the telegraph, telephone, and efficient mail service. At the same time, trade barriers were either modest or overwhelmed by the strong competitive advantages of the new large-scale firms.

The burst of globalization soon slowed, however. Most of the few industries that were global moved increasingly toward a multidomestic pattern. Multinationals remained, but between the 1920s and 1950 many evolved toward becoming federations of autonomous subsidiaries. The principal reason was a strong wave of nationalism and resulting high-tariff barriers, partly caused by the world economic crisis and world wars. Another barrier to global strategies, chronicled by Chandler in chapter 13, was a growing web of cartels and other interfirm contractual agreements. These limited the geographic spread of firms.

The early global competitors began rapidly dispersing their value chains. The situation of Ford Motor Company is no exception. While in 1925 Ford had almost no production outside the United States, by World War II its overseas production had risen sharply. Firms that first became multinationals during the interwar period tended to adopt country-centered strategies. European multinationals, operating in a setting where there were many sovereign countries within a relatively small geographical area, were very early to establish self-contained and quite autonomous subsidiaries in many countries. A more tolerant regulatory environment also encouraged European firms to form cartels and other cooperative agreements among themselves, which limited their foreign market entry.

Between the 1950s and the late 1970s there was a strong reversal of the interwar trends. As the outcome in Figure 1.1 implied, there have been very strong underlying forces driving the globalization of industries. The important reasons can be understood using the configuration/coordination framework. The competitive advantage of competing worldwide from concentrated activities rose sharply, while concentration costs fell. There was a renewed rise in scale economies in many activities because of advancing technology. The minimum efficient scale of an auto assembly plant more than tripled between 1960 and 1975, for example, while the average real cost of developing a new drug more than quadrupled. The pace of technological change has increased, creating more incentive to amortize R & D costs over worldwide sales.

Product needs have continued to homogenize among countries, as income differences have narrowed, information and communication has flowed more freely around the world, and travel has increased.[29]

Growing similarities in business practices and marketing systems (e.g., chain stores) in different countries have also been a facilitating factor in homogenizing needs. Within countries there has been a parallel trend toward greater market segmentation, which some observers see as contradictory to the view that product needs in different countries are becoming more similar. However, segments today seem based less on country differences and more on buyer differences that transcend country boundaries, differences such as demographic, user-industry, or income groups. Many firms successfully employ global segmentation strategies in which they serve a narrow segment of an industry worldwide, as do Daimler-Benz and Rolex.

Another driver of post–World War II globalization has been a sharp reduction in the real costs of transportation. This has occurred through innovations in transportation technology including increasingly large bulk carriers, container ships, and larger more efficient aircraft. At the same time, government impediments to global configuration have been falling in the postwar period. Tariff barriers have gone down, international cartels and patent-sharing agreements have disappeared, while regional economic pacts such as the European Community have emerged to facilitate trade and investment, albeit imperfectly.

The ability to coordinate globally has also risen markedly in the postwar period. Perhaps the most striking reason is falling communication costs, in voice, data, and travel time for individuals. The ability to coordinate activities in different countries has also been facilitated by growing similarities among countries in marketing systems, business practices, and infrastructure; country after country has developed supermarkets and mass distributors, TV advertising, and so on. Greater international mobility of buyers and information has raised the payoff to coordinating how a firm does business around the world. Increasing numbers of firms who are themselves multinational have created growing possibilities for differentiation by suppliers who were global. Growing volatility of exchange rates has raised the advantage of coordinating production in an international plant network.

The forces underlying globalization have been self-reinforcing. The globalization of firms' strategies has contributed to the homogenization of buyer needs and business practices. Early global competitors must frequently stimulate the demand for uniform global varieties, for example, as Becton Dickinson has done with disposable syringes (see chapter 15) and Honda did with motorcycles. Globalization of industries begets globalization of supplier industries. The increasing globalization of semiconductor manufacturers is a good example. Pioneering global competitors also stimulate the development and growth of international telecommunication infrastructure as well as the creation of global advertising media, for example, *The Economist* and *The Wall Street Journal*.

Japan has clearly been the winner in the postwar globalization of competition. Japan's firms not only had an initial labor cost advantage but the orientation and skills to translate this into more durable competitive advantages such as scale and proprietary technology. The Japanese context also offered an excellent platform for globalization in many industries, given postwar environmental and technological trends. With home market-demand conditions favoring compactness, a compelling need to cope with high energy costs, and a national conviction to raise quality, Japan has proved a fertile incubator of global leaders.

Japanese multinationals had the advantage of embarking on international strategies in the 1950s and 1960s when the imperatives for a global approach to strategy were beginning to accelerate, but without the legacy of past international investments and modes of behavior.[30] Japanese firms also had an orientation toward highly concentrated activities that fit the strategic imperative of the time. Most European and many U.S. multinationals, conversely, were well established internationally before the war. They had legacies of local subsidiary autonomy that reflected the interwar environment. As Japanese firms spread internationally, they dispersed activities only grudgingly and engaged in extensive global coordination. European and country-centered U.S. companies struggled to rationalize overly dispersed configurations of activities and to boost the level of global coordination among foreign units. They found the decentralized organization structures so fashionable in the 1960s and 1970s to be a hindrance.

STRATEGIC IMPLICATIONS OF GLOBALIZATION

When the pattern of international competition shifts from multi-domestic to global in an industry, there are many implications for the strategy of an international firm. At the broadest level, globalization casts new light on many issues that have long been of interest to students of international business. In areas such as international finance, marketing, and business-government relations, the emphasis in the literature has been on the unique problems of adapting to local conditions and ways of doing business in a foreign country.

In a global industry these concerns must be supplemented with an overriding focus on the ways and means of international configuration and coordination. In government relations, for example, the focus must shift from stand-alone negotiations with host countries (appropriate in multidomestic competition) to a recognition that negotiations in one country will both affect other countries and be shaped by possibilities for performing activities in other countries. In finance, measuring the performance of subsidiaries must be modified to reflect the contribution of one subsidiary to another's cost position or differentiation in a global strategy, instead of viewing each subsidiary as a stand-

Figure 1.6 Strategic Alternatives in a Global Industry

Geographic Scope

	Global Strategy	Country-Centered Strategy
Many Segments	Global Cost Leadership or Differentiation	Protected Markets
Few Segments	Global Segmentation	National Responsiveness

Segment Scope

alone unit. In battling with global competitors, it may be appropriate in some countries to accept low profits indefinitely—in multidomestic competition this would be unjustified.[31] In global industries, the overall system matters as much or more than the country.

Overall International Strategy

The most basic question raised by the globalization of an industry is what overall international strategy a firm should adopt. In a global industry, a global strategy that captures the particular advantages of configuration/coordination present in that industry is necessary to attain a leading position. The firm must examine each activity in the value chain to see if there is a competitive advantage to concentrating and/or to coordinating the activity globally in various ways. However, many firms may not have the resources or initial position to pursue a global strategy, particularly domestic competitors. It is important, as a result, to explore strategic options short of a full-blown global strategy that may be present in global industries.

Abstracting from the particular configuration/coordination a firm adopts for competing internationally, there are four broad types of possible strategies in a global industry, illustrated schematically in Figure 1.6. Any strategy involves a choice of the type of competitive advantage sought (low cost or differentiation) and the competitive scope within which the advantage is to be achieved.[32] In global industries, competitive scope involves both the industry segments in which a firm competes and whether it seeks the benefits of configuration/

coordination across countries or chooses instead a country-centered approach to competing. These dimensions lead to four broad strategies, illustrated in Figure 1.6:

Global Cost Leadership or Differentiation: seeking the cost or differentiation advantages of global configuration/coordination through selling a wide line of products to buyers in all or most significant country markets. Global cost leaders (e.g., Toyota, Komatsu) tend to sell standardized products and reap scale advantages in technology development, procurement, and production. Global differentiators (e.g., IBM, Caterpillar) often use their scale and learning advantages to lower the cost of differentiating (e.g., offering many models and frequent model changes) and exploit their worldwide position to reinforce their brand reputation and/or product differentiation with multinational buyers.

Global Segmentation: serving a particular industry segment worldwide, such as Toyota in lift trucks and Mercedes in automobiles. A variant of this strategy is competing in a subset of countries where the advantages of concentration/coordination are particularly great. In some industries, global segmentation is the only feasible global strategy because the advantages of a global configuration/coordination exist only in particular segments (e.g., high-priced business hotels). A global strategy can make entirely new segmentations of an industry possible, because serving a segment worldwide overcomes scale thresholds that make serving the segment in one country impractical.

Global segmentation, which captures the advantages of a global strategy but marshalls resources by focusing on a narrow segment, is frequently a viable option for a smaller multinational or domestic competitor. The strategy has been quite common among multinationals from smaller countries such as Finland and Switzerland. It is also frequently the first step in a sequenced strategy to move from a domestic to a global strategy. In industries such as motorcycles, farm tractors, and TV sets, for example, initial beachheads were established by Japanese firms following global segmentation strategies focused on the smaller-sized end of the product line, later expanded into full-line positions.

Protected Markets: seeking out countries where market positions are protected by host governments. The protected markets strategy rests on government impediments to global competition such as high tariffs, stringent import quotas, and high local content requirements, which effectively isolate a country from the global industry. Protected markets strategies usually imply the need for *early* foreign direct investment in a country and can encompass only a subset of countries, because if government impediments were pervasive the industry would be multidomestic. They are generally most feasible in developing countries with protectionist industrial policies such as India,

Mexico, and Argentina, though developed countries such as France and Canada offer havens for protected markets strategies in selected industries.

National Responsiveness: focus on those industry segments most affected by local country differences though the industry as a whole is global. The firm aims to meet unusual local needs in products, channels, and marketing practices in each country, foregoing the competitive advantages of a global strategy. The national responsiveness strategy may imply that a firm compete only in those countries where segments with unusual needs are significant in size. The national responsiveness strategy is based on *economic* impediments to global configuration/coordination, while the protected markets strategy rests on government impediments. National responsiveness and protected markets can be pursued simultaneously if government protection only covers certain segments.

Protected markets or national responsiveness strategies rest on the costs of global configuration/coordination that remain even in industries that globalize. They rely on careful focus on certain segments/countries to hold off global competitors, and represent natural options for domestic firms without the resources to become international as well as multinationals who lack the resources or skills to concentrate/coordinate their activities worldwide. The sustainability of a national responsiveness strategy depends on continued national differences in some segments as well as the price differential between locally tailored and global varieties. If the extra cost to buy a better performing global variety is small or the price premium to buy a tailored local variety is too great, global competitors may overtake country-centered ones. Moreover, there is a tendency for global competitors to widen their product lines over time as they overcome market-specific barriers to entry in a country, even into segments that appear subject to local differences. In motorcycles, for example, global Japanese competitors eventually entered the large bike segment even though it is insignificant in size in Japan and many other countries. They employed shared dealer networks, brand names, and production facilities built up through competing in the global small bike segment.[33]

The sustainability of the protected markets strategy rests on continued government impediments to global competitors as well as the sanctity of a firm's favored status. Governments often invite additional competitors into their markets as the markets grow, however, and also escalate their demands on a firm once it has sunk investments in a country. Because protected markets strategies lack a competitive advantage in economic terms, their choice depends on a sophisticated prediction about future government behavior.

In many industries, two or more of the strategies can co-exist.[34] Segments with strong national differences and/or countries with high levels of protection lead to situations where there are global competitors, country-centered multinationals, and domestic firms all competing in the industry. Chapter 2 explores some of these possibilities through a formal model. Timing plays an important role in the industry structures observed. Early entry by a global competitor often retards the development of country-centered multinationals and domestic firms. Conversely, first-mover advantages garnered by country-centered or domestic firms can erect country-specific entry/mobility barriers that offset the advantages of a global competitor. The importance of timing suggests that multiple outcomes may be possible.

FUNCTIONAL IMPLICATIONS OF GLOBAL COMPETITION

Competing internationally with global strategy creates unique challenges for each functional area of a firm when compared to country-centered or domestic strategy. I will sketch some of the most important issues here that global strategy raises for each function, including marketing, production, technology development, finance, and government relations. In global industries, government relations take on particular importance for firm success. The chapters that follow in this book examine each functional area in more detail from the perspective of global strategy.

Production and Global Strategy

There are a number of important production issues in a global strategy. One is the configuration of the global production system (including procurement), which itself can be broken into two areas of inquiry. The first is which activities within production to concentrate and which to disperse. A highly concentrated configuration is one extreme, in which all activities occur at one location and finished goods are exported around the world for local distribution, sales, marketing, and service. This approach is characteristic of Japanese companies. A highly dispersed production configuration is the other extreme, characterized by concentrating only a few activities such as the fabrication of key components, with the balance of operations including design modifications, fabrication, and assembly carried out in each major country. The considerations that bear on the choice between concentrated and dispersed configurations have been described previously.

The second issue in global production system configuration has to do with the path along which goods flow internationally. Historically, global production has meant a production system in which components and/or end products moved from the home base to foreign countries (in what might be termed a "hub and spoke" configuration). More recently, an alternative configuration is being employed as well, which I term a "networked" configuration. In it, components and/or end products are transshipped among specialized and dispersed production facilities located in different countries. There are a number of alternative ways of networking. One is to network by stage of the process (e.g., component and assembly plants). A firm locates one or more efficient-scale component plants and one or more efficient-scale assembly facilities in different countries. Components are shipped to assembly plants and finished goods are shipped to markets (including countries with component plants). Another approach is to network based on product varieties. Items in the line are produced in different plants that become worldwide sources for that product variety, with plants often located in countries where the product variety is particularly demanded. A good example of this approach is Stihl's production configuration in chain saws, in which a U.S. plant produces small saws for the world while European plants produce larger saws. A final networking concept, open to diversified firms, is to group products with similar manufacturing technologies in plants located in various countries.

A networked production configuration is a means to reap scale and learning economies while at the same time overcoming high tariff and nontariff barriers. Networking also allows activities in the value chain to be located where there is comparative advantage. For example, labor-intensive assembly might be located in low-wage countries, while skill- and scale-sensitive component fabrication or testing is located where appropriate skilled labor and infrastructure are present. Finally, networking allows local content *as well as* export potential in many countries. The networked configuration implies that many countries have both imports and exports depending on how they fit into the overall system, and the exports may be used to offset import restrictions. IBM, for example, seeks to configure its worldwide production activities so as to achieve a balance of imports and exports in each country.

The appropriateness of the networked configuration depends on low to moderate transport costs in components or finished goods and on the willingness of local governments to credit exports against imports. Networking also requires extensive coordination and increases risks of supply. Frequently, supply risk is mitigated by establishing two production sites for each component/product variety. Modern telecommunications and information systems along with lighter, more compact products are making networked configurations more feasible.

Configuration is only the first and in some ways the easiest issue in global production management. The second issue is the need for ongoing coordination of the global production system, involving such areas as scheduling, technical, and process coordination. Coordination is necessary to reap the advantages of worldwide production, but is made difficult by geographic distance, language differences, cultural differences, and so on. Another issue for production in a global strategy is the improvement and diffusion of the production process to multiple locations, an issue that also relates closely to the R & D function. Chapter 3 addresses these issues in some detail.

Marketing and Global Strategy

Many marketing activities are inherently tied to buyer location. However, there are opportunities in many industries for global coordination in marketing, in areas such as brand name, sales force, service network, and pricing. The product development function in global industries is particularly complex, because it requires the collection and coordination of information from around the world. This makes an already difficult coordination task between marketing and R & D even more difficult in global strategies.

These unique marketing issues in a global industry do not replace marketing's normal functions, but overlay them. Marketing must still understand local buyer needs, marketing systems, media, and so on, in not just one country but in many countries. As a result, marketing has perhaps the most acute need to both contribute to global coordination *and* respond to local market conditions. The role of marketing in global strategy is discussed in chapter 4.

Technology Development and Global Strategy

There is a technological dimension to competition in most global industries, which places demands on the technology development function. One increasingly complex issue is where R & D should take place. There is a body of literature that suggests broadly that R & D should take place in proximity to large (or potentially large) markets, and in proximity to "advanced" or sophisticated markets representing the cutting edge of industry development.[35] The global competitor has the option of performing technology development anywhere. Increasingly, the best place to do R & D is not necessarily the United States or advanced European countries, and the best place may differ for subtasks within the R & D function and for different products in the line. In copiers, for example, Xerox does research on small copiers in Japan, on medium-volume copiers in Europe, and on high-volume copiers in the United States. While this allocation may reflect the fact that Xerox has coalition partners overseas, it does appear that Japan is the most advanced market for low-volume copiers and the United States is the most advanced market for high-volume copiers. Similarly, a number of Japanese firms do R & D for medical products and semiconductors in the United States. Ronstadt's (1978) work has indicated that there are organizational pressures to enlarge foreign R & D activities once established and to direct them toward indigenous needs. Such pressures are typical of those in other activities and a global firm must organize to minimize them.

There are also many coordination issues involving technology development in global strategy. R & D must play its role in product development for worldwide markets, which requires that the R & D function have an unusual knowledge of technical issues and buyer needs globally. Similarly, process R & D is often crucial in global industries to facilitate the development of global-scale economies and learning to achieve consistent quality. Not only must R & D develop new products and processes, but new process technology must often be transferred to facilities around the world that operate under different economic and cultural circumstances. Sharing "best demonstrated practice" among facilities can be one of the major benefits of global coordination. Some considerations in coordinating technology development are discussed in chapter 3, while developing products for worldwide markets is discussed in chapter 4.

Finance and Global Strategy

Competing on a coordinated worldwide basis raises a variety of finance issues. The first is how to exploit a global presence in order to lower the overall cost of capital. Increasingly, global firms are raising capital in many countries. Other important issues in global strategy are the management of foreign exchange position and the related question of minimizing taxes. Tax regimes differ around the world, affecting global system configuration. Another way to affect the cost of capital is to take advantage of government financial incentives, prevalent in many global industries. How should a firm evaluate various types of financial incentives, and determine whether they contribute to global coordination or cause difficulties in doing so? Chapter 6 addresses the cost of capital differences among countries and the role of government incentives in some detail.

A global competitor typically has flows of products, components, and raw materials around the world and investments in facilities and working capital in many currencies. This creates more complex foreign exchange issues than for the firm that operates self-contained subsidiaries in many countries. A related question is the measurement of performance of individual plants or country operations in a global strategy. Global strategy implies linked investments rather than stand-alone ones, and the whole evaluation question is complicated by exchange rates. Firms often confuse nominal performance with true performance. The problems of exchange rate exposure and performance measurement in global competition are discussed in chapter 5.

Government Relations and Global Strategy

Because government can be both an obstacle and a benefactor to the global firm, the relationship between a firm and government takes on special importance in global strategy. An international competitor with a country-centered strategy must also deal with government, but the absence of global configuration/coordination simplifies the task. A country-centered competitor can view government relations in each country largely on a stand-alone basis, while a global competitor must respond to government requirements at the least possible compromise to its global strategy and entice government to enhance its global strategy rather than merely act as a force for dispersing more and more activities to the country.

Dealing with governments in a globally coordinated way is a skill just being developed in many companies. A firm must understand the significance of various government policy instruments for its ability to configure/coordinate, and the factors that will shape its long-term bargaining position with government. As governments get more sophisticated, the challenge facing firms becomes greater. Chapter 7 presents an overall perspective of the government-firm relationship in global industries. Chapter 8 addresses the bargaining with government over financial incentives and local requirements, while chapter 9 treats the organization of the government relations function in a global company.

Coalitions and Global Strategy

A coalition is a long-term agreement linking firms but falling short of merger. I use the term coalition to encompass a whole variety of arrangements that include joint ventures, licenses, supply agreements, and other kinds of interfirm relationships. International coalitions, linking firms in the same industry based in different countries, have become an important part of international strategy in the past decade.

International coalitions are a way of configuring activities in the value chain on a worldwide basis jointly with a partner. International coalitions are present in many industries, and are particularly common in automobiles, aircraft, aircraft engines, robotics, consumer electronics, semiconductors, and pharmaceuticals. While international coalitions have long been present, their character has been changing. Historically, firms from developed countries formed coalitions with firms in lesser-developed countries to perform marketing activities there. Today, we observe more and more coalitions in which two firms from developed countries are teaming up to serve the world, as well as coalitions that extend beyond marketing activities to encompass activities throughout the value chain and multiple activities.[36] Production and R & D coalitions are very common, for example.

Chapter 10 describes the strategic logic of coalitions and the choice of coalition partners, while chapter 11 presents evidence on the incidence of coalitions involving U.S. companies.

Organization and Global Strategy

The need to configure and coordinate globally in complex ways creates some obvious organizational challenges. Any organizational structure for competing internationally has to balance two dimensions: a country dimension, because some activities are inherently performed in the country; and a global dimension, because the advantage of global configuration/coordination must be achieved. In a global industry, the ultimate authority must represent the global dimension if a global strategy is to prevail. However, there are strong pressures within any international firm to disperse more activities once it disperses any. Moreover, forces are unleashed that lead subsidiaries to seek growing autonomy.

Chapter 12 describes the organizational challenges of managing a global strategy and some of the solutions. It stresses the need to go beyond purely structural solutions and modify the systems and management functions that may have become deeply embedded in historical modes of international strategy. Chapter 3 discusses the mechanisms for facilitating international coordination in operations and technology development. Flaherty stresses the importance of information systems and the many dimensions that valuable coordination can take.

THE FUTURE OF INTERNATIONAL COMPETITION

Since the late 1970s, there have been some gradual but significant changes in the pattern of international competition that carry important implications for international strategy. Foreign direct investment has been growing more rapidly and flowing in new directions, while growth in trade has slowed. For data on U. foreign investment, see chapter 14. This book's framework provides a template with which I can examine these changes and probe their significance. The factors shaping the global configuration of activities by firms are developing in ways that contrast with the trends of the previous thirty-years.

Homogenization of product needs among countries appears to be continuing, though segmentation within countries is as well. As a result, consumer packaged goods are becoming increasingly prone toward globalization, though they have long been characterized by multidomestic competition. There are also signs of globalization in some service industries as the introduction of information technology creates scale economies in support activities and facilitate coordination in primary activities. Global service firms are reaping advantages in hardware and software development as well as in procurement.

In many industries, however, limits have been reached in this scale economies that have been driving the concentration of activities. These limits grow out of classic diseconomies of scale that arise in very large facilities, as well as new, more flexible technology in manufacturing and other activities that is often not as scale sensitive as previous methods. At the same time, though, flexible manufacturing allows the production of multiple varieties (to serve different countries) in a single plant. This may encourage new movement toward globalization in industries in which product differences among countries have remained significant and have blocked globalization in the past. Another important change is the declining labor content in many industries due to automation of the value chain, which is reducing the incentive to locate activities in low-wage countries such as South Korea and Singapore.

There also appear to be some limits to further decline in transport costs, as innovations such as containerization, bulk ships, and larger aircraft have largely run their course. However, a parallel trend toward smaller, lighter products and components may keep some downward pressure on transport costs. The biggest change in the benefits and costs of concentrated configuration has been the sharp rise in protectionism in recent years and the resulting rise in nontariff barriers akin to the 1920s. As a group, these factors point to less need and less opportunity for highly concentrated configurations of activities and explain why growth in direct investment has been outpacing growth in trade. Falling labor content also suggests that more foreign investment will flow to developed countries (to secure market access) instead of low-wage countries.

When the coordination dimension is examined, the picture looks quite different. Communication and coordination costs are dropping sharply, driven by breathtaking advances in information systems and telecommunication technology. We have just seen the beginning of developments in this area, which are spreading throughout the value chain.[37] Boeing, for example, is employing computer-aided design technology to jointly design components on-line with foreign suppliers. Engineers in different countries are communicating via computer screens. Marketing systems and business practices continue to homogenize, facilitating the coordination of activities in different countries. The mobility of buyers and information is also growing rapidly, greasing the international spread of brand reputations and enhancing the importance of consistency in the way activities are performed worldwide. Increasing numbers of multinational and global firms are begetting globalization by their suppliers. There is also a sharp rise in the computerization of manufacturing as well as other activities throughout the value chain, which greatly facilitates coordination among dispersed sites.

The imperative of global strategy is shifting, then, in ways that will require a rebalancing of configuration and coordination. Concentrating activities is less necessary in economic terms, and less possible as governments force more dispersion. These forces are pushing firms to intermediate positions on the configuration axis as shown in Figure 1.7. At the same time, the ability to coordinate globally throughout

Figure 1.7 Future Trends in International Competition

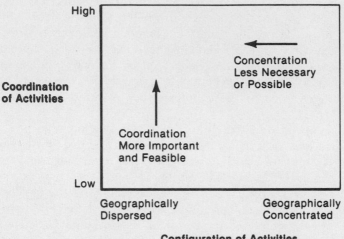

Configuration of Activities

the value chain is increasing dramatically through modern technology. The need to coordinate is also rising to offset greater dispersion and to respond to buyer needs. Moreover, intermediate configurations often require greater coordination, and coordination can neutralize some of the costs of dispersion forced on firms by governments. These considerations imply an upward movement in Figure 1.7. Thus, simpler first generation global strategies (e.g., concentration and export) seem to be giving way to more complex global strategies involving multiple though coordinated R & D activities, sophisticated networking of overseas plants, worldwide procurement, and so on.

Thus, today's game of global strategy seems increasingly to be a game of coordination—getting dispersed production facilities, R & D laboratories, and marketing activities to truly work together. Widespread coordination remains the exception rather than the rule today in many multinationals. Successful international competitors in the future will be those who can seek out competitive advantages from global configuration/coordination anywhere in the value chain, and overcome the organizational barriers to exploiting them.

NOTES

1. Intra-industry trade, where a country both exports and imports goods in the same industry, has grown markedly as well. The reasons will be made clear by the framework below.
2. United Nations Center on Transnational Corporations (1984).
3. For a survey, see Caves and Jones (1985).
4. See, particularly, the work of Hymer, Kindleberger, and Caves. There are many books on the theory and management of the multinational,

which are too numerous to cite here. For an excellent survey of the literature, see Caves (1982). A more recent stream of literature emphasizes how the multinational firm internalizes transactions to circumvent imperfections in various intermediate markets, most importantly the market for knowledge. Prominent examples of this work are Buckley and Casson (1976) and Teece (1981). For a survey and extension, see Teece (1985).

5. Knickerbocker's (1973) work on oligopolistic reaction adds an important dimension to the process of entering foreign markets through illuminating bunching in the timing of entry into a country by firms in an industry and relating this to defensive considerations. Vernon's product cycle of international trade combines a view of how products mature with the evolution in a firm's international activities to predict the patterns of trade and investment in developed and developing countries (Vernon 1966). Vernon himself, among others, has raised questions about how general the product cycle pattern is today.

6. There are some notable exceptions to the general paucity of thinking on the strategy of established multinationals. See, for example, Stopford and Wells (1972), Franko (1976), Stobaugh et al. (1976).

7. Porter (1980, 1985a).

8. The distinction between multidomestic and global competition and some of its strategic implications were first described in Hout, Porter, and Rudden (1982).

9. Perlmutter's (1969) concept of ethnocentric, polycentric, and geocentric multinationals is an interesting but different one. It takes the firm, not the industry, as the unit of analysis and is decoupled from industry structure. It focuses on management attitudes, the nationality of executives, and other aspects of organization. Perlmutter presents ethnocentric, polycentric, and geocentric as stages of an organization's development as a multinational, with geocentric as the goal. A later paper (Wind, Douglas, and Perlmutter 1973) tempers this conclusion based on the fact that some companies may not have the required sophistication in marketing to attempt a geocentric strategy. Products embedded in the lifestyle or culture of a country are also identified as less susceptible to geocentrism. The Perlmutter et al. view does not attempt to link management orientation to industry structure and strategy. International strategy should grow out of the net competitive advantage in a global industry of different types of worldwide coordination. In some industries, a country-centered strategy, roughly analogous to Perlmutter's polycentric idea, may be the best strategy irrespective of company size and international experience. Conversely, a global strategy may be imperative given the competitive advantage that accrues from it. Industry and strategy should define the organization approach, not vice versa.

10. Porter (1985a) describes value chain theory and its use in analyzing competitive advantage.

11. There is a growing globalization of service firm strategies, however, as service firms serve multinational buyers. Developments in information technology raise the importance of R & D, and automation pervades the primary activities of service firms. Service firms tend to draw advantages from a global strategy largely in the support activities in the value chain.

12. Buzzell (1968), Pryor (1965), and Wind, Douglas, and Perlmutter (1973) point out that national differences are in most cases more critical with respect to marketing than with production and finance. This generalization reflects the fact that marketing activities are often inherently country based. However, this generalization is not reliable because in many countries, production and other activities are widely dispersed.

13. In practice, a diagram such as Table 1.1 would involve each important discrete activity (not broad categories) and include all the countries in which a firm operates.

14. M. Therese Flaherty provided helpful comments that clarified the configuration/coordination distinction.

15. Here, the firm makes only a one-time transfer of knowledge in establishing each subsidiary, which gives it an advantage over local firms. Transaction costs dictate the multinational form rather than market transactions.

16. Strategic groups are described in Porter (1980), chapter 7.

17. For example, governments may desire national autonomy in decision making and the spillovers from domestic R & D and training of skilled workers.

18. A number of authors have framed the globalization of industries in terms of the balance between imperatives for global integration and imperatives for national responsiveness, a useful distinction. See Prahalad (1975), Doz (1976), and Bartlett (1979). I relate that distinction here to more basic issues of where and how a firm performs the activities in the value chain internationally.

19. Transactional failures make coordination between independent firms or coalition partners even more difficult than the initial transfer of knowledge in establishing a foreign subsidiary, not to mention ongoing coordination among subsidiaries.

20. Bartlett's chapter in this book provides a sophisticated treatment of the organizational issues in geographic coordination. The difficulties in coordinating across business units competing in different industries within the diversified firm as described in Porter (1985a), chapter 11.

21. For a discussion, see Porter (1985a), chapter 9.

22. Empirical research has found a strong correlation between R & D and advertising intensity and the extent of foreign direct investment (for a survey, see Caves 1982). Both these factors have a place in our model of the determinants of globalization, but for quite different reasons. R & D intensity suggests scale advantages for the global competitor in developing products or processes that are manufactured abroad either due to low production scale economies or government pressures, or that require investments in service infrastructure. Advertising intensity, however, is much closer to proxying the possibilities for the classic transfer of marketing knowledge to foreign subsidiaries. High advertising industries are also frequently those where local tastes differ and manufacturing scale economies are modest, both reasons to disperse many activities.

23. This description draws on a study of the incidence of multinationals in the hotel industry by Dunnina and McQueen (1981).

24. There is an analogy here between the Lawrence and Lorsch (1967) idea that differentiation of functions within a firm along with providing effective integration improves performance, a point suggested by M. Therese Flaherty.

25. It has been recognized that comparative advantage in different stages in a vertically integrated industry sector such as aluminum can reside in different countries. Bauxite mining will take place in resource-rich countries, for example, while smelting will take place in countries with low electrical power cost (see Caves and Jones 1985, p. 142). The argument here extends this thinking *within* the value chain of any stage, and suggests that the optimal location for performing individual activities may vary as well.

26. See Porter (1985b). The issues in this section are the subject of a major current research project involving nine countries.

27. See Linder (1961), Vernon (1966), and Gruber, Mehta, and Vernon (1967).
28. Where it does recognize scale economies, trade theory views them narrowly as arising from production in one country.
29. Levitt's (1983) article provides a supporting view. See also chapter 4.
30. Japan's limited prewar international sales were handled largely through trading companies. See Chandler, chapter 13. Trading companies still handled a good portion of Japanese exports in the 1970s but have become less important in newer and high-technology industries.
31. For a discussion, see Hunt, Porter, and Rudden (1982). For a recent treatment, see Hamel and Prahalad (1985).
32. For a discussion, see Porter (1985a), chapters 1 and 2.
33. A key consideration in the sustainability of national responsiveness strategies is the ability of broad-line competitors to share activities among segments. See Porter (1985a), chapter 7, for a generic treatment.
34. Mixed strategies are also observed in which a firm employs a global strategy in one group of countries and country-centered strategies in others. In the sewing machine industry, for example, otherwise global competitions product pedal-powered sewing machines that meet local needs in developing countries with high levels of protection.
35. See, for example, Hirsch (1970) and Ronstadt (1978).
36. Hladik's recent study of international joint ventures provides supporting evidence; see Hladik (1984).
37. For a discussion, see Porter and Millar (1985).

REFERENCES

Bartlett, C. A. "Multinational Structural Evolution: The Changing Decision Environment in the International Division." D.B.A. diss., Harvard Graduate School of Business Administration, 1979.

Buckley, P. J., and M. C. Casson. *The Future of the Multinational Enterprise*. London: Holms and Meier, 1976.

Buzzell, R. D. "Can You Standardize Multinational Marketing?" *Harvard Business Review* (November/December 1968): 102–13.

Casson, M. C. "Transaction Costs and the Theory of the Multinational Enterprise," in A. Rugman, ed., *New Theories of the Multinational Enterprise*. London: Croom Helm, 1982.

Caves, R. E. *Multinational Enterprise and Economic Analysis*. Cambridge, England: Cambridge University Press, 1982.

Caves, R. E., and R. W. Jones. *World Trade and Payments*, fourth edition. Boston: Little, Brown, 1985.

Doz, Y. "National Policies and Multinational Management." D.B.A. diss., Harvard Graduate School of Business Administration, 1976.

Dunning, J., and M. McQueen. "The Eclectic Theory of International Production: A Case Study of the International Hotel Industry." *Managerial and Decision Economics* 2 (December 1981): 197–210.

Franko, L. G. *The European Multinationals: A Renewed Challenge to American and British Big Business*. Stanford, Conn.: Greylock, 1976.

Knickerbocker, F. *Oligopolistic Reaction and Multinational Enterprise*. Cambridge, Mass.: Harvard University Press, 1973.

Gruber, W., D. Mehta, and R. Vernon. "The R & D Factor in International Trade and Investment of United States Industries." *Journal of Political Economy* (February 1967): 20–37.

Hamel, G., and C. K. Prahalad. "Do You Really Have a Global Strategy?" *Harvard Business Review* (July/August 1985): 139–48.

Hirsch, S. "Technological Factors in the Composition and Direction of Israel's Industrial Exports," in Vernon, R., ed., *Technological Factors in International Trade*. New York: National Bureau of Economic Research, 1970, 365–408.

Hladik, K. "International Joint Ventures: An Empirical Investigation into the Characteristics of Recent U.S.-Foreign Joint Venture Partnerships." Ph.D. diss., Business Economics Program, Harvard University, 1984.

Hout, T., M. E. Porter, and E. Rudden. "How Global Companies Win Out." *Harvard Business Review* (September/October 1982): 98–108.

Lawrence, P. R., and J. W. Lorsch. *Organization and Environment*. Boston: Division of Research, Harvard Graduate School of Business Administration, 1967.

Levitt, T. "The Globalization of Markets." *Harvard Business Review* (May/June 1983): 92–102.

Linder, S. *An Essay on Trade and Transformation*. New York: John Wiley, 1961.

Perlmutter, H. V. "The Tortuous Evolution of the Multinational Corporation." *Columbia Journal of World Business* (January/February 1969): 9–18.

Porter, M. E. *Competitive Strategy: Techniques for Analyzing Industries and Competitors*. New York: Free Press, 1980.

———. *Competitive Advantage: Creating and Sustaining Superior Performance*. New York: Free Press, 1985a.

———. "Beyond Comparative Advantage." Working Paper, Harvard Graduate School of Business Administration, August 1985b.

Porter, M. E., and V. Millar, "How Information Gives You Competitive Advantage." *Harvard Business Review* (July/August 1985): 149–60.

Prahalad, C. K. "The Strategic Process in a Multinational Corporation." D.B.A. diss., Harvard Graduate School of Business Administration, 1975.

Pryor, M. H. "Planning in a World-Wide Business." *Harvard Business Review* 43 (January/February 1965): 130–9.

Ronstadt, R. C. "International R&D: The Establishment and Evolution of Research and Development Abroad by Seven U.S. Multinationals." *Journal of International Business Studies* (Spring/Summer 1978): 7–23.

Stobaugh, R. B., et al. "Nine Investments Abroad and Their Impact at Home: Case Studies on Multinational Enterprise and the U.S. Economy." Boston: Division of Research, Harvard Business School, 1976.

Stopford, J. J., and L. T. Wells, Jr. *Managing the Multinational Enterprise: Organization of the Firm and Overlap of Subsidiaries*. New York: Basic Books, 1972.

Teece, D. J. "Multinational Enterprise: Market Failure and Market Power Considerations." *Sloan Management Review* 22, no. 3 (September 1981): 3–17.

———. "Transaction Cost Economics and the Multinational Enterprise: An Assessment." Working Paper IB-3, Business School, University of California at Berkeley, January 1985.

United Nations Center on Transnational Corporations, *Salient Features and Trends in Foreign Direct Investment*, United Nations, New York, 1984.

Vernon, R. "International Investment and International Trade in the Product Cycle." *Quarterly Journal of Economics* 80 (May 1966): 190–207.

Williamson, O. *Markets and Hierarchies*. New York: Free Press, 1975.

Wind, Y., S. P. Douglas, and H. B. Perlmutter. "Guidelines for Developing International Marketing Strategies." *Journal of Marketing* 37 (April 1973): 14–23.

2

Modeling Global Competition*

Pankaj Ghemawat
and
A. Michael Spence

INTRODUCTION

Our chapter resembles others in this book in that it compares global and country-centered strategies at the level of the individual industry. Unlike the others, however, we use a limited number of assumptions to deduce the way in which industry economics affect the relative viability of global and country-centered modes of competition.

Specifically, we focus on the interplay between drivers of and impediments to global coordination.[1] It is this interplay that complicates the choice between global and country-centered strategies; without the tug of opposed forces, the right choice would be obvious (and academic analysis dispensable). We invoke a particular mathematical form for this interplay and compute the "equilibrium." By equilibrium, we mean the set of country markets that global competitors will capture if every competitor, global or country-centered, independently tries to maximize its own profits. That set of countries turns out to be a general one; although we specify which economic parameters matter, we are not forced to fix the values that they can take.

Two objections may occur to our readers. First, isn't the imputation of rationality to all competitors psychologically and organizationally unrealistic? We do not regard this objection as a serious one. To quote a mathematician, "Experience shows [that] even though people do not always act very rationally...rational behavior is sufficiently common so as to make it imperative for all of us to understand

*Without implicating them in the views that we express, we would like to thank Richard E. Caves, M. Therese Flaherty, and Michael E. Porter for their comments on earlier drafts of this chapter.

what strategies are open to a rational opponent, and so as to make it extremely dangerous to underestimate an opponent's ability to act rationally" (Harsanyi 1982, p. 125). In other words, its prevalence and its normative content infuse rationality with interest. Even when rationality and reality diverge, rationality remains a useful benchmark for much the same reason that accountants compare actual costs with standard ones in order to understand cost behavior.

We are more sympathetic to the second potential objection: don't the other simplifying assumptions of our model sweep too much under the rug? Perhaps so. However, we should explain that we faced a choice between amassing detail in a model that would, at best, yield fragmentary insights *or* sticking to the essentials and searching for general patterns. The comparative advantage of mathematical models lies in the second, more abstractive approach.

That last avowal is fairly bald; it can be strengthened by comparing our model to a map. Very few maps are full-scale replicas of what they purport to describe. Instead, they usually condense some information and leave out the rest. A good map is one whose usefulness is not critically affected by this loss of detail. The test of usefulness is qualitative, but not entirely arbitrary; for instance, most map makers concur in leaving minor traffic arteries out of their highway maps.

What qualitative factors can we cite in favor of our highly selective model? First, as we have already discussed, rational, normative models are valuable even in settings where it is unreasonable to suppose total rationality. Closely allied to this point is the fact that rationality is a simple yet very powerful basis for deduction. As a result, the model pushes farther than sheer intuition would easily allow and sometimes yields "surprising" conclusions.

Second, many past researchers have framed their inquiries too narrowly by asking whether global competition or country-centered competition is going to "win out" in a particular setting. With a few exceptions (such as large commercial aircraft—see chapter 16) most of the industries that we call global are actually populated by a mixture of global and country-centered competitors. That our model allows and explicitly focuses on such intermediate outcomes should count as a strength.

We have already alluded to the model's third advantage: it systematically predicts the degree of globalization across a whole spectrum of industry economics. Case studies or simulations, by contrast, can be thought of as samples from individual points on that spectrum. Each approach has its distinct merits; systematic predictions will probably prove more important in any *synthesis* of knowledge about global competition.

Finally, the model encompasses customers' preferences as well as firms' economics. This lets us track worldwide welfare and assess whether market processes lead to too much or too little globalization according to that criterion. From the standpoint of national welfare, we can also establish some norms for governmental policies toward global industries.

We should remark that our analytic apparatus is borrowed from applied microeconomics.[2] The equations, terminology, and general methods of this chapter may impose some extra demands on readers unfamiliar with that discipline. We have, however, striven to avoid unintelligibility.

THE ANALYTIC APPARATUS

International integration of some value activities is the essence of global competition. The competitive advantages of international integration necessarily rest on economies of coordination that spill over national borders. Chapter 1 enumerates such economies; which ones, in practice, tend to be the most significant? A rather well-developed body of research on multinational enterprises is the best source of revealing clues; principally, it points a finger at intangible assets such as technological know-how, marketing expertise, and managerial skills that, once developed, can be put to work in extra countries at little incremental cost (Caves 1982, chap. 1). Intangible assets are a manifestation of economies of global scale; other plausible ones include bulk purchasing (to reduce procurement costs) and the achievement of efficient scales of production. For a more detailed discussion and arresting examples, see Flaherty, chapter 3. Therefore, economies of global scale seem a pervasive enough part of globalization to warrant our focus on them.

But the storyline cannot end there; if it did, it would predict total globalization of all industries even *tinged* with such economies. For counterpoise, we need impediments that can potentially block the forces driving toward globalization.

We return to Porter's list of impediments to global coordination in chapter 1: heterogeneous local conditions and needs, lead times, governmental policy, transactional costs, and organizational complexity. The first three impediments all pertain to the differences among countries; as an approximation we can think of them as factors that depress the average net revenue (or effective price) of global products relative to country-centered ones that have been tailored to a particular market. This is how we will model impediments to globalization.

This gives us the bones of a complete model: global competitors try to exploit the similarities across countries, while country-centered producers tend to be more responsive to the differences among them.[3] The schema now needs to be fleshed out with specific assumptions and some notation.

Suppose that there are n homogeneous customer segments in the world. For simplicity, assume a one-to-one match between customer segments and countries such that all N_i customers in country i share common preferences with each other but not with customers in any other country.[4] Demand is taken to be price-inelastic: each customer buys one unit of either the global product or the relevant country-centered one. Denote the gross benefit (i.e., the value of the product, gross of the price paid for it) that a representative customer in country i derives from the global product as u_i. We let the gross benefit to the same customer from the relevant country-centered product be $u_i + h_i$. The value of h_i is set to be greater than or equal to zero; it then captures the impediments to globalization that we discussed earlier. For expository purposes, we will refer to h_i as the country-tailoring premium.

Rational choice implies that customers in country i will purchase the country-centered product in preference to the global product if and only if

$$p_i < p_G + h_i , \tag{1}$$

where p_i is the price of the country-centered product and p_G that of the global product.

That completes the demand side of the model. On the supply side, we assume that there is, potentially, a different country-centered competitor in each country and that because it has chosen to tailor its product, it cannot serve countries other than the one it has targeted.[5] Therefore, if a country-centered producer were to supply country i, its total costs would be

$$C_i = F_i + c_i N_i , \tag{2}$$

where F_i is the country-centered producer's fixed cost and c_i its constant marginal cost.

There is just one global producer; in line with the earlier discussion of economies of global scale, its costs are assumed to behave somewhat differently. Let K be the set of countries that the global producer elects to supply, totally displacing the local country-centered producers. Then its total costs are

$$C_G = F_G + c_G\left(\sum_{k \in K} N_k\right) \tag{3}$$

where F_G denotes its fixed cost and c_G its marginal cost. The term within parentheses stands for the total number of customers in countries within the set K.

Finally, two behavioral assumptions are needed. First, the global competitor is not allowed to charge different prices for the same product in different countries. This can be interpreted as a consequence of antidumping legislation as well as of the typically low transshipment costs of successful global products. Second, the global producer acts as the industry price leader. For any given price that it announces, country-centered producers try to meet condition (1) without dipping into the red. Those that cannot make even zero economic profits drop out, abandoning their countries to the global product.[6]

Given these assumptions, the minimal price that the country-centered competitor in country i can charge without losing money is $F_i / N_i + c_i$. Its product will be demanded at this price only if

$$p_G > \frac{F_i}{N_i} + c_i - h_i .\qquad(4)$$

The right-hand side of inequality (4) is the average cost of the country-centered producer if it supplies its entire national market, minus the tailoring premium that it enjoys. For any particular p_G, the inequality is likely to be violated if the term on the right-hand side is large. Therefore, for each country i, we can define a "globalization index" of the form

$$G_i \equiv \frac{F_i}{N_i} + c_i - h_i .\qquad(5)$$

If the global producer charges a price less than or equal to G_i, the country-centered producer in country i will drop out. Consequently, if country j has a higher globalization index than country k, then country-centered production is less likely to prove viable in j than in k. If country-centered producers do survive in both countries, the one in country j will post a lower return on sales.

Examination of equation (5) confirms that country-centered producers are more likely to survive (and to earn high margins) in large countries with exotic tastes that can be satisfied relatively cheaply. In contrast, small countries whose tastes are relatively "metropolitan" yet expensive to satisfy will tend to purchase the global product.[7]

CALCULATING THE EQUILIBRIUM

In the last section, we identified tendencies but did not spell out what would actually happen. To calculate the equilibrium, we must figure out the level at which the global producer will optimally set its price, p_G.

The analysis can be simplified if, without loss of generality, we rearrange all n countries in *decreasing* order of their globalization indices. This convention, which will be used throughout the rest of this paper, ensures that

$$G_i \geq G_j \text{ if } i < j.\qquad(6)$$

As a result, if the global producer serves any countries at all, it will serve a continuous band of them with (reshuffled) indices ranging from 1 to an arbitrary k. This is useful because it tells us that out of the 2^n distinct sets of countries that the global producer might conceivably elect to serve, we have only to look at $n + 1$ sets to find the equilibrium outcome, that is, the set that maximizes the global producer's profits. With a total of ten countries, for example, this method reduces the number of sets that have to be scanned by 99 percent.

The globalization index approach can carry us somewhat farther. Let k be the marginal country (the country with the lowest globalization index) that the global producer serves at the equilibrium. In this case, it will set p_G equal to G_k. Pricing lower would serve no purpose because demand in countries k through n is price-inelastic and, by assumption, the global producer does not intend to supply country $k + 1$. Therefore, if the marginal country served is k, the global producer's total profits are

$$PR_G(k) = \left[G_k - \frac{F_G}{\sum\limits_{i=1}^{k} N_i} - c_G \right] \sum\limits_{i=1}^{k} N_i \qquad (7)$$

The term within brackets is the global producer's average profit per unit sold; the second term its total unit sales.

The global producer will choose the value k^* from the set $(1, 2, \ldots, n)$ that maximizes the expression in equation (7). If the maximized value, $PR_G(k^*)$, is greater than zero, the global producer will serve countries 1 through k^*. If the maximized value is less than zero, it will shut down and abandon all the markets to country-centered producers.

Although the number k^* can be calculated by plugging in specific values for the parameters, we cannot characterize it generally. The reason: we have to compare all feasible values of $PR_G(k)$ because the magnitude of $G_{k-1} - G_k$ does not disclose anything about the magnitude of $G_k - G_{k-1}$. In other words, the discreteness of countries allows jumps that make it impossible to use the methods of differential calculus.

To make further headway, the rest of this chapter adopts a "smoothed-out" model that approximates the structure we dealt with above. Array all countries, as before, in decreasing order of their globalization indices. For notational simplicity, posit that this establishes a one-to-one match between indices and countries, so that no two countries share the same index. If individual countries are small in relation to the global system then, as a mathematical idealization, we can view them as forming a continuum.[8] The globalization index, $G(s)$, is now defined over all real numbers, s, in the interval $[0, n]$. Make the additional assumption that $G(s)$ is a differentiable function of s, that is, that

Figure 2.1 The Global Producer's Choice

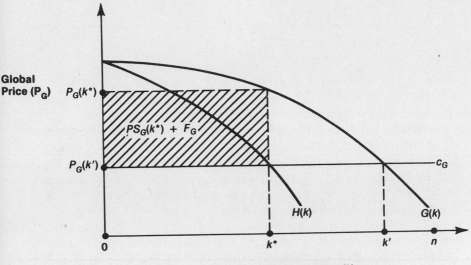

the continuum of globalization indices varies smoothly. This assumption will usually ensure that the components of $G(s)$, relabeled $F(s)$, $N(s)$, $c(s)$, and $h(s)$ are also differentiable.

The global producer's objective, depicted in Figure 2.1, is to pick k so as to maximize

$$PR_G(k) = \int_0^k [G(k) - c_G] \, N(s)ds - F_G.^9 \tag{8}$$

Two boundary solutions to the problem are theoretically possible. Subject to the constraint that its profits must be nonnegative, the global producer's optimal choice of k might turn out to be either 0 or n. These extreme cases are not particularly interesting, apart from the observation that *only* a boundary solution is possible if the $G(s)$ curve is flat. In other words, if countries' globalization indices are sufficiently alike, they will be subject to a "domino effect": either the global producer or the country-centered producers will win out across the board.

In order to guarantee interior solutions (equilibria in which global production coexists with some country-centered production), we need to impose some further restrictions. We will assume that $G(s)$ is concave (shaped like an overturned bowl) and that while $G(0)$ is sufficiently greater than c_G to allow *some* profitable global production, $G(n)$ is less than c_G.[10] Figure 2.1 anticipated these assumptions.

There will now be a unique solution to the global producer's maximization problem. Differentiation of equation (8) shows that it will satisfy the following first-order condition:

$$H(k^*) \equiv G(k^*) + \frac{G'(k^*)\int_0^{k^*} N(s)ds}{N(k^*)} = c_G, \tag{9}$$

where $G'(k^*)$ denotes the slope of the $G(k)$ curve at k^*. In words, the global producer will push its output up to the point where marginal revenue $[H(k)]$ equals marginal cost (c_G).

Because $G(k)$ decreases as k increases, $G'(k)$ is negative. Equation (9) then implies that the equilibrium price of the global product, $G(k^*)$, is greater than its marginal cost, c_G. Equivalently, from the standpoint of worldwide welfare, the global product is undersupplied at the equilibrium because it is not sold to some of the customers who would be willing to pay its marginal cost.

This undersupply is partly accounted for by the fact that our model lets one producer monopolize the market for the global good.[11] Because the global producer cannot price-discriminate, it avoids countries with globalization indices in the interval $[G(k^*),c_G]$: the price cuts needed to penetrate them would spread to the countries that it already supplies, hurting profitability. But that is not the only reason; the next section demonstrates that even with intensified competition to supply the global variety, a bias toward its undersupply will persist.

THE IMPACT OF COMPETITION ON GLOBALIZATION

As remarked in footnote 12, increased competition to supply a particular country-centered product fails to affect the degree of globalization. What happens when we increase the number of potential global producers?

If competition in the global segment is overhung by the threat of easy entry (because of low-entry barriers), then for any particular values of the parameters, the fixed cost, F_G, will impose a ceiling on the number of global producers that can profitably stay active. Call this number m. As the number of actual global competitors increases from 1 to m, the output of the global product will increase monotonically toward the level k' at which

$$G(k') = c_G. \tag{10}$$ [12]

Note that in terms of worldwide welfare, k' is the ideal level of supply of the global product because it would then have to be priced at marginal cost.

However, for any finite m, the left-hand side of equation (10) will continue to exceed the right-hand side. As a result, even though intensified competition to supply the global product *will* increase the degree of globalization, it will never quite redress the bias toward undersupply. Although both global producers and country-centered producers incur fixed costs, it is the fixed cost of global production (F_G) that causes a problem; that cost can (and should) be spread over a broader range of countries than market processes will permit.

For the rest of this chapter, we revert to the assumption that there is only one global competitor. This should not be too bothersome because of the monotonically increasing relationship between the number of active global competitors and the degree of globalization. The former number falls between 1 and m; the latter is no less than k^* (the monopolist's choice) but no greater than k' (the welfare-maximizing level). Consequently, if a particular parametric shift causes both k^* and k' to move in the same direction, that effect will generally hold up for any number of global competitors between 1 and m. The exceptions all relate to the possibility that a small change in the values of the parameters may, by affecting m, trigger a major change in competitive intensity. However, we will assume away such "knife-edge" effects.

THE IMPACT OF TECHNOLOGY ON GLOBALIZATION

This section looks at the effects of technological parameters on the degree of globalization at equilibrium. Our exposition revolves around the role of evolutionary processes in globalizing or deglobalizing an industry; however, the results also apply to cross-sectional comparisons of industries with different economies observed at the same point in time.

Scale Sensitivity

What happens if the scale sensitivity of all the production technologies increases, that is, if fixed costs bulk larger relative to marginal costs? (Note that decreases in scale sensitivity can be dealt with symmetrically.)

In tracing the effects of increased scale sensitivity, we have to guard against altering the values of extraneous parameters. At the initial equilibrium, the outputs of the global and the country-centered producers are uniquely determined. Hold each producer's total cost (or equivalently, its average cost) *at its original level of output* constant, but shift the technology so that fixed costs account for an increased fraction of average costs. What is the relation between the degree of globalization at the new equilibrium and at the old one?

Figure 2.2 supplies the answer. The parametric shift does not

Figure 2.2 Increase in Scale Sensitivity

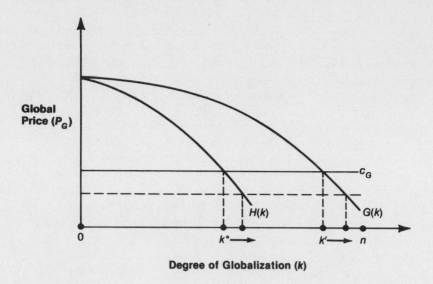

Degree of Globalization (*k*)

move the $G(s)$ curve at all (check equation [5]). However, it *does* shift the global producer's marginal cost curve, c_G, downward. This favors globalization: both k^* and k' (respectively, the monopolistic and the welfare-maximizing levels of output of the global product) are higher than before.

Intuitively, the global producer's competitive advantage derives from its ability to spread its fixed costs across different countries. As scale sensitivity increases, this advantage is amplified.

Cost Reduction

What happens if the average costs of the global product and all country-centered products fall by an equal absolute amount?[13] The effect, it turns out, depends on the degree to which fixed rather than marginal costs are affected.

Given our assumption of price-inelasticity, cost reductions that affect only marginal costs will have *no* effect on the degree of globalization. Figure 2.3a illustrates why. Equal absolute reductions in marginal costs simply translate the $G(s)$ and c_G schedules vertically downward by the same amount. This is just like relabeling the vertical axis. The horizontal axis is not affected; neither is the output of the global product.

The outcome is different if the cost reduction affects fixed costs. Then only the $G(s)$ schedule is translated vertically downward (see Figure 2.3b). This will reduce the equilibrium degree of globalization.

The results again highlight the strategic significance of fixed costs

Figure 2.3a Reduction of Marginal Costs

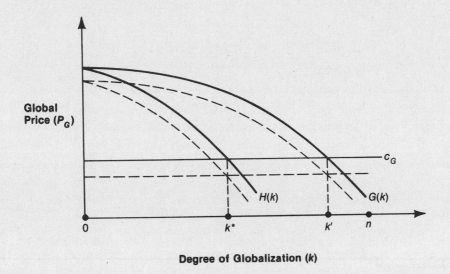

Figure 2.3b Reduction of Fixed Costs

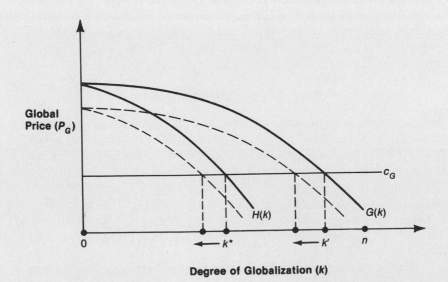

in our model. Fixed costs matter because the global producer and its country-centered competitors have implicitly chosen to cover them in two different ways (internationally versus intranationally).

THE IMPACT OF DEMAND PATTERNS ON GLOBALIZATION

It is also easy to use diagrams to trace the influence of shifts in the demand parameters. As in the last section, most of the exposition is couched in evolutionary terms; however, it can be reinterpreted cross-sectionally.

Demand Growth

In discussing the effect of demand growth, we have to distinguish between the degree of globalization, k, and the total output of the global product $\int_0^k N(s)ds$. The effect on the former is not obvious, meriting analysis.

Assume that aggregate demand increases in all countries, that is, the $N(s)$ schedule shifts upward. Figure 2.4 illustrates that this will lower the average cost of producing the country-centered varieties, shifting the $G(s)$ schedule downward. Because the global producer's marginal cost, c_G, stays put, the increase in demand hurts globalization (both k^* and k' are reduced).

Although this effect may come as a surprise, it can be explained intuitively. As markets expand, the importance of scale economies decreases; so does the value of the global producer's ability to spread its fixed costs across borders. This result is the counterpart of the one about scale sensitivity. Increasing scale sensitivity aids the global product because it raises the (average) significance of fixed costs; increasing market size hurts globalization by reducing their significance.[14]

Consolidation of Preferences

By consolidation of preferences we mean that the *number* of tailored products demanded worldwide decreases (although customers retain their preferences for tailored products over the global ones). A simple way to model this is to fix the total market size at $\int_0^n N(s)ds$ but decrease the number of different segments that it encompasses.

This effectively expands the market available to any tailored product, reducing its average cost. Figure 2.5 points out that this reduces both k^* and k' by shifting the $G(s)$ curve downward.

In other words, consolidation of this sort hurts global production

Figure 2.4 Growth of Demand

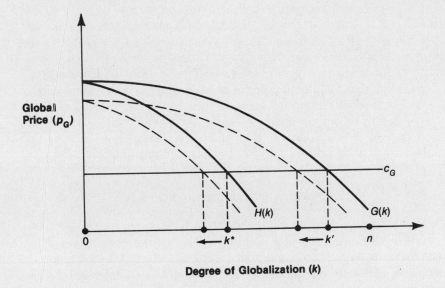

Figure 2.5 Consolidation of Preferences

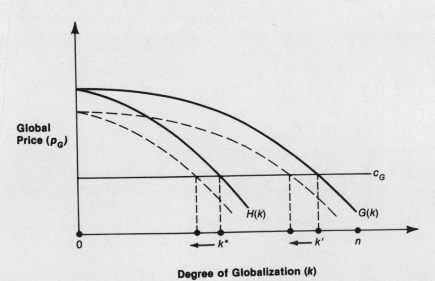

instead of helping it. As this conclusion is rather unexpected, its logic should be elaborated. As far as gross benefits to customers are concerned, we have assumed that the global product is nobody's first choice and everybody's second choice. Because consolidation leaves this ordering intact, it has absolutely no influence on the global competitor's supply curve for its product. It *does* improve the cost positions of tailored products—hence the reduced degree of globalization.

If, however, the global product represented some customers" first choice, consolidation might lead to an increase in the number of such customers, reducing the average costs of the global product as well as the tailored ones. In such a setting, the net impact of consolidation on globalization would depend on what the specific parameters were.

Convergence Among Countries

One familiar assertion about globalization is that it will always be favored by convergence across countries. There is an obvious sense in which this is true: If customers' needs—and their preferred tailored products—become the same, international differentiation will disappear and only one product will be supplied worldwide.

However, international commoditization is not the only way in which countries can become more alike: other methods include converging market sizes, equalizing income levels, and diffusion of production know-how across country-centered producers. These phenomena can flatten the $G(s)$ curve through their influences, respectively, on $N(s)$, $h(s)$, and $F(s)$ and $c(s)$. In the section on calculating the equilibrium, we have already remarked that equalization of globalization indices rules out interior solutions: only one mode of production will remain viable. The interesting point is that that mode need *not* be global production; depending on the parameters, equalization of the indices *might* lead to exclusively country-centered production.

Some notation will help pinpoint the outcome that is actually observed. Suppose that countries' globalization indices have converged to a common value, $\bar{G}$. If

$$F_G \le (\bar{G} - c_G) \int_0^n N(s)ds , \tag{11}$$

the global producer will win out in all the markets. On the other hand, if inequality (11) does not hold, only country-centered production will prove viable.

In other words, the outcome depends, in a very specific way, on the parametric values toward which countries are converging. The statement that convergence necessarily leads to globalization will not do.

Figure 2.6 Restriction of Trade

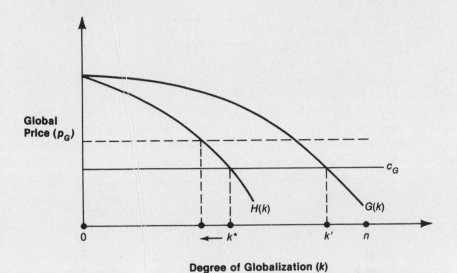

Degree of Globalization (k)

PUBLIC POLICY AND ECONOMIC WELFARE

So far, we have ignored the governmental dimension of globalization. National governments can—and often do—play a salient role in determining the degree to which an industry will globalize. Refer, for instance, to Doz's discussion in chapter 7. The most obvious weapon in their arsenal is the imposition of trade restrictions against inflow of the global product.

It is easy to check the effect of trade restrictions: the global producer's *effective* marginal cost of supplying the country in question is usually shifted upward. For instance, an across-the-board ad valorem tariff rate of t (expressed in fractional terms) changes the global producer's objective function from the one expressed in equation (8) to

$$PR_G(k) = \left[\frac{G(k)}{1 + t} - c_G \right] \int_0^k N(s)ds - F_G. \tag{12}$$

Compared to equation (8), this implies an increase of $tG(k)/(1 + t)$ in the global producer's effective marginal cost. Local content rules can act similarly by constraining the pursuit of economies of global scale.

Figure 2.6 makes the point that as trade restrictions raise the global producer's effective marginal cost, the degree of globalization, k^*, decreases. Because this shift is entirely the work of avoidable policy decisions, the *optimal* supply of the global good, k', holds steady. In other words, protectionism hurts worldwide welfare by exacerbating the undersupply of the global product.

However, a government is likely to be more concerned about national rather than worldwide welfare. Can the government in country s act unilaterally to increase its country's welfare? The answer depends on the relation between s and k^*.

First, consider countries that, in the absence of trade restrictions, consume country-centered products (i.e., countries such that s is greater than k^*). None of their governments can unilaterally influence the industry in a way that would improve their nation's welfare. Note that the only option open to such a government is to change the domestic consumption patterns by subsidizing the global product to such an extent that it supplants the country-centered product. But this doesn't make sense because customers' preferences for the country-centered product override the maximum cost savings from switching to the global product:

$$s > k^* \Leftrightarrow h(s) > \frac{F(s)}{N(s)} + c(s) - G(k^*). \tag{13}$$

Conversely, if s is less than k^*, it still doesn't pay for governments to shift their domestic patterns of consumption. The cost savings associated with the global product now outweigh customers' preferences for being supplied the country-centered product in its place.

However, if the global producer stands to make positive profits in the absence of governmental intervention, there *is* another range of choices available to the governments of countries in the interval $[0,k^*]$. Through tariffs, taxes, or other policy instruments, they can siphon off some of the profits of the global producer subject to two constraints: that the global producer can still make nonnegative profits and that despite a government's policies, it continues to supply the relevant country rather than ceding it to the country-centered producer.

Game theory does not uniquely specify the fraction of the global producer's profits that each country can thus hope to extract. However, most of the relevant solution concepts do lead to the prediction that larger countries will be able to extract greater fractions of the "rents" to global production than smaller ones. The intuition is straightforward. Because the global producer earns the same contribution $[G(k^*) - c_G]$ from every customer in each country that it serves, the only difference that it cares about among countries in the range $[0,k^*]$ is their relative size: the larger the country, the greater is its total contribution to covering the global producer's fixed costs, F_G. Hence, larger countries in the interval $[0,k^*]$ possess more bargaining power vis-à-vis the global producer than smaller ones do.

CONCLUSIONS

Our microeconomic model of global competition has yielded a number of conclusions. In the absence of governmental intervention, it is an easy matter to derive an indicator (the globalization index) of the degree to which customers in each country are prone to purchase the "compromise" global product rather than the locally tailored, country-centered one. This expedient tremendously simplifies the calculation of the equilibrium.

From the standpoint of global welfare, there is too much country-centered production at the equilibrium. The reason is that consumers of country-centered products do not internalize the higher average costs that their choices impose on the global producer. Competition to supply the global product increases its aggregate output but, in welfare terms, does not *quite* eliminate its undersupply.

Analysis of the equilibrium yields some additional insights. Globalization is aided by scale sensitivity but impeded by demand growth, segment consolidation, and cost reduction.[15] The impact of country convergence, which is frequently nominated as a cause of globalization, turns out to depend on what the countries in the global system are converging toward.

Trade restrictions reduce worldwide welfare by exacerbating the undersupply of the global product. Trade policy also hurts national welfare if it leads to a shift in the local pattern of consumption. The use of trade policy to increase national welfare is restricted to countries that, come what may, continue to consume the global products; their governments may then use trade restrictions as a way to extract some of the profits that would otherwise accrue to the global producer. Countries' bargaining power for such purposes depends directly on the relative sizes of their national markets.

Three broad suggestions for further research come to mind. First, the cost structure of the industry should be enriched. Statically, this would subsume phenomena such as country-specific setup costs for the global producer, and declining marginal costs. Dynamically, sunk costs might be allowed to influence industry evolution. Second, customers' preferences need to be generalized. A more general structure would allow product characteristics to be determined endogenously rather than set exogenously. To take one example, different global producers might then elect to supply different varieties of the "global" product. Another possible consequence is that a global producer could choose to supply a product that is tailored from the standpoint of one market but subject to differentiation penalties from the standpoint of others. Finally and most ambitiously, the importance of economywide factors such as exchange rates and input costs in shaping the pattern of international exchange implies that our analysis should be embedded in a framework that lets us calculate the multi-industry "general equilibrium" for entire countries.

NOTES

1. Our exposition skirts configurational (i.e., locational) issues. The practical reason is that impediments to centralization—such as transport costs—would complicate our model and obscure the broad patterns that can otherwise be identified. We *do* have a line of defense here: pure configurational advantages—such as the ability to tap cheap labor or raw materials—are an insufficient explanation for global competition because their exploitation does not require all value activities to be brought under the umbrella of a single enterprise (Caves 1982, chap. 1). In contrast, economies of coordination *are* sufficient to drive globalization. Therefore, if we have to choose between covering coordination and configuration, it seems reasonable to focus on the former.
2. Readers with a technical bent may wish to consult papers by Spence (1976) and Salop (1979) that focus on issues related to the one dealt with here. Similar but arguably simpler models of competition have also begun to crop up in international trade. See, for instance, the collection of papers in Kierzkowski (1984).
3. We are *not* asserting that global competitors are not or should not be responsive to the differences among country markets; empirical evidence suggests otherwise (see chapter 4). We simply want to point out that responsiveness is an unlikely basis for global competitors' advantages over country-centered ones.
4. The reason for this assumption is cosmetic: it simplifies the notation. International homogeneity could easily be dealt with by shifting the level of analysis from individual countries to groups of countries; intranational heterogeneity would require an analytic shift to individual segments. We perform some analysis along these lines in the section that looks at the impact of demand patterns on globalization.
5. Because this assumption may lead to some confusion, it is worth recapping. Basically, we have assumed that the global product is a "compromise" that is nobody's first choice (in terms of gross benefits) but everybody's second choice. This precludes intermediate products tailored to *clusters* of countries reducing the number of strategic alternatives that we have to track.
6. For such leadership to be feasible, we have to assume away sunk costs or reputational effects that might let firms precommit to continued operation. Sunk costs will help the competitor that is the first to enter a particular market (Ghemawat 1982, chap. 8).
7. Caves, Porter, and Spence (1980, chap. 1) informally reach similar conclusions.
8. Use of this device is fairly common in game theory (see Schotter and Schwodiauer 1980). But it does have two awkward aspects. First, the global producer's profits can no longer be compared with those for country-centered producers; their dimensions have diverged. Second, because countries have been taken to be individually insignificant, some configurational issues (such as the global producer's optimal choice of a "platform") become inaccessible.
9. Readers familiar with microeconomics will note that the global producer's choice of which markets to serve is now isomorphic to the more familiar one of a monopolist's optimal choice of output in *one* market.
10. Novshek (1985) discusses why these assumptions will suffice.
11. The local "monopolies" of country-centered producers are irrelevant because we have cast them as followers whom the global leader can discipline.

12. The monotonic approach toward k' depends on our assumption of a constant marginal cost, c_G (see Ushio 1983). With decreasing marginal costs, additional entry *could* lead to "congestion," raising average costs and decreasing the aggregate supply of the global product.
13. Of course, average costs could also increase. Those responsible might get sacked; with that exception, the outcome would be a mirror image of what happens when average costs decrease.
14. These opposed effects are captured by $F(s)/N(s)$ component of the globalization index, $G(s)$.
15. The last effect is contingent on *some* reduction in fixed costs. Refer to our earlier discussion of the impact of reduced costs.

REFERENCES

Caves, R. E. *Multinational Enterprise and Economic Analysis*. Cambridge, England: Cambridge University Press, 1982.

Caves, R. E., M. E. Porter, and A. M. Spence. *Competition in the Open Economy*. Cambridge, Mass.: Harvard University Press, 1980.

Ghemawat, P. "The Experience Curve and Corporate Strategy." Ph.D. diss., Harvard University, 1982.

Harsanyi, J. C. "Subjective Probability and the Theory of Games." *Management Science* 28 (February 1982): 120–25.

Kierzkowski, H., ed. *Monopolistic Competition and International Trade*. Oxford: Clarendon Press, 1984.

Novshek, W. "On the Existence of Cournot Equilibrium." *Review of Economic Studies* 52 (January 1985): 85–98.

Salop, S. C. "Monopolistic Competition with Outside Goods." *Bell Journal of Economics* 10 (Spring 1979): 141–56.

Schotter, A., and G. Schwodiauer. "Economics and the Theory of Games: A Survey." *Journal of Economic Literature* 18 (June 1980): 479–525.

Spence, A. M. "Product Selection, Fixed Costs, and Monopolistic Competition." *Review of Economic Studies* 43 (June 1976): 217–36.

Ushio, Y. "Cournot Equilibrium with Free Entry: The Case of Decreasing Average Cost Functions." *Review of Economic Studies* 50 (April 1983): 347–54.

II.

THE FUNCTIONAL AGENDA

3

Coordinating International Manufacturing and Technology*

M. Therese Flaherty

For many managers the term "global manufacturing" conjures up visions of consumers the world over driving identical, black Model Ts, eating the same cereal, and using computer keyboards with the same alphabets. In this vision one gigantic factory, with huge economies of scale, manufactures sufficient volume to supply the world market with a single design at low cost.

But in some technology-intensive business units global manufacturing also means something else: coordinating a number of plants internationally that may or may not make similar products. Proper coordination of these plants has the potential of reducing costs and enhancing the effectiveness of multiple manufacturing operations while preserving some diversity in final products and in location of manufacturing. For example:

- A U.S. heavy equipment manufacturer offered many options on its basic product line, which was manufactured at two plants in the United States and Europe. The business unit was able to

*I am indebted to managers in five U.S.-based manufacturing companies who generously shared with me many of their concerns and innovations in managing their international manufacturing operations. I am also indebted to Michael Porter for his support through the colloquium and his comments which helped me to focus my research. Robert Stobaugh's comments helped to clarify my thought as well as my expression. Also very helpful were the comments on drafts of this chapter by Robert Hayes, Richard Rosenbloom, Steven Wheelright, and Earl Sasser. Finally, I am indebted to the Division of Research of the Harvard Business School for financial support of this research. Of course, the responsibility for remaining errors, omissions, and misstatements is mine.

ship interchangeable products from both plants. This meant that the two-plant system could fill orders more quickly, shift some orders between plants in response to exchange rate fluctuations, and assure a steadily rising production rate for a third plant as it began operation.

- A U.S. chemical manufacturer acquired a plant in Europe that had been losing money for its original owner. As expected, specialists from the corporate technical group improved the operations of the new plant. But they also improved the manufacturing process of a plant in the United States by using knowledge gained at the European plant. The improved process enhanced the characteristics of the U.S. plant's product so as to appeal to a large and growing market in the United States.

- Two U.S. electronics manufacturers started systematic programs to purchase from vendors in several countries. As a result they saved up to 30 percent of the costs of purchased parts and materials for certain products.

The issue of coordinating international manufacturing has been given little attention by academics.[1] Until the 1970s most companies that had manufacturing facilities in several countries ran their manufacturing operations independently. To be sure, there had long been important exceptions: the major petroleum companies coordinated supply lines from the Middle East to their customers, and early in the twentieth century the Ford Motor Company supplied its European assembly plants with some parts from the United States.[2]

Coordinating international manufacturing is likely to become more important as companies adopt global strategies. Two academic developments would assist managers in designing and implementing global manufacturing strategies. One is a framework for thinking about coordination. The other is an understanding of the experiences of companies that seem to be good at it. These developments would help managers identify opportunities for coordination, evaluate the potential of particular coordination programs, and overcome problems likely to be encountered during implementation.

In this chapter I present such a framework and illustrate its use with examples of international manufacturing coordination from the experience of five U.S. companies. Two are primarily in chemicals, two in electronics, and one in heavy equipment. They are all reputedly well-managed, Fortune 500 manufacturing companies. They all serve industrial, rather than retail, customers. Each company has over 30 percent of its sales and assets outside the United States. Managers in all of them have devoted considerable attention to coordinating their international manufacturing operations. Within each company, I selected for study one technology-based business unit that was worldwide in its customer and manufacturing base. In discussing the experiences of these business unit, I refer to them as Chemicals A and B, Electronics A and B, and Heavy Equipment.

Many issues that arise in the coordination of international manufacturing are, of course, similar to issues that arise in the coordination of multi-site manufacturing operations located within one country. To the extent that the two sets of issues are the same, this chapter contributes to the management of multi-site operations in general. But some of these issues are of much greater significance in the international than in a single-country context. For example, geographic distance, divergence in customer requirements, and differences in company culture can all be much greater in international than in single-country manufacturing. Finally, other issues arise in international manufacturing that are simply not encountered in domestic manufacturing. For example, exchange rate fluctuations and national trade policies can be critical considerations in managing an international manufacturing system.

MANUFACTURING STRATEGY OF TECHNOLOGY-INTENSIVE BUSINESS UNITS

Multinational manufacturers in research-intensive industries, which include the five companies considered here, steadily accounted for most of the large and growing exports and foreign direct investment by U.S. manufacturing companies during the postwar period. Specifically, between 1962 and 1977, U.S. companies in the five most research-intensive industries accounted for over two-thirds of the exports and foreign direct investment made by U.S. manufacturing companies, but less than 40 percent of the total shipments from U.S. factories. Furthermore, between 1966 and 1978 the nominal stock of foreign direct investment in fixed assets by U.S. manufacturing companies, which had been accumulating since the nineteenth century, approximately doubled.[3] As Table 3.1 shows, companies in those industries—with the exception of the air transport sector of the transport industry—held at least 30 percent of their sales and fixed assets dispersed over several countries outside the United States.

Such companies, which base their competitive advantage largely on technology, depend on manufacturing in important ways. They earn profits on their technology largely by selling their products. The amount by which they profit from their technology depends on various factors; for example, on the time at which they introduce their products relative to the time that their rivals introduce their competing products, the availability of the products to customers in many locations, the conformance of the delivered products to specifications, and the design of the product.[4]

As these U.S. companies encountered more internationally competitive customers, rivals, and vendors during the 1970s and early

Table 3.1 Distribution of Sales and Assets of the Five Research-Intensive U.S. Industries over Different Geographic Areas, 1981

	U.S.	Canada	Western Europe	South America	Middle East	Asia	Total Non-U.S.
Chemicals SIC(28)							
Sales	63	8.6	16	3.3	4.7	0.0	37
Assets	68	8.9	15	3.4	0.0	3.6	32
Non-Electrical SIC(35)							
Sales	61	9.2	19	1.5	0.1	0.5	39
Assets	67	9.7	21	1.5	0.1	0.6	33
Electrical SIC(36)							
Sales	63	3.2	18	5.2	0.0	3.0	37
Assets	69	2.9	17	6.2	0.0	4.0	31
Transport SIC(37)							
Air Transport							
Sales	50	7.8	4.6	0.0	0.0	0.5	50
Assets	79	12	7.7	0.1	0.0	0.8	21
Non-Air Transport							
Sales	68	7.6	14	7.5	0.4	0.2	32
Assets	64	9.3	17	8.3	0.2	0.2	36
Instruments SIC(38)							
Sales	63	8.6	20	1.0	0.0	2.5	37
Assets	70	7.8	20	0.6	0.1	2.1	30

SOURCE: Data in Compustat II, Geographic Segments File.

1980s, they were particularly dependent on their international manufacturing. Many of these internationally competitive companies based outside the United States focused on different manufacturing tasks and used different manufacturing approaches than did their U.S. counterparts. The U.S. companies needed to learn about these approaches as part of their response to these new rivals. The U.S. companies also found that some of their most technologically sophisticated customers were for the first time located outside the United States. This meant that U.S. companies whose manufacturing and design employees interacted closely with customers had to work with companies outside the United States. And some U.S. firms found that the operations of their long-time U.S. customers had become international; those customers were demanding international service and products that could be used interchangeably regardless of where the products were manufactured. In meeting all these international challenges, U.S. managers had to devise new international manufacturing strategies.

In this chapter I define *manufacturing strategy* as the broad plan by which a company or business unit develops, introduces, and manufactures products in order to satisfy customers' needs better than competitors. Such strategies generally specify the decisions that will have long-lasting effects on the business and that usually require large financial commitments. Manufacturing strategies typically include:

- number, size, and location of plants
- technology and equipment choice
- assignment of materials, components, and products to be made by specific manufacturing facilities
- vertical span of the manufacturing process
- policies for manufacturing support activities
- policies for technology support activities[5]

The first four are decisions that require large lump-sum investments and that relate to the equipment and buildings that comprise the company's or the business unit's factories. Taken together, they define the set of plants and their manufacturing processes, along with the physical flows of material and products among them. I refer to this set of decisions as a *manufacturing configuration*. The business units that I studied with global manufacturing strategies all had plants located in a number of different countries.

In contrast, the last two categories of manufacturing strategy are policies that guide the daily activities of manufacturing and other technical employees located at geographically dispersed facilities.

Policies for manufacturing support activities encompass the daily activities that ensure the desired production is accomplished at the right time in the right place in the right way. These policies relate to procurement, production planning, and other activities listed in Table 3.2. Hayes and Wheelright call these the "infrastructure categories" and include them in manufacturing strategy because they can be as expensive and time-consuming to change as the first four categories.[6] I include them here for an additional reason. In globally competitive business units the strategic use of geographically dispersed facilities can be enhanced by the interaction of manufacturing support activities at one location with those at another.

For technology-intensive business units there is another category in the list of manufacturing strategy components: policies for technology support activities. These are also listed in Table 3.2 and refer to the design of new manufacturing processes and products and their introduction into manufacturing. One example is a policy requiring the use of common parts and processes in new product designs. Another is a policy requiring research on the basic manufacturing technologies used by a business. Such policies are the guides within which employees in technology and manufacturing develop the future manufacturing capabilities of the business unit. These policies require that the activities of employees in engineering and technical development be directed in part by manufacturing strategy. Manufacturing policies dealing with technology support activities typically require interac-

Table 3.2 Support Activities

Manufacturing Support Activities
• procurement
• aggregate production planning
• daily production planning and expediting
• quality assurance
• employee management and development
• manufacturing engineering
Technology Support Activities
• product design and improvement
• process design and improvement
• new product and process introduction

---

tions among technology and manufacturing employees, customers, and vendors that are located in widely dispersed facilities.

REASONS FOR THE GEOGRAPHIC DISPERSION OF MANUFACTURING FACILITIES

Each of the five business units I studied had developed a manufacturing strategy entailing plants in several countries. In several cases the managers intended to do further rationalization of the plants and reassignment of the products among plants within the following five years. But in all cases the managers intended to continue manufacturing in plants in several different countries. These strategies sacrificed some economies of scale and ease of management that would have been available had there been fewer plants for the same volume. They were designed to take advantage of major opportunities available to companies with internationally dispersed manufacturing facilities.

The key economic model of multinational expansion rests on two ideas. The first is that technology-intensive companies possess competitive advantages based on intangible (technology) assets that can be transferred within a company with ease, but outside a company only with more difficulty. The second is that using one's own technology in foreign manufacturing allows a company to earn a larger return on its technology than would be possible through an arm's-length sale of the technology.[7]

Business scholars, while recognizing the opportunities associated with establishing foreign manufacturing facilities, also emphasize the costs and risks involved. Their research suggests that U.S. managers prefer to locate manufacturing in the United States to avoid the cost and risk associated with the management of foreign manufacturing. Actions of competitors, however, which threaten their home market or foreign markets, are frequently sufficient stimuli to overcome managers' risk aversion.[8]

The benefits of foreign manufacturing for the five business units largely fell into five general categories, which relate closely to the general reasons for dispersion discussed in chapter 1. First, managers could enhance their long-term business relations outside the United States by- manufacturing abroad. For example, when Electronics A and B established manufacturing facilities in Europe, their managers found that they had made a believable commitment to serve local customers well over the long term. Furthermore, in all five business units local manufacturing allowed manufacturing and other technical employees to work closely with customers in order to better design customers' products and to identify problems after both had begun production.[9] This provided enhanced service and responsiveness to local customers' needs. Finally, managers in all five business units learned valuable lessons by operating manufacturing facilities abroad. They found, for example, that managing facilities in Japan allowed them to learn more effectively than they otherwise could have about Japanese manufacturing practices, the requirements of Japanese business customers, and the Japanese distribution system.

Second, managers could gain access to local, immobile factors of production by locating manufacturing outside the United States.[10] Electronics A and B, for instance, located their high-volume, labor-intensive operations in areas with low labor costs such as the Far East, Mexico, or the Caribbean. For other operations, they and the Heavy Equipment managers were attracted to locations with abundant, high-quality engineers or good industrial infrastructures. The relative costs of production and the pools of desirable immobile resources in different geographic areas were changing. For example, one manager of a new Electronics B plant located in the United States with participative work systems said that in 1984 his costs were competitive with those of offshore assembly plants.

Third, managers could reduce transport costs significantly by locating close to customers those manufacturing facilities that add bulk and weight. For instance, in part to avoid international shipment, Chemicals A had six geographically dispersed plants that manufactured products from locally available materials. Not surprisingly, transport costs were less of an issue for Electronics A and B than for the other business units I studied.[11]

Safety problems involved in transporting some chemicals also made multiple foreign manufacturing locations attractive for Chemicals A and B. In some cases, regulations explicitly restricted the movement of particular materials across national boundaries.

Fourth, managers could satisfy some demands of and gain benefits from local governments by locating manufacturing plants in their country. Some businesses received subsidies to locate in particular areas; others received protection from imports. In trying to respond to the demands of individual countries while preserving some economies of scale, Heavy Equipment and Chemicals A and B had adopted the strategy of building plants in one country and exporting from there to other countries in the region.

Fifth, managers could hedge against a number of location-specific risks by locating manufacturing facilities in several countries. Among these risks were local government instability and exchange rate fluctuations. Managers in Electronics A considered political stability when locating facilities in Asia. When the pound sterling appreciated relative to the U.S. dollar, Chemicals A closed a U.K. plant and transferred production to the United States. Later, partially in response to the strong U.S. dollar, Heavy Equipment increased production from a Latin American plant for export to the United States. All of these examples entail long-term adjustment of capacity to demand. None of the business units had moved production among countries in response to short-term exchange rate fluctuations, although managers in Chemicals B and Heavy Equipment were considering the possibility.

THE STRUCTURE OF GEOGRAPHICALLY DISPERSED MANUFACTURING

A business unit's manufacturing configuration is designed to capture specific benefits of internationally dispersed locations and it conditions the requirements and the opportunities for managing synergies among facilities.

Figure 3.1 illustrates the manufacturing configurations of the five business units. They have three to nine manufacturing plants (denoted by circles) and one to five warehouses (denoted by rectangles). The material flows are denoted by arrows. The circles are labeled with numbers to indicate the manufacturing process and products of the plant. Circles in one business unit labeled with the same number are plants that have similar products and more or less similar manufacturing processes. Warehouses are included in these configurations to indicate the flows between manufacturing plants and customers.

Three general characteristics of manufacturing configurations in global business units are suggested by these examples. The first characteristic is that in each business unit several plants have manufacturing processes that are more or less similar. This feature gives rise to opportunities for managing interactions among manufacturing plants. For example, improvements made at one plant can be used by another, and a given product can be made at more than one plant.

The second characteristic is that the pattern of material flows in each business unit is simple relative to the theoretical possibilities. In measuring simplicity it is difficult to be mathematically precise while being faithful to the managerial issues. But in this case there are two partially acceptable measures, both of which indicate simplicity.

The first indicates that there are few inter-plant shipments relative to the theoretical possibilities. There could, in theory, be two

Figure 3.1 Actual Material Flow Configurations

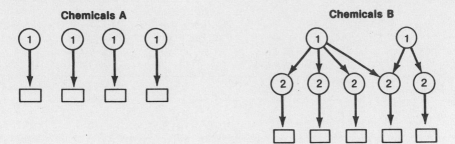

Chemicals A   Chemicals B

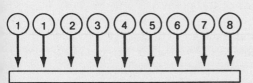

Electronics A

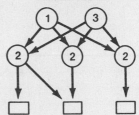

Electronics B

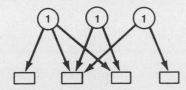

Heavy Equipment

Note: Circles represent manufacturing plants.
Rectangles represent warehouses.
The numbers in the circles indicate the kinds of manufacturing process and the products processed: if these are more or less similar in two plants in a business unit, then the plants are labeled with the same number; if not, then the plants are labeled with different numbers.

one-way material flows between any two facilities—plants as well as warehouses. The number of possible one-way flows of material and products among n facilities in one business unit is $n(n - 1)$. Electronics A, for instance, had nine manufacturing plants; theoretically it was possible for there to be seventy-two one-way material flows among them. Yet there were no material flows at all between the manufactur-

Table 3.3 Comparison of Actual with Possible Numbers of One-Way Material Flows between Plants in the Five Business Units

	Number of Plants Plus Warehouses	Possible Number of One-Way Material Flows	Actual Number of One-Way Material Flows	Actual as a Percentage of Possible
Chemicals A	8	56	4	7
Chemicals B	12	132	15	11
Electronics A	10	90	9	10
Electronics B	8	56	11	20
Heavy Equipment	7	42	8	19

ing plants in that business unit! Including Electronics A's single warehouse, ninety one-way materials flows were possible, but there were only nine. Similar calculations made for all the business units show that they used only 7 to 20 percent of the possible one-way material flows (Table 3.3). The simplicity of the material flows in the configurations is also indicated by a second measure. At most two manufacturing plants processed any particular material or subassembly before it reached a warehouse.

The third characteristic is closely related to the second. As managers developed global manufacturing strategies, they simplified their manufacturing configurations in order to make them more manageable. Managers at Electronics A, for example, introduced modular product designs and eliminated one assembly plant, and Electronics B decreased the number of plants that processed any given shipment.

THE NATURE OF COORDINATION

The managers of the business units I·studied had, during two or more decades of international operations, benefited from many of the advantages of internationally dispersed manufacturing discussed previously. But they had also forfeited economies of scale in plant and equipment and encountered considerable difficulty in managing their many manufacturing facilities to achieve synergies. They had managed their manufacturing plants located in different countries fairly independently of each other and of related technology support activities.

But, during the 1970s and early 1980s the managers responded to business crises by beginning a number of projects to capture synergies among manufacturing facilities. The projects reduced many of the problems, and suggest that the potential benefits of managing internationally dispersed plants interdependently could be significant. These projects involved various forms of coordination among dispersed plants. In discussing these projects, I use the term *coordination* to mean the sharing and use, by different facilities, of information about manufacturing and technology support activities. Most of the coordination projects, regardless of which activity was involved, shared several management characteristics. Their goals were set in terms of performance of manufacturing support activities, as opposed to advice for later action. They typically were performed by employees who were also responsible for the support activity, with minimal involvement from corporate staff. They required significant and new ongoing communication links among internationally dispersed sites. They were designed to fit and take advantage of the special circumstances of the business unit. Some projects directly supported material flows among plants and warehouses, but many were not associated with inter-site material flow at all.

As managers gained more experience with coordination projects, they found that projects and their effects interacted. Some projects were necessary before others could be undertaken. Some groups of projects had effects that, when taken together, made the operation much more effective than the sum of direct effects of the individual projects. Several projects, begun individually, seemed in retrospect to fit together as a program.

The coordination projects in these business units differed tremendously in their details, and the business units differed in the projects they undertook. But in all the business units, projects that focused on the same manufacturing or technology support activity fell into two or three well-defined categories. Within each such category the projects provided similar benefits and management challenges.

PROJECTS TO COORDINATE MANUFACTURING SUPPORT ACTIVITIES

Managers in the five business units considered here found significant opportunities for coordination projects in three of the six manufacturing support activities listed in Table 3.2: procurement, production planning, and manufacturing engineering.

Procurement is the obtaining of material, subassemblies, components, and equipment needed for manufacturing from outside vendors. In Heavy Equipment and Electronics A and B, international coordination projects in procurement seemed to provide significant benefits to the business, while there were fewer significant coordination projects in international procurement in Chemicals A and B.

Three categories of projects to coordinate procurement internationally appeared to lower cost and improve quality. First, procurement specialists at a plant in one country helped their counterparts at other, not necessarily similar, plants in other countries identify and negotiate with vendors in the first country. Electronics A and B and

Heavy Equipment, for example, all saved up to 30 percent of the local costs of the products (ranging from machined metal parts to printed materials) they purchased internationally, without sacrificing performance or conformance to specifications. Second, procurement specialists from similar plants in different countries brought the costs and reliability of their local vendors into line with those in other countries by quoting the contracts similar plants in the same business unit had made with vendors in other countries. This was especially effective if the similar plants had almost identical requirements and if the foreign vendors could supply all the plants. Indeed, one U.S. vendor to Heavy Equipment that used such information in a broad-based program improved methods and reduced manufacturing costs by one-third in one year. Third, in four of the five business units, procurement specialists at plants in Japan during the early 1980s arranged for a number of professionals from various plants in other countries to visit local vendors and learn about technical and management practice. During the early 1980s, this access to the managers of effective Japanese manufacturing operations was a major asset to the managers of U.S.-based manufacturing who were seeking rapid and far-reaching improvements in their own manufacturing practice.

Several considerations restricted the use of such international procurement projects. Managers felt they could only source high-volume parts with stable designs internationally. It was difficult, time-consuming, and not always feasible for distant, low-cost vendors to incorporate engineering or volume changes quickly. This appeared to be due in part to vendors being located so far from designers that rapid and broad-based communication relating to engineering specifications was difficult; in part to less extensive engineering support at remote vendors; in part to the vendors' production processes which, though labor-intensive, were best suited to long runs; and in part to the longer inventory pipeline required to source reliably at a distance. Furthermore, a local manufacturing plant appeared to be a major asset for a foreign plant in identifying and working effectively with local vendors. For example, Heavy Equipment and Electronics A and B all sourced from vendors located close to their international plants. Furthermore, Electronics B had found a corporate international purchasing group to be inadequate to facilitate local procurement on a continent where the business had no manufacturing plant. Even lead plants (responsible for engineering specifications of products for their own and several foreign plants) in the United States tended to focus on U.S. vendors and to ignore foreign vendors. Managers' personal experience in foreign manufacturing management seemed to increase the likelihood that a plant would procure outside its immediate locale. Finally, plants that were not themselves "in control," that is did not perform according to expectations on a daily basis, had difficulty using foreign vendors unless they built large buffering inventories.

While international coordination in procurement appeared promising for only three of the five business units, all five business units had begun international coordination projects related to aggregate production planning, as opposed to planning for shorter horizons. *Aggregate production planning* is the specification—usually monthly—of approximately what volume of which products will be manufactured at what date in a plant for the following period, usually a year.

The first type of international coordination project arose in direct support of material flows between related plants in manufacturing configurations in which one plant or warehouse processed the material or components made by others, as was the case with Chemicals B and Electronics A and B. Until the early 1980s, these flows had been managed at arm's-length with large inventories serving to decouple the plants' production schedules. But during the early 1980s, these technology-intensive business units encountered more competition, smaller manufacturing margins, higher interest rates, rising material costs, more rapid product changes, and pressure to reduce the inventory held between plants. This required closer coordination between the aggregate plans of the related plants, and it was managed differently by the business units. Electronics A began planning production of key products centrally at the business unit level with each plant receiving an order of precisely how much to deliver monthly; Chemicals B used a headquarters staff group in negotiation with plant planners to ensure that the monthly plans drawn up by the various plants were consistent; and Electronics B relied entirely on negotiations among independent plant schedulers who were under pressure to reduce inventories.

International sourcing from the business unit's own plants seemed to be limited by the same flexibility, cost, control, and responsiveness issues that restricted international procurement from independent vendors. It was more difficult and slower to introduce design changes to products assembled in offshore plants than to products manufactured in the United States. This was in part because of difficulties in rapid, complete, long-distance communication; in part because these factories (like many outside vendors in those geographic areas) found product changeovers and engineering changes difficult; and in part because the business units maintained ten weeks or more of extra inventory between the U.S. plants and related offshore plants. Unanticipated volume changes could also be difficult for remote plants to accommodate quickly, particularly if the plants were not "in control"; extra inventory costs, shortages, and delays in response at least the length of the inventory pipeline could ensue. Furthermore, the attention of distant management could be difficult to claim. In Electronics B, for example, offshore plants serviced several onshore business units; thus, they were faced with conflicting service requirements, all of which were impossible to meet. In contrast, Chemicals B plants' requirements of intermediate materials had unchanging specifications. For that business unit, inter-plant conflicts related to volume adjustments, and those conflicts had been largely eliminated after the source (which had been a joint venture) became a wholly owned subsidiary with the same incentive and administrative systems as the plants to which it shipped.

The second type of international aggregate planning arose in planning production schedules for one plant to ship products to customers of similar plants in other countries. Managers in all five business units did this to a significant extent, and they argued that the capability to transship products from international plants to customers in other countries could be very valuable. They could, for example, guarantee a smoothly rising output rate to a new plant during its start-up years; they could shift orders among plants internationally to hedge exchange rate fluctuations; and they could meet peak requirements in one plant with capacity elsewhere and conserve capacity in the long term.

The requirement that products made by different plants be interchangeable to customers severely limited this sort of transshipment for Chemicals A and B and Heavy Equipment. Engineers at similar plants had, for example, improved the process, used local vendors, customized product options for their customers, and changed packaging without complete documentation. So plants that had been established to make interchangeable products could not do so after several years. Indeed, engineers at corporate headquarters at Heavy Equipment, where custom products were important, designed an information and telecommunications system that would allow complete documentation of all existing parts, products, and their material content, as well as accommodate new parts and products. In contrast, managers at Chemicals A noted that between plants in different countries some product and process differences had arisen that resulted in product attributes that were not essential to customers, but that customers had accommodated in their manufacturing processes. Chemicals A gradually substituted a new, improved product line for the old one; the new process would be controlled at all plants to ensure that most customers could use products from all plants. Introducing the new, uniform product line required different operating procedures for each plant because the plants used basic equipment that had been built at different times for different volumes and that had useful economic lives of over thirty years.

The problems of maintaining the interchangeability of products with the same specifications that were manufactured at different plants without prohibiting improvements was difficult for the chemicals and electronics business units. Chemicals A was working to control the process in each similar plant within a very narrow range, or "window;" but this raised the prospect of stifling experiments that might lead to valuable innovations. Heavy Equipment controlled the process for making each part and product configuration within a very narrow window; but many product configurations could be designated by each plant, so each plant offered extended product variety. Projects to achieve the required similarity were undertaken by business unit-level engineering groups in all three business units.

I use the term "manufacturing engineering" here to include all the engineering activities located in a plant. These activities provide support for the manufacturing process and improve it. The three types of international coordination projects focusing on manufacturing engineering related to incremental changes in the process or products. They were: (1) transferring technological improvements developed at one plant to other similar plants; (2) transferring manufacturing responsibility and capability for one product from one plant to another; and (3) fixing problems that arise in one plant by changing the process at a related plant that processed the same product or material.

The opportunities for transferring technological improvements among similar plants located in different countries appear to be large. For example, Chemicals A found that for one product its European plant had improved costs by over 20 percent; its manufacturing specialist responsible for the improvements was able during several trips to institute comparable cost savings in two other plants. Electronics A and Heavy Equipment found regular meetings among engineers and managers at similar but geographically dispersed plants useful in initiating transfers of improvements. One impediment to these transfers was area managers' reluctance to invest their resources for the benefit of another area; in Chemicals A this reluctance was overcome by pressure from top business unit managers who knew all the people involved from their own earlier work experience in Europe. Another major impediment to the transfers was the reluctance of manufacturing managers to admit that they could learn from other plants.

The second type of coordination project arose in the two electronics businesses: transferring products and processes from production facilities focused on new, low-volume products in the United States to similar plants focused on high-volume products in the Far East or other low-labor cost regions. Manufacturing engineers in U.S. plants at Electronics A and B "stabilized" the process (to the point where there were few engineering changes each month in the United States). If the product turned out to sell in high volume, processes that were more efficient for high-volume production were developed; the products were then transferred to similar plants in the Far East. Engineers in the "lead plant" in the United States in one case in Electronics A developed a new assembly process that included some automation for a high-volume product and then moved with the process to the Far East for six months to ensure effective transfer. In contrast, Electronics B engineers from the Far East typically lived in the U.S.

lead plants for six months before accepting a new product responsibility. Both groups "debugged" all equipment in the U.S. lead plant, and both were satisfied with the effectiveness of their project.

The major limitations on the effectiveness of these transfers appeared to lie in the difficulty each offshore plant had in responding to the conflicting demands of several U.S. plants or businesses[12] and in the choice of products to be manufactured offshore. For example, one difficulty would occur when management of an offshore assembly plant needed to choose which of several products for different businesses to manufacture. Another would occur when the offshore facility was capacity-constrained and managers needed to choose between an old, high-volume product and a newer, potentially high-volume product whose price might be lowered and demand increased as a result of the transfer. The management of the shared offshore assembly plant by several plants and/or businesses inevitably was fraught with conflict and the possibility that suboptimal decisions would be made.

The third type of international coordination project in engineering was fixing technical problems that arose in one factory by making changes in another factory. Electronics B, for example, encountered this possibility as it introduced new products to production in the United States. In Electronics A similar possibilities arose in designing new products. In both businesses the main impediment to cooperation across plants was a formal management evaluation system in which the plant managers were judged independently as cost or profit centers. In both businesses top managers overcame the problem temporarily—but not permanently—by suspending the formal evaluation and incentive systems. I conjecture that these issues would arise more frequently in businesses with frequent new product introductions and in plants related by systems technology than in other businesses.

PROJECTS TO COORDINATE TECHNOLOGY SUPPORT ACTIVITIES WITH MANUFACTURING

Technology support activities located outside manufacturing contribute to the development of a business unit's future products and its future manufacturing capabilities. To be effective they require some coordination with manufacturing. Managers in the business units I studied were working to enhance the performance of their ongoing coordination projects in product and process design and improvement.

Many of these projects addressed the same issues addressed by single-site or single-nation manufacturing business units. For example, Chemicals A and Electronics B had discovered that some process technologies, which were being developed by competitors, had been ignored by their own technology support groups; they had no mechanisms to review systematically and regularly current process

technologies for possible opportunities. Both established formal processes to review process technology opportunities at the business unit
level. Another issue, which was not confined to business units doing
international manufacturing, was increasing the speed and improving
the quality of the new product design-to-market process. Electronics
A and B and Heavy Equipment were all addressing this issue by introducing manufacturing considerations into the design process earlier
and by extending the responsibility of design into manufacturing. Like
many other business units, in their first efforts they saw decreases in
design-to-market periods from, for example, seven years to three, and
improvements in their new products that were better designed for
manufacturability than earlier products. Like many single-nation business units, they found sophisticated telecommunications systems to
be a major asset in introducing new products.

Each business unit I studied, however, was also beginning coordination projects between technology support activities and manufacturing that were aimed at several related issues not encountered by
single-site or single-nation business units in anything like the same
form. These managers had decided that they would maintain multiple
similar plants making the same products rather than consolidate their
manufacturing operations into one "world plant." They continually
confronted the problem of "how similar" to make and maintain the
plants, products, and processes.

I previously defined similar plants loosely as those that manufactured the same products with more or less the same technology. Here
it is worthwhile to be specific. "Similar" covers a broad range. At one
extreme similar plants in a business unit produce overlapping parts of
the same product line with different processes for different business
missions. For example, among three plants of Electronics B, one was
focused on low cost, another on establishing a foreign market presence, and the third on new product introductions and technical leadership of the similar plants. In Heavy Equipment and Chemicals A
and B, similar plants focused both on serving their geographic areas
with some products based on the same designs and processes but
somewhat customized for each area, and on some products that served
the world and were identical throughout. In all the business units
similar plants produced products that had the same specifications, but
the plants used processes that differed by virtue of having, for instance, different vintages, different de-bottlenecking and improvement efforts by local engineering, and different vendors.

Increasing similarity seemed to make a larger degree of coordination possible. For example, similar plants in Heavy Equipment that
had different volume and parts requirements could work together to
identify vendors internationally, but only when they had virtually
identical vendor requirements could they use their contracts to help
make vendors in the United States more competitive with those lo-

cated in other regions. Chemical products that were more alike could be used by a wider group of customers; in this case increasing similarity of products increased the potential extent and benefits of plants' shipping to the customers of other similar plants. In Chemicals A, the more similar plants' processes were, the more process improvements discovered at one plant could be easily transferred to others.

The degree of similarity in product and process among a business's internationally dispersed plants also seemed to condition the extent and types of manufacturing coordination and technical support that were possible. In Heavy Equipment the similarity required to make international procurement projects worthwhile was considerably less than that required to make it possible for several plants to ship interchangeable products to customers. Similarly, transferring technological improvements among plants required more similarity of process and product in Heavy Equipment and Electronics A than the procurement projects, and in Chemicals A and Heavy Equipment shipping interchangeable products required still more similarity than many process transfers.

It also seems that business units based on different technologies and in different markets would require and benefit from different amounts of similarity of product and process. The Electronics business units, for example, shipped interchangeable products worldwide with apparently little concern for controlling for more similar processes. But Heavy Equipment required close control of specifiations for parts and product options to do that, and the Chemicals business units required close process control. For these three business units, the technology support problem of how similar to make the processes and products among plants was particularly difficult.

The new product and process design and introduction processes also appeared to be easier if the plants had similar products and processes, and if new products used parts and processes in common with existing ones. For example, in the Chemicals business units introducing a new product that would be made using each plant's existing equipment required that central engineering define different operating procedures for each plant; and the more divergent the process equipment the more involved the process of defining new operating procedures. Likewise in Electronics A if a new product used many of the same parts as existing products, then introducing it to manufacturing required less purchasing effort than if it used few common parts. Furthermore, if several plants manufactured the same products using common parts, then a new product required only one design and much less incremental purchasing, inventory, management, training, and equipment design. Common processes and parts also meant less confusion during manufacturing for any given product mix. It meant less changeover time between different products, less inventory, less new equipment, and better reactions to volume and mix changes.

Similar processes also meant that it was easier to communicate about new processes. This was particularly noticeable for business units using advanced communications systems. In Heavy Equipment, for example, employees in the European plant routinely at the end of their workday on Monday submitted a technical question via computer mail to their U.S. counterparts, had the U.S. employees process it during their workday, and received an answer at the beginning of the European workday on Tuesday. The managers attributed the speed of answer to both the communications system and the common technical contexts of the two plants.

There are, of course, potential disadvantages to close similarity in processes and products across plants. The first is the possibility that commonality would lead to excessive product homogeneity for customers. For Chemicals A and B, some product homogeneity across similar plants was acceptable to customers, and that was the business unit's goal. For Electronics A, products used in different countries had to accommodate different power supplies and had to have lengthy documentation in the local language. Modularizing manufacturing maximized the parts of the product that did not require customization and made clean interfaces with the parts of the products that did not achieve high process commonality while preserving the required heterogeneity for the customer. Heavy Equipment's customers required significant customization, on each order. There central engineering designed an information and communication system that required all similar plants to document their product, part, and material specifications for all to access so that any plant with a specification usable at one plant could make a product acceptable to the customer. In this case the information system—at a cost—gave the similar plants broad and identical potential product sets; but similar plants rarely manufactured the same products. These approaches suggest that some technologies allow plants to have process commonality with considerable product variety.

A second potential disadvantage to closely similar plants would be important if the control required to maintain close similarity would stifle innovation in plants. Individual plant improvements in process and product had been significant in all the business units. For example, Chemical A's plant in Europe had cooperated with the local applications engineering group and with local customers to refine their process, enhance product properties, and lower costs considerably relative to other plants in the business unit making the same product. In some regimes under consideration with common processes and control at all plants, the experiments that were formerly done quickly and informally would require the permission of central engineering; the bureaucracy and the difficulty of formally conducting the valuable experiments would be much greater. Managers in Heavy Equipment were also concerned that their comparatively much more permissive cross-plant process control through their information system would hinder local engineers in providing customers with custom designs.

Managers in all the business units encountered problems in implementing their plans for making processes and products more similar. The first was generally in getting central engineers' attention and effort. As in initiating coordination activities in manufacturing, crises and comparisons among plants were useful in this. Another problem was that the required engineering effort itself was large in business units like Chemicals A where many products and much capital equipment in several plants were redesigned. (The manufacturers also appointed a manufacturing manager at one plant to keep track of process performance monthly at all plants.) A third problem was particularly evident in the Electronics business units where engineering and manufacturing managers would have liked to coordinate across facility boundaries, but the formal incentive and evaluation systems discouraged them; in both cases the managers involved suspended the formal system and evaluated their subordinates with much more close attention and with, at least temporary, good effect. Electronics A managers, for example, mandated a change in engineering requirements and measurement of the number of new parts in a product; on the first new product, designers drastically reduced the number of new parts per product. A major difficulty in increasing the commonality of parts and processes is giving designers quick and easy access to parts and processes already in use. Group technology and computer aids to design were helpful in doing that for Electronics A and for Heavy Equipment. Finally, with the major technology support organizations for all five business units located in the United States, non-U.S. plants in several business units had different access to technology support than U.S. plants. This appears to have been an advantage for one plant, which as a consequence worked more closely with its local applications engineering group and made major process and product improvements. For the Electronics business units this, coupled with relatively low engineering support at low-cost/high-volume assembly plants, may have been responsible for the stop in cost-reductions related to "learning" when products were transferred from U.S. plants to those in the Far East.

MANAGING COORDINATION IN INTERNATIONAL MANUFACTURING

In all five business units individual coordination projects were undertaken in anticipation of their direct benefits. However, by 1984, managers in each business unit had also realized major indirect benefits of many of the successful projects. Indeed, in retrospect, in each business unit several projects seemed to form a coherent history as a program. The following brief histories describe several such interrelating projects in each of three business units.

- Between 1975 and 1982 central engineering in Heavy Equipment developed a common product classification system in which each product design and customizing change could be specified. Second, a different staff group independently developed a computer communications system to link all plants in one network. During the early 1980s, as both of these developments were put in use, a control system administered by central engineering was implemented. It required that plants could only institute a change in or an addition to the common product definition with central approval and that all changes would be instituted at all plants on the same day. For the first time this ensured that products made at one plant were, from customers' standpoints, interchangeable with those made at other plants and that customers' spare parts could be defined accurately. The computer communication system that linked all the plants allowed engineering changes to be processed rapidly enough to ensure that customer service was not sacrificed and that plants could proceed quickly without awkward delays in their designs of new product options.

  After this, Heavy Equipment introduced a monthly central aggregate planning function for the European, U.S., and Latin American plants. In this context, managers considered shifting production among the plants in response to different patterns of capacity requirements, plant development, and even such other phenomenon as exchange rate fluctuations. Further, introducing a new product to manufacturing in Europe proceeded much more smoothly and quickly in 1984 than it ever had before.

- In 1980 Chemicals A acquired a plant with a process related to processes the business unit had already established at other plants. Subsequently central engineering improved that process and made the acquired plant much more productive than it had been before. Central engineering then took some ideas from the acquired plant's process and introduced them to a U.S. plant. Managers at the U.S. plant were assisted in their efforts by the employees at the acquired plant. In the United States product attributes improved so much that demand increased substantially. This, in turn, justified developing a new, improved product line for all the plants worldwide.

- In 1983 a manager at a U.S. plant in Electronics A—who had previously worked at the Far Eastern plant—suggested that purchasing experts at the Far Eastern plant help identify local vendors. After the vendors were identified and contracts placed, the U.S. plant had saved 30 percent on the delivered costs of those internationally sourced items. Those particular items were also used—and consequently sourced from the Far East—by the business's European plant, whose engineering for that product was done by the U.S. plant. After that, the European plant began to use Far Eastern sources for products it had developed itself.

Clearly, in all three cases individual projects, which had been undertaken in anticipation of their direct benefits, turned out to have major additional and unanticipated benefits through interactions with other projects. The independent projects in Heavy Equipment, for example, turned out to allow central management to shift production orders among plants internationally at the notice of the aggregate plan rather than at the timing of strategy changes. In Chemicals A central engineering had improved the process at the acquired plant with no expectation of also improving the U.S. plant's process and ultimately developing a successful world product. In Electronics A the manager who began the Far Eastern plant did not expect to aid the business unit's international sourcing program so much. What began as isolated projects turned out to be the beginnings of longer-term programs to coordinate international manufacturing.

Certainly a limited and preliminary study such as this can make no pretense to presenting solidly grounded recommendations to managers of coordination projects. The applicability of my observations and their refinement are clearly areas for future research. But they do suggest several considerations for managing the coordination of international manufacturing. I explore those implications here.

The fact that in these instances groups of projects appear to be *interrelated* seems to have several implications for managing such coordination projects. It suggests that such groups of related projects should be managed centrally as programs. Evaluation of some projects that are not justifiable on the basis of their direct benefits—for example, projects to use common parts in design or to establish a telecommunications network for the business unit—should take into account their indirect effects in, among other areas, making new product introductions easier. Also, top management should overcome the inevitable organizational impediments.

In addition, in these instances some projects were more effective if certain other projects had prepared for them. Managers of such coordination projects should note that some projects should *naturally precede* others. Similarity of plants' processes and products, in particular, appeared to be natural precedent to many types of coordination projects. Similarity, as discussed previously, seemed to make more coordination possible in terms of both coordination focused on different support activities and higher degrees of coordination focused on one activity. For example, plants needed the capability to make interchangeable products before they could ship to each others' customers. Like similarity, business unit-specific international communication systems seemed to facilitate many other coordination projects. In evaluating projects that "naturally precede" others, managers should take into account the indirect benefits that result from the coordination projects for which they prepare.

Furthermore, many of these coordination projects seemed to have *major unanticipated consequences* that themselves led to later projects and benefits. This property, in contrast to the first two, seems to imply that such projects should be managed in a decentralized, ad hoc manner. This would allow those lower-level employees, who are located in internationally dispersed manufacturing and technology support facilities and who are most likely to recognize new opportunities, to act on them without extensive bureaucratic justification.

Finally, it appears that in these business units technology support projects were critical to obtaining the benefits of coordination. This was because the usual activities of technology support in designing and improving products and processes determined—within some limits determined by customers—the similarity and relatedness of products and processes among internationally dispersed plants. In turn the degree of product and process similarity among plants determined many of the opportunities for coordinating international manufacturing. Finally, in technology-intensive business units technology support and the effects of coordination on the speed and effectiveness of new product and process introduction and improvements can be critical to competitive success.

These observations suggest at least a two-pronged approach to managing the coordination of international manufacturing. Such an approach would assign responsibility for proposing and carrying out most coordination projects to independent, geographically dispersed manufacturing and technology support employees. It would also assign responsibility to top business unit managers for initiating the program, assuring that it has direction and scope appropriate to the manufacturing strategy and configuration of the business unit, and provide some aid in overcoming organizational impediments to coordination. A regular review of coordination projects would allow top business unit managers to capture the benefits of unanticipated opportunities identified by support employees, enabling them to take advantage of important interrelations among projects. Few additional staff employees should be required.

In this scheme lower-level manufacturing and technology support employees would propose, design, and execute coordination projects. They would need authority and resources to execute coordination projects involving several sites. These are the employees most likely to identify new, unanticipated follow-on coordination projects because they know their own projects, problems, and resources best. If they were also aware of what improvements similar plants were making, what coordination programs were being undertaken, and what resources other plants had, they could identify new opportunities even better.

Top business unit managers could facilitate such lower-level activities by, for example, increasing employee familiarity with projects and their counterparts at other sites, improving inter-facility communication facilities, and increasing the similarity of the products and processes among plants. For the first purpose several managers of these business units had instituted regular meetings (typically three or four times a year) among manufacturing support employees at similar plants. At the meetings support employees discussed their recent inter-and-intra-plant projects and proposals; follow-up visits among manufacturing sites were usual if opportunities were identified. While meetings improved awareness, sophisticated communication systems seemed to help geographically dispersed employees to keep in touch throughout the year and carry out the coordination projects themselves. Finally (as discussed previously), to the extent that plants had similar products and processes, support employees would find more opportunities for coordination projects among them.

Business unit or company managers themselves would be facilitators, protectors, and reviewers. They identified the crises that spurred the coordination projects, suspended formal incentive and evaluation systems when they contradicted the requirements of coordination, and overcame the impediments of top area managers. They also reviewed the progress of projects whose size might not ordinarily have brought them to the attention of the top management.

The regular reviews should serve to address difficult and broad issues like establishing a degree of familiarity among plants, improving the inter-plant communications system, considering the previous relations between projects, identifying large organizational impediments to coordination, or providing adequate technical support to manufacturing or manufacturing coordination. They should also be receptive forums to review and communicate unanticipated opportunities for coordination projects.

CONCLUSION

The managers of the five business units I studied each coordinated manufacturing and technology support activities to increase the effectiveness of their internationally dispersed operations. The particular support activities they coordinated and the extent of the coordination, as well as the benefits they derived from them, varied considerably from business unit to business unit. They ranged from sharing information about vendors located worldwide, to controlling production processes so that products with the same specifications would be interchangeable in customers' applications to improving the processes for manufacturing products by incorporating improvements made in several locations.

These observations suggest that companies derive greater value from coordinating manufacturing and technology support activities at different sites if the operations located at different sites are more similar. This follows first, because opportunites for coordinating support activities between two sites increase as the processes at the sites become more similar and second, because it is easier and cheaper to coordinate operations which have more in common. For example, two operations with very different products and processes could share vendors. But operations with processes which are tightly controlled so they are identical could manufacture products which would be interchangeable in users' applications, and share vendors. In particular, projects to make geographically dispersed operations more similar appear to have been prerequisites to some of the most valuable projects coordinating manufacturing and technology support activities.

Increasing the similarity of geographically dispersed operations was expensive and difficult, however, because each operation was unique because of its history and customers. Furthermore, the constituency served by each on-going operation had to be served continually by the business while the coordination in manufacturing and technology support was underway. Neither the ultimate expense nor the extent of such projects were known with certainty to the managers at the start. Consequently, even though some coordination projects proved surprisingly valuable, managers in most of these business units chose to eschew many types of coordination projects because the costs were perceived to outweigh the benefits.

Managers of the more extensive and successful coordination programs generally began with a group of apparently unrelated projects, each of which could improve the manufacturing or technology support activities located at at least one site. One of the basic projects typically addressed the similarity of several geographically dispersed operations. Over time, the managers found that some projects were in fact interrelated and provided extra benefits. They found that other projects needed to be abandoned or redirected. In general, it appears that the most successful approach to taking advantage of coordination possibilities is to set out in the general direction of coordination with a number of parallel projects in manufacturing and technology support, monitor them closely, and be willing to make mid-course corrections.

NOTES

1. There are a few notable exceptions that deal mostly with the frequency of cross-shipments rather than with the management of interactions

among manufacturing plants located in different regions. C. Pomper *International Investment Planning: Integrated Approach* (New York: North Holland, 1976) presents a plan for a United States–based chemical company's plants worldwide in which plants in Latin America regularly ship product to customers in Europe near another plant. J. Curhan, W. H. Davidson, and R. Suri *Tracing the Multinationals* (Cambridge, Mass.: Ballinger, 1977), 397, present tabulations of data on multinationals that reveal that in 1975 less than one-fifth of all the subsidiaries in their sample cross-shipped more than 10 percent of subsidiary sales. In "Influence in the Multinational Enterprise: The Case of Manufacturing" in R. Stobaugh and L. T. Wells, Jr., *Technology Crossing Borders* (Boston: Harvard Business School Press, 1984), 265–92, H. de Bodinat presents evidence that fewer than one-quarter of the 33 multinationals he studied had cross-shipments greater than 10 percent of subsidiary sales. He also addresses the question of how these flows would be managed by investigating the influence of headquarters in managing the flows. His investigations relate to the level of influence of the headquarters rather than the problem addressed here. F. M. Scherer et al., in *The Economics of Multi-Plant Operation* (Cambridge, Mass.: Harvard University Press, 1975), 397–98 conclude that there is little ongoing administrative coordination among the many multisite manufacturing operations he studied, but they expect such coordination to increase.

2. A. Chandler, in a private communication in April 1984, supplied these early examples of coordinating international manufacturing operations. But he agreed that such coordination was rare until the 1970s. M. G. Duerr and J. M. Roach *Organization and Control of International Operations* (New York: The Conference Board, 1973) also support this observation.

3. For the period until 1962 see W. Gruber, D. Mehta, and R. Vernon, "The R & D Factor in International Trade and Investment of United States Industries," *Journal of Political Economy* 75 (1967). For later periods see M. T. Flaherty, S. Ghoshal, and R. Stobaugh "Comparative Advantage versus Global Competition," manuscript, 1984. Of course, inflation during that period would tend to overstate the growth rate, and exchange rate fluctuations would distort it. But the general conclusion that foreign direct investment by U.S. manufacturers grew significantly seems warranted.

4. See M. T. Flaherty, "Market Share, Technology Leadership, and Competition in International Semiconductor Markets," in R. S. Rosenbloom, ed., *Research on Technological Innovation, Management and Policy* Volume 1 (Greenwich, Conn.: JAI Press, 1983) for evidence on this point from the semiconductor industry.

5. In "Manufacturing—Missing Link in Corporate Strategy," *Harvard Business Review* (May–June 1969), W. Skinner's early enunciation of manufacturing strategy differs from this one largely in that (1) it mentions management systems, but does not emphasize policies for manufacturing support; and (2) it classifies technology support activities as part of the business's resources, rather than as part of manufacturing strategy.

6. R. H. Hayes and S. C. Wheelwright, *Restoring Our Competitive Edge* (New York: Wiley, 1984).

7. R. E. Caves, *Multinational Enterprise and Economic Analysis* (New York: Cambridge University Press, 1982) provides a thorough statement of this argument and a survey of the relevant economics and business literature.

8. R. Vernon, *Sovereignty at Bay* (New York: Basic Books, 1971) 75, discusses the motives of manufacturing companies to establish foreign manufacturing subsidiaries in these terms. R. Stobaugh, *Nine Investments Abroad and Their Impact at Home* (Boston: Division of Research Harvard Business School, 1976), chap. 8, 187–91 reaches a similar conclusion about the companies he studied. F. T. Knickerbocker *Oligopolistic Reaction and Multinational Enterprise* (Boston: Division of Research, Harvard Business School, 1973) reaches a similar conclusion in studying a number of foreign investments in a given industry. R. W. Moxon, "Offshore Production in the Less Developed Countries—A Case Study of Multinationality in the Electronics Industry," *The Bulletin* (1974): 98–99, provides positive statistical evidence on this point.

9. R. Stobaugh, "Creating a Monopoly: Product Innovation in Petrochemicals," in R. S. Rosenbloom, ed., *Research on Technological Innovation, Management and Policy*, Volume 2 (1985) presents evidence that for petrochemical businesses, manufacturing in large markets fosters close contact with customers and facilitates innovation.

10. This is a well-researched phenomenon. Moxon, "Offshore Production," presents evidence that in the electronics industry going offshore for low-cost labor was necessary for many companies to meet competition.

11. R. Stobaugh, "Where in the World Should We Put That Plant?," *Harvard Business Review* (January–February, 1969) presents evidence that petrochemical products whose transporation costs relative to product value were higher were manufactured outside the United States earlier than those with lower relative transportation costs. Scherer et al., *Economics of Multi-Plant Operation*, also presents empirical evidence on the importance of relative transport costs for the location of production.

12. W. Skinner's "The Focused Factory," *Harvard Business Review* (May–June 1974), identifies many of the problems a manufacturing plant would be likely to encounter if it served several businesses that had different requirements.

4

Three Roles of International Marketing in Global Strategy*

Hirotaka Takeuchi
and
Michael E. Porter

INTRODUCTION

The internationalization of competition has become widely discussed in contemporary research on management. Though the concern with international issues is manifested in the marketing field, the view of marketing's role in international competition has been limited. Research in international marketing has long been concerned with the differences in marketing for foreign as compared to domestic markets. Recently, a controversy has arisen about whether or not markets are becoming global and product needs are becoming standard everywhere. In this debate and in the literature generally, however, little attention has been given to the broader role of marketing in international strategy.

In this chapter we argue that there are three central roles of marketing in a global strategy. The first relates to where various marketing activities—such as new product development, advertising, sales promotion, channel selection, marketing research, and others—should be performed around the world. We call this marketing *configuration*. Marketing activities can be performed either centrally at the corporate or regional headquarters or dispersed locally to country subsidiaries. While for the most part the configuration of marketing activities should and must be geographically dispersed, we show that certain activities can be concentrated to reap scale or learning economies.

The second role of international marketing is through the nature

*This chapter has benefited from comments by participants in the Mitsubishi Bank Foundation Seminar on Business Strategy and Technological Innovation in Ito, Japan.

and extent of *coordination* among marketing activities being performed in different countries. Marketing activities can be performed the same way across countries or modified to fit each country's (or region's) circumstances. Though the literature in international marketing has created a dichotomy between marketing standardization across countries and tailored marketing for each country, we show that the essential task is to do both simultaneously.

The third strategic role of international marketing is in its *linkage* to the rest of a firm's activities—especially technology development and manufacturing. Even when there are limits to international coordination (and standardization) in the marketing function, marketing can unlock possibilities for achieving competitive advantages through global configuration/coordination of other activities. We explore this linkage between marketing and other activities in the firm, and show how product development and product positioning can enhance global competitive advantage.

POLAR VIEWS OF INTERNATIONAL MARKETING

Past research in international marketing has generated two opposing views. The first view, held by a majority of practitioners and academicians, treats marketing as an inherently local problem. This stream of research emphasizes differences across countries in customers and marketing systems, and advocates a tailor-made marketing program for each country. The opposing view treats marketing as know-how that can be transferred from country to country. This research tends to emphasize the benefits gained from standardization, and argues in favor of a common marketing program across countries.[1] More recently, the homogenization of buyer needs around the world has been advanced as an additional reason for a global marketing approach.[2]

The Localized View of International Marketing

Those with the view that "everything needs to be local" point to a number of important differences across countries that affect marketing. Three categories of differences are identified. The first is differences in *market* characteristics among buyers. Even the most sophisticated marketers have at times experienced difficulties in foreign markets because they did not fully understand differences in buyer behavior or customs. For example:

- Campbell's canned soups—mostly vegetable and beef combinations packed in extra-large cans—did not catch on in soup-loving Brazil. A post-mortem study showed that most Brazilian housewives felt they were not fulfilling their role if they served soup that they could not call their own. Brazilian housewives had no problems using dehydrated competitive products (such as Knorr and Maggi), however, which they could use as a soup starter but still add their own ingredients and flair.[3]

- Johnson & Johnson's baby powder did not sell well in Japan until its original package was changed to a flat box with a powder puff. Japanese mothers feared that powder would fly around their small homes and enter their spotlessly clean kitchens when sprinkled from the plastic bottle. Powder puffs allowed them to apply powder sparingly.[4]
- Tandy Corp., which entered Europe with its Radio Shack stores in 1973, geared its first Christmas promotion in Holland to December 25, following the custom in the United States. Much to its dismay, the company discovered that the Dutch exchanged holiday gifts on St. Nicholas Day, usually celebrated on December 6.[5]
- Advertisers have encountered difficulty when using colors in certain foreign countries. For example, purple is a death color in Brazil, white is for funerals in Hong Kong, and yellow signifies jealousy in Thailand. In Egypt, the use of green, which is the national color, is frowned upon for packaging.[6]

Differences in per capita income, level of education, level of unemployment, and social norms across countries may also call for a localized approach toward international marketing. Consumer goods regarded as inexpensive staples in the developed countries may need to be marketed as "luxuries" elsewhere. Countries facing a high level of unemployment will be less willing to substitute labor for robots, numerical controls, or other automated equipment in the factory.

The second category of differences across countries is differences in the character of local *marketing infrastructure*. Differences in infrastructure—such as the transportation system or available media—may force a multinational to pursue marketing on a country-by-country basis. The most widely occurring differences from country to country include the following:

- *Media availability.* Commercial television spots are not available in Sweden, Norway, and Denmark. British public television slots are sold through a sealed-bid auction process, which makes advertising schedules highly uncertain. The ban on liquor television advertising in the United States by the National Association of Broadcasting, says the chairman of Suntory in Japan, serves as the main deterrent for this Japanese liquor manufacturer to enter the U.S. market in a big way.
- *Distribution system.* Some countries have much different channels of distribution for products than others. The distribution of goods in Japan, for example, involves a number of wholesale intermediaries. The ratio of cumulative wholesale to retail sales in Japan is 4:1 according to recent estimates, compared to 1.6:1 in the United States.

- *Legal restrictions*. Different countries impose different laws and regulations—for example, patent laws, trademark laws, antitrust laws, resale price maintenance, tariffs and taxes, and so on. These laws force differences in marketing practices from country to country. Japan, for example, does not accept the results of certain testing and certification procedures conducted outside Japan for some products, such as drugs. Tandy Corp. learned its lesson the hard way in Europe. It overlooked a Belgian law requiring a government tax stamp on window signs. It also violated a German sales law by giving away flashlights to promote the opening of its stores.[7]

- *Physical environment*. Country differences due to such physical and geographical factors as climate, topography, and electrical currency lead to required differences in products and marketing practices. Producers of refrigeration and air conditioning equipment experienced fungus problems in high humidity areas of Africa. Sand and ocean air have been found to cause maintenance problems in the Middle East countries as well. International companies selling products run by electricity must contend with differences in the cycles and voltages of the electrical power supply across countries.

- *Transportation and communications*. Differences among countries in the telephone system, road network, postal practices, and the like, may require modifications in marketing practices. Mail-order retailing is popular in the United States but is virtually nonexistent in Italy, for example, because of differences in the telecommunication and mail systems.

The third category of differences among countries is differences in the *competitive* environment. Under different competitive conditions in different countries, the marketing approach may need to be modified. Nestlé, for example, achieved more than a 60 percent market share in instant coffee in Japan, but less than 30 percent in the United States. Nestlé had to contend with two strong domestic competitors in the United States—namely General Foods, which markets the Maxwell House, Yuban, and Brim brands, and more recently Procter & Gamble, which markets Folgers and High Point—but with relatively weak domestic competitors in Japan. IBM, which is the leading computer company in the world, slipped to third place in the Japanese market in 1984, behind Fujitsu Ltd. and NEC Corporation, in terms of total revenues. Nestlé and IBM must reflect these differences in the competitive environment in such marketing choices as pricing, sales-force behavior, and advertising.

The Standardized View of International Marketing

In contrast to the view that marketing must be country-tailored is the school of thought that marketing skills or know-how can be transferred from country to country and that significant benefits can be achieved through standardization of marketing on a global basis. In the extreme, standardization would mean the offering of identical product lines at identical prices through identical distribution channels, supported by identical sales and promotional programs throughout the world. Although such an extreme case is rare, advocates of standardization point to numerous successful examples, many of which are in product categories that would seem quite susceptible to local differences in tastes and other conditions.

- Coca-Cola, which uses a common brand name and ingredients throughout the world, has been able to maintain over 50 percent of the worldwide carbonated soft drink industry.
- Esso successfully applied its common advertising theme, "Put a Tiger in Your Tank," in all of the countries in which it had a presence in the 1960s.
- Most of the early Japanese multinationals—such as Honda in motorcycles and Sony in consumer electronics—followed a similar market entry strategy in the United States and Europe. They initially pursued a niche at the low end and gradually upgraded their product offerings.[8]

In a study based on interviews with executives from twenty-seven U.S. and European multinationals (doing business in the food, soft drink, soap-detergent-toiletries, and cosmetics industries) in the early 1970s, Sorenson and Wiechmann found a high degree of standardization in marketing across European countries and the United States.[9] As shown in Table 4.1, standardization was particularly high with respect to brand name, physical product characteristics, the role of middlemen, and packaging.

More recently, several authors have emphasized the importance of capitalizing on a general drift underway toward the homogenization of needs and wants across countries. Levitt refers to this phenomenon as "globalization of markets" and describes it as follows: "Commercially, nothing confirms this as much as the success of McDonald's from the Champs Elysées to the Ginza, of Coca-Cola in Bahrain and Pepsi-Cola in Moscow, and of rock music, Greek salad, Hollywood movies, Revlon cosmetics, Sony televisions, and Levi's jeans everywhere."[10]

Companies that take advantage of this trend toward worldwide homogenization of needs and preferences can potentially realize economies of scale in sourcing, logistics, production, and marketing, as well as in the transfer of managerial know-how, which all can translate into reduced prices. The advantages of standardizing products across countries have been summarized by Channon:[11]

- It allows a common approach to a number of markets, helps create a uniform worldwide corporate image and reduces confu-

Table 4.1 Degree of Marketing Standardization among Selected U.S. and European Multinationals

Elements of Marketing Program	Degree of Standardization (%)[a]		
	High	Moderate	Low
1. Product characteristics	81	4	15
2. Brand name	93	—	7
3. Packaging	75	5	20
4. Retail price	56	14	30
5. Basic advertising message	71	6	20
6. Creative expression	62	4	34
7. Sales promotion	56	11	33
8. Media allocation	43	10	47
9. Role of sales force	74	10	15
10. Management of sales force	72	10	17
11. Role of middlemen	80	7	13
12. Type of retail outlet	59	7	34

SOURCE: Reprinted by permission of the *Harvard Business Review.* An exhibit from "How Multinationals View Marketing Standardization" by Ralph I. Sorenson and Ulrich E. Wiechmann, (May/June 1975). Copyright © 1975 by the President and Fellows of Harvard College; all rights reserved.
[a]Sums across to 100 percent.

sion, especially in consumer markets as increased market penetration takes place.

- It facilitates the development of a global marketing mix, in particular with respect to brand name, advertising message, after-sales service, sales training, and sales promotion. This may lead to lower costs and also facilitates ease of management.
- It permits economies of scale in production and stock control and opens up opportunities for tax saving, international production sourcing, and transfer pricing.
- It increases the prospect of rapid investment recovery because the risk of product failure is spread over a much wider geographic area.

Past research has also explored the benefits of a standardized approach to multinational advertising.[12] As with product standardization, advertising standardization helps to develop a consistent and universally recognized brand image and reduces the risk of consumer confusion. It also leads to cost savings in the production of art work, films, and other advertising materials.[13]

Limitations of Past Research

Most participants in the debate between the desirability of the locally tailored versus standardized approaches to international marketing would agree that neither extreme makes much sense. A totally localized approach yields no competitive advantage to a multinational in terms of scale economies, shared know-how, or worldwide brand recognition. On the other hand, a totally standardized approach does not appear to be practical given the country differences mentioned earlier. Some have argued that finding the "right balance" between the two extremes is desirable; yet, the factors that determine the right balance have not been developed, nor has the possibility that local responsiveness and standardization can be pursued simultaneously.

Perhaps we have been asking the wrong questions. The question, "Should we standardize our marketing activities or not?" may have led some researchers to take an either-or position. The real question is how a firm's approach to international marketing can lead to competitive advantage measured on a worldwide basis. As we have argued, the task is really to pursue both local responsiveness and standardization simultaneously, and to recognize how the approach to international marketing should vary across products and across various marketing activities. This is what the results in Table 4.1 were really saying.

Because standardization in international marketing has been often looked upon as an all-or-nothing choice, there has also been little systematic examination of the benefits of international coordination in individual activities within the marketing function. Past research on standardization has focused on product, pricing,[14] promotion, and distribution decisions. Researchers have tended to ignore such areas as service and sales force. In addition, much of the attention of past research has been directed at the benefits of commonality of approach across countries or the transfer of marketing know-how among them. Relatively little emphasis has been placed on identifying opportunities for actual sharing of marketing activities on a worldwide basis to reduce cost or raise differentiation.

Much research in international marketing (and, for that matter, in marketing generally) also appears to have been preoccupied with questions of marketing effectiveness—for example, how effective a standardized product would be in meeting the customer needs in different countries, how a successful advertising theme or sales promotion program in one country can be effectively transferred to other countries, how effective localized pricing would be in industries where transshipping is the norm, or how effective a direct distribution system would be in countries with multiple layers of wholesalers/distributors. Relatively little attention has been directed toward how international marketing policies contribute to efficiency, either directly in terms of marketing costs themselves or indirectly through marketing's potential effects on R & D costs, production costs, and so on.

Finally, much past research has examined a very limited group of industries. Most studies have examined consumer package goods firms, where products are particularly taste and image sensitive and marketing costs generally far exceed production and R & D costs. Consumer package goods exhibit but one of many patterns of international competition that must inform research on international marketing.

Most consumer package goods companies have historically pursued *country-centered* strategies in which firms compete with other multinationals and local competitors on a country-by-country basis. (See chapter 1 for a definition of a "country-centered" strategy.) Each subsidiary is treated as an independent profit center and power and authority rest with local managers. Such firms commonly transfer a unique product that has proven successful in the domestic market to other countries and quickly establish foreign production facilities. Once this occurs, the product is typically adapted to meet local needs. By looking at firms with country-centered strategies, researchers may have been led to conclude that the leverage from centralizing and coordinating international marketing was modest and confined to sharing know-how or product designs across countries.

What is needed in setting international marketing strategy is a framework that addresses the relationship between marketing and overall competitive strategy. Such a framework must also treat the role of marketing in determining relative cost position as well as its impact on differentiation. In addition, the framework must encompass the possibility that different elements of the marketing mix need to be treated differently in international marketing.

Marketing and International Strategy

International marketing is one component on a firm's overall international strategy. As discussed in chapter 1, the starting point for setting international strategy is the distinction between multidomestic and global industries. In a multidomestic industry, competition in each country (or small group of countries) is essentially independent of competition in other countries. Thus, international competition is much the same as domestic competition with the added complexities of doing business abroad. In global industries, competition in one country is strongly influenced by competition in other countries. International strategy must thus consider the interdependency among activities performed in different countries.

In multidomestic industries, international marketing should be tailored to local conditions as are other aspects of strategy such as production and R & D. A firm must recognize the particular characteristics and needs of each country in which it competes and set marketing policies accordingly. There is little payout to coordinating or standardizing international marketing in such industries, among them insurance and distribution. In such industries, it is counterproductive to pursue a global strategy.

In a global or globalizing industry, however, marketing has a potential role in contributing to overall competitive advantage if it is managed with a worldwide perspective. To see the role of marketing in a global strategy, the basic tool is the value chain (Figure 4.1). The international firm must decide where (i.e., configuration) and how (i.e., coordination) to perform each activity in the value chain. Concentrating an activity in one or two locations to serve the world can reap economies of scale, increase the rate of cumulative learning, simplify coordination with other activities, and reap benefits from performing the activity in a country with comparative advantage in that activity. Coordinating dispersed activities in various ways can lead to accumulation and transfer of knowledge, a consistent image with buyers, flexibility in competitive response, and other benefits. The factors that shape the coordination/configuration choice in general terms are described in chapter 1.

The same choices apply to where and how marketing activities are performed in different countries. There is, however, no simple one-to-one correspondence between international marketing strategy and global strategy. In some global strategies marketing should play the role of tailoring and not standardizing in order to support the overall global strategy. In other cases, standardized marketing may be in order.

THREE STRATEGIC ROLES OF INTERNATIONAL MARKETING

The value chain exposes three roles of international marketing in global strategy. The first relates to the configuration of marketing activities on a worldwide basis. While the need to perform marketing activities in all the countries means that many marketing activities should be dispersed, competitive advantage can be gained in some industries by concentrating globally such activities as production of promotional material, sales force, service support, training, and media selection.

The second role of international marketing in global strategy is through the coordination of marketing activities performed in different countries. Marketing coordination takes a number of forms, ranging from the use of similar methods across countries (e.g., common brand, product positioning, service standards), to the transfer of know-how among countries (e.g., market entry approach, customer/market information), to the integration of effort by marketing organizations across countries (e.g., international account management).

The third role of international marketing is through its linkage to the international configuration/coordination of other activities in the value chain.[15] Marketing plays a potentially powerful role in global strategy through unlocking opportunities for competitive advantage in upstream and support activities in the value chain. Marketing can unlock potential advantages in nonmarketing activities by supporting the development of universal product varieties that can be sold in many

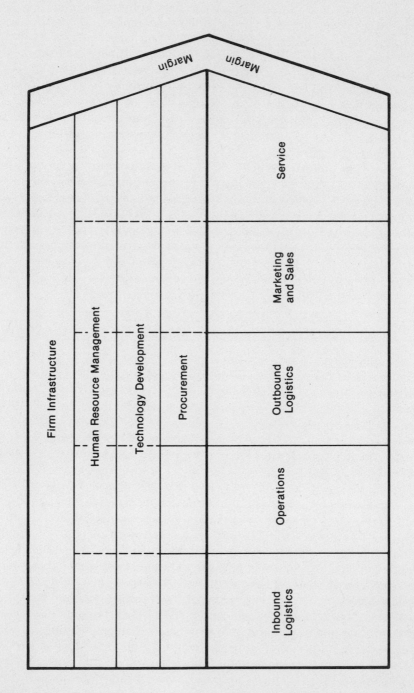

Figure 4.1 The Value Chain.

countries, creating demand for more universal varieties, segmenting the market to allow sale of universal varieties, and providing services or accessories that effectively tailor a standard physical product. These three roles of marketing in global strategy are not mutually exclusive and can be pursued simultaneously.

We examine each role below, making use of field interviews and survey data collected in the spring of 1984. We surveyed managers in seven large Japanese multinationals about various dimensions of the international industry environment and their marketing practices in forty-six product categories. These product categories spanned consumer nondurables, consumer durables, components, raw materials, and capital goods business. The survey data was supplemented by in-depth personal interviews. Because Japanese companies have been particularly successful in international marketing, they provided an interesting sample of experience from which to draw. Though the survey and interviews are not extensive enough to permit statistical findings at this stage in our research, they do provide some indication about how international marketing practices have been changing and are expected to change in the future. A list of the forty-six product categories is provided in the appendix at the end of this chapter.

International Configuration of Marketing Activities

Dispersion of marketing activities to each country in which a firm competes is usually necessary because many marketing activities are inherently tied to where buyers are located. Competitive advantage is gained by being responsive to local needs in performing such activities as pricing, distribution, advertising, and sales promotion on a market-by-market basis. This inherently local character of many marketing activities, in contrast to R & D, production, and finance, is one of the major reasons behind the view that marketing cannot be standardized internationally. According to this view, because marketing must be performed everywhere anyway, the benefits of responding to local conditions must surely outweigh those of standardization.

Performing marketing activities in many countries can be valuable in itself. International marketing presence may be seen as an indication of the firm's stature, and it may also benefit the recruiting of high-quality human resources from different parts of the world. Provided there is global coordination (see below) dispersed marketing can lead to other advantages as well. Insights gained from competing in many markets can refine a company's marketing process. An early warning system is created through the ability to spot changes in lead markets. Technology development is facilitated through relationships established with users/buyers in different countries.

But not all marketing activities have to be performed on a dispersed basis. In fact, competitive advantage—in the form of lower cost or enhanced differentiation—can sometimes be gained by performing selected marketing activities on a centralized or regional basis. Five types of marketing activities appear to offer the most potential for gaining advantage through concentrating the activities in one or a few locations: (1) production of promotional materials, (2) sales force, (3) service support organization, (4) training, and (5) advertising. Opportunities to gain advantage from centralizing marketing activities appear to be growing as a result of technological change, buyer shifts, and the evolution of marketing media.

Central Production of Promotional Materials

Centralized production of advertisements, sales promotion materials (e.g., brochures, posters, etc.), and user manuals can reap economies of scale in both development and production, as well as faster accumulation of learning, even if these materials are produced in a number of variations. The use of experienced art directors and producers may result in better TV ads being created at a greater speed or lower cost due to the learning curve effect. The use of centralized printing of materials may facilitate the adoption of a state-of the-art technology. For example, most of the basic film footage for Coca-Cola and Nestlé TV ads are produced in a single location. All of the photos used in BMW print ads and brochures are produced centrally and distributed worldwide. Canon produces its user manuals and product literature, which are printed in different languages, centrally as well.

Working against these advantages are some impediments. Transportation costs for some types of promotional material (e.g., bulky printed materials) may favor actually printing them in decentralized locations. Different product usage patterns in different countries may make the production of uniform user manuals impractical. Cultural differences can serve as a deterrent to the use of similar ads or brochures.

Central Sales Force

Another potential source of competitive advantage is a sales force partly or wholly based in one location and serving the world or large regions of it. A worldwide sales force or sales support group typically consists of a number of highly skilled sales specialists stationed in the home market or in a regional headquarters. These specialists provide support to local subsidiaries by traveling from the home market to the local markets.

The potential for achieving competitive advantage through a partly or wholly central sales force seems to be greatest when the following industry characteristics are present: (1) the complexity of the selling task is very high, (2) products are high ticket or large orders are placed at a single time, and (3) purchases are made infrequently.

To be effective in such industries, the quality of the salesperson must be extremely high, and direct contact between the salesperson and R & D and production personnel is essential. But the need to frequently travel to the buyer's locale is not that essential in such industries.

Central Service Support

In some industries, competitive advantage can be gained through a central service support group. Highly skilled service specialists, stationed at world or regional headquarters, can visit local subsidiaries to provide nonroutine service assistance. Defective parts or products may also be sent to a centralized technical service department for repair and/or for full examination of the causes of failure. This can reap economies of scale in complex repair functions as well as yield information of great benefit to design engineers. Finally, a central service support group can analyze field data from around the world and establish appropriate servicing procedures.

The impediments to maintaining a central sales force and a service support group are similar. They include: (1) the ability of highly skilled salespersons/service technicians to be well versed in the different sales/service requirements across countries, (2) travel time, and (3) transportation cost and time involved in delivering sales promotional items and parts. Industries where the advantages outweigh these impediments tend to be those with expensive products with complex service requirements. But despite these impediments, recent developments in information technology are making remote diagnosis and servicing more feasible. More and more companies will be able to benefit from the presence of central service groups with state-of-the-art technology to supplement field personnel.

Centralized Training

Centralized training in the marketing function is becoming an increasingly important tool to implement effectively a global strategy. Canon holds a "world meeting" twice a year in Tokyo for its overseas sales managers, while other firms conduct such meetings on a more ad hoc basis (e.g., Hewlett-Packard has been conducting a series of training programs for its marketing managers since it restructured the corporate organization in mid-1984).

Centralized marketing training can lead to (1) economies of scale in the production and delivery of training programs—advances in telecommunication technologies are making it easier for a multinational firm to hold centralized training sessions without having to assemble people in one location, and the use of worldwide "teleconferences" and centrally produced and distributed video programs for marketing training is also increasing; (2) faster accumulated learning as a result of having people with varied experiences assembled in one location; and (3) increased uniformity around the world in implementing marketing programs. Some of the impediments include: (1) language barriers, (2) travel time and cost, and (3) availability of training material and qualified training personnel.

Global Advertising

Although the bulk of advertising must be performed on a country-by-country basis, "global" or regional advertising is becoming more of a reality in a number of ways. First, a multinational may select one advertising agency to handle its international advertising, economizing in needed coordination and facilitating a consistent advertising approach worldwide. Second, it is more possible to advertise today in global media, such as *The Economist*, certain trade magazines, or at international sports events seen by viewers around the world. Who has not seen the brand names emblazoned on the walls of World Cup soccer stadiums, and on the clothing of top athletes? An increasing number of global media are resulting from the international strategies of publications and other media providers as well as from telecommunications technology (e.g., satellite broadcasting) that is tying the world more closely together. A third way to engage in global advertising, related to the previous one, is to advertise in media with relatively high international spillovers. Airport billboards, airline and hotel magazines, and numerous other media have a decidedly international reach. Some of the impediments to global advertising include: (1) rules and regulations governing national advertising, (2) distinctive national habits, (3) language problems in translating copy, and (4) absence of certain media.

International Marketing Coalitions

An alternative means of configuring international marketing open to a firm is to establish a marketing coalition with a foreign firm. A marketing coalition is a formal, long-term alliance between firms that links their marketing activities. Coalitions are discussed in more general terms in chapters 10 and 11. It includes, among others, distribution agreements, sales agreements, service agreements, brand name licensing, and marketing joint ventures.

International marketing coalitions are common, in part, because downstream marketing activities must usually be performed near buyers and often have to be tailored to individual country conditions. A coalition, under these circumstances, provides the firm with market access to particular countries in which its partner has more market knowledge or a stronger competitive position. Coalitions can also enable a firm to overcome market access barriers established by governments (in the form of tariffs, quotas, testing requirements, and other nontariff barriers, etc.) as well as a nationalistic purchasing policy prevalent in some countries. Coalitions open the door to effective "insider" positions, to use Ohmae's terminology.[16] Coalitions also reduce the risk of doing business on a worldwide basis and speed the accumulation of local know-how.

A number of marketing coalitions have been established recently by AT&T, for example, which was forced to sell its overseas assets to ITT in 1925. In order to become a global competitor, AT&T formed a joint venture with Philips of Holland in 1982. It also took a minor equity position in Olivetti of Italy in 1983. As a result of these coalitions, AT&T has gained at least partial access to the worldwide sales and distribution network of Philips and Olivetti.

While coalitions can be an effective way to configure marketing in countries where the firm is weak, they carry some considerable risks and management problems. Competing abroad through coalitions complicates the international coordination of marketing activities, as AT&T has discovered in its alliances. Marketing coalitions also sometimes stand in the way of linking marketing to nonmarketing activities in ways that create a competitive advantage on a global basis. These issues will be treated further below.

International Marketing Coordination

There are a number of ways in which marketing activities dispersed in different countries can be coordinated to gain competitive advantage. International coordination takes the following forms: (1) performing marketing activities using similar methods across countries, (2) transferring marketing know-how and skills from country to country, (3) sequencing of marketing programs across countries, and (4) integrating the efforts of various marketing groups in different countries. Coordinating international marketing does not necessarily mean standardizing it, nor is coordination equally valuable for all activities within the marketing function. Here we discuss each form of marketing coordination and the circumstances in which it leads to competitive advantage.

Similar Methods of Performing Marketing Activities

One form of marketing coordination is to perform activities within the marketing function identically or similarly in each country. This form of marketing coordination implies standardizing activities in favor of allowing local discretion. Employing similar methods among countries can lead to competitive advantage in a variety of ways. It can reinforce reputation or image when either buyers or information are internationally mobile. If a customer receives the same treatment by the salesperson anywhere, for example, this can reinforce the firm's differentiation. Even if buyers are not mobile, information today flows freely around the world through the media, scientific journals, word of mouth, and the like. A firm with similar marketing policies anywhere is best placed to benefit from this flow. Performing marketing activities the same or in a similar way anywhere can also allow economies in training and in purchasing the inputs used in marketing. It can also allow a firm to move more quickly down the learning curve if know-how is shared among countries.

The choice of whether to perform an activity in a similar way across countries must be made for each activity within the marketing function. The firm may choose to employ the same brand name, for example, while modifying substantially the selling approach and pricing structure. Against the benefits of similarity must be weighed any country differences that affect the particular activity. Country differences are frequently more significant with regard to some activities than others. A global brand name and a common worldwide warranty system, such as those offered by Canon or Caterpillar, may be more universally effective than common credit terms or the use of a particular advertising medium that may be absent in some countries.

Governments also frequently play a role in limiting the opportunities for standardization of some marketing activities, through such methods as constraints on the development of large-scale distribution outlets, regulations regarding price promotions, or codes regulating what can or cannot be shown on TV.

An example of the weighing of benefits and costs is the choice of whether to employ a common brand name worldwide. Common brand names are often used by companies pursuing global strategies; prominent examples include Shell in the petroleum industry, Kodak in film, Canon in cameras, IBM in computers, Intel in semiconductors, Boeing in aircraft, and others. Companies pursuing country-centered strategies or competing in a multidomestic industry, on the other hand, are more likely to use different brand names in different countries. The consumer packaged goods industry offers a number of examples in this regard. Nestlé used the Taster's Choice brand name in the United States, the Gold Blend brand name in Japan, and several variations of the Nescafé brand name in Europe and elsewhere for its freeze-dried instant coffee. Unilever does the same with its health and beauty aid products sold around the world.

The most obvious advantage of a common brand name is to lower the cost of advertising and promotion to mobile customers. Faced with the choice of filling up a car with Shell gasoline or an unknown local brand in South America, for example, a European traveler may be predisposed to selecting Shell because of prior media exposure back home. Firms with common brand names can also enjoy cost savings due to media spillovers. Kodak, for example, recently carried out a pan-European advertising campaign partly because it discovered that television broadcasts and cable services in Europe reach so many countries at the same time. A global brand name can also lead to differentiation through the operation of international word of mouth.

Sony, for example, has been utilizing "It's a Sony" campaign through-out the world to foster international word of mouth.

As industries, buyers, media, and information become increasingly global, companies are increasing their use of common brand names. Nissan Motors, for example, recently spent millions of dollars in an effort to establish "Nissan" as its common worldwide name. These same forces are working to enhance the benefits of standardization in other marketing activities as well.

Certain activities are easier to coordinate internationally than others from an organizational standpoint. Forms of coordination involving a one-time decision are easier to implement than forms of coordination requiring ongoing communication and monitoring. Adopting a common brand name throughout the world, for example, is easier to carry out than establishing a uniform sales-force approach throughout the world. Table 4.2 arrays some of the most common activities within the marketing function based on the ease or difficulty of international coordination, combining the organizational costs of coordination and the extent to which local country differences make standardization impossible or inappropriate.

Table 4.2 Ease/Difficulty of Standardizing
Marketing Activities across Countries

EASIER	MORE DIFFICULT
• Brand name	• Distribution
• Product positioning	• Personal selling
• Service standards	• Salesperson training
• Warranties	• Pricing
• Advertising theme	• Media selection

Our survey of forty-six product categories suggests that the degree to which worldwide standardization is carried out differs by marketing activity. Figure 4.2 illustrates that the firms in our sample, cutting across all types of products, were more likely to employ a common brand name worldwide, employ the same advertising theme, and offer the same service and product guarantee worldwide than they were to use the same pricing policy, employ the same sales promotion programs, or use the same distribution channels. The survey data also illustrate that except for brand name, most firms modify activities somewhat across countries rather than keep them the same. The stark dichotomy between standardizing and tailoring is a false dichotomy in practice, because many degrees of coordination across countries are possible.

Our field interviews, confirmed by Marquise Cvar's case studies described in chapter 15, suggest that leading global competitors often move proactively to standardize marketing activities even if local con-

Figure 4.2 Similarities/Differences across Countries on Marketing Programs

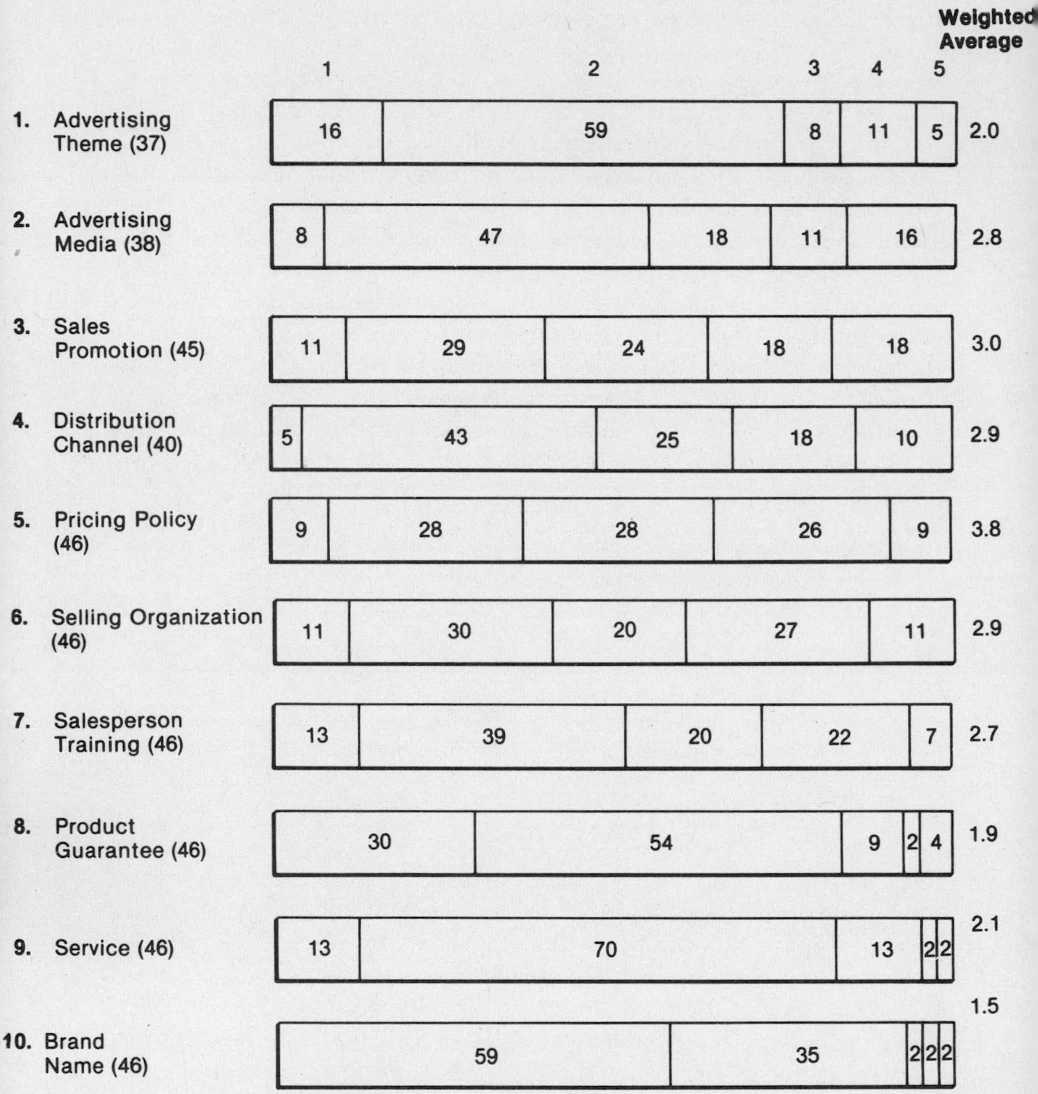

		1	2	3	4	5	Weighted Average
1.	Advertising Theme (37)	16	59	8	11	5	2.0
2.	Advertising Media (38)	8	47	18	11	16	2.8
3.	Sales Promotion (45)	11	29	24	18	18	3.0
4.	Distribution Channel (40)	5	43	25	18	10	2.9
5.	Pricing Policy (46)	9	28	28	26	9	3.8
6.	Selling Organization (46)	11	30	20	27	11	2.9
7.	Salesperson Training (46)	13	39	20	22	7	2.7
8.	Product Guarantee (46)	30	54	9	2	4	1.9
9.	Service (46)	13	70	13	2	2	2.1
10.	Brand Name (46)	59	35	2	2	2	1.5

Responses

1 Same throughout the world

2 Somewhat similar across countries

3 Cannot say one way or the other

4 Somewhat different across countries

5 Different from country to country

ditions have historically been diverse. Firms pioneer or encourage the development of distribution channels that have not previously been important, innovate in sales-force techniques, and so on. Success in global marketing coordination is not often the result of passive response to existing conditions but of active efforts to unleash the benefits of coordination by overcoming obstacles to it.

Transfer of Know-How

The second form of international marketing coordination is the transfer of know-how from one country to another. A number of different kinds of know-how can be transferred. Of particular importance are the transfer of a market entry approach that worked in one country to other countries, and the sharing of customer and market information. Transferring know-how does not necessarily imply the standardization of marketing activities, though standardization may make know-how easier to share.

Common market entry strategy: Companies have successfully utilized the same basic market entry strategy to penetrate a series of geographic markets. For example, BIC identified a market niche at the low-end of the ballpoint market in the late 1950s and developed an effective entry strategy that allowed it to penetrate every country selected as a target.

Shared know-how in entry strategy helps a firm gain competitive advantage in a variety of ways. Cost is reduced because the best demonstrated practice can be applied to a new geographic market. A global competitor has already learned how to overcome the difficulties encountered in entry and been exposed to a variety of competitive responses, giving it an advantage over domestic or country-centered competitors.

Our survey found that 65 percent of the products employed the same or a similar market entry strategy in all countries. In only 16 percent of the products did the firm employ a different entry strategy from country to country.

Sharing of Marketing Information: The ability to transfer customer and market information between countries and regions is one of the most important advantages of a global competitor. Useful information such as shifts in buyer purchasing patterns, recent trends in technology, life-style changes, successful new product or feature introductions, new point-of-purchase merchandising ideas or early market signals by competitors, can be passed quickly around the world and to headquarters.

A company with a presence in "lead" markets—or markets with the most demanding buyers or those buyers most likely to adopt innovations—has a particular advantage. Such presence plugs the firm

into the latest information on customer needs, technological developments, and competitive moves. The benefits of lead market presence
require that global competitors invest substantially to penetrate them.

In the past, the United States used to be the lead market for most
industries. In recent years, the lead market is becoming more varied
across industries. For example, Israel is now considered a lead market
in agriculture and Japan in electronics. Japan is also a lead market for
disposable diapers, a product developed in the United States. Procter
& Gamble tested its new line of improved disposable diapers in Japan
because it discovered that Japanese mothers are the most sensitive to
quality. The rationale for Procter & Gamble was simple: if a new product passes the scrutiny of the toughest customer, the likelihood is high
that it will be accepted anywhere in the world.

Despite the benefits of transferring know-how, marketing information does not flow freely among units in most companies. Without
mechanisms to overcome inertia and the parochialism of subsidiaries,
information is protected and not shared. Several organizational mechanisms can serve as facilitators of exchange. Hewlett-Packard, for example, publishes a quarterly magazine called *Intercom* to report on
the latest developments in its international operations. Canon's world
meeting facilitates information exchange and keeps its regional marketing managers abreast of developments elsewhere in the world.

Sequencing of marketing programs

The third form of marketing coordination, which implies the previous
one as well, is the sequencing of marketing programs in different
countries. New products or new marketing practices are introduced
in various countries in a planned sequence. Countries frequently differ to some extent in the desired product attributes, responsiveness
to particular advertising appeals, and so on. Country conditions, however, tend to evolve over time with economic development, per capita
income growth, and changing marketing infrastructure. The global
company recognizes this evolution and even encourages it by migrating product varieties and marketing programs to countries as they are
ready for them. A more advanced product that has been sold in Europe, for example, is introduced into Latin American countries as
their local manufacturers develop the technology to use it. Becton
Dickinson used this approach to its advantage in syringes, as chronicled in chapter 15.

The advantages of sequencing marketing programs across countries
can be substantial, especially if the global competitor pioneers the
new product or marketing program. By employing already developed
products or programs, the company can share costs with other regions
of the world. Such an approach also makes it difficult for domestic
competitors to respond since they lack a presence elsewhere in the

world. To reap the benefits of sequencing, a company must create organizational mechanisms to manage the product line from a worldwide perspective and to overcome country manager resistance to change.

Integration of Effort across Countries

The final form of international marketing coordination is integrating the activities of the various marketing groups located in different countries. The most common form of such integration is managing relationships with important multinational customers through systems commonly known as "international account management." International account management systems have long existed in service industries. For example, McCann-Erickson handles the Nestlé and Coca-Cola accounts on a worldwide basis. Bankers Trust, a wholesale bank, has account officers responsible for coordinating the service of its large corporate customers anywhere in the world.

Manufacturing firms are increasingly utilizing the international account management system as well. For example, Teradyne's Semiconductor Test Division, which manufactures a system to test memory devices, recently assigned international account managers to oversee the worldwide relationship with such corporate customers as Intel, Texas Instruments, Motorola, and others that were fast expanding their production facilities throughout the world. Another example is IBM, which has key account managers assigned to so-called Selected International Accounts, a category of IBM customers with locations worldwide. Account managers are stationed in countries where the headquarters of such customers are located.

Competitive advantage can result from international account management systems in a variety of ways. They can lead to economies in the utilization of the sales force if duplication of selling effort is avoided. They can allow a company to differentiate itself from its competitors through offering a single contact for international buyers. They can also leverage the skills of top salespersons by giving them more influence over the entire relationship with a major customer.

Some of the potential impediments to using international account management include increased travel time, language barriers, and cultural differences in how business is conducted. Dealing with a major customer through a single coordinator may also heighten the customer's awareness of its bargaining power.

Integration of effort across countries can also lead to competitive advantage in the area of after-sale service. Some international companies have come to realize that the availability of after-sale service is often as important as the product itself, especially when a multinational customer has operations in remote areas of the world or when the customer moves from country to country. For example, Caterpillar guarantees delivery of any part to any customer anywhere in the world within forty-eight hours or the parts are free. Caterpillar works closely with its 230 or so dealers scattered in different countries to meet this standard. Canon has a similar service in place. Its cameras, wherever they are purchased, are backed by the Worldwide Warranty (WWW) system, which guarantees camera owners with after-sale service anywhere.

Marketing Coordination in Practice

Our survey results indicate that 70 percent of the respondents were conscious of the need to coordinate marketing activities on a worldwide basis. Those products in the sample where marketing coordination was not deemed important today were print-out calculators, mobile telephones, projection televisions, room air-conditioners, elevators, and printing machinery for photosensitive resin. These are all products where buying decisions are highly localized.

The benefits of coordination are being enhanced by the globalization of media, the international mobility of buyers, the free flow of information around the world, and the growing number of firms with international production systems. This was confirmed by our survey. Eighty percent of the respondents answered that the need for coordination will increase in the future and 50 percent replied that the need "will increase substantially." No respondent believed that worldwide marketing coordination would become less important in the future.

As the benefits to coordination are increasing, so is the ability to coordinate growing. The transfer of data (e.g., results in consumer research, test marketing, focus group interviews, etc.), voice (e.g., message from the CEO at headquarters via teleconferencing), and visuals (e.g., use of videotex or facsimile) from one country to another has been greatly facilitated owing to recent developments in telecommunications and computers.

Marketing's Linkage to Nonmarketing Activities

Perhaps the greatest leverage from taking a global view of international marketing grows out of marketing's link to upstream and support activities in the value chain. In particular, marketing can unlock economies of scale and learning in production and/or R & D by (1) supporting the development of universal products, by providing the information necessary to develop a physical product design that can be sold worldwide; (2) creating demand for more universal products even if historical demand has been for more varied products in different countries; (3) identifying and penetrating segments in many countries to allow the sale of universal products; and (4) providing services and/or local accessories that effectively tailor the standard physical product.

Physical Product Differences among Countries

An increasing number of companies have come to realize the benefits of producing a "world" product, that is, a standardized product sold throughout the world. Indeed, world products exist in many different industries, ranging from hamburgers to cosmetics to vacation spots (Club Med). The concept of a world product seems to mean different things to different people, however. One view of a world product is a product that has standardized physical attributes (including packaging and brand name) in every country. Another view is a product where the product image or positioning is the same everywhere though there are physical differences across countries. Still another view of a world product is a product that is manufactured and assembled in many countries around the world (e.g., Boeing's 767 gets most of its wings, cockpit, and final assembly from North America, the rudder and fins from Italy, and the main body from Japan).

From a strategic point of view, the physical uniformity of the product is the most important attribute for defining a world product. Physical uniformity allows the achievement of economies of scale and learning in R & D and/or production activities. A common image or positioning across countries without physical uniformity may allow certain benefits in the marketing function, but generally has a lesser impact on cost position or differentiation. Where the physically uniform product is actually produced is a matter of optimizing the trade-offs among scale economies, comparative advantage, transport costs, tariffs, and other factors described in chapter 1.

The extent of physical product differences across countries can be arrayed along the following taxonomy:

Universal Product: The physical product sold in each country is identical except for such things as labeling and the language used in manuals. Many basic materials, components, high-technology products, industrial products, and even some consumer goods fall into this category. Some examples are steel, chemicals, plastics, ceramic casings used in memory chips, aircraft turbine engines, cameras, and sunglasses (e.g., Ray-ban).

Modified Product: The physical product sold in each country (or group of countries) is substantially similar, but the basic product is modified in areas that represent a modest percentage of total costs. Modifications include such factors as voltage, color, size (where size does not require significant production changes), accessories, and so on. Some modifications may be mandatory (e.g., government regulation on packaging and labeling or use of the metric system) while others are made to reflect local differences in taste, buying habit, climate, and usage conditions.

Industrial products such as CT scanners, broadcast video cameras, mainframe computers, copiers, precision-testing equipment, and large construction equipment fall into this category. Modified products also include consumer goods such as cars, motorcycles, calculators, and microwave ovens. Each of these products employs the same basic design and technology to produce the "core" product but relatively minor modifications are made to adapt to local requirements. Cars, for example, have a high degree of commonality in engines, drive trains, and other key components in order to maximize production scale economies and long production runs, but have customized accessories, options packages, paint, emission control devices, and seat-belt arrangements to meet local requirements.

The cost of modifying products has been decreasing due to flexible manufacturing systems and the embedding of software into products. Flexible manufacturing systems reduce the cost of producing many product varieties. Software embedded in the product allows its performance to be altered while keeping the hardware the same (e.g., in a telecommunication switch).

Country-Tailored Product: The physical product is substantially tailored to each country (or group of countries) in ways that affect a significant fraction of total costs. Many country-tailored products occur in consumer packaged goods, especially food items and household products. This is understandable because tastes and usage patterns vary from country to country. Nestlé, for example, has dozens of different formulations of instant coffee and bottle shapes to package it in for this reason. Also, because production costs associated with consumer packaged goods tend to be relatively small compared to marketing costs, there is less incentive to physically standardize them. Industrial products, on the other hand, tend to have cost structures more sensitive to scale economies in R & D and production.

Our survey found that physical product design was similar worldwide for 83 percent of the forty-six product categories surveyed (in 24 percent of the product categories, products were the "same throughout the world" category and in 59 percent "somewhat similar throughout the world"). To test respondents' definition of similarity, we also asked them to estimate the extent of physical product similarity across countries using value added as an indicator. Asked what percent of the product's parts was common across countries, 41 percent of the product categories surveyed had "over 95 percent common" across countries, 24 percent had "about 90 percent common," and 17 percent had "about 80 percent common."

Marketing's Contribution to New-Product Development

Given the link between physical product differences across countries and upstream and support activities, the ability of a firm to successfully sell a universal product anywhere is significant to competitive advantage. The achievement of economies of scale and learning is most significant with universal products, less so with modified products, and almost nonexistent with country-tailored products.

The first role of marketing in unlocking these advantages is through supporting the development of universal products or products that are inexpensively modified that will be salable. A multinational firm must address two basic questions in developing a new product: (1) what kind of product to develop, and (2) how to go about developing it.[17] In setting out to develop a universal product, there are two basic philosophies that can be employed. One is to develop a product that represents the "greatest common denominator"—it has all the features demanded anywhere in the world or in a region. The other philosophy is to develop a universal product with an optimized set of functions and features that balance market needs and cost.

This second philosophy was employed in the case of Canon's Personal Copier (PC). This case illustrates how adept global competitors often go to great lengths to devise ways of circumventing or adapting to local differences while preserving the advantages of the similarities. In Japan the typical paper size is bigger than American legal size and the standard European size. Canon's PC copier will not handle this size—a Japanese company introduced a product that did not meet its home market needs in the world's largest market for small copiers! Canon gathered its marketing managers from around the world and cataloged market needs in each country. They found that capacity to copy the large Japanese paper was only needed in Japan. In consultation with design and manufacturing engineers, it was determined that building this feature into the PC would significantly increase its complexity and cost. The feature was omitted because the price elasticity of demand for the PC was judged to be high. But this was not the end of the deliberations. Canon's management then set out to find a way to make the PC salable in Japan. The answer was to add another feature to the copier—the ability to copy business cards—which added little cost and was particularly valuable in Japan. This case illustrates the principle of looking for the similarities in needs among countries and in finding ways of creating similarities, not emphasizing the differences.

International marketing units play a vital role in the development of universal products by collecting information from around the world and putting designers and engineers in touch with customers in different countries. These inputs help to determine the new product concept and the actual design specifications. The decision to develop a universal product also shapes the manner in which the new product development process should be managed. Canon's experience in developing the AE-1 camera, which was introduced in 1976, provides insights into how marketing can work with R & D and production to bring about major breakthroughs in upstream activities and build organizational commitment for new products.

Based on several formal and informal market analyses, Canon's marketing group at headquarters took the initiative in establishing the target product—a quality, automatic-exposure single-lens reflex (SLR) camera in the 80,000 yen price range (the prevailing price level of a comparable SLR camera was over 100,000 yen). In addition, the new camera had to be compact, lightweight, and easy enough for anyone to use.

The development task force (consisting of design engineers, production engineers, and planners from every sector of the company, including people with business machine experience) established by Canon succeeded in meeting this ambitious target by incorporating several major breakthroughs in camera design and production: (1) introduction of an electronic brain consisting of integrated circuits custom-made by Texas Instruments, (2) modularized production,[18] which made automation and mass production possible, and (3) reduction in the number of parts by 30 to 40 percent. Because Canon intended the AE-1 to become a standardized world product, its marketing personnel presented the prototype to overseas managers at the semiannual "world meeting" in 1975, a year before planned market introduction. Managers from overseas subsidiaries exhibited strong initial resistance to the product because the previous SLR model was selling well overseas and because many felt the target sales volume for the AE-1 was too ambitious. The marketing group succeeded in enlisting subsidiary support by demonstrating how the success of the project was contingent on achieving worldwide volume (which led to larger production scale and lower unit cost). Several design modifications and feature additions that were suggested by the overseas managers at the meeting were also incorporated into the product. The AE-1 experience suggests that some tradeoffs have to be made to satisfy the greatest common denominator.

According to our survey, products were developed with the global market in mind from the start in 76 percent of the categories. In addition, market information from overseas was acquired during the product development process in 98 percent of the product categories studied. The top three sources of information used in new product development mentioned included (1) a firm's overseas subsidiaries, which confirms the extent to which information sharing was taking place, (2) outside research and consulting firms, and (3) personal visits and direct contacts with customers and others outside the firm.

The AE-1 experience suggests the importance of active participation by overseas subsidiaries during the early phase of the new product development process. Our survey found that (1) overseas subsidiaries participated in the product development process in half of the product categories surveyed, and (2) of these, 87 percent participated in the first (i.e., concept development) phase of the development process.

Creating Demand for More Universal Products

It is sometimes possible to create demand for a universal or inexpensively modified product where country-specificity has been the norm. While the initial marketing investment required to do so may be high, the potential impact on competitive advantage can be substantial. Both Clinique (a division of Estée Lauder producing skincare products) and Krugerrand, for example, created universal products out of product categories with deeply entrenched country differences through heavy advertising and promotion. Honda created demand in the United States for small motorbikes, giving it a preemptive volume and cost advantage that has led to industry leadership in the world. Cvar's case studies in chapter 15 provide further evidence of this phenomenon.

Opportunities to create demand for universal products appear to be growing as a result of the globalization of markets. This was the controversial thesis of Levitt's work, and was supported by Ohmae.[19] Ohmae's research suggests that the 600 million consumers in the United States, Japan, and the European community had strikingly similar needs and preferences. Homogenization of worldwide consumer wants and wishes is being facilitated by the rapid expansion of communication, travel, and spending power throughout the world.

While there has been little data on either side of the globalization of markets controversy, our survey provides some tentative support for the thesis that globalization is occurring. Respondents said that product standardization had been increasing in 74 percent of product categories (in 33 percent of products, standardization had "increased substantially" and in 41 percent, it had "increased somewhat"; only 6 percent said it had been decreasing). Moreover, respondents believed that product standardization would increase in the future in 74 percent of categories; only 13 percent forecast it would decrease. Categories in which standardization was expected to decrease were excavators, dot-matrix printers, portable generators, motorcycles, and desk-top professional personal computers.

Segmentation and Physical Product Design

Market segmentation is the third way in which a global approach to international marketing can facilitate the sale of physically similar products worldwide. There are three different approaches: (1) identifying segments present in many or most countries, (2) targeting differ-

Figure 4.3 Universal Segment Positioning across Countries

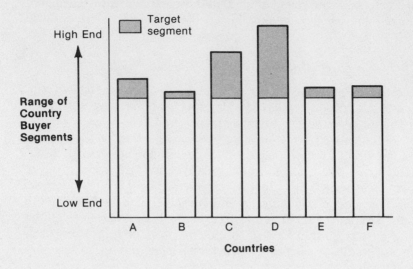

ent segments in different countries with the same product, and (3) identifying clusters of countries that demand similar products.

Selling to a Universal Segment across Countries: Although physical product needs overall vary among countries, there may be a segment of the market with identical needs in every country. This *universal* segment is most likely to be high-end consumers, multinational companies, or the most sophisticated business users because these groups tend to be the most mobile and/or the most likely to have extensive international contacts. For example, the very rich in Japan, Zaire, and Argentina all want a Mercedes because it is positioned as a top-of-the-line, high-performance product.

The universal segment approach is illustrated in Figure 4.3. Note that the size of the universal segment can be small, and its size typically varies among countries. Many Japanese companies employ the universal segment approach, gaining a small share of virtually every country market in the process.

Targeting Diverse Segments across Countries: Even if product needs vary among countries, a physically similar product can sometimes be sold everywhere if it is targeted at *different* segments in each country. This approach is illustrated in Figure 4.4. In this approach, marketing activities such as advertising channels, and sales-force operations are varied across countries to reach the different segments that demand the same physical product. Tailoring the way certain

Figure 4.4 Diverse Segment Positioning across Countries

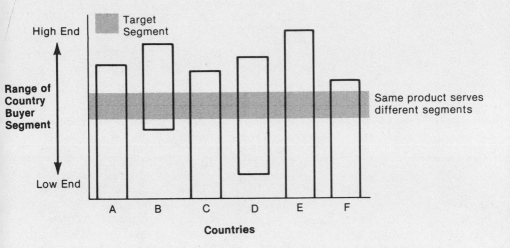

marketing activities are performed in each country thus makes standardization in upstream activities possible. As segmentation of needs within each country is increasing, this approach to international marketing seems to be becoming more prevalent.

The Canon AE-1 camera provides a good example of this international segmentation approach. The AE-1 was targeted toward young replacement buyers in Japan, upscale first-time buyers of 35mm single-lens reflex cameras in the United States, and older and more technologically sophisticated replacement buyers in Germany. Once such segments were identified, Canon's marketing group developed a marketing program best suited for each country. Three different marketing programs for AE-1 were developed for Japan, the United States, and Europe, as illustrated in Table 4.3.

A diverse segment positioning approach can also apply to modified products, such as automobiles. Honda, for example, sold its Accord primarily to the second or commuter car buyer segment in the United States, the family-car segment in Japan, the highly engineered sporty car segment in certain countries in Europe, and the status-seeking segment in certain less-developed countries. Honda manufacturers used creative but varying marketing programs to reach the various country segments.

Targeting Country Groupings: Another way of segmenting to allow the sale of physically similar products worldwide is on the basis of geography. Products rarely require modification or tailoring for every

Table 4.3 Diverse Segment Positioning of the AE-1

Marketing Activities	Japan	United States	Europe
Target audience	Replacement buyers among young people	First-time buyers of SLR cameras who can be converted from box cameras to SLR	Replacement buyers who can be converted from old-fashioned cameras to SLR
Advertising message	"Continuous-shooting SLR": single-lens reflex that allows sequences of two frames per second	"So advanced, it's simple": by using sports celebrities show the camera's ability to meet the challenge of fast-paced sport action and its suitability for non-professional photographers.	No catch-phrase used in Europe; ads stress techno-logical superiority result-ing from use of micropro-cessor in the central processing unit or "brain" of the camera as well as speed and ease of use
Advertising media	Newspaper, television, magazine	Even split between televi-sion and newspaper/maga-zine; also official sponsor of Winter Olympics Games, Avon Tennis, Championship Profes-sional Golfers Association, etc.; very substantial in-crease in promotional budget	Magazines, billboards, cinemas, bus/trains; sub-stantial increase in promo-tional budget
Distribution	Specialty stores	Use AE-1 as means of shifting distribution from specialty stores to mass merchandisers; extensive dealer promotions and dealer training programs	Multi-unit specialty chains; some dealer pro-motions
Price	Retail list price of 85,000 yen (with 50 Fl.4 lens and case) or U.S. $290 at time of introduc-tion	Determined locally; retail list price of $430 at time of introduction and actual selling price of below $300	Differed from country to country

single country, because groups of countries are often similar in their product needs. Relevant groups of countries may reflect similarities in climate, language, and state of economic development, or religious beliefs. Countries can also frequently be grouped on the basis of sim-ilarities in infrastructure (e.g., media availability, distribution chan-nels, etc.). An imaginative format for clustering countries may allow the sale of universal products within the group of countries and mod-ified products or country-tailored products across groups, or the sale of modified products within the group and country-tailored products across groups.

Understanding similarities among groups of countries may not only help unlock scale economies in upstream value activities, but may also allow a firm to better coordinate marketing via transfer of know-how or learning, or to sequence products and marketing programs. It may also suggest the best way to organize the marketing function.

The Segmentation Approaches Compared: Of the three segmentation approaches, universal segmentation usually leads to the greatest overall competitive advantage because not only can products be standardized but reputation is reinforced internationally and marketing know-how can be transferred among countries as well. Under the diverse segmentation approach, a firm must develop different marketing programs for different countries and its image in each country is somewhat different. The country segmentation approach lies somewhere in between.

Tailoring the Physical Product via Service and/or Accessories

A final means of facilitating the sale of physically similar products worldwide is to provide services and/or accessories that effectively tailor the product. Although the "core" product remains the same, country differences are embodied in the product through services and/or accessories. For example, Brother sells an electronic typewriter with replaceable daisy wheels worldwide. Replacing the daisy wheel allows users in different countries to type in their own language. Similarly, L. M. Ericsson of Sweden took advantage of the advent of electronic switching technology to develop a series of modular software packages that could be used in different combinations to meet the needs of diverse telephone systems throughout the world.

Integrating Physical Production Design and Segmentation

Our discussion of the role of marketing in shaping nonmarketing activities led us to identify three categories of products—universal, modified, and country-tailored—and three ways of using segmentation to allow the sale of physically uniform products worldwide even with country differences. These two variables define the matrix of possibilities shown in Figure 4.5. Examples of products are included in six of the cells for illustrative purposes. As discussed previously, different product segments within an industry may fit into different cells. Industries can also move from cell to cell. Telecommunications equipment, for example, is moving from cell 5 to cell 3 as technology shifts from electromechanical to electronic and the cost of modifying the product to meet country differences falls. Consumer packaged goods

Figure 4.5 Determinants of International Marketing Strategy

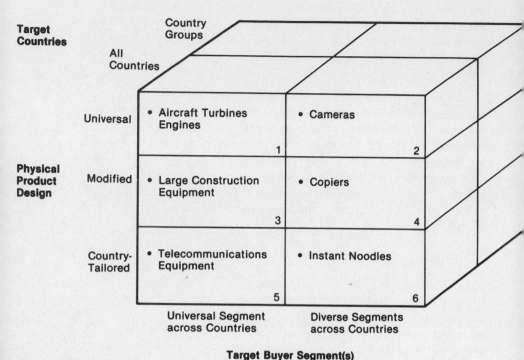

are becoming less country tailored and competitors are discovering more universal segments across countries.

The matrix provides a convenient way to summarize a number of important considerations for international marketing strategy that have not been described thus far:

1. The appropriate kind of international marketing coordination varies by cell. In the upper left-hand cells, strong linkage between marketing and upstream/support activities is present. The universal or modified products of these cells tend to be more susceptible to a common branding, and to the use of similar marketing approaches in different countries. In the lower right-hand cells, linkages between marketing and upstream/support activities are not as strong. Less coordination is needed or appropriate.

2. A product's position within the matrix can shift with industry evolution. Homogenization of preferences across countries or industry

maturation can move a product up. TV sets, for example, evolved from being country-tailored to essentially universal.

3. Finding ways of moving a firm position upward and leftward within the matrix increases competitive advantage. Of the two directions of change, greater advantage seems to be gained by an upward move because upward movement allows shared upstream activities. Leftward movement on the matrix allows more marketing coordination but only on downstream marketing costs.

4. Marketing innovations that move a product up the matrix take on high priority. Honda convinced middle-class Americans that riding motorcycles could be fun through innovations in advertising, promotion, and trade shows. It turned market preferences in a key country market toward the characteristics of its own products, thereby making mass production possible.

5. Reducing the cost of physically modifying a product can wholly or partly offset the need to reposition. Japanese firms frequently modify products, often with the help of local designers, but do so in ways that minimize the disruption to scale economies.

6. The position on the matrix carries implications for the organization of international marketing function. The organization of the marketing function should vary by cell because the nature and extent of required marketing coordination varies by cell. Centralization of authority over decision making in all international marketing units should usually increase as we move leftward and upward in the matrix. Product development also should be more centralized as we move upward.

SUMMARY

There is still a lingering controversy surrounding the appropriateness of globalizing the marketing function. Some are inclined to say "yes," citing the increasing homogenization of needs around the world. Others say "no," arguing that there is very little evidence of worldwide homogenization of needs but compelling evidence that country circumstances differ.

We have argued that standardization is too vague and narrow a concept with which to understand marketing's role in global strategy. While our data support the view that needs are globalizing, to frame the debate about international marketing strategy around this question misses the point. Instead, marketers must understand how to configure marketing activities worldwide, how and when to coordinate separate marketing groups in different countries, and how to use international marketing strategy to support a firm's overall global strategy. In these diverse ways, we find a compelling role for a global approach to international marketing that is likely to increase in the future.

APPENDIX
Product Categories Covered in the Survey

Raw Materials

1. Crystallized cellulose
2. Synthetic fibers

Components

3. Semiconductors
4. LCD panel displays
5. Mechanical parts for mini-printers
6. Floppy disk drives
7. Monitor displays
8. Black-and-white cathode-ray tubes
9. Color cathode-ray tubes

Machinery

10. Computer numerical control machine tools
11. Machining centers
12. Corrugating machinery
13. Iron/steel manufacturing machinery
14. Printing machinery for photosensitive resin
15. Industrial sewing machines
16. Mask aligners

Industrial Products

17. Forklift trucks
18. Excavators (power shovels)
19. Elevators
20. Marine diesel engines
21. Bulk/oil carrying vessels

Medical Products

22. CT scanners
23. Artificial kidney-related products

Office Products

24. Plain paper copiers (small-size)
25. Plain paper copiers (medium-size)
26. Printout calculators
27. Dot-matrix printers for office use
28. Mobile telephone sets
29. Electric key telephone systems
30. Desktop professional personal computers

Durable Consumer Goods

31. Color televisions
32. Projection televisions
33. Video-cassette recorders

34. Microwave ovens
35. Room air conditioners
36. Portable generators
37. Small-size tractors for home use
38. Cameras
39. Hand-held personal computers
40. Personal computers
41. Printers for personal computers
42. Audio products
43. Car stereos
44. Automobiles
45. Motorcycles
46. Off-the-road tricycles

NOTES

1. See R. D. Buzzell, "Can You Standardize Multinational Marketing?" *Harvard Business Review* (November–December 1968): 102–13, for an excellent discussion of these two opposing views.
2. See T. Levitt, "The Globalization of Markets," *Harvard Business Review* (May–June 1983): 92–102 and M. E. Porter, *Competitive Strategy* (New York: Free Press, 1980), chap. 13.
3. "Brazil: Campbell Soup Fails to Make It to the Table," *Business Week*, October 21, 1981, 66.
4. L. Kraar, "Inside Japan's 'Open' Market," *Fortune*, October 5, 1981, 122.
5. "Radio Shack's Rough Trip," *Business Week*, May 30, 1977, 55.
6. C. L. Lapp, "Marketing Goofs in International Trade," *The Diary of Alpha Kappa Psi* (February 1983): 4.
7. "Brazil," *Business Week*.
8. A description of this pattern of evolution by Japanese companies is given in P. Kotler, L. Fahey, and S. Jatusripitak, *The New Competition* (Englewood Cliffs, N.J.: Prentice-Hall, 1985).
9. R. I. Sorenson and U. E. Wiechmann, "How Multinationals View Marketing Standardization," *Harvard Business Review* (May–June 1975): 48.
10. Levitt, "The Globalization of Markets," 93.
11. Taken from D. F. Channon with M. Jalland, *Multinational Strategic Planning* (New York: AMACOM, 1978), p. 269. For further references in the product area, see W. Keegan, "Multinational Product Planning: Strategic Alternatives," *Journal of Marketing* (January 1969): 58–62; G. Leroy, *Multinational Product Strategy* (New York: Praeger, 1976).
12. See, for example, E. Elinder, "How International Can Advertising Be?" in *International Handbook of Advertising*, S. Watson Dunn, ed. (New York: McGraw-Hill, 1964); A. C. Fatt, "The Danger of 'Local' International Advertising," *Journal of Marketing* (January 1967): 60–62; E. S. Lorimor and S. W. Dunn, "Four Measures of Cross-Cultural Advertising Effectiveness," *Journal of Advertising Research* (December 1967): 10–13; R. T. Green, W. H. Cunningham, and I. C. M. Cunningham, "The Effectiveness of Standardized Advertising," *Journal of Advertising* (Summer 1975): 25–30; S. H. Britt, "Standardizing Marketing for the International Market," *Columbia Journal of World Business* (Winter 1974): 39–45; J. Hornik, "Comparative Evaluation of International vs. National

Advertising Strategies," *Columbia Journal of World Business* (Spring 1980): 36–45; M. Colvin, R. Heeler, and J. Thorpe, "Developing International Advertising Strategy," *Journal of Marketing* (Fall 1980): 73–79.

13. Buzzell, "Can You Standardize Multinational Marketing?," 105.

14. For a collection of articles on transfer pricing, see R. Murray, ed., *Multinationals Beyond the Market: Intrafirm Trade and the Control of Transfer Pricing* (New York: Halsted Press, 1981).

15. A linkage is a relationship between the way one activity is performed and the cost or effectiveness of other activities. For a discussion of the concept of linkages in value chain theory see Porter (1985a), chap. 2.

16. K. Ohmae, *Triad Power: The Coming Shape of Global Competition* (New York: Free Press, 1985).

17. See H. Takeuchi and I. Nonaka, "The New-New Product Development Game," *Harvard Business Review* (January–February 1986) for a more detailed discussion of how to manage the new product development process.

18. Modularized production is a system under which the camera is constructed with pre-assembled units or modules. The AE-1 had five major modules: the shutter, viewfinder, auto exposure mechanism, exposure control, and mirror unit.

19. Levitt, "The Globalization of Markets" and Ohmae, *Triad Power*.

5

Finance and Global Competition: Exploiting Financial Scope and Coping with Volatile Exchange Rates*

Donald R. Lessard

INTRODUCTION

The emergence of global competition represents a major threat to firms that have gained competitive advantage under the previous largely multidomestic rules. However, it also creates new opportunities for firms that can reconfigure their operations to exploit the leverage provided by global scope with managers who can shift their perspectives to cope with this more complex environment.

Finance plays a critical role in a firm's adaptation to this new competitive environment. In discussing finance under global competition, we define its role broadly,

- to provide a yardstick for judging current and prospective operations;
- to raise the funds required for these operations; and
- to add value in its own right by exploiting distortions in financial markets, reducing taxes, and managing the risks inherent in the firm's activities.

The larger stakes associated with world-scale operations require greater financial resources and flexibility. Further, global competition in product and factor markets reduces the ability of a firm to pass

*I am grateful to Carliss Baldwin, Gene Flood, Sumantra Ghoshal, Bruce Kogut, John Lightstone, Tom Piper, Michael Porter, David Sharp, Mark Trusheim, and Louis T. Wells for comments on earlier drafts; Alberto Boiardi, Yongwook Jun, Chartsiri Sophonpanich, David Sharp, and Mark Trusheim for allowing me to draw on their unpublished thesis research; and Nancy Dallaire for editorial assistance.

through to their customers any financing or tax costs in excess of those facing the lowest-cost producers. Thus, the firm must match its global competitors on these terms. Finally, volatile exchange rates create much greater challenges for a firm facing global competition than one operating largely in a multidomestic mode.

Under global competition, exchange rate fluctuations not only change the dollar value of the firm's foreign profits and foreign currency-denominated contractual assets and liabilities, such as accounts receivable and debt, they also alter the firm's competitive position and often call for changes in operating variables including pricing, output, and sourcing. These decisions are complicated by the fact that volatile exchange rates distort traditional measures of current and long-term profitability, creating illusions that depend on the currency in which alternatives are weighed and a manager's performance is judged.

A firm wearing "dollar-colored" eyeglasses or, for that matter, "yen-colored" eyeglasses will have a distorted view of its competitive position and is likely to make costly mistakes. A firm that sees through these effects will be in a much better position to judge its evolving competitive strengths. As a result, it will be more likely to make appropriate pricing, output, and sourcing choices in response to exchange rate shifts and will be in a better position to measure management's contribution to current performance, controlling for the macroeconomic situation.

These views are borne out by the experiences of 1978–79, when the weak dollar favored global competitors with U.S. production, and from 1981 through the present, when the strong dollar has had the opposite effect. In the first period, many firms were lulled into a false sense of security because the margins were holding up in the face of increasing Japanese competition, when in fact they should have been doing much better than normal. As a result, they were poorly prepared for the shift in competitive position vis-à-vis non-U.S. firms resulting from the dollar shock of late 1980. While it is impossible to forecast exchange rate movements, it is likely that extreme shifts such as these will reoccur, again altering international competitive positions and requiring major adjustments by firms.

This chapter is organized in four parts. In the first part I characterize changes in financial markets that have accompanied the shift to global competition. In the second I describe the changing role of finance in the context of global competition, and contrast it with finance under multidomestic competition. In the third I explore in greater depth the implications for the finance function of volatile exchange rates coupled with global competition, as well as the implications of a firm's financial perspectives for its competitive behavior under these circumstances. Finally, in the fourth part I summarize the themes developed in this chapter, briefly outline their implications for management practice, and suggest further lines of research.

THE NEW FINANCIAL ENVIRONMENT

The emergence of global competition has coincided with major changes in the international financial environment. These changes include an increased linkage of major financial markets, a counteracting increase in the use by governments of financial instruments in industrial policy, and a substantial increase in macroeconomic volatility as reflected in exchange and interest rates.

Increased International Linkage of Financial Markets

A major characteristic of the current financial environment is the increased linkage of national money and capital markets as the result of a variety of factors.[1] These include the dismantling of many restrictions on financial flows across national borders,[2] the deregulation of financial institutions both at home and abroad,[3] financial innovations that allow a separation of the choice of currency and other attributes of contracts from the jurisdiction in which they take place,[4] and increased corporate awareness of the intricacies of international finance.

This integration of financial markets is not universal, though. Many less-developed countries, in response to foreign exchange crises brought about by their own external borrowing coupled with the world recession, have imposed new or tighter exchange controls and other measures that isolate the domestic financial markets from world markets.[5] As a result, private firms based in these countries have seen their access to international financial markets cut back to pre-1970 levels. Nevertheless, financial markets are considerably more integrated on balance than they were in 1970.

This increased integration of financial markets, of course, implies an evening of the cost of funds in various countries and a consequent reduction in the benefits accruing to a firm from spanning national financial markets.[6] Increased global competition, though, puts more pressure on firms to take advantage of the remaining gains from global financial scope.

Increased Financial Intervention in Domestic Economies

Counteracting this trend toward a level international financial playing field are the increased uses by governments of financial interventions to favor home firms or home production. Credit allocation, with its implicit subsidies to firms with access to credit, continues in several industrialized countries and is the rule in most developing countries.[7] Many governments also offer concessional loans and explicit or implicit guarantees, to the point that these have become a major source of contention in international trade. Finally, most governments modify their basic tax structures by providing tax holidays, special deductions or credits, or the ability to issue securities exempt from personal tax to favor particular activities.[8]

These interventions lead to intense "shopping" for tax and financing benefits by firms as noted by Baldwin in chapter 6 and increasing competition among governments for projects as discussed by Encarnation and Wells in chapter 8. In many cases, access to these financial benefits is linked to performance requirements such as the location of the plant or the level of employment or exports.[9] However, the value of these incentives to the firm often depends on how it arranges its internal and external finances. For example, a firm with no need for borrowing in a country with cheap credit can shift its interaffiliate accounts so as to increase its apparent local borrowing requirements, while a firm investing in a start-up venture that will not break even for several years in a country offering a tax holiday can use transfer prices to shift profits from related operations to the tax-sheltered unit. Similarly, a firm engaged in overseas oil exploration may obtain a tax benefit from having operations in the United States because it can deduct these expenses from taxable profits in the United States, but not from profits in most other countries.[10] In the second section I show that the ability of the firm to exploit these conditions will depend on how many options it has for shifting funds and/or profits among subsidiaries across national boundaries, which in turn will depend on the number of places it operates and the magnitude and richness of the ongoing real and financial interactions among its component corporations. Thus, a firm's international financial scope is likely to be an important factor in its competitiveness.

Exchange and Interest Rate Instability

A major characteristic of the current world economy involving both the financial and real spheres is the extreme volatility of exchange and interest rates. This volatility is inextricably linked to differing degrees of integration internationally of finance, industry, and politics. Because of the high degree of integration among financial markets in major industrialized countries, factors influencing interest rates are readily transmitted across national boundaries. Given the lesser degree of integration in markets for goods and real factors of production, and the almost total lack of coordination in macroeconomic policies among nations, the result has been a high degree of volatility in nominal and real exchange rates.[11] This volatility, in turn, has led to sharp swings in the competitiveness of production facilities based in different countries.

In the short run, the volatility of exchange rates dominates longer-term trends, yet these trends are critical in the evolution of competitiveness. Over time, nominal exchange rates tend to adjust so as to offset cumulative differences in rates of inflation among countries.[12]

Changes in real exchange rates—defined as changes in nominal exchange rates relative to cumulative inflation differences—therefore, do not cumulate to nearly the same extent. As a result, in the long run, the competitive effects of cumulative movements in real exchange rates are likely to be swamped by microeconomic factors such as the firm's productivity growth compared to that of its host economy.[13]

This long-run tendency for exchange rates and inflation differentials to offset each other is illustrated by the circles in Figure 5.1, which depict cumulative changes in nominal (vertical axis) and real exchange rates (horizontal axis) from 1973 through the end of 1980. In the short run, though, when inflation differentials are small, both real and nominal exchange rates move together as shown by the points represented by squares (June 1982) and triangles (September 1983) in Figure 5.1

Resulting Threats and Opportunities

Global competition coupled with an increasingly integrated and volatile financial environment gives rise to both threats and opportunities for firms whose activities span real and financial markets in various countries. A major threat is the exposure to exchange rate volatility and its impact on the firm's competitive position. A closely related threat, which is more subtle and therefore more difficult to address, is the potential for management error due to illusions associated with short-run movements in exchange rates.

On the positive side, as Baldwin notes in chapter 6, exchange rate volatility provides an opportunity to exploit relative price shifts, but this requires production flexibility that is costly and organizational flexibility that is difficult to sustain.[14] Further, with the less than complete integration of financial markets and the significant degree of government intervention, firms continue to face opportunities to engage in arbitrage across financial markets and tax regimes via internal financial transactions. While there is reason to believe that these arbitrage opportunities may be more limited than before, global competition creates more pressure to exploit them because it shifts the incidence of differential taxes and financing costs to the firm. Thus, finance not only comes into play in addressing issues that arise because of global competition in product markets, but also becomes a direct factor in that competition.

Each of these threats and opportunities has significant implications for the finance function and its interaction with other aspects of the firm. In order to trace these implications I will review the role of finance in the corporation and then consider how this role is or should be changed in the context of global competition.

Figure 5.1 Real vs. Nominal Currency Movements Relative to U.S. Dollar—1973 Base

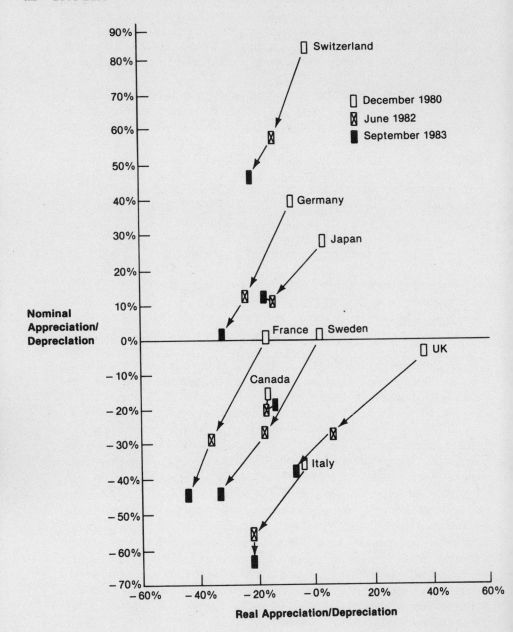

THE ROLE OF FINANCE IN THE CONTEXT OF GLOBAL COMPETITION

Notwithstanding the periodic attempts of conglomerateurs or asset strippers to create value by repackaging financial claims, finance derives most of its value from the real business operations it makes possible. In an idealized world characterized by complete information, perfect enforceability of all contracts, and neutral taxation, the role of the finance function would be to provide a yardstick for judging business options to insure that they meet the "market test" for the use of resources, raise sufficient funds to enable the firm to undertake all projects with positive present values, and return funds to shareholders when they cannot be reinvested profitably.

Of course, the world does not match this idealization. Managers often possess information that they cannot or will not disclose to investors, and investors often disagree among themselves as well as with managers regarding future prospects. As a result, defining and monitoring contractual relationships between managers and various classes of claimants is extremely complex and imperfect.[15] Further, taxes are not neutral and access to particular capital markets is often restricted in a discriminatory fashion. As a result, financial contracts at times are not fairly priced.

In such an environment, finance can contribute to the firm's value[16] in several ways in addition to its basic role of evaluating and funding investment opportunities. Finance can add value by permitting the firm to

- exploit pricing distortions in financial markets,
- reduce taxes, and
- mitigate risks and allocate them among different parties in order to:
  a. maximize diversification benefits,
  b. create appropriate managerial incentives, and
  c. reduce costs of financial distress.

What is of interest in this chapter is how the nature and potential contribution to value of each of these functions differ under conditions of global as opposed to multidomestic competition. Are the two environments really different from a financial perspective? Does finance play a different role in the two contexts? The nature and potential contribution of many of these functions would appear to depend on the firm's multinationality, that is, the extent to which it spans different currency areas or tax jurisdictions, rather than the degree of integration or coordination of the firm's primary activities such as manufacturing or marketing. Even the distinction of global versus multidomestic is vague from a financial perspective.

The finance function is an excellent example of the global-multidomestic continuum. Although much discussion treats the two as mutually exclusive categories, in practice firms can be a little bit global. A firm is global to the extent that it is structured and operates so as to realize benefits from international integration of particular activities (scale economies), coordination of activities (scope economies), and transnational learning (see chapter 1). Any multinational must achieve some such cross-border benefits to overcome the costs of operating at a distance.[17] At the multidomestic extreme of the continuum, integration typically is limited to indirect overhead functions including research and development and finance. At the global extreme, substantial portions of the direct value activities also are integrated or coordinated across borders. Further, it is likely that in such cases the indirect activities represent a larger fraction of value than in the multidomestic case. Thus, a multinational firm may be global in finance but not in other activities. On the other hand, merely being multinational does not guarantee that it will realize the benefits of global scope in even this one function. However, there are many reasons why the nature and potential contribution of the multinational financial function will differ in the context of global competition.

As noted in the introduction, the global operating environment is complicated by firms' differing exposures to volatile exchange rates, by the possibility that one firm will obtain a competitive advantage through access to favorable financing or fiscal arrangements, and by the proliferation of modes of international production accompanied by a veritable explosion of financing vehicles. Thus, finance not only comes into play in addressing issues that arise because of increased global competition in product markets, but also becomes a direct factor in that competition. Table 5.1 provides an overview of the changing nature of the finance function and its linkages to the firm's overall competitive position under international, multidomestic, and global competition.[18] I include tactical pricing and output changes to exchange rate changes, not strictly finance functions, because they are closely linked to exchange risk management and strongly influenced by a firm's currency perspective.

In the remainder of this section I review the implications of increased global competition coupled with the increased integration of financial markets for each of the major functions of finance identified earlier. In each case, I contrast this new context with the previous, largely multidomestic era, using the study of multinational finance by Robbins and Stobaugh (1973) as a base for comparison.

Evaluating Investment Opportunities

A clear implication of the current competitive and financial environment is an increase in the complexity of investment opportunities and the corresponding increase in the potential for management error. The estimation of incremental benefits from resource outlays must take into account increased international interdependence among the

Table 5.1 Implications of Global Competition for Finance Function

Nature of International Competition Function	Export/Import	Multidomestic	Global
Investment Evaluation	Domestic perspective, few "foreign" considerations	Yes/no decision to enter market or change mode to serve local market	Mutually exclusive global choices, currency, tax issues central
Funding Operations[a]	Meet domestic norms	Meet local norms	Match global competitors' cost of capital
Exchange Risk Management	Focus on exposure of foreign currency contracts	Focus on exposure of converting foreign profits into dollars	Focus on exposure of home and foreign profits to competitive effects of exchange rate shifts
Output/Pricing Responses to Exchange Rate Movements	No change in home currency price	No change in local currency price	Change in home, local price to reflect global competitive position
Performance Measurement	Measure all operations in dollars at actual rates	Measure foreign operations in local currency	Measure all operations relative to standard that reflects competitive effects of exchange rate changes

[a]The entries in this row reflect typical behaviors of firms. Clearly, firms can and some do pursue global cost-minimizing financing strategies regardless of global linkage of operations.

various activities of the firm in terms of the benefits of scale, scope, learning, and hence, future opportunities.

In analyzing alternative plant locations, for example, the firm must evaluate not only differences in the direct costs of operating in each location, but also the impact of different choices on other strategic factors such as access to particular markets and the scale and experience "platforms" that each alternative provides for future operations. Consider the case of the Korean consumer electronics industry whose U.S. operations appear to break even at best.[19] This poor financial performance is often taken as evidence of uneconomic behavior on the part of Korean firms or of extensive Korean government subsidies of its firms' operations abroad. Another explanation, though, is that the financial performance of the U.S. operations is only one component of their contribution to Korean firms' value. Others include the impact of unit cost reduction due to the scale made possible by entering the U.S. market on the profits of these firms in Korea, where they are oligopolists with substantial market power and the impact of learning from present U.S. operations on future investment opportunities in the United States and elsewhere. Choices among alternative product and marketing programs are even more complex, because gains in some product market segments will result in erosion in others, while in other cases there may be positive carryover.

Given the varying patterns of government intervention, choices among strategic alternatives are further complicated by the need to trade these direct and indirect benefits off against alternative packages of investment incentives and performance requirements, where the present value of each package will depend on the corporation's anticipated cash flow and tax position in various jurisdictions. While similar complications existed under multidomestic competition, in general they were less central because they influenced whether a firm should enter a particular national market rather than which (mutually exclusive) way they should serve a world market.

A further complication is the problem of the "bent measuring stick" identified by Robbins and Stobaugh. They noted that unless the firm conducts all interaffiliate transactions at "arm's-length," the profits (incremental cash flows) of any activity to any corporate unit will not equal the incremental flows to the corporation as a whole. They further noted that there are many reasons, such as minimizing taxes which I discuss later, that a firm will not want to adopt arm's-length transfer pricing as well as reasons why it may not be able to compute such prices even if it wants to. Under global competition, this problem is exacerbated not only by the increased interdependencies among the firms' operations, but by the overwhelming impact of exchange rate fluctuations on revenues, costs, and profits, a point I develop in greater detail in the section "Coping with Exchange Rate Volatility." In projecting future profits and cash flows, firms must see through the short-term impacts on profits of currency movements to focus on their evolving microcompetitiveness.

These complexities have contributed to a general view that discounted cash flow (DCF) techniques are no longer valid and that their use by U.S. management has contributed to the decline in America's competitive position.[20] Nothing could be farther from the truth. It is probably true that U.S. managers' overreliance on short-term return on investment (ROI) goals, coupled with a simplistic use of DCF techniques, result in a bias against projects with indirect future benefits.[21] When properly employed, however, DCF measures provide a powerful framework for combining the effects of scale, scope, and learning on present and future activities.[22] What is needed is a closer linkage of competitive analysis and DCF techniques rather than discarding these techniques in favor of more subjective approaches.

Funding Business Requirements

The increased scope of the competitive arena implies larger stakes for most major business gambles.[23] However, the increased integration of financial markets in different countries has enhanced firms' external financing capacity as well, especially for firms based in smaller countries with isolated capital markets.[24] Firms that consider themselves global competitors are broadening their funding bases to insure that they will not find themselves at a competitive disadvantage in this regard.[25] Even a multidomestic competitor is not safe; the emergence of a firm with a global financial advantage will alter the terms of competition in much the same way as would the emergence of a firm with globally integrated production in an industry hitherto characterized by production on a national scale.

Exploiting Financing Bargains

To the extent that financial markets are not fully integrated or that financing concessions differ among countries, multinational firms' ability to span these markets will not only increase its ability to fund global operations but also increase the likelihood that they can identify and exploit financing bargains.

If a firm can identify financial investment or borrowing opportunities that are mispriced, it can add value by engaging in arbitrage or speculation. In general, opportunities for such gains are rarer than for gains arising from real market advantages that are protected by barriers to entry, because there are likely to be fewer such barriers to financial transactions. This is the basis for Baldwin's skepticism regarding the alleged cost of capital advantages of Japanese firms (see chapter 6). However, such opportunities do exist from time to time, especially in capital markets that are distorted and isolated by controls on credit and exchange market transactions.

Because they are at once domestic and foreign, multinational firms are more likely to encounter exploitable distortions in financial markets than firms operating in single countries. They can often circumvent the credit market and exchange market controls that create these profit opportunities.[26] Firms' internal financial networks provide them with considerable latitude in the choice of *channels* through which they transfer cash and/or taxable profits among their various national corporate components as well as in the *timing* of interaffiliate transfers. A firm, for example, can advance funds to a subsidiary through an injection of funds in the form of equity or a loan, through a transfer of goods or intangibles such as technology at less than an arm's-length price,[27] or by providing it with a guarantee that enables it to borrow locally. Depending on how the subsidiary is funded, the firm then has a similar array of channels through which it can withdraw funds. It can accelerate or delay transfers by leading or lagging interaffiliate settlements relative to their scheduled dates, or if such behavior is prohibited, by shifting the timing of the shipment of goods within the corporation.

This discretion over the channels and timing of remittances

among related corporations is of little value within a single tax and monetary jurisdiction, because transfers among units typically involve little cost and have no tax consequences. However, when the firm operates across jurisdictions, certain channels may be restricted by virtue of exchange controls and the use of others will trigger additional tax liabilities. Under these circumstances, the firm benefits from "internalizing" these transactions.[28]

Robbins and Stobaugh, studying a set of multidomestic multinationals, showed that the gains from exploiting internal financial systems were often significant. However, they also found that larger firms tended not to fully exploit this potential because of external constraints (or self-policing to avoid sanctions) and organizational limitations. I suspect that the pressure to pursue such gains is much greater with global competition because it drastically reduces the ability of a firm to pass through any financing costs in excess of those facing the industry cost leaders. In a multidomestic context, in contrast, the competitive impact of these costs depends on the relative position of firms in each country.

Reducing Taxes

By appropriately "packaging" the cash flows generated by business operations, firms often can substantially reduce the present value of governments' tax take.[29] The simplest example in a single-country setting is the use of debt as a way to reduce corporate income taxes. Firms operating internationally may be in a position to shift income into jurisdictions with relatively low rates and/or relatively favorable definitions of income. While some of these profit shifts occur through transfer prices of real inputs and outputs, the pricing of interaffiliate financial transactions often provides the greatest flexibility.[30] In the current global competitive environment, though, a new factor is coming into play. As governments seek to actively manipulate their fiscal systems for nationalistic and/or distributional gains, firms "shop" fiscal regimes and actively bargain over the distribution of rents resulting from a given activity. This is especially true of facilities on a world scale which, by definition, are not premised on access to any single market.[31] In these cases, tax system arbitrage becomes an area of active bargaining as well as gaming of passive fiscal systems.

A final way that an international firm can reduce (the present value of expected) taxes is to structure interaffiliate commercial and financial dealings, as well as hedging the risks of individual units through external transactions, in order to minimize the chance that any of its corporate components will experience losses on its tax accounts and, as a result, have to carry forward some of its tax shields. Virtually all corporate income tax regimes are asymmetric in that they collect a share of profits but rebate shares of losses only up to taxes paid in the prior, say, three years. Otherwise, the losses must be carried forward with an implied reduction in the present value of the tax shields. In essence, the tax authorities hold a call option on profits. As a result, the expected tax rate is an increasing function of the variability of the taxable profits of each entity that comprises the firm.[32]

As with financing costs, global competitors will be under much greater pressure than multidomestic competitors to match the lowest tax burden obtainable by any firm in the industry while increasing their flexibility in where to locate and how to coordinate value activities. Thus, tax and financial management aimed at minimizing the firm's cost of capital will no longer be an optional activity pursued by a handful of sophisticated firms, but an integral element of global competitive strategy.

Managing Risks

A final, often critical role of finance in a firm is to mitigate particular risks inherent in its undertakings and/or shift them to other firms or investors. Global competition, for example, increases firms' exposure to exchange rate volatility, but the firm can to a large extent lay off this risk through hedging transactions including currency futures, swaps, options, or foreign currency borrowing. Some aspects of exchange risk can also be shifted to suppliers or customers through the choice of invoicing currencies. Alternatively, the firm can retain this risk and, implicitly, pass it on to its shareholders.

An important result in financial theory is that in an idealized perfect capital market the allocation of risks among firms, as well as the form in which it is passed on to investors, does not matter because investors can completely diversify their holdings and hence will be affected only by undiversifiable risks. Under these circumstances, hedging does not add value and, as long as prices are "fair," contractual risk sharing with suppliers or customers is of no consequence. However, in practice, firms devote a great deal of effort to risk allocation in the form of hedging and risk sharing. While much of this behavior can be traced to attempts by managers to look good within imperfect control systems, several recent analyses provide a rigorous basis, consistent with shareholder value maximization, for hedging under some circumstances.[33] In particular, as we have seen earlier, it can reduce the (present value of) taxes. It can also increase diversification benefits, improve managerial incentives, and reduce the costs of financial distress.

Although capital markets are becoming more integrated, there are barriers to cross-border investment in the form of taxes, controls on foreign investment, and political risks that have different impacts on domestic and foreign investors, particularly transfer risks. Because of these barriers, investors in various countries will differ in their scope for diversifying particular risks and, hence, will place different values on particular securities.[34] They may also differ in their ability to mitigate those risks that are at least in part the result of choices by governments or other firms. A firm may exploit this comparative advantage in risk bearing by issuing securities either directly or indirectly, that is, by contracting with a firm with a different set of investors, to the investor group who will value them most highly. A global firm will not constrain itself to any particular capital market base and, hence, will exploit this potential to the fullest.

Volatile earnings and cash flows may reduce a firm's ability to compete by distorting management information and incentives, hindering access to capital markets, and threatening the continuity of supplier and customer relationships. In the case of risks that are outside the control of individual firms, but that affect many firms, such as exchange rates or relative prices of key commodities, firms with large specific exposures will benefit by laying off these risks to other firms or investors that have smaller or perhaps even opposite exposures. To the extent that the risks affecting particular business undertakings are at least partially controllable by one or more potential participants, risk allocation to create appropriate strategic stakeholdings is likely to mitigate risk.[35]

Organizational Implications

Global competition results in a blurring of the boundaries between finance and operations. Investment choices involve tax and financing considerations that depend on the firm's overall cash and profit position. Exchange rate impacts, typically the realm of the treasury function, are critical factors in the shifting competitiveness of the firm's operations. Operating profitability cannot be separated from financing considerations and must be judged relative to the macroeconomic environment.

Further, just as global competition blurs national product market boundaries, it also blurs national boundaries in finance. The use of finance to offset exchange exposures and exploit distortions in financial markets requires a high degree of global coordination and centralization of decision making, and may interfere with the management of operations sensitive to local conditions, especially in cases where global optimization reduces the profits of a local affiliate. Already bent, measuring sticks used in evaluating the performance of operations in a multidomestic context will be further distorted.

A further consequence of global management of the finance function is that it may require affiliates to act in conflict with local national interests.[36] Robbins and Stobaugh, following the theme of Vernon's *Sovereignty at Bay,* cited the firm's ability to bypass financial controls by using its internal network as a key element in the weakening of sovereign control. In recent years, governments of major industrialized countries appear to have conceded the battle over the control of international capital flows and, as a result, have found themselves severely constrained in terms of policies to stabilize currency values. The battle is still being fought on fiscal terrain, but the advent of global competition and the resultant aggressive tax shopping by firms and fiscal promotion by particular countries is transforming the conflict from one between firms and nation-states to one among states. Attempts at cooperation (cartelization?) by governments, such as the EC code on investment incentives, will undoubtedly increase, but whether they succeed is an open question.

The Bottom Line

Many of the differences between finance under global and multidomestic competition are of degree rather than kind. Multinationality in terms of being able to span national financial markets confers financial benefits on firms whether they compete globally or multidomestically. However, the ability of the firm to pass on differential financing costs and taxes is reduced by global competition. Thus, to compete it will have to match its competitors' "cost of capital" and, as a result, the value of an effective finance function to a global firm is overwhelming.

Further, the greater currency volatility of the current period and its greater proportionate effect on firms' cash flows and profits, given global competition, increase the importance of effective foreign exchange management, both in terms of limiting risks and providing management information for tactical and strategic choices.

The biggest differences appear to lie in this latter area, the role of finance in evaluating business options. The boundaries between finance and competitive behavior are blurred, and appear to be becoming even more so.

COPING WITH EXCHANGE RATE VOLATILITY

Given the vital importance of exchange rate volatility in the new global environment, it is necessary to examine in greater depth how exchange rate volatility affects firms engaged in global competition and how these firms cope with this volatility. I focus on three specific issues arising from the coincidence of volatile currencies and global competition. These are (1) the impact of exchange rate fluctuations on competitiveness, (2) corporate management of exchange risk, and (3) the impact of firms' currency perspectives on their strategic and tactical choices.

The Impact of Exchange Rate Shifts on Competitiveness

A major difference between multidomestic and global competition is the impact of exchange rates on the competitiveness and, hence, profitability of a multinational firm. Under multidomestic competition, markets are national in scope and, typically, a substantial proportion of value added is local. Thus, exchange rate shifts do not significantly change the relative costs of firms operating in a particular market. As a result, firms' revenues and costs move together in response to shifts in exchange rates, and profits from foreign operations, when converted into dollars, move roughly proportionally with exchange rates.[37]

In contrast, under global competition, there will be a tendency toward world prices and larger proportions of firms' value added are likely to be concentrated in particular countries.[38] Thus, unless all firms have the same geographic patterns of value added, shifts in exchange rates will change their relative costs and profit margins. With the emergence of non-U.S. global competitors, this is almost bound to be the case.[39] In this case, the profits of foreign operations may respond either more or less than one for one with shifts in exchange rates, and the profits of operations in the United States will be affected as well.

The responsiveness of operating profits to shifts in exchange rates, then, is comprised of two effects: a *conversion effect* and a *competitive effect*. The conversion effect is the proportional adjustment of foreign currency operating profits into dollars. By definition, it applies only to foreign operations. The competitive effect, in contrast, is the response of local currency operating profits to exchange rate shifts resulting from the interaction of the various competitors' supply and price responses. It applies to both domestic and overseas activities.

These *operating exposures*—the sensitivity of a firm's operating profits (margins) measured in the parent currency to exchange rate movements—differ from *financial exposures*—the sensitivity of the parent currency value of its money-fixed assets and liabilities—in several ways. First, they are exposures to shifts in real exchange rates rather than in nominal exchange rates. Further, these operating exposures depend on the structure of the markets in which the firm operates and not necessarily on the country or currency in which the firm purchases or sells its product.

Consider the case of Economy Motors, a hypothetical U.S. manufacturer of small cars. Economy produces components and assembles its products in the Midwest and sells them throughout the United States. Its products sell in direct competition with Japanese imports, which dominate the market and are the price leaders. The shifting competitive position of Economy under different real exchange rate scenarios is illustrated in Figure 5.2.

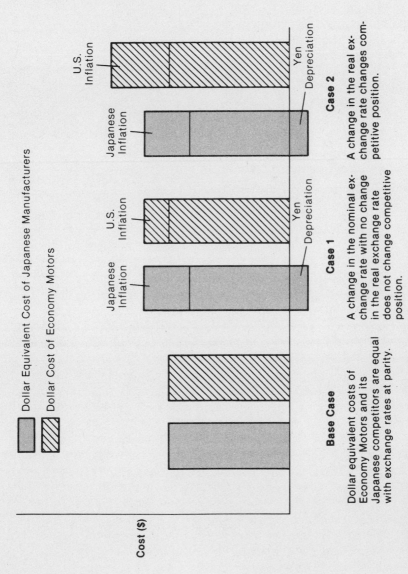

Figure 5.2 The Effects of Japanese Yen Depreciation on the Competitive Position of Economy Motors

In the base year, when the yen and dollar are "at parity," the Japanese set U.S. prices so that they (and Economy) earn normal margins. In some later year, if the yen strengthens in line with the difference in inflation between the two countries, Economy remains on par with the Japanese. However, if the yen weakens while Japan's inflation remains below that of the United States, the Japanese firms have lower dollar costs, they cut prices to gain share, and Economy faces reduced profits.

The reason Economy faces an operating exposure even though it operates entirely in its domestic market is that the market in which it sells its output is much more integrated globally than the markets in which it purchases its inputs.

The sensitivity of a firm's profits to shifts in exchange rates under global competition may be greater than one for one. Extending the Economy Motors example, assume that the operating margin under normal (parity) conditions is 15 percent, that all costs are in U.S. dollars, but that a 1 percent change in the real yen/dollar rate results in a .5 percent change in dollar prices of small cars in the United States. In this case, assuming that the optimal response to exchange rate changes involves matching price and holding volume constant, the sensitivity of profits would be 3.33 to 1.[40] In other words, a 10 percent change in the exchange rate would result in a 33 percent change in operating profits!

A useful way to think of the price effects of exchange rate changes is in terms of a currency habitat for each product or input. This *currency habitat* is defined as the currency in which the price of the good tends to be most stable.[41] The determinants of the currency habitat can be summarized in two dimensions illustrated in Figure 5.3: (1) the geographical scope of the product market, and (2) the relative influence of producer costs and characteristics of consumer demand on price in a given market.

The geographic scope of the market will depend on the ability of the firm, or its suppliers in the case of inputs, to segment national markets, either by limiting transshipment or by differentiating the products it sells in various markets. As product markets become more globally integrated, prices in various national markets tend toward a world price. The marginal pricing factor captures the relative importance of supply and demand considerations, which reflect among other things the competitive structure of the industry, the price elasticity of demand, the existence of complements and substitutes, and the structure of costs, in particular the level of nonrecurring costs.[42]

The two dimensions are not entirely independent because firms with significant market power will be able to discriminate among national market segments by "bundling" local services (e.g., warranties) with products or otherwise precluding transshipment by distributors or customers. The recent collaboration of Mercedes Benz and other

Figure 5.3 Determinants of Currency Habitat of Cost/Price

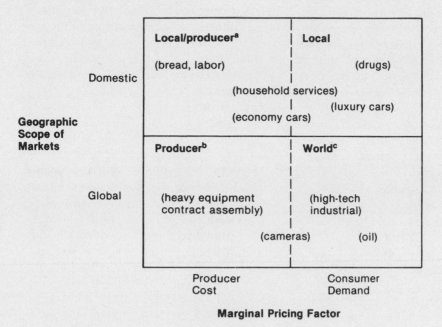

Marginal Pricing Factor

[a]Local if recurring costs of production are local.
[b]Currency of marginal firm/price leader depending on industrial structure.
[c]Basket weighted by relative importance (income and elasticity) of consumers. As a first approximation, this is the basket comprising special rights (Special Drawing Rights).

luxury auto manufacturers with the U.S. government in requiring the stamping of various component parts to reduce theft was squarely aimed at stamping out the gray market, as were MBZ's ads stressing that while they stood behind all their cars, they could only promise exceptional service to owners who had purchased their cars from authorized U.S. dealers. Quotas have performed the same role for Japanese manufacturers. An additional dimension that is important when there are few global producers is the level of operating margins (quasi-rents) in the industry, reflecting the relative importance of nonrecurring (capital and R & D) and recurring costs.

In the case of local markets (the upper half of Figure 5.3), the currency habitat will clearly be the local currency if costs are local as well, because in this case international supply and demand will play little or no role. The more interesting case for our purposes, though, is where a significant proportion of value added is global in nature, that is, where the degree of global configuration and coordination is high, but where producers have sufficient market power to engage in some price discrimination across borders. Because these firms can effectively segment national markets through their own market power and with the collaboration of regulatory authorities, they face local currency-denominated marginal revenue curves. If recurring costs are low, therefore, they will tend to maintain constant local prices in the face of exchange adjustments. If these costs are high, in contrast, they will adjust both local price and volume. Patented drugs represent one extreme in this regard, with local currency habitats, while in the absence of quotas, the price habitat of mid-range autos such as Toyota and Nissan will involve a combination of local and producer currencies. The currency habitat for luxury cars, which face less elastic demand because of greater product differentiation, and with higher margins of sales price over recurring costs, will also involve a mix of local and producer currencies, but with a much greater weight on the local currency.

In those cases where transshipment cannot be barred, in contrast, either because of the portability of the product, the inability of manufacturers to control distribution channels, or the power of key customers, prices will tend to a single world level (lower half of Figure 5.3). The camera industry is a case in point, with gray marketeers denying manufacturers the ability to fully segment national markets. The same is true of industrial equipment and components that are sold to sophisticated buyers who themselves are multinational. The currency habitat of these world prices will depend on the weighted importance of demand from various countries and the currency habitat of the costs incurred.

Foreign Exchange Risk Management under Global Competition[43]

Exposure to exchange rate movements is a serious problem for firms in the current environment, especially those that are global competitors. However, foreign exchange management as currently practiced is unlikely to help firms compete effectively and, in fact, is likely to provide misleading signals. There are two reasons for this. First, foreign exchange risk management is concerned primarily with deciding whether to hedge or retain particular exposures arising from operations rather than seeing to it that this exposure and its impact on expected operating profits have been factored into operating decisions. In fact, as practiced, it differs little from staking the assistant treasurer with a sum of money to be used to speculate on stock options, pork bellies, or gold. Second, it tends to focus on exposures that lead to identifiable foreign exchange gains or losses, contractual items as opposed to operating profit impacts.

Foreign exchange exposure can be defined as the sensitivity to shifts in exchange rates of either a firm's cash flows or its reported

Figure 5.4 Types of Foreign Exchange Exposures

		Contractual	Noncontractual	Fictitious
Accounting Exposures	Transaction	Contracts including accounts payable, receivable, and debt "closed out" during period	not applicable	not applicable
	Transaction	Contracts on books at end of period	not applicable	fixed assets
	Operating	Gains/losses on "unbooked" contractual items including backlogs, purchase contracts	gains/losses on items not contracted for (e.g., future revenues, expenses)	not applicable

Cash Flow Exposures

profits, or some subset thereof. While the cash flow perspective makes more economic sense, the reporting perspective also matters to the extent that it affects managerial decisions or financial market reactions.[44] Figure 5.4 shows the major categories of foreign exchange exposures on these two dimensions. Accounting impacts are classified in terms of their recognition in accounting reports.

Under current rules, transaction gains or losses are separately identified in earnings, translation adjustments bypass earnings and go directly to net worth, while operating impacts are mixed in with all other sources of variation in profits. Cash flow impacts are classified in terms of the nature of the cash flows in question, whether they are contractually fixed in some money or whether they depend on competitive interactions. The fictitious category refers to those accounting adjustments that have no cash flow counterpart.

The category that differs most under global, as opposed to multidomestic, competition is the operating/noncontractual cell that reflects the impact of exchange rate fluctuations on operating profits via adjustments in revenues and costs that have not been contracted for. This is what we refer to as operating exposure, consisting of both a conversion and a competitive effect. The conversion component is readily identifiable. However, the competitive component is much more difficult to isolate because it is mixed in with a host of other variables, both macroeconomic and microeconomic, that affect local operating profits. As a result, few firms have fully incorporated it into their foreign exchange management function, and they often do not take into account the impacts of these exposures on current and projected operating profits in making strategic and tactical choices. I will review each of these points in turn.

Measuring Operating Exposures

While most firms are aware of their operating exposures, it appears that few have defined or estimated them very carefully or developed explicit procedures for dealing with them. In reviewing the 1982 and 1983 annual reports of thirty firms, Trusheim (1984) found that while twenty-two mentioned the impact of the strong dollar, sixteen of them focused on the reduced dollar value of foreign revenues and only six discussed impacts of the strong dollar on their margins or overall competitive position.

While these external reports do not provide a full picture of internal procedures, they do show that the treatment of operating exposure by U.S. firms is less than complete. This is corroborated by more detailed reviews of the practices of a few firms. In in-depth interviews with three firms, Boiardi (1984) found that all three had a rough notion of their operating exposures, but none had acted on this estimate. In discussions with six firms, we have found the same thing, a growing awareness of the general concept, but little or no progress in addressing it.[45] One reason for this is the relative difficulty of assessing operating exposures. The second is the difficulty of managing them appropriately in the typical firm.

Managing Operating Exposures

Firms have both business and financial options for reducing exchange rate exposures. Three kinds of business options are available to the firm in managing operating exposure. These are:

1. configure individual businesses to have the flexibility to increase production and sourcing in countries that become low cost due to swings in exchange rates,
2. configure individual businesses to reduce operating exposure by matching costs and revenues, and
3. select a portfolio of businesses with offsetting exposures.

The first option, that of configuring operations to increase flexibility, can actually increase a firm's expected operating profits as well as reduce their variability. The other two can at best reduce variability with no reduction in expected operating profits and, often, will result in some reduction in expected operating profits. The reason for this in the case of configuring individual businesses to match the currency habitats or revenues and costs is that such matching typically will require some departures from the optimum configuration in terms of scale and locational advantages. In the case of selecting a portfolio of businesses with offsetting exposures, this is likely to be the case because of the increased administrative costs and reduced efficiency associated with managing diverse businesses without other synergistic linkages.

The firm also has several financial options available to it. These include long-dated forwards, swaps, or borrowing in foreign currencies as well as long-dated currency options. None of these is exact, because they are keyed to nominal rather than real exchange rates, but they have the advantage that when competitively priced they reduce the variability of operating profits with little or no reduction in the anticipated level of such profits.[46]

Given the magnitude of operating exposures and the fact that they do not necessarily have even the same sign as contractual exposures, firms that hedge only their contractual exposures may actually increase their total exposures.[47] If a firm does not understand its operating exposure, its best policy is not to hedge at all.

Strategic and Tactical Responses to Exchange Rate Volatility

Volatile exchange rates create havoc for operations in a globally competitive industry. Shifts in rates require decisions regarding pricing, output, and sourcing, and these decisions typically will involve a balancing act between vaguely understood limits to sustainable price differentials across countries and the impact of local currency price shifts on demand and hence profits. Further, given the emergence of global oligopolies in many industries, pricing decisions must reflect anticipations of competitor actions or reactions. Estimating these reactions is likely to be complicated by the fact that competitors differ significantly in the currency composition of their costs and, perhaps more importantly, in the currency eyeglasses they wear. Currency fluctuations also introduce noise into measures of current performance, reducing the firm's ability to monitor its evolving competitive position and distorting its results-based managerial incentives. If these distortions are significant, and if many key decisions are made on a decentralized basis, the firm's choices are likely to be distorted as well. Finally, the impact of currency fluctuations on current operations is likely to distort the perceived long-term profitability of strategic choices.

The finance function plays a key role in terms of the perspective it provides on these choices, though none involve finance in the classic sense of raising funds. This financial perspective on operating choices, and the rules of thumb that follow from it, are part of a firm's culture. The perspective is the result of corporate experience and is unlikely to change rapidly. Thus, given the drastic change in the competitive and financial environment over the last ten years, I expect that this perspective is only now catching up with the new reality. This is clearly borne out in the relatively slow evolution of corporate management of exchange risk, and I expect it to have major operational implications as well.

Currency Illusions and Pricing/Output Choices

A perennial pricing error that results from a currency illusion is the practice of setting foreign currency prices by multiplying the domestic price by the spot rate and, perhaps, adding an "uplift" for the extra costs of doing business overseas. The illusion is that the foreign currency proceeds can be converted into dollars at the spot rate, whereas in fact the prices quoted are for future payment and, hence, can be converted only at the forward rate (or expected future spot rate) corresponding to the time of cash payment.[48] Foreign currency receivables are often "booked" at spot rather than forward rates, with the result that operating profits are initially overstated in the case of strong currencies or understated in the case of weak and subsequently exposed to potentially large transaction gains or losses that on average will offset the initial error. Depending on when and at what rate these receivables are "handed off" to treasury, the true profitability of one or both functions will be misstated and management decisions are likely to be distorted.[49] If operating managers are not held responsible for the ultimate exchange gains or losses, their contribution will be systematically misstated; if they are held responsible, their contribution is likely to be buried in the noise created by exchange rate movements.

This illusion can be readily overcome by valuing all contracts at forward rates, but this requires an explicit recognition that generally accepted accounting rules are misleading and therefore require a shift in procedures.[50] While many firms have changed procedures to do this, what is surprising is how many have not. A survey of practices conducted by Czechowicz, Choi, and Bavishi (1982), for example, found that 55 percent of all firms included transaction gains and losses in measures of managers' performance.[51] This illusion affects all international transactions and is not unique to global competition. It does, however, illustrate how traditional perspectives can interfere with appropriate choices in a changing environment.

With global competition, the problem is compounded by the fact that pricing not only must take into account the relative value of future claims in various currencies, but also the possibly asymmetric impact of exchange rate shifts on the firm's costs and prices relative to competitors. If prices in local currencies are left unchanged subsequent to an exchange rate shift, prices will differ across countries, inviting transshipment and entry by competitors in "high-priced" markets. On the other hand, if prices in the parent currency are maintained by "passing through" the exchange rate variations to local customers, sales volumes may react abruptly.

Even with full information and a "rational" economic perspective, therefore, pricing adjustments to exchange rates will be extremely complex. In practice, though, I expect that choices will be strongly influenced by the firm's view of the world. The easiest response to a change with complex implications is to do nothing. Doing nothing, however, can be defined in many different ways. In the case of pricing responses to exchange rate changes, it could be either (1) maintaining parent currency (dollar) prices, or (2) maintaining local prices. Active responses, in turn, could involve either (3) maintaining market share, or (4) adjusting both price and volume to maximize long-term profit.

Under multidomestic competition, with its largely autonomous national operating units, the likely choice is for the firm to "do nothing" by maintaining local prices, although, as we see later in our discussion of control systems, the parent currency may play a role as well. With global competition though, firms' activities are more integrated or coordinated across national boundaries and, therefore, they are more likely to "do nothing" in terms of maintaining parent currency prices. This may be a reasonable approximation to the correct response for a firm that dominates world markets, but it will not be for a member of a global oligopoly with players based in several different countries and with different currency perspectives and exposures.

The heavy construction equipment industry, once dominated by a handful of U.S. firms but now including major Japanese and European players in global markets, is an excellent case in point. Sharp (1984) found that distributor prices of construction equipment sold in the United Kingdom by U.S. firms tended to remain stable in dollars through 1980, when they shifted abruptly in response to Japanese inroads, and subsequently appear to be sensitive to the dollar–yen relationship as well. His finding of different pricing responses to exchange rate changes for virtually identical products produced and sold in the United Kingdom by a U.S.- and a U.K.-based firm support the view that at least some of this effect can be traced to organizational factors rather than to technical demand or cost considerations.

An ironic example of this type of pricing is the reported satisfaction of many U.S. firms with their ability to hold their own and maintain dollar prices during the 1978–79 period, when in fact they should have been able to raise dollar prices given the general weakness of the dollar in that period. U.S. firms are not alone in this type of illusion. The Swedish auto firms, especially Volvo, nearly priced themselves out of U.S. markets in this same period. They apparently attempted to pass through to U.S. customers most of the appreciation of the krona, while they should have maintained relatively stable dollar prices.[52]

The picture is not all bleak, of course, Sharp's findings do suggest an awakening of U.S. firms to the realities of global pricing and Boiardi (1984) found that pricing decisions were consistent with market structures, although two of the three firms he studied faced multidomestic product market competition.

Interaffiliate Pricing

A large proportion of the production of firms engaged in global competition move through interaffiliate sales on their way to the final customer. Apart from their impact on taxes and tariffs, the transfer prices on these sales have no economic impact except through their effect on the behavior of managers. These behavioral impacts, though, are often substantial and represent a key determinant of the firm's pricing of final sales.

Firms with strong, centralized (or coordinated) production units often apply transfer pricing rules based on standard costs measured in the parent currency, imposing the full impact of currency swings on the downstream stages of the value-added chain. The shift to global competition strengthens this effect because the pursuit of global scale and scope economies requires greater integration and coordination of production.

There are several different ways to address this problem. The first is to create a mechanism whereby transfer prices are negotiated to approximate arm's-length prices, in essence forcing production and marketing to share the exchange rate impact. This clearly is most feasible where there are alternative sources of supply. The second is to leave the transfer prices as they are, but adjust the performance standards (margin or ROI) of the marketing units to reflect the baseline impact of the exchange rate shifts. This requires substantial prior analysis of exchange rate impacts and appropriate operating responses at the corporate and business unit levels. A third is to substitute narrower performance standards, for example, market share or some measure of production efficiency, for profits at one or more stages in the value-added chain. This approach, however, presupposes that the firm can specify such standards appropriately, which may be as complex as solving the cross-unit profit conflicts. This clearly is one of the most challenging issues arising in global competition and is likely to push key operating responsibilities up to higher levels within the firm.

Measurement of Current Performance

Currency fluctuations clearly have an impact on measured performance, and these measures presumably feed back to a host of operating choices. While there are many technical issues in measuring performance in the face of fluctuating exchange rates, the debate among practitioners appears to be centered on whether performance should be measured in local currency or parent currency terms. Under conditions of global competition, neither is appropriate.

An ideal performance measurement system should hold managers responsible for those aspects of performance over which they have substantial control, but should limit responsibility for performance shifts due to factors largely beyond their control. Of course, this ideal is seldom met because, for example, fluctuations in aggregate demand are inextricably linked with managerial success in producing and selling a product. The emphasis of many firms on market share, however, is an attempt to separate these two effects. In the case of currency fluctuations, some aspects of the problem are easily separable while others are not. Gains or losses on accounts receivable resulting from currency surprises, for example, are outside the control of operating managers and can be split out by transferring these claims to treasury at forward rates. If this is done, treasury's contribution through "selective hedging," actually speculation in the form of market timing, is fairly measured as well.

In contrast, with the competitive component of operating exposures, such a clear separation is not possible because managers can and should react to exchange rate shifts by altering prices, output, and sourcing. However, so long as there is some degree of global competition it should be recognized that profits in either local or parent currency should fluctuate in line with real exchange rates. A failure to incorporate this in the control system is likely to lead managers to "leave money on the table" when they are favored by exchange rates, and to sacrifice too much market share by attempting to hold constant dollar margins when exchange rates work against them.

What is required is a budgetary standard that adjusts for exchange rate impacts. The process of developing such a budget should involve a joint exploration by corporate and business unit managers of the impacts of and appropriate responses to exchange rate movements, thus providing a dress rehearsal of future tactics as well as a standard against which future performance can be judged.[53]

The controller of a U.S. firm's U.K. plant, in an interview with Sharp, stated that he would have no trouble in meeting his firm's goal of "cutting real *dollar* costs by x percent" because in the period since the program was announced the pound had already fallen by a large fraction of that amount relative to the dollar. His response would have been quite different if the corporation had demanded an x percent cut relative to costs *normalized* for exchange rate circumstances.

Assessment of Strategic Options

Just as currency fluctuations affect current performance, they also alter the attractiveness of the firm's strategic options. The long-run profitability of a given business unit will depend on its evolving competitive advantage, but in the short run its advantage can be swamped by exchange rate impacts. In some cases, the firm will be able to enhance its average profitability over time by building a degree of flexibility that allows it to shift sourcing and value-added activities as exchange rates move.[54] In general, though, it will have to look past the current circumstances to assess its long-run competitiveness. This requires a multistage procedure:

1. assess future expected cash flows conditional on purchasing power parity,[55] concentrating on microcompetitive factors such as the firm's likely experience gains relative to anticipated wage increases,
2. assess how these (conditional expected) cash flows would differ under alternative exchange rate scenarios, and
3. estimate expected cash flows across scenarios given their relative likelihood.

In general, it should choose the alternative with the highest (net present value of) expected cash flows, without regard for exposure to exchange rate movements, because as noted earlier these exposures can be offset by financial hedges that have little or no cost in present value terms.

While there have been several recent surveys of capital budgeting practice,[56] none have focused on this issue, so it is not clear whether academic observers are lagging behind practice or whether practice is lagging behind changes in the competitive environment. I suspect some of both.

CONCLUSIONS: IMPLICATIONS FOR MANAGERS AND FUTURE RESEARCH

The emergence of global competition, coupled with both increased integration of financial markets and continued exchange rate volatility represents a major threat and challenge to U.S. firms that have been accustomed to world market leadership under multidomestic competition.

I have argued that the finance function plays a critical role in meeting the challenge of global competition, both because of the demands globalization places on the finance function per se and its requirement for a much more sophisticated financial perspective on strategic and tactical choices. Because a firm's financial eyeglasses are part of its culture, these changes in outlook lag changes in the competitive environment. However, it does appear that many firms are rapidly moving down the "financial learning curve" and changing their standard operating procedures to accommodate global competition.

Within the traditional realm of finance—the treasury functions of raising funds externally and maneuvering them efficiently within the corporation—firms will find that, in order to compete globally, they must fully exploit the benefits of multinational financial scope to match their competitors' costs of capital and effective rates of taxation. The structure of external financing will have to become more global, shifting from primarily home currency borrowing at the parent level and local currency borrowing on the part of foreign subsidiaries to a more complex pattern recognizing the interaction between minimizing taxes, exploiting financial incentives and distortions in financial markets, and offsetting exchange rate exposures.

Even greater changes will be required in areas where finance interacts more closely with operations. One such area is in the management of foreign exchange exposures. Financial managers, with their knowledge of the dynamics of foreign exchange, must assist operating managers in configuring operations to cope with exchange rate volatility and responding to shifts as they occur. They also should provide internal hedging facilities (or contingent performance standards) to insulate operating managers from the inevitable exposures resulting from strategic bets to the fullest extent consistent with maintaining incentives for proper operating responses. At the same time, they must expand the scope of corporate exchange risk management to include operating exposures.

Another such area is the measurement of business unit performance. Not only must each unit's performance be measured relative to a standard that takes into account key changes in the macroeconomic environment, including but not limited to shifts in exchange rates, but also adjust for tradeoffs that improve corporate profits at the expense of one or more units. Firms will have to redefine business units along the dimensions where greatest coordination is required. However, because no structure can simultaneously capture geographic, product, and stage of value-added leverage points, they will also have to create more effective processes for mediating conflicts among units. This will, among other things, involve the substitution of relatively narrow measures of business performance, such as market shares and unit costs, for the bottom-line measures of financial profitability favored by most U.S. firms.

Regarding future research, we need to learn much more about how firms have reacted to the changed competitive and financial conditions and, especially, how these reactions have been colored by financial perspectives developed under other circumstances. Most normative statements regarding financial management assume that these perspectives play a critical role, but there is little sound evidence that they do.

Most recent academic research in finance has focused on the interplay between firms and capital markets. This research has provided a much better understanding on how investors value securities and hence how managers should judge whether their decisions add value. This valuation-based research must be extended in the international dimension to capture potential cost of capital differences due to differing institutional arrangements. However, most corporate decision makers operate in "internal capital markets" where there can be no direct capital market feedback. While research in the control area does focus on the organizational considerations that come into play in these internal systems, it often proceeds without a rigorous basis for judging value creation. Corporate finance should cover both aspects, linking capital market-based valuation theory with an understanding of the types of incentive and control mechanisms necessary so that managers will make appropriate decisions. How corporations cope with exchange rate volatility is a promising area for such boundary-crossing research. I hope that this discussion of some of the issues involved will be a useful starting point.

NOTES

1. For an overview of recent evidence on financial market integration see Kohlhagen (1983).
2. For recent studies of border controls and their effects on financial markets see Dooley and Isard (1980) and Otani and Tiwari (1981).
3. The deregulation of financial institutions first took the form of an escape from national regulations by banks operating "offshore" as described by Dufey and Giddy (1981), Grubel (1977), Kindleberger (1974), Tschoegl (1981) and others. Subsequently, partly in response to this offshore competition and partly to shifts in domestic considerations, it has taken the form of reduced regulation of financial intermediation within individual national markets.
4. For a review of recent financial innovations see Dufey and Giddy (1981) and Antl (1984).
5. For a review of exchange restrictions see International Monetary Fund (1985). Rosenberg (1983) discusses the (in)effectiveness of these controls given the mechanisms firms can use to circumvent them.
6. For overviews of the benefits to a firm of spanning national financial markets see Robbins and Stobaugh (1973) and Lessard (1979a).
7. There is an extensive literature on interest rate repression in developing economies (for example, McKinnon 1973), but less in the context of industrialized countries.
8. These include the ability to make use of tax-exempt bond issues, "80/20" offshore financing in the United States and similar measures in most other industrialized countries.
9. See Guisinger et al. (1985).
10. This has been given as one explanation of BHP's (Australia) recent acquisition of a U.S. exploration company.
11. For recent views of the determinants of exchange rates see Dornbusch (1983), Frenkel and Mussa (1980), and Stockman (1980).
12. This tendency, known as purchasing power parity, was first outlined by Cassel (1923). For a recent review of its various meanings see Shapiro

(1983). For evidence on how well it holds see Roll (1979), Frenkel (1981), and Adler and Lehman (1983).

13. For a discussion of the strategic implications of purchasing power parity in the long run see Kiechel (1981).

14. Also Kogut (1983).

15. Myers (1984) and Barnea, Haugen, and Senbet (1981) discuss the impact of these agency effects on financing choices.

16. Here we refer to the warranted (present discounted) value of the firm's shares, the most complete financial measure of a firm's performance.

17. This point was made as early as 1960 by Hymer (see Kindleberger 1985). It was further developed in Kindleberger (1969) and remains one of the central tenets of the theory of the multinational firm.

18. Export/import—predominately domestic value added in home country with some international sales and/or sourcing. Multidomestic—substantial value added in each country, little cross-border integration or coordination of primary value activities. Global—substantial cross-border integration and coordination of primary value activities.

19. This discussion draws on Jun (1985).

20. This theme is developed by Hayes and Abernathy (1980) and echoed by Hout, Porter, and Rudden (1982). Donaldson (1972) provides an earlier indictment of DCF techniques, but also indicates where the problems lie and suggests ways to overcome them.

21. Surveys by Schall, Sundem, and Geijsbeek (1978), Wicks (1980), and Oblak and Helm (1980) show that managers continue to favor DCF-rate of return calculations in spite of the clear superiority of additive present value calculations when a project gives the firm access to significant future growth options. Hodder and Riggs (1985) discuss how methodological biases distort decisions. Hodder (1984) finds substantial differences between the capital budgeting practices of U.S. and Japanese firms. U.S. firms appear to be more "number driven," but devote much less attention to alternative scenarios and strategic options.

22. One line of development of DCF techniques that is capable of taking many of these effects into account is the valuation by components method. Under this approach, cash flows are segregated into equity equivalents, debt equivalents, and option equivalents and each component is valued using techniques most appropriate to its characteristics. Developed by Myers (1974), it has been extended to the international context by Lessard (1979b, 1981). Recent work on valuing option equivalents in investment decisions by Brennan and Schwartz (1985) and Myers and Majd (1983) is particularly promising in the treatment of future options to invest, abandon, or receive various forms of government support. Booth (1982) and Lessard and Paddock (1986) discuss the advantages of valuation by components relative to the more traditional single discount rate approach.

23. Vernon (1979) argues that, in contrast to the 1960s, a much larger proportion of new product launches will be on a global scale with correspondingly larger outlays.

24. An interesting case in point is the Danish firm Novo whose entry into U.S. equity markets is chronicled by Stonehill and Dullum (1982). Firms such as Schlumberger and Ciments LaFarge have also shifted their funding from small home markets to integrated world markets and, most recently, Jardine-Mathieson is shifting its "window" on world capital markets from Hong Kong to Bermuda. Adler (1974) and Agmon and Lessard (1977) discuss the basis for such capital-market-seeking behavior of firms.

25. Hitachi, for example, recently announced the creation of five offshore financing centers for its worldwide business.
26. For a discussion of the relationship between credit market and exchange controls and pricing distortions in financial markets, see Dooley and Isard (1980) and Otani and Tiwari (1981).
27. The source of profit shifting in this case comes from manipulating the transfer prices among affiliates. See Brean (1985) for an in-depth discussion of financial transfer prices.
28. The concept of internalization has been extended to many other aspects of multinational firms' activities. See in particular, Buckley and Casson (1976) and Hennart (1982), and Rugman (1981).
29. Packaging can involve setting up tax-minimizing ownership chains as discussed by Rutenberg (1970) or choosing the nature of the parent's financial claim—equity, debt, or a claim on royalties—as discussed by Horst (1977) and Adler (1979).
30. Examples of the impact of interaffiliate financial transactions on a firm's taxes are presented by Horst (1977) and Brean (1985).
31. The industry studies in Guisinger et al. (1985) confirm that fiscal incentives are most important when several alternative sites provide access to the same (common or world) market.
32. This point is developed in Smith and Stulz (1985).
33. See for example, Barnea, Haugen, and Senbet (1985), Shapiro and Titman (1985), and Smith and Stulz (1985).
34. For an introduction to the impact of cross-border barriers on the valuation of securities see Stulz (1985).
35. See Blitzer, Lessard, and Paddock (1984).
36. See Robbins and Stobaugh (1973) for an early discussion of this point.
37. In more technical terms, given a change in the real exchange rate, the demand and supply curves facing the firm will remain unchanged in the local currency (adjusted for inflation). Hence the optimal output and local currency price will remain unchanged, as will local currency profit. From a dollar perspective, of course, both curves will shift by the same amount, and the dollar profit will change in proportion to the change in the exchange rate.
38. An exception may be IBM, which, because of its very large scale and its responsiveness to national goals, is able to balance global scale production of specific products with a matching of value added and sales in most major markets.
39. Under these circumstances, a change in the real exchange rate will result in a *relative* shift of demand and supply curves, regardless of the reference currency of the firm. This implies that the optimal price and volume will change as well.
40. If volume does not change, the sensitivity of operating profits can be defined as:

$$\text{sensitivity (profits)} = \frac{\text{sensitivity (revenues)}}{} \times \frac{\text{revenues}}{\text{profits}} - \text{sensitivity (costs)} \times \frac{\text{costs}}{\text{profits}}$$

See Levi (1982) and Flood and Lessard (1986) for a fuller explanation.
41. The term currency habitat is introduced by Flood and Lessard (1986). It has also been defined as the "currency of price (cost) determination." It may differ from the currency in which prices are quoted, invoices issued, or transactions settled. For example, the prices of various products are quoted in particular currencies, e.g., crude oil in dollars, certain chemicals in DM, etc. and as shown by Grassman (1973), Magee (1974), and

McKinnon (1979), certain currencies are favored in invoicing, but the prices of the products in these currencies are not necessarily independent of the exchange rate.

42. If nonrecurring costs, e.g., "up front" capital investment including R & D and capital equipment, are a large proportion of total costs, then the marginal unit costs of production will be small and pricing will be dictated primarily by demand considerations.

43. This section draws substantially on Lessard and Lightstone (1986).

44. For a discussion of why a firm should concern itself with managing foreign exchange risk see Logue and Oldfield (1977), Wihlborg (1980), Dufey and Srinivasulu (1984), Lessard and Shapiro (1984), and the references cited in note 33.

45. The same point is made by Waters (1979) and several corporate finance officers interviewed in "Coping with Volative Currencies: Multinationals Go for Safety First," *Business Week*, January 30, 1984.

46. Lessard and Lightstone (1986) describe an alternative hedge that is keyed to real exchange rates and, hence, is more appropriate for operating exposures.

47. This is especially likely for firms facing global competition that hedge their translation as well as transaction exposures, because under FAS 52 a foreign plant is often classified as a foreign asset, without regard to whether the prices of its inputs and outputs are determined locally, the prices of its inputs are determined locally but its outputs are priced internationally, or vice versa. While this contradiction can be resolved to some extent by clever choices of functional currencies, it is unlikely that any translation scheme will capture the exposure of a firm's future operating profits that is so important in the context of global competition.

48. For a recent example, see Hintz-Kessel-Kohl, a Harvard Business School case (#9-284-019) prepared by Professor Thomas Piper.

49. See Lessard and Lorange (1977) and Lessard and Sharp (1984) for further discussion of this point.

50. Strictly speaking, valuing contracts at forward rates only makes them comparable to contracts for future payment in the home currency. Both should still be discounted to reflect the time value of money measured in that currency.

51. The question asked does not quite address the issue I raised, because transaction gains/losses include anticipated gains/losses and surprises. I would contend, however, that neither component should be included in a manager's evaluation. See Lessard and Sharp (1984) for further discussion.

52. The reason why the dollar/krona relationship should have had little or no impact on dollar prices of Saabs or Volvos was that transshipment was limited and demand, presumably, relatively price elastic. Further, the effect of the exchange rate on short-run variable costs measured in dollars was quite small given that under Sweden's labor policies, wages are a fixed cost in the short run, and most other inputs are internationally sourced.

53. Lessard and Sharp (1984) discuss alternative ways that this recognition of exchange rate effects can be incorporated in the control system.

54. This point is discussed by Kogut (1983, 1985) and Baldwin (chap. 6 of this book).

55. As might be expected, there is no unambiguous measure of purchasing power parity. An instructive attempt to estimate parity rates, though, is provided by Williamson (1983). A further issue that has not been re-

solved in the literature is whether real exchange rates tend to return to parity or to move randomly. The results of Adler and Lehman (1983) and Roll (1979) support the latter view, but the macroeconomic models of Dornbusch (1983) and others suggest that there must be some type of adjustment over time.
56. See note 21.

REFERENCES

Adler, M. "The Cost of Capital and Valuation of a Two-Country Firm." *Journal of Finance* 29 (1974): 119–37.

———. "U.S. Taxation of U.S. Multinational Corporations," in M. Sarnat and G. Szego, eds., *International Trade and Finance*, vol. 2, Cambridge, Mass.: Ballinger, 1979.

Adler, M., and B. Dumas. "International Portfolio Choice and Corporate Finance: A Survey." *Journal of Finance* 38 (1983): 925–84.

Adler, M., and B. Lehman. "Deviations from Purchasing Power Party in the Long Run." *Journal of Finance* 38 (1983): 1471–87.

Agmon, T., and D. Lessard. "Financial Factors and the International Expansion of Small Country Firms," in Agmon and Kindleberger, eds., *Multinationals from Small Countries*. Cambridge, Mass.: MIT Press, 1977.

Antl, B. *Swap Financing Techniques*. London: Euromoney Publications, 1984.

Barnea, A., R. A. Haugen, and L. W. Senbet. "Market Imperfections, Agency Problems, and Capital Structure: A Review." *Financial Management* 10, no. 2 (Summer 1981): 7–22.

———. "Management of Corporate Risk." *Advances in Financial Planning and Forecasting* vol. 1. Greenwich, Conn.: JAI Press, 1985.

Blitzer, C., D. Lessard, and J. Paddock. "Risk-Bearing and the Choice of Contract Forms for Oil Exploration and Development." *The Energy Journal* 5 (1984): 1–28.

Boiardi, A. "Managing Foreign Subsidiaries in the Face of Fluctuating Exchange Rates." Master's thesis, MIT Sloan School of Management, 1984.

Booth, L. D. "Capital Budgeting Frameworks for the Multinational Corporations." *Journal of International Business Studies* 8, no. 2 (1982): 113–23.

Brean, D. J. S. "Financial Dimensions of Transfer Pricing," in Rugman and Eden, eds., *Multinationals and Transfer Pricing*. London and Sydney: Croom Helm, 1985.

Brennan, M. J., and E. S. Schwartz. "Evaluating Natural Resource Investments." *Journal of Business* 58, no. 2 (1985): 135–58.

Buckley, P., and M. Casson. *The Future of Multinational Enterprise*. London: Macmillan, 1976.

Carsberg, B. "FAS #52—Measuring the Performance of Foreign Operations." *Midland Corporate Finance Journal* 1, no. 2 (1983): 47–55.

Cassel, G. *Money and Foreign Exchange after 1914*. London: Macmillan, 1923.

Cornell, B., and A. C. Shapiro. "Managing Foreign Exchange Risk," *Midland Corporate Finance Journal* 1, no. 3 (Fall 1983).

Czechowicz, J., F. Choi, and V. Bavishi. *Assessing Foreign Subsidiary Performance: Systems and Practices of Leading Multinational Companies*. New York: Business International, 1982.

Donaldson, G. "Strategic Hurdle Rates for Capital Investment." *Harvard Business Review* 50 (March–April 1972): 50–55.

Dooley, M., and P. Isard. "Capital Controls, Political Risks and Deviations from Interest Rate Parity." *Journal of Political Economy* 88 (1980): 370–84.

Dornbusch, R. "Exchange Rate Economics: Where Do We Stand?" *Brookings Papers on Economic Activity* 1 (1980): 143–85.

————. "Equilibrium and Disequilibrium Exchange Rates." *Zeitschrift für Wirtschafts und Sozial-wissenschaften* 102 (1983): 573–99.

Dufey, G., and I. Giddy. *The International Money Market*. Englewood Cliffs, N.J.: Prentice-Hall, 1978.

————. "Innovation in the International Financial Markets." *Journal of International Business Studies* 7, no. 2 (1981): 33–52.

Dufey, G., and S. L. Srinivasulu. "The Case for Corporate Management of Foreign Exchange Risk." *Financial Management* 12, no. 4 (1984).

Dukes, R. "Forecasting Exchange Gains (Losses) and Security Market Response to FASB 8," in Levich and Wihlborg, eds., *Exchange Risk and Exposure*. Lexington, Mass.: Heath Lexington, 1980.

Flood, E. "Global Competition and Exchange Rate Exposure." Research Paper #837, Graduate School of Business, Stanford University, September, 1985.

Flood, E., and D. Lessard. "On the Measurement of Operating Exposure to Exchange Rates: A Conceptual Approach." *Financial Management* 15, no. 1 (Spring 1986): 25–36.

Frenkel, J. A. "The Collapse of Purchasing Power Parities During the 1970's." *European Economic Review* 16, no 1. (1981): 145–65.

————. "Flexible Exchange Rates, Prices and the Role of 'News': Lessons from the 1970's." *Journal of Political Economy*, no. 4 (August 1983): 665–705.

Frenkel, J. A., and M. Mussa. "The Efficiency of Foreign Exchange Markets and Measures of Turbulence." *American Economic Review* 70 (1980): 374–81.

Grassman, S. "A Fundamental Symmetry in International Payment Patterns." *Journal of International Economics*, no. 2 (May 1973): 105–16.

Grubel, H. "A Theory of International Banking." *Banca Nazionale del Lavoro Quarterly Review*, no. 123 (1977): 349–64.

Guisinger, S. E., et al. *Investment Incentives and Performance Requirements: Patterns of International Trade, Production, and Investment*. New York: Praeger, 1985.

Hayes, R., and W. Abernathy. "Managing Our Way to Economic Decline." *Harvard Business Review* 58, no. 4 (July–August 1980): 67–77.

Hennart, J.-F. *A Theory of Multinational Enterprise*. Ann Arbor: University of Michigan Press, 1982.

Hodder, J. E. "Evaluation of Manufacturing Investments: A Comparison of U.S. and Japanese Practices." Technical Report 84-8, Department of Industrial Engineering and Engineering Management, Stanford University, November, 1984.

Hodder, J. E., and H. E. Riggs. "Pitfalls in Evaluating Risky Projects." *Harvard Business Review* 85, no. 1 (January–February 1985): 128–35.

Horst, T. "American Taxation of Multinational Firms." *American Economic Review* 67 (1977): 376–89.

Hout, T., M. Porter, and E. Rudden. "How Global Companies Win Out." *Harvard Business Review* 60, no. 5 (September–October 1982): 98–108.

Hymer, S. *The International Operations of Multinational Firms*. Cambridge, Mass.: MIT Press, 1960.

Ijiri, Y. "Foreign Exchange Accounting and Translation," in R. J. Herring, ed., *Managing Foreign Exchange Risk*. New York: Cambridge University Press, 1983.

International Monetary Fund. *Annual Report on Exchange Arrangements and Exchange Restrictions*, 1985.

Jun, Y. W. "The Internationalization of the Firm: The Case of the Korean Consumer Electronics Industry," unpublished Ph.D. diss., Cambridge, Mass.: MIT Sloan School of Management.

Kiechel, W., 3rd. "Playing the Global Game." *Fortune* 104 (November 16, 1981): 111–26.

Kindleberger, C. P. *American Business Abroad*. New Haven: Yale University Press, 1969.

————. *The Formation of Financial Centers: A Study in Comparative Economic History*. Princeton Studies in International Finance, no. 36, 1974.

————. "Plus Ça Change—A Look at the New Literature," in Kindleberger, ed., *Multinational Excursions*. Cambridge, Mass.: MIT Press, 1985.

Kogut, B. "Foreign Direct Investment as a Sequential Process," in Kindleberger and Audretsch, eds., *The Multinational Corporation in the 1980's*. Cambridge, Mass.: MIT Press, 1983.

————. "Designing Global Strategies: Profiting from Operating Flexibility." *Sloan Management Review* (Fall 1985): 27–38.

Kohlhagen, S. "Overlapping National Investment Portfolios: Evidence and Implications of International Integration of Secondary Markets for Financial Assets," in R. Hawkins, R. Levich, and C. Wihlborg, eds., *Research in International Business and Finance*. Greenwich, Conn.: JAI Press, 1983.

Lessard, D. "Transfer Prices, Taxes and Financial Markets: Implications of Internal Financial Transfers within the Multinational Firms," in R. B. Hawkins, ed., *Economic Issues of Multinational Firms*. Greenwich, Conn.: JAI Press, 1979*a*.

————. "Evaluating Foreign Projects: An Adjusted Present Value Approach," in D. R. Lessard, ed., *International Financial Management*. New York: Warren, Gorham, and Lamont, 1979*b*.

————. "Evaluating International Projects: An Adjusted Present Value Approach," in R. Krum and F. Derkindiren, eds., *Capital Budgeting under Conditions of Uncertainty*. Hingham, Mass.: Martinus Nijhoff, 1981.

Lessard, D., and J. Lightstone. "Volatile Exchange Rates Can Put Operations at Risk." *Harvard Business Review* (July–August 1986): 107–114.

Lessard, D., and P. Lorange. "Currency Changes and Management Control: Resolving the Centralization/Decentralization Dilemma." *Accounting Review* 52, no. 3 (1977): 628–37.

Lessard, D., and J. Paddock. "Evaluating International Projects: Weighted-Coverage Cost of Capital versus Valuation by Components." *Journal of International Business Studies*, 1986 forthcoming.

Lessard, D., and A. Shapiro. "Guidelines for Global Financing Choices." *Midland Corporate Finance Journal* 1, no. 4 (1984): 68–80.

Lessard, D., and D. Sharp. "Measuring the Performance of Operations Subject to Fluctuating Exchange Rate." *Midland Corporate Journal* 2, no. 3 (1984): 18–30.

Levi, M. *International Finance*. New York: McGraw-Hill, 1982.

Logue, D., and G. Oldfield. "Managing Foreign Assets When Foreign Exchange Markets Are Efficient." *Financial Management* 7, no. 2 (1977): 16–22.

Magee, S. "U.S. Import Prices in the Currency Contract Period." *Brookings Papers on Economic Activity*, no. 1 (1974): 303–23.

Magee, S., and R. Rao. "Vehicle and Nonvehicle Currencies in Foreign Trade." *American Economic Review* 70 (1980): 368–73.

Mason, S., and R. C. Merton. "The Role of Contingent Claims Analysis in Corporate Finance," in Altman and Subrahmanyan, eds., *Advances in Corporate Finance*. Homewood, Ill.: Dow Jones-Irwin, 1985.

McKinnon, R. *Money and Capital in Economic Development*. Washington, D.C.: The Brookings Institution, 1973.

———. *Money in International Exchange: The Convertible Currency System*. New York: Oxford University Press, 1979.

Myers, S. "Interactions of Corporate Finance and Investment Decisions." *Journal of Finance* 29 (1974): 1–25.

———. "The Capital Structure Puzzle." *Journal of Finance* 39 (1984): 575–92.

Myers, S., and S. Majd. "Calculating Abandonment Value Rising Option Pricing Theory," MIT Sloan School of Management, Working Paper #1462-83, August, 1983.

Oblak, D. J., and R. J. Helm, Jr. "Survey and Analysis of Capital Budgeting Methods Used by Multinationals." *Financial Management* 9, no. 2 (Winter 1980): 37–40.

Otani, I., and S. Tiwari. "Capital Controls and Interest Rate Parity: The Japanese Experience 1978–1980." *Staff Papers* 28 (1981): 798–815.

Robbins, S., and R. Stobaugh. *Money in the Multinational Enterprise*. New York: Basic Books, 1973.

Roll, R. "Violations of Purchasing Power Parity and Their Implications for Efficient International Commodity Markets," in M. Sarnat and P. Szego, eds., *International Finance and Trade*, vol. 2. Cambridge Mass.: Ballinger, 1979.

Rosenberg, M. "Foreign Exchange Controls: An International Comparison," in A. George and I. Giddy, eds., *International Finance Handbook*, vol. 1. New York: John Wiley, 1983.

Rugman, A. *Inside the Multinationals: The Economics of Internal Markets*. New York: Columbia University Press, 1981.

Rutenberg, D. "Maneuvering Liquid Assets in a Multinational Company: Formulation and Deterministic Solution Procedures." *Management Science* 16, no. 10 (1970): B671–84.

Schall, L. D., G. L. Sundem, and W. R. Geijsbeek, Jr. "Survey and Analysis of Capital Budgeting Methods." *Journal of Finance* 33, no. 1 (1978): 281–87.

Schydlowsky, D. "Simulation Model of a Multinational Enterprise," in S. Robbins and R. Stobaugh, *Money in the Multinational Enterprise*. New York: Basic Books, 1973.

Shapiro, A. "What Does Purchasing Power Parity Mean?" *Journal of International Money & Finance* 2 (1983): 295–318.

Shapiro, A., and S. Titman. "An Integrated Approach to Corporate Risk Management." *Midland Corporate Finance Journal* 3, no. 2 (1985): 41–56.

Sharp, D. "Organization and Decision Making in U.S. Multinational Firms: Price Management Under Floating Exchange Rates." Diss., MIT Sloan School of Management, 1985.

Smith, C. W. Jr., and R. Stulz. "The Determinants of Firms Hedging Policies," *Journal of Financial and Quantitative Analyses* 20, no. 4 (December 1985): 391–405.

Sophonpanich, C. "Exchange Rates and Corporate Performance." Master's thesis, MIT Sloan School of Management, 1984.

Stockman, A. "A Theory of Exchange Rate Determination." *Journal of Political Economy* 88 (1980): 673–98.

Stonehill, A., and K. Dullum. *Internationalizing the Cost of Capital*. New York: John Wiley, 1982.

Stulz, R. "Pricing Capital Assets in an International Setting: An Introduction." *Journal of International Business Studies* 15, no. 3 (1985): 55–73.

Tobin, J. "A Proposal for International Monetary Reform." Cowles Foundation Discussion Paper 506, Yale University, 1978.

Trusheim, M. "An Exploration of Foreign Exchange Operating Expense." Master's thesis, MIT Sloan School of Management, 1984.

Tschoegl, A. *The Regulation of Foreign Banks: Policy Formation in Countries Outside the United States*. NYU Monograph series in Finance and Economics (1981–82).

Vernon, R. "The Product Cycle Hypothesis in a New International Environment." *Oxford Bulletin of Economics & Statistics* 41, no. 4 (1979).

———. *Sovereignty at Bay: The Multinational Spread of U.S. Enterprises*. New York: Basic Books, 1971.

Waters, S. "Exposure Management Is a Job for All Departments." *Euromoney* (December 1979): 79–82.

Wicks, M. E. *A Comparative Analysis of Foreign Investment Evaluations Practices of U.S.-based Multinational Companies*. New York: McKinsey and Co., 1980.

Wihlborg, C. "Economics of Exposure Management of Foreign Subsidiaries of MNCs." *Journal of International Business Studies* 6, no. 3 (1980): 9–18.

Williamson, J. *The Exchange Rate System*. Washington, D.C.: Institute for International Economics, 1983.

6

The Capital Factor: Competing for Capital in a Global Environment*

Carliss Y. Baldwin

INTRODUCTION: THE COST OF CAPITAL DOCTRINE

In recent years, a new doctrine has grown up in the United States. Our corporations, it is said, are at a disadvantage against foreign, especially Japanese, competition because the U.S. cost of capital is too high.[1] Lower costs of capital abroad have led to investment and capital formation "over there" and disinvestment, deindustrialization, and loss of jobs over here. As foreign companies use low-cost funds to penetrate markets that were once our own, managers at a number of companies are asking: How can U.S. corporations hope to succeed against competitors who do not have to meet the same standards of profitability and a fair rate of return?

Capital as a Competitive Weapon

There is a kernel of inconsistency in the "cost of capital doctrine" that needs to be resolved before we can proceed. A cost of capital that is artificially low represents a subsidy. Subsidization usually results in economic loss. How is it, then, that Japanese (and other) firms, by investing in losing projects, have actually managed to generate spectacularly high returns for their investors over the long run?[2]

*I have greatly benefited from the comments of Michael Porter, Richard Caves, M. Therese Flaherty, Richard Meyer, and Thomas Piper and the participants in the Colloquium on Competition in Global Industries. I would especially like to thank Donald Lessard for insights contributed in numerous conversations extending over several months. Thomas Montvel-Cohen and Rita Seymour provided invaluable research assistance. Any remaining errors or omissions are of course my own.

The resolution of this paradox lies in the difference between a subsidy and a speculation. A subsidized investment never generates a satisfactory return. In contrast, a successful speculation provides low returns for a period of time, but at maturity is transformed into a highly profitable economic swan.

The ability to sustain a speculation, holding near-term capital costs down in order to gain higher returns in the future, is a valuable competitive weapon. Lower short-run capital costs may allow a company to intensify R & D or marketing efforts in order to win a technology race or outlast its opponents in a price war. Access to "patient capital" is also valuable when investments are open-ended and each generation of technology qualifies the company for the next round. In such cases, a reputation for spending a lot to gain a little may deter rational, economically minded competition from investing in the next round or even entering the race in the first place. Thus, the belief among competitors that one's cost of capital is low and one's staying power unlimited is worth cultivating purely for its effect on competitors' behavior.

In summary:

- "Low-cost" capital provides a competitive advantage, but only if it is used to finance profitable, long-term speculations.
- Competitors' belief that they will be outspent acts as a deterrent, and therefore merely the reputation of having low-cost capital may increase long-run returns.

Companies with access to low-cost capital can thus outspend, undersell, and outlast their competition, and by these methods may come to dominate their product markets. But how does a cost of capital difference arise? And, more to the point, if such differences exist, how may a global corporation gain access to the low-cost funds?

Unfortunately, aggregate measures of corporations' costs of capital tend to be complicated and cumbersome. Frequently, the analysis runs to many pages of equations and definitions, which are then combined into a single number called the corporate or national cost of capital.[3] From a managerial perspective, there are two problems with this approach. First, because so much is packed into a single number, the overall analysis may be in error because of flaws in the component parts. Inexact measurement of one component—the cost of equity, for example—may significantly bias the final results. Managers are then faced with the unwelcome task of sorting through arcane methodological disputes before they can know if the final measure is reliable.

The second problem is that the final result usually does not offer much operational guidance. Most characteristics of the capital markets are outside the control of even the largest firms. Within the firm, opportunities to increase capital efficiency to get "more bang for the buck" usually occur at the level of individual projects or transactions, and hence may be swept aside in the calculation of a single corporate-wide cost of capital.

For these reasons, this chapter does not attempt to construct a single measure of a corporate or national cost of capital. Its aim instead is to describe the factors underlying capital costs, factors that taken together determine the "bottom-line" cost of capital to a global corporation. In the course of this analysis, the following questions will be addressed:

1. Where, and why, have national cost of capital differences arisen in the past?
2. What trends in global capital sourcing and utilization can be observed today?
3. How may a global corporation turn present trends and opportunities to its advantage?

The factors that influence a corporation's cost of capital include: national capital market structure, national tax policy, national systems of corporate governance as well as project-linked financing opportunities. Figure 6.1 provides an overview of the relationship of these factors to the capital flows of a global corporation. Initially, capital originates as savings within a national market. Corporations gain access to capital funds by borrowing from financial intermediaries and by issuing debt and equity directly into the market. Corporations in turn allocate their capital to individual projects. Home governments tax and regulate transactions between the corporation and the national capital market; host governments tax, regulate, and may subsidize flows between the corporation and individual projects.

At the national level, competitive forces of supply and demand determine the cost of capital within the marketplace. The following section describes how capital market segmentation and national policies with respect to taxation, securities laws, bankruptcy provisions, and so on can lead to cost of capital differences among firms with access to different national capital markets.

However, a dramatic development of the last ten to fifteen years has been the integration of world financial markets into one global "supermarket." Global corporations are particularly well positioned to gain access to this market and many are also prepared to profit from short-run disparities in the cost of funds between markets through financial arbitrage.[4] The third section describes some of the profit opportunities found in arbitrage of national capital markets, but goes on to argue that, as global corporations approach the point of having essentially equal access to all markets, national cost of capital differences (for example between the United States and Japan) will come to have less competitive significance.

Far more significant in years to come will be the opportunities to structure the financing of specific projects in order to make more effi-

Figure 6.1 Factors Affecting the Cost of Capital to a Global Corporation and its Projects

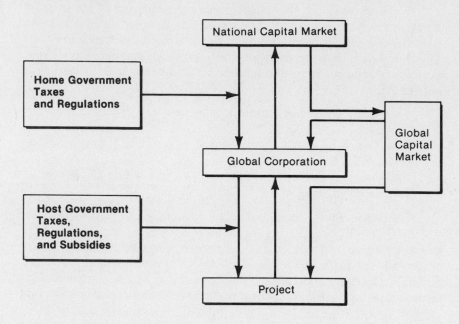

cient use of corporate capital resources. The final section argues that, for a global corporation, the classic dichotomy between investment and financing decisions makes little sense, because project values are almost always affected by project-specific financing opportunities. In part this is because host governments are in competition with one another for the job-creating investments that global corporations control. Informed by financial analysis, negotiations between a global corporation and a host government may be directed toward the goal of more efficient capital utilization and this, in turn, can provide the cost of capital advantage that a corporation needs in order to prosper in an increasingly integrated world economy.

COST OF CAPITAL DIFFERENCES AMONG COUNTRIES

In the U.S., Japanese, and Western European economies, which have highly developed capital markets (i.e., efficient banking institutions, investment intermediaries, and a stock market), corporations in the same industry normally have access to capital on equal terms. However, if capital cannot flow freely between countries, then costs of capital may be different for companies sourcing capital in different national markets. Thus, a key issue for firms engaged in global competition is: Does a competitor have access to capital at advantageously low rates?

A nation's capital markets, tax policies, and financial institutions all may affect its corporations' costs of capital. In order to show how national differences may lead to differences in corporate capital costs, I will compare costs of capital in the United States and Japan, currently the two largest national markets in the world.[5] These two markets provide an interesting contrast, for while the U.S. capital market is relatively open and representative of the world market, the Japanese capital market traditionally has been closed and subject to more active government intervention. Thus, it would seem possible for costs of capital in Japan to differ from those in the United States and the rest of the world. Such a difference would be of concern to global corporations because lower costs of capital in Japan would give Japanese corporations a competitive advantage and could contribute to their success in penetrating product markets outside Japan.

When capital flows freely from one location to another, competitive forces of supply and demand will quickly eliminate any price or rate of return disparities. Thus, cost of capital differences (other than those arising from differences in risk) cannot persist in an integrated capital market. For this reason, research in international finance has tended to focus on the question of whether international capital markets are integrated or segmented.

If capital markets are integrated, then economic theory suggests that short-term notes and bills and long-term bonds will be priced so that real interest rates are equal across nations. This condition, known as purchasing power parity, leads to a predicted equilibrium relationship involving exchange rates, interest rates, and expected inflation across countries. If rates should deviate from the predicted relationship, the theory states, international investors should be able to buy or sell securities in order to take advantage of the rate disparity. For example, if the real rate of interest in country A were too high, international traders should rush to purchase that country's bills and bonds: these purchases would quickly drive prices up and rates down to their equilibrium levels.

However, numerous tests of the purchasing power parity hypothesis indicate that deviations from strict parity are common and may endure for months or even years.[6] Although in the long run there seems to be a tendency for real interest and exchange rates to revert to parity, in the short run it is difficult to distinguish the dynamic behavior of real interest or exchange rates from a random walk.[7]

Further evidence of capital market segmentation may be found in the equity markets. In an internationally integrated market, investors would be expected to hold internationally diversified portfolios. In fact, most individuals' portfolios are concentrated within their national markets, even though the benefits in overall risk reduction of international diversification appear to be substantial.[8] In short, there is considerable evidence that national capital markets for both debt and equity are at best imperfectly integrated.

In Japan, government policy has tended to intensify the naturally existing degree of capital market segmentation. For example, until recently, foreigners could not buy Japanese bonds or equities and Japanese investors could not freely invest in the United States or Europe.[9] Such explicit restrictions on the free movement of capital could give rise to differences in required rates of return, which in turn would result in different costs of capital for U.S. and Japanese corporations.

The segmentation of U.S. and Japanese capital markets means that a difference in the cost of capital between them *might* exist, but the magnitude and direction of the difference remains in doubt. Two recent and widely cited studies, one undertaken by Chase Financial Policy[10] on behalf of the U.S. Semiconductor Industry Association and one by G. N. Hatsopoulos,[11] claim to have demonstrated that such a difference does exist and that it works to the advantage of Japanese firms. Unfortunately, both studies contain significant flaws that tend to cast doubt on their conclusions.

In the Hatsopoulos (1983) report, most of the calculated difference between the Japanese and U.S. costs of capital is due to the high cost of U.S. equity estimated for the period 1974–81. However, the method used to calculate the cost of equity is itself questionable. The report equates the cost of equity with the current corporate dividend yield plus an estimated long-term growth rate. It fails to recognize that corporations generally set dividends so that the probability of a future dividend cut is small.[12] Because dividends tend not to fall except in the direst circumstances, any negative shock that causes corporate market values to decline will cause dividend yields and hence the *apparent* cost of equity to rise. This is not a short-term effect: the bias will persist until market values regain their formal levels, and thus may endure for several years. For example, after the U.S. stock market collapsed in 1973–74, it did not regain its former level until 1978. Nevertheless aggregate corporate divident payments continued to increase over the period. Dividend yields, and thus the Hatsopoulos cost of equity rose.

The other major flaw in the Hatsopoulos study is its comparison of a weighted average cost of capital (a measure that combines the costs of debt and equity) in the United States with the cost of debt in Japan. Debt is much less risky than equity, and investors generally require lower rates of return on securities of lower risk. Thus, it comes as no surprise that a heavily equity-weighted measure[13] of the U.S. cost of capital is higher than a solely debt-based measure of the Japanese cost of capital.

The Chase study focuses on the U.S. and Japanese semiconductor industries. Its main weakness is that the U.S. and Japanese companies in the sample are fundamentally dissimilar and thus would not be expected to have equal costs of capital. The U.S. firms tended to be small and undiversified: semiconductors accounted for more than 70 percent of their sales. In contrast, the Japanese companies were, almost without exception, large, diversified producers of a variety of electric and electronic products: on average, semiconductors accounted for less than 7 percent of their sales.

Within a diversified corporation, risk and the cost of capital vary from business unit to business unit. The risk of the corporation as a whole is a weighted average of the individual risks of the underlying businesses. Because Japanese semiconductor manufacturers are buried within large, heterogeneous corporations (for example, Mitsubishi), their individual costs of capital are not directly observable. Semiconductor manufacturing is an extremely risky business;[14] therefore, one would expect the costs of capital to the parent companies to be lower than independently measured costs of capital to the subsidiaries.

Past research has failed to show conclusively that U.S. and Japan firms face significantly different costs of capital either on average or within particular sectors. Here I take a slightly different approach, which first compares the costs of capital adjusted for risk in the U.S. and Japanese public capital markets and then considers the impact of tax policies, financial institutions, and financing practices on the net cost of capital perceived by corporations.[15]

Market Costs of Capital in the United States and Japan

Most investors are risk-averse and thus require higher rates of return on securities of higher risk. Trading within a capital market determines the equilibrium between risk and return for that market. A cost of capital difference exists if securities *of the same risk* have different required rates of return.

Table 6.1 presents data on the nominal returns (i.e., returns not adjusted for inflation) on U.S. long-term bonds and stocks and Japanese bonds and stocks from 1960–80. It also shows the mean and standard deviation of the rate of inflation in the two markets.[16] The table indicates that U.S. and Japanese bonds have similar risk as measured by the standard deviation of annual holding period returns. Nominal returns were higher on Japanese bonds than on U.S. bonds, but the average rate of inflation was also higher in Japan. In the equity markets, Japanese common stocks exhibited higher average annual rates of return, but also much higher risk: the standard deviation of returns on Japanese equities was 27.98 percent as opposed to 17.68 percent for U.S. equities.

Because annual inflation rates were different in the United States

Table 6.1 Nominal Performance of U.S. and Japanese Bonds and Stocks (1960–80)

	Average (%)[a]	Standard Deviation (%)[b]
United States		
Bond Returns	4.31	5.39
Equity Returns	10.23	17.68
Inflation	5.33	3.81
Japan		
Bond Returns	7.73	5.04
Equity Returns	15.24	27.98
Inflation	7.31	4.80

[a]Arithmetic average of annual holding period returns.
[b]Square root of the mean square deviation from the annual average. For example, U.S. equity returns average 10.23 percent per annum plus or minus 17.68 percent.
SOURCE: Data in Ibbotson, Carr, and Robinson (1982).

Table 6.2 Real Performance of U.S. and Japanese Bonds and Stocks (1960–80)

	Average (%)	Standard Deviation (%)
United States		
Bond Returns	−0.82	6.56
Equity Returns	4.87	17.39
Japan		
Bond Returns	0.60	6.46
Equity Returns	8.05	28.35

NOTE: Annual real returns were calculated by deflating the nominal holding period yield by the concurrent rate of inflation. Specifically:

$$R_{real} = (1 + R_{nominal}) / (1 + \text{Inflation Rate}) - 1$$

Averages and standard deviations of the resulting series are reported above.

and Japan,[17] comparisons based on nominal returns may be misleading. Therefore, Table 6.2 computes returns and risks on bonds and stocks adjusted for inflation. The basic results are unchanged: differences in bond returns and risks are insignificant, and, although the average return on U.S. common stocks is lower than the average return on Japanese common stocks, Japanese stocks also exhibit higher risk.

Investors can control their overall risk by changing the proportions allocated to high- and low-risk securities in their portfolios. Consider two portfolios, one composed of U.S. bonds and equities, and the other composed of Japanese bonds and equities. If portfolio weights are selected so that the two portfolios are equally risky, we may ask: Which of the two obtained higher returns?

Figure 6.2 graphs the risk-return combinations that investors in the United States and Japan would have achieved by combining long-term bonds and equities in portfolios. The vertical distance between the two lines measures the difference in average rates of return for portfolios of the same risk. For all risk levels, *the difference is never greater than 1 percent*. Furthermore, the direction of the difference changes; whereas Japanese portfolios have higher rates of return than U.S. portfolios at low-risk levels, U.S. portfolios have higher rates of return at high-risk levels. Thus, based on the performance of market aggregates over the past twenty years, U.S. and Japanese portfolios of similar risk on average have obtained similar returns.

The preceding comparison is based on historical rates of return, although there is reason to believe that returns on risky bonds and stocks were unusually low in the period 1960–80.[18] The comparison is still valid, as long as macroeconomic factors tended to displace both sets of market returns in the same direction. The comparison would not be valid if the two series were biased in opposite directions, for example, if Japan experienced abnormally high real returns (relative to expectations and long-run averages) while the United States experienced abnormally low returns. Because the U.S. and Japanese economies are linked and have experienced similar macroeconomic pressures and shocks, the hypothesis of a consistent bias in average returns seems plausible.[19]

However, even if market rates of return and gross costs of capital (adjusted for risk) are similar in the United States and Japan, corporations in the two countries might still face different *net* costs of capital. Within an integrated capital market, differences in net costs of capital can arise if corporate income is taxed differently or if certain investments receive more favorable tax treatment (e.g., more accelerated tax depreciation allowances) in one country than another. In addition, national financial institutions and financing practices may expedite or hinder corporations' capital raising activities and thereby raise or lower the net cost of capital for specific new investments. Because their visibility is greater but their net impact probably smaller, I will take up the issue of corporate taxes first, before moving on to consider the impact of financial institutions and practices on costs of capital in the two markets.

Corporate Taxes and the Cost of Capital

For corporations doing business in many nations, host and home country tax laws interact in numerous complex ways. The difference between aggregate taxes due and tax payments calculated on a decentralized basis can be quite significant,[20] and therefore centralized tax planning and analysis are important aspects of a global corporation's financial activities.

Nevertheless, if taxes are managed appropriately, differences in

Figure 6.2 Combinations of Risky Portfolios: U.S. vs. Japan

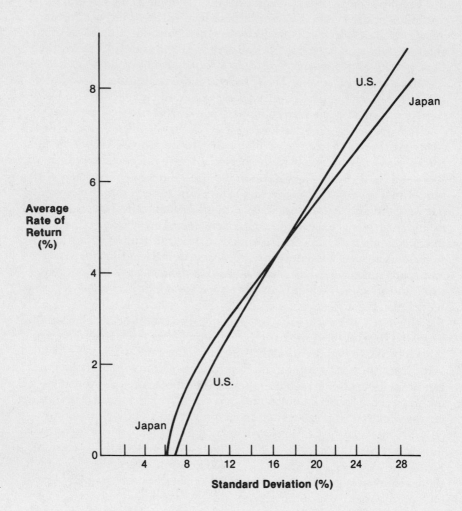

home country tax rates are not likely to have a significant effect on a global corporation's competitiveness. The impact of home country tax policies is diminished by:

- the (virtually universal) tax deductibility of interest;
- similarities in national systems of taxation of corporate income;
- for global corporations, control over the repatriation and taxation of foreign income; and
- offsetting foreign tax credits.

A corporation's cost of capital is a weighted average of the costs of debt and equity, with weights determined by the proportions of debt and equity used in its capital structure. Although interest is a tax deductible expense in almost every country in the free world, most countries maintain their right to tax corporate profits, which provide the return to equity. Home country taxes are thus most burdensome to companies that are all equity financed; their impact declines as the fraction of debt in a company's capital structure increases.

There are three types of corporate income or profits tax: each differs in its treatment of dividends paid out to investors.[21] In so-called classical systems, such as those found in the United States or the Netherlands, dividend returns are taxed twice: once as corporate income and again as individual income. In split rate systems, such as the one used in Japan, dividends are taxed at both levels, but the corporate tax rate on income paid out in dividends is *lower* than the rate on income retained in the business.[22] Finally, in imputation systems, such as are found in the United Kingdom, France, and Germany, corporations pay income tax, but individuals are allowed to take a fraction of corporate taxes as a credit against their personal income taxes. Given equal corporate tax rates, the classical system is theoretically the most burdensome; split rate and imputation systems partially offset the burden of double dividend taxation.

Table 6.3 presents estimates of effective statutory tax rates (national plus local taxes) for the United States and Japan. For comparison, similar estimates are presented for France, the United Kingdom, and West Germany. Notably, the total spread in tax rates on retained earnings among the five countries is only 6 percentage points; tax rates on dividends for all countries except West Germany are within 5 percentage points of each other.

Table 6.4 then calculates total tax rates in the United States and Japan for dividend payout ratios ranging from zero to 100 percent.[23] At all payout ratios, the tax rates in the two countries differ by only a few percentage points. Thus, differences in statutory rates or methods of taxation of corporate income do not appear to cause large differences in the costs of capital between the United States and Japan. Larger differences arise *within* the two countries among corporations with different dividend policies.[24]

In general, if market costs of capital and corporate tax rates are the same, more liberal deductions from corporate income or credits against corporate taxes result in lower effective taxes and thus a lower net cost of capital. Unfortunately, aggregate comparisons provide a very incomplete view of the impact of tax preferences and incentives on investment. Within specific sectors, tax deductions and credits may have a large effect on investment: for example, oil and gas investment in the United States has been greatly stimulated by generous depletion allowances and other specialized tax incentives. But, other than

Table 6.3 Effective Statutory Corporate Tax Rates (1979–80)

	Retained Earnings (%)	Dividends (%)
United States[a]	50.32	50.32
Japan[b]	52.60	47.00
France[c]	50.00	50.00
United Kingdom[c]	52.00	52.00
West Germany[c]	56.00	36.00

[b]Estimated by Touche Ross, International (1981). Includes a provision for local taxes. Tax rates are 1 to 2 percent higher in Tokyo.
[c]Estimated by Nobes (1980).
[a]SOURCE: U.S. Tax Code. Includes a provision for state taxes estimated at 8 percent of corporate taxable income (Hatsopoulos 1983). State taxes are deductible from federal taxable income.

Table 6.4. Marginal Tax Rates for Different Dividend Payouts

Payout Ratios (%)[a]	Effective Tax Rates (%)[b]	
	U.S.	Japan
0	50.32	52.60
20	55.29	56.78
40	60.26	60.96
60	65.22	65.14
80	70.19	69.32
100	75.16	73.50

[a]Equals dividends divided by net income.
[b]Includes corporate taxes at the statutory rate (see Table 6.3) plus personal taxes at 50 percent.

causing sectoral shifts in the allocation of capital, the impact of tax incentives on aggregate costs of capital is difficult to ascertain.[25]

Nevertheless, at the aggregate level, U.S. and Japanese investment tax credits and depreciation deductions are similar and if anything, the U.S. combination of incentives may be more generous. Through most of the seventies, Japanese corporations could write off many (but not all) forms of capital more rapidly than U.S. firms, but, except in a few special cases, Japanese firms did not have the benefit of the investment tax credit. Assuming similar nominal interest rates, the benefits of U.S. investment tax credits outweighed the benefits of Japan's more accelerated depreciation schedules: this was especially true after the United States adopted the Accelerated Cost Recovery System in 1981.

However, the total impact of tax credits and deductions depends on the interaction of the scheduled tax reductions with nominal interest rates at the time an asset is placed in service.[26] On average (as we have seen), Japanese nominal interest rates over the last twenty years have been higher than U.S. rates. However, during the late seventies and continuing to the present, Japanese nominal interest rates have tended to be *lower* than U.S. rates.[27] Lower nominal interest rates increase the value of depreciation tax deductions to Japanese firms and this, in turn, has tended to equalize the net benefit of tax incentives under the two systems.

Multinational corporations are even less exposed than domestic firms to adverse effects of home country taxation because a large fraction of their income is earned outside the home country. A home government usually does not have access to tax records in countries where the corporation's income is earned, and thus tax authorities must rely on the corporation itself to report its income. In such circumstances companies may be forgiven if they calculate income in a way that minimizes their tax liability.

In recognition of this fact, most countries that tax corporate foreign income also have provisions that reduce or defer the taxes actually paid. For example, subject to some limitations, a foreign subsidiary of a U.S. corporation may defer paying U.S. taxes until dividends are actually remitted to the parent.[28] Japanese corporations may establish tax deferred reserves for overseas market development. And finally, in both the United States and Japan, foreign taxes paid can be credited against corporate income taxes due.[29] Provisions such as these in effect exempt a portion of the income of overseas subsidiaries from taxation by the home country,[30] and thus tend to diminish cost of capital differences between global corporations of different national origins.

In short, if a global corporation uses all available tax minimization levers, its home country's ability to impair its competitiveness through tax policy is very limited. Interest tax deductibility, similarities among statutory rates, exemption from tax of unrepatriated earnings and foreign tax credits all tend to neutralize differences in home country tax policies and so give global corporations equal access to capital at prevailing world rates.

A last piece of evidence supporting the contention that home country taxes are not a major concern to most global corporations is the fact that few large corporations have seen fit to move in order to escape taxation. A number of small countries (Panama, Monaco, the Netherlands Antilles, etc.) do function as tax havens, and some industries, notably the shipping industry, have found it advantageous to identify such nations as their countries of origin. But movement by global corporations from one home country to another is rare. The moves that have taken place—for example, Jardine Matheson's impending move from Hong Kong to Bermuda[31]—appear to be motivated as much by political and strategic considerations as by specific concerns about confiscatory taxation.[32] Given the multiple methods available to reduce or defer home country taxes, the differences that do exist among home country tax systems do not seem large enough to induce significant numbers of global corporations to "vote with their feet" in favor of lower taxes.

Financial Institutions and Practices: Debt Utilization

Even in a globally integrated capital market, a corporation's cost of capital may be affected by the financial institutions and practices of its home country. One frequently cited example of a combined institutional and tax effect is the different patterns of debt and equity utilization prevailing in the United States and Japan.[33]

In both the United States and Japan (and, as was noted previously, most other countries), interest is a tax deductible expense, and therefore debt is theoretically a cheaper source of capital than equity.[24] (In effect, interest tax deductibility means that the government through tax reductions bears a portion of the interest expense.) Two questions arise: First, why are Japanese corporations better able (or American firms more reluctant) to use debt? Second, what impact does the difference in financing practices have on aggregate net costs of capital to the two groups of firms?

A partial answer to the first question may be found in the contrast between mechanisms used to resolve creditors' claims in the two countries.[35] In the United States, the various claimants on a firm— banks, bondholders, and equity holders—are separated and there is seldom much overlap between investor classes. If a corporation fails to meet its financial obligations, the conflicting claims among creditors and investors ultimately may be resolved through an adversarial proceeding in bankruptcy court. Out of bankruptcy, the creditors' role is sharply circumscribed.[36]

In contrast, in Japan (and some European nations such as West Germany), banks occupy a special place at the center of large groups of interrelated companies. The banks function as principal financiers to companies within their groups, holding not only short-term debt but also long-term bonds and equity. Banks and related companies may be actively involved in corporate policy formulation and management, and if a company experiences difficulties, its bank, acting in unison with other members of the group, may be able to replace management without going through formal bankruptcy proceedings.[37] The greater integration of debt and equity claims in Japan thus gives creditors more flexibility in dealing with a corporate borrower's failure to meet its financial obligations: this in turn may allow Japanese firms to borrow more in order to exploit more fully the tax advantages of debt.[38]

However, recent evidence suggests that *in aggregate* the magnitude of the tax advantage to debt is not as great as once was believed. Corporate tax deductions for interest paid are offset by investors' tax liabilities on interest received and this, in turn, increases the cost of taxable debt relative to tax-exempt debt and equity.[39] Recent empirical evidence[40] suggests that, at present, debt may only be 10 to 20 percent cheaper than equity (instead of 46 percent as an analysis limited to corporate taxes alone would suggest).

On average, large U.S. corporations today finance approximately 47 percent of their total capital[41] with debt, while the average debt-to-total-capital ratio for Japanese firms is on the order of 62 percent.[42] Using the Capital Asset Pricing Model and data on current interest rates, the weighted average cost of capital to a U.S. firm of average risk in 1984–85 is in the range of 15 to 17 percent. Moving from 47 to 62 percent debt would reduce the weighted average cost of capital by approximately one percentage point.[43]

Given the uncertainties that generally surround cash flow forecasts and project evaluations, a 1 percent change in the weighted average cost of capital is unlikely to make much difference to a corporation's investment decisions. However, such a change in the cost of capital can have a substantial impact on a corporation's market value. The leveraged buyout (LBO) form of capital structure is a recent U.S. innovation designed to push up a company's debt for a short period of time in order to take full advantage of the tax shields thereby generated.

The best leveraged buyout candidates are companies with low expected growth rates, stable cash flows, and dominant product market positions, which can afford to make substantial cash payments for a period of three to five years. A typical LBO capital structure initially may comprise 80–95 percent debt and as little as 5 percent equity. However, the so-called "mezzanine" level of subordinated debt,[44] which may account for 40–60 percent of total capital, is generally held by a single lender or a syndicate that also has a substantial equity interest in the LBO.[45] Thus, in the event of a default, the costly conflicts of interest between debt and equity holders, which ordinarily arise in bankruptcies and reorganizations, are avoided. The likelihood of default is itself reduced by limiting the company's new investments (for example, by prohibiting acquisitions) and by structuring managerial incentives so that the managers have reason to return cash to investors as quickly as possible.

The activity of "taking companies private" via leveraged buyouts has grown rapidly over the last seven years. In 1979 the capitalized value of all LBO transactions was less than half a billion dollars.[46] In 1985, a single transaction, the Kohlberg, Kravis, Roberts buyout of Beatrice Corporation had a capitalized value of over $6 billion.[47]

Leverage buyouts provide evidence that tax shield benefits and cost of capital advantages are associated with high levels of debt, if costs of financial distress, bankruptcy, and reorganization can be avoided. Ironically, however, companies taking on this structure are generally not in a position to use the lower cost of capital to improve their position in the product market position or opportunities. Instead, during the three to five years of very high leverage after the buyout, such companies must be managed very conservatively. All of management's attention and effort must be focused on the tasks of maximizing cash flow and servicing debt.

Financial Institutions and Practices: Equity Markets

In addition to patterns of debt utilization, other differences in financing practices may also have a significant impact on corporate costs of capital. For example, differences in methods of raising equity can result in higher or lower capital costs to corporations experiencing rapid growth.

For example, returning to the case of the U.S. and Japanese semiconductor manufacturers, recall that most of the U.S. companies in the industry were "stand-alone" companies with semiconductors accounting for 70 percent of their sales. In contrast, Japanese semiconductor manufacturers tended to be imbedded within larger corporations for which semiconductors represented on average only 7 percent of total sales. Business units that are subsidiaries of larger parent organizations have access to internal markets for equity capital: excess cash flow from mature businesses can be funneled into promising investments arising in immature high-growth sectors.[48] In contrast stand-alone businesses must rely on external equity markets to finance their growth.

Today there is mounting evidence that inefficiencies in the public equity markets can significantly raise the cost of capital for companies that need additional equity in order to grow.[49] The cost of external equity is high because, from the perspective of an outside investor, a firm may raise equity for two reasons: first, because it has valuable opportunities and needs capital to grow, or alternatively because it is about to encounter financial difficulties. Unfortunately, investors cannot perfectly discriminate between the two types of equity issuers, and thus the market's immediate reaction to the announcement of a new equity issue is to mark down the price of the stock. Recent empirical evidence indicates that, on average, the announcement of a new equity issue reduces the value of previously outstanding shares by 30 percent of the value of the issue.[50] There are even documented cases in which the decrease in company value exceeded the amount of new money raised.[51]

This reduction in value, which affects 80 percent of all firms raising equity, increases the net cost of capital applicable to new investment projects. For example, for a project of average risk the cost of external equity may be 50 *percent higher* than the cost of equity generated internally. (See Table 6.5 for details of this calculation.) The

Table 6.5. Impact of Equity Value Reduction on the Cost of Capital to New Investments

Project Life (yrs.)	Market Cost of Equity Capital (%)[a]	Project Cost of Equity Capital (%)[b]	Market Weighted Average Cost of Capital (%)[c]	Project Weighted Average Cost of Capital (%)[d]
5	20	33.0	15	22.8
10	20	28.5	15	20.1
15	20	27.0	15	19.2
20	20	26.5	15	18.9
30	20	26.1	15	18.7

[a]For purposes of the example, the market cost of equity capital is assumed to be 20 percent. This is consistent with a cost of equity calculated using the Capital Asset Pricing Model for a company or project of average risk ($\beta = 1$), given a risk-free rate of 10 to 12 percent and a market risk premium of 8 to 10 percent.
[b]A reduction of equity value of 30 percent is converted into an equivalent increase in the project cost of equity capital.
[c]For purposes of illustration, it is assumed that new projects will be financed 60 percent with equity and 40 percent with debt. The cost of debt is assumed to be 14 percent: this figure is consistent with long-term yields on investment grade bonds as of August 1984.
[d]Combines the cost of debt with the project cost of equity capital, assuming project capitalization is 40 percent debt, 60 percent equity.

difference in total costs of capital to a company with access to internal equity versus a stand-alone company is thus potentially quite substantial.

The implications of this recently documented inefficiency in public equity markets have yet to be fully explored. Many multidivisional U.S. corporations have internal capital markets, and there is no strong evidence that they consistently outperform stand-alone enterprises. Furthermore, capital market inefficiencies that hamper a firm at one stage of its development may be offset by financing practices that confer advantage at other stages: for example, Flaherty and Itami observed that although the U.S. capital markets appear weak with respect to financing emerging growth companies, they function more effectively than Japanese markets in raising funds for startups and new ventures.[52] Nevertheless, it is disturbing that U.S. firms, at a critical juncture in their development, may face a difficult choice between issuing costly equity or forgoing a promising investment opportunity.

In summary, segmented national capital markets, as well as differences in tax policies, financial institutions, and financing practices all may give rise to cost of capital differences among corporations from different nations. However, as companies gain access to international capital markets, national differences come to have less competitive significance. Thus, for global corporations one of the most important financial developments of the last twenty-five years has been the growth of a world capital market. Today this market provides corporations with an attractive source of low-cost funds as well as opportunities to profit by arbitrage of cross-border rate differences. International arbitrage of financial markets by global corporations is in turn driving rates within national markets toward a common global standard.

THE GLOBAL SUPERMARKET

Today, competitors of Japan are accusing it of regulating financial markets in order to maintain a domestic cost of capital lower than the world standard. Ironically, the international capital market, which presently is based in London, Zurich, Singapore, and various other cities around the world, had its origins in an attempt by the U.S. government to maintain an artificially low domestic cost of capital during the period 1964–74.

After World War II, the U.S. dollar became the world's chief reserve currency, and the U.S. capital market (based in New York) was acknowledged to be by far the largest and most efficient capital market in the world. Thus, it was natural for foreign issuers, both governments and corporations, to raise capital through the New York market. Between 1946 and 1963, about $14 billion of debt capital was raised by foreign borrowers in the U.S. market.[53]

During the latter part of this period, persistent balance of payments deficits led foreigners to hold large quantities of dollars. Foreign investors thus became a major source of funds for dollar-denominated foreign issues, and the possibility then existed of short-circuiting the New York market by matching European investors with European issuers directly. The actual impetus for the development of an offshore market was provided by the Interest Equalization Tax (IET) of 1963. The IET was designed to raise foreigners' cost of borrowing in the United States by 1 percent: U.S. domestic issuers would enjoy a 1 percent cost of capital advantage over foreign issuers of comparable securities.

The interest equalization tax effectively halted foreign issues in the United States but failed to halt the flow of U.S. dollars overseas. The ever-growing pool of dollars held by foreigners, U.S. multinational corporations, and the foreign branches of U.S. banks funded the newly organized Eurodollar money and bond markets. Rather than coming to New York, foreign borrowers instead sought financing in the offshore, dollar-denominated capital market whose primary geographical base was the city of London.

In 1967, the interest equalization tax was increased to 1.5 percent. At the same time, U.S. bank loans to foreign companies were penalized, and the Office of Foreign Direct Investment imposed mandatory controls on transfers of capital from U.S. corporations to their foreign subsidiaries. These measures not only increased the disadvantage to foreigners of borrowing in the United States, but also discouraged investors from repatriating dollars to U.S. territory once they were held offshore. At the same time, the United States continued to run a balance-of-payments deficit, and the pool of funds available for investment overseas continued to grow, reaching a peak in 1972.

In 1973–74, the end of the Bretton Woods fixed exchange rate system coupled with the first oil crisis created a severe but temporary setback for the offshore capital markets. To assist in the recycling of petro-dollars, the U.S. government in 1974 repealed the interest equalization tax. Although total Eurodollar issues decreased significantly in 1974, their volume recovered in the following year. Eurodollar bond issues grew from a low of $1 billion in 1974 (down from $4 billion in 1973) to $39 billion in 1982. It is estimated that the volume of issues will exceed $100 billion in 1986.

Increasingly, the borrowers in the international markets have been U.S. corporations, which, although they have access to the U.S. domestic capital market, find they can borrow abroad at lower rates. Thus, in contrast to its initial role as a means for international banks, global corporations, and foreign investors to avoid returning dollars to the United States, the Eurodollar market now is a means for U.S. corporations to raise low-cost funds to finance domestic operations.

In recent years, interest rates in the Euromarket have tended to be .5 to .75 percent below rates on comparable U.S. domestic issues. Prime international credits have even found it possible to borrow at rates lower than those paid by the U.S. Treasury. For example, in 1982, the Coca-Cola Company, an AAA credit with high name recognition overseas, was able to issue $100 million of 5½ year bonds at 10.5 percent or 40 basis points (.4 percent) below the then-prevailing rate on U.S. Treasury bonds of similar maturity.

The low rates in the international markets are believed to arise because investors in those markets are not subject to the same taxation or government scrutiny as investors in national capital markets. For example, U.S. citizens report and pay taxes on interest and dividend income according to their individual tax status; until 1984, foreign investors were subject to a 30 percent withholding tax on U.S. interest and dividend income. In contrast, securities issued in the offshore market are not subject to tax; moreover most Eurobonds are issued in bearer form so that no record is kept of the identity of the purchaser. Investors' reporting of income to their respective tax authorities is therefore strictly voluntary.[54]

From a corporate treasurer's perspective, the low rates in the international capital market provide not only a means of reducing the corporation's cost of capital, but also the opportunity to profit through arbitrage of the rate differential between the international and domestic markets. Arbitrage in its purest form consists of the simultaneous purchase and sale of securities of similar risk at different prices. For example, in 1985, Exxon Corporation purchased $175 million of U.S. Treasury thirty-year zero coupon bonds yielding 8 percent, and simultaneously sold $200 million of thirty-year zero coupon Eurobonds priced to yield 7.6 percent.[55] The future proceeds from the Treasury bonds exactly offset Exxon's liability on its own issue. The rate differential and Exxon's ability to span the international and domestic markets thus resulted in a $25 million profit to the company on the transaction. (According to Exxon, when the time comes to use the $175 million, the company can simply sell the Treasury bonds instead of issuing new securities.)

Although dollar-denominated securities comprise the largest segment of the offshore capital market, there are active markets in yen, Deutschemark, and sterling securities as well. Arbitrage opportunities may arise in any of these sectors, and global corporations are generally well positioned to take advantage of them. Thus, in 1984, three U.S. corporations (Pepsico, Baxter Travenol Laboratories, and Sterling Drug) profited by a maneuver known as "midnight-to-morning" defeasance: each issued Deutschemark denominated bonds in the Euromarket and on the same day purchased like amounts of German government securities paying higher rates.[56] Because the companies placed the government bonds in irrevocable trusts as security for their own issues, under then-prevailing Financial Accounting Standards Board rules, the companies did not have to report the debt on their balance sheets but could immediately record the profits on the transactions.

However, international arbitrage carries the seeds of its own destruction. The profit opportunities presented to global corporations are themselves incentives to bid up underpriced securities and bid down overpriced securities until the rate differential disappears. The Deutschemark defeasance just described is one example of such a self-liquidating opportunity: after the three transactions described, German government rates fell and corporate rates rose to make the morning-to-midnight transactions no longer profitable.

In many ways, Japan's position in 1986 is similar to that of the United States in 1966. Although the Japanese government today may be attempting to hold down the domestic cost of capital, its attempts are being subverted by its own financial institutions and global corporations which, together with the rest of the global financial community, are attracted by the profit opportunities implicit in the difference in rates.

Figure 6.3 indicates the difficulty of maintaining a low domestic cost of capital when both global corporations and financial intermediaries are doing business in world markets. If domestic rates are lower than foreign rates, then there are many avenues by which corporations and intermediaries may realize profits. Foreign investments will offer higher returns than domestic investments, and financial intermediaries and global corporations will have incentive to borrow at home in order to invest in offshore assets. Although some investments may take the form of direct ownership of foreign subsidiaries, there will be equal or even greater incentive to invest in foreign securities, such as bank deposits, debt, and equity. Through the mechanism of financial intermediation, these funds in turn become available to all capital market participants at prevailing world market rates. Meanwhile, the increased demand for funds in the domestic market tends to put upward pressure on domestic rates until they reach an equilibrium with the world standard.

In the case of Japan, from 1945–75, government regulations effectively created a closed capital market. However, for most of this period, rates of return on domestic opportunities were probably *above* the world rates, and capital controls were necessary to keep foreign funds from flowing into Japan.[57] During this period the Japanese government sought to maintain some domestic interest rates at artificially low levels: these attempts resulted in a dual-rate structure and capital rationing in the corporate bond market.[58] Taking advantage of their multiple financial relationships with corporations, banks used compensating balances on loans to offset the low mandated interest rates and increase total rates of return on their combined loan and bond portfolios.[59]

Today, capital is no longer in short supply to fund Japan's purely domestic opportunities,[60] and as Japanese corporations and financial intermediaries enter the world capital markets, it is becoming commensurately difficult to maintain domestic interest rates below the world standard. Even as this book goes to press some sectors of the Japanese capital market appear to have reached parity with international markets while others are rapidly approaching that point. For example, in 1982, Otani and Tiwari examined the behavior of short-term rates on overnight deposits in Tokyo (where the Bank of Japan can influence the market) and yen deposits in Europe (an unregulated market). In all time periods, the differences between domestic and Euroyen rates were very slight, and there was no evidence of consistently lower rates in the domestic market.[61]

In the long-term markets, the May 1984 accords between the United States and Japan have recently led the Japanese government to grant permission to a number of U.S. and European companies to issue yen-dominated securities. These securities may be purchased by Japanese institutions who at the moment are reputed to have "hundreds of billions" of dollars in surplus funds to invest.[62] U.S. firms that have issued yen-denominated bonds include McDonald's Corporation, Anheuser-Busch, Honeywell, and the credit corporations of

Figure 6.3 Transmission of Financial Claims to Offshore Investments

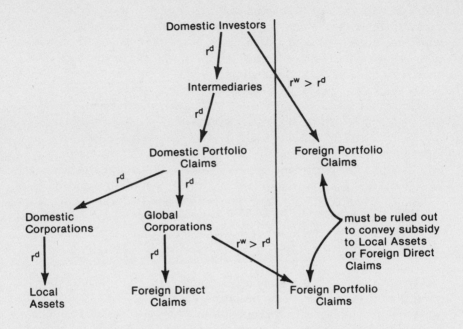

Note: Assume $r^d < r^w$.

Westinghouse Corporation, and the Ford Motor Company. Most of these issuers have not used their yen, but instead have swapped yen for dollars with a Japanese corporate counter-party.

The fact that such swaps are profitable is evidence that a cost of capital difference currently exists between Japan and the rest of the world in the long-term, fixed-income market. The magnitude of the difference can be gauged by comparing interest rates on the dollars obtained through dollar-yen swaps with rates on other dollar-denominated domestic and international issues. Market participants estimate that Japanese funding provides approximately a 25 basis point (.25 percent) savings on the overall cost of the financing, but there continue to be persistent rumors that the rate differential is due partly to aggressive pricing by Japanese merchant banks jockeying for position in this new market.[63]

In summary, numerous forces in the world economic environment continually operate to drive costs of capital toward the world market rates. As national costs of capital converge, opportunities to profit by "playing the spread" between markets decrease. Global corporations must then focus on building competitive advantage through selection of superior investment opportunities and more efficient allocation of limited capital resources. The allocation of capital to individual projects is the subject of the final section of this chapter.

PROJECT-BASED FINANCING AND INVESTMENT OPPORTUNITIES

In a global network, many factors affect the value of an individual capital project, among them:

- operating linkages between geographically separate facilities;[64]
- host country taxation;
- project-specific financing opportunities; and
- special incentives negotiated with host governments.

Thus, in contrast to purely domestic projects, the value of an international project can seldom be analyzed separately from its taxation or its financing. The need to analyze jointly the operating, tax, and financial dimensions of an international project has spurred the development of new evaluative methods that are at once more comprehensive and more flexible than the traditional techniques based on segregation of investment and financing decisions.

The "present value by components" approach[65] is a flexible tool that allows many different sources of value to be evaluated within a single framework. The approach breaks a project down into discrete components (direct capital and income flows, tax payments, value of project specific finance, etc.) and can be used to show operating linkages as well as financial transfers between different parts of a global network.

As an example of the method's application to an international project,[66] suppose ABC Corporation plans to manufacture a new product in Country Y. The product will then be sold by ABC marketing units throughout the world. Transfer prices permit marketing units to earn profits of 5 percent on net revenues and these profits are taxed at an average rate of 50 percent. Table 6.6 presents a present value by components analysis of the project. The table breaks down negative and positive contributions to project value according to the organizational

Table 6.6 Intra Corporate Chart of Value for a Hypothetical Project

Components	Present Value of Cash Flows[a]			
	Corporate Headquarters ($000)	Country Y Mfr. Division ($000)	Marketing Divisions ($000)	Total ($000)
Capital Outlays	(2,690)			(2,690)
Operating Cash Flow after Tax[b]	—	8,390	—	8,390
Gains to Affiliates	—	—	630	630
	(2,690)	8,390	630	$6,330

[a]All flows were initially projected in local currencies and converted to the base or home country currency at the appropriate forward rates. The resulting flows were then discounted by a rate that reflected the current risk-free rate plus a risk premium corresponding to the systematic risk (β) of the *business unit* relative to the *world market portfolio*. (Because the risk–return tradeoff in the world market has not been fully calibrated, the U.S. equity market is often used as a proxy for the world market. This practice is sound if the industry is similarly represented in the world and U.S. markets, but may be misleading in cases where the industry accounts for different proportions of the world and U.S. portfolios. For example, U.S. copper company betas are significantly different from world copper betas, due to the underrepresentation of that industry in the U.S. portfolio.)

[b]Excludes the value of tax incentives and project-specific financing opportunities.

unit that contributes capital or receives cash returns. Here the parent company is assumed to allocate $2,690,000 from general funds to the investment; the required rate of return on the funds is the corporation's weighted average cost of capital at world market rates. Country Y's manufacturing division captures the present value of operating cash flows after local taxes. Marketing divisions receive the present value of differences between their selling prices and the transfer price from Country Y.

The basic chart of Table 6.6 can easily be expanded to reflect capital transfers and project-related financing opportunities. For example, suppose the capital outlays of the project are financed as follows:

- two-thirds with blocked funds[67] on deposit at local banks and earning interest at 5 percent (versus a 10 percent rate prevailing in world markets); and
- one-third with borrowing from local banks, supported by a parent company guarantee.

Table 6.7 shows the impact of this financing on the overall investment opportunity. One column must be added to represent the value of payments to and from the local banks. The fact that this column sums to zero indicates that the borrowing takes place at market rates: that is, the value realized by the banks (including the value of the

Table 6.7. Impact of Financing on the Chart of Value for a
Hypothetical Project

Components	Corporate Headquarters ($000)	Country Y Mfr. Division ($000)	Marketing Divisions ($000)	Country Y Banks ($000)	Total ($000)
(1) Capital Outlays		(2,690)			(2,690)
(2) Operating Cash Flow after Tax		8,390			8,390
(3) Gains to Affiliates			630		630
(4) Blocked Funds Used		1,790			1,790
(5) Opportunity Cost of Blocked Funds[a]		(1,240)			(1,240)
(6) Borrowed Capital		900		(900)	0
(7) Borrowing Supported by Project		(500)		500	0
(8) Value of Parent Company Guarantee[b]	(400)			400	0
Total	(400)	6,650	630	0	6,880

[a]The opportunity cost of blocked funds is calculated as the value of interest payments of 5 percent ($89,500 per year) for ten years (the project's assumed life) discounted at 10 percent (the market discount rate).
[b]Loan guarantees may be valued using contingent claims analysis. Mason and Merton (1985) discuss the application of this technique to parent company guarantees of the debts of subsidiaries.

parent company's guarantee) exactly equals the value of funds borrowed.

The table indicates that capital is no longer being provided from general corporate funds, but instead the project is being financed by the division: capital outlays are thus moved from the corporate to the divisional column (line 1). As before, the manufacturing division receives the benefit of operating flows from the project, and marketing divisions get the value of their sales, net of the transfer price (lines 2 and 3).

The table further shows the manufacturing division using $1,790,000 in blocked funds to finance the new project (line 4). Because these funds are earning less than the current market rate, their opportunity cost is only $1,240,000 (line 5). The difference of $550,000 enhances the value of the project. The remaining capital outlays of $900,000 are borrowed from local banks under a guarantee from the parent company: although no money changes hands, the guarantee in effect transfers value from the parent company to the banks (line 8).

The column totals reflect the fact that the project's net present value has been increased by $550,000 through the use of blocked funds. Moreover, a far greater proportion of the cost of the project is being absorbed at the divisional and country level, as opposed to the corporate or global level. This pattern is typical of corporations with mature overseas operating divisions, whereas Table 6.6 is characteristic of corporations that are in the process of moving their production overseas.

Host Government Financial Incentives

Through tax subsidies, loans, equity, and guarantees, host governments can have a significant impact on a project's economic value. Because host governments are increasingly using financial incentives to attract investment to their jurisdictions, a global corporation must have the ability to evaluate complex financial contracts with governments in countries where it does business. The value implicit in host country incentives must then be incorporated into the evaluation of the proposed investments, to allow the corporation to make an informed and efficient capital allocation decision.

Within the generic value-added chain,[68] host country financial incentives are most likely to be available for (1) technology development, and (2) operations. That is, incentives are usually designed:

- to promote technological advancement within a region, or the relocation of research or design facilities to a region; or
- to influence global corporations' siting of new manufacturing facilities.[69]

A sampling of the incentive packages offered by host governments indicates their diversity, complexity, and potential importance to a project:

- When it located assembly operations in the United States, Volkswagen received subsidies with an estimated value of over $50 million from local, state, and federal governments. It also negotiated wage concessions valued at over $40 million from the UAW.
- John DeLorean's ill-fated venture was financed by almost $100 million in loans and equity from the government of Northern Ireland. Puerto Rico and Detroit had earlier offered packages each valued at approximately $60 million.
- Both national and regional governments are generally eager to promote high-tech industry and R & D. For example, in Canada, the province of Quebec offers a 10 percent tax credit on salaries paid to research workers. This credit can be transformed into a cash subsidy if the corporation fails to have taxable income.[70]

Government financial subsidies can reduce a corporation's net capital contribution to new projects, and increase returns (the ROE or ROI) on corporate capital. But subsidies may also involve the company in complex, many-sided negotiations with numerous governmental agencies and interest groups.[71] An analysis of subsidies broken down according to the key players is often a useful way to summarize the status of bargaining at any point in time; it can also provide a framework in which concessions made on one dimension may be traded off against benefits received in another. Finally, depending on the corporation's relations with its host government, an analysis of subsidy value can serve as a "single negotiating text"[72] to assist parties in discussion and bargaining over individual items in the package.

Volkswagen's experience in locating a plant in the United States illustrates the complexity of negotiating a comprehensive subsidy package. Key players in the process were Volkswagen, the state government of Pennsylvania, and the United Auto Workers (UAW). The Federal government was also involved, both as the ultimate source of much of Pennsylvania's bounty and because actions by the Environmental Protection Agency (EPA) substantially increased the final cost of the plant.

Table 6.8 presents an analysis of subsidy values for the Volkswagen Westmoreland facility.[73] (The figures are estimates based on publicly available information, and may be subject to omissions on that account.) The largest component in the package was the UAW's $1.00 per hour wage concession. The remaining elements were divided between Pennsylvania and the Federal government (through municipal interest tax subsidies, foreign trade zone tax subsidies, and CETA grants).

Clearly illustrating the difficulties of dealing with multiple governmental bodies is the fact that although through most of the negotiations the Federal government acted merely as a passive provider of tax subsidies, after negotiations between Volkswagen and Pennsylvania were complete, the Federal EPA took back significant amounts of value through an unfavorable regulatory interpretation. The EPA's ruling occurred before construction on the plant commenced, and because Volkswagen threatened to pull out, the cost of satisfying the EPA was borne by Pennsylvania.[74]

The Value of Options

Although Pennsylvania undertook to pay the cost of the EPA's negative ruling, the cost of a subsequent adverse ruling by another Federal agency, the Interstate Commerce Commission, was borne by Volkswagen. This sequence illustrates the shift in bargaining power that typically occurs as a company reduces its options by becoming increasingly committed to a particular site.

An understanding of option values is useful in both internal corporate deliberations and negotiations with host governments. For example, Volkswagen's Westmoreland plant involved both location and timing options. Lower costs might have been obtainable in regions besides southwestern Pennsylvania. On the other hand, the move oc-

Table 6.8. Volkswagen of America—Westmoreland Plant Chart of Subsidy Value
(millions of dollars)

Subsidy	Local	State	Federal	Union	To VW
Purchase & Renovation of Chrysler Plant[a]		(11.8)	(8.8)		20.6
Transport Improvements (Highway & Rail)[b]		(22.7)	(7.3)		30.0
Employment & Training[c]			(2.8)		2.8
Foreign Trade Zone[d]			(4.5)		4.5
Wage Concession[e]				(46.6)	46.6
Tax Abatement[f]	(4.5)				4.5
EPA[g]	-	(xxx)	(xxx)	-	-
Totals	4.5	34.5	23.4	46.6	109.0
% of Total	4.1	31.6	21.5	44.7	100.0

[a]*Plant Purchase and Renovation*—The Pennsylvania Industrial Development Authority (PIDA) floated bonds to raise cash to loan VW. PIDA lent VW $40 million, which was repaid over thirty years. For the first twenty years, the interest rate was 1.75 percent. For the last ten years, the rate was 8.5 percent. PIDA's cost of borrowing was 6 percent. VW's cost of funds, had they issued A-rated bonds, would have been 9 percent. Source: *The Wall Street Journal*, June 16, 1976.
[b]*Highway and Rail Spur*—Financed by $30 million, thirty-year General Obligation bonds of the state of Pennsylvania (*The Wall Street Journal*, June 2, 1976). Subsidy total of $30 million allocated between the State and Federal governments based on the interest differential between taxable and tax-free bonds.
[c]*Employment and Training Funds*—The State provided $4 million over four years. This is assumed to be a pass-through of Federal CETA funds. Source: *Industrial Development*.
[d]*Foreign Trade Zone*—Federal tax break valued at $1 million a year for six years. Source: *Distribution*, October 1982.
[e]*Labor Subsidy*—A "lower-bound" estimate calculated by taking 5000 workers times 52 weeks × 40 hours × $1/hour. This was the differential *before* UAW—Big 3 renegotiations in late 1978, which would widen the gap. Source: *The Wall Street Journal*, October 20, 1978.
[f]*Tax Abatement*—Estimated at $1 million a year for six years, discounted at 9 percent.
[g]*EPA*—After the contract between Pennsylvania and Volkswagen had been finalized, the EPA, noting that Pennsylvania was far behind in its progress towards Clear Air Act standards, ruled that the plant could not be built unless offsetting pollution reductions could be found. Volkswagen claimed that because the issue was not addressed in the contract, the responsibility for finding "offsets" rested solely with Pennsylvania. Fearful that Volkswagen would take its business elsewhere, the state took the then-revolutionary step of seeking reductions in its own polluting activities. Pennsylvania agreed to switch to a low-polluting asphalt mixture in sixteen counties in southwestern Pennsylvania, and on that basis, the EPA allowed plant construction to proceed. The cost Pennsylvania incurred by the switch is unknown.

curred during a period of low dollar–Deutschemark exchange rates, and thus the company was under pressure to act quickly in order to take advantage of a potentially temporary exchange rate window.

Because of its ability to scan international markets,[75] and time and locate investments, a global corporation generally controls numerous valuable options.[76] As investments move through the stages of proposal, planning, location, design, construction, and operation, these so-called "real" or "operating" options must be identified, evaluated, and ultimately exercised in an optimal way.

In general, operating options fall into the following categories:

- *Location Options.* A global corporation can scan the world to determine the optimal location of any particular activity. For example, in choosing the location of new production capacity, electronic equipment manufacturers such as Texas Instrument or Hewlett-Packard, may compare sites in the Far East, North and South America, and Europe to see which offers the best cost configuration (including the impact of taxes and financial incentives).

- *Timing Options.* A global corporation may also time its moves to take advantage of transient cost and exchange rate disparities. For example, the growth of Volkswagen's U.S. markets in the sixties and early seventies made the location of production facilities in the United States an attractive long-run proposition. However, the optimal time for the move was when the Deutschemark was overvalued relative to the dollar.

- *Technology (Flexibility) Options.* Operating costs may vary across countries or within countries over time. Flexible technologies allow corporations to take advantage of short-run price movements. For example, one multinational tire company built extra capacity in several European plants, and schedules extra shifts at the plant currently having the lowest unit cost. (Plant unit costs may deviate in the short run because of exchange rate fluctuations.)

- *Growth or Staging Options.* Once a global corporation has established a presence in a particular country, it may be able to introduce new products or expand capacity by building on its existing base. These opportunities for downstream investment enhance the value of the initial capital: they also allow the company to fine-tune subsequent moves in response to changing market conditions. For example, in its heavy oil investments in Canada, Exxon Corporation has defined ten to twelve project phases: as each phase is complete, the corporation has the option of waiting or proceeding to the next round. At each point, a decision can be made based on the prevailing price of oil as well as technological knowledge from the previous phase.[77]

The optimal management of options brings an added dimension of complexity to the task of evaluating, selecting, and implementing investment programs within a global system. Option values often can be the difference between a winning or losing project. Moreover, options become increasingly valuable as the volatility of prices, exchange rates, or demand rises. Given the increase in variability in both product and financial markets worldwide, in the future, companies that recognize option values and build a degree of flexibility into their investments are likely to be at a significant advantage relative to companies that fail to take account of option benefits in the design and evaluation of capital project.

CONCLUSION

Today's global corporations must compete for capital and investment opportunities within a complex and fast-evolving system of international markets. They have the advantage of being able to scan numerous locations and technologies in order to determine the most productive match of resources and activities. But they themselves are being scanned by increasingly sophisticated international providers of capital.

The evolving international "supermarket" for capital presents global corporations with an attractive source of low-cost funds as well as opportunities do profit by arbitraging cost-of-capital differences between national markets. However, cross-border arbitrage by corporations and financial intermediaries inevitably tends to drive costs of capital in all markets toward a common global standard, and thus, opportunities to profit by pure financial arbitrage are decreasing. In the future, only highly specialized financial intermediaries may be able to sustain a competitive advantage based on superiority in trading across national and international capital markets.

Nonfinancial corporations are more likely to create positive value by applying financial tools of analysis to the structuring of their product market investments. International investments are complicated by operating linkages between units, home, and host country taxes, project-specific financing opportunities, and host government financial incentives. Individual investments may also create or extinguish important options affecting the location, timing, flexibility, and growth of future operations. Given the intrinsic complexity of international investment decisions, sound project evaluation and capital allocation policies can lead to superior investment decisions, which in turn may be the basis of more sustainable competitive advantage than results from transitory financial transactions.

Over the longer term, resources in the form of capital and credit inevitably will flow to corporations that demonstrate the ability to create value within the changing global environment. In support of this goal, finance provides a comprehensive framework that can be used to analyze the components of value inherent in capital transactions and investment opportunities. By identifying the major elements of value in its projects and its financial structure, and by incorporating these assessments into its decisions, a corporation can greatly enhance its knowledge of its opportunities, and thus lower the cost and increase the efficiency of the capital it deploys.

NOTES

1. The view that U.S. corporations are at a cost of capital disadvantage has been espoused by groups ranging from the largely Republican President's Commission on Industrial Competitiveness (1985), to Democratic industrial policy proponents (e.g., Magaziner and Reich 1982), to labor spokesmen (e.g., Bluestone and Harrison 1982). It is a commonly cited "fact" in the public press (e.g., *Business Week*, "Fighting Back: It Can Work," [May 26, 1985]). However, as I hope this chapter may show, the truth underlying the cost of capital doctrine is not as simple nor as clearcut as press reports would indicate.
2. For example, from 1960 to 1980 the average annual return on a diversified portfolio of Japanese common stocks was 15.24 percent as compared to 10.23 percent on a similar portfolio of U.S. common stocks.
3. See, for example, Hatsopoulos (1983).
4. Arbitrage involves the simultaneous purchase and sale of securities in two markets to take advantage of rate differential.
5. In 1980 the market value of traded U.S. equities amounted to U.S. $1,187.5 billion. U.S. government and corporate bonds accounted for another $1,111.7 billion. The value of traded equities in Japan was almost a third as large ($357.0 billion) as the value of U.S. equities and the Japanese bond market was half as large ($544.6 billion) as the U.S. bond market. The European markets in total were larger than the Japanese market, but the largest national market in Europe was only about half as large as the Japanese market (Ibbotson, Carr, and Robinson, 1982).
6. Despite its recent drop, many observers believe that in 1985 the U.S. dollar is overvalued by as much as 20 to 30 percent. This apparent deviation from parity has persisted for over four years, despite numerous predictions of the dollar's imminent decline (e.g., *The Economist*, "A Levitating Dollar Confounds Soothsayers," [December 17, 1983]; *Business Week*, "Why the Dollar Seems to be Topping Out at Last," [February 20, 1984]; "The Dollar's Mystique Starts to Fade" [April 15, 1985]). For discussion of the economic theory and empirical tests of the parity hypothesis, see: Frankel (1981), Aliber (1978), Levich (1978), Cornell (1979). For recent evidence on parity in the United States and six European nations, see Mishkin (1983) and Cumby and Mishkin (1984).
7. Adler and Dumas (1983).
8. Lessard (1976), Solnik (1974). However, international portfolio diversification is on the increase as institutions are increasing their investments overseas and as investment managers offer products (e.g., international mutual funds) that facilitate cross-border asset ownership.
9. Restrictions on securities transactions between Japan and the rest of the world in the sixties and early seventies are described in Suzuki (1980). Beginning in 1971, many of the controls have been relaxed so that both Japanese investment in foreign securities and foreign investment in Japanese securities are increasing. These trends have accelerated since the U.S.–Japan Accords of November 1983 (finalized in May 1984).
10. Chase Financial Policy (1980).
11. Hatsopoulos (1983).

12. Lintner (1956).
13. In Hatsopoulos's calculation of the U.S. cost of capital, the cost of equity enters with a weight of approximately .75; the cost of debt receives a weight of only .25.
14. As evidenced by the systematic risk (betas) of U.S. semiconductor companies. For firms with a majority of their business in semiconductor operations, equity betas in 1980 ranged from 1.27 (Intel) to 2.07 (Intersil) with a mean of 1.68 (Chase Financial Policy 1980). Unlevered asset betas ranged from 1.19 to 1.93 with a mean of 1.42. The average equity beta for all U.S. firms is 1.0: assuming a tax advantage to debt of about .2, the average unlevered asset beta is around .6. High levels of systematic risk commonly occur in businesses like semiconductors, whose values depend heavily on future growth and the exploitation of investment opportunities.
15. The approach of this chapter is to look at risk-adjusted costs of capital for the U.S. and Japanese markets as a whole. A different but equally valuable approach is taken by Ando and Auerbach (1985) who consider costs of capital for a matched sample of nineteen U.S. and twenty-one Japanese firms. In contrast to the Chase and Hatsopoulos studies, Ando and Auerbach do not find grounds to conclude that the cost of capital in Japan is significantly lower than in the United States.
16. Data on holding period yields on each class of security were obtained from Ibbotson, Carr, and Robinson (1982). Each series is based on a very broad market-value-weighted portfolio of the securities in the class.
17. Inflation in Japan was higher than in the United States during most of the sixties. In 1975–80, inflation in Japan increased significantly, while in the United States it continued to rise. The years of peak inflation in the United States were 1979–80 (13.3 percent and 12.4 percent); inflation rates in Japan in those years were 4.9 percent and 7.1 percent respectively (Ibbotson, Carr, and Robinson 1982).
18. From 1960–80, average real returns on long-term bonds were negative in the United States and very close to zero in Japan. In the United States, the long-bond yield was lower than the average real return on less risky, short-term debt instruments. Furthermore, average real returns on U.S. common stocks amounted to only 4.87 percent over the period. Long-run historical surveys indicate that the expected real return on a diversified common stock portfolio is on the order of 8 to 10 percent. These estimates are plausible and tend to be corroborated by independent comparisons of market risk and investors' risk tolerance. (See Merton 1980).
19. A different hypothesis would require market benchmarks based on more than twenty years of data. Such benchmarks exist for the United States, but cannot be developed for Japan because mature capital markets are a relatively new phenomenon in that country. Merton (1980) has proposed an alternative approach that is applicable over shorter time spans, if observations are frequent. Given daily or weekly data on market performance, his approach offers the best hope of refining cost of capital comparisons to permit identification of transient as well as long-term differences.
20. See Robbins and Stobaugh (1973), Horst (1977), or Lessard (1979a) on opportunities to reduce taxes within the global network.
21. The literature on corporate taxation in the United States and abroad is vast. On the U.S. tax system as it affects global and multinational corporations, a good starting point is Rodriguez and Carter (1979), appendix 1. Business International Corporation (1983) provides a useful overview

of current tax codes in the United States and Japan. See also Touche Ross, International (1981). Nobes (1980) compares tax systems within the European Economic Community.

22. The tax reform plan proposed by the Reagan administration in May 1985 provides for differential taxation of dividends and earnings. This would shift the United States from a classical to a split-rate system.

23. It is not possible to present comparable figures for the Western European countries, because the intricacies of their systems of personal income taxation make it difficult to estimate effective marginal tax rates on investment income. Marginal tax rates on investment income for individuals in both the United States and Japan are approximately 50 percent.

24. Table 6.4 probably overstates the differences in effective tax rates due to different dividend policies because (1) not all investors are in the 50 percent tax bracket, and (2) high bracket investors may be able to shelter part of their dividend income. (On methods of sheltering dividend income, see Miller and Scholes 1978). In general, tests of the hypothesis that high-dividend-paying stocks have higher before-tax required rates of return (and hence higher costs of capital) have proved inconclusive. See, for example, Hess (1982) and Litzenberger and Ramaswamy (1982).

25. Specialized tax incentives need to be analyzed on a case-by-case basis. Frequently tax incentives are a part of a comprehensive package of financial incentives offered in order to attract a specific project to a particular location. See Guisinger (1983) on the increased use of such subsidies and their relation to the GATT.

26. See Baldwin and Ruback (1982) for details.

27. Japanese inflation rates have also been lower in this period.

28. Rodriguez and Carter (1979), appendix A summarizes the limitations on deferrals under the U.S. Tax Code.

29. U.S. foreign tax credits are limited to 50 percent of a corporation's net taxable income.

30. Deferral of tax reduces the present value of the corporation's ultimate payments to the home country. This has the same effect as exempting a fraction of current income from taxation altogether.

31. *The Wall Street Journal* (March 30, 1984).

32. Of course, ultimately taxation is a reflection of the prevailing political climate. In this context it is interesting to note that several firms that have recently shifted their headquarters or drastically reoriented their activities are French; for example, Schlumberger (France to the United States) and Ciment LaFarge (France to North America).

33. Hout (1972) was among the first to recognize the potential connection between capital structure and cost of capital differences in the United States and Japan. On the evolution of corporate capital structures in the United States, see Taggart (1983); in Japan, see Kurosawa (1981), Hodder (1985), or Kester (1985). On the implications of the modern theories of capital structure for U.S. and Japanese costs of capital, see Ando and Auerbach (1985) and Hodder and Tschoegl (1985).

34. The theory of capital structure is attributed to Modigliani and Miller (1958, 1963). Since their correction of the original model, it has been generally accepted that debt is a cheaper source of funds than equity. However, recently the magnitude of the tax advantage to debt has become a matter of some debate. Breaking with his coauthor, Miller (1977) has gone so far as to argue that for an individual firm, there is no advantage to debt finance. Most other researchers would probably concede that whereas there is a cost advantage to debt, it is less than the 46

percent implied by the corporate statutory rates. For further discussion
on the "modern" theory of capital structure and empirical evidence on
the magnitude of the effect, see deAngelo and Masulis (1980) and Masulis
(1980).

35. For a four-country comparison of the process of resolving creditors'
claims in large corporate failures, see Reich (1985).

36. If a creditor becomes too closely involved in the management of a company that subsequently goes bankrupt (for example, if a bank oversees or
reviews corporate policy), the creditor may be charged with responsibility for managerial actions and forfeit the seniority of its claim. Thus creditors, even if they are aware of a deteriorating situation, may hesitate to
take action for fear of jeopardizing their legal status.

37. Because large corporate bankruptcies are rare in Japan, the recent (August 1985) collapse of Sanko Shipping Co. was especially noteworthy.
Among the casualties was Toshio Komoto, the largest shareholder and a
prominent politician who resigned from the cabinet to accept "political
responsibility" for the failure. See *Business Week*, "In the Wake of Shipping's Biggest Failure" (August 26, 1985); *Fortune*, "Japan's Lone Wolf
Sinks Alone" (September 26, 1985).

38. In line with this hypothesis, Kester (1985) finds that, in Japan, large firms
make heavy use of debt finance, whereas small- and medium-size enterprises that do not have such close relationships with banks have capital
structures much closer to their U.S. counterparts.

39. The personal tax offset to corporate interest deductibility was first analyzed by Miller (1977) who concluded that debt is not a cheaper source
of funds than equity. For a model incorporating personal taxes but providing for a (reduced) tax advantage to debt, see deAngelo and Masulis
(1980).

40. Masulis (1980).

41. Total capital equals debt (both long- and short-term) plus equity.

42. Sarathy and Chatterjee (1981). Exact percentages tend to change slightly
from year to year in response to the business cycle. Utilization of debt
by U.S. firms increased during the late sixties and early seventies, but
has been relatively stable over the last decade (Taggart 1983, S & P
Compustat Services).

43. Details of this calculation are available from the author. The result is
roughly consistent with that obtained by Ando and Auerbach (1985) for a
matched sample of large U.S. and Japanese corporations.

44. "Mezzanine" debt is subordinated to the claims of senior lenders, but
carries interest and principal obligations. A typical LBO has about as
much senior debt as would be found in an ordinary company's capital
structure (30 to 40 percent); the remainder of its funding is in the form
of subordinated debt, with equity accounting for only a small sliver (5 to
10 percent) of total value.

45. Note the similarity to Japanese banking practices.

46. Includes transactions valued at $10 million and up: Golden (1984).

47. *The Wall Street Journal*, "Beatrice Accepts Kohlberg, Kravis's Sweet-
ened Offer of $50 a Share or $6.2 Billion, to Take Firm Private" (November 15, 1985). Kohlberg, Kravis, Roberts & Co. is a privately held firm
that specializes in promoting leveraged buyouts.

48. This approach to corporate finance and strategic planning was first developed by the Boston Consulting Group (BCG). See, for example, Henderson (1970, 1973). For a critical appraisal of the BCG model, see Hax
and Majluf (1983).

49. Theoretical models of this phenomenon may be found in articles by Miller and Rock (1985), and Myers and Majluf (1984). For an overview and synthesis of work in this area, see Myers (1984).
50. Asquith and Mullins (1986).
51. Such examples include John Deere's equity issue of April 1981 (announced in January); ATT's issue of March 1983 (announced in February).
52. Flaherty and Itami (1982).
53. Salomon Brothers, *International Bond Manual*.
54. In the United States, the IRS's view of voluntary reporting is such that citizens are prohibited from purchasing Eurobonds in a public offering.
55. *Institutional Investor,* "Borrowing as a Profit Center," (August 1985).
56. *Institutional Investor,* "Clouds over Morning-to-Midnight Defeasance," (June 1984).
57. Suzuki (1980).
58. Before 1970, the Council for the Regulation of Bond Issues (Kisai Chosei Kyogikai) determined the amount to be issued in each rating category during the fiscal year.
59. According to Suzuki (1980), "the reason why city banks could absorb a certain amount of corporate bonds at sub equilibrium yields is that a number of the companies are loan clients of the banks. . . . the banks can therefore . . . take [the bonds] into account when computing the required compensatory deposits to give the effective interest rate."
60. Japan is now an exporter of capital (*International Financial Statistics,* 1984).
61. Otani and Tiwari (1981).
62. *The New York Times,* "Tapping into Japanese Capital Markets," (October 17, 1985).
63. *Business Week,* "The Yen Revolution Is Still a Long Way Off," (January 21, 1985).
64. On the increasing importance of operating linkages in global manufacturing, see Flaherty (chap. 3 of this book).
65. The present value by components or "adjusted present value" (APV) approach to capital budgeting was initially developed by Myers (1974). See Lessard (1979b) and Lessard and Paddock (1980) for expositions of the method in the context of international capital budgeting.
66. The example is based on a case study by Ornstein and Vora (1978).
67. Blocked funds are those that because of currency controls or withholding taxes, may be reinvested within a country but cannot be reallocated across national boundaries.
68. On the value-added chain for a global corporation, see Porter (chap. 1 of this book) figure 1.1. On the goals of host governments in providing financial incentives, see Doz (chap. 7 of this book).
69. The specific targeting of financial incentives to R & D and manufacturing may be understood as a governmental response to a global corporation's *options.* The interaction of investment options and host country incentives is further discussed later.
70. Advertisement, *Boston Globe,* sponsored by the Ministry of Science and Technology, Government of Quebec.
71. Some governments are organizing themselves to provide "one-stop shopping," but many-sided negotiations are still the norm. See Encarnation and Wells (chap. 8 of this book).
72. For a discussion of single text negotiation, see Raiffa (1982).
73. Based on a case study by Montvel-Cohen (1984).

220   II. The Functional Agenda

74. The EPA's requirements were satisfied by a change in the asphalt mix used to maintain roads and highways in western Pennsylvania.
75. The ability to be informed about conditions in more than one market in order to select the best opportunity is an economy of scope that accrues to multinational and global enterprises.
76. The value of financial options was first rigorously characterized by Black and Scholes (1973) and Merton (1973). More recently, the options associated with "real" (i.e., nonfinancial) investments have come under investigation. A nontechnical introduction to real options is found in Myers (1983). On the multinational firm as a collection of options, see Kogut (1983).
77. Kester (1983) provides a nontechnical discussion of the values inherent in growth options or opportunities. For a comprehensive analysis of staging options for a large construction project, see Majd and Pindyck (1985).

REFERENCES

Adler, M., and B. Dumas. "International Portfolio Choice and Corporation Finance: Synthesis." *Journal of Finance* 38, no. 3 (June 1983): 925–84.
Aliber, R. L. *Exchange Risk and Corporate International Finance* London: MacMillan, 1978.
Ando, A., and A. Auerbach. "The Corporate Cost of Capital in Japan and the U.S.: A Comparison." Mimeo, May 1985.
Asquith, P., and D. W. Mullins. "Equity Issues and Stock Price Dilution." *Journal of Financial Economics* 15, no. 1/2 (January/February, 1986): 61–90.
Baldwin, C. Y., and R. S. Ruback. "Inflation, Discrete Replacement and the Choice of Asset Lives." Harvard Business School Working Paper 83–05, August 1982.
Black, F., and M. Scholes. "The Pricing of Options and Corporate Liabilities." *Journal of Political Economy* 81, no. 3 (May/June 1973): 637–59.
Bluestone, B., and B. Harrison. *The Deindustrialization of America*. New York: Basic Books, 1982.
Business International Corporation. *Investment, Licencing and Trading Conditions Abroad* (multiple issues).
Chase Financial Policy. "U.S. and Japanese Semiconductor Industries: A Financial Comparison." Report prepared for the Semiconductor Industry Association, July 1980.
Cornell, B. "Relative Price Changes and Deviations from Purchasing Power Parity." *Journal of Banking and Finance* 3, no. 3 (September 1979): 263–79.
Cumby, R. E., and F. S. Mishkin. "The International Linkage of Real Interest Rates: The European–U.S. Connection." NBER Working Paper No. 1423, 1984.
deAngelo, H., and R. Masulis. "Leverage and Dividend Irrelevancy under Corporate and Personal Taxation." *Journal of Finance* 35, no. 2 (May 1980): 453–64.
Flaherty, H. T. and H. Itami. "Financial Institutions and Financing for the Semiconductor Race," in D. Okimoto, et al, eds., *Competitive Edge*. Stanford: Stanford University Press, 1984.
Frankel, S. "Flexible Exchange Rates, Prices and the Role of News: Lessons from the 1970's." *Journal of Political Economy* 89, no. 4 (August 1981): 665–705.

Golden, W. J. "Leveraged Buyouts as a Corporate Planning Tool." *Impact* Cambridge, Mass.: Arthur D. Little, 1984.

Guisinger, S. "Investment Incentives and Performance Requirements." Report prepared for the World Bank, 1983.

Hatsopoulos, G. N. "High Cost of Capital: Handicap of American Industry." Report sponsored by the American Business Conference and Thermo-Electron Corporation, April 1983.

Hax, A. C., and N. S. Majluf. "The Use of the Growth-Share Matrix in Strategic Planning." *Interfaces* 13, no. 1 (February 1983): 46–60.

Henderson, B. D. "The Product Portfolio." *Perspectives,* no. 66. Boston: Boston Consulting Group, 1970.

————. "The Experience Curve Reviewed. IV: The Growth Share Matrix of the Product Portfolio." *Perspectives,* no. 135. Boston: Boston Consulting Group, 1973.

Hess, P. J. "The Ex-Dividend Day Behavior of Stock Returns: Further Evidence of Tax Effects." *Journal of Finance* 37, no. 2 (May 1982): 445–56.

Hodder, J. E. "Corporate Capital Structure in the U.S. and Japan: Financial Intermediation and Implications for Financial Deregulation." Mimeo, April 1985.

Hodder, J. E., and A. E. Tschoegl. "Some Aspects of Japanese Corporate Finance." *Journal of Financial and Quantitative Analysis* 20, no. 2 (June 1985): 173–91.

Horst, T. "American Taxation of Multinational Firms." *American Economic Review* 67, no. 3 (June 1977).

Hout, T. M. *The Cost of Capital in the Japanese Economy and Petroleum Industry 1970–1985.* Boston: Boston Consulting Group, 1972.

Ibbotson, R. G., R. C. Carr, and A. W. Robinson. "International Equity and Bond Returns." *Financial Analysts Journal* (July–August 1982): 61–83.

International Monetary Fund, *International Financial Statistics* 37, no. 7 (July 1984).

Kester, W. C. "Capital and Ownership Structure: A Comparison of United States and Japanese Manufacturing Corporations." Mimeo, January 1985.

Kogut, B. "Foreign Direct Investment as a Sequential Process," in Kindleberger and Audretsch, eds., *The Multinational Corporation in the 1980's.* Cambridge, Mass.: MIT Press, 1983.

Kurosawa, Y. "Corporate Financing in Capital Markets." Japan Development Bank Staff Paper, September 1981.

Lessard, D. R. "World, Country and Industry Relationships in Equity Returns: Implications for Risk Reduction through International Diversification." *Financial Analysts Journal* (January/February 1976): 2–8.

————. "Transfer Prices, Taxes and Financial Markets: Implication of Internal Transfers within Multinational Firms," in R. B. Hawkins, ed., *Economic Issues of Multinational Firms.* Greenwich, Conn.: JAI Press, 1979a.

————. "Evaluating International Projects: An Adjusted Present Value Approach," in D. R. Lessard, ed. *International Financial Management.* New York: Warren, Gorham and Lamont, 1979b.

Lessard, D. R., and J. Paddock. "Evaluating International Projects: Weighted Average Cost of Capital vs. Valuation of Components." *Journal of International Business Studies,* 1986 forthcoming.

Levich, R. M. "Tests of Forecasting Models and Market Efficiency in the International Money Markets," in Frankel and Johnson, eds., *The Economics of Exchange Rates.* Reading, Mass.: Addison-Wesley, 1978.

Lintner, J. "Distribution of Incomes of Corporations among Dividends, Re-

222   II. The Functional Agenda

tained Earnings and Taxes." *American Economic Review* 46, no. 2 (May 1956): 97–113.

Litzenberger, R. H., and K. Ramaswamy. "The Effects of Dividends on Common Stock Prices: Tax Effects or Information Effects?" *Journal of Finance* 37, no. 2 (May 1982): 429–44.

Magaziner, I. C., and R. B. Reich. *Minding America's Business: The Decline and Rise of the American Economy.* New York: Harcourt Brace Jovanovich, 1982.

Majd, S., and R. Pindyck. "Time to Build, Option Value and Investment Decisions." Mimeo, revised November 1985.

Mason, S. M., and R. C. Merton. "The Role of Contingent Claims Analysis in Corporate Finance," in E. I. Altman and M. G. Subrahmanyam, eds., *Recent Advances in Corporate Finance.* Homewood, Ill.: Richard D. Irwin, 1985.

Masulis, R. W. "The Effects of Capital Structure Change on Security Prices: A Study of Exchange Offers." *Journal of Financial Economics* 8, no. 2 (June 1980): 139–78.

Merton, R. C. "The Theory of Rational Option Pricing." *Bell Journal of Economics and Management Science* 4, no. 1 (Spring 1973): 141–83.

——— "On Estimating the Expected Return on the Market: An Exploratory Investigation." *Journal of Financial Economics* 8, no. 4 (December 1980): 323–62.

Miller, M. H. "Debt and Taxes." *Journal of Finance* 32, no. 2 (May 1977): 261–75.

Miller, M. H., and K. Rock. "Dividend Policy Under Asymmetric Information." *Journal of Finance* 40, no. 4 (September 1985): 1031–52.

Miller, M. H., and M. Scholes. "Dividends and Taxes." *Journal of Financial Economics* 6, no. 4 (December 1978): 333–64.

Mishkin, F. S. "Are Real Interest Rates Equal Across Countries?" NBER Working Paper No. 1423, 1983.

Modigliani, F., and M. H. Miller. "The Cost of Capital, Corporation Finance and the Theory of Investment." *American Economic Review* 48, no. 3 (June 1958): 261–97.

——— "Corporate Income Taxes and the Cost of Capital: A Correction." *American Economic Review* 53, no. 3 (June 1963): 433–43.

Montvel-Cohen, T. "Volkswagen of America." Unpublished research report, Kennedy School of Government, Harvard University, 1984.

Myers, S. C. "Interactions of Corporate Financing and Investment Decisions: Implications for Capital Budgeting." *Journal of Finance* 29, no. 1 (March 1974): 1–25.

——— "Determinants of Corporate Borrowing." *Journal of Financial Economics* 5, no. 2 (November 1977): 147–76.

——— "Finance Theory and Financial Strategy." *Interfaces* (1983).

——— "The Capital Structure Puzzle." *Journal of Finance* 39, no. 3 (July 1984): 575–92.

——— and N. Majluf. "Corporate Financing and Investment Decisions When Firms Have Information Investors Do Not Have." *Journal of Financial Economics* 13, no. 2 (June 1984): 187–222.

Nobes, C. W. "Imputation Systems of Corporation Tax with the EEC." *Accounting and Business Research* (Spring 1980): 221–31.

Ornstein, J. A., and K. T. Vora. "Valuation of Foreign Investment Projects for Multinational Corporations: A Case Study." Master's Thesis, Sloan School of Management, MIT, 1978.

Otani, I., and S. Tiwari. "Capital Control and Interest Rate Parity: The Japanese Experience, 1978–1981." *IMF Staff Papers* 28 (1981): 798–815.

President's Commission on Competitiveness. "Global Competition: The New Reality." January 1985.

Raiffa, H. *The Art and Science of Negotiation*. Cambridge, Mass.: Harvard University Press, 1982.

Reich, R. B. "Bailout: A Comparative Study in Law and Industrial Structure." *Yale Journal of Regulation* 2, no. 2 (1985): 163–224.

Robbins, S. M., and R. B. Stobaugh. *Money in the Multinational Enterprise: A Study in Financial Policy*. New York: Basic Books, 1973.

Rodriguez, R. M., and E. E. Carter. *International Financial Management*, 2nd ed. Englewood Cliffs, N.J.: Prentice-Hall, 1979.

Salomon Brothers. *Industrial Bond Manual*, 1983.

Sarathy, R., and S. Chatterjee. "Japanese Corporate Financial Structure: A Canonical Correlation Analysis." Paper presented at the Academy of International Business meeting, Montreal, October 1981.

Solnik, B. H. "Why Not Diversify Internationally Rather than Domestically?" *Financial Analysts Journal* (July/August 1974): 48–54.

Suzuki, Y. *Money and Banking in Contemporary Japan*, trans. by G. Greenwood. New Haven: Yale University Press, 1980.

Taggart, R. A. "Secular Patterns in the Financing of U.S. Corporations." National Bureau of Economic Research, Cambridge, Mass., 1983.

Touche Ross, International. *Business Study: Japan*, 1981.

Wellons, P. A. "Competitiveness in the World Economy: The Role of the U.S. Financial System," in B. R. Scott and G. C. Lodge, eds., *U.S. Competitiveness in the World Economy*. Boston: Harvard Business School Press, 1985.

7

Government Policies and Global Industries*

Yves L. Doz

GOVERNMENT POLICIES AND GLOBAL INDUSTRIES

Multinational companies (MNCs) have long been of concern to host and home government officials. Foreignness has always been a source of tension and foreign investments have been regulated and controlled in almost all countries. Control over trade policy is also a long-established government prerogative; debates between advocates of free-trade, mercantilism, and protectionism fill the literature on economic history.

A global pattern of industry competition draws both types of concerns. Domestic firms are exposed to international competition in the form of trade flows, *and* the industry is also populated by subsidiaries of a few large MNCs. Furthermore, governments find that existing MNCs in global industries aim increasingly to develop intrafirm trade among their affiliates to gain the benefits of configuration described in the opening chapter of this book. Thus, as industry globalization increases, MNCs also account for a growing share of international trade in the products of their industries.

Confronted with industry globalization and growing MNC presence, governments have developed and implemented a wide array of

*The author is indebted to Professors Edith Penrose and José de la Torre, both at INSEAD, for their comments and criticisms of earlier drafts, as well as to the participants in the Harvard Business School Colloquium on Competition in Global Industries. Financial support from the Harvard Business School and from INSEAD is gratefully acknowledged; it made the research supporting the argument developed in this chapter possible.

policies and actions designed to influence the structure of industries and to impact both the nature of competition and the types of firms that participate in them. Government intervention in global industries is not limited to developing countries nor to countries whose ideology implies state-control of the economy. Regulation and protection extend to traditionally liberal countries such as the United States and other OECD members.

Over the last few years, governments have shown growing ingenuity in intervening in global industries. The highly concentrated nature of many global industries, in some cases populated by but a handful of global competitors, has also shifted the context of the interface between governments and business from regulation to negotiation.*

Government intervention can be pervasive enough to substantially modify the set of strategic options available to global competitors. It creates both constraints and opportunities, and also modifies the relative attractiveness of various options. Governments also have a sufficient impact on the evolution of industry structures, and on the nature of rivalry within industries to make a careful consideration of their actions—current and potential—of critical importance in formulating and implementing global strategies.

To allow such careful consideration, the argument in this chapter will develop in four sections. First, I will outline the typical sources of host government concerns, as they apply both to industry globalization and to the presence of MNCs in global industries. Second, I will review the policies usually followed by host governments to act upon these concerns, and analyze how these policies broaden or limit the range of options available to MNCs. Third, I will discuss the interaction between specific government policies and MNC global strategies, with a view to identifying conditions that lead to mutuality of interest or to conflict. Finally, a fourth section will draw some practical managerial implications to guide the choice of strategy to be followed and to prepare MNCs to cope effectively with government policies.

GOVERNMENT CONCERNS ABOUT GLOBAL INDUSTRIES

Government concerns about global industries tend to focus on selected issues that result from industry globalization. First, the growth

---

*When competitors are few, and global oligopolistic rivalry prevails, direct negotiations between specific host governments and individual MNCs may allow both sides to develop relationships that serve both the policies of the host government and the competitive advantage of the MNC. Across the board regulation of foreign investments by host governments would ignore the differences between the competitive positions of firms and lead to suboptimal choices for governments and MNCs.

in trade that characterizes industry globalization makes felt acutely and quickly the need for economic adjustment. The first set of government concerns thus stems from adjustment issues. Global competitive pressures may also question the survival of independent national suppliers of strategic goods, such as specialty metals, computers, and combat aircraft. Concerns also focus, therefore, on strategic industries. Further, concerns differ somewhat with the patterns of industry globalization, in particular with the absence or presence of MNCs, and with their choices of resource configuration and coordination. This section identifies and reviews these various sources of concern and describes how governments have usually articulated them.* I will begin with the general concerns toward interdependence and industry globalization and later move to the specific concerns that MNC configuration and coordination patterns elicit.

The growing international interdependence that results from industry globalization is the starting point for most government concerns, particularly when interdependence involves the presence of integrated multinational companies rather than market forces alone. Concerns about the extent of global interdependence—mainly via trade—and about the identity of the specific trading agents and commodities are not unrelated phenomena. Trade in goods, technology, and capital are complementary or alternative conduits for interdependence that governments may seek to influence jointly in order to develop a coherent industrial policy. Indeed, partly in response to government policies, the relative importance of various conduits for interdependence shifts over time. One may recall, as an example, how increased Japanese investments in the U.S. TV set industry and the surge in imports from Southeast Asian and Latin American countries followed government-sponsored "Orderly Marketing Agreements" between the United States and Japan in 1976.[1]

Growing international interdependence puts a greater burden of adjustment on the national economies: in an international environment of freer trade and freer investment their structure must adjust more quickly to relative changes in the competitiveness of various national industries. Yet, rigidities have severely limited the adjustment capabilities of Western economies. Groups that the costs of adjustment fell on have successfully defended their interest, while the broader groups that would benefit from faster adjustment have not been able to put their benefits forward with equal strength. Local

---

*While strong national idiosyncrasies remain critical and cannot be ignored in developing specific global strategies (e.g., from Malaysia's ethnic composition to France's Gaullist heritage or to Mexico's all-encompassing "Institutional Revolution Party"), this section focuses on the *common core of enduring concerns* shared by OECD countries and by NICs, whose governments want them to play a significant role in global industries.

firms and local workers are well-organized, whereas consumers at large and the increasing number of unemployed workers, who would benefit from adjustment, are not organized. Therefore, at least until the early 1980s, rigidities and protection in the labor market have made adjustment slow and difficult, particularly in Western Europe.[2]

Faced with the difficulties of adjusting their economies to global competitive demands, governments have become increasingly concerned with the competitiveness of their economies under conditions of high international interdependence when their industries face strong adjustments needs. First, they are concerned with the equity and efficiency of adjustment processes in declining industries: what the least cost adjustment path is and how the costs should be shared. Second, some governments have also shown concern toward the development of new industries. Government officials fear that faster industry life cycles call for early identification and targeting of emerging industries, and believe that cooperative state–private sector institutional arrangements can perform these tasks more effectively than private firms acting alone. Economies of scale in data gathering and analyses, joint discussion of such analyses among business and government officials, and integration into a consistent strategic framework may decrease both the cost and the uncertainty for private firms of committing resources toward new emerging industries. To a large extent, this is the function of MITI's "10-year visions" in Japan.[3] Economic and technical uncertainties, high interest rates, and adverse fiscal conditions are viewed as discouraging private long-term strategic investment in emerging industries, and therefore may call for specific state action to support the development of such industries, from R & D subsidies and investment incentives to the provision of state-controlled "first-users" markets.[4]

Interdependence and Strategic Industries

Industry globalization also raises host government concerns about the specialization of their national economy, particularly when it affects strategically salient industries. Since the early theories of comparative advantage, it has been recognized that specialization goes with globalization. Recent evidence on intra-industry trade and international specialization, some gathered at the initiative of governments, only reinforces the awareness that the most successful countries—measured by GNP growth—are also the most specialized in their participation in the world economy.[5] Such specialization nurtures a fear of dependency: each country depends on the others for the wide range of goods it does not produce any longer. Well-known incidents of a sovereign state influencing another through such dependency, from the export of automobiles from Argentina to Cuba by a U.S. MNC subsidiary to the famous Soviet gas pipeline embargo, fuel government concerns toward the globalization of strategically significant industries.[6]

Government concerns toward global industries are therefore not undifferentiated; they focus on specific issues raised by the growing international interdependence, and the needs for economic adjustment that result. Adjustment needs are most clearly felt around maturing and declining industries—with the social woes that result—around emerging industries, and around industries that question the wisdom of globalization in light of their strategic significance.

Government Concerns and the Pattern of Global Competition

Not all kinds of global industries create similar concerns on the part of governments. Some concerns relate to the volume of international trade, even in the absence of MNCs, while others stem from the presence of MNCs, even when they operate as "multidomestic" entities in the absence of trade. Both sets of concerns overlap, and some new ones appear in true global industries, with both global trade competition and globally integrated and coordinated competitors.

These differences are captured graphically in Figure 7.1, along the dimensions of trade and MNC presence. The horizontal dimension separates "multidomestic" from truly "global" competition, while the vertical axis separates MNC presence (typically where intangible assets play a key role in multidomestic industries and where benefits of coordination are high in global industries) from MNC absence (typically in internationally traded commodities, where transaction costs are low and the superiority of MNC coordination over market mechanisms not compelling). These differing patterns of international competition implied in each cell are described in chapter 1.

Government concerns differ predictably according to these categories. Leaving aside type 4 industries (multidomestic with predominantly local competitors), which are beyond the scope of this book, I will review quickly the government concerns in each category.

Concerns regarding Global Competition without MNCs

The simplest and most sharply focused set of concerns apply to global industries without MNCs (type 3 industries in Figure 7.1). Stemming from the general concerns about interdependence and adjustment summarized earlier, the government concerns about such industries focus on whether to regulate the extent and speed of exposure of national producers and markets to international competition and, therefore, to manage the adjustment process of their economy. The choice is partly one of producers' versus consumers' interests: weak national producers benefit from protection while consumers benefit from the ability to purchase from the most efficient suppliers. It is also partly one of international interdependence: whether to accept the high de-

Figure 7.1 A Classification of Global Industries

Importance of International Trade

	High	Low
Dominant	TYPE 1: *Truly Global Competition among Integrated MNCs,* Strong Advantages to Configuration and Coordination (e.g., automobiles, computers, consumer electronics, petroleum, pharmaceuticals)	TYPE 2: *Multidomestic with MNCs Exploiting Intangible Assets* (Technology, Know-How, Brand Names, Management Skills, etc.) (e.g., prepared food products, most beverages, services, cosmetics, etc.)
Marginal	TYPE 3: *Global Competition, But No MNCs* Advantages of Configuration, But No Advantage of Coordination (e.g., bulk grains, textiles, steel, shipbuilding)	TYPE 4: *Multidomestic with Local Firms* No Advantages of Configuration or Coordination (e.g., construction, most furniture, most staple food, etc.)

Role of MNCs as Competitors

gree of specialization of the national economy that is likely to follow from the free play of global competition.

Concerns regarding Multidomestic MNCs

Government concerns about multidomestic industries populated by MNCs vary with the degree of coordination implied by MNC strategies. When MNCs invest in a country to serve its national market discretely, with no interaffiliate coordination beyond that needed to transfer intangible assets to the country effectively, this is usually of only minor concern to host governments. The behavior of the local affiliate is likely to be primarily determined by local factors, and thus to be predictable and rather similar to that of local firms. Only in some respects, such as the amount of risk that a subsidiary may be willing to take, is the existence of a global parent company portfolio of investments likely to induce behavior at the subsidiary level much different from that of a local firm.[7]

Yet, as stressed in chapter 1, managing international affiliates as mere portfolio investments ignores sources of competitive advantage that accrue from multinationality. More often than not, therefore, global competitive rivalry, rather than specific national market characteristics, may determine the MNC investments. MNCs may participate in some markets not because of their intrinsic interest, but because they can provide leverage against competitors. The objectives such an MNC assigns to its affiliates are then likely also to be driven by global competitive rivalry rather than by local conditions alone. Such strategic coordination of affiliates raises additional concerns for host governments. MNCs may disrupt competition in their country, for example, through pricing policies, and, for instance, eliminate local competitors through low prices. The actual target may be another MNC using the country as a source of cash flow to feed active competition elsewhere, and not the local firms, but the local firms are still likely to be the first casualties. For these reasons, strategic coordination, even in the absence of actual logistics integration, is a major source of government concern about MNCs. As competitors come to recognize global competitive interactions in a growing number of so far primarily multidomestic industries (e.g., tires, industrial gases, beer,) such concerns are bound to grow.

Concerns regarding Integrated MNCs

As the product flows are added to cash flows across borders (moving from "coordinated" type 2 to "integrated" type 1 along the horizontal axis of Figure 7.1), new host government concerns are also added. International, rather than local conditions, weigh more heavily on MNC decisions about their affiliates.

First, governments are concerned that integrated MNCs may quickly respond to shifts in the relative factor cost competitiveness of various manufacturing locations by relocating their manufacturing facilities in different countries. Global scanning capabilities of MNCs, according to some concerned governments, will even give them advanced notice of and plentiful information on shifts in competitiveness. Their multinational nature will let them relocate easily without showing particular commitment to any country, except maybe their home base—although relocation of activities abroad may be necessary and not adversely affect the domestic economy.[8] Whether such behavior on the part of integrated MNCs is widespread or not, or distinguishes them much from local firms' outsourcing, is irrelevant; the mere fear that it might occur is sufficient to heighten government concerns. Even within single regions, such as the EC, the MNCs are often rationalizing their manufacturing networks and closing down some subsidiaries as a response to competitive pressures, as observed in the mechanical, instrument, and electrical engineering industries.[9] Some moves across regions, for example, General Electric's relocation of small appliance manufacture from the United States to Brazil and Singapore were widely heralded, but aggregate data on their frequency remain scanty.[10]

A second concern of governments relates to the taxation of integrated MNCs: in industries where direct costs are small in relation to allocated costs, integration offers the MNCs the opportunity to bias financial results of subsidiaries to decrease the total MNC tax exposure. Transfer pricing and subsidiary remittances (royalties, fees, etc.) allow the transfer of income from high- to low-tax countries, in ways that are difficult for government officials to detect.

Third, host governments are also concerned with integrated MNCs retaining key competencies outside of host countries—typically at the center in the home country—and farming out to subsidiaries only the menial tasks that contribute little to the development of knowledge and skills in the host country.[11] Even when MNCs locate knowledge-intensive activities in host countries, such as R & D centers, they are often confined to adapting global products to local markets, or else they report directly to global headquarters and seldom contribute to the overall technological development of the country or provide the host government with responsive technological capabilities for national projects.[12]

More generally, governments also worry about the network of relationships that influence the subsidiaries of integrated MNCs. Some government officials feel that the response of integrated MNCs to their policies is particularly difficult to predict, or even understand, because these relationships make reactions of MNCs quite different from those of national firms producing and selling the bulk of their goods in only one country. MNC affiliates are but a piece of an intensely coordinated globally optimized system. This generates much frustration among government officials about integrated MNCs.

An added irritant—and a corollary of global integration—is the disappearance of national decision centers in MNCs. When negotiating with the managing director of an MNC affiliate in a multidomestic industry, government officials rightly believe that they have in front of them someone who can make most critical decisions affecting the future of the subsidiary, and in particular, its relations with the host government. Not so in an integrated MNC: local managing directors seldom have direct responsibility of more than the operating management decisions. Strategic decisions result from more complex interfaces and decision processes.[13] Government officials do not know at which levels to interact with MNC executives, between the local subsidiary level and the CEO, nor do they usually understand the structure of the MNC decision processes. Frustrations result from the local managers only being able to act as conduits for information, not as decision makers. In sum, both the determinants of integrated MNC responses to their policies, and the processes through which such responses are developed, are rather opaque to host governments.

This is all the more important as MNC coordination and integration shift the very nature of their relationships with host governments from regulation to negotiation. In industries where oligopolistic competition prevails on a global scale, and where multinational competitors are asymmetric in their existing resource deployment, the same set of terms and conditions from a host government may be given very different values by different competitors. In the mid 1970s, for example, Ford valued investing in Spain highly: it lacked a low labor-cost manufacturing location from which to export small cars to the very price-competitive markets of France and Italy. Also it needed to expand capacity anyway, and was not yet assembling cars in Spain, contrary to its major European competitors. The Spanish investment was all the more valued because competitors would not follow suit quickly: the terms provided by the Spanish government deterred other competitors from building a world-class plant in Spain. To other competitors, in particular to Ford's European competitors, investing further in Spain was at best of marginal interest. While the Spanish decrees were cast in "regulation" terms, they followed months of detailed, but informal, negotiation with Ford, and were quickly dubbed by observers the "Ford laws."[14] The point here is that by not shifting from regulation to negotiation, host governments lose the opportunity to find the most mutually beneficial agreement with individual MNCs, and thus may incur a significant opportunity cost. Yet, to civil servants used to issuing regulations, or used to negotiating with well-known domestic firms, having to negotiate step by step with individual MNCs may be disconcerting and difficult.

MNC integration not only creates a need to shift the host government–MNC relationship from regulation to negotiation, it also forces a much sharper recognition of relative bargaining power and of the evolution of relative power over time. Prior to a new investment several alternative locations can be considered by the MNC to serve the same group of markets. Potential host governments may be led to waive the usual performance criteria and to outbid each other for incentives, thereby giving excessively good terms and to outbid each other for incentives, thereby giving excessively good terms to the MNC. While this may create instability later on, with the government tightening its terms, it is difficult, under pressures from unions and public opinion, not to sweeten the initial terms. Once the investment is made, relative bargaining power is usually more balanced. A new plant that belongs to a global network is of limited value to the host government should the links with the MNC system be severed. Yet, although it is not in its interest, the host government has the power to bring down at least part of the MNC system by paralyzing or disconnecting one of its critical components. Drastic action thus has negative consequences for both sides, a situation that leads to moderation, while bargaining takes place only at the margin, on the sharing of the economic value created by the investment. Over time, the government is thus likely to try to take small steps to increase its benefits, from increased taxation to the imposition of partly local ownership, but both parties agree on the need to keep the investment going. Data on patterns of ownership and expropriation of manufacturing MNC subsidiaries in Latin America support the strength of integration as a source of bargaining power—integrated MNC subsidiaries were much less frequent targets for nationalization than self-standing ones.[15] While extractive industries were frequent targets for expropriation, control of international trade and distribution—the equivalent of an integrated network in manufacturing—became a potent deterrent to further expropriation.

Industry globalization raises one last major issue for national governments: national firms that produce and sell mainly in their domestic market may have to become global or disappear.[16] However, the resources needed to become an effective global competitor may be beyond the reach of most national firms, unless they specialize in narrow segments. Specializing in narrow segments may not satisfy the host government's concerns for national independence (how useful is it, in national security terms, to be a world leader in one type of computer peripheral equipment when the country can no longer design and build whole systems?) nor provide a sound basis for maintaining competitive advantage. Indeed, in industries where hardware, software, and system skills and products are tightly coupled, such as in the information technology industry, picking narrow global segments may not provide competitive strength. Similarly, in distribution-intensive industries, such as consumer electronics, it may not be possible to maintain effective global distribution with a narrow product range. The need to be global and to cover a broad scope of related products further increases the resource and skills requirements, and makes the transition from national to global even more difficult. The plight of national companies such as Bull and ICL in the computer industry is a constant reminder of these difficulties to host government officials.

To the MNC executive formulating a global strategy for a business, a first step in incorporating host governments in his or her analysis is to identify the likely sources of host government concerns, both toward the industry in which his or her business competes, and toward the specific actions that the strategy may entail. The preceding section has summarized the most usual concerns raised with host government officials by industry globalization, MNC presence, and the shift in MNC strategies from multidomestic approaches to strategic coordination and to operational integration. Once an understanding of existing and likely concerns is developed, the second step is to analyze how these concerns are likely to be translated into concrete policies. This is the focus of the following section.

GOVERNMENT POLICIES IN GLOBAL INDUSTRIES

The concerns raised by global industries create difficult policy trade-offs for governments about the conditions under which their national economies will participate. Not participating or seeking to insulate the country from global industries to maintain long-term economic autarky, while in principle a feasible option, has been followed by very few governments (probably because of its high opportunity cost) and will be considered here only insofar as governments have selectively followed this policy in a few strategically significant industries. Participation in global industries may take place through various means. While the specific arrangements are innumerable, three broad modes of national economy participation seem to be characteristic:

1. *Integrated subsidiaries of major MNCs.* Usually, integrated subsidiaries are set up in a country when its government bargains access to its large domestic market for an investment that has favorable balance of payment and positive employment effects. The Brazilian automobile industry is a case in point, with most MNCs committing themselves to substantial exports in order to obtain or maintain access to a promising domestic market. Sometimes the host country's government adds incentives to make investing even more attractive to MNCs.

2. *Internationally competitive national firms that actively participate in global industries.* At first, national firms are protected—along the usual "infant industry" terms—and later assisted to participate in international markets, and finally, when competitive, left on their own. The well-known development of the automobile and consumer electronic industries in Japan provides textbook examples of this policy of active national firms' participation in global industries.

3. *International coalitions.* As described in chapters 10 and 11 of this book, such coalitions abound in global industries. They involve joint R & D, coproduction, and reciprocal marketing in a multitude of combinations. They are often seen by governments as a compromise between the advantages of effective participation in global industries and their desire to maintain a measure of national control and influence.[17]

These three modes of participation are not mutually exclusive. France, for instance, offers a choice market for IBM, provides state support for national producer Bull in the hope of seeing it become internationally competitive, and encourages international coalitions and partnerships (such as those between MATRA and Norsk Data, and MATRA and Harris Semiconductors, all in the computer industry).

Yet, these three modes of participation in global industries represent clear tradeoffs among concerns and priorities, and imply different, but consistent sets of national policies toward global industries. This section will first make explicit key dimensions of these tradeoffs and then will compare them.

The Tradeoffs Implied by Each Mode of National Participation

Integrated Subsidiaries of Major MNCs

Integrated subsidiaries may offer host countries a short-cut to participate in global industries. In industries that are difficult to enter (e.g., because of technology, minimum size, limited access to distribution), they allow national economies to circumvent entry barriers. From a national policy standpoint, relying on integrated MNC subsidiaries makes sense when the issue is to leverage quickly a national comparative advantage. Countries that enjoy a factor cost advantage in labor, energy, or raw material, but whose firms lack the necessary skills and capabilities to leverage that advantage globally are best served by integrated MNC subsidiaries. The factor cost advantage should entice MNCs to turn the country into an "export platform," to the mutual benefit of the MNCs and the countries. The MNC has access to low-cost factors, while the country leverages those on the worldwide market. A number of smaller, rapidly industrializing countries, from Ireland to Singapore, have followed this approach. This usually involves subsidizing the cost of labor to attract MNC investment and increasing its productivity via training and controlled labor relations.

Although this approach offers smaller developing countries a way to participate efficiently in global industries and to leverage their comparative factor cost advantage, it offers little control. While integrated MNCs may abide by set rules (e.g., on export ratios) they are unlikely to let any national government gain a say in how they run their operations, within the framework of pre-negotiated and agreed-upon guidelines. Governments are therefore likely to tolerate, or even encourage, the presence of integrated MNC subsidiaries mainly in industries where their concerns about integration apply least. This implies that issues of local decision making, autonomous development, transfer of advanced technology, and so on, are not seen as critical.

Governments will also tolerate integrated MNC subsidiaries more easily in industries that are difficult to de-integrate vertically, in which MNCs provide process and product technology and worldwide distribution, that would be difficult for local firms to pursue on their own. Typical examples of such industries are automobiles, consumer electronics, or computers. Governments that call in integrated MNCs in such industries are clearly more interested in the macroeconomic benefits of participating (via exports) in global industries than in the industry itself. In sum, the tradeoff made by governments in favoring integrated subsidiaries goes for efficiency at the expense of control.

The cost, beyond the immediate loss of control, is also longer-term vulnerability. Unless the government manages the evolution of its industry structure and relative factor cost positions together, the country may find itself with a portfolio of aging MNC investments, likely to lose their competitiveness on world markets and to result in large-scale MNC exodus. To a large extent, a string of MNC divestments in the United Kingdom can be seen in that light: traditional plants, from Singer's sewing machine plant in Scotland to Caterpillar's tractor plants, lost their competitiveness, and Britain was comparatively slow in attracting MNC investments in newer industries where it could still provide a competitive location. Conversely, albeit in a much simpler city-state, the government of Singapore has carefully managed jointly the evolution of its work force (wages, form of unionization, training level, etc.), the composition of its industrial base, and the incentives provided to and performance requirements demanded from MNCs to adjust quickly to its shifting competitive position vis-à-vis other developing countries.

In addition to the tradeoffs involved in accepting or seeking new integrated MNC investments, host governments also face difficult issues when well-established MNCs integrate their operations in maturing or declining industries, when confronted with international competition. These issues revolve around two types of action: (1) locally based companies, not MNCs, developing global outsourcing networks, and (2) integrating local subsidiaries of foreign MNCs into a global network. While national unions may try to stall relocation of manufacturing by domestic firms, and usually succeed in delaying it, governments seldom oppose them, given the alternatives. Integration of local MNC subsidiaries into a global network may raise more difficult issues.

Mature global industries populated by MNCs are often characterized by complex manufacturing processes, sensitive to economies of scale and experience. The most logical MNC competitive response to maturity is to integrate operations across borders, in particular when such operations were initially sized to serve separately small discrete national markets.[18] Integration raises difficult managerial issues that may stall its implementation.[19] It has also usually been resisted by trade unions and often opposed by host governments.[20] Yet, postponing such integration may cost dearly, and lead to complete, rather than partial, divestiture on the part of the MNC. Integration usually leads to the closing of the marginal plants in the emerging integrated network and the concentration of production into the most efficient, larger, and better-located plants. Integration therefore raises difficult social issues, but it often constitutes the only possibility for the MNC to continue operations.

MNC integration may often conflict with parallel efforts, on the part of national governments, to consolidate the national industry. Whether integration takes place nationally or internationally seems to depend on the existence of a potential "national champion" around which to regroup other companies and on an assessment, on the part of the host government, of the risk to national independence of losing control of the industry. A government may decide to consolidate the electrical engineering or the telecommunications equipment industry along national lines, for example, but let the automobile or the ball-bearing industries consolidate into integrated MNCs.

Again, the central tradeoff is efficiency versus control. If there are national firms that can efficiently consolidate the industry along national lines, there is no point in letting the MNC integrate and thus lose control. Yet, if no credible national firms exist, it is better to let MNCs integrate, rather than to totally lose out to exports.

In global industries not characterized by strong MNC presence, the issues are parallel, but protection is an easy temporary solution, as witnessed in steel, clothing, or in the auto industry vis-à-vis Japanese exporters. Affected competitors are distant, and little retaliation is to be feared. Competitors from threatened countries may themselves become global in their sourcing and in their marketing, thus trying to capture the competitive advantage enjoyed by competitors from developing countries.

Using the format of Figure 7.1, the policy choices of governments toward maturing industries in which their country is losing its competitive advantage can be outlined, as in Figure 7.2.

Internationally Competitive National Firms

The policies governments use to promote the domestic development of internationally competitive national firms in new industries are well known. First, the domestic market is closed to imports, to create a large repressed domestic demand, then an "infant industry" is promoted and protected. In some cases, the state administers the acquisition and diffusion of foreign technology, and several domestic competitors may be supported. Rapid growth of the domestic market allows national firms the opportunity to achieve competitiveness. Competition among them selects winners and weeds out losers. Protection of domestic producers is then decreased, and successful ones are poised to achieve international competitiveness. The development of the Japanese automobile or computer industries are good examples of this scenario. Such policy is sketched in simplified form, over time, in Figure 7.3.

Despite the striking success of Japan in pioneering the develop-

Figure 7.2 Policy Choices toward Mature Global Industries

Importance of International Trade

		High	Low
Role of MNCs as Competitors	Dominant	• Allow cross-border rationalization within MNCs? • Rationalize the number of firms in the national industry? • Allow moves offshore	• If new technology justifies it, let MNCs integrate across border to cut costs • Manage decline independently in each country
	Marginal	• Temporary protection to allow: —Move offshore —Orderly withdrawal —Repositioning, of technology, market segments, etc. • Permanent protection	• Manage decline dependently in each country • Often a large number of small firms as in the construction industry

ment policy outlined, the implementation difficulties of this approach should not be underestimated. This policy assumes both that vested interest can be made to converge and that timing can be controlled. It also assumes that foreign markets can be penetrated.

First, this policy corresponds to a tradeoff favoring collective long-term interests over short-term interests of specific groups. In the short term, it serves nobody's interest: consumers are deprived of imported products; investors might individually prefer the short term, but certain profits of import to the long term are an uncertain pay-off of building a stronger national industrial trade basis. The unusual industry structure of Japan with its major industrial trading and banking groups, as well as cultural traits of subordinating individual motives to group interests, have allowed this policy to succeed.

Intense competition among domestic suppliers in a country is also unusual. The emergence of a single "national champion" is more frequent. The absence of domestic competition and the dependence of this single national company on the state may deter it from developing the capabilities and skills needed to succeed in competitive interna-

Figure 7.3 Accelerating the Development of a Competitive National Position in a Global Industry

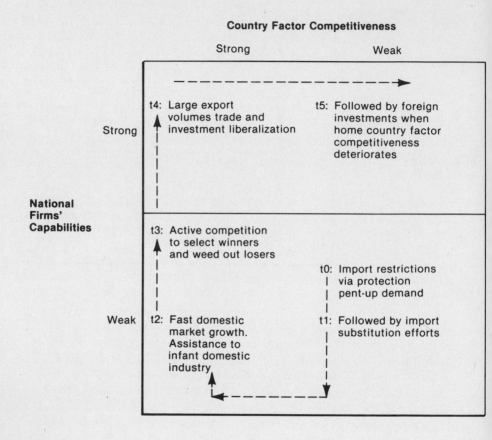

tional markets. In this case, the policy of assisting national champions to develop a competitive participation in a global industry becomes self-defeating.[21]

Second, the success of this policy of self-development of internationally competitive industries is critically dependent on its timing. Success is first dependent on the rapid growth of a large domestic market, which provides domestic manufacturers with sufficient volume to quickly decrease their costs and perfect their manufacturing methods. Low costs and high quality first achieved in serving the domestic market will then catapult them toward international competitiveness. Again, Japan may be somewhat unusual in how fast and sequentially consumer goods markets developed. Successive waves of demand for TV sets, cars, stereo sound, and VCRs, allowed the very rapid accumulation of manufacturing experience in each of these products. Most other countries whose governments aspire to see them play a leading role in global industries have smaller, less controlled* domestic markets, which would drastically reduce their opportunity to encourage international competitiveness through domestic demand growth. Japanese entries into industries often preceded their globalization, and sometimes acted as a catalyst toward globalization. This often gave the Japanese a prime mover advantage over competitors hamstrung in social and political difficulties (e.g., Philips in consumer electronics) or lacking in acumen, resources, or competencies to develop and carry out global strategies (e.g., General Electric in household appliances).[22]

Third, the autonomous development policy assumes that technology can be obtained unbundled from abroad. While this may be true in relatively mature industries, such as automobiles where Korea could develop successful products and efficient productive processes from piecemeal imports of technology, it is less and less true in more advanced industries. All too aware of such precedents as the transfer of TV tube and microelectronics technology to Japan, leading manufacturers in technology-intensive industries now limit transfers of technology overseas, often with the active support of their home government. The tightening U.S. policy toward exports of technology and advanced products under the Reagan administration is a case in point.

Finally, this autonomous development policy assumes that foreign markets are easily penetrable. The full benefits of the policy are obtained via exports that require that other countries and companies abandon their markets to imports. Despite the well-known examples of the motorcycle, photographic equipment, and consumer electronics industries, matters are seldom so simple. First, established competitors fight back, including on the home base of the fledgling newcomers. IBM not only fights back the Japanese mainframe manufacturers in the United States, but also in Japan. General Motors not only hopes its new "Saturn" subsidiary, with its technological and managerial innovations, will wipe out Japanese car makers' cost advantages, it also competes in Japan via its investment in Isuzu. Second,

*"Controlled" here denotes not only formal import protection but also the power of manufacturers to time the development of markets via their control of distribution and prices, as well as strong social norms that facilitate the fast diffusion of new consumer goods throughout the population.

distribution networks are seldom so easy to penetrate as those of mass merchandisers. Even when penetrated by OEM imports, channels may remain under control of domestic manufacturers that see OEM imports as a temporary palliative only. IBM, for example, sees purchases of printers from Seiko, or components from Matsushita, for its personal computers as a temporary expedient in establishing cost competitiveness. Third, protectionism may prevail and blunt the success of autonomous development policies.

In summary, the policy to develop autonomous internationally competitive national firms represents a tradeoff favoring long-term, potentially very high benefits, against short-term facility. Its success is predicated on a few critical domestic and international conditions. On the domestic side, it assumes a capability to first constrain and then to mobilize domestic demand to the advantage of national producers, to mix government assistance and exposure to competition in the development of national firms, to guide domestic markets toward the rapid diffusion of new products, and to develop labor skills and management practices that allow the maintainance of efficiency and quality through rapid scale-ups in production volume. On the international side, the policy assumes that critical technology can be imported and absorbed piecemeal and unbundled (rather than in the bundle provided by MNC investment), and that foreign markets can be penetrated without strong competitive retaliation or forbidding protectionist policies from other governments.

When actively pursued, and meeting with some success despite their intrinsic difficulty, such development policies do have significant implications for participants in global industries. First, they close some large potential markets to global competitors, when pent-up demand is created and released in favor of domestic suppliers.[23] Second, they may—when successful—nurture new global competitors. Third, these competitors may have access to financing on preferential terms, or not be subject to the same performance criteria as established ones.[24] These competitors may therefore be more aggressive in international markets and make a successful response to their inroads difficult for established competitors, who may hurt themselves severely in trying to quench new competition.

International Coalitions and National Independence

Governments have prevented the globalization of strategically critical industries, although on economic and competitive grounds alone global competition and MNC integration would have prevailed in these industries. Defense industries, such as combat aircraft, provide good examples of this policy. Some countries such as Britain and France have continued to independently develop and produce most advanced warplanes (e.g., the Mirage 2000 in France, the Harrier in the United Kingdom), others undertake the costly license production of U.S. types (e.g., the F 15 in Japan, the F 16 in the Benelux countries), and countless light-strike aircraft are designed, developed, and produced the world over, from Argentina to Indonesia, Brazil, Chile, Spain, Italy, Yugoslavia, Rumania, Poland, India, Israel, Taiwan, and several other countries. The opportunity cost of such fragmented design, engineering, development, and production efforts is staggering, in fully accounted unit cost terms, when compared to efficiently mass-produced aircraft in the United States and the Soviet Union. Telecommunication equipment, in particular digital switching, is also characterized by the costly multiplication of rather parallel national development efforts, most of which have only a remote probability of ever breaking even. Chapter 16 in this book analyzes the comparable phenomena that have long characterized the civilian aerospace industry.

Governments have increasingly recognized the very high opportunity cost of protecting strategic industries. While some have encouraged exports, sometimes with little discrimination but significant successes, as the French with the Mirage fighter planes, exports are only a palliative: volumes are often insufficient and prices are almost always depressed. Yet, protecting national independence in strategically critical industries at an affordable cost is increasingly important as national budgets are tightened and new technology costs escalate (the full development costs of a new digital switching system or a new fighter plane are estimated at around $1 billion). Global industries imply national specialization among industries or within each industry; they limit the independence of each country, because it now has to procure from abroad a substantial part of the goods it needs. While this is nothing new (witness the efforts of European countries to gain independent access to spices, coffee, and tea in the sixteenth century), it raises difficult issues in critical industries. Trying to remain competitive, independently, across a broad product scope in an industry whose technology evolves rapidly may be a self-defeating effort beyond the means of a single country, as the French discovered painfully with computers and the British with civilian airliners.[25] Specialization would not satisfy dependency concerns because excelling in one small global segment does not eliminate dependency in others. Relying on MNCs does not eliminate dependency either, since they are likely (1) to keep their most advanced research at home; (2) specialize their activities by country and; (3) try to avoid the diffusion of the technology to the host countries.

The need to be global, not specialize, and retain control has driven government officials to encourage transnational coalitions. The role of coalitions in international strategy is discussed in chapters 10 and 11. To governments, they offer a better choice (than purely national efforts) to participate successfully in global industries at an affordable cost, while hopefully letting them retain the measure of national control that they need in strategic industries. While agreement is not always easy between governments (e.g., Britain's initial nonparticipation in the Airbus launch) nor between national firms (e.g., the withdrawal of France's Dassault from the "Future European Combat Aircraft" coalition in 1985), while coordination and management costs are high, and while national prestige often prevents the adoption of the most efficient production system (e.g., by maintaining multiple assembly lines in different countries), such coalitions represent a healthy compromise between costly national efforts and efficient but hard to control MNC investments.

Comparing the Modes of Participation in Global Industries

So far this section has discussed *from the point of view of governments* the pros and cons and implicit tradeoffs corresponding to each mode of national participation in global industries. It is now possible to relate these modes to the broader conditions of national firms' and governments' likely choice of modes of participation in global industry as a function of national production factors and firms' competitiveness.

This process is obviously facilitated by the pre-existence of process-diversified firms, even if their initial position in a new industry is weak. Japan's industrial groups, or Korea's diversified groups not only can manage dynamically a portfolio of activities in industries at various stages in the evolutionary process described previously, they also provide a professionally run institutional context to lift specific activities quickly along the vertical axis of Figure 7.4. If the building of a modern firm must coincide with the development of a new industry (new to the country), a problem faced by most least-developed countries, chances of success are severely curtailed, and continued reliance on foreign MNCs may be the only appropriate policy. In some countries with a relatively strong industrial base, but a weak locally owned institutional base of modern diversified firms, the resulting frustrations, among government officials, intellectuals, and local entrepreneurs may be high.

Obviously, the picture presented in Figure 7.4 is not static. Over time, as the individual industries mature, and as individual countries develop, the structure of national economies shifts with resources being transferred from sectors where countries lose competitiveness to industries where they gain competitiveness.

Unless it is the initial innovation in the development of a new industry, a country is likely to start with both its factor and firm competitiveness being weak, and to move clockwise on Figure 7.4, through inward investments (which may be required to take the form of joint ventures to assist rather than thwart the development of domestic firms), through the development of internationally competitive

Figure 7.4 Likely Government Policies as a Function of National Firms'
and National Factors' Competitiveness

Factor Competitiveness

	Strong	Weak
Strong	Assistance to the autonomous development of internationally competitive national competitors, export development policies; temporary protection of domestic market	Assistance to the multinationalization of national firms, encouragement to outward investment in offshore sourcing plants
Firms' Potential Competitiveness	Reliance on inward foreign investments, with export performance requirements and export-oriented incentives	Imports, no national production, unless the industry is strategically important
Weak	Government-sponsored coalitions in strategic industries	

exporters, to finally the multinationalization of national firms and the location of their manufacturing offshore where production factors are now more competitive than in the home country.

Independent development of a national industry also requires a large domestic market. Smaller countries trying to accelerate their development may have no choice but to attract MNC subsidiaries. Attractiveness is based not only on factor competitiveness, but also on privileged access to larger markets. Membership of the EEC, for example, made Ireland a much more attractive location. So did ASEAN for Singapore. Larger countries may benefit most from global industries by retaining, and bargaining, access to their domestic markets, while smaller countries benefit most from free trade. Small countries lack bargaining power vis-à-vis MNCs, and they need to offer better incentives than larger countries and impose fewer performance requirements in order to attract MNC investments. They also tend to rely more on factor protection rather than on commodity protection in their incentive package, which is the contrary of the favored tool of larger countries.[26]

Although government preferences for one mode or another are likely to vary over time in predictable fashion, governments may also see advantages in having several modes of participation coexist, in the same industry, at a given point in time. Several modes allow governments to maintain competitive variety in an industry by encouraging competitors following fundamentally different strategies to coexist and compete one against another. Investments by integrated MNCs, such as Ford's investment in Spain, may allow host governments to jolt complacent protected national industry into shaping up. In general, the threat of introducing MNCs can be used to stimulate efficiency and productivity by the national producers. Conversely, the existence of credible national suppliers provides bargaining strength to host governments in their negotiations with MNCs: should negotiation fail, or the MNC pull out, the government can fall back on local suppliers. Plausible evaluations or partnerships can similarly increase the government's bargaining power.

Variety between MNCs can be relied upon to the same effect. Multidomestic MNCs, whose main concern is to be responsive to national conditions—including government demands—can be played off against integrated MNCs in negotiation. MNCs that try to reconcile the flexible national responsiveness with the competitive advantages of integration in a Janus-faced "multifocal" strategy can also be relied upon as an alternative to coalitions between national companies: they offer host governments a rather similar tradeoff.[27]

Governments are thus likely to weigh the benefits of maintaining competitive variety against those of a tighter fit between national conditions and participation modes. In the following section we will see that MNCs themselves are usually quite willing to contribute to competitive variety as well, their choices mirroring those of host government policies.

CORPORATE RESPONSES TO GOVERNMENT POLICIES: COMPLEMENTARY OR CONFLICTIVE

The typical host government policies outlined in the prior section create conditions that allow cooperation or lead to conflicts with MNCs depending partly on the strategic choices of the individual MNCs affected by government policies. In this section we review possible corporate responses to host government policies toward specific industries. These responses are typically conditioned by broader choices of strategic posture in how a given MNC competes internationally in a given industry, or in a particular subsegment of that industry. These broader choices of strategic posture are reviewed first in this section. Both these choices and the appropriate specific responses to host government policies are also dependent on the relative competitive position of individual MNCs in the same industry. Leading global competitors and weaker multinationl firms are unlikely to react to host government policies in similar fashion. This section then proceeds to describe interactions between these competitive positions and MNC strategic responses to host government policies.

The Typical MNC Strategies in Dealing with Host Governments

Integration strategies seek to create, via the higher efficiency provided by integration, an economic rent of a monopoly nature. Such rent is then shared between the MNC, which achieves the efficiency, and the host governments that make such rent possible by granting the integrated MNC continued license to operate in their territory. The exchange of value is essentially economic. The host governments share the rent, but are dealt with by the MNC at the margin: their ability to influence MNC operations, and their ongoing bargaining power is quite limited. The strategic choices of the MNC remain quite independent from direct host government influence. The strategic autonomy of the MNC is justified by its managers as a necessary condition of rent creation. Governments trade a measure of control for better economic performance. The sharing of the rent can take multiple forms beyond the payment of taxes by the MNC, and is usually a compromise along multiple dimensions that results from negotiations between the MNC and individual host governments. MNCs' managers may consider such sharing as "citizenship costs" to maintain the good will of the government and of the host country in general.

Multifocal strategies seek accommodation with governments while preserving the benefits of integration. They are predicated on a different exchange of value: the MNC allows some influence on its strategic choices to national partners and government authorities in exchange for support from the host governments. Rather than only the sharing of rents, the strategy of the MNC itself becomes an item for negotiation. To some extent, the MNC, with the support of host governments, still attempts to achieve integration, but in a way negotiated to satisfy the various governments. To avoid possible conflicts between governments the company may want to team up with a single national partner—as Honeywell did in France—and to appear as an integrated global competitor in other countries. Or it may attempt to allocate responsibility for R & D, manufacturing, and sometimes sales of its various product lines to various countries in a way most congruent with host government needs, as Philips did with semiconductors.

National responsiveness strategies go beyond a merely multidomestic approach in differentiating the MNC approach to national markets: they seek to position the MNC as a partner of host governments and of host country firms in developing the national economy.

They are predicated on a clear exchange of value: the nationally responsive MNC brings its worldwide skills to the service of the host country, but requires preferential treatment, against MNCs that follow an integrated or a multifocal strategy in dealing with host countries. Typically, this involves acting as a good partner, not merely a good citizen, being traded off against strong product protection (e.g., preferential public sector purchasing, tariffs, and quotas, etc.) when the economic penalty of fragmenting the world market is not judged excessive by either the MNC or the host government. When the economic penalty of market fragmentation is deemed excessive, factor protection (e.g., via subsidies for R & D or for exports) is substituted for product protection. In both approaches, national responsiveness strategies provide the host government with a flexible multinational partner, usually at the cost of economic efficiency. There are, in any case, limits to the extent of government influence; for instance, MNC managers are unlikely to let their various subsidiaries compete independently for exports with no coordination.

We can now analyze where the choice of one or another of the three MNC strategic approaches to global competition and to relations with host governments leads to complementarity or conflict with host government policies.

Corporate responses to Government Choices to Rely on Integrated MNC Subsidiaries

Where host governments decide to rely on subsidiaries of integrated MNCs the conditions of collaborative relationships are relatively obvious. First, neither national firms nor nationally responsive MNCs are given much of a chance, unless the government wishes to maintain a heterogeneous industry structure, and this severely restricts the access of the integrated MNC's subsidiary to the domestic market. This can take the form of domestic market share limits and of mandatory export-to-domestic sales ratios. For instance, both these constraints were imposed on Ford by the Spanish government in the early years of Ford's investment in Spain. To ensure that such constraints will be enforced, national firms can "cry wolf" and mobilize domestic political support. Further, they can, as can also nationally responsive MNCs, point out the benefits of maintaining a heterogeneous industry structure in order for the government to have bargaining power over the integrated MNC without having to resort to the brinkmanship of threatening expropriation. All these actions were undertaken in Spain by Ford's established competitors, with some measure of success.

Second, the issues between the integrated MNC and the host government are relatively straightforward. The integrated MNC will bargain initially to ensure (1) that a strong economic rent is indeed created, and (2) that it is shared in ways that guarantee the MNC sufficient future returns. Creating a strong economic rent involves ensuring that the conditions provided by the government allow the plant to be effectively competitive against global competitors, not just local ones. This typically involves negotiations along a whole range of cost items: energy prices, labor training, transportation and shipping facilities, financing of the investment at preferential rates, waiving of certain local content regulations to allow the MNC to procure components at the lowest world prices, and so forth. Sharing the rent in a mutually agreeable way, once the investment has been made, also involves negotiating on a variety of items, which are costs to one side and revenues to the other: tax concessions, credit terms, the treatment of intersubsidiary remittances, and other such matters. While the MNC will try to front-load incentives to minimize the pay-back of its investment, the government typically will try to stretch it out, not so much to decrease the profits of the MNCs as to guarantee a longer-term stability to the investment, other social benefits of such stability often outweighing direct financial and fiscal considerations.

The stance taken in negotiations with host governments by integrated MNCs is also likely to depend on their competitive positions. Intense competition among closely matched competitors (e.g., Ford and General Motors in Europe) may make each a tougher bargainer with host governments. Unless some unique benefit—not available to competitor(s)—is provided by the country, neither firm may be willing to compromise its rent-generating potential, nor to share its rent, because it fears being thereby put at a competitive disadvantage. Only the ability to execute a unique pre-emptive move that competitors cannot match (e.g., Ford investing in Spain in full knowledge that GM would not be allowed to follow suit for a few years) will lead a MNC to be flexible when it faces direct rivals. A single leading competitor (e.g., IBM in the computer industry) may refrain from exercising its full bargaining power for fear of alienating host countries, and, paradoxically, be a more pliable partner. Because its rent-generating capability is less directly threatened by competition, such a company may be less concerned about sharing rents or configuring its network less than optimally, in order to accommodate demands of host governments. Such a company has a lot more to lose by alienating its relationships with host governments than by lowering its (high) economic returns somewhat to satisfy governments' demands. Corporate values and styles may also play a role: some may encourage "good citizenship" and implicit gentlemen's agreements with governments (at the cost of oversatisfying government demands) rather than project an image of a tough hard-nosed bargain hunter. As long as slack is available, such a posture may be maintained. When competition toughens, however, it may become less tenable.

The sharing of rent between the MNC and the host government depends partly on the alternatives open to each party. By explicitly considering alternative investment sites from which to access the same markets, the MNC (e.g., an automobile manufacturer in the EC) can maximize its bargaining power and limit the share of rent it gives to any host government. Provided that several geographic alternatives yield comparable benefits to the MNC, the choice can plausibly be presented to host governments as a function of their incentives. Conversely, if a country offers access to a large, lucrative market (e.g., via protection) and there are a number of potential MNC investors, bargaining power favors the country. MNC concentration, globally and in a particular country, has been identified as a source of MNC bargaining power toward that country, while market size was confirmed as a source of national bargaining power.[28]

Yet, a responsible MNC negotiator may not use the bargaining power he enjoys to its fullest extent prior to an investment decision. A deal too slanted in favor of the MNC in the short term would compromise its long-term viability and remain constantly exposed to host government renegotiation efforts. Both the MNC and the host government parties may want to create the conditions for a stable bargain over time. Typically, the bargaining power of the MNC is eroded once its has committed resources, which lead it to request the government to provide immediate incentives at the outset of an investment rather than over its life. Conversely, benefits to the host country accrue only over the life of the investment, which may encourage the government to build incentives for the MNC to stay in the country. Because trust may not fully exist at the onset of negotiation, timing of incentives and performance requirements may be critical. Different utility functions and discount rates between MNCs and governments may allow an agreement to be reached more easily, however. Social cost benefit analysis may help governments assess and compare the value of alternative investments.[29] Performed by the MNC, it may help its managers determine the reservation price of the host government, that is, the minimum level of its total share of rent at which the government would accept the investment.[30]

Because aspects of relative bargaining power and of negotiation tactics between MNCs and host government is covered in depth by Encarnation and Wells in chapter 8, I will not push the analysis of this field further here but rather will turn to other types of interfaces between host governments and competitors in global industries. The main points of the preceding subsection are summarized graphically in the first row of Figure 7.5.

Corporate Responses by MNCs to the National Autonomous Development of Internationally Competitive Firms

As I discussed in the previous sections, government efforts to assist in the development of effective independent global competitors from a

Types of MNC Corporate Strategic Responses

Types of Host Government Policies	Nationally Responsive MNC Strategy	Multifocal MNC Strategy	Integrated MNC Strategy
1. *Reliance on integrated MNC subsidiaries—bargaining of a mix of incentives and performance requirements*	• Put forward advantages of heterogeneous industry structures • Limit integrated MNC's access to domestic market	• Put forward their ability to offer the best of both worlds	*AGREEMENT* *Negotiations on:* • conditions that allow sustained creation on an economic rent • sharing of the rent
2. *Efforts to develop independent national global competitors*	• Invest early in the country, be co-opted as a partner by the national govt.	• Be co-opted as a partner superior both to local firms and to integrated MNCs	Increase the cost to national government and national firms • Technology retention • Pre-emptive partnerships and OEM supply agreements • Control of market access
3. *Government-sponsored transnational coalitions and partnerships*	• In general avoid them (can gain most of the advantages sought by coalition on its own, and joining forces with national firms may create conflicts between the MNC subsidiaries)	• Become partner with selected local firm in exchange for privileged local market access and subsidies	• Generally similar to policies toward independent national efforts to develop independent internationally competitive national competitors

Figure 7.5 Conditions for Mutuality of Interests and Conflicts between MNCs and Host Governments

protected domestic base raise difficult issues for MNCs, particularly as these efforts give birth to dangerous new competitors. After a period of benign neglect toward new competitors from Asia and other developing countries, U.S. and European competitors have now awakened to the threat they constitute.

Integrated MNCs can react to these efforts by making them more costly, that is, by making the conditions for success outlined previously (see the section "International Coalitions and National Independence") less likely and more costly. First, as already discussed, MNCs, or for that matter leading exporters from other countries, may make access to their technology more difficult. This involves much tighter conditions for selling licenses than in the past, or a careful retention of their technology. Companies may do more and more of their own manufacturing process and machinery development in-house, and keep it proprietary. The shift in attitude of semiconductor equipment manufacturers from easy selling of equipment to all new semiconductor producers to a more restrictive policy is characteristic of these concerns. Similarly the recent publicity given to IBM's legal actions toward Japanese computer makers and former IBM employees to prevent the spread of its new products' operating software and architecture data shows a similar concern to stifle the efforts of independent national competitors to gain access to the industry leader's technology.

Second, industry leaders may try to enter into "partnerships" with fledgling national producers. Such partnerships, while offering the national firms an easy way to participate quickly in global industries may perpetuate their dependence on the leading MNC, and pre-empt their options. Although such motives would hardly be admitted publicly, there is some evidence that at least some of the collaborative agreements between large global MNC competitors and smaller national firms are not meant to succeed: they correspond to a tacit collusion between both partners. The MNC pre-empts the options of the smaller competitors and makes other more productive coalitions involving the same national competitors impossible. The local company uses the existence of the partnership as an alibi not to do anything else in a particular field rather than commit resources to what may be a priority area for the government but a cash drain for the local company.

Third, industry leaders may try to get into new country markets early, even at a cost penalty, as a way to stifle an independent national industry. If they are already well-established in a country—particularly via manufacturing operations that are costly and troublesome to dislodge—the attractiveness to the government of developing an independent national industry is usually lessened: it looks both less necessary and more costly. In fact, many of the early investments made by MNCs following nationally responsive strategies in industries where national markets are fragmented by barriers to trade and government purchasing preference toward local production correspond to this desire, on the part of MNCs, to occupy the ground before local companies could grow into viable competitors providing a genuine alternative to reliance on MNCs. Again, Japan was somewhat unusual after World War II in protecting its market early, even for products that the government had no intention to let the national industry produce in large numbers.*

Short of producing themselves in the country early, MNCs may let the local industry develop but in a truncated way. MNCs may, for instance, use local national companies as subcontractors, but retain control on their access to global markets. OEM supply contracts fit this policy, particularly when they apply to components and subsystems that are difficult to sell to end users independently from the MNC. This policy may placate governments, letting them successfully develop an export-oriented industry earning foreign exchange, but still guarantee the MNC against the irruption of new independent competitors on the world markets.

More generally, control of foreign market access is a strong leverage point for MNCs to prevent the independent development of globally competitive national producers. Asymmetries in bargaining power between producers and distributors in various markets, worldwide, make this policy more or less feasible. To take the extreme cases, the existence of large powerful mass merchandisers in the United States, such as Sears and Montgomery Ward, made the initial Japanese penetration of the U.S. durable consumer goods markets easy, while Matsushita's and other local manufacturers' control over their distribution in Japan makes it next to impossible for foreign suppliers to penetrate the consumer electronics market in Japan. A shift in Japan toward large independent mass merchandisers would be likely to make market access easier to foreign producers.

In some industries, where barriers may be more political (e.g., formal trade barriers) than institutional (e.g., the structure of distribution), lobbying and political pressure for equalization of terms may be useful and lead to some results, although in such areas as public sector purchasing, practices change quite slowly.

Finally, integrated MNCs can make their presence more desirable

---

*It is ironic to recall in passing that the limitation to trade in cars to the very low level of three thousand per year between Japan and Italy was negotiated in the late 1940s at the request of the Japanese government, then concerned with seeing the Japanese market flooded by cheap Italian cars! It is also interesting to recall that the Japanese car industry initially developed against the wishes of MITI, whose officials contested the need for a passenger car industry in Japan given urban congestion, scarcity of farm land, difficulty of terrain, and the excellence of public transportation.

by increasing the level of citizenship costs they are willing to incur. This contributes to making the autonomous national development option more costly, relative to the continuation of reliance on existing MNCs. The integrated MNC may also make itself more responsive to local market conditions and more sensitive to host government concerns, taking itself closer to a multifocal approach. This allows both to counter attack new competitors emerging on their home turf—where they have most to lose—and to make the MNC a better alternative, for the government, than to support the national competitors. An excellent example of these policies is IBM's efforts in sensitive countries such as Japan, France, and Germany to position itself as both a globally integrated MNC and a nationally responsive one.

MNCs following multifocal strategies may argue the advantages of being Janus-faced: on the one side, they can offer host governments some measure of control on their operations—and thus probably remove one of the host government's motives in developing an independent locally owned industry; on the other side, they can offer host governments the benefits of already being global, that is, market access worldwide, global capabilities for competitive retaliation, and possibilities to leverage new technologies on a global scale.

The mix of possible MNC corporate responses to government policies of autonomous development of national competitors is sketched in Figure 7.6 along two critical dimensions: time and exposure. The time dimension captures the key choices open to MNCs against fledgling national competitors: to try to nip them in the bud, or even to deter governments from sponsoring their development, or to control them later once they are established in their country and attempt to develop internationally. The exposure dimension captures the choice of battleground: in the host country, or on the international markets. The MNC can either establish advanced positions in the country to deter or stifle the emergence of new competitors, or establish its defense line around its established markets, which do not necessarily encompass the country where the new competitor is emerging. Obviously the two positions are not mutually exclusive, and an MNC that has both advanced and defensive positions has many more strategic options than one that concentrates on defensive positions only. The choice between a more advanced or a more defensive position may be based on an assessment of the likelihood of the new competitors to reach global competitiveness, compared to the cost of investing early in the country and engaging in vigorous competition there. This trade-off may be quite different from country to country: in Japan and Korea, the danger may be great and the cost of early investment minimal; in many developing countries aspiring to elbow into global industries, the choice may well be the opposite. The technical and managerial capabilities may not exist to a sufficient extent in the local firms, while the cost to an MNC of creating and nurturing a subsidiary

Figure 7.6 Choices of MNC Strategic Responses to Government Policies to Develop Independent New Global Competitors

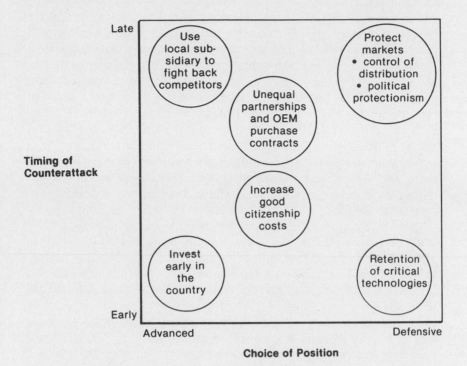

in an otherwise rather unattractive market may be high (low profitability, exposure to financial and political risks, managerial cost of relating to headquarters, etc.).

The key features of the interactions between government policies to develop new independent global competitors and likely MNC corporate responses are summarized on the second row of Figure 7.5.

Corporate Responses to Government-Sponsored Transnational Coalitions

To a large extent, integrated MNCs take a view of government-sponsored coalitions similar to the view they take of national development: participation in coalitions, while potentially attractive, leads to such a loss of strategic freedom as to ultimately threaten the efficiency of their integrated network, their ability to reconfigure it at will, and to coordinate its activities without direct external interventions. Thus, except when the government-sponsored partnership can be easily bounded (e.g., a specific European upstream research project in computer mathematics) or restricted to a single nation (e.g.,

IBM's access to and participation in various Japanese research programs) integrated MNCs tend to shy away from participation in transnational government-sponsored coalitions.

In general, as well, large globally integrated MNCs have less to benefit from partnerships than their smaller, less-global rivals (as discussed in chapter 10, which treats the economies of international coalitions in detail). The combination, on the part of globally integrated MNCs, of both lesser needs for coalitions and greater concern about government intervention in decisions affecting the very structure of their networks, makes them unusual partners in complex forms of coalitions. This, obviously, does not exclude them from specific contracts, or even specialized joint ventures, with other companies (such as major auto manufacturers jointly manufacturing components or acting as OEM supplier to one another) but makes them less likely partners in more extensive coalitions, where, for example, whole product ranges are shared.

While it may be more difficult to prevail over the combined forces of several governments and national companies, the policies of integrated MNCs toward international coalitions are often similar to those they adopt against individual national efforts to support new competitors. These policies have been described in the previous section and will not be reiterated here.

Nationally responsive MNCs could engage more flexibly in partnerships and coalitions at the level of each subsidiary. Yet, as soon as such coalitions have international ambitions, they put the MNCs in the awkward position of seeing them compete against their other subsidiaries or product lines. ITT, for instance, was involved in the late seventies in developing one digital switching system (System 12) on its own through a joint project between its various subsidiaries, and another such system (System X) in the United Kingdom through a partnership between ITT's British affiliate Standard Telephones and Cables (STC), and two independent British firms, Plessey and GEC. British hopes for exporting System X conflicted with ITT's preference for its own system. STC first left the System X coalition, and was subsequently partly divested by ITT and merged with the British computer manufacturer, ICL. Unless the top management of the MNC accepts such competition, which it may to hedge its bets on new technologies or market access or to stimulate internal competition, even nationally responsive MNCs may find it difficult to participate in coalitions, unless they do not compete with their own products in the same markets.

Further, even nationally responsive MNCs can often obtain on their own many of the advantages provided by coalitions. R & D can be shared between different affiliates, coordinated, and its cost can be amortized on the total worldwide sales volume of all affiliates. As long as economies of production warrant it, and this does not conflict too much with the nationally responsive image of the firm, nationally responsive MNCs can also combine and integrate the production of some components and subsystems. Finally, almost by definition, a nationally responsive MNC has good market access in a number of countries.

National partnerships with the aim of serving the national market are, on the other hand, quite acceptable to the nationally responsive MNC. Its management may see collaboration with local firms—whatever legal framework under which such collaboration takes place—as a way to further its national responsiveness image, to create joint interests with local partners who have the ear of government officials, and to minimize its exposure in the national market.

Still, MNCs following multifocal strategies may be the most willing to engage in government-sponsored coalitions with individual national partners. They may not engage in coalitions involving other partners from multiple countries, for the same reasons that make both the integrated and nationally responsive MNCs avoid them. But a single national partner can be quite valuable. First, it may provide privileged access to a particular country market or even to third-country markets (to Honeywell, French computer affiliate C21 Honeywell Bull not only allowed privileged access to the French public sector markets, but also to African countries where Bull was strong and to which France extended tied-in aid, as well as to the Eastern European market where the French affiliate provided a convenient non-American "front" behind which to sell equipment that might have been more difficult to export from the United States). Second, government R & D subsidies are almost always welcome. Third, as long as the coalition does not include third parties, and thus remains bilateral, the MNC can continue to follow an integration strategy to the mutual benefit of its privileged host government and of itself. For example, Honeywell could be nationally responsive in France, and compete as an integrated MNC elsewhere in the world.

Figure 7.5 summarizes, in the bottom row, the typical responses of MNCs to transnational coalitions. Clearly these coalitions more often regroup the nationally supported "underdogs" in global competition than the leading MNCs, except when their scope is contained to limited product supply or cross-licensing agreements on specific technologies that can be transferred from one competitive area to another.

The contents of Figure 7.5 are but a broad empirical generalization, and thus should be taken neither as universal MNC behavior, nor as prescriptive implications. The variety of specific cases of cooperation and conflict between MNCs and host governments defies simple classification into a few categories. Figure 7.5 should be thought of, thus, more as a possible way to structure alternative modes of collaboration or confrontation with governments, which outlines typical responses brought by MNCs following different types of strategies to the government policies described in the earlier section "Government Policies in Global Industries."

CONCLUSIONS AND IMPLICATIONS FOR MNC MANAGERS

The clearest conclusion for strategy choices in global industries to be drawn from the preceding sections is that an analysis of government policies should be an integral part of strategy making. While this has long been obvious to MNCs involved in industries such as weapon systems, telecommunications equipment, or even computers, it may not have been so obvious in other industries. Governments modify both the option set available to global competitors, according to the specific policies these governments follow, and the relative attractiveness of various feasible options to specific MNCs.

At the first and best-recognized level, government policies affect the mode of entry of MNCs by trade and investment policies.[31] Alternatives between exports, investments, coalitions with local partners, technology transfers, and just ignoring the national market are strongly influenced by government policies.* These policies have been analyzed in the preceding sections. They can best be understood through an analysis of government concerns and policy alternatives, and of the pattern of choices governments make between inviting MNC subsidiaries, supporting the development of national competitors, and sponsoring transnational coalitions. These policies directly affect the opportunities for MNC configuration of resources and investment.

Second, and sometimes less well-recognized, governments also affect coordination within the MNC.[32] By demanding responsiveness—mainly through public sector purchasing policies—they may exclude integrated MNC subsidiaries from the public sector market. In particular, the responsiveness demands of governments are usually much more extensive than those of users. While users are typically interested in commercial performance (quality of products, service,

---

*A "middle level" analysis is required to understand these policies and try to anticipate them. Merely studying their explicit manifestations— codes, laws, regulations, and the like—would ignore the opportunity to anticipate and even to influence them by studying their dynamics and understanding the concerns, motives, and logic of government intervention. Moving too much into national politics, sociology, and culture, while useful, may have diminishing returns to the cost of information in MNCs. First, the political and social analysis is more difficult to gather and analyze meaningfully in a way directly related to the MNC's activities. Second, if the MNC wants to use that information to influence its environment, it may be taken outside the realm of corporate competition into mingling in the domestic politics of the host country (e.g., ITT in Chile in the early 1970s).

application support, etc.), governments are mainly interested in social and political performance (autonomous local decision making, safety of supply, localization of technology to cover risks of embargo, etc.). Centrally coordinated MNCs can easily provide the responsiveness demanded by users provided they are sensitive to their needs (see chapter 4 by Takeuchi and Porter), they may even provide for certain government demands (such as export performance requirements to offset imports), but they cannot yield to demands for local control, except for some activities that are taken "off" the main business (e.g., IBM's military equipment divisions in some European countries provide much responsiveness to the local military, but this activity is not part of IBM's mainline worldwide business).[33]

As they exclude subsidiaries of integrated MNCs from certain government contracts and other protected markets, governments also make it possible for second-tier competitors to succeed in these protected markets. Not only local producers, but smaller MNCs, or even large MNCs which used for a long time to operate in a nationally responsive way (which would find the shift to global integration organizationally difficult anyway) and thrive on these protected markets. In a given industry, there appears a two-tiered structure, with integrated MNCs serving leading international customers, and nationally responsive MNCs serving national customers. When competitive pressures become too strong, weaker integrated MNCs are willing to de-integrate selectively some of their activities to enlist government support, while national firms band together into coalition to overcome diseconomies of scale in research and development and in manufacturing, and to pool their domestic markets. A 1979 study of the strategies followed by MNCs in selected industries in the EC supports this interpretation. This study identified the dominant coordination patterns in forty-eight multinational businesses* in eleven industries in the EC.[34] Technical and economic characteristics alone strongly favored integration strategies for all these businesses. Yet, as government control over their market—measured by the share of sales in these businesses to the public sector customer—increased, the competitors with the smaller relative marketshares increasingly followed multifocal strategies and coalitions with local partners. As government shares of sales increased further to become predominant, local responsiveness strategies became the exclusive type of strategy followed. Sample businesses were chosen so that government control over their markets would vary widely, while economic, technical, and competitive forces would consistently pull toward integration.

The results of this study are presented in summary form in Figure

*"Business" denotes here a set of related products that would have both a specific "business" strategy and a dedicated management structure. In diversified MNCs, it refers to such sets of products as, for instance, jet engines within General Electric, heavy electricity generation equipment in Brown Boveri, TV sets and tubes within Philips, and so on.

7.7. On the horizontal axis, the various businesses are arrayed according to the percentage of their total sales accounted by public sector customers. The vertical axis measures the relative European market-shares of various competitors. In the area to the left, above the two S-shaped curves, integration strategies predominate, that is, major competitors in businesses with low or moderate levels of sales to public customers. In these businesses, even smaller competitors integrate their operations and have to treat their business as global. In the area between the two S-shaped curves, multifocal strategies predominate. MNCs in this area follow multifocal strategies (e.g., Philips in micro-electronics) or form coalitions between global and national suppliers (e.g., General Electric–SNECMA in jet engines) or still, develop international partnerships between national firms (e.g., Airbus Industrie). To the bottom right of the S curves, national responsiveness MNC strategies and national competitors prevail.

In summary, policies constrain the strategic options open to integrated firms, to the point where they make it difficult for such firms to participate in certain markets, in particular those for defense-related strategic goods. They may also impose such performance requirements as to make participation unattractive to integrated MNCs. Government policies may also widen the options for weaker global competitors by offsetting some of the competitive disadvantages they would suffer in a competitive and homogeneous global industry.

The important implication from the preceding study is that choices of *configuration and coordination have to be made jointly*, not only as a function of economic and competitive dynamics, but also as a function of government policies. Insofar as government policies help maintain competitive variety within an industry and require from MNC active competitive responses (such as those outlined on Figure 7.6), they have to be integrated in the analysis.

The diversity of host country policies complicates the managerial task greatly. First, in a diversified MNC, businesses are likely to be subject to different host government demands as exemplified in Figure 7.7: companies such as Philips, Siemens, or General Electric participate in a whole range of businesses—from TV tubes to electrical power equipment—with very different government demands. Businesses thus have to be managed differently. While this is clear in terms of government relations (and the findings of the Mahini and Wells study on centralization and specification of government relation tasks in MNCs reported in chapter 9 are consistent with the analysis and the empirical evidence summarized here), it also has extensive implications for the organizational and managerial issues (see Bartlett, chapter 12).[35]

Matters are further complicated as government policies toward subsegments of an industry may differ greatly. For instance, governments may demand local responsiveness for large switching systems

Figure 7.7 Comparative Patterns of Strategy and Competition in Selected European Industries 1978–79

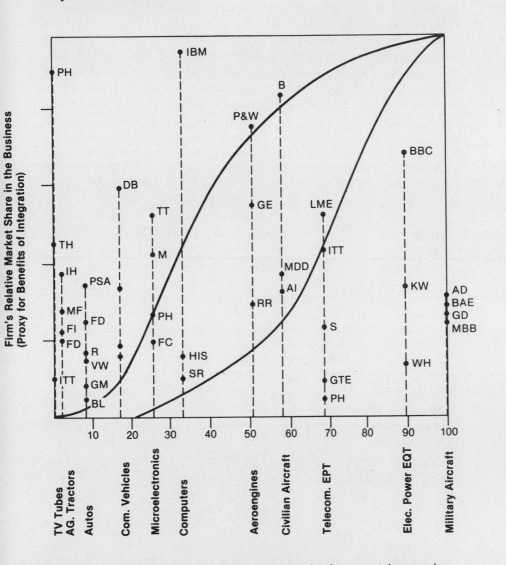

SOURCE: Reproduced from Yves L. Doz, "International Industries, Multinational Companies and Host Government Control: A Framework," in Walter H. Goldberg, ed., *Governments and Multinationals: The Policy of Control vs. Autonomy* (Cambridge, Mass.: Oelgeschlager, Gunn & Hain, 1983).

(including large private branch exchange systems), but leave the markets for telephone set and small console private exchanges open to global competition or, at least, to imports by MNCs that manufacture other equipment locally.

Changes in technology, as they modify the value chain of a business, may also trigger shifts in government policies: they make one or another policy option more or less attractive to a government. For example, in telecommunications switching, the emphasis of government policies has shifted from local manufacturing—when the technology was relatively static, and the manufacture of electromechanical systems was labor-intensive—to collaboration and coalitions in R & D, now that the shift to digital electronic technology has shrunk manufacturing costs and shifted manufacturing value-added to electronic components' suppliers but has much increased the complexity and cost of R & D. Shifts in technology may thus modify both the government policies and the MNC strategies and put to question an existing mutuality of interest between MNCs and host governments. This provides an entry opportunity for new competitors in a government-controlled industry, or on the contrary, leads to the eviction of existing competitors. While the success of new entrants is mixed, and existing nationally responsive competitors have shown great resilience, the telecommunications switching industry currently witnesses some changes of this nature.[36]

Within a business, or a business segment, national policies are likely to be different, based on the factors discussed in the second section of this chapter. This calls for a differentiated approach by MNCs. Broadly, one may think of at least three types of national markets:

1. *Strategic countries,* either because they are a key linchpin in a regional or global MNC strategy, or because they give birth to new competitors. Examples would include Spain for Ford and General Motors in passenger cars, Germany for Philips in "professional" electronics, Japan for IBM and Caterpillar, or still the United States for Daimler Benz or Honda. Strategic markets may play different roles in a MNC strategy (profit sanctuary, sourcing platform, blocking positions for competitors, etc.). An analysis of these is outside the scope of this chapter, and is treated elsewhere.[37] Yet, for these markets, an understanding of government policies is critical to MNC success, and resources ought to be devoted to these. Changes in government policies in these markets are likely to have system-wide impact on integrated MNC operations and on those of competitors.

2. *Tactical markets,* which are typically either markets served by imports or by nationally responsive autonomous subsidiaries. Changes in government policies in these markets may affect the conditions and

attractiveness of one or another strategic options for serving these markets, but are unlikely to have significant system-wide effects in the MNCs.

3. *"Opportunistic" markets*, where no commitments are made, but which can be served on a marginal basis, as the opportunity arises, usually through agents. These government policies matter only insofar as they affect foreign exchange and trading conditions.

The attention devoted by the MNC management to national policies in various countries must reflect, in its priorities, some categorization such as the one just outlined. The degree of centralization and decentralization and of standardization or adaptiveness (the issues considered by Mahini and Wells) in managing government relations must also reflect such differences. Finally, such diversity questions the role of area managers: adjacent countries—such as Singapore, Malaysia, and Indonesia, for instance, may well belong to different categories for a given business, and not to the same category for each business (Singapore, for instance, may be a strategic country for General Electric's consumer electronics businesses—a large sourcing platform—and for General Electric's jet engine business—a large fledgling national airline with ambitions in aircraft maintenance—but may be an "opportunistic" market for electrical equipment).

Government-imposed interdependencies between businesses add to this difficulty. The most usual form of government-imposed interdependencies is offset agreements, whereby the MNC has to engage in counter-trade to offset, via exports, its imports into the country. When General Electric sold jet engines for fighter planes to the Canadian armed forces, no fewer than fourteen business units, unrelated to jet engines from a competitive, market, and technology standpoint, had to become involved in exploring potential offsets for the sale of jet engines. Governments may also impose a less direct form of offset agreements, for instance, a commitment to maintain employment in a business with a local plant, in order to continue importing equipment made by another business not producing in the country.

One critical implication, thus, in addition to those that stem directly from the analyses in the preceding sections, is to understand that the diversity of conditions that are imposed on MNCs, or that MNCs find to their advantage in dealing with host governments, much complicate the task of top management. External variety has to be matched by internal variety in order to be addressed successfully. Yet, internal organizational variety comes at a high cost and is not easy to trade off against management's desire for control and uniformity.[38] The true challenge raised by host governments to MNCs in the 1990s may thus well be more organizational than economic: the days when governments discussed whether (and how) to ban MNCs are gone, but the organizational difficulties of dealing with very complex and differentiated conditions for resource configuration and coordination may impose their own limits to MNC growth and success.

NOTES

1. See J. E. Millstein, "Decline in an Expanding Industry: Japanese Competition in Color Television," in J. Zysman and L. Tyson, eds., *American Industry in International Competition, Government Policies and Corporate Strategies* (Ithaca: Cornell University Press, 1983), 138. Also M. Radnor, et al., "The U.S. Consumer Electronics Industry and Foreign Competition" (Washington, D.C.: U.S. Department of Commerce/Economic Development Administration, May 1980).
2. For a summary, see Organization for Economic Cooperation and Development, Special Group of the Economic Policy Committee on Positive Adjustment Policies, "Positive Adjustment Policies Final Report," mimeo (Paris, 1982).
3. See Ministry of International Trade and Industry, "The Vision of MITI Policies in the 1980s" (Tokyo, MITI, March 1980). Also, C. Johnson, *MITI and the Japanese Miracle* (Stanford: Stanford University Press, 1982); and G. C. Allen, *The Japanese Economy* (London: Weidenfeld and Nicolson, 1981).
4. For an example, that of the semiconductor industry, see James M. Utterback and A. E. Murray, "The Influence of Defense Procurement and Sponsorship of Research and Development on the Development of the Civilian Electronics Industry" (Cambridge, Mass.: MIT Center for Policy Alternatives, CPA 77-5, June 30, 1977).
5. See, for instance, the influential study in France: Groupe d'Etudes Prospectives Internationales, *Croissance Mondiale et Stratégies de Spécialisation* (Paris: Centre Français du Commerce Extérieur, 1976).
6. See R. Vernon, "Storm over the Multinationals" (Cambridge, Mass.: Harvard University Press, 1977); also Detlev F. Vagts, "The Host Country Faces the Multinational Enterprise," *Boston University Law Review* 53, no. 2 (March 1973): 261–77.
7. See R. A. Caves, "Causes of Direct Investment: Foreign Firms' Shares in Canadian and United Kingdom Manufacturing Industries," *Review of Economics and Statistics* 56 (August 1974): 273–93; and R. A. Caves, "Multinational Firms, Competition and Productivity in Host Country Industries," *Economica* 41 (May 1974): 176–93.
8. For some evidence on this, see R. Stobaugh et al., *Nine Investments Abroad and Their Impact at Home* (Cambridge, Mass.: Harvard University Press, 1976).
9. See N. Owen, "Scale Economies in the EEC: An Approach Based on Intra EEC Trade," *European Economic Review* no. 7 (February 1976): 143–63. See also N. Hood and S. Young, *European Development Strategies of U.S.-Owned Manufacturing Companies Located in Scotland* (Edinburgh: Her Majesty's Stationery Office, 1980).
10. See B. D. Wilson, "Foreign Divestment in the Multinational Investment Cycle," *Multinational Business* no. 2 (1978).
11. See W. Warren, *Imperialism: Pioneer of Capitalism* (London: NLB & Verso Editions, 1980), chap. 7 in particular; and A. Fishlow et al., *Rich*

and Poor Nations in the World Economy (Washington, D.C.: Council of Foreign Relations, 1978).

12. See J. N. Behrman and W. A. Fischer, "The Coordination of Foreign R & D Activities by Transnational Corporations," *Journal of International Business Studies* 10, no. 3 (Winter 1979): 28–35.

13. See Y. L. Doz, "Strategic Management in Multinational Companies," *Sloan Management Review* 21, no. 2 (Winter 1980); and Y. L. Doz, *Strategic Management in Multinational Companies*, chap. 7 (Oxford: Pergamon Press, 1985).

14. See Y. L. Doz, "Ford in Spain (A)," Harvard Business School Case Services, 4-380-091, 1979.

15. See N. Fagre and L. T. Wells, Jr., "Bargaining Power of Multinationals and Host Governments," *Journal of International Business Studies* 13, no. 2 (Fall 1982): 9–24.

16. G. Hamel and C. K. Prahalad, "Creating Global Strategic Capability," in N. Hood, D. Schendel, and J.-E. Vahlne, eds., *Strategies in Global Competition* (forthcoming).

17. D. Morris, research in progress, at INSEAD.

18. See S. Young and N. Hood, *Dynamic Aspects of U.S. Multinational Operations in Europe* (Farnborough: Saxon House, 1981).

19. See Y. Doz, "Managing Manufacturing Rationalization," *Columbia Journal of World Business* 13, no. 3 (Fall 1976).

20. See J. Rojot, *International Collective Bargaining* (Deventer, N.L.: Kluwer, 1978).

21. See J. Zysman, *Political Strategies for Industrial Order: The French Electronics Industry Between the Market and the State* (Berkeley: University of California Press, 1976).

22. G. Hamel and C. K. Prahalad, "Do you really have a global strategy?" *Harvard Business Review* 63, no. 4 (July–August 1985); and G. Hamel and C. K. Prahalad, "Creating Global Strategic Capability," in Hood, Schendel, and Vahlne, eds., *Strategies in Global Competition*.

23. See I. C. Magaziner and T. M. Hout, *Japanese Industrial Policy* (London: Policy Study Institute, 1980).

24. See E. Sakakibara, R. Feldman, and Y. Horada, "Japanese Financial System in Comparative Perspective" (Harvard University, Center for International Affairs, Working Paper, 1980). See also J. Monson and K. D. Walter, *Nationalized Companies: A Threat to American Business* (New York: McGraw-Hill, 1983).

25. See C.-A. Michalet and M. Delapierre, "Impact of Multinational Enterprises on National Scientific and Technical Capacities: Computer and Data Processing Industries" (Paris: OECD, 1977); and "European Aerospace Industry: Competitiveness and Market Share," *Interavia* no. 6 (1977): 587–94.

26. See S. Guysinger et al., "Investment Incentives and Performance Requirements," unpublished monograph, World Bank, 1984.

27. See Doz, "Strategic Management."

28. Guysinger et al., "Investment Incentives"; and Fagre and Wells, "Bargaining Power."

29. See L. T. Wells, "Social Cost-Benefit Analysis for MNCs," in *Harvard Business Review* 53, no. 2 (March–April 1975) 40–50.

30. See L. T. Wells, "Negotiating with Third World Governments," *Harvard Business Review* 55, no. 1 (January–February 1977): 72–80.

31. J. Dunning, *Multinational Enterprises, Economic Structures and International Competitiveness* (New York: John Wiley & Sons, 1985).

32. Doz, "Strategic Management;" and Doz, *Strategic Management*.
33. See Y. L. Doz, et al., "Competition in the European Information Technology Industry: The Role of the Foreign Multinationals," discussion paper, INSEAD, 1984.
34. See Y. L. Doz, "International Industries, Multinational Companies and Host Government Control: A Framework," in Walter H. Goldberg, ed., *Governments and Multinationals: The Policy of Control Versus Autonomy* (Cambridge, Mass.: Oelgeschlager, Gunn & Hain, 1983); and Doz, "Strategic Management."
35. See C. A. Bartlett, Y. L. Doz, and C. K. Prahalad, "Global Competitive Pressures vs. Host Country Demands: Managing Tensions in Multinational Corporations," *California Management Review* 23, no. 3 (Spring 1981).
36. Doz, *Strategic Management*.
37. See Y. L. Doz and C. K. Prahalad, *The Work of Top Management* (New York: Free Press; C. Bartlett and S. Ghoshal, "Tap Your Subsidiaries for Global Research," *Harvard Business Review* (November–December 1986).
38. See Doz, Bartlett, and Prahalad, "Global Competitive Pressures vs. Host Country Demands. See also Y. Doz and C. K. Prahalad, "Patterns of Strategic Control in MNCs," *Journal of International Business Studies* 15, no. 2 (Fall 1984). Also see, Y. L. Doz and C. K. Prahalad, "Quality of Management: An Emerging Source of Global Competitive Advantage?," in N. Hood et al., eds., *Strategies in Global Competition* (forthcoming).

8

Competitive Strategies in Global Industries: A View from Host Governments

Dennis J. Encarnation
and
Louis T. Wells, Jr.

During the summer of 1978, no fewer than a dozen government agencies visited a single Cupertino, California, computer manufacturer. The agencies hailed from three continents. Singapore's Economic Development Board and Taiwan's Foreign Investment Board stood out among the Asian representatives. From Europe, principal promoters included the Irish Development Authority and the Scottish Development Agency. Even North America was represented: the Puerto Rican Investment Council arrived shortly after the Massachusetts Development Board. The objectives of all of these agencies were the same: to get the management of Apple Computer to consider a new plant location in their jurisdictions. The job of these contenders would not be easy. Apple's management was not actively considering expanding to a new site. Yet three years later Apple had established two new plants: one in Ireland, the other in Singapore.

As this illustration suggests, corporations are not alone in devising competitive strategies in global industries. Indeed, competition among governments for foreign investment involves strategies that are as complex as those adopted by private firms. Whether the contest pits California against Massachusetts, Scotland against Ireland, Singapore against Taiwan, the story remains the same: numerous governments on all continents are actively vying to attract foreign investors who serve their development objectives. In a study surveying seventy-four foreign manufacturing investments on four continents, for

This paper has benefited from comments by Christopher Bartlett, Michael Porter, and other participants in seminars preceding the Colloquium.

example, Guisinger and associates found that over two-thirds received government incentives that, according to business managers, directly influenced their location decisions.[1]

For both multidomestic and global enterprises, these government incentives can be lucrative. To illustrate, a financial executive from a European multinational that operated in over sixty countries reckoned that the share of his group's total investment accounted for by grants and other investment incentives had doubled in value over the five years through 1982, from 2 to 4 percent.[2] For specific projects, the impact can be far greater. Baldwin (chap. 6 of this book), for example, shows that auto-manufacturing plants are among the most sought-after investments, with incentives ranging in value from $50 million to upward of $150 million.

Such inducements, however, are often accompanied by constraints that national governments place on domestic and global decision making. Limits on ownership in local subsidiaries, rules on how much they must export or buy locally, whom they must employ, and how they must finance their operations apply almost everywhere. These so-called performance requirements can impose significant costs on a firm facing global markets, as governments try to ensure that the firm provides desired benefits to the host country.

Potential benefits, generating employment, increasing foreign exchange earnings, building national champions, and other development objectives are typically cited by governments as reasons to seek foreign investment. To these ends, governments have tried to diversify their sources of investment. They have increasingly substituted foreign commercial debt for direct investment. Even among direct investors, gone are the days when Latin America was the territory of only North American firms; European and Japanese multinationals are interested and can be attracted. Similarly, ex-colonies that once looked to Britain or France for investment now look elsewhere as well, both because firms' horizons have broadened, and because the countries want to loosen their dependence on one or two sources of funds and know-how.

But during this decade, patterns of foreign investment have been changing. Foreign commercial lending to most developing countries has no longer been available to cover shortfalls in domestic savings. To make matters worse, the flow of new foreign direct investment has also begun to fall off. Not only have growth rates in total stock declined, but much of the new investment made by multinationals during the 1970s came from retained earnings. In other words, supplies of new foreign direct investment and its potential substitutes have diminished, while demand has at least remained constant—and probably intensified. Given these conditions, the specter of "foreign investment wars" looms ever larger.[3] Governments try to outbid their "competitors" with packages of investment incentives and other inducements that have important implications for multinational investors as well as host governments.[4]

For these governments, increased competition for foreign investments may impose huge costs.[5] Incentives offered may exceed the minimum necessary to attract foreign firms, for example, or may even exceed the social (economic) benefits generated by the project. On the other hand, the incentives offered may be too small to attract the desired investment. Or the time consumed by long negotiations with government agencies to secure those incentives may repel attractive investors.[6] In short, host governments face strong pressures to devise appropriate competitive strategies—as well as structures to carry out these strategies. But, first, governments must identify the "market" in which they compete.

THE MARKET FOR GLOBAL INVESTMENTS

Although no formal "market" for foreign investment exists, governments behave as if there were one, analogous in many ways to a product market.[7] Just as producers compete for market shares of consumer expenditures, so too countries compete for market shares of new foreign investment ventures. Consistent with this analogy, firms seeking a plant location abroad can be characterized as "buyers," while countries and other jurisdictions (e.g., American states) that are possible sites for the investment assume the role of "sellers." In short, the market for foreign investment has many of the same characteristics as product markets.

Many observers of this market for foreign investment have characterized it as a bilateral oligopoly and, therefore, have concentrated their attention on the relative bargaining power of "buyers" and "sellers." Research on the outcomes of international business negotiations has contributed much to our understanding of this nexus. Generally, a foreign firm's bargaining power relative to the host government is likely to increase if the enterprise is in a global industry, and

- exports a large part of its output and is able to control the market downstream from the production site;[8] and
- utilizes factors of production (e.g., unskilled labor) that are easily substitutable across countries.[9]

Such bargaining power is not limited to global industries, but may also be shared by a firm in a multidomestic industry if that firm

- occupies a monopolistic or dominant oligopolistic position in its industry;[10]
- utilizes a relatively "high" technology in its operations or requires large capital outlays, all with few substitute sources;[11]

- produces highly differentiated products that require large marketing or research and development expenditures;[12] and
- does not require large capital investments that once in place are difficult to liquidate or move.[13]

Similarly, a government's bargaining power is a function of the extent to which it can control through regulations and its own enterprises access to product markets, investment finance, and production technology.[14] Governments typically control access to the domestic market, and try to generate, both internally and externally, alternative sources of finance (e.g., domestic savings, foreign commercial loans) and technology (e.g., licensing agreements, indigenous technology).

Control over access to product markets is so important in determining bargaining power that differences in the final destination of a project's output create three distinct segments in the competition for foreign investment. That is, the relative bargaining power of a country and a corporation depends upon whether the proposed investment is (1) principally oriented toward a large domestic market in a single host country, as part of an investor's multidomestic strategy; (2) principally global, oriented toward the worldwide export market; or (3) some combination of the two, like investments oriented toward a common market.

For example, governments such as India and Mexico with large home markets are able to exercise some monopoly power by limiting foreign access through trade or investment. The foreign firm that wants to supply that market typically cannot do so by locating in another jurisdiction. By contrast, governments in Singapore and elsewhere without a domestic market of significant size face high entry barriers if they enter into competition for domestic-oriented investments. The hold over a large domestic market gives a host government a monopsony position that is similar to that held by a government if it controls desirable raw materials that are in very limited supply.[15]

Competition among governments for investments that supply a domestic market is significantly different from competition for export-oriented investments in global industries. In the latter, the competitive position of a government is strongly influenced by its factor endowments, and by its ability to differentiate the country's endowments from those of its competitors. For example, a jurisdiction with high labor costs will find that these serve as significant barriers if it tries to enter the market for export-oriented manufacturing investment. The large number of low-wage countries worldwide assures vigorous competition for this type of investment.

Barriers to entry encountered by countries that are in free trade areas such as the European Common Market are more complicated. Individual governments have limited control over access to their own product markets because trade within the regional market is supposed to be unrestricted. Investors can go to other member countries and supply the entire free trade area, or selected markets in that area. A government's rivals, however, are limited to other member governments if barriers to foreign trade are high enough to prevent imports.

In summary, investments designed to service multidomestic, global, and common markets are so different that governments behave as if they were three distinct market segments.[16] Because the structure of each segment differs substantially from the others, the intensity of competition among governments—and the competitive strategies of these governments—vary widely according to the segment they find most attractive.

COMPETITIVE STRATEGIES OF HOST GOVERNMENTS

Competition among governments in the market for foreign investment is analogous, we have argued, to competition among producers for market share. Just as corporations formulate and implement strategies designed to gain a relative advantage over competitors, governments adopt strategies to attract politically valued or socially profitable foreign investment projects. As in product markets, some "buyers" (foreign investors) are very sensitive to "price"; others, to the distinctive features of the "product" (the investment site).

Pricing Plant Locations

By offering cash grants, tax holidays, tariff protection, and other inducements, countries engage in "price" competition designed to increase their share of the available supply of foreign investment. These inducements are often designed to offset and exceed the potential costs associated with a variety of performance requirements. In fact, the analogue of price in product markets is the total incentive offered by government, reduced by the value of all government-induced disincentives. Financial incentives are given to encourage behavior whose social profitability or political value is positive, but where private profitability relative to other investment sites is inadequate to induce investment. For the investor, such incentives can reduce the effective cost of new capital projects and thus greatly increase the leverage of the global corporation's limited capital pool (see Baldwin, chap. 6 of this book). For the host country, these incentives can increase the country's market share of new foreign investment.

Seeking to attract firms sensitive to price, Singapore exemplifies a country that has adopted an aggressive pricing strategy, stating frankly its intention to meet any competitive offer for investments that greatly aid its export performance. This was certainly Singapore's strategy in the computer industry, where Apple was a principal beneficiary. It was also true in petrochemicals, where the government actively courted a reluctant Sumitomo Chemicals, beginning in the late 1970s. Singapore invariably practiced price discrimination, giving different net incentives to different firms. The government targeted incentives selectively to priority industries such as computers, and to specific firms like Apple within those industries. The incentive package offered to Apple was relatively straightforward. Although large in value, the incentives that made up the package were few, their mechanics were simple, and many were automatic. Even those incentives whose levels were negotiated rather than automatic were largely based on simple and known criteria. Singapore was not alone in adopting this strategy. A similarly aggressive, discriminating, simple, and predictable pricing strategy was adopted in Ireland. In both countries, investments in export-oriented global industries were the principal targets.

Aggressive pricing strategies were not limited to such export-oriented firms. Foreign investors entering the U.S. market, for example, encountered American states and localities eager to influence their final choice of a plant site.[17] Here, competition proved intense, especially because Ohio and other industrialized states of the Northeast and Midwest looked to foreign investment as one way to defeat economic stagnation. And throughout the country, every community wanted more jobs, stirring up even more competition.

Ohio, for example, beat out several contenders by offering Honda in 1981 an incentive package that included a $2.5 million grant to develop a local site; a $90 thousand reduction in annual property taxes; designation of the site as a foreign trade subzone with reduced duties; a guarantee that the federal government would make railroad improvements valued at $300 thousand; free English tutoring for Japanese expatriates and their children at a nearby state university. At roughly the same time, Ohio's neighbor and competitor, Tennessee, proposed a comparable incentive package to Honda's rival, Nissan. Among many inducements, Tennessee spent $12 million for new roads to the Nissan plant, and $7 million to help train workers, while the county government reduced property taxes by another $1 million over the first five years of the project. Just a few years earlier, Pennsylvania had offered Volkswagen an incentive package valued by Baldwin (chap. 6 of this book) at over $50 million. In all, these states, like other governments in the United States and elsewhere, tailored a package of incentives to the needs of each investor.

In marked contrast to the aggressive behavior of some American states—not to mention Singapore and Ireland—other governments followed more passive pricing strategies. Consider, for example, Indonesia. While the government ostensibly targeted incentives to priority industries, within an industry there was seemingly no discrimination among firms in terms of incentives to attract a particular investor. Striking was the very large number and variety of incentives and restrictions that were potentially available to foreign investors. In government negotiations with Toyota and Nissan over domestic automobile production, Indonesia, for example, altered the net benefit to the investor, using varying combinations of incentives that were linked to performance requirements stipulating local content and local ownership. Because the Indonesians are principally seeking domestic-oriented investment for their large market, they usually face no direct competition from other host countries for these investments. Still, they feel compelled not to pursue a strategy totally independent from their neighbors.

There is considerable evidence concerning the impact of price competition on the location decisions of foreign firms.[18] The general conclusion is that such competition among countries does little to increase the overall supply of investment, although it may increase the share held by a particularly aggressive government. Tariff and tariff-equivalent trade barriers are particularly effective in the location of investments designed to service a domestic or common market. On the other hand, for these investments, tax and other incentives may influence the final location within a national or regional market, but not the prior decision to enter that market. By contrast, for export-oriented investments, especially investments characterized by mobile factors of production, tax and other incentives may be more effective in determining the initial choice of location sites.

One response of governments to what appears to be counterproductive price competition is to negotiate an understanding with competing governments to refrain from price competition. Within the European Community (EC), for example, agreements exist on the maximum "grant equivalent" that may be offered to attract investors. Similarly, the Andean Group has set bounds on offers to investors. Agreements among countries seeking to limit competition for foreign investment are, however, particularly difficult to reach and to enforce. Even in the face of explicit agreements among countries to limit competition, as in the EC, segments of the market remain intensely competitive because of the relative magnitude of the stakes. Moreover, the number of potential tools is so great that agreements are usually quickly undermined.

Only the Japanese have been relatively successful in curbing price competition. The Japanese central government long considered competitive bidding among prefectures for investment to be counterproductive, and negotiated an implicit understanding with potentially competing prefectural governments to refrain from competition—in marked contrast to the policy of benign neglect practiced by the U.S. federal government in relation to American states.[19] To promote accord, the Japanese government exercised further control over the incentive packages offered by the prefectures. Again, in contrast to American states, these packages—while large in value—were few in number, and their mechanics were well understood. Within each of the regional development authorities, the central government dispatched personnel on two-year assignments, ostensibly to aid the investment promotion process. Those personnel helped coordinate policy nationwide, as did special loans to foreigners available from central government institutions. A supplementary goal was the subsequent curtailment of competition.

Differentiation

Bidding with financial incentives has not been the only competitive strategy employed by governments. Indeed, governments often try to avoid the costs of price competition, and have been successful in attracting investors for whom such incentives are less important. Moreover, they have sought investors by creating images of attractive business climates—a strategy that parallels efforts used by private firms to differentiate their products from those of their competitors. For example, governments have introduced industrial parks and export processing zones to appeal to a narrow segment of global investors. They also market possible location sites through media advertisements, promotional and "sales" offices, and overseas missions sent in search of new investors.

Occasionally, such differentiation substitutes for bidding, as in the case of Japan. The "Technopolis" program, for example, has allowed certain regional governments to target investment in high-technology industries (the computer industry, for example) while at the same time drawing attention to that region's peculiar advantages. In addition, rural prefectures helped foreigners to get loans from local banks, secure land, and qualify for central government licenses. Still, differentiation among prefectures was limited. Instead, agencies of the central government coordinated impartially much of the direct "marketing" of investment sites available in the country, and reported available incentives. So, in Japan, differentiation—like bidding—was constrained.

More frequently, governments try various combinations of pricing and differentiation to achieve the investments they desire. Singapore, already known for its aggressive pricing strategy, devoted even more effort to differentiating itself from the other newly industrialized countries of East Asia. The Economic Development Board (EDB) was viewed by many observers as the "marketing arm" of the Singapore government. Its agents not only granted incentives, but also conducted careful marketing operations. Domestic marketing efforts were supplemented by offices in Europe, Japan, and North America that were tightly integrated with the home office. EDB's internal incentive structures were consistent with its marketing orientation: "performance evaluations" were used by EDB directors to reward personnel for their success in attracting target amounts of investment in selected sectors. In addition to Singapore, Ireland and several American states combined aggressive pricing and differentiation.

Elements of price competition and differentiation were also inextricably intertwined in certain enclaves of national economies—notably the export processing zones of developing countries. In India, Mexico, and elsewhere, the strategies pursued by the export processing zone authorities were not characteristic of the strategies their governments adopted toward foreign investment as a whole. The distinguishing strategic feature of these export zones is their packaging of financial incentives with government investments in infrastructure. Recognizing the possible advantages of packaging incentives aggressively, at least for a narrow subset of investment proposals, other countries have imitated their potential rivals. For example, Indonesia's current proposal to establish a large zone trails by several years the establishment of export zones in other ASEAN member states. By 1982, there were eight export zones in the Philippines, and four each in Malaysia and Thailand. Singapore could even be considered to be one large zone.

Outside of export zones, most governments—especially those in developing countries—feel more ambivalent about their dual roles as regulator and promoter of foreign investment. Indonesia's coordinating board, for example, devoted little of its resources to investment promotion. Screening projects appeared to be its principal function, evidenced by its long application form and lengthy approval procedures. In India, a comparable tension between regulation and promotion resulted in the establishment of a separate promotion board operating parallel to the existing regulatory structures. This separation of marketing from negotiations stood in marked contrast to Singapore. Even when efforts were made to integrate regulation and promotion in a single body, as in the Philippines, the results were considerably less concerted and coordinated than in Singapore.

Finally, in the market for foreign investment, another form of differentiation includes a country's efforts to "service" investors during negotiations and afterward. Consider, for example, policy implementation. The way a government implements the terms of a contract is central to a firm's prior evaluation of investment opportunities and to the government's success in competing for foreign investment. The failure of some government agencies to provide adequate service by honoring contractual arrangements leads investors to believe that the terms as negotiated are not likely to be implemented fully once the firm begins operations.

Central to this perception are organizational considerations. The agencies that implement government decisions are often different from the agencies that negotiate prior to investment, especially in developing countries. Nowhere is the disjuncture between negotiations and implementation more apparent than in India, Mexico, or Indonesia—large countries where diffused authority extends the number of potential agencies involved in decision making. In India, for example, no fewer than forty administrative departments in upward of twenty-six central government enterprises could be involved in either negotiations, or implementation, or both. Such involvement makes use of the expertise—and accommodates the political interests—found in various government agencies charged with performing different functions. Not surprisingly, policies that govern the initial entry of a firm can differ from those that govern the implementation of agreements that have been concluded. In sharp contrast to India is a small country like Singapore, where there is virtually no difference between policies negotiated and implemented. To guarantee these results, the EDB is empowered not only to negotiate policy but also to monitor and facilitate the implementation of policy through contact with relevant ministries. Most other countries lie between these two extremes.

COMPETITIVE STRUCTURES OF HOST GOVERNMENTS

Whether for promotion, screening, or implementation, governments must not only design strategies for attracting and shaping the actions of foreign investors. Governments must, in addition, establish institutional arrangements and management practices to carry out these strategies. The structures chosen by a host government to deal with foreign firms are themselves a part of that government's strategy in the competitive market for foreign investment. To differentiate their countries, for example, governments may create "one-stop" investment boards and other institutional arrangements to improve "customer service" at various stages of the investor's operations, from entry negotiations to the actual implementation of the terms negotiated. Yet, like firms investing overseas (see Mahini and Wells, chap. 9 of this book), governments find these organizational tasks to be particularly perplexing.

First, policy makers must decide how centralized to make the negotiating process. There are a number of possibilities, and each has its advantages and disadvantages. Some government organizations, for example, that might be particularly effective in negotiating with investors for the most favorable terms and in screening unattractive proposals are likely to discourage would-be investors. As we saw earlier, few countries have established a single organization that was effective both in screening out "bad" proposals and in promoting foreign investment.

In a study of the organizations used by government to promote investment, evaluate proposals, and negotiate with foreigners, we found considerable variation across countries, across industries, and over time in the organizational choices of governments.[20] The same country was likely to use different approaches for different industries at any one time; its approach for the same industry also could change over time; and different countries could adopt similar approaches to deal with investors in the same industries. These patterns of choice were not random, but were influenced primarily by three identifiable variables. The choices reflected, first, a country's general development strategy and the role of foreign investment in that strategy; second, the salience of a particular industry in the development plans of that country; and, third, the degree of competition that the country faced in attracting particular kinds of investors.

Approaches to Promoting, Screening, and Negotiation

In our in-depth study of four countries (plus a quick review of several others), we observed four basic ways of handling the tasks of promoting foreign investment, screening subsequent foreign investment proposals, and negotiating the terms under which projects would be accepted.

The first option, an unusual one for most countries, was a "policy approach." Countries following this approach did not, in fact, conduct individual negotiations with investors over important issues. Rather, they had determined in advance general policies that specified, at least for the majority of investors, the industries in which they would be accepted or excluded, and the terms under which they could operate. Such policies might be lenient toward foreign investment, excluding few potential projects, or they might be very restrictive, virtually closing the country to foreign investment. Hong Kong and the U.S. Federal government illustrate the first type; Burma and Albania are examples of the second. Moreover, in a few other countries, for example, Singapore, a policy of nonnegotiation is offered to all foreign investors who do not seek host-country incentives.

Among the benefits of nonnegotiation is the greater predictability of the process and outcome for both government and investor, compared to the inevitably more ambiguous negotiations associated with selective policies. Such predictability may be reflected in the standardization of terms, in the reduction of time consumed, and in the agencies involved in the negotiation. Consequently, the potential costs for the firm considering entry are likely to be low. But, in the presence of price distortions resulting from tariffs, subsidies, and limited competition, a very "open door" policy of nonnegotiation will result in the entry of projects that are not socially profitable—that is, projects that use local resources in ways that yielded less goods and services for the host country than those resources cost the country.[21]

Equally problematic, a government's fear of these social costs may generate simple exclusionary rules that keep out many investments that would be beneficial to the country. Short of adopting simple rules that either promote or discourage investment indiscriminately, project-by-project screening may be necessary if the host country is to extract all the potential social benefits from each prospective investment. Such screening, however, is a second-best solution, but one that is easier to implement than eliminating those subsidies that reduce social rates of return.

Once a government adopts public policies that require negotiations with prospective foreign investors, its subsequent approach to negotiating with these investors is likely to fall on a continuum that has a decentralized approach at one extreme, and a centralized one at the other. Under a decentralized regime, a foreign investor typically must conduct a series of difficult negotiations dispersed across several ministries, agencies, and enterprises whose operations and interests would be affected by the investment—for example, the ministries of industry, trade, and finance, the central bank, and perhaps a state enterprise in the sector. Virtually all countries adopted this approach at some point in their histories, and for many—especially India, Mexico, and other developing countries—it still continues in some industries.

On the other extreme, authority to negotiate with an investor is concentrated in one organization that has the full authority to accept or reject an applicant, and to conclude the terms that will govern the investor's sojourn in the country. Along the continuum between centralized and decentralized structures lie various coordinating mechanisms. All of these structures offer quite different advantages and disadvantages to the host country (see Table 8.1).

Advantages and Disadvantages

A decentralized approach, for example, is attractive for several reasons. First, enterprises can muster the technical expertise necessary to evaluate proposals for a specific industry. Tax expertise is likely to be concentrated in the finance ministry; knowledge of labor laws and issues, in the labor ministry; technical skills for the relevant industry, in the ministry of industries; and so on. Second, these units of government are likely to be the same agencies that will eventually have to administer the terms of any agreements that might be reached. Having these agencies conduct the relevant part of the negotiations is likely to generate terms that can be effectively administered with available resources. Further, if the administrators are the negotiators, there is a reasonable chance for learning from past successes and mistakes. Indeed, when the same people are regularly assigned to foreign investment negotiations, technical skills and, in some cases, longevity

Table 8.1. Strengths and Weaknesses of Patterns and Structures of Decision Making

Patterns and Structures of Decision Making	Strengths/Benefits	Weaknesses/Costs
A. Abstention: no structures or procedures	a. Predictability for investors b. No administrative costs c. Speed of response	a. Unrestricted entry: entry of firms inconsistent with national interest b. Autarchy: excludes socially beneficial investments

B. Decentralization
  1. Government functional agencies
  2. State-owned enterprises
	a. Can muster technical expertise for specific industry
	b. Results in high organizational learning on part of government
	c. Agencies that negotiate often same that implement policies
		a. Little evaluation of overall net benefits: focus on technical feasibility
		b. Little consideration of larger policy issues
		c. Little consideration of impact of decisions on other investors
		d. Little promotion of national investment opportunities
		e. High negotiating costs to investors
		f. Disjuncture between policy as negotiated and policy as implemented because implementers are multiple

C. Coordination
  1. Permanent interagency board
  2. Ad hoc interagency committee
	a. Both: reduce investor's negotiating costs
	b. Both: reduce interministerial conflict
	c. Both: improve monitoring of international environment
	d. Permanent: considers larger policy issues and issues' impact on other investors
	e. Permanent: greater promotion of investment opportunities
	f. Ad hoc: masters industry expertise
		a. Permanent: little in-depth industry knowledge
		b. Permanent: disjuncture between policy as negotiated and policy as implemented because implementation occurs outside the new structure
		c. Ad hoc: little organizational learning
		d. Ad hoc: little consideration of impact on other investors or larger policy issues
		e. Ad hoc: little promotion of investment opportunities

D. Delegation
  1. Industry-specific agencies and state-owned enterprises
  2. Broadly defined development authorities
	a. Both: reduce investor's negotiating costs
	b. Both: policy negotiated is policy implemented
	c. Both: greater promotion of investment and greater scanning of environment
	d. Both: improved organizational learning
	e. Broad authority: consider larger policy issues and impact on other investors
		a. Industry agency: larger policy issues and impact on other investors ignored
		b. Broad authority: little in-depth industry knowledge
		c. Broad authority: loss of personnel to industry
		d. Both: ignore interests of other agencies and their constituencies

SOURCE: D. J. Encarnation and L. T. Wells, Jr., "Sovereignty en Garde: Negotiating with Foreign Investors," *International Organization* 39 (Winter 1985): 76–77.

of employment enable such specialized units to learn and retain lessons that may enhance the government's negotiating skills in the future.

At the same time, a decentralized approach may cause serious problems. First, the involved agencies and ministries are likely to have little technical knowledge or limited experience with the industry or with foreign investors generally. They may insist on performance requirements (e.g., minimum exports, local content) that repel an otherwise desirable investor, for example, without even caring about or understanding the full implications of their demands. Second, diffuse units operating autonomously also have little ability to evaluate overall net benefits in light of larger policy issues. For example, a ministry of labor is likely to support a project for the employment it generates whatever the cost in terms of foreign exchange, foregone tax revenues, or plant efficiency. As a consqunce, too little or too much may be offered to the potential investor. Moreover, an individual government unit has no incentive or mechanism to consider the wider implications of its actions on potential foreign investors in other industries. As a result, inappropriate precedents may be established.

Finally, a decentralized approach is likely to be costly to the foreign investor. The period of negotiation tends to be longer and the results unpredictable at the outset. The potential investor with only marginal interests will probably go elsewhere. In fact, the pool of investors applying to a country with a decentralized process might well be less than for a similar country that is quicker and promises more predictable outcomes for the investor. In the countries that we studied, it was the effect on investors that led governments to abandon the decentralized process for a more centralized approach. The organizational change was part of each country's overall strategy to attract foreign investors.

Centralized bodies are of two distinct types, each with its own particular benefits and disadvantages. Both have a common objective to reduce the high costs to potential foreign investors otherwise associted with decentralized negotiations.

One type of centralized body can be found in Ireland, Singapore, and a few other countries that have concentrated in one autonomous body negotiations with the vast majority of foreign investors. This approach directly addresses the problem of greatest concern to most countries that abandoned a decentralized approach in an effort to please would-be investors: quick negotiations and predictable patterns of outcomes. It also offers other advantages. An autonomous body that covers a wide range of negotiations can consider the overall impact of a project on the country, and it can weigh the total package of incentives and performance requirements to determine what is required to attract a desired investor. Moreover, it is very likely to consider carefully issues of precedent in its negotiations and decisions.

Still, such a centralized body has its problems. It leads to a separation of negotiation from implementation. Implementation usually remains the problem of the relevant technical ministries. The distance between negotiator and administrator can lead to terms that may well be difficult to administer. Moreover, broad autonomous units pose one additional problem. The breadth of the task assigned to such an agency almost assures that it will not have in-depth expertise in industry-specific issues.

To overcome this latter problem, governments have established a separate type of centralized body with specialized expertise, a body that covers only a single industry or a single type of investment. For example, oil agreements might be negotiated by a particular state enterprise, as in Indonesia or Mexico. Or agreements with potential exporters might be the sole responsibility of an export-processing zone authority, as in the Philippines or India. Like the autonomous unit with authority for a wide range of industries, this more specialized agency was also likely to conduct quick and reasonably predictable negotiations. But, unlike its more broadly defined counterpart, industry-specific organizations rarely took into account the impacts of their agreements on the other investment negotiations outside of their area of authority. This created problems. State oil companies, for example, were unlikely to worry about the impact that the terms of their petroleum agreements had on discussions with mining or manufacturing firms. Moreover, the single-industry organization was likely to ignore other larger policy issues, including the net national benefit of the investment.

Finally, both types of centralized organizations also imposed a major political cost on the host country. Establishing such organizations required the government to "disenfranchise" agencies that expressed interest in the outcome of negotiations and sought to participate. Centralization meant, for example, that tax matters were decided outside the ministry of finance; foreign exchange issues, outside the central bank; and so on. It was this reason that made broad-based, autonomous agencies for foreign investment so unusual, except in a few small countries or in selected industries. Governments were not willing to incur the political costs of centralization without strong reason.

Unwilling to incur such costs, and displeased with the operation of decentralized approaches, many countries have tried to combine some of the advantages of each. In particular, they have attempted to coordinate the activities of various government agencies involved earlier in a decentralized negotiation process. They do this without going to the extremes of centralization.

This intermediate step of coordinating government screening and negotiation also took at least two forms. Most common was the investment coordinating board, which was run jointly by a number of ministries whose interests were typically affected by foreign investment. Virtually every developing country has one, from India to Mexico, Philippines to Peru, Liberia to Indonesia. Like other organizational responses to foreign investment, coordinating boards have had their advantages and disadvantages as well. Unlike industry-specific bodies, however, they did provide a mechanism for examining the overall benefits and costs of proposed projects, and for weighing the total package of incentives and performance requirements. Moreover, coordinating boards considered the precedents that were generated by individual negotiations. Particularly important, they did, when they worked well, reduce the costs of negotiation for the investor.

Rarely, however, did coordinating bodies work as well as intended. First, they typically developed little expertise in particular industries or policy areas. Even worse, powerful ministries often refused to cooperate in the coordination effort. Those ministries might not honor the agreements reached by the coordinating board, or they might slow down the negotiating process by sending low-level personnel—or no one at all—to meetings. Wise investors then learned to negotiate with the separate ministries regardless of the existence of coordinating boards. Those that did depend on the coordinating board found their agreements not honored; the experience of these investors further damaged the investment climate of the host country. Such faults often meant that coordinating boards often failed to accomplish the country's goal of attracting more investment.

In an effort to overcome these weaknesses of interministerial boards, governments sometimes took another approach to coordination. They formed special ad hoc coordinating committees to deal with particular investments. Except for their shorter duration, these project-specific committees were quite similar to the industry-specific centralized bodies noted previously. Politically, these ad hoc bodies sought to minimize through co-optation a ministry's possible effort to sabotage negotiations; administratively, they sought to assemble a special team with in-depth knowledge of the industry involved. Like their centralized counterparts, such committees generally paid little attention to matters of precedent and overall policy; even worse, they could rely little on institutional learning.

Given these several problems with each approach to screening and negotiation, few countries adopted a single approach for all industries. Most established a portfolio of approaches that reflected the various types of investment under consideration. Thus, in the 1970s, Indonesia negotiated with most investors through the BKPM, a coordinating board that represented such ministries as trade, industry, and finance. At the same time, however, a state enterprise, Pertamina, had almost full effective authority to negotiate oil and gas agreements. Simultaneously, negotiations for a large petrochemical project were handled by an ad hoc committee with representation from several government agencies, including Pertamina and the ministry of industries. Moreover, some consideration was being given to the creation of new export processing zones where the authority for negotiation might, like other countries in the region, be centralized in an organization solely responsible for the operation of the zone. Indonesia's experience was not unique; it was replicated in various ways in India and Mexico, for example.

Factors Affecting the Choices

The choices that countries made when they established negotiating structures followed quite regular patterns, influenced by three sets of variables. First, a country's general development strategy and, thereby, its attitude toward foreign investment determined the approach that would govern its negotiations with most would-be investors. Countries that were not eager to attract foreign investment, such as India for much of its history, tended to choose more decentralized approaches. On the other hand, Ireland and other countries that desired more foreign investment tended to establish more centralized organizations; in larger countries, this typically meant some kind of coordinating body. In making its choice, the country had to weigh the political cost incurred by centralizing the negotiation process against the high costs that decentralized processes imposed on would-be investors. Only countries that evidenced a strong desire for more investment were willing to pay the costs of disenfranchising ministries otherwise involved in more decentralized negotiations.

This relationship between strategy and structure was also apparent within a single country. Changes in attitude toward foreign investment frequently preceded changes in a country's screening processes. Indonesia required investors to negotiate with a large number of government agencies in the Sukarno days, when it was particularly suspicious of the supposed benefits from foreign investment. Under the Suharto regime, however, attitudes changed. Eager to attract foreign investment, the government moved toward coordinating the negotiation process. Complaints about the effectiveness of coordinating efforts led to an increase in the role of the coodinating board in the mid-1970s. By the 1980s, the desire to promote exports led to consideration of a centralized, autonomous authority to handle investments entering a proposed export processing zone.

Whatever the choices countries make for negotiating with the majority of investors, they tend to make special arrangements when the industry is particularly important, or "salient"—a second variable influencing the choice of negotiating structures. Such salience may be based on the size of the project (as in petrochemicals), its presumed employment effects (autos), its R & D intensity (computers), and its relationship to basic needs (pharmaceuticals). All are typically global industries. For most of these industries, countries have been unwilling to live with the possibility that a decentralized approach would result in a poor agreement, or none at all. And they have not been willing to live with the lack of industry expertise that typically characterizes a broad coordinating board or investment authority. The most suitable approach for countries facing a particularly salient project has been to vest power to negotiate in a specialized state enterprise, or to create a special ad hoc coordinating committee if no relevant state firm existed. Either approach offered the prospect of speedy negotiations, the possibility of weighing the incentives and performance requirements as a package, and, most important, the potential for bringing to the negotiations a good deal of industry expertise.

There were other special cases when governments decided not to use the negotiating approach that they used for most investors. These special arrangements were generally established when the competition among countries for particular kinds of investors was particularly intense—a third and final set of conditions influencing the choice of negotiating structures. Examples commonly involved export-oriented projects, especially those utilizing factors of production that were easily substitutable across countries. Although a country, especially one with a large domestic market, could attract foreign investors for the local market (i.e., multidomestic firms) by offering protection from import competition, this most effective incentive was not available for firms—typically in global industries—that wanted to set up facilities for export. Such firms could locate their plants in any of a number of countries that offered cheap production resources. In most cases, they needed only inexpensive labor, sufficient infrastructure, and good transportation and communication facilities. Many countries viewed these kinds of investment as attractive, largely because they consistently increased national income, while at the same time they increased foreign exchange earnings.

As a result, the competition for these "footloose" investors was usually quite intense. Fearful of losing the battle for such investors, many countries have centralized in one unit negotiations for such firms. The goal of centralization was to create an organization that could act quickly and decisively, thereby increasing the attractiveness of the country to global investors. Accordingly, in many countries—from Mexico to the Philippines to India—potential investors for export plants have had the option of investing in export processing zones. Not only do these zones offer infrastructure, but they are generally run by an organization that is fully vested with authority to reach agreements quickly.

Even beyond these global industries, governments may also compete for foreign investment in multidomestic industries if they are members of an effective free trade area (e.g., the EC). Firms that are interested in producing for one member country (say, Germany or France) are free to locate elsewhere in the area (say, Ireland or Britain) to supply the larger Common Market. Thus, when deciding on where to locate, many of these multidomestic investors are more mobile than they would be in the absence of the free trade area. A member country is, therefore, in competition with other countries for a much wider range of investors—both global and multidomestic—that may not limit their sales exclusively to the domestic market or to export markets. Rather, those investors may service both markets to varying degrees. Limited evidence from countries in the EC suggests that the degree of competition among members is high, creating pressure to adopt centralized negotiating structures if foreign investment is strongly desired. The Irish Development Authority is the best example of a centralized body in Europe.

CONCLUSIONS

Firms enter a highly competitive market when they look for foreign production sites. Much has been made of the increased competition among companies in the international market. No longer do U.S. firms hold the same sway over the market for investment that they once did. In many cases, European, Japanese, and even third-world multinationals compete with them for the favors of governments. But relatively little has been said about the intense competition among governments for foreign investment. When a firm has something special to offer—capital, technology, or access to controlled foreign markets—numerous governments are eager to attract its investment and to offer a wide range of incentives in exchange.

Like any customer facing competitive sellers, firms can benefit from intense competition among suppliers. Price competition means that governments offer grants or loan guarantees that decrease the costs of foreign investment. Tax incentives may increase the returns to the firm. And protective tariffs can also increase returns and dramatically lower risks. The variety of vehicles for price cutting and the intensity of competition among countries, at least for certain kinds of investments, means that efforts on the part of governments to limit price wars are unlikely to be effective. Ultimately, the would-be investors benefit (see Baldwin, chap. 6 of this book).

Further, efforts by governments to attract investments by differentiating their location sites are also likely to benefit investors. Attempts by governments to maintain images of stability and to make sure that expectations are not spoiled at the implementation stage reduce the risks for the foreign firm. Moves to make the negotiating process quicker and more certain mean that corporate management can save valuable time otherwise wasted from drawn-out negotiations that often lead to unacceptable terms.

For countries, the intense competition may be quite destructive. Price wars are rampant, with little balancing of costs against benefits. None of the countries that we examined was conducting economic (social) cost-benefit analyses of proposed projects. In fact, one of the reasons given by government officials for the lack of economic analysis was the fear that the analysis would drive away would-be investors, so severe was the perception of competition. Yet, data that we collected suggest that governments were offering costly incentives for many projects that were, in fact, likely to be harmful for economic growth.[22]

Still, despite such competition, governments are usually portrayed as impediments to the global operations of multinational firms. With their focus on the national interest, governments try to impose restrictions on the activities of the international manager. Indeed, for many firms, government barriers to imports were the factors that led the multinational enterprise to abandon concentrated production and its accompanying economies in order to manufacture abroad. The first step in response to government restrictions has generally been foreign assembly, with an effort to retain significant production economies in component production. But government policies have often gone farther by requiring that certain components be manufactured locally, or that exports account for a certain portion of the firm's total sales.

When they emphasize import substitution policies, governments limit a firm's ability to choose the cheapest site for manufacturing each of its products to meet its global competitors. But that constraint does not necessarily negate the ability of a firm to follow a global strategy. Some multinational enterprises have based a large part of their world-wide strategy on responding to such policies. Although they sacrifice the gains that might accrue from a policy of integrated manufacturing operations (see Porter, chap. 1 of this book), they are still likely to be able to use know-how from centralized product, production, or advertising development. If host governments continue to provide protection from import competition, the higher costs associated with scattered production facilities are of little consequence to local sales. In the firm's response to such government policies, an important task of management becomes that of assuring the continued pleasure of host governments and, thus, continued protection. Such firms are usually extremely accommodating in their dealings with governments (see Mahini and Wells, chap. 9 of this book), emphasizing their willingness to participate in joint ventures with local partners, to develop local suppliers of inputs, and so on.

But the impact of governments is not always of this restrictive nature. An increasing number of countries have become disenchanted with the high costs associated with import substitution policies. Especially for small countries, such inward-looking policies have meant inefficient use of domestic resources, with limited opportunities for exports from the manufacturing sector. As the penalties of withdrawing the domestic market from efficient global competitors have become clearer, a number of countries have moved toward more open borders, either across the board or through common market arrangements. In so doing, they have slowly moved toward the kind of competition that is increasingly familiar to firms in the global market.

In an effort to gain economies of scale and to obtain associated cost reductions, as well as to earn foreign exchange, governments have had to adopt more outward-looking development policies. These policies include less protection of firms from imports. To continue to attract investment, they search for other incentives to offset the lack of tariff protection. Grants, subsidized loans, tax holidays, free sites, quick negotiations, and other policies supplement their promotional efforts to attract investors to manufacture in their countries at world scale. The intense competition among countries for certain investors means a spread of information that itself encourages global thinking by managers. Apple Computer, with which our chapter started, was induced to become more global in its consideration of plant sites partly because of the actions of such governments.

When governments surrender import protection as a tool for attracting investment, they have given up the most powerful investment incentive that they can offer. Without being able to isolate their markets, they are themselves in increasingly tough global competition for foreign investments, a point that has been made repeatedly in this chapter. To succeed in that competition, they must be responsive to the desires of the firms they wish to attract. Moreover, much like private firms, governments that compete in this open market for investment cannot isolate themselves from their competitors, but must take into account the strategies of other countries that are eager to attract the activities of the same set of enterprises. This worldwide competition among countries has imposed tight limits on the restrictions that governments can impose on those firms that can choose among a range of production sites. For example, requirements for local participation in equity begin to disappear as governments see the opportunities to induce firms to manufacture at world scale and export. Governments can hardly afford policies that are in strong conflict with the strategies that firms in global competition must follow to survive in world markets.

There are clear pitfalls for companies. Managers have tended to view governments as monolithic entities. Our research has shown that they consist of many agencies often with quite different interests with respect to foreign investors. Sometimes governments can resolve their internal differences and negotiate with one voice with foreign investors. In most cases, they cannot.

We have concluded that a particular government, like the multinationals in the previous chapter, has an array of negotiating structures from which to choose. These range from diffuse, through coordinated, to delegated. A large number of investors are handled by a single, common method in a particular country. This approach is determined by the role that foreign investment plays in the country's development strategy. But different approaches are used when an industry is politically salient or when competition for investment is particularly severe.

The wise investor carefully examines the process he or she is likely to face in a particular situation. Experience in one industry in a country is not likely to serve as an accurate guide for another industry. Nor is the investment literature prepared by the host government of much help for the would-be investor. Both lead to misunderstandings. For example, a U.S.-based oil company spent months negotiating with a state enterprise for a contract involving the mining of a hard mineral. The fact that the state firm had no power to reach an agreement was not understood by the investor, who had simply extrapolated from the firm's experience in oil in the same country. In that instance, the state oil firm could conclude agreements. Such misunderstandings cost this U.S. multinational time and money.

Remember the similarity between governments' choices and those of the multinational firms. Both may leave negotiations to individual parts of the organizations; or they may try to coordinate the activities of subunits; or they may assign authority to a particular unit of the organization that is supposed to develop special skills and knowledge and to consider the impact of negotiations on the overall organization.

The manager can understand the factors that influence the choices of governments because they are so similar to those that affect the decisions of firms. If overseas activities are relatively unimportant to firms, or foreign investment plays only a minor role in a country's development strategy, diffuse approaches to negotiations are the likely choice. As foreign investments become more important, attempts to coordinate grow in both kinds of organizations. For the firm, of course, integration of activities in different countries accelerates the process. Further, political salience pushes both types of organizations toward concentrating authority in a single unit to develop skills, capture learning, and reduce squabbling.

NOTES

1. S. Guisinger et al., *Investment Incentives and Performance Requirements* (New York: Praeger, 1985), 49; for an earlier study with comparable findings see G. L. Reuber et al., *Foreign Private Investment in*

Development (Oxford: Oxford University Press for the Organization of Economic Cooperation and Development, 1973), 120–32.

2. *The Economist*, February 19, 1983, 86.
3. C. F. Bergsten, "Coming Foreign Investment Wars," *Foreign Affairs* (October 1974): 135–52.
4. For a good examination of the role of incentives and performance requirements in shaping foreign investment in one global industry, see H. P. Gray and I. Walter, "Investment-Related Trade Distortions in Petro-chemicals," *Journal of World Trade Law* 17, no. 4 (1983): 283–307.
5. With regard to economic costs, the frequency to unattractive investments in LDCs is suggested in Reuber, et al. *Foreign Private Investment*, 17–39, and in S. Lall and P. Streeter, *Foreign Investment, Transnationals and Developing Countries* (Boulder, Colo.: Westview, 1977). For more recent evidence employing social cost/benefit analysis of data covering fifty foreign investment decisions, see D. J. Encarnation and L. T. Wells, Jr., "Evaluating Foreign Investments," in T. H. Moran, ed., *Investing in Development: New Rules for Private Capital?* (Washington, D.C.: Overseas Development Council, May 1986).
6. See S. J. Kobrin, *Managing Political Risk Assessment* (Berkeley: University of California Press, 1982), 109–24.
7. See Guisinger et al., *Investment Incentives*, 1–18.
8. G. Gereffi, "Drug Firms and Dependency in Mexico: The Case of the Steroid Hormone Industry," *International Organization* 32 (Winter 1978): 237–86; N. Fagre and L. T. Wells, Jr., "Bargaining Power of Multinationals and Host Governments," *Journal of International Business Studies* 13 (Fall 1982): 9–23.
9. Reuber et al., *Foreign Private Investment*, 120–32.
10. F. T. Knickerbocker, *Oligopolistic Reaction and Multinational Enterprises* (Boston: Harvard University, Graduate School of Business Administration, 1973), 1–12.
11. J. M. Grieco, "Between Dependence and Autonomy: India's Experience with the International Computer Industry," *International Organization* 36 (Summer 1982): 609–32; Fagre and Wells, "Bargaining Power."
12. Fagre and Wells, "Bargaining Power"; D. J. Encarnation and S. Vachani, "Foreign Ownership: When Hosts Change the Rules," *Harvard Business Review* (September–October 1985): 152–60.
13. T. H. Moran, *Multinational Corporations and the Politics of Dependence: Copper in Chile* (Princeton, N.J.: Princeton University Press, 1974); D. A. Lax and J. K. Sebenius, "Insecure Contracts and Resource Development," *Public Policy* (Fall 1981): 417–36.
14. D. J. Encarnation, *Bargaining in the Uneasy Triangle: A Study of Multinationals, the State, and Local Enterprises in India*, book manuscript, forthcoming, 1987.
15. D. Smith and L. T. Wells, Jr., *Negotiating Third World Mineral Agreements* (Cambridge, Mass.: Ballinger, 1976).
16. Guisinger et al., *Investment Incentives*, 12–17.
17. The following discussion of the competitive strategies of American states and Japanese prefectures is from D. J. Encarnation, "Cross-Investment: A Second Front of Economic Rivalry," in Thomas K. McCraw, ed., *America versus Japan* (Boston, Mass.: Harvard Business School Press, 1986).
18. For an early review of this literature, see Reuber et al., *Foreign Private Investment*, 120–32; for a more recent review, see Guisinger et al., *Investment Incentives*, 47–54.
19. See note 17.

20. D. J. Encarnation and L. T. Wells, Jr., "Sovereignty en Garde: Negotiating with Foreign Investors," *International Organization* 39 (Winter 1985): 47–78.
21. Encarnation and Wells, "Evaluating Foreign Investments."
22. Ibid.

9

Government Relations in the Global Firm

Amir Mahini
and
Louis T. Wells, Jr.

The globalization of industries introduces new problems for firms, and some old problems take on new dimensions. For firms with overseas operations, among the most perplexing of these problems is that of relations with host governments. Government policies toward industrialization may support the firm's strategy in serving global markets, or they may prove to be the undoing of that strategy. Governments may prohibit the foreign firm from establishing particular operations within their borders. They may offer tax incentives or other subsidies that are critical to a project's success. The outcome of government negotiations in one country may affect the firm's operations in other countries, as the following examples from our research illustrate:

- After much pressure, a U.S. industrial company agreed to build an additional plant to manufacture certain product components in a European country. This decision was made despite the existence of excess capacity in other plants of the company in Europe producing similar components that could supply this market. Management was aware that, from a narrow cost perspective, a single supply source for Europe would probably have been the most efficient. Corporate management could not, however, afford to ignore the implicit risk that such a "request" posed to the sales of other product lines in that country, for which public agencies and state-owned companies were major customers.
- In 1977, IBM was faced with a critical decision on a decade-old Indian government demand to reduce its ownership of local operations to a minority status. Rather than compromise its con-

sistent worldwide policy of 100 percent ownership and set a precedent for its operations elsewhere in the world, IBM decided to withdraw from India.

- A pharmaceutical firm was introducing a major new product in a particular European country. The firm launched a massive advance publicity campaign targeted at doctors and hospitals and announced a release date. It could not, however, reach agreement with the government concerned regarding pricing for the new drug. The price suggested by the government was regarded by the firm as inadequate. Given the important worldwide precedent-setting nature of new drug pricing, the firm was faced with a dilemma. Submitting to the government's price would leave the firm vulnerable to not recovering its large R & D investment; withholding the introduction of the drug could result in straining relations with the government and jeopardizing the goodwill of medical professionals who were looking forward to the drug. The firm decided to distribute the product free, pending agreement with the government on a price the company found acceptable.

- In another multinational enterprise, the manager in one of the firm's Latin American subsidiaries had taken a strong position to local government officials against proposals to reduce tariffs under the Latin American Free Trade Agreement (LAFTA) arrangements on a component that was being used by the subsidiary's customers and being produced on a small scale by the subsidiary. The manager of one of the multinational's subsidiaries in another Latin American country had taken an equally strong position supporting the proposed tariff reduction, in the hopes of capturing the whole LAFTA market by taking advantage of that subsidiary's lower cost resulting from its larger scale manufacture.

The task of our research has been to determine where in the enterprise decisions on government relations issues, such as those in the illustrations, are and should be made. We were *not* concerned with the outcome of negotiations, that is, what the company should decide. We were concerned with, for example, whether decisions should be left to the manager of the subsidiary abroad; whether the decisions should be made entirely at regional headquarters or higher in the multinational; or whether there are other, more appropriate ways of handling such issues. Further, we wanted to know whether the increasing globalization of industries and business strategies affects how firms handle international government relations.

How multinational enterprises should, and do, resolve such cases is a subject that has received little study, in spite of the critical role of government to the success of global strategies.[1] The few attempts to make recommendations have usually sought some ideal solution that would be appropriate for all multinationals. Our research suggests that such an ideal solution does not exist. Rather, as with other organizational problems, the appropriate approach to organizing for government relations depends at least partly on the business strategy that the firm is pursuing. Strategy and structure are, as in so many other cases, intimately linked.

It turns out that the problem of managing relations with multiple foreign governments is related to the issues that managers confront in other tasks. First, some of the issues in the choices for managing foreign government relations are quite familiar to managers, from their constant struggles to make reasonable tradeoffs in other organizational decisions between the advantages of decentralization versus those of centralization. A number of the issues in global government relations, however, go beyond the centralization/decentralization debate. They are of a special type, typical of those that arise when a complex organization must negotiate important issues with another organization, such as the problems that a large corporation faces when it negotiates with a labor union.[2] Management must decide how much to involve the subunits of the enterprise in negotiations and how to resolve conflicts when the interests of different subunits are not the same (see Bartlett, chap. 12 of this book). Further, the management problems with which firms must deal in deciding how to handle issues involving governments have close analogies in the problems that governments face when they structure their approaches to negotiating with multinational enterprises. Thus, a thorough understanding of the firm's alternatives, and the advantages and disadvantages of each, helps the manager to understand the government team on the other side of the bargaining table (see Encarnation and Wells, chap. 8 of this book, for an analysis of the parallel issues facing governments that serve as hosts to multinational enterprises).

THE CORE OF THE PROBLEM

If negotiations with an individual government could be managed without concern for the impact of the outcome of those negotiations on the operations of parts of the firm located elsewhere, the task of government relations in the multinational would differ little from the problem of managing government relations at home for the purely domestic firm. The local subsidiary manager could simply be given responsibility for local government relations. In fact, many of the multinationals that we studied had handled their overseas government relations exactly that way in their early days.

There are some clear reasons why top management might want to delegate relations with a local government to the subsidiary manager. The subsidiary manager is likely to be most intimately familiar with the local environment. That manager is likely to know early when issues are arising and to understand the political environment in which decisions will be made by the government. As Daniel Sharp of Xerox put it: "Our best sources are the local managers. They are better educated about their environments than anyone here at staff headquarters. Often, they went to school with those who run the government and other important institutions in their countries."[3] Further, the local manager is likely to be the most affected by the outcome of negotiations. Consequently, that manager should have an incentive to handle the relations in a way that is beneficial to the subsidiary's interests. And, because the manager has to live on a day-to-day basis with the government, the power to conduct major negotiations and make decisions may increase his or her ability to deal with the government on minor issues. Moreover, management evaluation and motivation are easier if the subsidiary manager is responsible for government relations. In most cases, the subsidiary manager is to be evaluated on the performance of the subsidiary. If that manager does not have authority over government relations, the enterprise is likely to face problems of performance evaluation and motivation.

If the local manager is responsible for government relations, however, the implications of government relations in one country on operations of the enterprise elsewhere are likely to receive scant attention. Few multinational enterprises can safely ignore those implications. The actions of one government can affect other parts of the firm in three ways. First, in some multinationals, matters of importance to one government have a *direct impact* on the operation of subsidiaries located in other countries. For example, if an automobile firm agrees to satisfy desires of one government for more local content by manufacturing locally parts that it had been importing from an affiliate elsewhere, that decision will affect the capacity utilization of the multinational's affiliates located elsewhere. Second, in perhaps rarer instances, the multinational firm can find itself confronting *contradictory orders* or desires from governments. A government may, for example, wish a subsidiary located within its borders to export products to a particular country, while the government with jurisdiction over another part of the enterprise attempts to forbid those exports as part of a boycott. Third, a particular decision in one country can affect operations in another country through a *less direct route*. The path may go from government to government, and then to the firm. If a multinational petroleum company agrees to a production-sharing agreement in Indonesia that yields the government an abnormal share of production, within days governments in other OPEC countries will know of the deal. They are likely to put pressure on the multinational's subsidiaries in those countries to grant them similar arrangements. Thus, in all three types of cases, seemingly local issues become issues that can affect the interests of parts of the multinational enterprise located in countries other than those in which the government issue first arose.

The need for the manager to take into account the global implications of certain government relations decisions generates a great deal of pressure for top management to vest authority for government relations in a level higher than the country subsidiary. If worldwide government relations were centralized, for example, management could be sure to take into account the global implications of a decision involving any one government.

The wider impact of government relations issues is not the only pressure for centralization. In many cases, the manager of an overseas subsidiary has little training or experience in government relations. The manager was originally assigned to the position because of his or her skills in marketing production, or some other functional area. Only rarely did the manager's background include experience in government relations. This seemed to be the case especially if the manager was transferred from domestic operations in the United States. Further, unless special efforts were made in the firm, subsidiary managers seemed to have little chance to learn about government relations problems and approaches from the experience of managers in the same firm in other countries. On the other hand, centralized authority for government relations means that specialists can handle the problems and can learn from all the firms' experiences around the world.

Like many of the other problems addressed in this book, the task of managing international government relations becomes partly one of balancing the advantages of centralization with those of decentralization, those of integration with those of differentiation. Or, in the language used in thinking of global strategy, the advantages of globalization versus those of a country-centered approach.

METHODOLOGY

To determine how multinational firms actually manage their international government relations, we examined the practices of the thirteen U.S.-based enterprises listed below. In all, some one hundred eighty interviews were conducted and analyzed. In most firms, the interviewees included senior executives, product or division executives, and major functional and country managers.

Figure 9.1 Companies included in the Study

Atlantic Richfield Company (Arco)
Conoco, Incorporated
Cummins Engine Company, Incorporated
Eli Lilly and Company

Exxon Corporation
Ford Motor Company
Gulf Oil Corporation
IBM Corporation
International Harvester Company
ITT Corporation
Mobil Corporation
Standard Oil Company of California (Socal)
Xerox Corporation

To a degree, in all the firms studied, responsibility in government-related issues is dispersed through the various functional, product, and area parts of the organization. Few executives, therefore, had any more than the most general notions of the abstraction that we called "management of government relations" in their firms. For some managers, a study in this area conjured up images of investigative journalism into international corruption scandals; others saw management of government relations as an extension of the public relations function of the firm. Not a few executives were extremely sensitive to discussing the issues involved under the rubric of government relations. To them, the area represented a potential minefield where anything said could violate important confidences or reveal deep embarrassments.

To illuminate the methods actually used to decide on major business–government issues, we focused questions on a few issues or events that management considered important and that were within the recent experience of the executives being interviewed. To understand how different firms might deal with a common set of issues and to cover a variety of issues, we prepared a set of hypothetical scenarios in a number of issue areas. If an issue area appeared in the interviews to be one that was of importance to the firm, we asked how the company would handle the hypothetical case and for examples of similar problems that the company had recently encountered.

The areas included government requests for increases in local value-added and in exports (relevant for all firms except petroleum enterprises), government pressure on product pricing policies (relevant to pharmaceutical companies), demands for local ownership in subsidiaries (relevant to International Harvester and IBM), transfer pricing disputes (relevant particularly to pharmaceutical companies), issues involving downstream operations (especially important for petroleum companies), and renegotiations of basic operating terms (again, particularly relevant for petroleum companies).

THE APPROACHES ENCOUNTERED

The firms included in our study managed their government relations in strikingly different ways. Four approaches could be identified, although some firms used combinations of these types. Moreover, some of the firms had recently made, or were in the process of making, changes in the way they managed relations with foreign governments.

The four approaches that we observed were:

- Policy
- Centralized
- Diffuse
- Coordinated

In the *policy approach*, the firm decided in advance of individual negotiations what its position would be on issues of major importance to the enterprise. Managers had little or no freedom to depart from company policy on these critical matters. Thus, there was little to negotiate.

Of the companies that we studied, IBM was the one that managed issues of government relations in a way that could best be described as a policy approach. On matters of great importance to the enterprise, such as ownership of foreign subsidiaries, trade among affiliates, and location of R & D facilities, IBM had strict policies that were not subject to negotiation with host governments. IBM had decided, for example, that it would not yield to government pressures to share ownership in its overseas manufacturing subsidiaries with local investors. Similarly, pressures to export more from a particular operation and to import less were countered by an overall policy of balancing trade of a particular operation with the rest of the world. Although sites for computer R & D were selected almost without regard to government pressures, the company provided widespread R & D facilities for activities that were not at the core of its business.

IBM was generally "proactive;" that is, it usually identified areas of potential conflict (ownership, balance of payments, employment, transfer pricing, and so on) and took steps to implement its solutions in possible confrontations with host governments even before governments raised the issues.

The *centralized approach* was, in one important aspect, quite similar to the policy approach. Under the centralized approach, authority was largely removed from the subsidiary or other frontline managers and was placed instead at a high level in the firm. Companies that used the centralized approach placed negotiations in the hands of a specialized unit, usually located at headquarters. Although the subsidiary manager might well be present at negotiations, his or her position was subordinated to that of representatives of the specialized government relations unit. The principal difference between firms that followed the policy approach and those that used the centralized approach was that, in the former, top management decided most important issues in advance while, in the latter, headquarters was more willing to negotiate. Consequently, they then had to create centralized structures for this purpose.

The term proactive, used to describe the stance of the policy-oriented firms toward government relations, applied to the firms using the centralized approach as well. In fact, the stance toward government relations in such companies was an integral part of their overall international strategy. Consequently, the company's very top level of management generally played a role in the process. The formal government relations unit was closely supervised by top management; sometimes top-level management even participated directly in particular negotiations.

The six international oil companies in our sample all followed a centralized approach to international government relations. They were remarkably similar to each other in the structures that they used, although their policies on particular issues could be quite different. All had specialized staffs to handle government issues. The most important staffs were attached to the exploration and production division and had general responsibility for company–government negotiations throughout the world. They usually took the lead role in negotiations for new exploration and production contracts. For example, Arco's chief negotiator in Dubai, when new exploration and production rights were under discussion, was the head of the E & P division's government negotiations staff. His team included an assortment of technical specialists, engineers, and economists from the division, along with legal and tax specialists from corporate headquarters. His bargaining limits were defined, however, by senior management. On the other hand, regional management (from the geographic division) usually took the lead in renegotiations. Nevertheless, in many renegotiations, senior management was directly involved. In the 1974 renegotiations in Indonesia, Arco's team was headed by the Eastern Operating Group president with help from the division and corporate negotiations specialists.

The companies that centralized government relations in corporate specialists usually also had formal arrangements to coordinate positions when different stages of a vertically integrated operation were involved. The permanent staff organizations were supplemented by ad hoc teams and working groups to reconcile interdivisional interests, especially when refining and transport activities were at issue. Further, corporate tax and legal staffs were likely to be involved in all major negotiation teams.

At the opposite end of the scale from the firms just described were those that followed the *diffuse approach*. In these firms, major issues of government relations were left to lower level managers, sometimes actually at the foreign subsidiary, but at other times located in regional units or in functional parts of the organization such as marketing or manufacturing. The designation of who would handle a particular issue was ad hoc and generally depended a great deal on who seized the initiative. Few limits were placed on the freedom of the manager to respond in ways that he or she deemed appropriate to demands of the host government.

The general stance of companies in this mode was typically a reactive one as opposed to the proactive stance of the firms at the other end of the scale. In the firms that followed the diffuse approach, management waited for issues to arise and then dealt with them without planned procedures or responses.

Two companies in our sample illustrate this approach to government relations: International Harvester in the heavy equipment industry and Cummins in diesel engine manufacturing.

In International Harvester, country managers were lords of their fiefdoms prior to 1977. Their power included local government relations. With the formation of three worldwide product divisions in 1977, the general locus of decision-making power moved up the corporate ladder to the divisional level. But little attention was paid to the handling of government relations. Such issues were dealt with on an ad hoc basis. In one case that we discussed with managers, country management in Mexico was completely bypassed by division management. Simultaneously, similar negotiations in Canada were being handled solely by subsidiary management. International Harvester had no specific mechanisms and procedures for the coordination of issues between product divisions. When there were several country managers for various product lines in a single country, it was unclear who represented the company to the government. The manager with the largest subsidiary was designated as "Mr. International Harvester" for the entire country, but it was not unusual for one subsidiary manager to refuse to recognize the preeminence of another in relations with the host government.

The influence of frontline managers in government negotiations at Cummins is illustrated by the way some other Latin American issues were handled. In 1976, Cummins was attempting to establish facilities in the Andean Pact countries. Negotiations waxed and waned with changes of Latin American marketing managers. A few years later, at roughly the same time, the company found itself in negotiations with Brazil and Mexico involving exports and expansion of existing capacity and production lines. These negotiations involving major operations decisions were focused in the corporate manufacturing staff, but with others involved in uncoordinated ways from time to time. Eventually, the Mexicans began negotiating with General Motors. When the threat to Latin American expansion became clear, top management assigned responsibility for both Latin American cases to a senior executive, a lawyer, who was recruited to head the international marketing division.

Some firms tried to avoid the extremes of the centralized or policy approaches and the diffuse approach. Under the *coordinated approach* to government negotiations, the goal of the company was to design a mechanism that clarifies who is responsible for government relations and that leaves most of the authority for negotiations in the hands of the subsidiary or other frontline managers. At the same time, management attempted to create a structure that would enable and encourage responsible managers to coordinate local decisions with the interests of other subsidiaries. The designers of such systems hoped to reduce the reactive nature of government relations that seems inherent in the diffuse approach and substitute some degree of initiative, or at least of forecasting, in government relations. In sum, management tried to retain some of the advantages of involvement by frontline managers, yet gain some of the advantages of centralization.

Firms in our sample used different methods to coordinate their global government relations. One approach is illustrated by Xerox, a company that seemed to be in transition between a diffuse approach and a more formal, coordinated approach. In one of its regions, the company had instituted a rather formal program for government relations. Each country manager was responsible for preparing quarterly reports on government issues in his or her country. These reports were then discussed with regional management, in order to determine a list of proposed objectives for government relations. By integrating these objectives into the company's management-by-objectives systems, the country manager's handling of government issues were explicitly included in the annual performance review. Further, every quarter, regional management and country managers of neighboring countries met as a group to discuss the impact of possible outcomes of one subsidiary's actions on the interests of all and to share experiences. These sessions helped develop a convergence of views among country managers as well as between them and the regional functional staffs. By the end of the session, each subsidiary manager was to have objectives that were acceptable to him or her and to regional management.

A number of other firms in the sample had some mechanisms for coordinating government relations activities. ITT's was similar to Xerox's in its emphasis on ensuring a major role for the subsidiary manager. In addition, ITT relied a great deal on special committees, joint task forces, and working groups to supplement monthly meetings between country managers in order to ensure some coordination on government relations matters.

Ford and Eli Lilly followed similar approaches that were rather different in their detail from those of Xerox and ITT. Both placed more emphasis on permanent coordinating bodies that played a staff role within the corporate organization. Ford, for example, had a special international business planning staff attached to the office of the president of the international division. The staff dealt primarily with issues

Table 9.1. Location of Decision-Making Enterprise and Stance in Negotiations

	Location in Enterprise		
Stance	Periphery (usually subsidiary level)	Periphery coordinated, perhaps with participation of center	Center
Predetermined policies on many issues	X	X	Policy
Most issues may be negotiated	Diffuse	Coordinated	Centralized

that arose in response to new government demands in one country or region and that affected the operations of subsidiaries in another region. Although Eli Lilly placed general responsibility for pricing issues in the central marketing staff of the domestic pharmaceutical division, which had a worldwide mandate, special arrangements were required to handle global government relations. The need to take into account the policies of national pricing boards and the differences in government sensitivities toward new drug pricing led to the formation of a special committee outside of the regular corporate structure to bring together area executives from the international division and the central marketing staffs. Area executives were thus able to bring to bear their intimate knowledge of a country's regulatory environment in combination with the global functional perspective of the staff. The company also made constant use of a special standing committee to resolve the delicate and highly political issue of drug transfer pricing.

The four approaches that firms used to conduct government negotiations are summarized in Table 9.1. The policy approach is the only approach we encountered in which the stances of the enterprise toward government–business issues were determined in advance and were largely nonnegotiable. Consequently, none of the companies in our sample falls in the first two cells in the top row of the table. It is, of course, difficult to conceive of an enterprise with predetermined policies that were set at the periphery of the enterprise. One might, with some effort, imagine a firm that set policies in advance through the use of a coordinating mechanism, but we did not uncover any such enterprise.

With one exception, all the firms that we examined fell in the bottom row of the table. They were willing to negotiate almost any issue with a government, but they differed substantially in where the responsibility for the negotiations lay in the enterprise. At one extreme were the firms that followed the diffuse approach, leaving negotiations to the periphery of the enterprise; at the other extreme were the firms that delegated negotiations to a body at the center of the firm.

In spite of the varying patterns, and the changes being made by the multinationals, we believe that we have been able to link the approach used by a firm with the international strategy being followed by that enterprise with certain characteristics of the firm's industry. The choice of approach to government relations is not, we are convinced, a random one; the experiences of the firms that we studied provide guidelines for other firms to examine the practices that they are currently following and to design approaches for the future.

COMPANY STRATEGY AND THE APPROACH TO GOVERNMENT RELATIONS

The dilemmas facing the firms in this study are familiar ones, much like those associated with other choices of centralized versus decentralized decision making. Not surprisingly, we found that the approaches chosen by the firms reflected the strategies and structures of the industries in which they operated. Four variables seemed largely to determine how the firms handled international government negotiations: the firm's bargaining power in dealing with governments; the significance of international operations to the enterprise; the degree of interdependence of the subsidiaries; and the political salience of the industry.

The Policy Approach

Perhaps all firms would like to be in the position of establishing policies covering major issues that the company is likely to confront in government negotiations. If governments request the subsidiary to share ownership with local partners, a company policy might simply forbid it. Or, if the government requests local purchases of certain ingredients for the final product, company policy might insist on purchase from affiliated plants in the home country. Such a policy approach avoids the need for government negotiations on issues of major importance to the firm. Despite the seeming attractiveness of the approach, as we have pointed out, only one firm in our sample, IBM, relied on overall, rigid policies for major business-government issues.

Only those firms in a very strong bargaining position can impose their will on governments to the extent required to avoid the need for negotiations on important issues. Bargaining power is principally the result of the need that a government feels for the resources a company can bring and of the number of companies that can offer similar resources.[4] Among the companies that we studied, IBM stood alone in its bargaining power. Many governments consider computer technology to be an essential input into the development of their industries.

For a number of years, IBM was one of the very few companies with sophisticated know-how in the field and extensive interests in international operations. In the face of strong demand for its know-how and little competition, IBM could long insist that governments accede to its preferences with respect to issues it considered of strategic importance.

That is not to say that IBM had no mechanism for considering the requests of host governments. Changes in policy or exceptions to existing policy were handled by much the same process in which the policy had come into existence in the first place—through the corporate management committee, which was made up of the top five corporate executives. If conflicts seemed sufficiently important, possible exceptions to government relations policy could work their way up to and be reviewed by the corporate management committee. When India, in the mid-seventies, informed the company that it would have to reduce its 100 percent equity ownership to 40 percent in accordance with the Foreign Investment Review Act, it was to this committee that the decision was referred.[5] Although Indian operations were only an insignificant part of IBM's activities, a great deal of management time was devoted to this issue within the company. IBM finally offered certain compromise proposals, but kept its policy of complete ownership of its manufacturing subsidiaries intact. Rather than yield to India's continued pressure, IBM responded to its fear of setting a precedent that would undermine its policies elsewhere and withdrew from India. Soon thereafter, with less internal turmoil, the company withdrew from Nigeria over the same ownership issue. The policy had been tested and retained. Presumably, it will remain intact until IBM's bargaining power has weakened to the point that it has to negotiate such important issues on a case-by-case basis.

The Centralized Approach

The oil companies, in their choice of a centralized approach, seem to have been influenced by one of the characteristics that pushed IBM toward a policy approach: the activities of the firms were of great importance to host countries. In the major oil-producing countries, the operations of the companies accounted for the major part of foreign exchange earnings and of government revenue. The actions of oil firms have a dramatic impact on the economy. They were, in the terminology of the political scientist, "politically salient."

On the other hand, the oil companies were quite different from IBM in another important aspect. They did not have the bargaining power in government negotiations that IBM did. At one time, their position may indeed have been similar to IBM's, but their hold over technology and access to markets had weakened in recent decades.[6] Consequently, the oil companies have faced many international competitors, and a number of host country governments believe that their state oil companies could, if necessary, continue oil operations without the presence of the international firms.

Interdependence of Subsidiaries and the Choice of Approach

The oil companies differ not only from IBM, but also from Cummins and International Harvester, which were following a diffuse approach to government relations. The oil companies had established a large network of overseas affiliates, many of which were closely tied to the activities of others through vertical integration. Producing affiliates supplied transportation affiliates. Transportation affiliates supplied refining operations, which, in turn, supplied the distribution system. Thus, overseas operations were both important to the companies' overall profits and closely integrated globally. A change in any one piece of the system was likely to have ramifications in other parts of the multinational enterprise.

The extreme political salience of oil assured that decisions made in one subsidiary would affect not only others in the vertical chain, but also subsidiaries at the same level in other countries. If one affiliate signed new terms for exploration and development, the new terms would be known very quickly by the governments of other countries in which the firm was producing. If the terms were more favorable to the host government than the previous agreements, other governments would insist on renegotiation.

When the firm's strategy involves interdependent affiliates (a global strategy with geographically dispersed units) and the industry is so salient that the negotiations in one country almost certainly set precedents for the demands imposed on affiliates in other countries, the multinational firm finds it extremely difficult to leave local government negotiations to onsite subsidiary managers. In fact, coordination is likely to be insufficient. Coordination is generally regional, given limits imposed by travel needs and by the requirement that coordinating groups include a manageable number of units. But the impacts of negotiations in oil companies are likely to extend far beyond the region in which the negotiations occur. Not surprisingly, perhaps, the oil companies conducted most government negotiations through specialized headquarters units. These units were in a position to take into account the impact of actions in one country on the activities of affiliates in all other countries in which the company had interests. In so doing, they could concentrate scarce expertise in dealing with government relations issues that were of critical importance to the firms.

The choice of a centralized approach to negotiation means almost completely disenfranchising the subsidiary or other frontline manager from the process. This is not a decision to be taken lightly, given the responsibility of subsidiary managers for profits, their knowledge of local conditions, and the fact that undermining the subsidiary managers' apparent authority might have an impact on the day-to-day tasks of working with government officials in host countries. Thus, the centralized approach is likely to be characteristic of only those few companies whose activities are particularly salient politically and whose operations are closely interlinked in a dispersed global network.

The Diffuse Approach

The firms that followed a diffuse approach to negotiations stood at the opposite end from the oil companies. Rather than designing a formal structure to handle negotiations, these firms let the assignments fall in an ad hoc way, though frontline managers were usually the major decision makers. These firms chose not to take steps to regularize and coordinate their government relations. To capture the advantages that accrue from the involvement of the managers with the most direct interest in particular government relations issues as well as the benefits associated with matching authority and responsibility, some firms were willing to sacrifice the ability to take into account the impact of actions in one subsidiary on activities elsewhere in the enterprise. Without any formalized effort to regularize government relations and without clear assignments of responsibility, those firms could not easily institute mechanisms to encourage managers to learn from the experience of managers in other countries where similar problems might have arisen.

The two firms that chose the diffuse approach to government relations were both companies with strategies that emphasized national responsiveness rather than global coordination. Their strategies were country-centered. Consequently, the impact of decisions taken in one subsidiary on the activities of other subsidiaries were not likely to be great. Further, in neither firm did overseas profits account for a large fraction of total profits, and the number of overseas operations was small. Consequently, any gains from a more formal approach to government relations may not have seemed worth the cost in management attention. With hindsight, it is not surprising that it was in these companies that we had the most difficulty identifying government issues that were viewed as very important by management at headquarters.

The Coordinated Approach

Where the problems of the diffuse approach are significant, but the extreme of the centralized approach is also unattractive, companies seek a middle ground that involves efforts to *coordinate* government relations while still leaving a major role for the frontline manager. Two of the companies that tried to coordinate their government relations, but without delegating them to a specialized unit, were in industries that were quite salient politically: pharmaceuticals[7] and automobiles.[8] Government had a considerable interest in the activities of these firms and sought to impose conditions on their operations.

Although neither of the industries had the extreme political sensitivity of petroleum, and neither faced an organization such as OPEC that would assure that terms negotiated in one country were immediately known in other countries, coordination of approaches to governments could be important. In the case of Ford, recent experience in soliciting bids from a European government to obtain incentives for the location of a new facility demonstrated the potential payoff from coordination. Governments wanted automobile plants and were willing to bid hard. Ford sought to capitalize on this interest by following a strategy that emphasized long-term agreements at the preinvestment stage when its bargaining strength was highest.[9] While agreeing to time-phased targets on such issues as exports and local value-added requirements, the company sought to retain flexibility in determining the specific products to be included under the arrangements. For Lilly, government concern about the pricing of pharmaceuticals could easily spill over borders, as Hoffmann-LaRoche's conflict in Britain had shown.[10]

The political salience of the industry was not the only similarity between the oil companies and Ford and Eli Lilly. Ford, particularly, and Eli Lilly, to some extent, were following global strategies that emphasized integration of activities in various countries. Ford had gone a long way toward integrating the manufacturing operations of, especially, its European plants. Trouble in a German plant could quickly spill over to cause problems with production in Britain where Ford's plant used some German parts. Eli Lilly maintained a network of formulating and finishing plants with a considerable degree of mutual dependence, but not to the extent of Ford's network. For both firms, however, there was reason to believe that decisions in one country might have an impact on company operations elsewhere. In response to the political salience of their industries and the integration of their activities, Ford and Eli Lilly took major steps to coordinate their global government relations. In fact, Ford had begun to adopt an increasingly proactive stance by providing expertise to governments in Latin America to help them develop their national automotive industry policies.

Neither ITT nor Xerox had gone as far as Ford and Eli Lilly with coordination of their government relations, but both had taken some steps. A look at their industries and strategies suggest some reasons why they differed. Telecommunications is as politically salient an industry as automobiles and pharmaceuticals. Thus, there was pressure on ITT to coordinate the activities of its country units. On the other hand, ITT's strategy did not emphasize integrated activities across its operations. Manufcturing in one country tended to be rather independent of that in other countries, and thus the need to coordinate and preserve an integrated global strategy was less than for Ford and Eli Lilly. Consequently, ITT seemed to have made only weak attempts to coordinate international government relations.

Xerox, which had only recently begun coordination and only in some of its activities, probably faced the least pressure to move away from the diffuse approach. Its traditional business did not carry the political salience of the other firms, and there had been until very recently relatively little integration among Xerox's subsidiaries. Interestingly, the first steps toward coordination in government relations began in a region where a common market had threatened the independence of decisions in different countries. One of the issues that had influenced the change in approach involved conflicting positions in different subsidiaries with respect to tariffs. Proposed reductions in tariffs would have forced Xerox to shift manufacturing and trade patterns in the region.

Further, for Xerox, overseas operations were not as important in overall profitability as they were for the oil companies and for Eli Lilly, Ford, and ITT. Most overseas profits had come from Xerox's joint ventures in Japan and the United Kingdom; there was little interdependence between them. Jolted by a worsening profit picture at home and responding to increasing interest in establishing a strong foothold in the European automated office equipment market, however, Xerox was beginning to pay greater attention to its overseas operations. In marketing sophisticated office products such as telecopiers and Ethernet (its coaxial cable network), Xerox found itself confronting different national technical standards and great interest on the part of European governments in developing a national position in the "informatics" industry. This new environment and strategy resulted in the first steps toward coordinating government relations among some countries. Xerox, it seemed, was a company in transition, responding to its growing need for global coordination because of its increasing dependence on profits from abroad and the greater political salience of its new businesses.

Thus far, we have treated the approaches to government relations of the firms we examined as falling into four distinct types. In practice, the approaches lie on a continuum, with the diffused approach at one end and the policy and centralized approaches at the other. Various efforts to coordinate subsidiary management fall within the range between these extremes. In addition, firms do not always follow a single approach for all issues. Rather, they have a portfolio of tools to deal with government relations. What we have described are the approaches that they use for issues that are of most importance to the strategy of the enterprise.

Problems of Transition

It appears that most multinational firms started by leaving government relations issues primarily to subsidiary managers. (We are less certain about the early history of the petroleum firms. For these firms, overseas production operations were linked to downstream operations in other countries at the outset; and the industry was politically salient to both host and home countries even in the industry's early days. Consequently, the history of the oil companies might well be different from that of other firms. But those early days were too far back for our interviewees to be very helpful in telling us how overseas government relations were handled.) As firms' strategies became more global, certain issues in government relations in one country began to affect other parts of the enterprise. As this began to happen, management initiated attempts to coordinate responses to these types of issues, moving the firm along the continuum away from the diffuse approach. Nevertheless, many issues in government relations have little impact beyond the particular subsidiary. Firms generally left the handling of such issues largely to subsidiary managers, although the efforts to coordinate major issues did lead to some efforts at creating mechanisms to transfer experiences across subsidiaries even on minor issues. Thus, a particular firm might coordinate responses to government demands for more exports, if yielding to those demands would affect other parts of the enterprise, but it might leave the subsidiary manager free to negotiate labor policies with the local government if those policies were not likely to affect other parts of the firm.[11]

It was apparent from the interviews that the move away from a diffuse approach has not been an easy one. Local managers typically saw the change as eroding their authority and, therefore, consciously or unconsciously made the shift difficult. During, and even after, such a change the firm remained dependent on local managers to provide information about government issues. The local manager was likely, however, to bring to higher management only those issues that he or she chose to. For example, if coming pressures from government were likely to benefit his or her subsidiary, the manager perhaps would not give early notice to headquarters. In a number of cases, local management and local government appeared to be allied against what higher-level management saw as the interests of the firm as a whole. Information that might make the local manager look bad was likely to go unreported. With the exception of the oil companies, many of which had developed extensive organizations at headquarters for political analysis, top management in all the companies we studied remained very dependent on local management to identify emerging issues and to provide information to higher management.

Gaps in Our Knowledge

In our research, we studied government relations only in each firm's principal industry. Thus, we could not establish whether large, diversified firms such as ITT employed different patterns in the different industries in which they operate, reflecting company strategies and political salience. Nor did our research address the extent of coordination across lines of business. For some firms, such coordination is likely to be very important. Diversification is likely to provide both a large advantage and a significant disadvantage to some firms in their relations with governments. If the firm is able to coordinate its government relations, it may be able to draw on the important skills it can offer to a government in one line of business to increase its bargaining power in another line. On the other hand, once the company has several businesses in place in a country, the government may hold one of those businesses hostage to the demands it places on another of the firm's activities.

There are other important gaps in our research. We included in our sample no marketing-oriented firms in the consumer goods sector because we suspected at the outset that such firms would face less conflict than other firms over global government issues. Because such industries are generally less politically salient than the ones that we examined, the pressures to coordinate government relations might well be small. On the other hand, the strategies of consumer goods firms differ considerably, even among those that are strongly marketing-oriented. Some firms are very much concerned about the impact of product design and quality, prices, and advertising in one market on the image of the firm's products in other markets. Thus, on certain issues, there may be pressures to centralize government relations so that uniformity can be maintained across borders. Answers to how marketing-oriented consumer goods firms manage global government relations will have to await studies of firms such as General Mills, Coca-Cola, and Procter & Gamble.

In addition, the small sample of the firms examined leaves other questions beside the obvious ones of statistical significance. We simply cannot know whether we have covered the full range of approaches that are used by U.S. multinationals (even excluding those mentioned in the previous paragraph), much less the range used by non-U.S. firms. One can imagine quite different patterns. Our own suspicion, however, is that we observed the range of approaches typical of U.S.-based multinationals. On the other hand, we suspect that we have not explored the full richness of how the approaches are managed.

Table 9.2. Factors Determining Approach to Global Government Relations

Approach to Relations	Industry Conditions	Strategy
Policy	High political salience, strong bargaining position for the firm	Globally integrated operations
Centralized	High political salience, weak bargaining power	Foreign operations important Little global integration
Diffuse	Low political salience	Foreign operations minor Integrated operations
Coordinated	Medium-high political salience	Foreign operations important

CONCLUSION

In spite of the questions remaining, we believe that the framework developed from this research can be useful for management when considering the problem of government relations in a multicountry framework. Moreover, the framework suggests the directions in which managers are likely to have to move in the face of increasing global competition.

The research suggests that a company's approach to the conduct of government relations in the multinational firm is a function of company strategy and industry structure. Only if a firm is in a very strong bargaining position vis-à-vis host governments can it follow a policy approach. Only firms that have small, country-centered overseas operations are likely to follow the diffuse approach. Increasing integration and greater political salience of their industry are likely to move companies to coordinate their global government relations. At the extreme, they delegate the relations to a special unit at the center of the enterprise. (These relations are summarized in Table 9.2.)

The increase in global competition in a wide range of industries is likely to mean that few firms will be able to manage their government relations with a policy approach. As long as a firm has a monopoly position with respect to important technology or major markets, its bargaining position is likely to be high. It may well choose to exploit this position in the way it manages government relations. But the time period during which such monopolies dominate seems to be shrinking. Gone are the days in which U.S. firms held sway for long periods over critical know-how. As bargaining power declines, the ability of the firm to manage government relations with a policy approach diminishes.

The pressures from global competition drive many firms to integrate the activities of their foreign subsidiaries. In many industries, country-centered strategies are yielding to strategies that involve integration on a regional or global basis. As this happens, the costs to the multinational system of leaving government relations to the local managers grow. Thus, the pressures to abandon the diffused approach increase.

As governments themselves become more active in the global market for investment (see Encarnation and Wells, chap. 8 of this book), they increase their ability to monitor terms that firms agree to in other countries. The chances of the events in one country affecting a multinational's affiliate in another country expand. Further, governments' offers in bidding for investment increase the opportunities for profits for firms. As governments become more active in an industry, the costs to the firm of uncoordinated government relations grow.

Globalization of industries will tend to push many companies toward efforts to coordinate or even to manage their global government relations through central institutions. In our samples, the petroleum firms have long managed in a global industry and have established strong centralized government relations units. Xerox was in the middle of changes in strategy and its handling of government relations in response to the globalization of its industry. Cummins and International Harvester, at least in fairly recent years, still operated in industries that were not globalized and managed their government relations accordingly.

Coordination or centralization is not an easy move for firms, as we have pointed out. It means removing authority from subsidiary managers who are likely to cling to it. Further, because those managers remain the principal source of intelligence required for overseas business–government relations, they have a great deal of ability to impede change. Coordination adds to the complexity of management. Motivation, performance evaluation, and control become increasingly difficult with centralization. Management becomes even tougher. That, we suspect, is an inevitable consequence of globalization.

NOTES

1. See, for example, J. N. Behrman, *U.S. International Business and Governments* (New York: McGraw-Hill, 1971); J. Fayerweather, ed., *International Business-Government Affairs: Toward an Era of Accommodation* (Cambridge, Mass.: Ballinger, 1973); T. N. Gladwin and I. Walter, *Multinationals Under Fire* (New York: John Wiley & Sons, 1980); Y. Doz, *Strategic Management in Multinational Companies* (Oxford: Pergamon Press, 1986); J. L. Bower and Y. Doz, "Strategy Formulation: A Social and Political Process," in Schendel and Hofer, eds., *Strategic Management: A New View of Business Policy and Planning* (Boston: Little, Brown, 1979); S. J. Kobrin, *Managing Political Risk Assessment* (Berkeley: University of California Press, 1982).

2. See, for example, R. E. Walton and R. B. McKensie, *A Behavioral Theory of Labor Negotiations* (New York: McGraw-Hill, 1968).
3. Quoted in "The Multinationals Get Smarter About Political Risks," *Fortune*, March 24, 1980.
4. See N. Fagre and L. T. Wells, Jr., "Bargaining Power of Multinationals and Host Governments," *Journal of International Business Studies* 13 (Fall 1982): 9–23. See also Encarnation and Wells, chap. 8 of this book.
5. For an excellent account of the events, particularly from the Indian government's perspective, see J. M. Grieco, "Between Dependence and Autonomy: India's Experience with the International Computer Industry," *International Organization* 36 (Summer 1982).
6. For a description of the change, see R. Vernon, ed., *The Oil Crisis in Perspective*, special volume of *Daedalus* 104, no. 4 (Fall 1975).
7. See, for example, J. E. Schnee, "International Shifts in Innovational Activities: The Case of Pharmaceuticals," *Columbia Journal of World Business* (Spring 1978).
8. For historical surveys of international business–government issues in the automobile industry, see M. Wilkins, "Multinational Automobile Enterprises and Regulation: An Historical Overview," in W. Abernathy and D. Ginsburg, eds., *Government, Technology, and the Automobile Industry* (New York: McGraw-Hill, 1980); and L. T. Wells, Jr., "Automobiles," in *Big Business and the State* (Cambridge, Mass.: Harvard University Press, 1974).
9. For a description of the "obsolescing bargain," see R. Vernon, *Sovereignty at Bay* (New York: Basic Books, 1971), 46–59.
10. See "F. Hoffmann-LaRoche & Co. A.G.," 9376055. Boston: Harvard Business School, 1975.
11. One can certainly imagine cases when labor policies would affect other parts of the firm: for example, in industries with strong attempts on the part of labor unions to coordinate across borders the activities of national unions or when the same union operates in two or more countries in which the firm has subsidiaries (as does the UAW in the United States and Canada.)

III

ORGANIZATIONAL FORMS AND CHALLENGES

10

Coalitions and Global Strategy*

Michael E. Porter
and
Mark B. Fuller

The globalization of industries has created a new set of strategic problems for managers, and they have responded by employing some distinctive tools. One of the most prominent is what we term "coalitions." Coalitions are formal, long-term alliances between firms that link aspects of their businesses but fall short of merger. They include joint ventures, licensing agreements, supply agreements, marketing agreements, and a variety of other arrangements. The motives for coalition formation are varied, and include the reduction of risk, the search for economies of scale, the need for technology or market access, and response to government pressure.

Coalition formation seems particularly related to the process of industry and firm globalization. When AT&T began to look outside its traditional U.S. market, for example, alliances with Olivetti and Philips were among its first moves. In the automobile industry, coalitions are widespread and include links between General Motors and Toyota and Isuzu, Ford and Toyo Kogyo, Chrysler and Mitsubishi, and American Motors and Renault. In commercial airframes and engines, coalitions involve virtually every significant industry participant.

While coalitions are not new in international competition, their character seems to be shifting. Coalitions are becoming more strategic, through linking major competitors together to compete worldwide. More traditional coalitions were often tactical, involving tie ups with local firms to gain market access or to transfer technology passively to regions where a firm did not want to compete directly. The

*This chapter has benefited from research by Richard Rawlinson and comments by Pankaj Ghemawat and John Stopford.

widespread incidence of coalitions and the growing need to integrate them into global strategies has increased the need to understand the role of coalitions in international strategy.

This chapter examines one important class of coalitions—international coalitions among firms that compete in the same industry. Most academic authors have examined piecemeal a particular subset of coalitions, based on the legal form of the coalition agreement (e.g., joint ventures). Our research frames coalitions more broadly as a range of agreements intimately related to a firm's competitive strategy. After reviewing the literature on interfirm agreements, we present a framework that relates coalitions to global strategy. The actual pattern of coalition activity from 1970 to 1982 is investigated in chapter 11.

PAST RESEARCH ON COALITIONS

The literature on coalitions has split into a series of largely independent streams of research on various types of coalitions delineated by the legal form of the coalition agreement. Past research concentrated primarily on joint ventures and licensing. Domestic joint ventures have been treated separately from international joint ventures. Recently, a few studies have taken a broader view of coalitions.

Firms view coalitions as among the strategic alternatives in competing internationally. The legal form of coalition chosen is related to the competitive conditions facing a firm, but also reflects country-specific legal and tax considerations. There is no simple relationship between the legal form of coalitions and the purposes they are designed to achieve. For example, a cross-licensing agreement may have much the same purposes as an R & D joint venture. Similarly, the legal form of the agreement says little about the contribution of each partner. A partner's contribution to a joint venture may range from cash to staffing and ongoing management. We treat all types of coalition as a class of transactions here, and analyze them based on purpose rather than legal form.

Past research on coalitions has frequently mixed diversifying coalitions with coalitions among firms in the same industry, because the literature has been heavily concerned with the transactional or contractual difficulties of forging and managing any interfirm agreement. However, the strategic purposes of diversifying coalitions are quite different than for horizontal coalitions, and mixing them complicates both theory and empirical testing. We do not treat diversifying coalitions in this and the next chapter for this reason and because international diversifying coalitions are not common in practice. A final characteristic of the writing on coalitions is that coalitions have usually been viewed as individual, stand-alone choices. In practice, any particular coalition can only be understood in the context of a firm's overall global strategy, which may involve multiple coalitions.

Domestic Joint Ventures

In 1958, Fusfeld initiated what has been a continuing discussion of the anticompetitive effects of horizontal joint ventures (between firms in the same industry). Fusfeld hypothesized that the management of joint ventures could be the forum for more general discussion between competitors, that common sourcing could lead to common cost structures and identical pricing, and that joint ventures could be the mechanism through which emerging industries such as titanium could be dominated by existing large firms in related industries. This line of analysis was also advanced by Dixon (1962) and Boyle (1968).

West (1959) made an early attempt to identify other reasons for joint-venture formation besides limiting competition, such as diversification, capital constraints, government pressure in overseas operations, and pooling of know-how. He believed that pooling of know-how was becoming more important and that it explained the growing number of joint ventures in the oil, steel, nonferrous metals, and chemical industries. He also noted the operational difficulties of joint ventures, stemming from the need to keep two masters happy and the reluctance of the parents to delegate full authority to joint-venture managers.

More systematic efforts sought to test the hypothesis linking joint ventures and competition. Pate (1969) found that 80 percent of all joint ventures were between firms in the same two-digit SIC category or in a buyer–seller relationship. Pfeffer and Nowak (1976a, b) found that the proportion of a given industry's joint ventures represented by joint ventures with another industry was correlated to the extent of transactions links with that industry (derived from input–output tables), and to the proportion of scientists and engineers in total industry employment. Given that market transactions and coalition agreements are alternatives, it makes sense that joint-venture formation is related to the existence of market links between industries.

The technological rationale behind domestic joint ventures has provided ammunition for those trying to refute the anticompetitive taint of joint ventures and other interfirm agreements. Berg and Friedman (1978) identified at least one prima facie innocent class of joint ventures by showing that the more "technological" a given industry group's joint ventures were, the more dispersed were the industries with which joint ventures formed. Berg and Friedman argued that the absence of transactions interdependence between two industries did not foreclose technical interaction (even if it made it less likely) but should completely rule out collusive interaction. Friedman, Berg, and Duncan (1979) found evidence that joint ventures substituted for internal R & D activity. Firms that had engaged in joint ventures had lower R & D to sales ratios than those in the same industry that had not formed joint ventures.

Berg, Duncan, and Friedman (1982) fitted a regression equation to predict industry joint-venture participation rates. While their equation explained a relatively modest proportion of the variation, they found that large average firm size and rapid growth in industry capital expenditures were significant predictors of joint-venture activity, as was average R & D intensity for technologically oriented joint ventures. Joint ventures are mechanisms for achieving competitive advantage in a variety of ways. Attempts to explain a broad cross section of joint ventures are likely to achieve limited success. Berg, Duncan, and Friedman recognized this in part by making a distinction between technological and nontechnological joint ventures.

International Joint Ventures

The literature on international joint ventures divides into two streams, each with concerns that are quite different from those of writers on domestic joint ventures. The largest body of literature examines joint ventures between multinationals and local partners. The other stream investigates joint ventures between two or more firms from developed countries.

Stopford and Wells (1972) and Franko (1971) established the basic analytical framework for examining joint ventures between multinationals and local partners. Stopford and Wells model joint-venture formation as an underlying tradeoff between "the drive for unambiguous control" and "the quest for additional resources." Local partners offer multinational access to resources such as indigenous management, local legitimization, market access, and knowledge of local conditions. On the other hand, the presence of a local partner can complicate the integration of the joint-venture entity into the multinational's worldwide strategy. Willingness by multinationals to enter into joint-venture agreements should be inversely related to the degree to which their overall global interests diverge from the interests of the local partners in optimizing the joint ventures' strategies as stand-alone operations. Examining a sample of 187 U.S.-based firms, Stopford and Wells detected the expected relationship. Strategies that emphasized marketing techniques, rationalization of production, or control over sources of raw materials, as well as those based on product innovation, led firms to avoid joint ventures. Those firms that aimed to adapt their products to local markets, that could retain control of all vertical stages of their industry by dominating one stage, or that had an exceptional need to spread the risk of their expansion, were all more likely to participate in joint ventures with local partners. Franko's (1971) study established a connection between a firm's organizational evolution to an area or area-functional management structure and the dissolution of joint ventures.

These studies were based on thorough questionnaire and interview research. The joint ventures they attempted to explain are only a subset of all coalitions, and recent evidence (Hladik 1984) suggests that the nature of multinational–local joint ventures may be evolving toward more equal partnership. Gullander (1976a) studied joint ventures in manufacturing industries in developed European countries. The coalitions in Gullander's sample were much more diverse than those examined by Stopford and Wells and Franko, and he identified a broader range of motives behind them. Among the causes of joint-venture formation he proposed were nationalism, achievement of economies of scale or experience, creation of a balanced set of skills, trading resources not exchanged in conventional markets, establishing collaborative frameworks for managing interdependencies with suppliers, buyers, and competitors, and diversification. Gullander subscribed to Stopford and Wells's view that the impediments to joint-venture formation stemmed primarily from issues of control and organization, though he also noted legal, fiscal, and antitrust obstacles.

In Gullander's view, an industry leader endowed with a variety of advantages would have only a political incentive to enter joint ventures. Gullander's framework for analyzing corporate strategies rests heavily on the assumption that joint ventures are second-best alternatives to either arm's-length markets or integration within the single firm. It does not accommodate linkages between firms that have an enduring value even to substantial competitors, and whose rationale would be defeated by full merger between the parents. As Richardson (1972) pointed out, such links are in fact quite common. Rolander (1983) applied the Gullander approach to horizontal cooperative ventures in the world car industry. Rolander concluded that these ventures were a phenomenon of adjustment where government intervention has impeded exit from the industry.

International Licensing

The literature on licensing has viewed it as yet another alternative for exploiting a foreign market opportunity, though little research has examined licensing in combination with joint ventures and other vehicles for entering foreign markets. However, a few studies have begun to fill the gap. Davies (1977) examined the differences between licensing and joint ventures as means of transferring technology from British to Indian firms during the period 1963–69. He concluded that joint ventures afforded closer interfirm links and were more likely than licensing agreements to entail comprehensive support through the provision of managerial personnel, skills, and information. There are many reasons to suspect that Davies' assertion may not apply more generally, however, and that licensing can be a permanent basis for continuing technology transfer.

Telesio (1979) identified and examined two different motivations for international licensing: entering a foreign market and reciprocal access to technology. When licensing was used as a means of entering a foreign market, Telesio found correlations between licensing activity and five explanatory variables: firm diversification, R & D spending as a percentage of sales, small relative size, lack of foreign experience, and the intensity of competition. Telesio found that companies with more foreign experience tended to license less (though as Caves [1982] pointed out, the measure of overseas experience used—the percentage of total sales manufactured by controlled subsidiaries abroad—biases the test toward confirmation of the hypothesis). Telesio also found the unexpected but statistically significant result that non-U.S. firms appeared to have relatively more licensee sales and more royalty income than U.S. firms. He could not find statistically significant confirmation for his other hypotheses. In particular, he expected but did not find the R & D as a percentage of sales variable to be a determinant of licensing.

Broader Studies

A number of writers have tried to draw broader attention to the existence of forms of organization that fall between the poles of arm's-length markets and merger. For example, Richardson (1972) analyzed cooperative agreements, and more generally the division between markets and administrative coordination, in terms of the need to coordinate discrete economic activities, either because they need to be joined together to produce a product (complementary activities) or because of shared skills or costs (similar activities). Richardson's basic analytical approach is an apt one, but he applies it primarily to the division of vertical stages in an industry.

A more recent attempt to examine a broad range of interfirm transactions was made by Mariti and Smiley (1983). They identified all long-term, explicit agreements among firms reported in the European financial press during 1980 and interviewed firms that had actively participated in coalitions. The legal form was a joint venture in 55 percent of the cases, a bidding consortium in 29 percent, and in the remainder some other arrangement or no legal contract. The most active two-digit industries in establishing cooperative agreements were electrical and electronic appliances and telecommunication equipment, chemicals, electronics, automobiles, and oil refining (the latter particularly for bidding consortia).

The categorization of motivations for the agreements the authors identified is given in Table 10.1. Transaction cost reduction was universally dismissed as a motivation by their interviewees. In automobiles managers identified the reasons for coalition formation as cost reduction through scale economies, in metals the control of excess

Table 10.1. Motivations in the Sample of
Seventy Cooperative Agreements

Motivation	(%)
Technology Transfer	29
Technological Complementarity	41
Marketing Agreement	21
Economies of Scale	16
Risk Sharing	14

SOURCE: Mariti and Smiley (1983).

capacity was deemed important, and in computers the speed and diffusion of technical development was the key motivation. Although their identification of motivations for agreements was relatively broad, Mariti and Smiley did not explore why cooperative agreements are preferred to mergers, nor provide a conceptual framework for understanding them.

COALITIONS AND INTERNATIONAL STRATEGY

Coalition formation can only be understood in the context of a firm's overall strategy for competing internationally in an industry. As discussed in chapter 1, two key dimensions of international strategy are the international configuration of a firm's activities (where and in how many places they are located) and the extent to which activities located in different countries are coordinated (how do they relate). Coalitions are a means of performing one or more activities in combination with another firm instead of autonomously—they are thus a means of configuration. The choice of a coalition implies that it is perceived as a less costly or more effective way to configure than the alternatives of on the one hand developing the skills to perform the activity in-house or on the other hand of merger to gain the capability to perform the activity or to buy products or skills in arm's-length transactions.

Just as a coalition changes the global configuration of an activity, it also complicates the ability to coordinate that activity with others. This is because a coalition links a firm to another independent firm with potentially different motivations. A coalition in one activity may also limit a firm's ability to configure others. For example, a local joint-venture partner may seek to broaden the activities performed in the venture instead of accepting a configuration that is globally determined.

Coalitions and the Value Chain

The benefits and the costs of coalitions in both configuration and coordination can be understood by relating coalitions to the activities a firm performs. Chapter 1 described the concept of the value chain, which disaggregates a firm into the discrete activities performed in developing, producing, marketing, selling, and servicing after sale a product or service (see Figure 10.1).

Coalitions can potentially be formed to perform any activity or group of activities in the value chain. Coalitions arise when performing an activity with a partner is superior to performing the activity internally on the one hand, and to reliance on arm's-length transactions or merger with another firm on the other. The benefits and costs of coalitions versus other forms will depend on the value activity involved. We employ a simplified value chain in this chapter that groups activities into three categories: operations and logistics; marketing, sales, and service; and technology development (see Figure 10.2).

Each of the three groupings of value activities tends to have different economic characteristics, with important implications for the pattern of international competition and for the nature and benefits of coalitions. In technology development, fixed costs and the resulting importance of global scale are often high. In contrast, marketing, sales, and service activities must generally be performed within each country. Thus, the cost of marketing, sales, and service tends to be influenced by country scale and other attributes of the firm's position in each country rather than by the firm's overall global scale or position. Operations and logistics activities generally fall somewhere in between in terms of scale sensitivity, though there are wide variations among industries. These differences imply that we must investigate both the generic purposes of coalitions and also how these generic purposes relate to the activity groupings.

Strategic Benefits of Coalitions

Coalitions will be preferred when the coalition form unlocks benefits that cannot be obtained either by internal development, merger, or arm's-length transactions. Coalitions may allow a firm to reap four classes of benefits in an activity.[1] The first is gaining *economies of scale or learning* by concentrating the activity within one entity to serve both firms. Pooling volume raises the scale of the activity or the rate of learning about how to perform it compared to that of each firm operating separately. Renault and Peugeot, for example, have formed a coalition in which one or the other makes various automotive components.

The second class of benefit of coalitions is in acquiring, pooling, or selling *access* to the knowledge or ability to perform an activity where there are asymmetries between firms; one firm has already incurred the cost of developing the ability, enjoys a preferred position in the activity, or has superior resources. Coalitions for access seek such things as distribution channels, local legitimacy, technology or

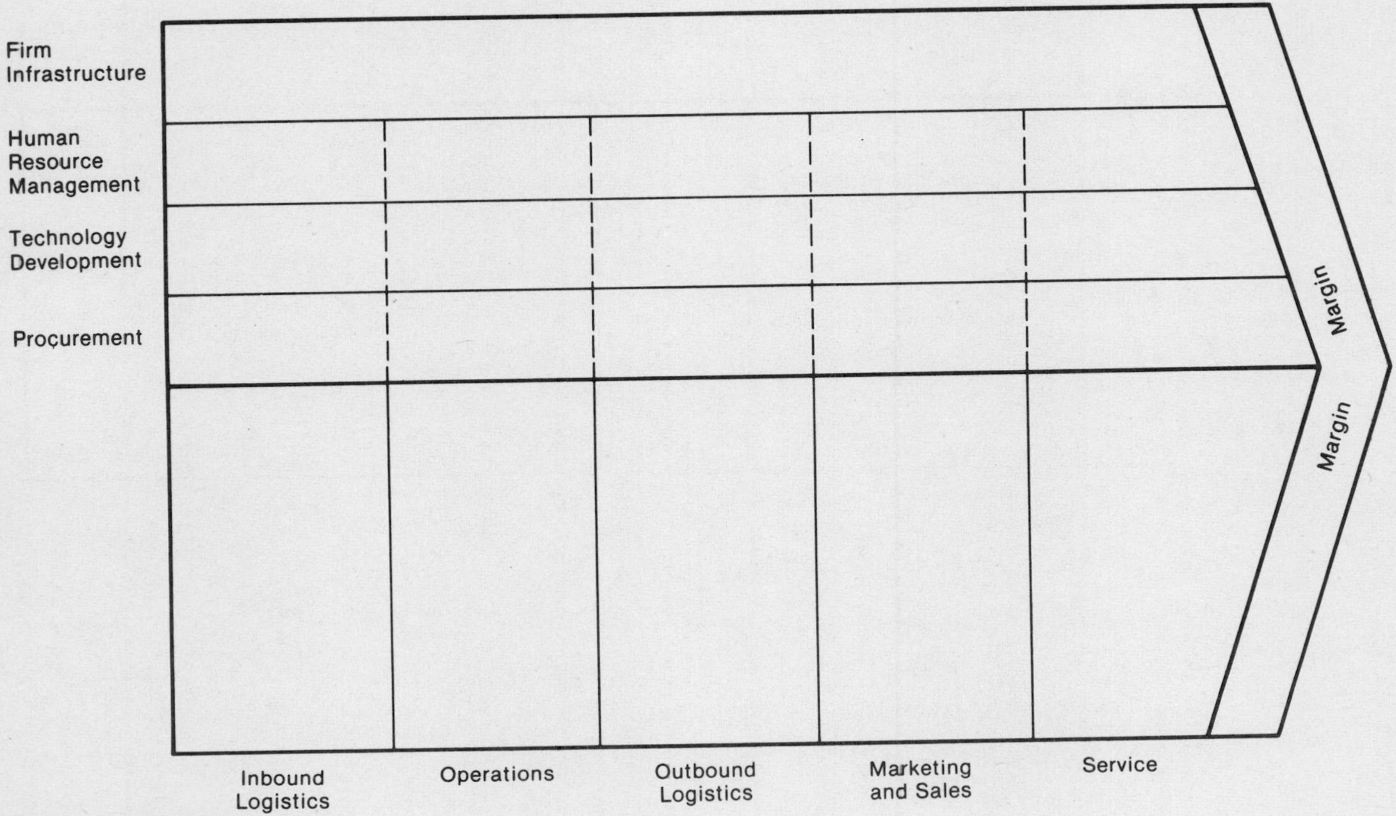
Firm Infrastructure
Human Resource Management
Technology Development
Procurement
Margin
Margin
Inbound Logistics
Operations
Outbound Logistics
Marketing and Sales
Service

Figure 10.1 The Value Chain

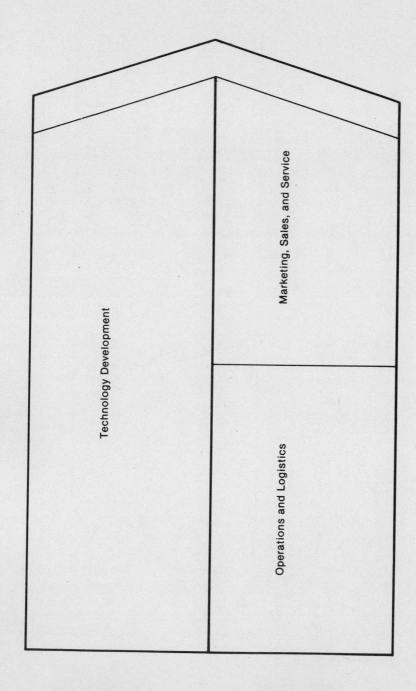

Figure 10.2 Simplified Value Chain

innovative ability, specialized know-how, and capital. Coalitions for access generally grow out of either first-mover effects (e.g., one firm is way ahead on the learning curve or has preempted scarce resources); comparative advantage effects (a country is a preferred location for performing an activity); desire for local ownership; or a combination of the three. Access coalitions either lower the cost of or, importantly, reduce the time required to achieve competence in the activity.

The third class of benefit of coalitions is *reducing risk*. Coalitions are an attractive mechanism for hedging risk because neither partner bears the full risk and cost of the coalition activity. For example, where the absolute size of the variance of return from some activity is very large in relation to optimal firm size in other activities, firms form coalitions to spread risk. In oil, firms often join together in exploration purely to spread risk without any thought of improving the management of the exploration activity or raising its scale.

A fourth class of benefit of coalitions is *shaping competition*, because coalitions can influence who a firm competes with and the basis of competition. This fourth motivation for coalition has been framed narrowly in the literature, primarily in terms of facilitating collusion. In practice, a firm may employ coalitions to facilitate entry of other firms into an industry in order to develop a technology, to affect its competitors' cost structure by influencing key costs or ensuring that competitors employ a particular technology, and to shape competition in its favor in a variety of other ways. Coalitions formed for other reasons may also have an adverse impact on industry structure and competition. We will examine this when treating the costs of coalitions.

A coalition in one activity may require specialized adjustments in other activities—e.g., a technology agreement may require modification of the after-sale service network. This may inhibit coalition formation or cause the span of the coalition to spread. Multiactivity coalitions are common and will be discussed further below.

Both partners to a coalition must gain benefits for the coalition to be the preferred option, though these benefits need not be the same. The benefits of coalitions do not correspond in any simple way to the form of coalition adopted. Economies of scale or desire for access may be reflected in either joint ventures, cooperative agreements or licenses, for example. The legal form of the coalition is more a function of the relative positions of both partners and tax and regulatory considerations than it is of the underlying purpose of the agreement, though the form of the agreement has a strong influence on the allocation of risk. Data presented in chapter 11 illustrate that many coalitions do not take the form of licenses or joint ventures but of agreements of various types. This diversity of forms is further evidence that the form of agreement is tailored to the circumstances rather than vice versa.

Strategic Costs of Coalitions

Coalitions involve potential costs to a firm that must be offset against their benefits. The costs of coalitions fall into three categories: coordination, erosion of competitive position, and creation of an adverse bargaining position. Coalitions require ongoing coordination between the partners that involves management time and money. In addition, divergent interests between coalition partners may complicate the pursuit of a global strategy. The partners may not agree on the best way to configure an activity worldwide, because both partners typically want to play a bigger role. Coordination among dispersed units may also be impeded if different units have different ownership. For example, a joint-venture plant in a developing country may resist standardizing procedures or sharing expertise with the foreign partner's other units or vice versa. Coalitions may also make it more difficult to achieve linkages among separate activities in the value chain because linkages require system optimization that crosses activity boundaries and may raise the cost of the coalition activity.[2] For example, a firm may not be able to persuade its partner in a manufacturing coalition to perform enough inspection, because after-sale service costs fall outside the coalition.

The extent of coordination costs will depend on the degree of similarity of partners' interests and the extent to which the coalition is part of a global or country-centered strategy. As Stopford and Wells (1972) pointed out, the need to integrate the coalition into other activities (signaling the presence of a global strategy) raises the costs of a coalition versus a wholly owned unit. In global strategies, coalitions will involve greater costs if high levels of ongoing coordination are required; a global approach to configuration or coordination in one-time forms, such as a standardized product design, creates less of a need for fluid interaction with the coalition partner than does the need for ongoing coordination in areas such as know-how transfer or scheduling. (See chapter 1 for a discussion of these different forms of coordination.) The similarity of partners' interests will be greater if both are pursuing global strategies than if one is not. Here they will both gain advantage from linking the coalition's activities to others within their organizations. Coalitions involving two multinational firms may well be less costly for this reason, as opposed to coalitions involving a multinational and a domestic firm.

The competitive costs of coalitions grow out of their potential to dissipate sources of competitive advantage and undermine industry structure. Coalitions may create a competitor or make an existing competitor more formidable through the transfer of expertise and market access. Closely related to this, coalitions can lower entry barriers into an industry and worsen other elements of industry structure. In aluminum, for example, the willingness of the majors to enter into joint ventures has made it much easier for a variety of new players such as Royal Dutch Shell and AMAX to get in the industry. Joint ventures have also exacerbated pressures for oversupply because all partners in a venture must agree to reduce its operating rate or pay a penalty.

The presence of competitive costs of coalitions may raise the coordination costs of managing them. Because the partners do not trust each other's long-term motives, they may be wary of coordination that will speed the dissipation of their individual advantages. Similarly, forms of beneficial coordination that make the partners dependent on each other may be avoided.

Coalitions also require that the firm divide the benefits with the coalition partner. Coalitions can expose one or both partners to extraction of profits by the other because it is in an adverse bargaining position. One partner may be able to capture a disproportionate share of the value created by the coalition, because the other partner has made specialized and irreversible investments or the contribution of the partner would be difficult to replace. Such circumstances can eliminate the possibility of reaching an agreement to form the coalition in the first place.

The costs of coalitions are likely to change over the life of the coalition for several reasons. Coordination costs may fall as the partners gain experience in working with each other and trust is established. Similarly, competitive costs may fall if the coalition proves mutually profitable and the likelihood of the partners proceeding on their own decreases. Coordination costs will rise, however, if one or both partners' interests and goals shift. Competitive costs may also rise if one partner gains much of the expertise or position in its own organization that it sought through the coalition and the continuing contribution if the other partner falls.

The learning effect of working with a coalition partner both in ongoing coordination and in discerning partner motives implies that one successful coalition with a partner often begets another coalition with that partner. Partner-specific learning is transferrable across coalitions as long as the relative contributions of the partners remain comparable. In addition, participation in multiple coalitions with a partner can reduce the risk that the partner will behave opportunistically.

Coalitions versus Other Forms

Coalitions must always be compared to other forms of transaction to determine if they are the preferred option to achieving the desired benefit. Compared to arm's-length relationships between firms, coalitions can ease transactional or contractual difficulties. Coalitions usually involve complex areas in which the future is difficult to foresee. Arm's-length transactions or contracts would face difficulties in providing for all the contingencies, while a coalition through sharing profits or otherwise linking firms for the longer term allows both sides to bear risks. In achieving the benefits that coalitions seek, arm's-length transactions also often suffer from impacted information (one side has difficulty learning the value of what is exchanged). For example, the value of a technology is difficult to communicate convincingly without disclosing proprietary information.

Another problem is great uncertainty about the value of what each partner contributes, which leads to coalitions to transfer valuation decisions to the market. In a marketing agreement, for example, sharing profits over a defined period is a way of letting the market decide what the value of market access is rather than agreeing on a price. Similarly, though benefits of shared learning could in principle be achieved if one party allowed the other to perform an activity and purchased its output in return for a payment compensating for the learning benefits the other party gained, determining the size of such benefits beforehand is extremely difficult.

A third transactional issue that makes coalitions sometimes preferable to arm's-length transactions is the problem of creating the proper incentives. A long-term coalition gives each side ongoing incentives to perform, for example, while an arm's-length sale of services or technology may not. Without a coalition, these problems would lead to a lower benefit from the transaction or require high costs of monitoring and control. Another reason to employ coalitions rather than arm's-length transactions is to mitigate the risk or lengthen the period before the other party in the transaction may become a competitor. A coalition also allows the negotiation of terms that limit the activities of the other party, such as defined marketing territories and the like, which raise the firm's long-term profitability.

The other forms of transaction that can achieve the same benefits as coalitions are internal development and merger. Compared to internal development, coalitions are often a more rapid means of repositioning. The time required to build expertise or gain market share internally is likely to exceed the time required with a coalition. As product life cycles have shortened and competitive rivalry has intensified, the timing advantages of coalitions are increasingly important. Coalitions may also be less costly than internal development because partners enjoy first-mover advantages which makes it more expensive to duplicate the benefits sought, and/or partners may price the benefits sought on incremental cost, below the cost of development. Coalitions may also involve a less irreversible commitment than internal development if the coalition can be terminated more easily than a firm could eliminate employees or otherwise change its own course because of the presence of exit barriers.

Coalitions can be preferred to merger because the cost of acquiring a compatible firm is high. Not only may merger premiums be substantial, but retaining management with new found wealth may be difficult. Coalitions also preserve independence for management teams compared to merger, particularly for the partner that is smaller and whose management is likely to be demoted. Home governments also often have an interest in keeping local firms independent instead of having them absorbed by foreign firms. Finally, coalitions can be preferred to merger because they represent a less irreversible commitment where there are uncertainties about the most appropriate partner.

Forming a coalition, then, is a way of achieving the desired benefits with enough assistance from the partner to make the gaining of the benefits practical and timely, with enough permanence to make the gaining of the benefits feasible, but without the finality of making the arrangement completely inflexible. Coalitions are a more rapid means of repositioning than internal development and are often less costly and involve a less irreversible commitment than merger. Where market transactions are difficult to consummate but firms would benefit from collaboration, coalitions are a means of permitting collaboration without sacrificing independence.

The speed of coalitions as a means of repositioning implies that they will be particularly likely to occur during period of rapid and significant structural change in an industry, particularly structural change involving rising economies of scale. Structural change frequently erodes the existing sources of competitive advantage of some firms and creates new bases of advantage. Firms seek coalitions in order to respond quickly and without the expense of acquisition while retaining independence. This implies that some coalitions may be transitional devices that ultimately dissolve or lead to merger.

Coalition Stability

The role of coalitions as a transitional device as well as the fact that coalitions have costs suggest that it is important to understand what makes a coalition stable. Coalitions involving access to knowledge or ability are the most likely to dissolve as the party gaining access acquires its own internal skills through the coalition. Coalitions designed to gain the benefits of scale or learning in performing an activity have a more enduring purpose. If they dissolve, they will tend to dissolve into merger or into an arm's-length transaction. The stability of risk-reducing coalitions depends on the sources of risk they seek to control. Coalitions hedging against the risk of a single exogenous event will tend to dissolve, while coalitions involving an ongoing risk (e.g., exploration risk for oil) will be more durable.

Coalition agreements require that each party contribute to the coalition and receive benefits that exceed those of alternative forms. Partner contributions can each be in the same activity or the coalition can involve complementary contributions by the partners in two or more activities. A firm's contribution to coalitions in an activity can take three forms that are not mutually exclusive: (1) access (e.g., knowledge, market position), (2) volume of throughput independent of access, and (3) capital. Capital is a form of access (access to resources) that is usefully separated from others for present purposes. Firms may *pool* contributions in these forms (e.g., both contribute knowledge about how to perform an activity and comparable volume of throughput) or one firm may contribute in one way (e.g., volume and/or capital) while the other firm contributes in other ways. Coalitions also frequently arise as well when one partner provides one form of access (e.g., technology) while the other provides another (e.g., market access). In some complementary coalitions, the coalition spans several activities and partners make differing contributions in each one.

The stability of coalitions rises when partners make balanced or complementary contributions in forms that are not one-time or self-liquidating. Hence, for example, a coalition based on an essentially one-time transfer of knowledge in return for capital will tend to be less stable than one in which both firms contribute volume of throughput and pool their technical staffs. The latter coalition, if it dissolves, will more likely lead to merger. Similarly, a technology-licensing agreement to hedge risk will be most stable if both partners are engaged in active R & D work (cross-licensing) than if one firm is principally contributing capital to buy the results of the other's R & D.

FORMS AND TYPES OF COALITIONS

The generic motivations for coalitions translate into more specific reasons underlying coalitions, in particular value activities or spanning particular groups of countries.

Technology-Development Coalitions

The nature of technology-development activities make the relative importance of coalitions benefits different for technology-development coalitions than in other activities. Chapters 1 and 3 have illustrated how technology is essential to international competition, yet it changes rapidly and unpredictably. Moreover, the costs of technology development often have a large fixed component regardless of a firm's sales volume and market share.

The large, fixed component of technology-development cost leads to frequent coalitions to achieve economies of scale or learning. In many industries, such as computers, telecommunications, and aircraft, for example, the absolute size of technology-development cost has been increasing rapidly. This raises the incentive to pool R & D despite transaction and coordination difficulties. European computer companies have been active participants in collaborative research efforts, for example. Siemens and ICL both have links with Fujitsu, while ICL, Siemens, and Machines Bull have formed a joint research institute in West Germany to pool their basic research. In the United States, fourteen computer and semiconductor firms formed the Microelectronics and Computer Technology Corporation in 1983 to develop advanced computer and software technology.

The large, fixed-cost component of technology development also leads to coalitions to gain access to technology when one firm has advanced far beyond others. Either through licenses or joint development agreements, technological leaders can transfer to followers technology that would be prohibitively expensive to develop internally even if followers pooled their efforts. The joint-development agreement between Boeing and a number of Japanese firms is one example. Similarly, in the pharmaceutical industry, coalitions in the form of patent licenses for new products allow firms to overcome irreducible delays in developing and testing products in-house. The motivation for leaders to transfer technology is usually capital or market access.

Coalitions in technology development can also be a way of gaining access to innovations that would be hard to replicate internally even if spending on technology development was high. Innovative technological development may require different managerial skills than commercialization. Small entrepreneurial firms may be good innovators, but need assistance in commercialization and are reluctant to lose their independence. For example, the scientific entrepreneur, Stanford Ovshinsky repeatedly employed this strategy. In semiconductors and microfilm technology, he formed coalitions with IBM, Eastman Kodak, 3M, Agfa-Gevaert, and Asahi Chemical.[3]

The unpredictable and risky nature of technology development makes the hedging of risk a prominent motivation for coalitions in this activity as well. Coalitions hedge against the risk that a firm misses out on important innovations. Coalitions allow more technological avenues to be pursued and provide an easier mechanism than mergers for switching partners (and thus research capability and strategy) over time. In the pharmaceutical industry, for example, competitors have traditionally been willing to cross-license new products. The number of licenses has proliferated as the cost of product development has risen and firms have felt the need to hedge, particularly in the biotechnology field. Shared research efforts or other coalitions between firms widen access in an industry to new innovations. An assessment of the social effect of such coalitions must balance any reduction in competition involved against wider access to innovations.

Coalitions in technology development are also an important means for shaping industry structure. Coalitions that diffuse a technology may aid in developing the market, achieving technological standardization, or providing buyers a second source.[4] Coalitions that encourage new competitors may block other more threatening entrants. Coalitions that diffuse technology within the industry may elevate competitor cost structures to lock in an advantage for the firm. They may also give one partner the ability to monitor development efforts by competitors.

Technology coalitions are often preferable to arm's-length market transactions because stable, long-term relationships can be vital in technology exchange. The cost of switching to other technologies is often high because other activities in a firm are configured for a particular technology. A firm becomes dependent on the continued supply of developments from its technology supplier, placing the firm in an adverse bargaining situation. In addition, transferring technology between separate organizations usually requires prolonged interaction between personnel of the two firms that is not feasible without a long-term contractual framework. For example, in the marine diesel engine industry, designers maintain engineering staffs permanently on the premises of their licensees and offer extensive training programs. Diesel engine designers also need feedback from their licensees on problems encountered in manufacturing and in operational service. A coalition is a necessary framework for this uninhibited cooperation.

Coalitions in technology development are often preferred to arm's-length transactions because technology is kept out of the open market, preserving entry and mobility barriers. Market transactions involving technology also involve significant contractual difficulties. The seller of a technology knows much more about it than the potential buyer; if the seller tells the buyer everything before the sale the buyer need not buy. A coalition does not completely solve this problem, but it can make it less necessary to agree in advance on the value of a technology. If firms form an equity joint venture, for example, they need agree only on the relative contribution of each to its success; the overall size of the profits can be left to the market to determine. Unless the coalition partners are successful at predicting how their mutual interests will evolve, however, coalitions raise the risk of an agreement that one or both parties find inappropriate in the future.

Operations and Logistics Coalitions

Coalitions in operations and logistics activities are frequently motivated by the search for ongoing scale and/or learning economies. Two particular situations are often associated with their formation. When process change increases the minimum efficient scale in an industry in activities such as component fabrication, assembly, or logistical infrastructure, firms may be unable to attain the new scale internally, and may face substantial difficulties in gaining the market share necessary to justify expansion because other competitors are attempting to do the same thing. Coalitions can allow the partners to exploit scale economies in an activity with little disturbance to the rest of their value chains, while preserving independence.

Coalitions in operations and logistics also grow out of needs for access. Coalitions may be used to transfer manufacturing know-how. A prominent example is the production joint venture in California between General Motors and Toyota.[5] Another access motivation for coalitions in operations and logistics is the result of pressure from host governments for local manufacturing. Government pressure is often greatest in labor-intensive activities such as assembly. In some countries, local partners are mandated by government. In other circumstances, global competitors may join together in a local facility to both gain access and achieve scale efficiencies in serving a country. For example, coalitions in automobile assembly produce several rivals' cars for the local market in some highly protected countries. Coalitions can thus facilitate responsiveness to government at less cost than alternative arrangements.

Coalitions in operations and logistics may also be motivated by the desire to gain access to comparative advantage in performing activities in a country. A coalition either pools the cost of establishing facilities in a country or taps the prior investment in the country by a local firm. Coalitions in operations and logistics are proliferating today with firms in Pacific rim countries such as Korea, Taiwan, Singapore, and Hong Kong for this reason, as the data in chapter 11 will illustrate.

Operation and logistical coalitions are rarely formed to hedge against risk, though this motivation may grow more prevalent as exchange rate fluctuations continue to persist. In a world of fluctuating exchange rates, coalitions in manufacturing in several countries may be a form of hedging. Such coalitions may also hedge against shifts in overall competitiveness among countries, reflecting shifts in relative labor and resource costs.

Operations and logistical coalitions can play a role in shaping competition, though generally a less important one than coalitions in technology development or in marketing, sales, and service. Coalitions in operations and logistics may play the role of promoting retirement of capacity when demand falls. Coalitions that allow rationalization of plants can allow the partners to share in the benefits of higher capacity utilization.

Marketing, Sales, and Service Coalitions

The character of coalitions in marketing, sales, and service (MSS) reflects the fact that these activities usually must be performed near buyers and often must be tailored to individual country conditions. The costs of MSS are therefore often sensitive to scale in a country or to relative country market share.

MSS coalitions can allow the partners to reap economies of country scale or learning, particularly coalitions between foreign firms to serve a country. Even more prominent are MSS coalitions to achieve access to local know-how, local legitimacy, government blessing, and strong local market positions gained through first-mover effects. MSS coalitions are infrequent for purely risk-hedging purposes. However, they can be an important tool for shaping competition through neutralizing potential competitors.

Now entrants into an industry sometimes form MSS coalitions with established firms as an entry strategy. For example, Western Union purchased 25 percent of Vitalink Communications Corporation.[6] "As a small company there were questions about whether we could meet customers' long-term demands for [communications] capacity," said Vitalink's president. "So we needed a relationship with a [larger] company." This variant of coalition, between a firm in an emerging industry and one in the industry for which it is substituting, allows a newcomer to tap the distribution channels and reputation of the established firm (access motive) and permits the established firm some measure of protection against substitution (hedging motive) while reducing the threatened industry's resistance to substitution (shaping competition motive).

MSS coalitions may be particularly unstable, however, because they frequently are formed because of the access motive on one or both sides. For example, one partner needs market access while the other needs access to product. As the foreign partner's market know-how increases, there is less and less need for a local partner. Even MSS coalitions formed for scale or learning motives can be unstable. If markets grow larger, the incentive of each partner to integrate forward may rise. If distinctive national requirements in a country become less important, the need for a nationally oriented marketing organization may fall and diminish the need for a coalition. A local partner naturally has no incentive to promote this process, and instead is more interested in increasing the backward vertical integration of local operations. Conflict between the partners may therefore tend to increase over time and cause the coalition to dissolve.

Multiple-Activity Coalitions

Coalitions may cover more than one value activity. Multiple-activity coalitions arise for two different reasons. Activities may be so inexorably linked that forming a coalition in one forces a similar arrangement in the other. The connections among activities may involve such things as the need for close coordination or the requirement to invest in specialized assets in other activities because of how one activity is performed. The need for specialized investment would place the firm involved in an adverse bargaining situation to the coalition partner in the linked activity and hence the coalition is broadened to include both. For example, in countries where automobile companies have formed coalitions for local production, marketing links usually follow because of the need for coordination and investment in specialized service facilities.

Multiple-activity coalitions also arise when there are incentives for coalition formation in several activities and either (1) agreement is easier to achieve overall rather than for each activity separately, (2) there are coordination problems in working with multiple-coalition partners simultaneously, or (3) both. The partners' strengths in different value activities may be different and complementary. For instance, if one is strong in technology development and the other in MSS, a coalition that covers both sets of activities establishes a mutuality of benefit that makes the coalition attractive and potentially more stable. If the firms viewed each activity separately, however, the stronger party in each would have little incentive to enter a coalition. An interesting implication is that coalitions have an element of exclusivity. Forming one coalition with a partner may lead to a more extensive coalition, a tendency reinforced by the coordination benefits of dealing with one partner.

An example of a coalition strategy embracing both multiple-value activities and multiple-coalition partners is Montedison in the polypropylene business.[7] Montedison began with a joint research agreement with Mitsui Petrochemical covering polypropylene. This project produced a number of proprietary catalysts that were exploited in the U.S. market through licensing agreements. When Montedison decided to reenter the U.S. market directly, it was able to lever its newest catalyst into a U.S. presence by use of a more extensive coalition. Its coalition partner was Hercules, which had a large (13 percent) but unprofitable share of the world's polypropylene capacity, an excellent U.S. marketing organization, and the objective of reducing its involvement in commodity chemicals. Hercules and Montedison merged their worldwide polypropylene resin businesses in a 50–50 joint venture. Montedison contributed its new technology and about $100 million in cash, while Hercules contributed the bulk of the venture's manufacturing capacity and its U.S. marketing arm. A major reason why both companies were willing to enter such an extensive coalition was a history of successful joint ventures between them. They had shared the operation of an Italian polypropylene plant for over twenty years, and also had a jointly owned drug company in the United States.

Firms' positions in different value activities may evolve differently over time. In a coalition that embraces both technology development and MSS, for example, the benefit of the technology link might diminish if the rate of technological change slows while the marketing link remains important. If value activities covered in a coalition evolve in different ways, friction between the partners is likely to arise and it may be difficult to renegotiate the coalition to both parties' satisfaction.

Single-Country and Multicountry Coalitions

Coalitions can cover a single country or many countries. The geographic scope of a coalition reflects its motivation. Single-country coalitions are formed for reasons that are inherently country-specific, often to gain access to a particular country as a market, as a local production site or in response to government pressure or the presence of comparative advantage. The link between Honda and British Leyland (BL) in the United Kingdom, for example, allows Honda to tap BL's dealer network and production facilities, thereby leapfrogging its stronger Japanese competitors, while BL obtains the latest technology faster and more economically than it could develop it internally. At the same time, the coalition heads off damaging government action against Japanese imports.

Single-country coalitions are most frequently in the MSS activities because these are most closely tied to individual countries. Here, a firm may construct a network of such coalitions involving different partners around the world. Multicountry coalitions are typically formed in activities that can apply to many countries, such as operations and logistics and technology development. The activity covered by a coalition need not be conducted in many countries, but its output serves many countries. Multicountry coalitions should become more prevalent the more global the pattern of competition in an industry becomes.

X and Y Coalitions

There are two types of coalitions that involve any value activity: coalitions across the borders of activities (X coalitions) and coalitions within activities (Y coalitions). In X coalitions, firms divide the activities within an industry between themselves (for example, one partner manufactures while letting the other market). In Y coalitions, the firms *share* the actual performance of one or more value activities (for example, a joint marketing agreement). The distinction between X and Y coalitions is important because their strategic motivations differ as well as their costs.

The essence of an X coalition is that the partners contract with each other for the performance of activities. A coalition provides a tighter coordinating mechanism than an arm's-length transaction, but does not go as far as vertical merger. Forming X coalitions involves identifying the activities in which a firm is well positioned, and "purchasing" through the coalition activities that the firm cannot perform effectively or efficiently. Conversely, a firm may contract to perform an activity for another firm to reciprocate for the other firm performing a different activity, to generate cash, or to strengthen the activity by increasing scale.

Thus X coalitions usually imply that firms have asymmetric positions in an activity: one is strong and the other is weaker. A tighter coordinating mechanism in the exchange than the open market is needed (particularly when national borders are crossed) for administrative convenience, and more importantly, because both buyers and sellers of an activity are often committed to each other once capacity has been put in place. X coalitions normally take the form of long-term supply agreements, licenses, or marketing agreements, though they can be joint ventures in which one partner contributes primarily money.

Y coalitions, in contrast to X coalitions, change the way an activity is performed because the partners work together on a continuing basis to perform it. Y coalitions are aimed at improving firms' joint positions in a value activity rather than parceling out the activities that they individually perform. Sharing or combining may allow the achievement of scale economies, the reduction of excess capacity, transfer of knowledge, or risk pooling. Y coalitions tend to result when the partners are more similar in strengths, weaknesses, and objectives. Y coalitions are also more effective mechanisms for learning from partners, because they imply close and constant contact with them. Y coalitions frequently take the form of joint ventures, but they also include technology sharing, cross-licensing, and other cooperative agreements.

X coalitions result from complementary dissimilarity between the partners' value chains. An X coalition allows a partner to specialize in value activities where it is strongest. In Y coalitions, on the other hand, the partners tend to be more similar and neither by itself can satisfactorily perform an activity, even with the increased volume gained if it performed the activity for the other partner. The best solution, therefore, is for both partners to participate in managing the coalition activity so that both can contribute to its effectiveness. The greater similarity between partners' positions in Y coalitions means that they should be more stable than X coalitions, other things being equal.

The bargaining positions of partners in X coalitions depend on the industry structure. The relative importance to competition of the coalition activities will determine bargaining power. Bargaining power is greater when a firm has strength in important activities for competition in which few coalition partners are available. Relative bargaining power in Y coalitions depends more on the economics of the value activity covered by the coalition. In a manufacturing joint venture, for example, bargaining power is a function of relative sales volume if the activities covered are scale sensitive.

The intermingling of an activity between partners in Y coalitions has important implications for the bargaining positions of the partners

Figure 10.3 Patterns of International Strategy

		Geographically Dispersed	Geographically Concentrated
Coordination among Activities	High	foreign investment with strong central control	simple global strategy
	Low	country-centered multinationals or domestic firms	export-based strategy

Configuration of Activities

both before and after the coalition is formed. It is generally harder to switch partners in Y coalitions than it is in X coalitions. In X coalitions, a firm must induce a new firm to play the same role as the old partner. In Y coalitions, terminating a relationship may require a buy-out by one partner and the other partner starting from scratch, relying only on what has been learned through the coalition. In a Y coalition, therefore, the alternative for each partner tends to be complete integration, whereas in an X coalition the alternative is more likely to be replacing one partner with a new one.

The Pattern of Coalitions and International Strategy

Chapter 1 described how configuration and coordination were the two important dimensions of international strategy. These were combined into a matrix on which different patterns of international strategy can be positioned (see Figure 10.3). Coalitions are a means for implementing each pattern of international strategy with the help of a partner. In a highly dispersed configuration, for example, a firm can use local coalitions to adapt to country requirements. Dispersed configurations involving modest coordination among countries will tend to be associated with the presence of many single-country coalitions. Firms with highly integrated international strategies will tend to get involved in multicountry coalitions, particularly in operations and logistics and technology development. Firms in the upper-right-hand corner of the matrix will resort to single-country coalitions only under government pressures.[8]

Two or more firms with incomplete global networks may join through coalitions to build a more complete global strategy. Typically, such coalitions involve multiple value activities or multiple geographical markets. For example, the partners may agree to market each other's products in parts of the world where they have offsetting strengths. Frequently, technology is shared between the two. The firms do not merge completely because the benefits of a global strategy are confined to a few value activities, and there may also be a strong desire for independence. If industry structure continues to move toward globalization and the coalition is judged a success by the firm, the impediments to merger may fall over time and the partners may unite.

While coalitions can be a powerful tool in global configuration, however, they have important effects on a firm's ability to change configuration and to coordinate that has been described earlier. Coalitions, once established, can limit feasible future configurations. Having coalition partners can make it difficult to pursue a concentrated configuration. Partners may prefer to increase the span of activities they perform rather than give up some activities for the sake of overall global cost position or differentiation. They may exaggerate the desire of local governments for local content, as well as the need to adapt products for local market needs. This can severely impede the transition to a fully global strategy.

Coalitions also often make coordination more difficult because they involve a partner in the value chain with independent and potentially different motivations (this is the familiar complaint of multinationals about joint-venture partners). In some value activities (frequently MSS), less global coordination may be needed than in other activities because of local differences. Single-country coalitions in such activities can help global competitors respond to country-specific conditions.

Firms in the lower left-hand corner of Figure 10.3 should be relatively willing to form single-country coalitions, because they suffer little from the coordination problems raised by coalitions or from the pressures created by coalition partners against concentrated configurations. Provided partners' international strategies remain unchanged, coalitions among them can be enduring. The noted instability of joint ventures seems to reflect more a trend for multinationals to change their overall strategies from uncoordinated to coordinated than a change in the method of implementing an uncoordinated strategy.

IMPLEMENTING COALITION AGREEMENTS

Identifying coalition partners is perhaps the single most important issue in establishing a successful coalition. Prospective partners must be carefully assessed both in terms of their contribution to the success of the coalition and the risks of forming links with them. A partner's contribution depends on both its capabilities as well as its incentive to harness those capabilities in a way that allows the firm to achieve its objectives from the coalition. An important risk in coalitions is that one partner will use the coalition to strengthen its own position while holding back benefits that would strengthen the other partner. The partner with the most to offer in a coalition is often the one that poses the greatest long-term competitive threat. This implies that European forms may want linkages with U.S. or Japanese firms for their technology, but prefer alliances with other European firms from a competitive standpoint.

In selecting coalition partners, it is important to predict how the partner's contribution and the partner's strategy will evolve over time. A continuing convergence of interests is necessary, as well as the willingness of each partner to work consciously to do its share of tasks that may be incompletely specified in the legal agreements. Because coalitions are difficult to untangle, it is important to avoid coalitions for short-term expediency that will foreclose preferable alliances later on. It is also highly desirable that the negotiations to form a coalition are perceived as fair, because of the continuing coordination required in a coalition.

The transactions costs of negotiating and managing coalitions are a significant barrier to coalition formation. Coalitions tend to consume a great deal of management time because they are transnational, often important, relatively complex, and frequently somewhat inflexible once they have been established. The managers involved in supervising coalitions are often very senior because of the need for high-level involvement when dealing with independent firms in long-term agreements.

Managing coalitions is facilitated if the partners' organizational structures and procedures are similar. This makes the partners' motivations both more compatible and more understandable to each other. Organizational similarity tends to be greater when the partners are of similar size, growth prospects, and international experience. Negotiating and managing coalitions often seem to follow a life-cycle pattern. In the initial courtship phase, the potential partners gather information about each other to identify whether their goals are congruent and their capabilities complementary. In the negotiation stage that follows, expectations are defined and the coalition's legal structure is established. In the start-up phase, the functions of courtship and negotiation are continued, but in a more intimate fashion. Practical details are settled, and a pattern for operating the coalition falls into place, from which changes are hard to achieve. Nonetheless, revisions of the coalition agreement are sometimes inevitable or a coalition will dissolve. The most difficult renegotiations are those in which the partner's needs or contributions have diverged.

If a coalition outlives its usefulness, the manner of its dissolution can be important to the partners. Disagreements between the partners can destroy the economic assets that a coalition has created. Market positions are particularly vulnerable to erosion by a messy divorce, as buyers lose confidence. A coalition may simply be dissolved (firms cease to share their research results with each other, for example), be absorbed entirely by one partner, or become a separate entity distinct from both the parents. The contingency of dissolution should be examined and provided for before a coalition agreement is signed.

SUMMARY

The discussion in this chapter suggests six criteria for selecting a long-term coalition partner:

- *Possession of the desired source of competitive advantage*. The partner must possess the scale, technology, market access, or other contribution that the coalition seeks. Conversely, the combination of the two weak partners does not necessarily make a strong coalition unless the combination results in the possession of all important sources of competitive advantages.
- *The need for a complementary or balanced contribution from the firm*. The partner must not be so strong, or so weak, that the coalition is or becomes unstable, or that the partner can extract too large a proportion of the profits.
- *A compatible view of international strategy*. The partner's view of international strategy must support the required coordination.
- *Low risk of becoming a competitor*. In part because of the firm's enduring contribution and in part because of the partner's goals and strategy, it is unlikely to seek to dissolve the coalition in favor of competing independently.
- *Preemptive value as a partner vis-à-vis rivals*. The partner would provide a major source of advantage to threatening rivals that would seriously undermine the firm's position, so that preempting it carries defensive value.
- *Organizational compatibility*. The partner's organizational style and norms are similar enough to allow ongoing collaboration.

In choosing a temporary or transitional partner, the first and fifth criteria become dominant. Here the firm may deliberately select a partner with whom a coalition has a high level of instability so as to lower the cost of parting once the benefits of the coalition have been achieved.

Coalitions represent an important strategic option in international competition. While they have long been common and offer benefits even in country-centered strategies, the benefits of coalitions are enhanced by several industry characteristics also associated with global competition. Substantial R & D expenditures, economies of scale and learning, and differing patterns of country comparative advantage among activities all tend to make competition more global at the same time as they create incentives to use coalitions to deal with it. Coalitions involving multiple activities and multiple countries become increasingly likely as competition globalizes, as do coalitions among firms from developed countries (in contrast to coalitions between developed country firms and local partners). Particularly as industries evolve to a global pattern of competition, coalitions may be resorted to frequently as a transitional device. The growing government impediments to global strategies are heightening the incentives for, and in some cases forcing, firms to employ the coalition option as well.

Coalitions also create difficulties that are exacerbated by global competition. Coalitions clearly complicate the process of global coordination as well as the adjustment of global configuration to changing circumstances. Coalitions also have a greater likelihood of creating a competitor or eroding industry structure when competition is global than if it is multidomestic and the coalition partner is a foreign firm. Finally, coalitions are frequently unstable and difficult to manage. They can be disruptive to a firm's strategy.

Coalitions should be approached with a full view of their costs as well as their benefits. We believe that coalitions in the most vital activities of a firm's value chain should be resorted to only rarely. A firm must ultimately master such activities itself if it is to sustain a competitive advantage in its industry. The widespread coalitions in Europe in recent years are unlikely to be the "solution" they have frequently been perceived to be. However, coalitions can be a valuable tool in many aspects of global strategy and the ability to exploit them will be an important and probably growing source of international competitive advantage.

NOTES

1. Many of the benefits of coalitions, such as market access or economies of scale, have been discussed in the literature on specific forms of coalitions.
2. See Porter (1985), chap. 2 for a discussion of linkages.
3. *Business Week* (1976).
4. For a discussion of these and other benefits of competitors, see Porter (1985), chap. 6.
5. Operations know-how is also often part of a license or joint-venture agreement in technology development.
6. *Business Week* (1983).
7. *Chemical Week* (1983).
8. Stopford and Wells's (1972) pioneering work on joint ventures supports this interpretation.

REFERENCES

Berg, S. V., J. Duncan, and P. Friedman. *Joint Venture Strategies and Corporate Innovation*. Cambridge, Mass.: Oelgeschlager, Gunn & Hain, 1982.

Berg, S. V., and P. Friedman. "Technological Complementarities and Industrial Patterns of Joint Venture Activity, 1964–1975." *Industrial Organization Review* 6 (1978): 110–16.

Boyle, S. E. "An Estimate of the Number and Size Distribution of Domestic Joint Subsidiaries." *Antitrust Law and Economics Review* 1 (1968): 81–92.

Business Week. "The Race for a New Market in Microfilm." April 5, 1976, 44–49.

Caves, R. E. *Multinational Enterprise and Economic Analysis*. Cambridge, England: Cambridge University Press, 1982.

Chemical Week. "Two Hands Are Joined in Polypropylene." May 25, 1983, 10–11.

Davies, H. "Technology Transfer Through Commercial Transactions." *Journal of Industrial Economics* 26 (1977): 161–75.

Dixon, P. R. "Joint Ventures: What Is Their Impact on Competition?" *Antitrust Bulletin* 7 (1962): 397–410.

Franko, L. G. *Joint Venture Survival in Multinational Corporations*. New York: Praeger, 1971.

Friedman, P., S. V. Berg, and J. Duncan. "External vs. Internal Knowledge Acquisition: Joint Venture Activity and R & D Intensity." *Journal of Economics and Business* 32 (1979): 103–10.

Fusfeld, D. R. "Joint Subsidiaries in the Iron and Steel Industry." *American Economic Review* 48 (1958): 578–87.

Gullander, S. "Joint Ventures in Europe: Determinants of Entry." *International Studies of Management and Organizations* 6 (1976a): 85–111.

———. "Joint Ventures and Corporate Strategy." *Columbia Journal of World Business* 11 (1976b): 104–14.

Hladik, K. J. "International Joint Ventures: An Empirical Investigation into the Characteristics of Recent U.S.-Foreign Joint Venture Partnerships." Ph.D. diss., Harvard University, Graduate School of Business Administration, 1984.

Hlavacek, J. D., B. H. Dovey, and J. J. Biondo. "Tie Small Business Technology to Marketing Power." *Harvard Business Review* 55, no. 11 (January/February, 1977): 106–16.

Mariti, P., and R. H. Smiley. "Co-operative Agreements and the Organization of Industry." *The Journal of Industrial Economics* 31 (1983): 437–51.

Pate, J. L. "Joint Venture Activity, 1960–1968." *Economic Review,* Federal Reserve Bank of Cleveland, 1969, 16–23.

Pfeffer, J., and P. Nowak. "Joint Ventures and Interorganizational Interdependence." *Administrative Science Quarterly* 21 (1976a): 398–418.

———. "Patterns of Joint Venture Activity: Implications for Antitrust Policy." *Antitrust Bulletin* 21 (1976b): 315–39.

Richardson, G. B. "The Organization of Industry." *Economic Journal* 82 (1972): 883–96.

Rolander, D. "Horizontal Cooperative Ventures in the World Car Industry—Driving Forces and Effects." Stockholm School of Economics, Institute of International Business, 1983.

Stopford, J. M., and L. T. Wells, Jr. *Managing the Multinational Enterprise*. New York: Basic Books, 1972.

Stuckey, J. A. *Vertical Integration and Joint Ventures in the Aluminum Industry*. Cambridge, Mass.: Harvard University Press, 1983.

Telesio, P. *Technology Licensing and Multinational Enterprises*. New York: Praeger, 1979.

West, M. W., Jr. "The Jointly Owned Subsidiary." *Harvard Business Review* 37, no. 4 (July/August, 1959): 31–34, 165–172.

Williamson, O. E. *Markets and Hierarchies: Analysis and Antitrust Implications*. New York: Free Press, 1975.

11

Patterns of International Coalition Activity

Pankaj Ghemawat, Michael E. Porter,
and
Richard A. Rawlinson

This chapter assembles evidence about the extent of international co-alition activity, its distribution across industries, countries, and types of firms, and its purposes. Coalitions represent a taxonomically novel category and, as chapter 10 argues, a strategically meaningful one. Therefore we should expect to learn a substantial amount through an integrated, rather than piecemeal, examination of them. We employ a new dataset to do so, which is more current and comprehensive than those available to previous researchers.

Our principal goal in this chapter is to provide a factual picture of international coalition activity and partial tests of its variation across countries, industries, and firms. Easily testable hypotheses about the incidence of the coalitions are difficult to come by, and hence our study stops short of full-blown verification or falsification of theories of coalition incidence.[1] An example may help clarify the difficulty. Case studies suggest that coalitions are often formed in order to pool R & D efforts. Should we therefore expect a higher incidence of coalitions in R & D–intensive industries? Not necessarily—in very R & D–inten-sive industries, the forces driving toward integration might be so strong that firms rely on internal development rather than coalition. By implication, if coalitions abound in industries with intermediate R & D intensities, the *average* R & D intensity of those industries could be either higher or lower than the average across low R & D industries (market by market intermediation) and high R & D indus-

We are indebted to Richard E. Caves, John M. Stopford, and Louis T. Wells, Jr., for helpful comments. U. Srinivasa Rangan provided able re-search assistance.

tries (marked by integration). A similar problem—that coalitions represent an intermediate choice between two polar forms of economic organization—dogs many of the other hypotheses about coalition incidence that have been floated in past research. Particularly in light of these problems, an in-depth look at the actual patterns of coalition activity should help both to clear the air about the phenomenon and lay a foundation for future research.

RESEARCH DESIGN

The principal database for this chapter comprises *all* the international coalitions formed between 1970 and 1982 that were reported in *The Wall Street Journal*. The sample included joint ventures, licenses, supply agreements, and other long-term interfirm accords; we did, however, leave out agreements—such as hotel management contracts—that appeared to be routine industry practices. We focus in this chapter on the *flows* of new coalitions rather than the total *stock* of existing coalitions. Stocks, although of direct interest, are hard to measure because of the paucity of data sources and the reportedly wide variations in coalition longevity. We make the assumption that firms *tend* to form coalitions in settings congenial to them. By implication, new coalitions, as (partial) adjustments toward optimality, will be concentrated in coalition-prone settings, and the incidences of stocks and flows will be correlated positively.

Flows of new coalitions are easier to measure than stocks; when tracked over a suitably long period, they also capture most of the stock in existence at the end of it. A bit of arithmetic will clarify. Assume that the proportion of all new coalitions recorded by *The Wall Street Journal* has been constant over time and that existing coalitions decay exponentially (i.e., at a constant rate). If the stock of coalitions at the end of 1969 is not greater than the stock at the end of 1982, we can calculate the *minimal* proportion of the latter that we pick up by looking at the flow of coalitions over the 1970–82 period. The results, portrayed in Figure 11.1, merit some explanation. If the expected duration of a coalition is five years, then at least 84 percent of the coalitions in existence at the end of 1982 were formed between 1970 and 1982. Even if the duration is as long as twenty years, coalition formation between 1970 and 1982 still accounts for at least 36 percent of the 1982 stock. The coverage would exceed these minimum figures to the extent that the 1982 stock is greater than the 1969 stock. Hence our sample is likely to capture a significant fraction of the stock of coalitions in existence in 1982.

For each of the 1,144 coalitions in our *Wall Street Journal* sample, we compiled information on the following variables:

- The date the coalition was cited in *The Wall Street Journal* (as a proxy for the year in which it was formed).

Figure 11.1 Coverage of Coalition Stocks[a]

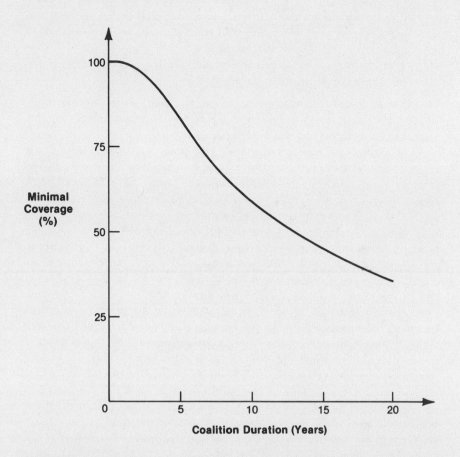

Minimal Coverage (%)

Coalition Duration (Years)

[a]Coverage refers to the percentage of coalitions in existence over 1982 that were formed over the 1970–82 period. The assumptions underlying this calculation are discussed in the text.

- The names of the parent firms and of the coalition (where applicable).
- The countries in which the coalition and the parents' head-offices were located.
- Four-digit SIC codes for the coalition and the parents. Parents were categorized by the principal SIC code of the ultimate holding company. This information was derived mainly from the *DISCLOSURE* database and Dun & Bradstreet's *Principal International Businesses*.
- The purpose of the coalition for each of the parents. The coding reflected both the value activity performed by the coalition and the role of the parent in its performance. Thus, an operation and

logistics coalition was distinguished from a technology development coalition, for example, while a parent contributing technology was distinguished from a parent that acquired technology. A separate category was established for coalitions that
spanned multiple value activities.
- The contractual form of the coalition: joint venture, license, supply agreement, or other agreement.

In order to gauge parents' purposes in forming coalitions, we consulted other articles in the business press and, on occasion, supplemented that information with our judgments.

The advantages of this database—compared to those used by past
researchers—include a consistent sample selection criterion, broad
coverage, large sample size, and relatively current data. However, we
also have to recognize three limitations of our sample. First, reliance
on *The Wall Street Journal* probably implies that coalitions with some
U.S. connection are overrepresented in our sample: for instance 78
percent of the coalitions in our sample have at least one U.S. parent.
We attempt to counteract this bias by reporting how our results would
change if we confined our analysis to coalition or parents located in
the United States, or if we excluded them entirely.

Second, *The Wall Street Journal* is more likely to report alliances
between corporate whales rather than minnows. We do not account
for this potential source of bias; note, however, that the fixed costs of
international, interfirm agreements seem to deter small companies
from participating in coalitions.[2] The final problem, of course, is that
we are measuring numbers of coalitions rather than the amount of
economic activity they represent. Again, the fixed costs of forming
coalitions should help bound variations in coalition size.

To investigate *The Wall Street Journal* sample, we also draw on
Harvard Business School's PICA database. PICA contains data on a
large number of U.S. industries and on the publicly held companies
that participate in them. Its major attraction for us is that its concor-
dances allow us to piece together data from a variety of primary
sources that use different classification schemes. Particularly noteworthy in this regard are PICA's matched industry and company data,
which we shall make heavy use of in profiling coalition parents. Note
that we use U.S. data on industries' technological attributes and structural characteristics as proxies for the conditions that exist overseas.
This technique is common in research on industrial organization because interindustry differences along these dimensions seem to outweigh international ones.[3]

EMPIRICAL RESULTS

This section describes the patterns observed in the formation of international coalitions over the 1970–82 period. We examine several di-

Figure 11.2 Contractual Forms of Coalitions

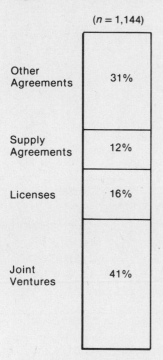

(*n* = 1,144)

Other
Agreements   31%

Supply
Agreements   12%

Licenses   · 16%

Joint
Ventures   41%

mensions of coalition activity: contractural form, trends over time, geographic locus, industry attributes, coalition purpose, parental characteristics, and parental contributions.

Contractual Form of Coalitions

Figure 11.2 classifies our sample of 1,144 coalitions by their contractural form. The striking conclusion is that only 57 percent of all coalitions in the sample were either joint ventures or licenses, the two forms that have been studied the most extensively in the past. Even when supply agreements are added to joint ventures and licenses, the residual ("other agreements") still amounts to nearly one-third of our sample. Thus, the data confirm that the contractual form of international link-ups between firms varies widely.

Trends in Coalition Activity over Time

Figure 11.3 traces coalition formation over the 1970–82 period. The flow of new coalitions fluctuates conspicuously from year to year; its coefficient of variation is 0.23. Our data do *not* bear out the popular belief that coalition activity has increased recently;[4] to the extent that there is a trend, it is downward, albeit very weak. Further analysis

Figure 11.3 Trends in Coalition Formation

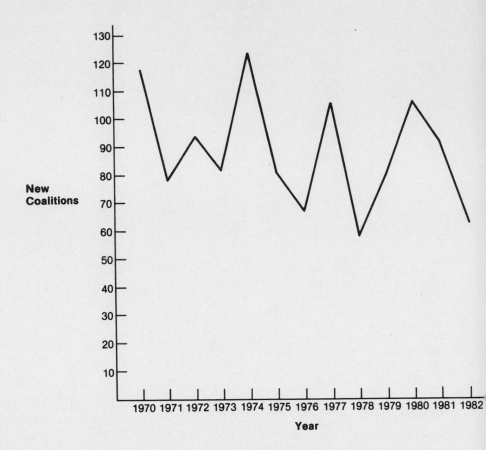

showed that time trends were also absent for coalitions involving U.S. parents and for coalitions between U.S. and Japanese parents.

Geographic Distribution

How are international coalitions, and their parent companies, distributed internationally? In answering this question, we needed to be responsive to the U.S. bias of our sample. In order to control (roughly) for international differences in the opportunities to form coalitions, we supplemented measures of the *absolute* incidence of coalitions with data scaled relative to the gross domestic products (GDP) of the countries involved. To facilitate our review, we aggregated countries into the groups listed in Table 11.1.

Turning first to coalition location, 75 percent of the coalitions and

Table 11.1 Geographic Distribution of Coalitions and Parents

	Coalition Location		Parent Location	
Country Group	Number	Index Relative to GDP[a]	Number	Index Relative to GDP[a]
Developed				
United States	124	.5	910	1.4
Canada	46	1.8	101	1.3
United Kingdom	31	0.9	126	1.4
France	32	0.7	129	0.9
West Germany	14	0.3	84	0.4
Other Western Europe	93	0.8	208	0.7
Japan	117	1.4	332	1.4
Australia, New Zealand, and South Africa	33	1.6	37	0.7
Developing				
Latin America	94	1.6	90	9.6
Middle East	53	1.5	59	0.6
ASEAN, South Korea, and Taiwan	64	2.8	55	0.8
Other LDCs	70	1.5	67	0.5
Eastern Europe	40	—	53	—
Multi-Area	46	—	2	—
Unclassifiable	287	—	135	—
Total Number	1,144	1.0[b]	2,388	1.0[b]

[a]GDP denotes gross domestic product in 1976 as reported in *International Financial Statistics*.
[b]The total is a weighted average across developed and less-developed countries.

94 percent of the parents in our sample proved classifiable by area. We note that although developed countries (DCs) account for a larger number of coalition sites than less-developed ones (LDCs), the coalition-to-GDP ratio is over 100 percent higher for LDCs than for DCs.[5] Coalitions apparently represent a greater proportion of economic activity in LDCs than in DCs. Among the LDCs, East Asian countries are especially coalition-prone; among DCs, Canada leads, perhaps because of its close integration into the U.S. economy, combined with a government policy that has historically placed a high weight on Canadian ownership.

If we turn to the location of coalition *parents*, the picture reverses itself; DCs have an 81 percent higher parent-to-GDP ratio than LDCs.[6] The DCs with the highest parent-to-GDP ratios are, as one would expect, advanced countries with strong technological bases that own relatively high stocks of assets overseas: the United States, the United Kingdom, and Japan.

The broad message from Table 11.1, then, is that while LDCs tend to be relatively abundant in coalitions, the parents are over-

352   III. Organizational Forms and Challenges

Table 11.2 Geographic versus Sectoral Distribution of Coalitions

Sector	Industry Group	DCs (%)	LDCs (%)	Eastern Europe (%)	Multi-Area (%)	Total (%)
Primary	Agribusiness	4	8	15	2	4
	Metals and Minerals	11	8	3	2	9
	Energy	9	29	8	0	15
	Construction	2	5	5	0	3
	Textiles, Clothing, and Leather	2	1	5	0	2
	Paper and Wood Products	3	1	3	0	2
	Chemicals	14	9	15	20	13
Secondary	Computers and Semiconductors	5	2	3	15	4
	Other Electronics	3	1	5	11	3
	Other Electrical	3	1	3	0	2
	Automobiles	6	6	8	4	6
	Aerospace	3	1	0	2	2
	Other Machinery	7	8	8	28	9
	Other Manufacturing	13	8	8	2	10
Tertiary	Transportation	1	2	0	2	2
	Communications, Publishing, and Recreation	2	1	0	0	1
	Distribution	4	3	8	0	4
	Finance	5	6	0	4	5
	Services	4	5	5	7	4
Total Number		453	260	39	46	798

NOTE: Columns sum vertically to 100 percent.

whelmingly concentrated in the DCs. This can be checked by comparing the assignments of coalitions and parents to DCs and LDCs: the DCs account for just 64 percent of the coalitions but for 87 percent of the parents.[7]

Coalitions located in DCs differ in some important respects from those located in LDCs. Table 11.2 cross-classifies 70 percent of the coalitions in our sample in an attempt to compare their sectoral distribution across countries. The classification of sectors into primary, secondary, and tertiary is derived from development economics; typically, as a country develops, the bulk of its labor force shifts from primary to secondary to tertiary activities.[8] The broad sectoral distributions of coalitions almost coincide across DCs and LDCs. Differences between DCs and LDCs show up, however, if we move down to the industry level. Energy and construction account for 34 percent of all LDC coalitions but only 17 percent of DC coalitions. By implication, coalitions located in DCs tend to be more concentrated in manufacturing than those located in LDCs, a result that makes sense given the greater technological abilities of DCs and their larger market sizes for manufactured goods.

Table 11.3. Coalitions by Industry Group

	1970–82	1970–73	1974–76	1977–79	1980–82
Agribusiness	4	3	6	3	3
Metals and Minerals	8	12	7	9	3
Energy	13	8	15	12	19
Construction	3	2	4	3	1
Textiles, Clothing, and Leather	2	4	2	1	2
Paper and Wood Products	2	4	2	1	0
Chemicals	13	10	15	13	16
Computers and Semiconductors	6	3	5	6	10
Other Electronics	4	2	2	6	5
Other Electrical	2	3	3	1	3
Automobiles	5	6	5	7	4
Aerospace	2	4	1	1	2
Other Machinery	12	11	10	12	13
Other Manufacturing	8	8	8	11	8
Transportation	2	3	3	2	0
Communications, Publishing, and Recreation	2	2	1	1	3
Distribution	3	5	2	2	2
Finance	4	5	3	3	3
Services	5	6	5	5	2
Total Number	1,050	346	253	218	233

NOTE: Columns sum vertically to 100 percent.

Industries

The distribution of the full sample of coalitions across industry groups is reported in Table 11.3. It is, of course, dominated by coalitions that have at least one U.S. parent; if one digs a bit deeper, one finds that coalitions without any U.S. participation are more frequent in agribusiness, energy, chemicals, "other machinery," and "other manufacturing." Some intertemporal shifts in the overall distribution are also apparent. Metal and minerals coalitions have declined in frequency, while energy coalitions have surged after each of the two oil crises. The percentage of coalitions in chemicals, computers, and other electronic products—all of which are very R & D–intensive—has drifted upward over the 1970–82 period.

For the rest of this section, we will pass from the two-digit SIC group level to the less-aggregated, four-digit SIC industry level that better defines strategically distinct businesses. We were able to identify the four-digit SIC locus (the "industry") of 95 percent of the coalitions in our sample. Nearly one-third of all four-digit industries—321, to be exact—reported at least one coalition. However, the distribution of coalitions across these 321 industries was far from even; the top 50 industries accounted for 54 percent of the classifiable coalitions (see Table 11.4).

One could, of course, march down the roster of the industries in

Table 11.4. Top Fifty Coalition SIC Codes

SIC Code	Industry	Number of Coalitions
1311	Crude Petroleum and Natural Gas	90
3711	Motor Vehicles and Passenger Car Bodies	34
3573	Electronic Computing Equipment	28
2834	Biological Products	25
3674	Semiconductors and Related Devices	18
3714	Motor Vehicle Parts and Accessories	18
2869	Industrial Organic Chemicals, Not Elsewhere Classified	17
3079	Miscellaneous Plastics Products	16
3519	Internal Combustion Engines, Not Elsewhere Classified	15
2821	Plastics Materials, Synthetic Resins, etc.	14
2911	Petroleum Refining	14
3312	Blast Furnaces, Steel Works, and Rolling Mills	14
2819	Industrial Inorganic Chemicals, Not Elsewhere Classified	13
3662	Radio and Television Transmitting, etc. Apparatus	13
6020	Commercial Banks	13
3443	Fabricated Plate Work (Boiler Shops)	11
3861	Photographic Equipment and Supplies	11
2809[a]	Petrochemicals	10
2810	Industrial Inorganic Chemicals, General	10
5812	Eating Places	10
3523	Farm Machinery and Equipment	9
7011	Hotels, Motels, and Tourist Courts	9
1211	Bituminous Coal and Lignite	8
1629	Heavy Construction, Not Elsewhere Classified	8
3680[a]	Electronic Goods, Unspecified	8
3681[a]	Robotics	8
3724	Aircraft Engines and Engine Parts	8
3229	Pressed and Blown Glass and Glassware, Not Elsewhere Classified	7
3570	Office, Computing, and Accounting Machines, General	7
3728	Aircraft Parts and Auxiliary Equipment	7
6552	Real Estate Subdividers and Developers	7
8911	Engineering, Architectural, and Surveying Services	7
1011	Iron Ores	6
1061	Ferroalloy Ores, Except Vanadium	6
1094	Uranium-Radium-Vanadium ores	6
3011	Tires and Inner Tubes	6
3721	Aircraft	6
4411	Deep Sea Foreign Transportation	6
6211	Security Brokers, Dealer and Flotation Companies	6
1000	Unspecified Metal Mining	5
1499	Gypsum	5
2111	Cigarettes	5
2328	Men's, Youth's, and Boy's Work Clothing (Jeans)	5
2822	Synthetic rubber	5
2824	Synthetic Organic Fibers, except Celluosic	5
2865	Cyclic (Coal Tar) Crude, Intermediates, Dyes, etc.	5
2891	Adhesive and Sealants	5
3140	Footwear, Unspecified	5
3411	Metal Cans	5
3511	Steam, Gas, and Hydraulic Turbines and Turbine Generator Sets	5
	TOTAL	584

[a]Codes added for analytical purposes by the researchers.

Table 11.4 and discuss the characteristics that made each of them coalition-intensive. However, we will try to be more systematic by splitting our sample into coalition-intensive and coalition-extensive industries and then comparing industry attributes across the two groups. Given the data available from PICA, we could perform this comparison only for manufacturing industries. However, manufacturing industries do account for over half the coalitions in our sample; thus, the results hold considerable interest.

Whittling the sample universe down to manufacturing left us with 588 coalitions in 169 four-digit manufacturing industries; 281 manufacturing industries reported no coalitions. We searched inductively for differences between these two groups.[9] Table 11.5a contains the statistical results and Table 11.5b supplies definitions for each industry variable analyzed. We will discuss only the variables that expose significant differences between coalition-intensive and coalition-extensive industries.

The first set of variables pertains to market size and structure. The average value of SALES is significantly higher for industries reporting coalitions; note, however, that this may partly be the handiwork of *The Wall Street Journal*'s reporting criteria. The number of companies per industry, NENT, is also higher for coalition-intensive industries; this is consistent with its expected association with SALES, as well as with the notion that NENT proxies the number of foreign partners potentially available for the formation of nondiversifying coalitions. Finally, the four-firm concentration ratio, C4, is also significantly higher in industries reporting coalitions: this suggests that on balance, coalition-intensive industries are marked by greater economies of scale than coalition-extensive ones.

The second set of variables concerns the international exposure of industries. U.S. export-intensity, EXP, is significantly higher for industries reporting coalitions. Because our sample disproportionately contains coalitions of U.S. parentage, we surmise that coalition formation complements normal export activities.

The third set of variables uses FTC line of business data to compare the relative importance of different value activities across coalition-prone and coalition-free industries. The results suggest that coalitions abound in relatively scale-sensitive industries: industries with coalitions tend to have higher R & D intensities (RDCI and RDOI) and lower intensities of purchased materials (MTLI) than industries without any coalitions.[10] (Fixed costs predominate in R & D while purchased materials are largely a variable cost.) A summary measure, OPVAI (roughly, manufacturing value added or the degree to which purchased inputs are transformed) points in the same direction: it is significantly higher for industries reporting coalitions.

The fourth and final set of variables is a miscellaneous one. The asset-to-sales ratio, ATS, is significantly higher in industries with coa-

Table 11.5a Manufacturing Industries Classified by Coalition Incidence

	Coalition Incidence		
Variable (Mean)	0 (n = 281)	1 (n = 169)	t-Statistic
A. U.S. Market Size and Structure			
SALES	0.51	2.60	4.40[a]
NENT	5.4	12.3	8.52[a]
NEST	763	810	0.27
C4	36.3	40.8	2.26[b]
B. International Exposure			
EXP	6.6	10.6	3.78[a]
IMP	11.6	10.2	−0.60
TTRADE	19.2	21.5	0.85
DUTY	17.1	7.2	−1.44
C. Value Activities			
a. Activities			
MTLI	47.5	45.5	−1.61
LABI	20.7	20.8	0.23
RDCI	0.87	1.77	6.84[a]
RDOI	0.11	1.95	2.83[a]
ADI	1.38	1.22	−0.65
OSI	7.33	7.07	−0.46
GAI	6.49	6.35	−0.39
b. Summary Measures			
OPVAI	28.7	30.9	2.22[b]
OPCOSI	76.2	76.4	0.28
OPROS	8.48	8.69	0.49
OPROA	13.9	13.0	−1.40
c. Scale Economics			
RME	3.27	3.37	0.28
CDR	0.995	1.002	0.55
MDIST	492	543	1.75[c]
D. Miscellaneous			
ATS	62.2	69.4	3.85[a]
SDP	3.22	4.11	2.10[b]

NOTE: Tests of significance of differences between means assume identical (underlying) variances for the two samples. The t-statistics involve subtracting the mean value for industries reporting no coalitions from the mean value for industries with at least one each. The levels of significance, computed on all observations available for each variable, are for two-tailed tests: a = 1 percent, b = 5 percent, c = 10 percent.

litions, supporting the "capital-pooling" rationale for their formation. A measure of business risk, SDP, also turns out to be significantly higher in coalition-prone industries. This underpins the "hedging" rationale for the formation of coalitions. Lastly, MDIST, a measure of "effective" economies of scale once transport costs have been factored in, is also greater for industries that report coalitions.

Coalition Purposes

Following the discussion in chapter 10, we divided the parents' purposes in entering coalitions in terms of activities into three: technol-

Table 11.5b Definitions and Data Sources for Table 11.5a

Variable	Definition	Source
ADI	Media advertising expense as a percentage of total sales, 1976 (or 1975 or 1974).	FTC
ATS	Total assets as a percentage of total sales, 1976 (or 1975 or 1974).	FTC
C4	Percentage of industry shipments accounted for by the four largest producers, 1977.	Census of Manufactures
CDR	Value added per worker in the smallest establishments accounting for (approximately) half of industry shipments divided by value added in the remaining, larger establishments, 1977.	Census of Manufactures
DUTY	Duty assessed as a percentage of imports' FOB value, 1976	USCEXIM[a]
EXP	Exports as a percentage of total shipments, 1976.	USCEXIM[a]
GAI	General and administrative expense as a percentage of total sales, 1976 (or 1975 or 1974).	FTC
IMP	Imports as a percentage of total shipments, 1976.	USCEXIM[a]
LABI	Payroll expense as a percentage of total sales, 1976 (or 1975 or 1974).	FTC
MDIST	Mean miles shipped, 1972.	WEISS (1972)
MTLI	Materials expense as a percentage of total sales, 1976 (or 1975 or 1974).	FTC
NENT	Number of large companies with operations in the industry, 1976 (or 1975 or 1974).	FTC
NEST	Number of establishments classified to the industry, 1977.	Census of Manufactures
OSI	Selling expense other than media advertising as a percentage of total sales, 1976 (or 1975 or 1974).	FTC
OPCOSI[b]	Cost of operating revenues as a percentage of total shipments, 1976 (or 1975 or 1974).	FTC
OPROA	Operating income as a percentage of total assets, 1976 (or 1975 or 1974).	FTC
OPROS	Operating income as a percentage of total sales, 1976 (or 1975 or 1974).	FTC
OPVAI[b]	Cost of operating revenues minus material intensity of total sales, 1976 (or 1975 or 1974).	FTC
RDCI	Company-financed R & D as a percentage of total sales, 1976 (or 1975 or 1974).	FTC
RDOI	R & D billed to outsiders as a percentage of total sales, 1976 (or 1975 or 1974).	FTC
RMES	Average shipment per plant in the median and all higher classes as a percentage of total industry shipments, 1977.	Census of Manufactures
SALES	Industry shipments in billions of dollars, 1976 (or 1975 or 1974).	FTC
TTRADE	Exports and imports as a percentage of total shipments, 1976.	USCEXIM[a]
SDP	Standard deviation of annual profit before taxes as a percentage of owners' equity, 1965–72 (1966 data not available).	IRS

[a]USCEXIM denotes *U.S. Commodity Exports and Imports as Related to Output*, published by the Bureau of the Census.
[b]OPCOSI and percent gross margin add up to 100. OPVAI equals OPCOSI minus MTLI.

Table 11.6. Coalition Purpose versus Location

| | Coalition Location | | | |
Parent Purpose	DCs (%)	LDCs (%)	Eastern Europe (%)	Unclassifiable (%)
Technology				
Development	13	30[a]	26	19
Operations and Logistics	41	47	60	36
Marketing, Sales, and				
Service	31	11	7	23
Multiple Purposes	15	13	7	21
Total Number of Cases	985	593	84	590

NOTE: Columns sum to 100 percent.
[a]A significant fraction of this figure is accounted for by exploration activities.

ogy development (including exploration); operations and logistics; and marketing, sales, and service. We also included multiple purpose coalitions as a separate category.

Of the 2,388 instances of parentage in our sample, 94 percent proved classifiable in terms of parents' purposes in entering coalitions. Technology development was the governing motivation in 20 percent of the cases, operations and logistics in 42 percent, and marketing, sales, and service in 22 percent. The remainder (16 percent) involved multiple value activities.[11]

Table 11.6 arrays the parents' purposes in the coalition against the countries in which the coalitions were located. The results are striking. Coalitions located in LDCs overwhelmingly involved upstream value activities; coalitions located in DCs were more heavily slanted toward the downstream value activities of marketing, sales, and service. Coalitions in Eastern Europe predominantly involved operations and logistics.

Table 11.7 presents a different mapping: coalition purposes versus industry group. Two clear patterns emerge. First, in industry groups that involve mining (metals and minerals and energy), technology development (i.e., exploration) is the primary motive for coalition formation. Second, in the tertiary sector (transportation, communication, distribution, finance, and services) marketing, sales, and service are the value activities most often addressed by coalitions. These relationships tend to support the hypothesis that coalitions in a particular industry group are likely to involve the value activities that are the most critical to competitive advantage in them.

However, a more detailed study of coalitions in manufacturing industries suggests that it is not simply the relative costliness of activities that determines coalition incidence. Advertising intensity, ADI, is *not* significantly higher in industries reporting at least one market-

Table 11.7. Coalition Purpose versus Industry Group

| | Parent Purpose | | | | |
| | Technology Development (%) | Operations and Logistics (%) | Marketing, Sales, and Service (%) | Multiple Purposes (%) | No. of Parents |
Industry Group					
Agribusiness	12	47	22	19	74
Metals and Minerals	41	44	10	6	199
Energy	65	29	3	3	298
Construction	7	75	9	9	57
Textiles, Clothing, and Leather	0	40	25	36	45
Paper and Wood	10	69	10	10	39
Chemicals	9	58	23	10	292
Computers	17	31	25	28	127
Other Electronics	5	33	33	29	76
Other Electrical	10	40	34	17	48
Automobiles	5	63	17	16	112
Aerospace	31	35	19	15	52
Other Machinery	4	39	32	26	248
Other Manufacturing	8	59	17	16	177
Transportation	0	41	50	10	42
Communications, Publishing, and Recreation	22	33	17	28	36
Distribution	0	24	60	16	50
Finance	9	16	53	23	88
Services	13	38	38	12	95
Total Number of Cases	423	929	475	328	2,155

NOTE: Rows sum to 100 percent.

ing, sales, and service coalition (versus industries not reporting any); other selling expenses, OSI, are actually lower.[12] Marketing, sales, and service coalitions are evidently driven by the need for access as much as by the size of marketing cost. Industries with operations and logistics coalitions report lower materials and labor intensities, MTLI and LABI, than industries without such coalitions. The implication is that operations and logistics coalitions are driven by comparative advantage effects to only a limited extent. R & D intensity is significantly higher in industries marked by technology-development coalitions; however, this pattern is repeated for operations and logistics coalitions and for marketing, sales, and service coalitions, suggesting that R & D intensity is associated with a high incidence of *all* types of coalitions.

Coalition Parents

How do coalition parents compare to nonparents? Do parents tend to be leaders or followers in the industries in which they form coalitions? How important are these industries within parent portfolios?

Although these questions go to the heart of the link between coalition formation and competitive strategy, there has been virtually no previous research on them. In trying to answer them, we will rely heavily on the company–industry linkage data in PICA. Accordingly, that dataset bears description.

PICA contains a snapshot of the participation of U.S. firms in U.S. manufacturing industries in 1972. The companies for which participation data were available were matched carefully to those in COMPUSTAT, yielding a set of 1,159 "linkage set" companies for which industry data, as well as the COMPUSTAT company data, were available. Because these 1,159 companies were relatively large—their revenues in 1972 averaged $590 million—the coverage of the manufacturing sector was substantially greater than their number might suggest: cross-checking revealed that they accounted for 48 percent of U.S. manufacturing output in 1972.[13]

We first split the linkage set companies according to whether or not they had participated in at least one of the coalitions in our sample. This yielded 270 "parents" and 889 "nonparents." Table 11.8a compares these two categories of companies. The parents turn out to be significantly larger than nonparents, and to derive a larger fraction of their revenues from foreign markets. In other words, companies that form international coalitions tend to be relatively experienced at competing internationally. Parents' profitability is also slightly (but insignificantly) lower than nonparents'; this may reflect, inter alia, the former group's greater exposure to international competition.

Table 11.9a concentrates on the parents from the linkage set that formed at least one coalition in manufacturing; it compares the manufacturing industries in which they formed coalitions with the manufacturing industries in which they operated but did not form coalitions. Limiting the group to manufacturing coalitions leaves us with a total of 189 companies to analyze; unfortunately, 121 of these companies formed at least one coalition in an industry in which, according to the linkage set, they did not participate domestically in 1972. As a result, we report two types of measures: one (prefixed by "A") includes these zero-participation industries in computing the group averages while the other (prefixed by "B") excludes them.[14]

The results suggest the strategic importance of coalitions as described in chapter 10. Companies tend to have larger market shares in the industries in which they form coalitions than in the ones in which they do not. Furthermore, the industries in which coalitions are formed account, on average, for a larger fraction of total company sales. These findings fly in the face of the view that parents use coalitions to shore up weak competitive positions in industries of peripheral strategic importance. Instead, when a firm engages in an international coalition, the industry involved is likely to be one of strategic importance in which it holds a (relatively) strong domestic position.

Table 11.8a Linkage Set Companies Classified by Coalition Incidence

Variable (Mean)	Nonparents (n = 889)	Parents (n = 270)	t-Statistic
REV	330	1,431	9.40[a]
ROE	20.4	16.3	−0.94
ROA	11.5	11.4	−0.20
FSHARE	15.9	25.1	4.18[a]

NOTE: Tests of significance of difference between means assume identical (underlying) variances for the two samples. The t-statistics involve subtracting the mean value for nonparents from the mean value for parents. The levels of significance, computed on all observations available for each variable, are for two-tailed tests: a = 1 percent, b = 5 percent, c = 10 percent.

Table 11.8b Definitions and Data Sources for Table 11.8a

Variable	Definition	Source
REV	Revenues in Millions of Dollars, 1972	COMPUSTAT
ROE	Net Income as a Percentage of Shareholders' Equity, 1972	COMPUSTAT
ROA	Earnings before Interest and Taxes as a Percentage of Total Assets, 1972	COMPUSTAT
FSHARE	Revenues from Exports and International Operations as a Percentage of Total Revenues, 1977	SEC

By implication, coalitions may be critical to the firm's drive to extend its scope internationally.

Parent Contributions

Our last set of results compares the contributions of parents to the coalitions that they form. Following the typology of chapter 10, we classified coalitions into X-types and Y-types: 32 percent of the coalitions in our sample turned out to be of the X-type, 53 percent to be of the Y-type, and 8 percent to be unclassifiable. In other words, over the sampled period, parents tended to pool similar rather than dissimilar contributions. Although the ratio of X-type coalitions to Y-type coalitions fluctuated considerably from year to year, no overall time trend was discernible.

Figure 11.4 sorts the coalition types by the contractual forms chosen for them. Y-type coalitions tend, disproportionately, to be organized as joint ventures, while X-type coalitions are usually structured as license or supply agreements. The hypothesis that a coalition's contractual form is independent of its type can be rejected, via a chi-squared test, at the 99 percent level of significance.

Table 11.9a Parents' Positions in Coalition and Noncoalition Manufacturing Industries

Variable (Mean)	Noncoalition Industries (n = 189)	Coalition Industries (n = 189)	t-Statistics
ASHARE	2.35	3.24	1.95[b]
BSHARE	2.35	5.86	5.78[a]
BRANK	.512	.274	−10.60[a]
AINDP	11.0	21.9	4.76[a]
BINDP	11.0	36.8	10.28[a]

NOTE: Tests of significance of differences between means assume identical (underlying) variances for the two samples. The t-statistics involve subtracting the mean value for parents' average position in noncoalition industries from the means of their average positions in coalition industries. The levels of significance, computed on all observations available for each variable, are for two-tailed tests: a = 1 percent, b = 5 percent, c = 10 percent.

Table 11.9b Definitions and Data Sources for Table 11.9a

Variable[a]	Definition	Source
ASHARE BSHARE	Parents' Market Share, Averaged across a Particular set of Industries (Coalition or Noncoalition)	Linkage set
BRANK	Parents' Market Share Rank Divided by Number of Reported Competitors, Averaged across a Particular Set of Industries (Coalition or Noncoalition)	Linkage Set
AINDP BINDP	Percent of Parents' Shipments Accounted for by Each Industry, Averaged across a Particular Set of Industries (Coalition or Noncoalition)	Linkage Set

[a]Variables prefixed by "A" are computed over all industries in a particular set; variables prefixed by "B" exclude, from the coalition industry set those industries in which the parent's domestic participation was reported to be zero in 1972.

SUMMARY

Our study has identified some characteristics of international coalition activity that can be summarized as follows:

1. There has been no clear increase or decrease in coalition activity over the 1970–82 period.

2. Although LDCs tend to be relatively abundant in coalitions, the coalition parents are overwhelmingly concentrated in DCs.

3. Coalitions located in DCs tend to be more concentrated in manufacturing and more slanted toward downstream value activities than coalitions located in LDCs.

Figure 11.4 Contractural Forms of X and Y Coalitions

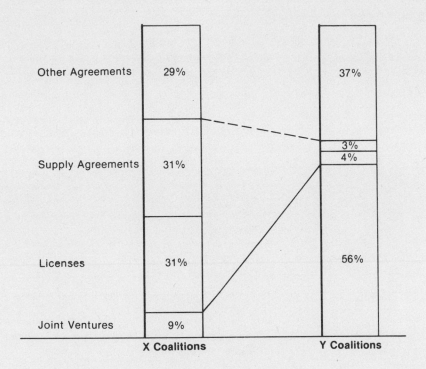

	X Coalitions	Y Coalitions
Other Agreements	29%	37%
Supply Agreements	31%	3% / 4%
Licenses	31%	56%
Joint Ventures	9%	

4. Within the manufacturing sector, some of the attributes of coalition-intensive industries differ significantly from industries in which coalitions are sparser. In particular, the former tend to be larger, more R & D–intensive and characterized by higher assets-to-sales ratios than the latter.

5. There is no clear link between the relative cost of value activities in manufacturing industries and the value activities that coalitions in those industries are likely to address.

6. U.S. companies that form international coalitions tend to be larger and more experienced internationally than U.S. companies that do not.

7. U.S. companies tend to form coalitions in industries in which they hold relatively stiong domestic positions.

8. Coalitions in which parents pool similar contributions (Y-types) are much more frequent than coalitions in which parents' contributions are dissimilar (X-types). No trend is apparent in their relative frequencies.

9. Y-type coalitions tend, disproportionately, to be organized as joint ventures, while X-type coalitions tend to be structured as license or supply agreements.

These findings cast considerable light on the nature and purposes of international coalition activity. We intend to develop them in future research in order to propose and test formal hypotheses about coalitions.

NOTES

1. In other words, our methodology is adductive. For a discussion of adduction, see Black (1970).
2. See, for example, Teece (1977) and Finkel (1986).
3. See, for example, Pryor (1972) and Caves, Porter, and Spence (1980).
4. See, for example, Boston Consulting Group (1985).
5. The figure for LDCs is 80 percent higher than for DCs if we knock the United States out of the DC sample.
6. That figure drops to 53 percent if we exclude U.S. parents from the sample.
7. Excluding the United States, the figures are, respectively, 57 percent and 78 percent.
8. See, for example, Kindleberger and Herrick (1977), 164–170.
9. We tried two other definitions of coalition intensity: industries reporting at least two coalitions and industries reporting at least one that involved a U.S. parent. The results for both dichotomizations paralleled the ones reported in Table 11.5a.
10. The negative relationship between MTLI and coalition intensity is almost significant; it attains significance at the 5 percent level if we divide industries into those reporting less than two coalitions and those reporting at least two.
11. If we restrict our attention to coalitions that involved at least one U.S. parent, the figures become, respectively, 20 percent, 49 percent, and 14 percent. In other words, U.S. parents are more prone than others to form coalitions in order to address operations and logistics.
12. The variables referred to in this passage are all defined in Table 11.5b. The details of the comparisons can be secured from the authors.
13. For details, see PICA (1983), section 2.
14. In the case of company rank within the United States, we report only the B-type measure; the A-type measure is not meaningful there.

REFERENCES

Black, M. *Margins of Precision: Essays in Logic and Language*. Ithaca: Cornell University Press, 1970.
Boston Consulting Group. "Strategic Alliances." Perspectives No. 276, Boston, 1985.
Caves, R. E., M. E. Porter, and A. M. Spence. *Competition in the Open Economy*. Cambridge, Mass.: Harvard University Press, 1980.

Finkel, M. "Overseas Research and Development by U.S. Multinationals." Ph.D. diss., Harvard University, 1986.

Kindleberger, C. P. and B. Herrick. *Economic Development*. New York: McGraw-Hill, 1977.

PICA, "Integrated Industry—Company Database Researcher's Notebooks." Volume IIB, Harvard Business School, 1983.

Pryor, F. L. "An International Comparison of Concentration Ratios." *Review of Economics and Statistics* 54 (May 1972): 130–40.

Teece, D. J. "Technology Transfer by Multinational Firms: The Resource Cost of Transferring Technological Know-how." *Economic Journal* 87 (June 1977): 241–61.

12

Building and Managing the Transnational: The New Organizational Challenge

Christopher A. Bartlett

ORGANIZATIONAL INFLUENCES AND CHALLENGES FOR MNCS

The globalization of industry structures and the accompanying changes in competitive behavior have created a need for fresh approaches and new strategies in most multinational corporations (MNCs). But for many companies, deciding *what* strategic response is required has proven less difficult than understanding *how* to implement such global strategies. The focus of this chapter will be on the difficulties facing MNC managers as they create the organization structures and the administrative processes that allow them to establish and maintain effective control of operations spread around the globe.

The Traditional Approach: A Point of Departure

Because the choice of a basic organization structure has such a powerful influence on the management process in an MNC, much of the early attention of managers and researchers alike was focused on trying to find which formal structure provided the right "fit" for which MNCs, and under which conditions. The most widely recognized study on this issue was John Stopford's research on the 187 largest U.S.-based MNCs.[1] His work resulted in a "stages model" of international organization structure that became the benchmark for most work that followed. Figure 12.1 summarizes his findings.

Although it was developed as a descriptive model, the findings were soon being applied in a prescriptive manner by consultants, academics, and managers. The debate was often reduced to simplistic

Figure 12.1 Stopford's International Structural Stages Model

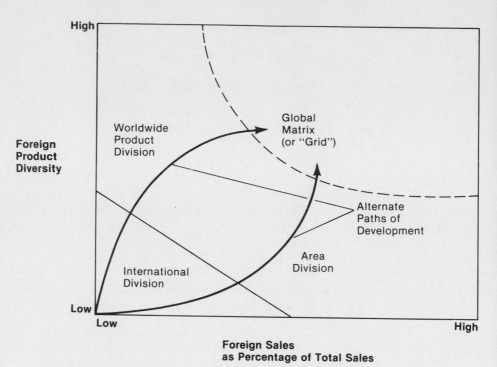

choices between "centralization" and "decentralization," or to generalized discussions of the values of product- versus geographically
based structures. But managers soon recognized that serial structural
reorganization as prescribed by the stages model was not solving their
global management problems. The simplicity of these either/or organizational choices stood in glaring contrast to the complexity of the
international environmental demands and strategic choices. There
was a need to think about the problem in other terms.

The major limitation of the stages model and other such simple
characterizations of the organizational task is that they purport to provide universal simple solutions to diverse and complex problems. A
company cannot develop an organization that can sense, analyze, and
respond to the complexity of the international environment on the
basis of a simple rule of thumb relating to product and geographic
diversity. There are some broader influences and constraints that must
be understood before deciding how to organize and manage a company's international operations:

- First, managers must develop a thorough understanding of the
  company's critical task demands as defined by its industry characteristics and strategic position.

- Second, they must recognize that their organizational choices will be constrained by the company's administrative heritage and its existing structure and processes.

The Influence of Task Demands on Organization

Because many of the forces that shape MNC task demands have been discussed in detail in chapter 1, there is no need to review them here. Suffice to say that there are multiple economic, political, social, and technological forces whose influence, separate and interactive, shapes the operating environment differently in each industry.

Although the forces themselves are diverse and complex, their organizational effects can be thought of more simply. Some, such as the increasing manufacturing economies associated with global or regional scale demand, or the need to spread escalating technological development costs over shorter product life cycles, tend to create the need for greater global coordination of effort and integration of operations. Other forces, such as national differences in consumer taste and market structure, or host government protectionism or regulation, increase the need for more local differentiation and responsiveness. It is the balance and interrelationship of these two forces that is influential in shaping the organizational task of the MNC.

Figure 12.2 illustrates how the intensity and balance of the forces for global integration and national responsiveness vary from one industry to the next.[2] While this classification is considerably richer than the simple categorization of an industry as "global" or "national," it is clear that it still greatly oversimplifies the diversity of industry characteristics. In any industry there are many activities in the value-added chain, each of which may have an intrinsic capability to benefit from global coordination or from national differentiation (see chapter 1). Yet, by charting the "center of gravity" of these activities (as in Figure 12.2), one can gain a sense of the way in which industry forces influence the nature of the organizational task.

- For example, the cement industry would seem to offer little incentive to build global scale plants due to logistical barriers, and limited ability to differentiate the product or operations nationally due to the mature commodity nature of the product.
- By contrast, the radio, TV, and hi-fi businesses were transformed with the advent of the transistor and the subsequent electronics revolution. Scale economies in product development and particularly in manufacturing became important sources of competitive advantage. Sony's ability to flood world markets in the early 1960s with a standard-design inexpensive transistor radio (a feat it repeated two decades later with the Walkman) demonstrated the low need for national product differentiation.
- Many branded packaged goods (foods, soap, cigarettes) bene-

Figure 12.2 Industry Characteristics: Global Integration/National Responsiveness Grid

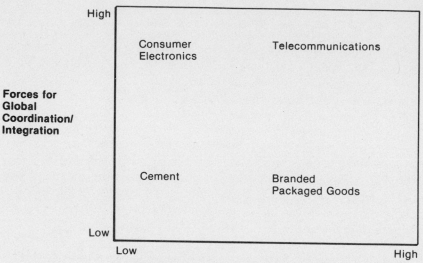

fited by nationally differentiated strategies, not only due to variations in local tastes and habits, but also because of differences in distribution channels and media. This gave a competitive advantage to those who were skilled in the downstream parts of the value-added chain (e.g., sales and distribution), tailoring such activities to local market differences. Few benefits accrued to those seeking global scale economies.[3]

- In the telecommunications industry, only a global-scale company can afford the $500 million or more it costs to develop a new digital switch. Yet, these companies must also respond to the demands for local concessions and modifications made by the various national governments who are the customers for switches and exchanges.[4]

Within any industry however, companies can and do respond in many different ways to the diverse and often conflicting pressures to coordinate some activities globally, and to differentiate others locally. It is important to recognize how a company's strategic choices also influence the nature of the organizational task. I will use the diversity of strategies in the auto industry in the mid-1970s not only to illustrate the way in which companies develop strategic postures that emphasize different parts of the value-added chain, but also to clarify some definitional terms that will be used throughout the chapter (see Figure 12.3).

Figure 12.3 Strategic Positions in Auto Industry
Global Integration/National Responsiveness Grid

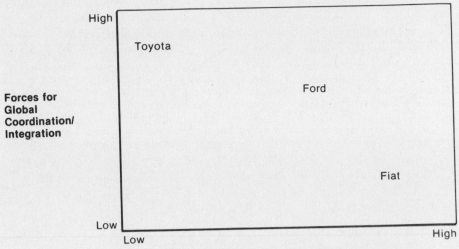

Toyota capitalized on the industry's huge potential for manufacturing scale economies, leading it to develop a tightly coordinated, centrally controlled operation that emphasized worldwide export of fairly standardized models from global-scale plants in Toyota City, Japan. The world-oriented strategy that seeks competitive advantage by capitalizing on the economies associated with a standardized product design, global-scale manufacturing, and centralized control of worldwide operations, I term "global strategy."*

At the other extreme was Fiat, which built its international operations on various governments' interest in developing national automobile industries. The company grew and prospered by negotiating with host governments for protection from more efficient global competitors in exchange for establishing local joint ventures and licensing agreements. Variants of the Fiat automobile have been built under such arrangements in Spain, Turkey, Russia, Poland, and Yugoslavia. This country-centered strategy that is based on a company's ability to differentiate its products to meet local needs and to respond to diverse national interests, I will term a "multinational strategy."†

Ford's strategy evolved to a different point than Toyota's or Fiat's.

*This is equivalent to Porter's definition of a pure global strategy (see chap. 1 of this book).
† Porter prefers the terms multidomestic or country-centered (see chap. 1 of this book).

Although Henry Ford's objective was to manufacture a standard world model and export from Detroit, he was soon forced to compromise. Rising tariff barriers in the 1920s and 1930s forced Ford to establish manufacturing plants abroad. U.S. auto designs were found unsuitable or unpopular in many foreign markets and the company began modifying basic designs and eventually developing totally national models. The need for strong local distribution networks further strengthened the role of local companies, as the company developed a truly multinational strategy. It was only in the 1970s that Ford renewed its objective to develop more standard "world" designs and to specialize and integrate its worldwide manufacturing operations.

The cross-country coordination of national operations that aims to capture the scale economies beyond those that can be supported by a single market, while simultaneously retaining the ability to respond to national interests and preferences, I term "transnational strategy."* (Ford would admit that at present such a strategy is still an overall objective rather than a broadly achieved reality.)

Influence of Administrative Heritage

While industry analysis can reveal the potential for global scale, a company's existing asset configuration, its historical distribution of responsibilities, and the ingrained management norms will greatly influence—and often constrain—its ability to fulfill that promise. A company's organization is shaped not only by its external task environment, but also by what I term its administrative heritage. I define this as the path by which the company's international operations were developed (its organizational history) and the ingrained values, norms, and practices of its management (its management culture).

Chandler presents extensive evidence on the developmental history of MNCs and shows how differences in national origin and developmental patterns have influenced the management processes and indeed the strategies of these companies (see chapter 13). Drawing on Chandler's work, my purpose in examining a company's administrative history is simply to illustrate its importance in shaping a company's current structure and in constraining its future organizational options.

The importance of a company's administrative history can be illustrated by contrasting the development of a typical European MNC whose major international expansion occurred in the interwar years with that of a Japanese-based company that made its main overseas thrust in the 1960s and 1970s. Even if these companies were in the same industry, the combined effects of the different historical contexts in which they developed and the disparate internal cultural norms

*This corresponds with many of the characteristics Porter classified as a "complex global strategy" or a "foreign investment–based global strategy."

that influence their management processes would almost certainly result in the development of very different international organizational models.

Expanding abroad in a period of rising tariffs and discriminatory legislation, the typical European company found its budding export markets threatened by local competitors. To defend its various market positions, it was forced to build local production facilities. With their own plants, various national subsidiaries were able to modify products and marketing approaches to meet local market differences. The increasing independence of these fully integrated national units was reinforced by the transportation and communications barriers that existed in that era, limiting central management's ability to intervene in the management of its spreading worldwide operations.

The emerging configuration of distributed assets and delegated responsibility fit well with the ingrained management norms and practices in many European companies. Chandler has shown that because of the important role of owners and bankers in corporate-level decision making, European companies, particularly those from the United Kingdom and France, developed an internal culture that emphasized personal relationships rather than formal structures, and financial controls more than coordination of technical or operational detail (see chapter 13). This management style, philosophy, and capability tended to reinforce companies' willingness to delegate more operating independence and strategic freedom to their foreign subsidiaries. Highly autonomous national companies were often managed more as a portfolio of offshore investments rather than as a single international business.

The resulting organization and management pattern was a loose federation of independent national subsidiaries, each focused primarily on its local market. This "decentralized federation" organization model is represented in Figure 12.4.

In contrast, the typical Japanese company, making its main international thrust in the postwar years, faced a greatly altered external environment and operated with much different internal norms and values. With limited prior overseas exposure, it chose not to match the well-established local marketing capabilities and facilities that its European competitor had built up. (Indeed, well-established Japanese trading companies often provided it with an easier means of entering foreign markets.) However, it had new efficient, scale-intensive plants, built to serve its rapidly expanding domestic market, and it was expanding into a global environment of declining tariffs. Together these factors gave it the incentive to develop a competitive advantage at the upstream end of the value-added chain. Its competitive strategy emphasized cost advantages and quality assurance, and required tight central control of product development, procurement, and manufacturing. A centrally controlled, export-based internationalization strat-

Figure 12.4 Decentralization Federation Model

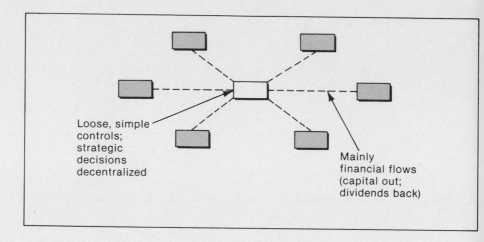

egy represented a perfect fit with the external environment and the company's competitive capabilities.

Such an approach also fit the cultural background and organizational values in our emerging Japanese MNC. At the foundation of the internal processes were the strong national cultural norms that emphasized group behavior and valued interpersonal harmony. These values had been enhanced by the paternalism of the *zaibatsu* and other enterprise groups. They were also reflected in the group-oriented management practices of *nemawashi* and *ringi* that were at the core of Japanese organizational processes. By keeping primary decision making and control at the center, the Japanese company could retain this culturally dependent management system that was so communications-intensive and people-dependent.

Cultural values were also reflected in one of the main motivations driving the international expansion of Japanese MNCs. As growth in their domestic market slowed and became increasingly competitive, these companies needed new sources of growth so they could continue to attract and promote employees. In a system of lifetime employment, growth was the engine that powered organizational vitality and self-renewal. It was this motivation that reinforced the bias toward an export-based strategy managed from the center rather than the decentralized foreign investment approach of the Europeans.

The basic structural configuration and management pattern adopted by these companies is one that I term the "centralized hub" (see Figure 12.5). The key parts of the company's value-added chain, typically upstream activities like product design or manufacturing, are retained at the center, or are tightly centrally controlled.

Figure 12.5 Centralized Hub Model

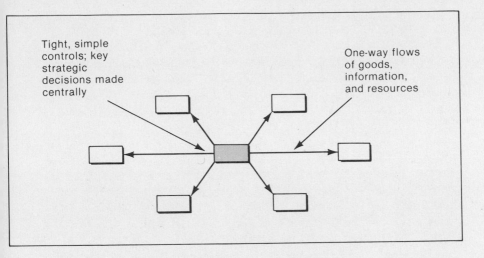

This brief comparison of the differences between the developmental histories of European and Japanese MNCs should illustrate that the organizational task facing MNC managers is not simply responding to environmental task demands. They must do so within the context of the company's administrative heritage—its inherited configuration of assets and resources, its historical distribution of tasks and responsibilities, and the ingrained organizational norms and values. For any established MNC, the concept of a zero-based organization is naive and usually quite infeasible.

Organizational Demands in the 1980s

I have suggested that one can think of the complexity of diverse environmental pressures and demands as divided into two basic, but often conflicting organizational forces—those that require companies to coordinate activities on a global basis, and those that benefit from a greater degree of national differentiation and responsiveness. In earlier periods, we have observed that one or the other of these sets of forces tended to dominate the organizational task facing most MNCs. In the interwar years, rising tariffs, national differences in consumer preferences and market structures, and logistical and communications barriers provided an environment in which relatively independent foreign national organizations could flourish. In contrast, the international environment in the immediate postwar decades was dominated by free-trade agreements, declining international transport costs and communication barriers, and developments in manufacturing processes and technology that increased the minimum efficient scale in many industries. In this environment, companies with tightly coordinated and centrally controlled global operations made huge advances.

By the late 1970s, however, some important changes were taking place. The rapid expansion and increased worldwide control of MNCs in the post–World War II era caused one prominent scholar to declare that by the late 1960s they held "sovereignty at bay."[5] However, it was the very success of the emerging global companies that caused the situation to change. As host countries became increasingly concerned about the impact these companies were having on their balance of trade, their national employment levels, and, indeed, on the international competitiveness of their economies, they began to reassert their sovereign powers more forcefully. Protective trade barriers were raised not only in the developing world but also in most OECD countries. When MNCs replaced their exports with direct investments, they found they were tightly regulated and controlled by increasingly widespread and sophisticated national industrial policies. By the late 1970s, sovereignty was no longer at bay.

Other forces were also appearing in the late 1970s and early 1980s to offset or counterbalance the globalizing influences that had dominated earlier decades. For example, flexible manufacturing processes employing robotics, CAD/CAM, and other emerging technologies not only reduced the minimum efficient scale in many industry segments, but also broadened the product variations that could be produced efficiently. In the words of C. J. van der Klugt, chairman of Philips's Board of Management, "The debate about global products will be short-lived when flexible automation becomes the dominant production methodology. Basic models that achieve the requisite scale economies will easily be able to be translated into more individualized products."[6]

Van der Klugt's comment hints at another countertrend of the 1980s, one that relates more to marketing than manufacturing. As the importance of software increased for a growing number of industries (from telecommunications to computers to consumer electronics), many companies recognized the need to adapt standard products into more flexible, differentiated, and responsive systems and services. Even in basic hardware, there was an emerging market reaction to standardized and homogenized global products. Larger segments of consumers demanded products more tailored to their local needs. A Matsushita manager explained that in response to a consumer preference shift away from mass-produced items, the company was producing more models in smaller runs. "We are having to grasp the consumer not en masse but as target groups—even down to the individual," he said.[7]

The net result is that during the 1980s, while the forces for global integration have remained important, there has been a reemergence

Figure 12.6 New Forces Impact on Integration/Differentiation

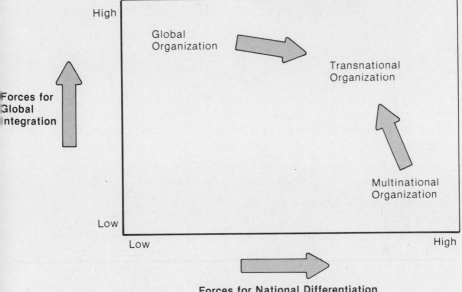

of several influences that require companies to be more nationally responsive. Today, not only are both these forces much stronger than they were twenty or even ten years ago, but they also affect a much broader cross section of industries. In our classically multinational branded packaged goods industry, companies are coordinating product development, marketing approaches, and overall competitive strategy across previously independent national organizations; in the consumer electronics industry, global companies have been forced to replace exports with local manufacture and to develop more locally differentiated products.

As a consequence, a large number of MNCs operating in today's environment are being forced to develop the organizational capabilities to respond to diverse national interests and demands while *simultaneously* coordinating and controlling these activities to allow the companies to act as efficient and effective global competitors. This theme is echoed in nearly every chapter of this book. To manage this way, MNCs require a very different kind of internal management process than existed in the relatively simple multinational or global organizations they may have had previously. I term this the "transnational organization" (see Figure 12.6). Learning how to create and manage the transnational organization could be the major challenge for MNC managers in the next decade, and the balance of this chapter will be devoted to describing the task.

THE TRANSNATIONAL ORGANIZATION: DEVELOPING AND MANAGING THE KEY CHARACTERISTICS

There are three important organizational characteristics that distinguish the transnational organization from its multinational or global counterparts: it builds and legitimizes multiple diverse internal perspectives able to sense the complex environmental demands and opportunities; its physical assets and management capabilities are distributed internationally but are interdependent; and it requires a robust and flexible internal integrative process. In the following paragraphs I will describe and illustrate each of these characteristics.[8]

Multidimensional Perspectives

Managing in an environment in which strategic forces are both diverse and changeable, transnational companies must develop the ability to sense and analyze the numerous and often conflicting opportunities, pressures, and demands it faces worldwide. Having a limited or biased management perspective through which to view developments can constrain a company's ability to perceive and respond to some potential problems or opportunities. This has been a major limitation of the multinational and global forms as the following examples illustrate:

- When the giant Swiss MNC Brown Boveri found it was losing market share to more efficient Japanese and Eastern Bloc small motors manufacturers, it tried to specialize and coordinate the activities of its numerous full-line national plants. However, a long history of local autonomy had vested considerable power in the hands of national subsidiary managers, and the relatively weak corporate-level product and functional managers were unable to enforce the necessary program of plant specialization and product transshipping.[9]
- In the late 1960s and early 1970s, there was growing concern in many Southeast Asian countries about the social, economic, and political insensitivity of strongly centralized Japanese MNCs. In many companies, the local manager's primary responsibility was to his business or functional group in Japan, and his views on the local environment were not considered very important. One study showed how this led to economic and sociocultural friction, resulting in widespread local resentment.[10] The Tanaka riots of 1974 were seen by many as a reaction to some companies' insensitivity to local needs.

The transnational organization must have broad sensory capabilities able to represent the diverse environmental opportunities and demands in the internal management decisions. Strong national subsidiary management is needed to sense and analyze the changing needs of local consumers and the increasing pressures from host governments; capable global business management is required to track the strategy of global competitors and to provide the coordination necessary to respond appropriately; and influential functional management is needed to concentrate corporate knowledge, information, and expertise, and facilitate its transfer among organizational units.

To eliminate biases built into the decision-making process, management must build up the capability, credibility, and influence of underrepresented organizational views and perspectives—the product and functional groups in Brown Boveri, for example. However, changing the established power structure, and decision process of a company can be a very traumatic occurrence unless handled gradually and sensitively. The most effective changes involve changes in three aspects of the underrepresented groups: upgrading the personnel, broadening their responsibilities, and increasing their power. An example may illustrate how these changes are implemented in an incremental and iterative manner:

- When top management at Baxter Travenol decided to counterbalance the dominant strength of its country managers by upgrading the global business perspective, they first appointed some of their fast-track MBAs to the international division's product management positions that had been held by more experienced but less analytical exsalesmen. This change allowed the positions to be enlarged from a purely sales support role to one also responsible for monitoring and analyzing worldwide product performance and trends. New information systems by product line were developed, and these gradually evolved into control tools. Furthermore, the more broadly defined roles required product managers to spend time in the field at the country subsidiary level, often to report on a specific issue raised by senior management.

  With increased market knowledge, access to current data, and power gained through the evolving control role, the international product manager position was ready for the next upgrading iteration. More senior and experienced managers from domestic product divisions and country subsidiaries gradually replaced the younger MBAs. Again, the opportunity was used to broaden the product managers' responsibilities and power base. The new appointees were given major roles in the budgeting and strategic planning process, enabling them to make powerful representations concerning the management of their lines of business worldwide. The increasing credibility and power base of this management group soon allowed them to stake out a legitimate coordination role on issues such as global product policy or sourcing decisions, and an important linkage role as knowledgable spokesmen and defendants of the overseas perspective within the headquarters organization.

Through this process, the classic line-staff distinctions began to blur, and management was able to reduce its dependency on a single, often parochial, view of its business.

Distributed, Interdependent Capabilities

Having sensed the diverse opportunities and demands it faces, the transnational organization must then be able to make choices among them and respond in a timely and effective manner to those that are deemed strategically important. When a company's decision-making process and organizational capabilities are concentrated at the center as they are in the global organization's centralized hub configuration, it is often difficult to respond appropriately to diverse worldwide demands. Being distant from the front-line opportunities and threats, the central group's ability to act in an effective and timely manner is constrained by its reliance on complex and intensive international communications. Furthermore, the volume and diversity of demands made on the central group often result in central capabilities being overloaded, particularly where scarce technological or managerial resources are involved.

- In the late 1970s, when NEC made a commitment to establishing a U.S. operation to sell its central office telephone switches, all product development, including systems engineering was done in Japan. After several years, it was decided to transfer software development responsibility to the United States, primarily because of the difficulty in responding appropriately to customer needs that were very different in the United States than in Japan, but also because NEC was finding it increasingly difficult to recruit and train sufficient software engineers in Japan to meet worldwide needs.

On the other hand, multinational organizations with their response capabilities spread throughout the decentralized federation of independent operations, suffer from duplication of effort (the "reinventing the wheel" syndrome), inefficiency of operations (the "local-for-local scale" problem), and barriers to international learning (the "not invented here" model).

- Until the early 1970s, Philips operated as a classic multinational organization, with independent national organizations (NO) responsible for much of their own product development, manufacturing, and marketing. The major inroads made by Japanese competitors during the next decade highlighted the inefficiencies of this system, and Philips acknowledged the need to pro-

Figure 12.7 Integrated Network Model

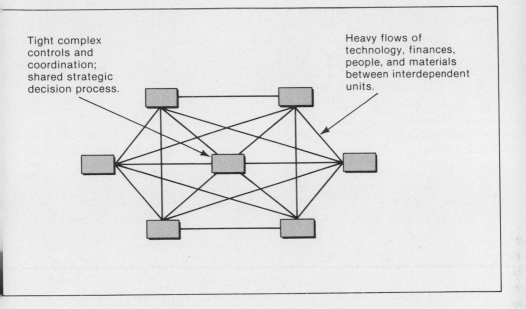

Tight complex
controls and
coordination;
shared strategic
decision process.

Heavy flows of
technology, finances,
people, and materials
between interdependent
units.

vide better global coordination of product design and to rationalize manufacturing on a regional and even a worldwide basis.

In transnational organizations, management breaks away from the restricted view that activities for which global scale or specialized knowledge is important must be centralized. They ensure that viable national units achieve global scale by making them the company's world source. Similarly, if important technological advances, or market developments are occurring in locations far from the company's headquarters, they work to secure the cooperation and involvement of the relevant national units in the development of the company's technology, its new products, and even its marketing strategy.

With a distribution of assets and responsibilities, the interdependence of worldwide units increases. Simple structural configurations like the decentralized federation and the centralized hub are inadequate for the task facing the transnational corporation. What is needed is a structure I term the "integrated network" (see Figure 12.7).

In the integrated network configuration, national units are no longer viewed only as the end of a delivery pipeline for company products, or as implementers of centrally defined strategies, or even as local adapters and modifiers of corporate approaches. Rather, the assumption behind this configuration is that management should consider each of the worldwide units as sources of ideas, skills, capabilities, and knowledge that can be harnessed for the benefit of the total organization. Efficient local plants may be converted into international production centers; innovative national or regional development labs may be designated the company's "center of excellence" for a particular product or process development; and creative subsidiary marketing groups may be given a lead role in developing worldwide marketing strategies for certain products or businesses. The company becomes a truly integrated network of distributed and interdependent resources and capabilities.

As the NEC and Philips examples illustrate, the task of developing such an organization is very different for a company with a classic global organization compared to one that has developed more closely to the multinational model. But for both this is a difficult transition, and in seeking to implement it many companies compromise their existing organizational assets and capabilities. Turning first to the task facing global companies, they must upgrade the role of national units from that of implementer or adapter of centrally directed policies and strategies, to that of contributor and partner in the development and execution of the company's worldwide strategies. However, in doing so, the challenge is to avoid compromising the efficiency that may have been achieved through global strategy and operations, or undermining the capabilities and legitimacy of the strong headquarters management group.

The problem is best illustrated by those global companies that responded to demands for more local responsiveness by adopting aggressive "localization" policies—taking on local equity partners, making local content commitments, replacing expatriate managers with nationals, and adapting products to local preferences. While such policies are both responsive and responsible, they are often implemented without keeping in mind the need to retain a coordinated and interdependent network. Without such an objective, localization policies frequently serve to isolate the national unit strategically, not only weakening its role in the parent company but also reducing its potential contribution to the host country.

To develop the organizational and strategic capabilities of its national units while retaining them in an integrated network of global operations, the manager must make the changes gradually and iteratively, as in the development of the multiple management perspectives. The three most important tasks to be undertaken involve the transfer of assets and resources to the country level, the transfer of knowledge and skills to use them effectively, and the transfer of tasks and responsibilities to allow the local unit to develop its potential and contribute to the worldwide network.

The transfer of one component without the others will not be effective. Simply shifting assets and resources to the national units will not build a transnational organization. Without the simultaneous transfer of the required knowledge and responsibilities, the company will simply evolve to a global organization with local assembly plants, satellite development labs, and branch office marketing operations, all still directed and controlled from the center. The way in which the three tools are used together to develop the national organizations is discussed in more detail in a separate paper,[11] but can be illustrated by describing the process through which NEC built its U.S. software capabilities:

- Having recognized the need to develop the systems engineering capabilities of its U.S. company and reduce its dependence on the parent company, NEC began a seven-year program to undertake the transition. An initial transfer of responsibility for "patching" software problems was successfully undertaken. Soon, the existing small group of U.S. engineers had proven their ability by developing an innovative process for fixing minor software faults from a central terminal hooked into all customers equipment rather than making expensive site visits to deal with such problems. (The innovation was subsequently adopted by the parent company to be designed into the core software of future NEC central office switches.) To take the next step in developing U.S. software engineering capability, NEC appointed as engineering vice president for the U.S. company the manager who had been responsible for the software design of the company's latest switch. Over the next two years, he recruited and trained ten engineers specifically for software development. During that time he kept asking headquarters for increasingly more important projects to be transferred from Japan. In early 1985, he hired an experienced director and created a separate design engineering department. Plans were authorized to expand the department from twenty to fifty engineers in the first year and to one hundred in the second.

  In seven years, the U.S. engineering group had evolved from a local implementer and deliverer of centrally developed products and policies to an innovative and responsive unit, able to tap the valuable local technical resources, sense and interpret local needs and opportunities, and develop innovative responses that could be used in other parts of the organization. It had evolved from a local dependency role to a contributor role in the total corporate system.

The task of developing distributed interdependent capabilities in a multinational organization is quite different from that of the global company. It involves creating the ability to coordinate, integrate, and control the diverse and often quite independent operations of a decentralized federation configuration, while protecting the capabilities and vitality of the national units on which the company's international business has been built. Too drastic a move to standardization, rationalization, or centralization may have the effect of disenfranchising the national units, demotivating their management, and compromising the valuable organizational assets that these responsive and entrepreneurial units often represent.

There are two important parts to this major organizational change. To minimize problems such as duplication of effort, suboptimal levels of operation, internal competition, and overlap of responsibility that often develop in organizations built around independent national units, the roles and responsibilities of the various national units must be rationalized. This is achieved by gradually realigning the tasks and responsibilities of national companies, building on the special competences and competitive advantages of each to create more specialized and focused operations.

Simultaneously, management must work to break down extremes of subsidiary independence and autonomy and replace any parochial attitudes with an identity and role in the new integrated worldwide operations. Although this task is achieved in part by the redistribution and specialization of roles just described, it also requires important changes in individual attitudes and interpersonal relationships. To ensure that local capabilities are enhanced, instead of depleted, and that the entrepreneurial spark is fanned not doused, the challenge is to co-opt rather than to subjugate the national units into a global role.

Again, a detailed description of this important change process is contained in another paper,[12] but an elaboration of the transition made by Philips will illustrate the broad thrust.

- Having recognized the need to better coordinate its independent national organizations (NOs), Phillips's product division management responsible for television took steps to standardize product lines, rationalize facilities, and centralize control. However, they soon recognized that central management's ability to sense and respond to increasingly rapid changes in market demands was limited, and that their attempts to control activities too tightly at the center were resulting in considerable frustration and demotivation in the NOs due to their depleted role.

  The company began to modify its approach and tried to involve local management more in its coordination efforts. It was clear that some NOs were of major strategic importance due to their position in large markets (like the United States), competitively important locations (like Japan), or technologically innovative environments (like the United Kingdom). Other NOs were important due to their internal capabilities (e.g., an efficient plant, innovative lab, or creative marketing group). There grew an internal realization that improved global competitiveness could be achieved by working through these key locations and building on existing competencies. For example, recognizing that four key countries represented the lead markets for new trends in television, division management invited product managers from these countries to be members of the corporate product development and marketing strategy committees. In addition, individual NOs were given world leadership roles in the development, manufacture, or marketing of individual global products. For example, because of the "champion" role it played in sensing and advocating the development of teletext TV sets, the United Kingdom's product development group was designated the corporate center of competence and given the mandate to coordinate the development of the company's teletext TV product line. The United Kingdom was also nominated as the company's international production center for these products. In this way, Philips was gradually co-opting the innovative capabilities of its NOs into an integrated and interdependent network of worldwide operations.

Flexible Integrative Process

Having established management groups representing multiple perspectives to reflect the variety of environmental demands and pressures, and a configuration based on distributed and interdependent assets and organizational capabilities, the transnational organization requires a management process that can resolve the diversity of interests and perspectives and integrate the dispersed responsibilities. But it cannot be bound by the symmetry of organizational process that follows when the task is seen in simplistic or static terms (e.g., "Should responsibilities be centralized or decentralized?"). It is clear that the benefits to be gained from central control of worldwide research or manufacturing activities may be much more important than those related to the global coordination of the sales and service functions. We have also seen how the pattern of functional coordination varies by business and by geographic area (aircraft engine companies need central control of more decisions than multinational food packagers; operations in developing countries may need more central support than those in advanced countries). Furthermore, all coordination needs change over time due to changes in the international operating environment, the life cycles of products and technologies, or the company's stage of development.

Thus, management must be able to differentiate its operating relationships and change its decision-making roles by function, across businesses, among geographic units, and over time. The management process must be able to change from product to product, from country to country, and even from decision to decision.

This requires the development of rather sophisticated and subtle decision-making machinery based on three different but interdependent management processes. The first is a self-regulatory capability in which top management's role is to establish an appropriate organizational context for delegated decisions;[13] the second is a managed organizational process in which the key management task is to structure roles and relationships in specific key decisions and the third is a supportive but constrained escalation process that allows top management to intervene directly in the content of certain decisions.

Managing the Context

Let us first examine the task of developing a self-regulatory organizational context. In an organization characterized by diversity and change, the ability of top management to be directly involved in the content of most decisions decreases dramatically. Even the demands of acting as the arbitrator of differences or coordinator of diverse activities quickly exceeds management's capacity to respond. It soon becomes evident that the primary responsibility of top management is not to manage such activities directly, but to create and manage an organizational context that will provide the means for the appropriate resolution of decision and coordination of activities.

There are many ways in which this task can be undertaken, and I will highlight only three of the most important: the establishment and communication of clear objectives and priorities; the development in key management positions of individuals with broad perspectives, open minds, and good interpersonal skills; and the promotion of explicit norms and rules relating to the required organizational process.

Particularly in an organization where managers are so widely separated by distance and culture as well as by organizational perspective and responsibility, it is important to develop a clear sense of purpose and direction, and a shared understanding of current objectives and priorities. To the extent top management can communicate such a unified vision, it will provide the common touchstone for the resolution of conflict and the glue to help coordinate and integrate actions. To the extent it can interpret the goals and overlay them with current priorities, it can affect the shorter-term direction and focus management attention.

- In Komatsu, the Japanese construction equipment company, a consistent sixty-year commitment to "overseas orientation and user perspective" has given the organization a unified view of a strategy driven by geographic diversification and led by consumer-oriented product development. Top management supplements this broadly articulated and widely understood purpose with specific medium-term objectives, usually captured and communicated in simple slogans ("Maru C" or "Encircle Caterpillar" is the most recent). These strategic objectives become the basis for a series of specific short-term projects that represent the means of achieving the objective. Again the organization's attention and efforts are united to achieve the current priorities (e.g., the V-10 campaign was a company-wide project to reduce costs by 10 percent).

The second important tool through which top management can shape the organizational context of the transnational is its ability to appoint and develop key managers. To operate effectively in a transnational, a manager needs more than just good analytical and operational skills. Key positions must be staffed by people with broad perspectives, open minds, and good interpersonal skills. This demands the selection of managers not only on the basis of their experience and technical skills, but also on their ability to see problems from different points of view and their willingness to negotiate openly on important issues. Further, it requires that managers be consciously developed to broaden their perspectives and build their key relationships. An example illustrates some of the ways this can be done.

- As a normal part of international career development, managers in Eli Lilly were routinely transferred from staff to line positions, from one product line to another, and from headquarters to national subsidiaries. Regular meetings on regional product and functional issues further broadened perspectives and developed relationships. One manager stated, "These [individuals] had far better information sources than computer reports, and more important, they developed the kind of influence that comes from being known, understood, and respected."

But even those who have developed broad perspectives and flexible management style need ongoing guidance and support to help them behave in a consistently appropriate manner, and this brings us to the third way in which context is developed in a transnational. Although clear communication of common organizational objectives can provide a good basis for unified organizational action, the diverse perspectives and interdependent activities built into a transnational organization ensure that many individual issues will still need to be resolved. To avoid disruptive conflict or unnecessary escalation of unresolved decisions, there is a need for clear norms and rules that define expectations of management behavior and organizational practices, and for a culture that supports efficient and legitimate resolution of differences.

There are numerous ways in which top management can foster the organizational norms and interpersonal values that are necessary in a transnational organization. The most obvious is to ensure that there is a statement of organizational expectations that is as clearly articulated and as well communicated as the strategic objectives. This is particularly important in the international environment, because individual manager's assumptions and behaviors may have been shaped by diverse national cultural backgrounds. Typical norms and values in a transnational organization would include free interchange of information, open-minded negotiation of issues, and a commitment to broad corporate objectives above individual parochial interests.

These expectations can then be reinforced and institutionalized by the company's formal and informal reward systems. In our Eli Lilly example, good communications and open-minded negotiating were reinforced by changing the management evaluation process to include formal inputs from those colleagues with whom an individual required strong and cooperative relationships.

One of the most effective ways top management can maintain the desired organizational behavior is through its own role model of how managers should relate and how decisions should be taken. Philips's long-held tradition of having issues resolved through negotiation between top-level commercial and technical managers did much to establish the strong corporate norm of intensive communication and negotiation before decisions are taken.

By establishing clear corporate objectives, developing managers with broadly based perspectives and relationships, and fostering supportive organizational norms and values, management can create a decision-making context that encourages resolution of conflict and coordination of activities at an appropriate level within the transnational organization. By focusing these activities on key senior-level positions in national units, product divisions, and corporate staffs, management can avoid the problems associated with forcing the conflict to low levels where they can result in inefficiency and organizational stress, or elevating too many issues to an overloaded and often underinformed top management. The overall objective of such activities is to create what one manager termed "matrix organizations inside the heads of a key group of senior managers" to allow the majority of issues to be resolved without resorting to formal structural means or top management intervention.

Managing the Process

Although management can shape the broad organization direction and define the ongoing management process through its control of various context variables, there are some issues it may be reluctant to delegate to the ongoing organization process. For poorly defined or emerging issues, changes in direction or priority, particularly sensitive decisions, or highly complex problems, top management may want to monitor closely their analysis and resolution. Management knows in advance that these kinds of issues may not be appropriately resolved if left to the contextual influences that define the organization's "auto pilot," and that they will need to exercise a more direct and active form of influence and control over the decision-making process.

The simplest way to do so is for management to monitor the particular issue more closely so that it can intervene if necessary. This can be done by such basic means as asking the manager most directly responsible to make regular direct reports on the issue. However, one of the biggest barriers to effective monitoring of key issues is that those with relevant information often have a vested interest in the issue in question. In such instances, top management must build supplementary information channels and sources of analyses to help them understand the situation properly.

- During a period of organizational transition at Corning Glass Works several problems arose due to real or perceived overlaps or conflicts in responsibilities among subsidiary managers or between subsidiary and central product managers. Top management had difficulty resolving the differences because its primary information source was the parochial advocacy positions of the competing managers. By legitimizing and strengthening the links among functional managers, top management created a valuable new information channel that gave it an independent view of the issues being sent up to it for resolution. Furthermore, these "functional analogs," as they were called, became neutral arbiters who were able to help resolve the differences. The system was so successful in preventing problems from escalating and reducing the need for headquarters to reach down into the organization, the information channeling and arbitrating role became an important ongoing part of the functional managers' task.[14]

Although some issues can be resolved by such minor interventions or modifications of the basic ongoing organization process, others are too complex or too disruptive to be handled in this way. For such issues, management has the alternative of removing them from the mainstream and structuring them in an "off-line" decision forum like task forces or committees.

In isolating the issue in this way, one can have much more direct influence on the processes that lead to its resolution. By controlling the composition and leadership of such off-line decision forums, defining their mandate, and determining the duration of their existence, top management can exercise considerable influence and control over the decision process, and thus the eventual outcome. In effect, a series of "mini matrix" organizations are created, whose purpose is to isolate the intense and often disruptive management process, yet at the same time legitimize it. Some examples will clarify the nature and use of these off-line forums.

- When the International Division president at Warner Lambert began considering the need to rationalize the company's numerous inefficient local plants, he set up a task force of geographic and functional managers to review capacity needs. During an eighteen-month study, the views of the headquarter's manufacturing finance and marketing managers on the team convinced the regional managers of the need to rationalize and coordinate operations, an idea they had resisted prior to the study.
- Philips understands better than most the problems that arise by giving a single management group the dominant role in product development. As a result, the company consciously seeks to retain the involvement and commitment of its R & D specialists who bring technical expertise, its product division staff who bring a global competitive perspective, and managers from key national organizations who bring these and immediate market knowledge. By creating product-development councils with this diverse constituency of managers it carefully removes the intensive discussion and debate associated with these decisions from the day-to-day operations.
- After decades of allowing each national subsidiary to decide its own product market strategy, top management at Procter & Gamble decided it was necessary to develop a more coordinated Europe-wide approach to product development and marketing strategies. Because this represented a major strategic shift that had the potential to cause considerable organizational trauma, special teams were created to manage the new EuroBrand strategies. Management had multiple objectives in establishing such teams: to co-opt the national subsidiaries into the decision, thus gaining their commitment to its implementation; to isolate the complex and controversial discussions from the ongoing decision process to minimize organizational disruption and distraction; and to allow closer monitoring and control of the process and its eventual outcome.

Managing the Content

No matter how sophisticated or well developed the organizational decision context, no matter how closely involved management is in structuring decision processes through its control of supplemental channels and forums, not all the conflicts will be appropriately resolved, and not all the activities will be adequately coordinated through these two processes. Indeed, the organization should be able to ensure that unresolved problems and inadequately developed solutions be escalated for review, arbitration, or resolution. On these types of decisions, top management must be involved in the content of the issues.

The critical requirement is for a supportive organizational environment that legitimizes the existences of differences and disapproves of any proposal to paper over problems or horse-trade for solutions. This requires well-established corporate norms that allow conflict to be dealt with openly and constructively, accept the fact that not all issues can be dealt with through negotiation, and provide clearly defined procedures for escalating issues for final decision.

- Although Procter & Gamble's EuroBrand team for the new liquid detergent Vizir had considerable freedom in developing the strategy for the new product, clearly defined corporate procedures ensured that when they started planning substantial investments and discussing the product launch, these decisions were automatically sent to top management for approval. Furthermore, because of P & G's well-established internal norms that emphasized the importance of thoroughly analyzing problems and the acceptability of escalating problems or conflicts up the chain of command for resolution, the team had no concern about raising for top management's attention any issues on which it remained deadlocked and all proposals on which they had doubts or concerns. For example, they involved top management in the resolution of the issue whether all country subsidiaries should be required to launch Vizir as part of a united European strategy, or whether local doubts or problems should be allowed to override the EuroBrand strategy.[15]

Through the various means of developing and managing the context, process, and content of decision making, management can create the kind of flexible integrative process required in a transnational organization. The purpose of developing such a process is twofold: to ensure that the large and complex task of coordinating and integrating the operations of a transnational organization does not exceed the organization's processing capacity; while also providing management with the means of differentiating its management processes and responding to the diversity and changeability of its task.

The first of these objectives will be recognized as important to anyone with experiences in companies in which formal global matrix structures have just been installed. In such companies, disputed decision and overlapping responsibilities are inevitably forced up for resolution, and top management quickly finds itself swamped by issues for which it has neither the expertise nor the capacity to resolve. By carefully constructing a more selective decision process in which differences are resolved and operations integrated at lower levels, managers of transnational companies can avoid such problems of top level overhead.

Perhaps more fundamental is the fact that through its management of context, process, and content, management can develop a portfolio of management processes that facilitates the task of managing different businesses functions and tasks in different ways. This is at the very heart of transnational management.

IMPLICATIONS FOR MANAGEMENT: NEW TASKS AND TOOLS

The kind of organization I have described as a transnational clearly represents something quite different from its predecessors, the multinational and the global organizations. Building such an organization requires much more than chosing between a product or a geographic organization structure; and managing it implies much more than centralizing or delegating decisions.

To provide a richer understanding of the nature of the transnational, in this final section I will describe some of the important management implications of this different form of organization. Of the many distinctive issues that have been raised in our earlier descriptions, two stand out as being particularly significant from a managerial perspective. First, the tools and techniques employed in developing and managing this kind of organization are different in kind and application from those typically used in global or multinational organizations. Second, the tasks and responsibilities of key managers in this kind of an organization differ considerably from those of other international organizations.

In describing each of these important management implications, we will be able to stand back from the previous description of the transnational and explore its attributes and operations.

Different Tools

By viewing this challenge as one of creating and managing a decision process that responds to the company's critical task demands, the MNC manager is forced to adopt a very different approach from someone who defines the problem as one of discovering and installing the ideal structure. But if the structural stages model no longer provides a helpful description of international organization development, we need a different way to conceptualize the more complex array of tools and processes discussed in our earlier descriptions of the transnational organization.

The simple but useful framework adopted here is to describe the organization in terms of a physiological model. This analogy helps emphasize that while formal structure is critical in defining the basic anatomy, its role is by no means dominant. To be effective, anatomical changes must be accompanied and complemented by appropriate adaptations to the physiology (the organization's systems and decision processes), and to the psychology (the organization's culture and management values). The different tools and processes used to build and manage the transnational will be described using this physiological model.

Structuring the Organizational Anatomy

The traditional approach to MNC organization problems not only had a strong structural bias, but it also took a very narrow view of formal structure as a management tool: the prescribed organizational forms tended to be defined in *macro* terms that focused on dominant *line* relationships. Thus, they focused on simple but rather superficial choices, such as the classic product versus area structure debate.

As we have seen in the previous section, the development of a transnational organization needs a different approach. It requires management not only to define the characteristics of the dominant line organization, but emphasizes the importance of designing and developing a surrounding structure that ensures that the innate power of the line structure does not lead to unidimensional management of multidimensional problems. Having carefully defined the structure and responsibilities of all management groups, the next challenge is to ensure that particularly those without line authority have appropriate access to and influence in the mainstream of the management process. This is difficult to achieve using only the powerful but blunt instrument of macro structure. Much more effective in achieving this task are *micro*-structural tools such as task forces or committees that become important supplemental decision-making forums. It is in these micro-structures that nonline managers can assume responsibility and be given authority in a way that is not possible within the formal line organization.

Where once task forces and special committees were considered ad hoc, or quick-fix devices useful primarily in reacting to short-term problems, companies pursuing transnational strategies have used them as legitimate and important structural tools that can provide top management the ability to modify or fine-tune their basic structure. To stretch our anatomical analogy, if the formal line structure is the organization's backbone, then the nonline structure is its ribcage, and these micro-structural tools are the muscle and the cartilage that give the organizational skeleton its flexibility.

Developing an Organizational Physiology

With its ability to shape classic hierarchical line relationships, dotted-line staff relationships, and off-line decision forum relationships, it is clear that management has the means available to influence the structure of the communication channels through which much of the organization's decision-making process operates. Yet, by adapting the various administrative systems, hierarchical channels, and informal relationships, they can exert an even more extensive and direct control over the volume, content, and direction of information flows. I term this flow of information that is the basis of all management processes the "organizational physiology."

Many researchers have shown the linkage between the need for information and the complexity and uncertainty of the tasks to be performed.[16] In the integrated network configuration, task complexity and uncertainty are very high. Operating an interdependent system in an environment of diverse, changeable, and often contradictory needs for national responsiveness and global coordination requires large volumes of complex information to be gathered, exchanged, and processed. We have seen a great deal of evidence that transnational organizations need a large number of sophisticated administrative, operational, and strategic systems. But it is equally clear to those in such organizations that formal systems alone cannot support their information processing needs. Again, managers have been forced to look beyond the traditional tools and the conventional approaches in order to develop and manage their new organizational form.

For years managers have recognized that a great deal of information exchange and even decision making—perhaps the majority—occurs through informal channels and relationships. Yet this part of the management process has often been dismissed as either unimportant ("office gossip" or "rumor mill") or unmanageable ("disruptive cliques" or "unholy alliances"). In the management of transnational organizations, such biases need to be reexamined. Not only is it more important for managers of international operations to exert some control and influence over informal systems, in most cases it is also more feasible to do so.

The highly complex and uncertain management processes in a transnational organization require more information than can be reasonably channeled through the formal systems. Furthermore, because organizational units are widely separated and because information is scarce and uncertainty is high, informal systems become an important source of information (and often, misinformation). But the widespread distribution of organizational units and the relative infrequency of direct contacts means that management has a better opportunity to shape and manage the informal systems in an international organization. Top managers are increasingly aware that it is legitimate and often important for them to try to do so.

Doing so is often remarkably easy, requiring only the thoughtful application of their daily involvement in the ongoing management processes as a means to shape the nature and quality of communications patterns and relationships. By influencing the timing frequency and agenda of management trips, corporate meetings, or committee assignments, or by defining an individual's career development process, a manager can greatly influence the development of informal relationships. It can also recognize, legitimize, and co-opt existing informal relationships to contribute to the corporate objective, as illustrated by the development of "functional analogs" at Corning Glass Works.

Organizational Psychology

In addition to an anatomy and a physiology, each organization also has a psychology (i.e., a set of explicit or implicit corporate values and shared beliefs) that greatly affect the way it operates. For companies operating in an international environment, this is a particularly important organizational attribute for a couple of reasons. With employees coming from a variety of different national backgrounds, management cannot assume that all will share common values and relate to common norms. Furthermore, in an operating environment in which managers are separated by distance and time barriers, shared management understanding is often a much more powerful tool than formal structure and systems in coordinating diverse activities. Yet, managers faced with the task of organizational change tend to reach for the more familiar and tangible tools of structural reorganization and systems redesign.

Of the numerous tools and techniques that can affect an organization's psychology, our review of transnational organization has highlighted three that are particularly important. The first is the need for a clear shared understanding of the company's mission and objectives. Matsushita's 250-year vision of its role in a world society, NEC's commitment to Communications and Computers (C & C), and Komatsu's objective to surround Caterpillar ("Maru C") represent variants of this approach applied at different strategic and operational levels.

The second important tool is the visible behavior and public actions of senior management. Particularly in a transnational organization where other signals may be diluted or distorted by the sheer volume of information being sent to foreign outposts, top management's actions speak louder than words, and tend to have a powerful influence on the company's culture. They represent the clearest role model of behavior and a signal of the company's strategic and organizational priorities. When Sony Corporation founder and CEO, Akio Morita relocated to New York to build the company's U.S. operations personally, he sent a message about Sony's commitment to its overseas businesses that could not have been conveyed as strongly by any other means.

The third and most commonly used set of tools for modifying organizational psychology in the transnational organization are those nested in the company's personnel policies, practices, and systems. A company can only develop a multidimensional and flexible organization process if its personnel systems develop and reinforce the appropriate kinds of people. In Eli Lilly we saw a good example of such an approach. Its recruiting and promotion policies emphasized the importance of good interpersonal skills and flexible, nonparochial personalities; its career path management was needed not only to develop skills and knowledge, but also to broaden individual perspectives and interpersonal relationships; and its measurement and reward systems were designed to reinforce the thrust of other organization-building efforts.

Although the process of adapting an organization's culture, values, or beliefs is slow and the tools and techniques are subtle, this tool plays a particularly important role in the development of a transnational organization, because changes in the organizational anatomy and physiology without complementary modifications to its psychology can lead to severe organizational problems.

Different Tasks

The transnational organization's unique structures and processes imply the need for management tasks and roles that are different from those in the traditional global or multinational organizations. The differences can be seen in the responsibilities or managers at the center and the country level of such organizations.

Headquarters Management Tasks

In global companies, headquarter managers were usually involved in developing the strategic and operating direction to the worldwide operations, and providing assistance and support from specialized headquarter staffs. In the multinational company, the primary task of managers at the center was typically to monitor and control the results of its foreign operations.

In the transnational organization, these roles remain an important part of headquarter management's responsibility, but are modified by the existence of multidimensional management perspectives, dispersed responsibilities and capabilities, and a flexible and integrative management process. While strategic direction still comes from the center, in the transnational it is explicitly developed on the basis of inputs and representations of multiple groups located throughout the organization. While the central support role to worldwide operations remains important in transnationals, the wide distribution of key resources and capabilities creates a greater interdependency between headquarters and national units. While the central control role remains, it is viewed much less in a mechanistic or hierarchical sense in a transnational organization, because headquarter management's objective is to co-opt the national organization's capabilities and commitment rather than to subjugate such operations to the parent company's control.

Because of the complexity of the structural configuration and the subtlety of the decision process, top management's attention moves from controlling the strategic content to managing the organizational process. The task of establishing, monitoring, and maintaining the legitimacy of multiple diverse perspectives, the linkages among dispersed interdependent capabilities, and the viability of a flexible integrative process is difficult and time-consuming. It implies a decrease in the center's capacity to direct, support, and control operations worldwide. As part of this change in focus, headquarter management's key role tends to evolve into a more sensitive coordinating task in which it builds and maintains the complex linkages required in a transnational.

Among the numerous coordination tasks we have described for headquarters managers, three stand out as key. First, they must coordinate strategic objectives and operating policies across business, functions, and geographic units, so that the dispersion of responsibility and the multidimensional decision-making processes do not deteriorate into organizational anarchy. In doing so, we have seen how they use management systems more as instruments of strategic coordination than as tools of administrative control. Through the planning and budgeting systems, they ensure that the corporate objectives are communicated and that the diverse organizational interests are resolved appropriately; through the information and control systems, they ensure that plans are implemented and that operating policies are not in conflict across organizational units.

Second, headquarter management must be responsible for the coordination of flows of supplies, components, and funds through the organization. The difficulty and importance of this task increases geometrically with the number of alternative production sources, potential markets, cost differences, lead times, supply conditions (e.g., local content percentages, export quotas, etc.), inventory levels, capacity utilization, and many other variables.

The third important type of central coordination relates to the collection, storage, and redistribution of the company's accumulated knowledge, information, and experience. We have noted that the MNC's global scanning capability represents one of its key competitive advantages. Headquarter management must also act as the central monitor of worldwide developments, the repository of useful knowledge and experience, and the transfer agent of that accumulated wisdom to offer parts of the organization.

Country-Level Management Tasks

Just as the tasks of headquarter managers change in a transnational organization, so too do the roles and responsibilities of managers in the national organizations. In the global organization, their task is primarily to act as the implementers and perhaps the adapters of corporate directives and policies. The country management identify with the company's global interests and will generally compromise local parochial interests in order to achieve corporate objectives.

In the multinational, country management's role is to sense and respond to the demands and opportunities of the local environment. These managers tend to have strong national interests and good local contacts and relationships. Their local autonomy often allows them to develop organizations that are responsive and entrepreneurial.

Despite the apparent conflict, the transnational organization requires both of these sets of management characteristics in its national organizations. The willingness and ability of national units to implement global directives must be achieved without compromising the sensitivity, responsiveness, or entrepreneurial spark of the front-line management.

In addition to these important tasks, the transnational organization demands that country management adopt an additional role of great strategic importance. Unlike their counterparts in global organizations, these managers do not have clear explicit strategies and objectives imposed on them from above. But neither do they have the strategic freedom of those in the country subsidiaries of multinational companies. In the transnational, the country manager takes on an important role in the company's strategic process as communicator of opportunities and threats in the local environment, defender of the national perspective, and advocate of the country organization's interests. In the kind of multidimensional and flexible strategic process that exists in a transnational, such a role is critical.

Furthermore, the national-unit managers must be willing to implement part of a total corporate strategy that may imply a responsibility that stretches well beyond the national boundaries. The country's plant may be designated as a regional source for a particular product or its technical group may be asked to play a key role as the company's competence center in developing a certain technology. Despite his or her position when exercising the advocacy role in the strategic process, the country manager must be willing to accept these additional roles as part of a worldwide operation. In brief, country management must learn to take a more central role in the company's strategy, participating in its development and contributing to its implementation.

CONCLUSION

What, then, is the transnational organization? At one level, the multidimensional management perspectives, the interdependent operations, and the flexible integration organization process might be taken as evidence that it is some kind of worldwide matrix. Such a conclusion would miss the central point of the argument, however.

I have suggested that particularly for managers operating in the international environment, it is important not to reduce the complex organizational task to the simplistic structural terms that have dominated earlier approaches to these issues. The objective must be seen not as one of finding and installing the right structure, but as a challenge to understand and develop an organization process that reflects the company's external task demands and internal administrative heritage. This means that one cannot think of creating a transnational organization through an overnight reorganization. A much more subtle and gradual approach is required to reshape the organization's anatomy, physiology, and psychology over a period of time measured in years rather than weeks.

One final question that must be answered is whether this form of organization is appropriate for all companies. To answer that question, one must first recognize that the transnational is not so much a type of structural configuration as a management mentality. Transnational management acknowledges the complex, diverse, and changeable nature of its environment and reflects those characteristics in its organization's multidimensional perspectives, dispersed capabilities, and flexible process. Rather than reducing the environmental complexity through simple structures or universal solutions, they hope that by capturing the complexity they can become more responsive to it.

It must be recognized, however, that the cost of developing the prescribed organization configuration, decision processes, and coordinating mechanisms is high, and the administrative complexity of operating in such an organization is very demanding of management's time, skill, and attention. Although the simpler organizations such as the more traditional global or multinational forms may compromise management's ability to sense and respond to the complex environment, many companies have chosen to retain such organizations. For them, the strategic disadvantage is more than offset by the administrative advantage of a simpler decision-making process and a less costly organizational overhead.

For some companies, there is little choice, however. Recalling our earlier example, those in the telecommunications industry without the capability to be responsible to diverse national environments while simultaneously obtaining global-scale efficiencies will probably not survive. Increasingly, in industry after industry, we have seen the development of organizations of forces that tend to move companies from their simpler global or multinational stances. While Philips is finding it must coordinate its diverse independent national organizations globally, Matsushita has been struggling with the challenge of transferring more responsibilities and capabilities to its overseas operations.

Obviously, I am not suggesting that all industries are destined to be plotted in the top right quadrant of the global integration/national responsiveness matrix. I have argued, however, that most industries are moving in that direction. The classic global and multinational organizations will find themselves increasingly less able to deal with the multiple and often conflicting political, economic, technological, and social forces, and to a greater or lesser extent, most companies will be forced to develop at least some of the multidimensional and flexible characteristics of the transnational organization.

History has shown that organizational capability has greatly affected companies' ability to survive and succeed. Chandler even termed the creation of an appropriate and effective administrative organization "the most important entrepreneurial act of the founders of an enterprise."[17] Today, most companies have begun to appreciate the nature of their strategic challenge in the global environment. What they need is the organizational capability to implement their strategy.

In the emerging international environment, a company's ability to be simultaneously nationally responsive and globally integrated may well represent the distinctive competence that separates the successful competitors from the mere survivors.

NOTES

1. J. M. Stopford and L. T. Wells, Jr., *Managing the Multinational Enterprise* (New York: Basic Books, 1972).
2. This framework is a derivative of the differentiation–integration concepts developed in P. R. Lawrence and J. W. Lorsch, *Organization and Environment* (Boston: Harvard Business School, Division of Research, 1967). The framework was originally adapted by Prahalad (see C. K. Prahalad, "The Strategic Process in a Multinational Corporation," diss., Harvard Graduate School of Business Administration, 1975). The framework was further applied and modified by Doz and Bartlett (Y. Doz, *Government Control and Multinational Strategic Management: Power Systems and Telecommunications Equipment* [New York: Praeger, 1979]; C. A. Bartlett, "Multinational Structural Evolution: The Changing Decision Environment in International Divisions," Ph.D. diss., Harvard Graduate School of Business Administration, 1979).
3. T. Horst, *At Home Abroad* (Cambridge, Mass.: Ballinger, 1974).
4. Doz, *Government Control*, gives a good description of the economic and political factors facing MNCs in the telecommunications industry.
5. R. Vernon, *Sovereignty at Bay* (New York: Basic Books, 1971).
6. C. J. van der Klugt, "Penetrating Global Markets: High Technology Companies," paper presented at Going Globe Conference sponsored by Economist Conference Unit, June 1985.
7. R. Snoddy, "How Matsushita Averted an Impending Crisis," *Financial Times*, June 6, 1985, 12.
8. For additional descriptions of the way in which such characteristics are developed, see C. A. Bartlett, "How Multinational Organizations Evolve," *Journal of Business Strategy* 1, no. 3. (Summer 1982); and

"MNCs, Get off the Reorganization Merry Go Round," *Harvard Business Review* (March–April 1983).

9. Y. Doz, "Brown Boveri & Cie," Case 9-384-027. Boston: Harvard Business School, 1976.

10. T. Ozawa, *Multinationalism, Japanese Style* (Princeton, N.J.: Princeton University Press, 1979).

11. C. A. Bartlett and H. Yoshihara, "New Challanges for Japanese MNCs," Harvard Business School Working Paper 9-786-032.

12. C. A. Bartlett and S. Ghoshal, "The New Global Organization: Differentiated Roles and Dispersed Responsibilities," Harvard Business School Working Paper 9-786-013.

13. The importance of shaping decisions through the management of the structural context is argued clearly in J. L. Bower, *Managing the Resource Allocation Process* (Homewood, Ill.: Richard D. Irwin, 1972).

14. C. A. Bartlett and M. Y. Yoshino, "Corning Glass Works: International," Case 9-381-160. Boston: Harvard Business School, 1981.

15. C. A. Bartlett, "Procter and Gamble Europe: Vizir Launch," Case 9-384-139. Boston: Harvard Business School, 1981.

16. J. Galbraith, *Organization Design: An Information Processing View* (Reading, Mass.: Addision-Wesley, 1974).

17. A. Chandler, "The Evolution of Modern Global Competition," chap. 13 of this book.

IV

EMPIRICAL EVIDENCE OF GLOBAL COMPETITION

13

The Evolution of Modern Global Competition

Alfred D. Chandler, Jr.

THE MULTINATIONAL AND THE TRANSFORMATION OF INTERNATIONAL TRADE

International trade and with it competition for distant markets has, of course, existed for centuries. But the global competition on which this colloquium concentrates is entirely modern. Until the last decades of the nineteenth century, international competitors were merchants and traders of different nationalities who purchased their goods from manufacturers and often from other intermediaries, usually wholesalers. Over the past century, international trade has been increasingly carried on by manufacturing enterprises that marketed their goods through their own salaried sales force operating from their own office in foreign lands. Many of these enterprises established their own manufacturing establishments abroad. Still others set up or acquired integrated foreign subsidiaries with personnel and facilities for marketing, purchasing, and R & D as well as for production.

The new multinationals not only transformed international trade but also the relationship between private business enterprise and public institutions. Trade across borders coordinated by a single administrative hierarchy carrying different economic functions and often handling several different product lines could not be regulated by those traditional means that had regulated market-coordinated flows between merchants and manufacturers of different nations. Moreover, the economic power of the multinationals continued to increase. Changing technologies and expanding markets enhanced the advantages of managerial coordination and at the same time intensified the competition between such managerial enterprises. As the technologies of production and distribution and the markets for products became more homogeneous, such competition forced the multinationals to acquire a broader, more global perspective.

An understanding of the evolution of modern global competition requires, therefore, a description and analysis of the evolution of this new species of business enterprise, the new player in international trade—the integrated, diversified multinational. This chapter attempts to provide such historical background by reviewing why the modern multinational appeared when it did, became located in the industries that it did, and grew to large size by the processes that it did. Once the similarities in the beginnings and early growth of the new institution are examined, the review considers, even more briefly, the significant differences that occurred in this evolutionary development in four of the world's leading industrial nations—the United States, the United Kingdom, Germany, and Japan. Next it examines the ways these similarities and differences shaped global competition in the period between the two World Wars. Finally it outlines basic factors that have transformed the nature of that competition in the years following the World War II.

THE BEGINNINGS OF THE MODERN MULTINATIONAL INDUSTRIAL ENTERPRISE

Let us begin by stressing once again that the large multinational administered by a hierarchy of salaried managers is an entirely modern phenomenon. Until the last decades of the nineteenth century, production and distribution of goods was carried on by small, personally managed enterprises. The rapid expansion of trade and markets in the eighteenth and early nineteenth centuries brought specialization in both the production and distribution. By the mid-nineteenth century, business enterprise normally operated a single unit of production (a farm, mine, mill, or shop) or a single unit of distribution. The latter normally handled a single function (wholesaling, retailing, importing, or exporting) and usually handled a single line of products (textiles, apparel, hardware, furniture, tobacco, drugs, jewelry, and the like). The flow of goods between these enterprises was coordinated by market mechanisms, which in turn were often affected by tariffs, subsidies, and other regulations decreed by nation states. At that time, owners, either as individuals or partners, managed their enterprises. Where salaried managers were employed, they were few in number and worked directly with the owners. As yet there were no middle managers who supervised junior managers and reported to senior ones. Nor were there enterprises administered through hierarchies of managers comparable to that depicted on Figure 13.1.

Technological innovation transformed such personally managed, single-unit, single-function enterprises into multiunit, multifunctional

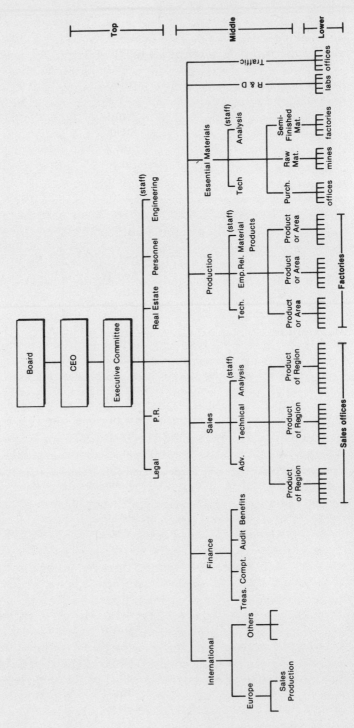

Figure 13.1 Multiunit, Multifunctional Enterprise

ones administered through a hierarchy of salaried managers. New technologies of production and distribution made possible historically unprecedented increases in the volume of output that a single unit of production could process and the volume of transactions that a single unit of distribution could handle. The resulting enormous expansion in the flow of goods in domestic and international trade was in large part not the result of the first industrial revolution that began in Britain at the end of the eighteenth century; that is, it was not entirely the result of the initial application of the new sources of energy (fossil fuel, coal) to the processes of production. It resulted much more from the coming of modern transportation and communication. The railroad, telegraph, steamship, and cable made possible the modern mass production and distribution that was the hallmark of the second industrial revolution of the late nineteenth and early twentieth centuries. These new high-volume technologies could not be effectively exploited unless the massive flows of materials were guided through the process of both production and distribution by teams of salaried managers.

Thus, the first such managerial hierarchies appeared during the 1850s and 1860s to coordinate the movements of trains and the flow of goods over the new railroad networks and messages over the new telegraph system. The management of the new mass retailing establishments—the department stores, mail order houses, and chains or multiple shops—whose existence the railroad and telegraph made possible, also required the creation of teams of salaried managers. Such a managerial organization permitted Sears Roebuck's mail order store in Chicago by 1905 to fill 100,000 orders in a single day—more than the average earlier U.S. merchant filled in a lifetime.[1] These administrative hierarchies grew to a still much greater size in industrial enterprises that integrated mass production and mass distribution within a single business enterprise, again on the basis of modern transportation and communication.

The integrated industrial enterprises have had much in common whether they were U.S., European, or Japanese. They appeared in the 1880s and 1890s in the United States and Europe and a little later in Japan, only because Japan was later to industrialize. They clustered in much the same types of industries; and, finally, they grew in much the same manner. In nearly all cases they became large, first, by integrating forward—that is, investing in marketing and distribution facilities and personnel—and by moving backward into purchasing and control of raw and semifinished materials; then, though less often, by investing in research and development. In this way they created the multifunctional organization that is depicted in Figure 13.1. Many of these new enterprises began in the 1880s and 1890s to make direct investments abroad, first in marketing and then in production facilities and personnel. Such enterprises were the first modern industrial multinationals. Many of these pioneers are, a century later, still major players in today's global competition.

Although not all such integrated industrial enterprises became multinationals, nearly all industrial multinationals evolved from such enterprises. From their beginnings in the 1880s and 1890s, these integrated managerial enterprises have clustered in industries with high-volume processes of production whose output was distributed to national and international markets. Tables 13.1 to 13.5 illustrate this point. Table 13.1 indicates the location by country and by industries of all industrial corporations in the world that in 1973 employed more than 20,000 workers. (The industries are those defined as two-digit industrial groups by the U.S. Census's Standard Industrial Classification [SIC]). In 1973, 263 (65 percent) of the 401 companies were clustered in food, chemicals, oil, machinery, and primary metals. Only 21 companies (5.5 percent) were in apparel, lumber, furniture, leather, publishing and printing, instruments, and miscellaneous. Just under 30 percent were in three-digit subcategories of the other of the census's two-digit groups, such as cigarettes in tobacco; tires in rubber; newsprint in paper; plate glass in stone, glass, and clay; cans and razor blades in fabricated metals; and mass-produced cameras in instruments.

A second point that Table 13.1 illustrates is the predominance of U.S. firms among the world's largest industrial corporations. Of the total of 401 companies employing more than 20,000 persons, over half (212, or 52.6 percent) were U.S. The United Kingdom followed with 50 (12.5 percent), Germany with 29 (7.2 percent), Japan with 28, (7.0 percent) and France with 24 (6.0 percent). Only in chemicals, metals, and electrical machinery were there as many as 4 or 5 more non-U.S. than U.S. firms. In the other groups, U.S. firms total as many or more than those of all other nations.

Table 13.2 shows that in the United States the large industrial corporations had clustered throughout the twentieth century in the same industries in which they were concentrated in 1973. The pattern, depicted on Tables 13.3, 13.4, and 13.5, is much the same for Britain, Germany, and Japan. The U.S. firms were larger, as well as more numerous, than those in other countries. For example in 1948, only 70 to 80 of the British firms had assets comparable to those of the top 200 in the United States. In 1930, the number was about the same. For Germany and Japan it was smaller. Well before World War II, the United States had many more and many larger managerial hierarchies than did other nations—underlining the fact that managerial capitalism first emerged in that nation.

An Explanation of the Beginnings

Why have these large, integrated, hierarchical, and increasingly multinational enterprises appeared in some industries but rarely in oth-

Table 13.1 The Distribution of the Largest Industrial Enterprises with More Than 20,000 Employees, by Industry and Nationality, 1973

SIC		U.S.	Outside of the U.S.	U.K.	Germany	Japan	France	Others	Grand Total
20	Food	22	17	13	0	1	1	2	39
21	Tobacco	3	4	3	1	0	0	0	7
22	Textiles	7	6	3	0	2	1	0	13
23	Apparel	6	0	0	0	0	0	0	6
24	Lumber	4	2	0	0	0	0	2	6
25	Furniture	0	0	0	0	0	0	0	0
26	Paper	7	3	3	0	0	0	0	10
27	Printing and Publishing	0	0	0	0	0	0	0	0
28	Chemical	24	28	4	5	3	6	10	52
29	Petroleum	14	12	2	0	0	2	8	26
30	Rubber	5	5	1	1	1	1	1	10
31	Leather	2	0	0	0	0	0	0	2
32	Stone, Clay, and Glass	7	8	3	0	0	3	2	15
33	Primary Metal	13	35	2	9	5	4	15	48
34	Fabricated Metal	8	6	5	1	0	0	0	14
35	Machinery	22	12	2	3	2	0	5	34
36	Electrical Machinery	20	25	4	5	7	2	7	45
37	Transportation Equipment	22	23	3	3	7	4	6	45
38	Instruments	4	1	0	0	0	0	0	5
39	Miscellaneous	2	0	0	0	0	0	0	2
	Diversified/ Conglomerate	19	3	2	1	0	0	0	22
	Total	211	190	50	29	28	24	59	401

NOTE: In 1970 the one hundred largest industrials accounted for more than one-third of net manufacturing output in the United States and over 45 percent in the United Kingdom. In 1930 they accounted for about 25 percent of total net output in both countries.
SOURCE: *Fortune*, May 1974 and August 1974.

ers? Why did they appear at almost the same historical moment in the United States and Europe? Why did these industrial enterprises in advanced economies grow in the same manner, first by integrating forward into volume distribution, then taking on other functions, and finally becoming multinational by investing abroad first in marketing and then in production?

Because these enterprises initially grew larger by integrating mass production with volume distribution, answers to these critical questions require a careful look at both these processes. Mass production is an attribute of specific technologies. In some industries the primary way to increase output was to add more workers and machines; in

Table 13.2 The Distribution of the 200 Largest Industrial Enterprises in the United States, by Industry[a]

SIC		1917	1930	1948	1973
20	Food	30	31	26	22
21	Tobacco	6	5	5	3
22	Textiles	5	3	6	3
23	Apparel	3	0	0	0
24	Lumber	3	4	1	4
25	Furniture	0	1	1	0
26	Paper	5	7	6	9
27	Printing and Publishing	2	3	2	1
28	Chemical	20	18	24	27
29	Petroleum	22	26	24	22
30	Rubber	5	5	5	5
31	Leather	4	2	2	0
32	Stone, Clay, and Glass	5	9	5	7
33	Primary Metal	29	25	24	19
34	Fabricated Metal	8	10	7	5
35	Machinery	20	22	24	17
36	Electrical Machinery	5	5	8	13
37	Transportation Equipment	26	21	26	19
38	Instruments	1	2	3	4
39	Miscellaneous	1	1	1	1
	Diversified/ Conglomerate	0	0	0	19
	Total	200	200	200	200

[a]Ranked by assets.

others it was by improving and rearranging the inputs, by improving the machinery, furnaces, stills, and other equipment, by reorienting the process of production within the plant, by placing the several intermediate processes of production required for a finished product within a single works, and by increasing the application of energy (particularly fossil fuel energy). The first set of industries remained "labor-intensive;" the second set became "capital-intensive." In this second set of industries the technology of production permitted much larger economies of scale than were possible in the first. That is, it permitted much greater reduction in cost per unit of output as volume increased. So in these capital-intensive industries with large batch or continuous process production technologies, big factories or plants, operating at minimum efficient scale (scale of operation that brought the lowest unit costs) had a much greater cost advantage over small works than was true with labor-intensive technologies. Similarly costs per unit

Table 13.3 The Distribution of the 200 Largest Industrial Enterprises in the United Kingdom, by Industry[a]

SIC		1919	1930	1948	1973
20	Food	63	64	52	33
21	Tobacco	3	4	6	4
22	Textiles	26	24	17	10
23	Apparel	1	3	2	0
24	Lumber	0	0	0	2
25	Furniture	0	0	0	0
26	Paper	4	5	6	7
27	Printing and Publishing	5	10	6	7
28	Chemical	11	9	19	21
29	Petroleum	3	3	3	8
30	Rubber	3	3	2	6
31	Leather	0	0	1	3
32	Stone, Clay, and Glass	2	6	7	16
33	Primary Metal	35	18	24	14
34	Fabricated Metal	2	7	9	7
35	Machinery	8	7	10	26
36	Electrical Machinery	11	18	12	14
37	Transportation Equipment	20	14	20	16
38	Instruments	0	1	1	3
39	Miscellaneous	3	4	3	1
	Diversified/ Conglomerate	0	0	0	2
	Total	200	200	200	200

[a]Ranked by sales for 1973 and by market value of quoted capital for the other years.

rose much more rapidly when volume of production fell below minimum efficient scale (of say 80 to 90 percent of rated capacity) than was true in labor-intensive industries.

What is of basic importance for an understanding of the coming of the modern managerial industrial enterprise is that the cost advantage of the larger plants cannot be fully realized unless a constant flow of materials through the plant or factory is maintained to assure effective capacity utilization. The decisive figure in determining costs and profits is, then, not rated capacity for a specified time period but rather throughput, that is, the amount actually processed in that time period. Throughput relative to rated capacity is the proper economic measure of capacity utilization. In the capital-intensive industries the throughput needed to maintain minimum efficient scale requires not only careful coordination of flow through the processes of production but also the flow of inputs from the suppliers and the flow of outputs to the retailers and final consumers. Such coordination cannot happen

Table 13.4 The Distribution of the 200 Largest Industrial Enterprises in Germany, by Industry[a]

SIC		1913	1928	1953	1973
20	Food	23	28	23	24
21	Tobacco	1	0	0	6
22	Textiles	13	15	19	4
23	Apparel	0	0	0	0
24	Lumber	1	1	2	0
25	Furniture	0	0	0	0
26	Paper	1	2	3	2
27	Printing and Publishing	0	1	0	6
28	Chemical	26	27	32	30
29	Petroleum	5	5	3	8
30	Rubber	1	1	3	3
31	Leather	2	3	2	1
32	Stone, Clay, and Glass	10	9	9	15
33	Primary Metal	49	47	45	19
34	Fabricated Metal	8	7	8	14
35	Machinery	21	19	19	29
36	Electrical Machinery	18	16	13	21
37	Transportation Equipment	19	16	14	14
38	Instruments	1	2	4	2
39	Miscellaneous	1	1	1	1
	Diversified/Conglomerate	0	0	0	1
	Total	200	200	200	200

[a]Ranked by sales for 1973 and by assets for the other three years.

automatically. It demands the constant attention of a managerial team, or hierarchy. Thus, scale is only a technological characteristic. The economies of scale, measured by throughput, require organizational input. Such economies depend on knowledge, skills, and teamwork— on the human organization essential to exploit the potential of technological processes.

Explanatory Generalizations Illustrated

A well-known example illustrates these generalizations. In 1882 the Standard Oil "alliance" formed the Standard Oil Trust.[2] The purpose was not to obtain control over the industry's output. That alliance, a loose federation of forty companies each with its own legal and administrative identity but tied to John D. Rockefeller's Standard Oil Company through interchange of stock and other financial devices, already controlled close to 90 percent of the U.S. output of kerosene. Instead the Trust was formed to provide a legal instrument to rationalize the industry and to exploit more fully economies of scale. The Trust provided the essential legal means to create a corporate or central office that could, first, reorganize the processes of production by shutting down some refineries, reshaping others, and building new ones,

Table 13.5 The Distribution of the 200 Largest Industrial Enterprises in Japan, by Industry[a]

SIC		1918	1930	1954	1973
20	Food	31	30	26	18
21	Tobacco	1	1	0	0
22	Textiles	54	62	23	11
23	Apparel	2	2	1	0
24	Lumber	3	1	0	1
25	Furniture	0	0	0	0
26	Paper	12	6	12	10
27	Printing and Publishing	1	1	0	2
28	Chemical	23	22	38	34
29	Petroleum	6	5	11	13
30	Rubber	0	1	1	5
31	Leather	4	1	0	0
32	Stone, Clay, and Glass	16	14	8	14
33	Primary Metal	21	22	28	27
34	Fabricated Metal	4	3	6	5
35	Machinery	4	4	10	16
36	Electrical Machinery	7	12	15	18
37	Transportation Equipment	9	11	18	20
38	Instruments	1	1	3	5
39	Miscellaneous	1	1	0	1
	Diversified/Conglomerate	0	0	0	0
	Total	200	200	200	200

[a]Ranked by assets.

and second, coordinate the flow of materials, not only through the several refineries, but from the oil fields to the refineries and from the refineries to the consumers. The resulting rationalization made it possible to concentrate close to a quarter of the world's production of kerosene in three refineries, each with an average daily charging capacity of 6,500 barrels with two-thirds of their product going to overseas markets. (At this time the refined petroleum products were by far the nation's largest nonagricultural export.) Imagine the diseconomies of scale (that is, the great increase in unit costs) that would result from placing close to one-fourth of the world's production of shoes, textiles, or lumber into three factories or mills!

This reorganization of the Trust's refining facilities brought a sharp reduction in its average cost of producing a gallon of kerosene. It dropped from 1.5 cents a gallon before reorganization to 0.54 cents in 1884 and 0.45 in 1885—costs far below those of any competitor. However, maintaining this cost advantage required these large refineries to have a continuing daily throughput of from 5,000 to 6,500 barrels, or a three- to four-fold increase over earlier 1,500 to 2,000 barrels daily flow. This required concomitant increases in transactions handled and in the complexity of coordinating the flow of materials through the process of production and distribution.

The Trust quickly recruited the managerial team essential to coordinate the flow through the new refineries. Then in the 1880s, it built a marketing network that quickly covered the world and so became one of the very first modern giant industrial multinationals. As late as 1910, Standard Oil still enjoyed 75 percent of the European markets for kerosene and lubricating oil despite the efforts of the Nobels, the Rothschilds, and such enterprises as Royal Dutch and Shell to reduce Standard's share in that rich market.

The Standard Oil story was by no means unique. In the 1880s and 1890s new mass production technologies—those of the second industrial revolution—brought a sharp reduction in costs as plants reached minimum efficient scale. In many industries the level of output was so high at that scale that a small number of plants were able to meet existing national and even global demand. The structure of these industries quickly became oligopolistic. Their few large enterprises competed worldwide. Many of the first enterprises to build a plant with a high minimum efficient scale and to recruit the essential management team have remained until this day leaders in their industries. A brief review of the industries listed in Tables 13.1 to 13.5 in which the large enterprises have always clustered illustrates this close relationship between scale economies, the size of enterprise, and industrial concentration.

In groups 20 and 21—food, drink, and tobacco—the adoption of brand new production processes brought rapid reduction of costs in the refining of sugar and vegetable oils, in the milling of wheat and oats, and in the making of cigarettes. In cigarettes, for example, the invention of the Bonsak machine in the early 1880s permitted the first entrepreneurs to adopt the machine—James B. Duke in the United States and the Wills brothers in Britain—to reduce labor costs sharply, in Wills's case from 4 shillings per 1,000 to 0.3 pence per thousand.[3] Understandably Duke and Wills soon dominated and then divided the world market. In addition most companies in group 20, and also those producing consumer chemicals, such as soap, cosmetics, paints, and pills, pioneered in the use of new high-volume techniques for packaging their products in small units that could be placed directly on retailers' shelves. The most important of these was the "automatic-line" canning process invented in the mid-1880s, which permitted the filling of 4,000 cans an hour. The names of these pioneers, Campbell Soup, Heinz, Bordens, Carnation, Nestlé, Cadbury, Cross and Blackwell, Lever, Procter & Gamble, Colgate, and others are still well known today.

In chemicals, group 29, the new technologies brought even sharper cost reductions in industrial than in packaged consumer products. Large-scale production of synthetic dyes and synthetic alkalis began in the 1880s. It came a little later in synthetic nitrates, synthetic fibers, plastics, and film. The first three firms to produce the new synthetic blue dye, alizarin, dropped production costs from 200 Reich-marks per kilo in the 1870s to 9 Reich-marks by 1886; and those three firms—Bayer, BASF, and Hoechst—are still, a century later, the three largest German chemical companies.[4]

Rubber production, group 30, like oil, benefited from scale economies, even more in the production of tires than rubber footwear and clothing. Of the ten rubber companies employing over 20,000 workers in 1973 (Table 13.1) nine built their first large factory between 1902 and 1908.[5] Since then the Japanese company, Bridgestone, has been the only major new entrant into the global oligopoly.

In metals, group 34, the scale economies made possible by maintaining a high-volume throughput were also striking. Andrew Carnegie was able to reduce the cost of making steel rails by the new Bessemer steel process from close to $100 a ton in the early 1870s to $12 by the late 1890s.[6] In the refining of nonferrous metals, the electrolytic refining process patented in 1886 brought even more impressive cost reductions, permitting the price of a kilo of aluminum to fall from 87.50 francs in 1888 to 47.50 francs in 1889. After the new plants went into full operation, the price fell to 19 francs at the end of 1890, and 3.75 francs in 1895.[7]

In the machinery-making industries, groups 35–37, new technologies based on the fabricating and assembling of interchangeable metal parts were perfected in the 1880s. By 1886, for example, Singer Sewing Machine had two plants—one in New Jersey and the other in Glasgow, each producing 8,000 machines a week.[8] Maintaining an output that satisfied three-fourths of the world demand required an even more tightly scheduled coordination of flow of materials into, through, and out of the plant than did the mass production of packaged goods, chemicals, and metals. By the 1890s, a tiny number of enterprises using comparable plants supplied the world demand for typewriters, cash registers, adding machines, and other office equipment; for harvesters, reapers, and other agricultural machinery; and for the newly invented electrical and other volume-produced industrial machinery. The culmination of these processes came with the mass production of the automobile. By installing the moving assembly line in his Highland Park plant in 1913, Henry Ford reduced the labor time used in making a Model T from twelve and one-half man hours to one hour and thirty-three minutes.[9] This dramatic increase in throughput permitted Ford to drop the price of the touring car from over $600 in 1913 to $490 in 1914, to $290 in the 1920s; to pay the highest wages; to dominate the global market for low-priced automobiles; and to acquire one of the world's largest fortunes in an astonishingly short time.

On the other hand, in the SIC classification of Tables 13.1 to 13.5, the areas where few large firms appeared—that is, in the older, technologically simple, labor-intensive industries such as apparel, textiles, leather, lumber, and publishing and printing—neither technological nor organizational innovation substantially increased minimum efficient scale. In these industries, large plants did not offer significant cost advantages over small ones. In these industries, the opportunities for cost reduction through more efficient coordination of high-volume throughput by managerial teams remained limited.

The differences in potential scale economies of different production technologies indicate not only why the large hierarchical firms appeared in some industries and not in others, but also why they appeared suddenly in the last decades of the nineteenth century. Only with the completion of the modern transportation and communication networks—the railroad, telegraph, steamship, and cable—could materials flow into a factory or processing plant and the finished goods move out at a rate of speed and volume required to achieve substantial economies of scale. Transportation that depended on the power of animals, wind, and current was too slow, too irregular, and too uncertain to maintain a level of throughput necessary to achieve modern economies of scale.

However, such scale economies measured by throughput do not in themselves explain why the new technologies made possible by the new transportation and communication systems caused the new mass producers to integrate forward into mass distribution. Coordination might have been achieved through contractual agreement with intermediaries, both buyers and sellers. Such an explanation requires a more precise understanding of the process of volume distribution; particularly why the wholesaler, retailer, or other commercial intermediaries lost their cost advantage vis-à-vis the volume producer.

The intermediaries' cost advantage lay in exploiting both the economies of scale and what has been termed the "economies of scope." Because they handled the production of many manufacturers, they achieved a greater volume and lower per-unit cost than any one manufacturer in the marketing and distribution of a single product. Moreover, they increased this advantage by the broader scope of their operation; that is, by handling a number of related products through a single set of facilities. This was true of the new volume wholesalers in apparel, dry goods, groceries, hardware, and the like and even more true of the new mass retailers—the department store, the mail order house, and the chain or multiple shop enterprise.

The commercial intermediaries lost their cost advantages when manufacturers' output reached a comparable scale. As one economist pointed out: "The intermediary will have a cost advantage over its customers and suppliers only as long as the volume of transactions in which he engages comes closer to that [minimum efficient] scale than do the transactions volumes of his customers or suppliers."[10] This rarely happened in retailing, except in heavily concentrated urban markets, but it often occurred in wholesaling. In addition, the advantages of scope were sharply reduced when marketing and distribution required specialized, costly, specific facilities and skills that could not be used to handle other product lines. By investing in such product-specific personnel and facilities, the intermediary not only lost the advantages of scope but also became dependent on what were usually a small number of producers to provide those suppliers.

All the new volume-producing enterprises created their own sales organization to advertise and market their products nationally and in most cases internationally. From the start, they preferred to have a sales force of their own to advertise and market goods. Salesmen of wholesalers and other intermediaries who sold the products of many manufacturers, including those of their competitors, could not be relied upon to concentrate on the single product of a single manufacturer with the intensity needed to attain and maintain market share necessary to keep throughput at minimum efficient scale.

As important, mass distribution of these products often required extensive investment in specialized, product-specific facilities and personnel. This was because nearly all of the products were either entirely new, or greatly improved versions of existing ones. They were, to use an economist's term, highly differentiated. Some required costly, specialized distribution facilities if they were to be marketed in the volume at which they were produced. Others called for demonstration, installation, after-sales service and repair, extensive consumer credit, and other specialized marketing services. Wholesalers hesitated to risk the investment needed to handle such new and often untested products. Even when they were willing to accept that risk, they hesitated to make the costly investments in facilities and personnel that could be used for only a handful of specialized products processed by a handful of producers on whom they would become dependent for the supplies essential to make the investment pay. After all, their business and profits rested on handling related products of many manufacturers.

Of all the new mass producers, those making packaged food products and consumer chemical products—cigarettes, matches, breakfast cereals, canned soups, milk, meat, soap, pills, and paints—required the least in the way of product-specific distribution facilities and personnel. However, the new canning and packaging techniques did immediately eliminate one of the major functions of the wholesaler—that of converting large bulk shipments into small packages. Because the manufacturers now packaged, they, not the wholesaler, began to brand and then to advertise on a national and global scale. Their sales forces now canvassed the retailers. But because mass sales of these branded packaged products demanded little in the way of specialized facilities and personnel, their processors continued to use the wholesaler to distribute physically the goods for a fixed markup or commission until the manufacturers' output became large enough to cancel out the scale advantages of the wholesalers who handled the products of many firms.

All other industrial groupings in which the large firm clustered required major investments in either specialized distribution facilities or specialized personnel and often of both. The distribution of perishable products and those produced by the new mineral and vegetable oil refining processes required a massive investment in facilities if their sales were to be high enough to keep the processing plants at minimum efficient scale. In the 1880s, the meat packers built and operated fleets of refrigerated cars and established refrigerated storage facilities in every city and major town in the United States. Soon they had ocean-going refrigerated ships and storage areas in the ports of Britain and continental Europe.[11] Also in the 1880s, Standard invested in a fleet of railroad tank cars and storage depots as it built its national marketing organization. As its marketing became global, so too did its ocean-going tanker fleet and its intercontinental network of storage depots.[12] American Cotton Oil made comparable investments at home and abroad, including a major storage unit in Rotterdam to facilitate its European deliveries.

When the coming of the automobile required still another costly distribution investment in pumps and service stations to provide roadside supplies to motorists, wholesalers were even less enthusiastic about making the necessary investment. On the other hand, the refiners, by making the investment, were not only assured of being able to control the scheduling of throughput necessary to maintain their high minimum efficient scale but were more certain that the quality of the product was not adulterated, as it might have been if it were packaged by independent wholesalers. In the case of gasoline, in order to avoid the costs of operating the pumps and service stations, most oil companies preferred to lease the equipment they purchased or produced to franchised dealers. A comparable situation occurred in tires, whose mass production benefited from the economies of throughput and whose mass sales required a specialized product-specific distribution network. Again, although tire companies occasionally owned their retail outlets, they preferred to rely on franchised retail dealers.

The mass marketing of newly invented machines that were mass-produced through the fabricating and assembling of interchangeable parts required a greater investment in personnel to provide demonstration, after-sales service and repair, and consumer credit than that required for product-specific facilities.[13] The mass distribution of sewing machines (for households and for the production of apparel), typewriters, cash registers, adding machines, mimeograph machines, and other office equipment; harvesters, reapers, and other agricultural machines, and, after 1900, automobiles and the more complex electrical appliances all required such services. Because these machines were so new, few existing distributors had the necessary training and experience to provide these services or the financial resources to extend long-term consumer credit.

On the other hand, the manufacturer had every incentive to do both. The provision of repair and service helped assure the product performed as advertised. As important, if they owned and operated a wholesale organization they were more certain of assured inventory as well as quality control. Moreover, as many retailers were needed to cover the national and international markets, these machinery manufacturers preferred to rely on, as did the oil and tire companies, franchised dealers. The retail dealers, who sold their products exclusively, were supported by a branch office network that provided the credit, delivered supplies on schedule, and had trained mechanics and special equipment to assure after-sales service and maintenance. Only the makers of sewing machines, typewriters, and cash registers went so far as to invest in retail stores. They did so primarily in concentrated urban areas where, before the coming of the automobile, only such stores were able to provide the necessary services and credit on a neighborhood basis.

The makers of heavier but still standardized machinery for industrial users often required even more in the way of demonstration, installation of the new machines, continuing maintenance and service, and consumer credit. In providing such service to purchasers of these technologically complex new or greatly improved shoe machines, turbines, pumps, boilers, elevators, telephone equipment, and the machinery to generate, transmit, and use electric power, manufacturers' agents and other intermediaries rarely had the training or the capital required. For the makers of industrial chemicals, volume distribution demanded investment in product-specific distribution facilities, as well as salesmen with specialized skills. Dynamite, far more powerful than black powder, required careful education of customers, as well as specialized storage and transportation facilities. So, too, did the new synthetic dyes and synthetic fibers whose use had to be explained to manufacturers and whose application often required new specialized machinery. On the other hand, metals produced by processes with a high minimum efficient scale required less investment in distribution. Even so, to obtain and fill volume orders to precise specifications on precise delivery schedules called for a trained sales force and for close coordination between production and sales managers.

It was this investment in costly, product-specific distribution facilities that carried the pioneering volume-producing manufacturers of new or greatly improved products abroad, that is, that led the large industrial firm to become multinational by making direct investments abroad in marketing. For a U.S. manufacturer located, let us say, in New York, little more effort was needed to set up branch offices with distribution facilities and personnel in Britain and Europe than it was to do so on the U.S. West Coast. Where transportation or tariffs substantially increased cost and where local markets were large enough to justify the building of plants sizable enough to achieve the cost advantages of scale, these companies built, or occasionally purchased plants to supply their marketing organizations. If these foreign markets continued to expand, the distant subsidiary often began to purchase its supplies as well as selling finished products locally. In this way, the foreign subsidiary became as integrated as its parent.

In nearly all the new volume-producing industries, the pioneers continued to dominate for decades. Investment in plants of minimum efficient scale, the building of a marketing and distribution network, and the recruitment of managerial hierarchies to administer and coordinate production and distribution created powerful barriers to entry. Late comers had to build plants of comparable size if they were to be competitive in costs and to set up comparable sales forces if they were to have a share of the market large enough to maintain that scale. Moreover, where the first movers were often able to finance continued expansion from retained earnings, the newcomers had to finance a much larger initial investment in both production and distribution and therefore paid higher financing costs. Finally, the new set of managers had to learn their trade while competing with experienced rivals. Competitors did appear, but they were few in number. From almost their beginnings these industries were oligopolistic. In most cases the oligopoly was international.

In these ways and for these reasons, the large industrial firm that integrated mass production and mass distribution appeared in industries with two characteristics. The first and most essential was a technology of production in which the realization of potential scale economies and maintenance of quality control demanded close and constant coordination and supervision of material flows by trained managerial teams. The second was that volume marketing and distribution of their products required investment in specialized, product-specific human and physical capital.

Where this was not the case, that is, in industries where production technology did not have a potentially high minimum efficient scale, where coordination was not technically complex, and where mass distribution did not require specialized skills and facilities, there was much less incentive for the manufacturer to integrate forward into distribution. In such industries as publishing and printing, lumber, furniture, leather, and apparel and textiles, the large integrated firm had few competitive advantages. In these industries, the small, single-function firm continued to prosper and to compete vigorously.

In industries that had the two critical characteristics, the most important entrepreneurial act after the initial investment in the new production technology was the creation of an administrative organization. This entailed the recruitment of a team to supervise the process of production, then the building of a national and normally international sales network, and finally the setting up of a corporate office of middle and top managers to integrate and coordinate the two. Only then did the enterprise begin to make direct investment abroad in production facilities. Such investment followed—almost never preceded—the building of an overseas marketing network. So, too, in the technologically advanced industries, the investment in research and development came after, not before, the creation of a marketing network. In these firms, the linkage between trained sales engineers, production engineers, product designers, and the research laboratory became a major impetus to continuing innovation in the industries in which they operated. The result of such growth was an enterprise whose organization is depicted in Figure 13.1. The continuing growth of the firm rested on the ability of its managers to transfer resources in marketing, research and development, and production (usually those that were not fully utilized) into new and more profitable related product lines, a move that carried the organization shown in Figure 13.1 to that illustrated by Figure 13.2. If the first step—that of integrating production and distribution—was not taken, the rest did not follow. The firms remained small, personally managed producing enterprises buying their materials and selling their products through intermediaries.

National Differences in the Growth of the Multinational Enterprise

The large managerial enterprise evolved in much the same way in industries with much the same characteristics in the major modern economies. However, there were striking differences in the pace, timing, and specific industries in which the new institution appeared and continued to grow in each of these economies. These differences reflected differences in technologies and markets available to the industrialists of the different nations, differences in their entrepreneurial and organizational skills, and differences in laws, cultural attitudes, and values. These dissimilitudes can be pinpointed by very briefly reviewing the historical experiences of the two hundred largest industrial enterprises in the United States, the United Kingdom, Germany, and Japan.[14]

The United States

In the United States, the completion of the nation's basic railroad and telegraph network and the perfection of its operating methods in the 1870s and 1880s opened up the largest and fastest growing market in the world. Its population, which already enjoyed the highest per capita income in the world, was equal to that of Britain in 1850, twice

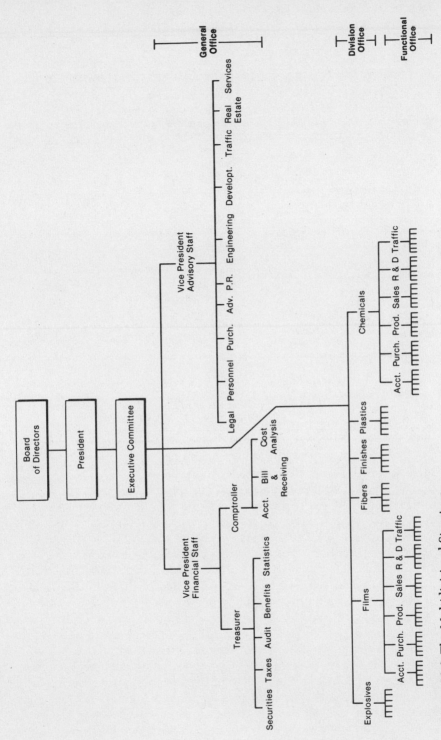

Figure 13.2 The Multidivisional Structure

Table 13.6. Multinational Companies in 1914[a]

Groups 20 & 21: Food and Tobacco	Groups 35, 36, & 37: Machinery and Transportation Equipment
American Chicle	American Bicycle
American Cotton Oil	American Gramophone
Armour	American Radiator
Coca-Cola	Chicago Pneumatic Tool
H. J. Heinz	Crown Cork & Seal
Quaker Oats	Fort Motor
Swift	General Electric
American Tobacco	International Harvester
British American Tobacco	International Steam Pump (Worthington)
	Mergenthaler Linotype
Groups 28, 29, & 30: Chemicals &	National Cash Register
Pharmaceuticals, Oil and Rubber	Norton
	Otis Elevator
Carborundum	Singer Sewing Machine
Parke Davis (drug)	Torrington
Sherwin-Williams	United Shoe Machinery
Sterns & Co. (drug)	Western Electric
United Drug (drug)	Westinghouse Air Brake
Virginia-Carolina Chemical	Westinghouse Electric
Du Pont	
Standard Oil of N.J.	*Others*
U.S. Rubber	
	Alcoa (33)
	Gillette (34)
	Eastman Kodak (38)
	Diamond Match (39)

*U.S. companies with two or more plants abroad or one plant and raw material producing facilities.
SOURCE: Mira Wilkins, *The Emergence of Multinational Enterprise* (Cambridge, Mass.: Harvard University Press, 1970) 212–13, 216.

that in 1900, and three times that in 1920.[15] U.S. entrepreneurs quickly made the investment in plants large enough to exploit the cost advantages of scale, recruited the managerial teams in production necessary to exploit scale economies, and made the investment in distribution necessary to market their volume-produced goods at home and abroad. They did so in all the industries in which large industrial firms would cluster for the following century. Most of these firms quickly extended their marketing organizations overseas, and then became multinational by investing in production facilities abroad, playing an influential role in a global oligopoly. Table 13.6 lists the U.S. industrial firms with production facilities abroad in 1914. By that date, the value of direct foreign investment by U.S. multinationals equaled 7 percent of the gross national product. That figure was still the same in 1966.[16] In some cases, particularly in mass-produced light machinery, the United States enjoyed close to global monopoly well before the outbreak of World War I. By that time too, multinationals in the more technologically advanced industries had begun to invest personnel and facilities in R & D.

In industries where several entrepreneurs simultaneously adopted new technologies to produce new or greatly improved products, the large enterprise initially came into being through mergers and acquisition. In such industries, manufacturers both in Europe and the United States responded to excess production capacity by cooperating with each other to control competition through a variety of contractual forms. U.S. manufacturers first attempted such cooperation by forming trade associations to control output and prices or to allocate marketing territories.[17] However, because of the existing common law prohibition against combinations in restraint of trade, these associations were unable to enforce their rulings in courts of law. So manufacturers turned to the holding company device. Members of their association exchanged their stock for that of a holding company, thus giving the central office of the new holding company legal power to determine output, prices, and marketing areas for the subsidiary firms.

However, for some, like John D. Rockefeller, such legal consolidation became the first step for rationalizing the resources of an enterprise or even an industry in order to exploit more fully potential scale economies. Even before the enforcement of the Sherman Antitrust Law in the early twentieth century made contractual cooperation by means of a holding company legally suspect, a number of U.S. enterprises had been transformed from a holding company into an operating one, by consolidating the factories of their subsidiaries into a single production department and unifying the several sales forces into a single sales department. Rationalization of personnel and facilities followed legal consolidation and administrative centralization. Some plants were shut down, others enlarged, and new ones were built in a way to exploit most effectively the cost advantages of scale in production. The sales network was reshaped to handle existing and forecasted sales requirements. Then, though less often than not, investment was made in research and development. In this way, a loose federation of operating companies was transformed into a single centralized enterprise as depicted on Figure 13.1. Whether an enterprise reached this form after merger and acquisition or by continuing reinvestment in its own production, distribution, and research facilities and personnel, these large managerial enterprises had become firmly entrenched in major sectors of the U.S. economy by the coming of World War I.

Great Britain

This was certainly not the case in Great Britain. As late as World War I, the large integrated industrial enterprise administered through an extensive managerial hierarchy was still the exception. Nearly all of the two hundred leading industrials in Britain had integrated production with distribution, but in a great number of these, owners remained full-time executives. They managed their enterprises with the assistance of a small number of "company servants" who only began to be asked to join boards of directors in the 1930s. In Britain, at the time of World War II, most of the top two hundred consisted of two types of enterprise, neither of which existed among the U.S. top two hundred at the time of World War I. They were either personally managed enterprises or federations of such enterprises. The exceptions were, of course, Britain's largest and best-known industrial corporations—those that represented Britain in their global oligopolies. However, as late as 1948, these numbered less than 20 percent of the top two hundred enterprises.

Large hierarchical enterprises did come when British entrepreneurs responded to the potential of new high-volume technologies by making the necessary investment in production facilities, creating management teams for production, and investing in distribution and research personnel and facilities. Between the 1880s and World War I, such individual entrepreneurs responded in this way in the production of several branded packaged products (like soap, starch, biscuits, and chocolates) as well as rayon, tires, plate and flat glass, explosives, and synthetic alkalis. For example, Courtaulds, the first to build a plant with a high minimum efficient scale in rayon, became and remained the largest producer of the first synthetic fiber, not only in Britain but also in the United States.

But where British industrialists failed to grasp the opportunity to make the investment and build the hierarchies, they not only lost the world market but the British home market itself. This was particularly striking in machinery, both light and heavy, and in industrial chemicals. The U.S. firms quickly overpowered the British competitors in the production and distribution of light mass-produced machinery, including sewing, office, and agricultural machinery, automobiles, household appliances, and the like. The Germans as quickly dominated the synthetic dye business so critical to Britian's huge textile industry, while both the Germans and Americans moved into Britain's electrical machinery industry. In 1912, two-thirds of the output of the electrical equipment industry within Britain was produced by the British factories of the U.S. General Electric and Westinghouse and the German Siemens.[18] Even those few firms that achieved and maintained their position in the British market and the global oligopoly created smaller hierarchies and had more direct owner management than did their U.S. counterparts.

After World War I, a few British firms in these new capital-intensive industries began to challenge their U.S. and German competitors, but they did so only by making the necessary investment in nonmanufacturing personnel and facilities and by recruiting managerial staffs. This was the case for Anglo-Persian Oil Company (it became

British Petroleum), for British General Electric, and Imperial Chemical Industries in each of their industries, for Metal Box in cans and for Austin and Morris in automobiles. Nevertheless, the transformation from personal or family management to one of salaried managers came slowly and grudgingly. Even in the largest enterprises—those with sizable hierarchies such as Courtaulds, British Celenese, Pilkington, Metal Box, Reckitt, Cadbury, Rank, and others—the owners continued to have a much greater say in the top management decisions than did their U.S. counterparts.

Why was this the case? The answer is complex. It lies in Britain's industrial geography and history, in its educational system, in the lack of antitrust legislation, and in a continuing commitment to personal and family management. Because Britain's domestic market was smaller and growing more slowly than that of the United States, British industrialists had less incentive than their U.S. counterparts to exploit scale economies. Moreover, Britain was the only nation to industrialize before the coming of modern transportation and communication. So its industrialists had become tuned to a slower, smaller-scale process of industrial production and distribution.

Nevertheless, precisely because it was the first industrial nation, Great Britain also became the world's first consumer society. The quadrangle bounded by London, Cardiff, Glasgow, and Edinburgh remained for almost a century after 1850 the richest and most concentrated consumer market in the world. British entrepreneurs quickly began to mass produce branded packaged consumer goods. (Of all the new industries these required the least in the way of specialized skills in production and specialized services and facilities in distribution.) But in other of the new industries, it was foreign, not British, entrepreneurs who responded to the new opportunities. Even though that golden quadrangle remained the world's most concentrated market for mass-produced sewing machines, shoe machinery, office equipment, phonographs, batteries, automobiles, appliances, and other consumer durables as well as electrical and other new heavy machinery and industrial chemicals, Germans and Americans were the first to make *within Britain* the large investment required to exploit the new technologies fully, to establish the product-specific distribution services and facilities, and to recruit the essential managerial staff. Apparently British industrialists wanted to manage their own enterprises rather than turn over operating control to nonfamily, salaried managers. They seemed to regard their companies as family estates to be nurtured and passed down to their heirs rather than mere money-making machines. As a result, they and the British economy as a whole failed to harvest many of the fruits of the second industrial revolution.

The commitment to family control was reflected in the nature of British mergers. As in the United States, many British firms grew large by merger and acquisition. As in the United States, holding companies were formed to control legally the output, price, and marketing arrangements of hitherto small competing enterprises; but in Britain, unlike in the United States, holding companies remained federations of family firms. Until after World War I, no British industrialist viewed merger as forerunner to the rationalization, consolidation, and centralized administration necessary to exploit the potential scale of economies. Indeed, the very first merger to centralize and rationalize in Britain came in 1920 at Nobel Explosives, the forerunner to ICI, which borrowed the necessary organizational techniques directly from its overseas ally, the Du Pont company of Wilmington, Delaware.[19] As late as 1928, Lever Brothers, one of Britain's largest enterprises, had forty-one operating subsidiaries and thirty-nine different sales forces. For these reasons, then, the founders of most large British enterprises continued to manage their enterprises directly. Hierarchies remained small and controllable. Sons, grandsons, and grandsons-in-law continued to move into the top offices. Britain continued until World War II to be the bastion of family capitalism.

Germany

In Germany, unlike Britain, there were integrated industrial firms that were as large as those in the United States well before the coming of World War I. They were, however, fewer in number and were concentrated in metals and the technologically advanced machinery and chemical industries. Among the top two hundred German firms during the interwar years, there were very few producing branded packaged products, except for the regional breweries. One can only locate two chocolate and confectionary and two drug companies among the top two hundred. The remaining few were subsidiaries of Nestlé's, Lever Brothers, and the two Dutch margarine makers that joined Lever in 1929 to become Unilever. Nor did the large German firms manufacture light mass-produced machinery in the U.S. manner. Singer Sewing Machine long remained the largest sewing machine maker in Germany. Well before World War I, the factories of National Cash Register and American Radiator and the sales office of International Harvester and Remington Typewriter dominated the German market for their products. In automobiles in 1929, the year when General Motors produced 1.6 million and Ford 1.5 million cars, only one Germany car company made more than 10,000, and that firm, Adam Opel, which produced 25,000, had just become a General Motors subsidiary. Even in standardized industrial machines, U.S. firms such as Mergenthaler Linotype (in printing presses) and Norton and Carborundum (in abrasives and grinding machines) dominated German markets.

The Germans did, like the British, have their one large representative in the global rayon, rubber, and oil oligopolies. (The last,

EPU, was dismembered during World War I.) It was in complex ma-chinery and chemicals, however, that the Germans made their global mark. In giant production works, German machinery and chemical enterprises produced in quantity a variety of complex machines and chemicals. Managerial hierarchies even greater in size than those of the production departments of U.S. firms guided the complicated flow of materials from one intermediate process to the next. In the 1880s and 1890s, enterprises—such as Bayer, Hoechst, BASF, AGFA, and Deugssa in chemicals; Merck, von Heyden, and Schering in pharma-ceuticals; Siemens and AEG in electrical equipment; AFA in storage batteries; and Metallgesellschaft in copper—built extended networks of branch offices throughout the world to market their products, dem-onstrate their use, install them where necessary, provide continuing after-sale service, and give customers the financial credit they often needed to make such purchases. Once established abroad, they built or acquired branch factories. Finally, they invested, usually more heavily than the Americans in research and development.

At home these large integrated enterprises reduced competition by making contractual arrangements for setting price and output and allocating markets. Because such arrangements were in Germany le-gally enforceable in courts of law, the arrangements became quite for-mal and elaborate. The I.G., a legal form that is best translated as the "community of interest," became the closest to that of the British and the U.S. holding company. The difference between the British hold-ing company and the German community of interest was that the lat-ter involved large hierarchical firms rather than small family enter-prises. Their extensive investment in marketing and distribution and in research and development permitted these firms to dominate the negotiations setting up cartels or associations both at home and abroad and provided them with the power essential to implement and enforce the contractual arrangements.

Finally, the capital requirements of these capital-intensive pro-ducers of industrial products were far greater than those of the U.S. and British makers of branded packaged products or the U.S. mass producers of light machinery. Because there were no highly devel-oped capital markets in Germany comparable to those of London and New York, German banks became much more involved in the financ-ing of large hierarchical enterprises than was true in Britain and the United States. Although the representatives of banks rarely sat on the Vorstand, the central administrative body of top managers, as did the founder and often full-time family executives, they did become important members of the Aufsichtsrat, or supervisory board.

Why was it that the large German industrial enterprises were con-centrated in metals and complex industrial products rather than branded goods or light mass-produced machinery? Why did the Ger-mans build large hierarchical organizations when the British did not?

Manufacturers in the new German empire of the 1870s, at the time when the transportation and communication revolution was nearing an end, enjoyed neither the rapidly growing continental market of the United States nor the concentrated consumer market of Britain. Because per capita income was lower in Germany than in the two Anglo-Saxon countries, and because Germany was neither a large importer of foodstuffs like the United Kingdom nor an exporter like the United States, neither the markets nor the availability of supplies for mass producing and mass distributing branded packaged products was comparable to those in Britain and the United States. On the other hand, the rapidly growing industrial markets in Europe, including Britain and Germany itself, created a powerful growing demand for the new specialized industrial machinery, including electrical equipment, and new industrial chemicals, including synthetic dyes. In building their technical sales and research organizations—their basic weapons in international competition—the Germans had the advantage of what had become the world's best technical and scientific educational institutions. Therefore, despite the defeat in two wars, the German strength in international competition still rests on the performance of their science-based industries.

Japan

The evolution of the large industrial enterprises in Japan differed greatly from those in the West. For Japan was just taking the first steps toward modern industrialization in the same decades that the new transportation and communication revolution was spawning the second industrial revolution in Europe and the United States. Indeed, Japan's first steel mill only went into operation in 1902. Only in the years after World War II was the economy large and strong enough to support modern mass production and mass distribution. Yet even before that war managerial hierarchies had appeared to exploit new technologies and to reach new markets.

In the early years of this century, Japan's domestic and foreign markets were totally different. At the time of the Meiji Restoration, Japanese manufacturers enjoyed a highly concentrated domestic market, comparable to Britain's during its early industrialization, with long-established channels for distribution of traditional consumer goods. As a result, only a few Japanese firms (and no foreign companies) began to create marketing networks to distribute branded packaged products within the country. By World War II, a small number of makers of branded packaged products such as confectionary, soy sauce, canned sea food, beer, and soap, who advertised nationally and had their own extensive sales forces, were listed among the largest two hundred Japanese industrial enterprises.

On the other hand, the Japanese had had no overseas commercial contact at all, even with the nearby Asian continent, for the more than two hundred fifty years of the Tokuagawa rule. Manufacturers using imported processes to produce textiles, fertilizers, ceramic, and metal products sought overseas as well as domestic markets, particularly in nonindustrialized East and Southeast Asia. Overseas they rarely set up their own branch offices. They had neither the volume nor the distribution needs to require large product-specific investments in distribution. They relied instead on allied trading companies to assure coordination of the flow of goods from factories to Japan to customers abroad, and also to those at home, and the flow of essential materials and equipment from overseas to the producing facilities. These trading companies set up branch offices in Japan and in all parts of the world as well as building a large central office in Tokyo or Osaka. That is, they invested in an extensive marketing and distribution organization that coordinated flows, provided marketing services, and generated information, thus lowering marketing and distribution costs. The trading companies became the linchpins of groups of single-product manufacturing enterprises, each group having its own banks and trust companies, as well as its own trading and warehouse concerns.

The close relationship between the managers of the manufacturing companies and those of the trading firms, either within the giant *zaibatsu* or between cooperating manufacturers in less formal groups, permitted the Japanese to capture an increased share of world trade, particularly in the relatively low-technology industries. However, where marketing and distribution did require product-specific skills, services, and facilities, enterprises set up their own distributing network and operated outside of the *zaibatsu* and other group enterprises. Before World War II, only a small number of such enterprises had appeared, primarily in industrial machinery, particularly electrical. The latter was especially important, for until the 1950s, Japan relied heavily on hydroelectric power for its energy. Only after the war, with the rapid growth of the domestic market did the makers of automobiles, electric appliances, radio, and television build comparable organizations. In the postwar years, these enterprises increasingly invested in distribution abroad and operated through extensive managerial hierarchies comparable to those of the West.

GLOBAL COMPETITION DURING THE INTERWAR YEARS

This review of the growth of the modern integrated industrial multinational provides the data necessary to understand the changing nature of competition among such enterprises in international trade. These changing patterns of competition can be most precisely presented by reviewing, first, competition during the years between World War I and World War II and, then, by examining the ways in

which changing technologies and markets within a changing system of
nation states helped to transform such competition in the post–World
War II years.

In the international markets of the interwar years, even after the
onslaught of the Great Depression, multinationals played an increasingly significant role. They grew both in numbers and in size. In these
years U.S. multinationals continued to be more numerous in more
industries and in some industries larger in size than those of other
nations. They divided fairly evenly between those producing and distributing consumer goods and those handling industrial products.
British multinationals concentrated more on the production of consumer goods, particularly branded packaged products; while the
strength of the German multinationals lay in the technologically advanced industrial chemicals, machinery, and metal products. The Japanese still played a minor role in international competition.

In these industries the first movers continued to maintain their
competitive advantage. But challenges did appear, and market share
in these global oligopolies rarely remained stable. The Americans continued to dominate in light machinery, becoming even stronger in appliances and automobiles. They remained strong in heavy machinery
and also in tires.[20] In oil the successors to Standard Oil (which was
dismembered in 1911 by a Supreme Court antitrust decision) were
increasingly challenged by Anglo-Iranian Oil (British Petroleum),
Royal Dutch Shell, Texaco, and Gulf. In branded packaged products,
such companies as Corn Products, General Foods, National Biscuit,
Wrigley Chewing Gum, Procter & Gamble, Colgate, and American
Home Products made direct investments in manufacturing to support
their sales organizations. The major expansion of British multinationals came in the production of branded packaged products including
consumer chemicals.[21] They continued to concentrate on the European and imperial markets. The Germans were severely hurt by
World War I, for the British, French, and Americans expropriated
subsidiaries of their chemical, pharmaceutical, electrical and nonelec-
trical machinery, copper, and oil multinationals. Nevertheless, most
of these firms quickly recovered from wartime losses. They soon began to regain market share, particularly in Eastern and Southern Europe but also in the wider international markets including chemicals
in the United States.[22] Nevertheless, the confiscation of overseas manufacturing and other properties during World War I discouraged them
from making capital investments abroad in the interwar years comparable to those made before 1914. In Japan, whose trade had benefited
greatly from World War I, the trading companies of the *zaibatsu* not
only expanded their activities primarily in the nearby markets of East
Asia, but also enlarged the size and number of their branch offices in
the United States and Europe.[23]

The growing economic autocracy of the leading nation states during the interwar years encouraged expansion abroad. Tariff barriers became increasingly higher and trade restrictions and currency controls increasingly rigid. Nevertheless, the desire to protect existing markets and to move in the new ones probably remained an even more powerful motive than tariff jumping for direct investment abroad.

In these years, differences in the ways of international competition reflected not only those in the technologies of production, but also differences in the patterns of competition and cooperation developed in various domestic markets. These differences in competition at home in turn reflected differences in the size of the domestic markets and in national laws affecting interfirm competition. In the United States, the large and rapidly growing domestic market permitted several enterprises to operate plants at minimum efficient scale. In Europe, on the other hand, domestic markets could rarely support more than one or two such enterprises. U.S. government legislation penalized monopoly but not oligopoly. European governments remained much more lenient toward monopoly.

Oligopolistic competition in the United States was rarely based on price alone. Usually the largest, which was often the oldest, became the price leader. The firms did, however, compete, often forcefully, for market share and profits by what can be termed functional and strategic efficiency. That is, they competed by becoming more efficient in carrying out the several processes of production and distribution, by developing and improving both product and process through systematic research and development, by locating new and more suitable sources of supply, and by providing more effective marketing services and carrying out more forceful marketing campaigns. With such functional efficiencies they maintained or improved their competitive advantages of cost and product differentiation. In addition, by more careful planning and resource allocation they moved more quickly than competitors into new and expanding markets and out of old and declining ones.[24]

Antitrust legislation encouraged this form of competition. As interpreted and enforced by the Federal courts, monopoly remained illegal; but oligopoly was sanctioned, depending in part on what the Supreme Court determined to be reasonable competition. The new competition did result in gains and losses, occasionally quite dramatic ones, in market share and in rate of return for the leaders in such major industries as steel, oil, rubber, glass, agricultural machinery, meat packing, and automobiles during the years between the turn of the century merger movement and World War II.

In Europe, much smaller domestic markets and the lack of antitrust legislation meant that market power was achieved and maintained in the domestic market far more by contractual cooperation than through functional and strategic efficiencies. In those British industries where a single firm did not dominate, federations of relatively small, usually family enterprises, normally in the form of holding companies, maintained agreements as to price, output, and marketing territory. In Germany, where cartel agreements were legal and could be enforced in courts of law, market control through contractual cooperation was even more effective.

In international competition, however, such contractural cooperation was much more difficult to enforce. No international courts existed to bring cheaters on the cartel into line. Nor was the holding company as effective across borders as it was within a single national legal system. Thus, by the interwar years, international competition became patterned more on the U.S. style of oligopolistic competition than on the European brand of monopoly. Nevertheless, in industries, particularly those producing industrial goods where technologies of production brought an extremely high throughput and so permitted a very small number of firms to dominate world production and where these few were primarily European firms, global cartelization did occur, but rarely on a permanent basis.

Industry Differences in Interwar Global Competition

During the interwar years, the ways of reflected differences in technologies of production in different industries as well as differences in national laws and traditions relating to competition helped to shape the organizational structure of the competing firms. In branded packaged food, tobacco, and chemical products (groups 20 and 21 and consumer products in group 28) the United States and Britain continued to dominate international markets. The Americans appear to have been more agressive in competing in Britain and the Continent than were the British in the United States. The U.S. companies' abilities to increase market share abroad rested on the transfer of marketing and distribution skills developed at home. The British preferred to concentrate more by expanding within their empire, that is, India and particularly the white commonwealth countries where they sold to transplanted Britishers.[25] The British may have been handicapped in direct competition with the Americans because their firms lacked a strong central office to direct the development and transferal of specialized marketing and distribution skills.

In these consumer goods industries, scale economies were less pronounced. Therefore, there was less competitive advantage to concentrating production in large plants, and local tastes directly affected sales because there were relatively few major advantages in coordinating flows on a global scale. Both British and U.S. multinationals producing such branded packaged products operated through decentralized federated structures. The British firms that had smaller corporate offices gave less direction to their foreign subsidiaries and monitored their activities less carefully than did the Americans. Within their local, usually national, markets they competed functionally and strategically. Although some of the large British firms worked together closely in obtaining supplies, and even in sharing the domestic market, there was little evidence of contractural cooperation in the packaged goods industries among international rivals in the marketing and distribution of their products abroad.

In the oil and rubber industries (groups 29 and 30) scale efficiencies resulting from administrative coordination of the flow of relatively homogeneous products to and from refineries and processing plants brought central control. In oil the global oligopoly was quickly dominated by three firms. By the early 1920s, Anglo-Iranian (British Petroleum) and Shell created managerial hierarchies comparable to those of Standard Oil (New Jersey, now Exxon).[26] By the 1930s, four other U.S. firms were competing in the oligopoly. These global leaders had heavy investments in pipelines, tanker fleets, and railroad cars, the use of which was carefully coordinated. Because of their much greater scale economies, oil companies were slower to build overseas processing plants than were the producers of branded packaged products. When they did, the output of one foreign refinery tended to serve several nations in one large region. Once established, decisions of local managers had to be integrated with those of the corporate staff at the home office if production and distribution efficiencies were to be assured. The following statement on the functions of the corporate Coordination Department at Jersey Standard written in October 1927 makes this point effectively.

> In general, the Department assists in currently determining the policies to be adopted so far as the activities of the producing, transportation and manufacturing branches of the Company are concerned, and cooperates with the subsidiary companies to see that these policies are carried out. This entails arranging for refinery Crude supplies; Crude transportation and allocation; production, purchases and movements of certain finished products (i.e., naphthas [gasoline], refined oil, gas, and fuel oils); coordination of refining manufacturing operations from the standpoint of Crudes run and products required, stocks on hand, etc., and the allocation of business among the various subsidiary companies.[27]

After spelling out the complexities of global coordination in crude oil production, transportation, and refining, the memorandum reviewed the intricacies of coordinating globally the distribution of refined products.

Because of comparable scale economies in the production of tires and to a lesser extent in rubber boots and shoes, the pattern was somewhat the same in rubber. Members of the global oligopoly—four U.S. firms (Goodrich, Goodyear, Firestone, and U.S. Rubber) and one from each major industrial nation—concentrated production in a few plants, brought raw materials from vast distances and marketed worldwide. As the volume of output was smaller and sources of supplies and centers of distribution somewhat fewer, coordination in rubber required less careful scheduling than it did in oil. Nevertheless, the overall corporate structure was much more a centralized than federated one.

In both industries during most of the interwar years, these large mass producers of primarily consumer goods competed functionally and strategically for market share in the U.S. style. In the late 1920s, the opening of vast new oil fields in Texas, California, and Iran threatened overproduction of crude oil. The three largest companies, Jersey Standard, Shell, and Anglo-Iranian, signed the well-known Achnacarry, or "as is" agreement, which attempted to maintain stability by reducing competition for market share.[28] As the Great Depression dampened demand, the smaller of "the Seven Sisters"—Texaco, Gulf, Standard Oil of New York (now Mobil), and Standard Oil of California—joined the enlarged general agreement. Nevertheless, few specific arrangements as to actual price and output were reached and still fewer of those created enforcing agencies.

No such agreements were attempted by the rubber manufacturers. The only significant agreements in that industry were between rubber-producing nations that restricted crude rubber production. These agreements were strongly opposed by the members of the rubber oligopoly as it forced those that had not already integrated backward into owning and operating distant rubber plantations to do so.

In mass-produced light machinery, where the United States continued to dominate international markets until well after World War II, there were even fewer attempts at contractural cooperation. U.S. makers of sewing machines, office and agricultural machinery, automobiles, and such appliances as washing machines, vacuum cleaners, and electric stoves relied on their own extensive marketing organizations to demonstrate, install, service, repair, and provide consumer credit. By 1930, nearly all had enlarged the plants they had operated before the war. Many built and purchased new ones. When competition did come, as it did in automobiles in Britain, it came usually because of the failure of the U.S. home office to adjust to basic local market requirements.

In the fabricating and assembling industries (groups 35, 36, and 37) the choice of direct investment abroad in production often rested on whether scale economies were greater in the fabricating or in the assembling of the parts. In automobiles, and to some extent in agricultural and light construction equipment, scale economies were best achieved by concentrating fabricating in a small number of large plants, usually at home, while having the assembling of parts scattered in a large number of smaller plants closer to markets. To operate both fabricating and assembling plants at minimum efficient scale required careful centralized coordination of product flow. On the other hand, in the mass production of sewing machines, typewriters, and other office equipment, such economies in fabricating were less pronounced than in automobiles, so manufacturers normally built plants abroad that both fabricated and assembled. In such cases, production was usually concentrated in a very few large plants that sourced from and sold to large usually multinational regions. Therefore, central coordination was less essential. The regional subsidiary coordinated product flow with little consultation from the home office. However, basic product and process design as well as continuing research on process and product continued to be carried out in the home country, usually close to corporate headquarters.

Even where the coordinating role of the home office was more critical to achieving production economies in both fabricating and assembling, the differing strategies of the different firms affected their organization structure. Thus, coordination by the Detroit office at Ford, where growth resulted from direct investment in assembling plants, was tighter than it became at General Motors, which in the late 1920s shifted to an expansion strategy of purchasing existing integrated enterprises.[29] Nevertheless, General Motors's corporate officers in Detroit determined manufacturing, design, and product policies for its major foreign subsidiaries, Opel in Germany and Vauxhall in Britain.[30]

In the production and distribution of industrial goods—chemical, electrical, and other heavy machinery—where production normally required the coordination of several intermediate processes, the Germans and Americans who dominated the international markets usually unified these processes within a single large plant or works. Therefore, when they went abroad, they normally set up a complete works that sourced and sold regionally with managers of the subsidiary handling day-to-day activities. However, in these industries the corporate office continued to control basic price and output policies more tightly than those producing consumer products.

The volume producers of industrial goods attempted much more than did producers of automobiles, light machinery, rubber, and oil to control international markets through cartels. In electrical equipment the four leaders of the global oligopoly, two U.S. and two German firms, had patents and licensing agreements with each other and with smaller companies in other nations—agreements that allocated markets as well as pooling patents and providing for technical information. The same was true for German and U.S. producers of storage batteries and other more specialized electrical products. Nevertheless, because the market for such equipment was until the 1930s growing rapidly and because the opportunity for technological innovation remained high in both product and process, the smaller, although still quite large, British, Swiss, and Swedish electrical manufacturers were able to increase output and market share. They did so, however, only after they had developed production, distribution, and research facilities and skills comparable to those of the four leaders.

Comparable patents, exchange of technical information, and market allocating agreements were significant in the chemical industries. There global cartels of a small number of large firms were relatively effective in glass, rayon, explosives, synthetic nitrates, dyes, pharmaceuticals, and films.[31] In the most technologically advanced organic and inorganic chemical industries, the Germans who had built the most efficient plants and created the most effective worldwide marketing organizations continued to have a major say in the drawing up of agreements and continued to have the economic power to enforce them. The Americans, because of the antitrust laws, rarely joined agreements to set price and output; but they did, through patent and licensing arrangements, agree to stay out of Europe if European firms, with some exceptions, stayed out of the U.S. markets. As in machinery, research and development continued to be done at home.

In the production of metals, both ferrous and nonferrous (group 33) the massive throughput needed to maintain minimum efficient scale kept the leading enterprises highly centralized. These firms rarely found it economical to build plants abroad, even though tariff barriers and transportation costs were high. The construction of costly plants in foreign economies at such a scale usually so expanded local capacity that existing demand was not enough to maintain a throughput necessary to achieve a competitive advantage. These firms, however, had branch offices abroad and employed a small professional international sales force to obtain orders with precise specifications to be delivered on a precise schedule.

Because this highly concentrated production in these industries with cyclical demand often brought the threat of global overcapacity, contractual cooperation by means of formal cartels became prevalent. However, cartels in iron and steel were rarely successful, even though in Europe they had the support of their national governments and even though the U.S. producers had withdrawn from the European markets.[32] The number of firms may have been too numerous and the products too differentiated to enforce effectively the agreements reached. On the other hand, in nonferrous metals—copper, nickel, and aluminum—such contractual agreements were more successful and longer lived. Far fewer firms were involved. In addition, the enormous scale economies generated by electrolytic refining technologies provided the pioneers with the economic power to enforce agreements, as their unit costs usually remained well below their somewhat smaller competitors.

In these ways, the strategies and structures of multinational companies competing for shares of the global markets reflected during the interwar years the cost advantages of scale, the pace of technological change, the existing restrictions to trade, and the contractual arrangements between a small number of competitors to set price and output and to allocate markets. In some cases, scale economies inherent in different technologies of production encouraged centralization, in others decentralization of decision making within multinational enterprises. Tariff barriers often hampered the rational exploitation of scale economies, led to building smaller plants for national markets, and often further decentralized decision making. On the other hand cartel arrangements usually centralized decisions as to price, output, and markets.

THE POST–WORLD WAR II ENVIRONMENT: MARKETS, TECHNOLOGY, AND MANAGEMENT

The underlying institutional framework within which global competition was carried on, created in the last decades of the nineteenth century and firmly established during the interwar years, has remained intact until today. Even the trauma of World War II did not alter basic patterns of international business. U.S. firms, of course, came out of the war with an enhanced position. Nevertheless, the devastated European and Japanese economies recovered with impressive speed. In both areas, the same large integrated multinational enterprises continued to dominate in the same industries for much the same reason. Even the German chemical and machinery firms, whose facilities were often totally destroyed and personnel scattered and whose homeland was divided, soon had positions in national and global markets almost as strong as they had been in the 1930s.

Indeed, in the postwar global setting there was more of a change in the number and activities of the nation states than in those of the multinational enterprises. While the United States and the countries of Western Europe continued to dominate world trade, with Japan as the one new challenger, a host of new nations, many former colonies or dependencies of the dismembered empires, appeared. Nearly all hoped to industrialize and to achieve economic growth by adopting the new technologies of production and distribution. Moreover, the world was quickly divided between the East and West—the Communist and non-Communist—with very little trade between the two. The key actors remained much the same, but the environment in which they operated changed swiftly. This transformation rested, as it had in the past, on expanding markets and continuing technological change.

Changing Markets

During the two decades after 1950, both domestic and international markets expanded at a faster rate than at any time since the 1880s.

Not only did population increase, but of most importance, so did per capita output and income.[33] The continuing rapid migration from the country to the city rapidly increased the numbers of customers for processed and manufactured products.

During these same decades of U.S. hegemony, traffic and other barriers that divided markets melted away. When trade restrictions lingered, they were often the result of legislation to encourage economic growth and health. In the 1950s and 1960s, the economic autocracy of the interwar years all but disappeared. The formation of the European Community (EC) by the Treaty of Rome in 1957 created a domestic market for European manufacturers that was large enough and growing fast enough to permit scale economies in production comparable to those that had long existed in the United States.

The decline in trade barriers was accompanied by a breakdown of prewar cartels and other interfirm contractual agreements. Free trade and competition, basic tenants of the U.S. economic creed, were exported abroad. The victorious U.S. authorities dismantled the cartels in Germany and dismembered the *zaibatsu* in Japan. Then, in 1956, the British Parliament passed the Restrictive Practices Act, the first Parliamentary legislation to challenge the legal and economic validity of maintaining market power through contractual cooperation.[34] Soon the EC began to develop a body of legislation that did much the same for the new broad continental market.

Even earlier, during and immediately after the war, the U.S. Justice Department had moved successfully against U.S. firms that through patent and license agreements had been able by legal means to allocate markets abroad and otherwise maintain their position in international trade. The Department court rulings prohibited the making of such agreements even with foreign affiliates in which they held a substantial, often controlling share (but less than 50 percent), of the voting stock.[35] These rulings at home, plus the new legislation abroad, weakened the position of U.S. machinery makers, particularly the manufacturers of electrical equipment in foreign markets. On the other hand, they opened the European market to the U.S. chemical companies. Thus, by the end of the 1950s, competitors in the enlarged and rapidly growing global markets no longer relied on contractual cooperation to maintain market power. Competitors in nearly all the global oligopolies now competed functionally and strategically for market share.

Technological Change

As important as expanding markets in shaping the global competitive environment was the diffusion of existing technologies and the development of new ones, particularly the new communications and information technology. The rapid transfer of highly product-specific production technologies during and after World War II eroded U.S. strength in international markets in light machinery, automobiles, and other vehicles and the German position in the technologically complex industrial, chemical, and machinery markets. Especially striking was the loss of U.S. dominance in the production of automobiles and commercial vehicles. Although Morris and Austin in Britain and Renault and Citroën in France had adopted U.S. production techniques during the interwar years, they had by 1939 gained only a tiny share of the international markets.[36] In Italy and Germany, such methods first appeared with the opening of the large Fiat plant in 1936 and the Volkswagen works in 1940, too late to affect prewar global competition. After the war, such companies quickly expanded output to meet domestic and then European demand. For example, by 1960, Volkswagen and Mercedes had joined Ford and General Motors's Opel as the dominant German firms, the four accounting for 87 percent of the nation's automobile output. In the next decade, the United States rapidly lost market shares to new competitors abroad and then in the 1970s at home. To a somewhat lesser extent, the same pattern occurred in the production of sewing, office and agricultural machinery, and consumer appliances. In electrical machinery and other volume-produced industrial equipment some of the major firms voluntarily, though temporarily, withdrew from the European markets partly because of the Justice Department's antitrust drive.

Far more dramatic was the new competition from Japan. As Hirschmeier and Yui noted in their *Development of Japanese Business 1969–1973:*

> Between 1950 and 1967 Japanese industry set records of technological transfers. A total of 4,135 licenses were purchased by Japanese industry, mainly from the USA, over half in the field of machinery construction and about 20% in the field of chemical industries. During the same time exports of licenses amounted to only about 1% of the money spent on imports of patents and licenses.[37]

This unprecedented transfer of technology and the rapid growth of the Japanese domestic market permitted that nation to adopt for the first time the new processes of mass production and mass distribution that have been at the center of Western industrial economies since the turn of the century. As a result, the Japanese firms, particularly in mass-produced automobiles and appliances, moved into existing global oligopolies. For example, the Japanese market, which absorbed less than 500,000 new cars in 1964, took 1.13 million in 1967, 2.38 in 1970, 2.93 in 1973, and 3.10 million in 1979.[38] Where in 1960 there were 5 passenger cars in Japan for every 1,000 inhabitants, by 1973 there were 185 passenger cars per 1,000. This expanding market in turn permitted scale economies based on the newest production technologies to reduce costs enough so that the large Japanese firms (by 1974 there were only five major manufacturers) were able to move decisively into world markets. Their great success was in mass-produced consumer durables where managerial efficiencies in manufacturing and distribution were particularly pronounced. In branded packaged food and consumer products, in chemicals, oil, and even rubber the Japanese challenge was less formidable.

The coming of new technologies may have had an even more direct impact on global competition than did the rapid transfer of existing ones. Of paramount importance were the innovations in the compilation, collation, and communication of business and industrial information. If the revolution in transportation and communications of the mid-nineteenth century created modern global competition, the second communications revolution of the mid-twentieth century has probably been the major force in shaping its current configuration. The railroad, supplemented by the truck, and the ship still carry the bulk of the world's goods. (The substitution of oil for coal as an energy source has not significantly changed the speed or regularity of land and sea transportation.) But in communications the jet plane, the new telecommunications technology, and the computer have achieved in Raymond Vernon's words, "The spectacular shrinkage of space."[39] The coming of the teleprinter made cable communication more effective. In 1956, the first trans-Atlantic telephone cable went into operation, greatly improving the speed and reliability of overseas telephone communication, which since 1927 had depended on radio transmission. In 1965, global communication was further improved when the first commercial communications satellite went into operation. In the 1950s, the introduction of the jet airplane for commercial travel greatly expanded the possibility of face-to-face communication. By 1960, international commercial flights already logged 26 million passenger miles. In 1974, the figure had reached 152 billion.

Even more impressive has been integration of the computer into the new international communications networks. In the late 1950s, the computer was being rapidly adapted for a multitude of business purposes. Then, in 1963, Honeywell demonstrated its potential for international coordination by placing a terminal in Britain to control a computer at a plant in Massachusetts with control signals being sent by the standard Telex line.[40] At first the new transborder computer networks were used largely by service companies for hotel and airline reservations, stock market quotations, and banking and insurance transactions. By the 1970s, multinational industrials were, according to one authority, increasingly relying on such computer data, usually through leased lines, "to coordinate production and marketing, to coordinate financial management, to share data-processing resources, to reduce costs of telephone circuits; to share scientific and technical research; [and] to improve accuracy and security of information transfer (e.g., by using standard message formats and data encryption techniques)." By the mid-1970s, such international computer communication was becoming an integral part of the control and information systems of British and European multinational enterprises, though possibly less so for their Japanese counterparts.[41]

The Transfer of Managerial Methods

The 1960s and early 1970s were not only the years of technological innovation and diffusion, but they were also those of the diffusion of management techniques. The United States had pioneered in the development of administrative and financial controls and overall management structures essential to the effective operation of a giant multinational enterprise. This was because, in part at least, U.S. firms competed more aggressively, both functionally and strategically, for market share than did those in Europe. It was these administrative skills and procedures that J. J. Servan-Schreiber had in mind when he wrote *The American Challenge*. The opening sentence of that book published in 1968 reads, "Fifteen years from now it is quite possible that the world's third greatest industrial power, just after the United States and Russia, will not be Europe, but American industry in Europe. Already, in the ninth year of the Common Market, this European market is basically American in organization." For Servan-Schreiber, the U.S. challenge was not one of U.S. financial power, nor the European "technological gap." "On the contrary, it is something quite new and considerably more serious—the extension to Europe of an *organization* that is still a mystery to us."[42]

It did not remain a mystery long. When Servan-Schreiber wrote, the transfer of techniques was already well under way. By 1970, for example, over half of the largest one hundred industrials in Britain had used the services of a single U.S. firm, McKinsey & Company, to reorganize their management structures. In most cases such reorganizations meant a transformation of a holding company into a modern multidivisional enterprise by rationalizing the operations of subsidiaries and by building a large corporate office.[43] In Germany, the growth and diversification of large firms brought to a lesser extent the adaptation of the similar structure; while in Japan came a rapid adaptation of quality, inventory, and other U.S. control systems as well as the importation and improvement of overall management structures worked out in the United States.

In the 1970s, then, the global environment in which the United States had dominated in the 1950s and 1960s was rapidly transforming. The two major sets of actors remained the same as they had been for almost a century. There were more nation states, but only one, Japan, had acquired industrial strength comparable to that of the United States and Western Europe. Nor was there a large turnover among the multinationals. They still clustered in much the same type of industries, and in most of these industries the leaders in the first decade of the century were still the leaders in the ninth decade. What makes Servan-Schreiber's prophecy so ironic today is that continuing changes in markets, technology, and managerial methods transformed the environment in which the multinationals competed and eroded the historical competitive advantages of U.S. firms.

CONCLUSION: THE CHALLENGE OF THE NEW COMPETITION

Because of these changes, the number of global competitors in the industries dominated by large enterprises increased and the competition between these players became based much more on functional and strategic competition than was true earlier. The U.S. firms lost their technological edge in many industries. At the same time they lost their managerial advantage. These losses were particularly serious in the mass-produced machinery industries—automobiles, appliances, and office, sewing, agricultural, and other light machinery. The leaders in these industries failed to maintain the functional and strategic competitiveness that won them global superiority early in the century. On the other hand, oil and rubber companies that continued to think in global terms and the chemical and pharmaceutical firms that further honed their functional and strategic skills as they made their initial moves into European markets were less adversely affected by the new competition.

At the very moment the United States was losing its technological and managerial advantages, the new communications and information technologies were permitting managerial teams to coordinate the flows essential to exploit fully the scale economies of global markets. The newcomers, with a smaller investment in older plants and equipment and with less of a commitment to specific established administrative practices and procedures, were able to move more quickly to exploit the cost-reducing possibilities of the new telecommunications and computer technologies. The United States was paying the price of early success. It faced a new environment with a huge investment in increasingly outmoded capital equipment and with inevitable institutional rigidities resulting from decades of successful competition under different conditions.

Moreover, the challenges of this new environment came at a time when the United States relied far more on global markets to provide the volume necessary for profitable operations than it had earlier in its history. For three decades after 1940, U.S. industrial enterprises had steadily increased their working force. The unprecedented war demands were followed by almost a quarter of a century of the greatest expansion of the domestic market ever witnessed. When the growth of the U.S. economy began to slow down in the early 1970s, U.S. firms, in order to maintain scale economies, responded by expanding rather than contracting their overseas activities. The direct investment by U.S. enterprises abroad rose from $75.5 billion in 1970 to $227.3 billion in 1981.[44] At the same time, foreign direct investment in the United States rose from $13.3 billion to $89.8 billion. Thus, as global markets have become increasingly vital to the United States, so U.S. markets have become more important to foreigners. Such global competition has become increasingly based on functional and strategic efficiencies in situations in which the U.S. firms no longer have a technological or managerial edge. The resulting challenge is the greatest challenge the modern U.S. industrial enterprises have had to face since the beginning of this institution a century ago.

This review has touched only on the major factors that helped to shape the modern global competition since it came into being in the late nineteenth century. It has only hinted at the variations and the subtleties in the constantly changing pattern. In each industry, the multinational enterprise operated with somewhat different technologies of production and different methods of distribution. Each nation state, as a result of its past history and current economic situation, has faced different issues and challenges in working out relationships with both home-based and foreign multinationals.

NOTES

1. A. D. Chandler, Jr., *The Visible Hand: The Managerial Revolution in American Business* (Cambridge, Mass.: Harvard University Press, 1977), 230–32.
2. Details and documentation are given in a case by A. D. Chandler, Jr., on "The Standard Oil Company: Combination, Consolidation and Integration," in A. D Chandler, Jr. and R. S. Tedlow, *The Coming of Managerial Capitalism: A Case Book in the History of American Economic Institutions* (Homewood, Ill.: Richard D. Irwin, 1985).
3. B. W. E. Alford, *W. D. & H. O. Wills and the Development of the U.K. Tobacco Industry* (London: Methuen, 1973), 143–49. Also Chandler, *The Visible Hand*, 249–58. For similar new high-volume technologies in the production of other branded packaged products see Chandler, chap. 9.
4. S. Kaku, "The Development and Structure of the German Coal-Tar Dyestuffs Firms," A. Okochi and H. Uchida, eds., *Development and Diffusion of Technology* (Tokyo: University of Tokyo Press, 1979), 78.
5. This statement is based on a review of histories of and annual reports and pamphlets by the leading rubber companies.
6. H. Livesay, *Andrew Carnegie and the Rise of Big Business* (Boston: Little, Brown, 1975), 102–6, 155. When in 1873 Carnegie opened the first works directed entirely to producing rails by the Bessemer process he dropped cost to $56.64 a ton. By 1889, with increase in sales the costs fell to $25 a ton.

7. L. F. Haber, *The Chemical Industry During the Nineteenth Century* (Oxford: Clarendon Press, 1958), 92.

8. Chandler, *The Visible Hand*, 302–14.

9. A. Nevins, *Ford: The Times, the Man, the Company* (New York: Scribner, 1954), chaps. 18–20 (esp. 473, 489, 511). A. D. Chandler, Jr., ed., *Giant Enterprise: Ford, General Motors and the Automobile Industry* (New York: Harcourt Brace & World, 1964) 152.

10. S. J. Moss, *An Economic Theory of Business Strategy* (Oxford: Robertson, 1981), 110–11.

11. Chandler, *The Visible Hand*, 299–302, 391–402.

12. Standard Oil only began to make an extensive investment in distribution after the formation of the Trust and the resulting rationalization of production and with it the great increase in throughput—H. F. Williamson and A. R. Daum, *The American Petroleum Industry: The Age of Illumination, 1859–1899* (Evanston, Ill.: Northwestern University Press, 1959), 687–701. For investment in gasoline pumps and service stations H. F. Williamson, et al., *The American Petroleum Industry: The Age of Energy, 1899–1959* (Evanston, Ill.: Northwestern University Press, 1963), 217–30, 466–87, 675–85.

13. Chandler, *The Visible Hand*, 402–11.

14. The analysis of these differences is based on detailed research by the author of available histories, company and government reports, business journals, and internal company documents dealing with these many enterprises. These four countries were chosen because they represent the most influential nation states in the evolution of global competition. Britain, the first industrial nation, was surpassed by the United States and Germany during the second industrial revolution, and these two have only recently been challenged by Japan.

15. W. S. Woytinsky and E. S. Woytinsky, *World Population and Production: Trends and Outlook* (New York: The Twentieth Century Fund, 1953), 383–85.

16. M. Wilkins, *The Emergence of Multinational Enterprise: American Business Abroad from the Colonial Era to 1914* (Cambridge, Mass.: Harvard University Press, 1977) 201, 212–13. Firms with one plant overseas in 1914 included Burroughs Adding Machine, Electric Storage Battery, Goodrich, Pittsburgh Plate Glass, Gramaphone Company, and American Rolling Mill among others. Nearly all firms with overseas factories also had plants in Canada.

17. Chandler, *The Visible Hand*, chap. 10.

18. I. C. R. Byatt, *The British Electrical Industry, 1875–1914* (Oxford: Clarendon Press, 1979), 150.

19. For Nobel, W. J. Reader, *Imperial Chemical Industries: A History*, Vol. 1 (London: Oxford University Press, 1970), 388–94; for Lever Brothers, C. H. Wilson, *History of Unilever*, Vol. 2 (London: Cassell, 1954), 302, 345.

20. From an analysis made by P. Williamson for a sample of 701 firms in the Harvard Multinational Enterprise databank at the Harvard Business School; also Wilkins, *Emergence of Multinational Enterprise*, chaps. 4, 7.

21. As indicated in B. R. Tomlinson, "Foreign Private Investment in India, 1920–1950," *Modern Asian Studies* 12 (1978): 655–77, esp. the table on 676–77; S. J. Nicholas, "British Multinational Investment before 1939," *The Journal of European Economic History* 11 (Winter 1982): 613.

22. This expansion is best described in chaps. 5 and 6 on Mannesmann and I.G. Farbenindustrie A.G. in A. Teichova and P. L. Cottrell, *Interna-*

tional Business and Central Europe, 1918–1939 (Leicester, England: Leicester University Press, 1983).

23. The expansion of the Mitsubishi Trading Companies is indicated by comparing two of the company-written pamphlets, Mitsubishi Sha, *The Mitsu Bishi Goshi—Kwaisha* (Tokyo: Mitsubishi Sha, 1910) and *An Outline of the Mitsubishi Enterprises* (Tokyo: Mitsubishi Sha, 1935).

24. The nature of such functional and strategic competition is suggested by the content of courses in production, marketing, purchasing, control, and policy that have been taught in U.S. business schools for decades. M. Porter, *Competitive Strategy: Techniques for Analyzing Industries and Competitors* (New York: Free Press, 1980) for a comprehensive and penetrating analysis of current functional and strategic competition. For European and U.S. comparisons see A. D. Chandler, Jr., "The M-Form: Industrial Groups, American Style," *European Economic Review* 19, no. 23 (1983) and A. D. Chandler, Jr., "Technology and Industrial Organization," in S. Bruchey and J. Colton, eds., *Essays in Technology and Social Structure* (forthcoming).

25. Nicholas, "British Multinational Investment before 1939," 625. In the interwar years 58 percent of British direct investment was in the Empire (up from 52 percent in the prewar years) and 21 percent on the Continent (down from 25 percent) as compared to 9 percent in the United States (down from 11 percent in the prewar period).

26. For the activities of the Anglo-Iranian company see R. W. Ferrier, *The History of the British Petroleum Company,* Vol. 1 (Cambridge, England: Cambridge University Press, 1982), esp. chaps. 8 and 11.

27. Memorandum on "Responsibilities and Duties of the Coordination Committee Department," October 28, 1927 written by O. Harden and quoted in A. D. Chandler, Jr., *Strategy and Structure: Chapter in the History of the Industrial Enterprise* (Cambridge, Mass.: MIT Press, 1962), 190.

28. M. Wilkins, *The Maturing of Multinational Enterprise: American Business Abroad from 1914 to 1970* (Cambridge, Mass.: Harvard University Press, 1974), 87–8 for oil agreements and 98–101 for rubber.

29. M. Wilkins and F. Ernst Hill, *American Business Abroad: Ford on Six Continents* (Detroit: Wayne State University Press, 1964), chaps. 3, 5, 7, 9, 11, and appendix 2, 434–35. Although some fabrication of parts was carried on in Canada and England, Ford did not begin large-scale manufacturing overseas until the early 1930s when a large plant near London and smaller ones in Germany and France were built to manufacture as well as to assemble the Model A, 185–200, 206–7, 232–41.

30. A. P. Sloan, Jr., *My Years with General Motors* (Garden City: Doubleday, 1963), 327–28, also 271.

31. The operations of several of these cartels are described in W. F. Reader, *Imperial Chemical Industries: A History,* Vol. 2 (London: Oxford University Press, 1975), D. C. Coleman, *Courtaulds: An Economic and Social History* (Oxford: Clarendon Press, 1969); G. W. Stocking and M. W. Watkins, *Cartels in Action* (New York: The Twentieth Century Fund, 1946); and R. A. Brady, *The Rationalization Movement in German Industry* (Berkeley: University of California Press, 1933).

32. J. C. Carr and W. Taplin, *History of the British Steel Industry* (Cambridge, Mass.: Harvard University Press, 1962), chap. 44.

33. S. Kuznets, *Economic Growth of Nations* (Cambridge, Mass.: Harvard University Press, 1971), chap. 1, esp. table 4.

34. L. Hannah, *The Rise of the Corporate Economy,* 2nd ed. (London: Methuen, 1983), 148.

35. Wilkins, *Maturing of Multinational Enterprise*, 291–300. Companies successfully brought to court by the Justice Department included General Electric, Timken Roller Bearing, Electric Storage Battery, Du Pont, and National Lead.

36. J. M. Laux, et al., *The Automobile Revolution: The Impact of an Industry* (Chapel Hill, N.C.: University of North Carolina Press, 1982), chaps. 7 and 9, esp. 145, 172 and 184; Wilkins, *Maturing of Multinational Enterprise*, 403–5. In 1950 total output of French automobiles was 260,000 as compared to Britain's 500,000 and 6.6 million for the United States (Laux, 172–73, 175).

37. J. Hirschmeier and T. Yui, *The Development of Japanese Business 1969–1973* (Cambridge, Mass.: Harvard University Press, 1975), 258.

38. Laux, *Automobile Revolution*, 199, also 182–83.

39. R. Vernon, *Storm over Multinationals: The Real Issues*, Cambridge, Mass.: Harvard University Press, 1977), 1–3. The quotation is from 3.

40. R. H. Veith, *Multinational Computer Nets*, (Lexington, Mass.: Lexington Books, 1981), 15–19. The quotation is from 17–18.

41. C. Antonelli, "The Diffusion of a New Information Technology as a Process Innovation: International Data Telecommunications and Multinational Industrial Companies," an unpublished paper completed at the Center for Policy Alternatives, MIT. I am greatly indebted to Dr. Antonelli for the most valuable information he provided on this subject. His findings have recently been published in *Cambiamento Tecnologico e Impresa Multinazionale* (Milan: Angeli, 1984), esp. chaps. 2 and 3.

42. J. J. Servan-Schreiber, *The American Challenge* (New York: Atheneum, 1968), 3, also 10–11.

43. This can best be documented by reviewing the references to McKinsey & Company as listed in the index to D. F. Channon, *The Strategy and Structure of British Enterprise* (Boston: Harvard Business School, 1973), 254; also B. Scott, "The Industrial State: Old Myths and New Realities," *Harvard Business Review* 51 (March–April 1973): 133–48.

44. *Economic Report of the President, February 1983* (Washington, D.C.: Government Printing Office, 1983) Table B 105, 281. U.S. receipts from overseas investment rose from 1.0 percent of GNP in 1960 to 2.9 percent in 1980 and foreign receipts from direct investment in the United States rose from 0.2 to 1.7 percent in those same years. Inflation had, of course, a major impact on the direct investment figures.

14

Entry of Foreign Multinationals into U.S. Manufacturing Industries*

Richard E. Caves
and
Sanjeev K. Mehra

As firms increasingly compete with global strategies, one of their most important choices is that of entry into foreign markets. Because of the size and importance of the U.S. market, entry into the United States takes on particular significance for foreign enterprises. The explosive increase during the last decade in foreign direct investment in the United States—year-end (nominal) book value increased by 230 percent from 1976 to 1982—can tell us much about how foreign multinationals respond to changing market opportunities and coordinate their newly configured investments.

This chapter reports two statistical studies of the entry and expansion of foreign multinationals in the United States, a process little explored heretofore.[1] The first analyzes the rates at which foreign-controlled subsidiaries have been expanding their shares of activity in U.S. manufacturing industries. Their expansion rates depend on both the short-run opportunities at hand and the long-run factors that favor serving the U.S. market through local production that is coordinated with the global parent's overseas activities. The second study addresses the choice of the foreign multinational between acquiring a going concern and building a new plant when it first enters the U.S. market. This choice turns out to depend strongly on the entrant's configuration of activities outside the United States and the prospects for coordinating its new U.S. facilities with its overseas units.

*Research for this project was supported by the Division of Research, Harvard Business School, and the General Electric Foundation. We are grateful to Michael Hemesath for research assistance and to Michael E. Porter, Robert Stobaugh, and Louis T. Wells for comments and suggestions.

EXPANSION OF FOREIGN-CONTROLLED ESTABLISHMENTS IN U.S. MANUFACTURING INDUSTRIES

The general public sometimes sees the multinational enterprise (MNE) as a U.S. invention sent out to colonize the economies of other countries. That view has proved increasingly false during the decades since World War II, as the MNEs based in other industrial countries have typically grown faster than those based in the United States (Rowthorn 1971). The U.S. share of the book value of all foreign investment is by now probably no higher than the U.S. share of the aggregate gross national product of the industrial countries. Nonetheless, shares of U.S. markets held by foreign MNEs have remained on average much smaller than MNEs' shares of markets in other industrial countries. In 1975, foreign-controlled establishments accounted for only 3 percent of employment in the average U.S. manufacturing industry, while a comparable figure might be 40 percent in Canada and 15 percent in Britain.[2] However, a considerable rise in foreign participation in U.S. markets has been in the cards. The convergence of income and productivity levels among most industrial countries, the rapid growth of foreign MNEs, and the end in the early 1970s of the previous decade's overvaluation of the U.S. dollar all favored an expanded foreign presence in U.S. manufacturing industries. Indeed, the mean share of plant employment held by foreign-controlled establishments rose from 3.05 percent in 1975 to 7.43 percent in 1981.[3]

In this section we analyze the determinants of the changes between 1975 and 1981 in foreign-controlled establishments' employment in seventy-five U.S. manufacturing industries. The model that we employ rests on two considerations. First, expansion of employment in foreign-controlled plants reflects the investment decisions made by foreign MNEs to enlarge their asset holdings in these industries. We assume that these changing commitments were driven by the factors that made foreign MNEs anticipate increased global profits from enlarging their production facilities in the United States. Second, MNEs do not hold all the advantages against national-market firms, nor is foreign investment always preferable to serving a country's market through exports or licensing. Therefore, one can think of the advantages of MNEs relative to other firms reaching a stand-off at some "interior" margin, which gives rise to a long-run equilibrium market share for the foreign investors. That share differs predictably from market to market with the structure of the industry and of the ambient national economy. The rapid expansion of foreign investment in U.S. manufacturing industries may reflect adjustment toward these steady-state shares.[4] Our cross-sectional regression model embodies both of these elements.

Hypotheses about Capacity Expansion

Economic analysis has evolved a standard approach to analyzing business investment decisions. Investment outlays move the firm's capital stock to (or toward) a preferred level determined by its cost of capital and the volume of output that it expects to sell. Because the MNEs that we observe were making their decisions at the same time, their capital costs are assumed to differ little[5] and hence to explain little of the interindustry differences in investment rates. The critical determinants of foreign MNEs' decisions are the factors driving their expectations about profitable levels of future output.

In order to explain our approach, we make the assumption (dropped in the empirical analysis) that production facilities in the United States serve only the domestic market. We suppose that foreign MNEs predicted the changes in the sizes of U.S. industrial markets during 1975–81 as best they could and, as a first cut, planned to invest enough to maintain their 1975 market shares. But they also expanded or contracted those shares to the extent warranted by other factors. Let ΔFES_i stand for the growth of sales in 1975–81 planned by foreign MNEs. Let ΔQ_i equal the change that they anticipated in the size of the U.S. market. Our basic model is

$$\Delta FES_i = A\Delta Q_i e^{\Sigma b_j X_{ji} \varepsilon_i} \tag{1}$$

where the $\Sigma b_j X_j$ represents a series of influences on the long-run steady-state share of each market commanded by foreign MNEs, and ε_i is a disturbance term. We can think of foreign enterprises claiming a common fraction A of the incremental sales in each market, but with the fraction modified by the forces pulling each observed share toward its industry-specific long-run steady-state value. This approach to combining the influence of short-run "stock" influences on their market shares has the advantage that it can readily be estimated in logarithms:

$$In\ \Delta FES_i = In\ A + In\ \Delta Q_i + b_i X_{j1} + \ \dots$$
$$+ b_i X_{ji} + \dots + u_i \tag{2}$$

This handy formulation does have the disadvantage that the logarithmic variables must be defined in ways to provide them with positive values.[6]

We have yet to specify ΔQ_i and explain why, in its context in equation (1), it captures the cash-flow expectations of foreign investors in the U.S. market. Investment models for the firm in a purely competitive industry emphasize the firm's adjustment toward (or to) a capital stock warranted by the relationship between the market price of its output and the user cost of capital. We assume that industries with substantial foreign-investor populations are subject to some product differentiation, and possibly to small numbers (oligopoly) as well. Then the firm's preferred capital stock depends not directly on a market price but on the position of its own individual demand curve, which for the "representative" firm changes mainly with the size of the total market. Therefore, we expect the MNE's desired capacity to vary with the changes it anticipates in the size of the U.S. market, subject to foreign-trade and other influences described later, and the factors affecting its profitability relative to its domestic competitors (the X_{ji}).[7]

On this reasoning, the change of employment in foreign-controlled establishments reflected decisions that foreign MNEs have made about expected profit-maximizing levels of production and sales in the U.S. market. The activity changes for 1975–81 that we observe reflect plans that firms made based on somewhat earlier data. Therefore, we construct the dependent variable as a planned output change, expressed as the actual change in employment blown up by a projected rate of industry productivity growth:

> $FCSCG$ = change in foreign-controlled establishments' employment, 1975–81, multiplied by one plus the rate of labor of productivity growth observed in the U.S. industry during 1972–77.[8]

$FCSCG$'s logarithm is the dependent variable in the following analysis.

Hypotheses about Investment Flows: "Keeping Up" Variables

Our model calls for a group of variables associated with ΔQ_i, called "keeping up" variables, and another set called "long-run share" or global-strategy variables. We must recognize that foreign MNEs produce in the United States either to sell in the U.S. market or to export to other markets (or to overseas affiliates). Production in the United States may serve the firm as an alternative to exporting goods to the U.S. market from abroad, but imports to the United States may instead be complementary when the U.S. subsidiary serves as a sales agency for both its own output and imported components of its foreign parent's line. These choices represent central elements in the global strategy of the MNE, so our statistical indicator of expected market growth must incorporate these decisions into the specification of ΔQ_i. As a first approximation, we assume that expected market growth can be expressed as a projected growth of total shipments (domestic plus export), expressed in employment units (for comparability to $FCSCG$):

> $TSCG$ = industry employment in 1975 multiplied by the 1972–77 average compound rate of growth of real output, blown up to a six-year growth rate.

That is, $TSCG$ represents the change in industry output that MNEs expected for 1975–81 (if they projected 1972–77 output growth rates), and $FCSCG$ represents the change in output that the MNEs planned to provide (if they projected productivity to grow at its 1972–77 rate); both changes are expressed in employment units by means of the industry's employees/output ratio for 1975.

We expect foreign MNEs to react differently to growth prospects for export and domestic sales. The variable $TSCG$ can be factored into those components by defining:

$XSCG$ = expected 1981 export shipments minus 1975 export shipments, both measured in employment units.

Expected 1981 exports are constructed by adding $TSCG$ to 1975 industry employment and multiplying the result by the actual exports/shipments ratio for 1978.[9] Subtracting $XSCG$ from $TSCG$ gives $DSCG$, expected growth of domestic shipments expressed in employment units. Because $XSCG$ has negative values for some industries, we factor ΔQ_i into its export and domestic components not by using $DSCG$ and $XSCG$, but rather by constructing $DMSH = DSCG/TSCG$ and adding $DMSH$ to the model along with $TSCG$. If $FCSCG$ were regressed directly on $DSCG$ and $XSCG$, we would expect positive coefficients for both but a larger one for $XSCG$. With $ln\ TSCG$ and $ln\ DMSH$ employed instead, we expect a positive coefficient for the former and a negative one for the latter.

Because for some MNEs, imports to the U.S. market may be good alternatives to domestic production, we expect plans for foreign investment to be more sensitive to the competitive position of imports than is the output of the typical domestic firm.[10] Increases in government restrictions on imports, both actual and threatened, should have focused MNEs' attention on investment to replace imports. Given the expected growth of domestic shipments, already defined, we therefore expect a larger expansion of employment in foreign-controlled establishments where imports' share of the market is decreasing. This variable can be measured analogously to $XSCG$:

$MSCG$ = expected 1981 import shipments minus 1975 import shipments, both measured in employment units.

The case for commensurable units is not so strong here as with $XSCG$, and so we also employ:

$IMGRO$ = ratio of imports to domestic shipments in 1976 divided by the ratio of imports to domestic shipments in 1972.

For use in equation (2), $IMGRO$ has the advantage over $MSCG$ of taking only positive values. We expect either variable to bear a negative relationship to $FCSCG$.

An influence that belongs in the model is the extent of excess capacity present at the beginning of the period. Excess capacity discourages acquiring new capacity to serve anticipated growth of the market. We expect MNEs to plan smaller increases in output; the larger is:

$EXCAP$ = industry employment in 1975 divided by $U/(1 - U)$
where U is the average of the ratios of actual output to preferred operating capacity in the years 1975–78.

The coefficient of $EXCAP$ should take a negative sign.

A final influence on the short-run inflow of foreign investment comes from the cost side. The foreign MNE establishing or expanding its U.S. capacity can either build new facilities or acquire existing plants or companies. We have assumed that MNEs in all industries face a common price level for capital funds and capital equipment. However, that is not necessarily the case for the buyer of controlling equity in existing companies, because the price of corporate shares may diverge from the cost of new corporate assets. That is, MNEs' shares may expand because they can pick up bargains on the market for corporate control, relative to the cost of adding new capacity. That relative cost is not directly observable, but the average of market-to-book-value ratios for companies classified to each industry serves as a rough approximation. Specifically, we use:

$AVEMB$ = average of ratios of market to book value for companies classified to the industry for the years 1974–79. Market values are the average of the year's high and low figures.

One's expectations of a negative coefficient for $AVEMB$ are very modest, for the reason that arbitrage in financial markets tends to eliminate just this kind of bargain, and there is no specific reason why market-to-book ratios should be observed sufficiently out of line to give a substantial opening to foreign MNEs. Indeed, the dispersion of an industry's market-to-book ratios might be a more appropriate indicator than its mean.[11]

Hypotheses about Long-Run Shares

We now turn to the hypotheses represented by the $b_j X_j$ terms in equation (2), which incorporates the long-run determinants of the opportunities for firms to employ global strategies, and hence equilibrium shares of MNEs vary from market to market. One may certainly suspect that the recent burst of foreign investment in the United States represents in part a catch-up process, as the MNEs emergent abroad in recent decades seized opportunities in the U.S. market like those that U.S. MNEs earlier exploited abroad. We employ two strategies to test this hypothesis. The first approach relies on the following simple line of reasoning: industries differ in their degrees of affinity for foreign investment, and those differences should be clearly revealed in a setting where firms have had ample time to exploit the available opportunities for foreign investment. The obvious choice for indicating this long-run equilibrium is the extent of foreign-investment activity by U.S. companies classified to each industry, to which we can compare the share of foreign investment in the U.S. industry at the start of our period. Specifically, we formed the variable:

USFI = ratio of overseas assets to total assets of domestic companies classified to the industry, 1972, minus the ratio of employment in foreign-controlled establishments to total employment in the U.S. industry, 1975.[12]

A significant positive regression coefficient of this variable would confirm the hypothesis that the growth of foreign MNE employment has been in part an adjustment toward a long-run equilibrium.

An alternative to using USFI as an instrument is to employ the variables predicted by economic analysis to influence the equilibrium market shares of MNEs.[13] This list has been winnowed by a number of investigators, so these industry characteristics can be presented with only a brief discussion of their rationales:

RND = company-financed R & D spending as a proportion of sales, average 1974–76;

MAD = media advertising outlays as a proportion of sales, average 1974–76;

MGT = managerial and kindred personnel as a proportion of total employees, 1970;

MLTP = numbers of plants in the industry operated by each of its largest four companies, 1977;

KBE = capital cost of an efficient-scale plant (proxied by the size of the plant that in 1977 accounted for the industry's 50th percentile of output when plants are arrayed from largest to smallest);

NTF = nominal rate of tariff protection adjusted for nontariff barriers, 1972 (effective rates of protection are designated by EFT);

NTR = cost of ocean transportation for U.S. imports classified to the industry, expressed as a proportion of f.o.b. value of imports. The variable is analogous to a nominal tariff rate (the equivalent analog to an effective tariff rate is designated ETR).[14]

Each is expected to wield a positive influence on the steady-state share held by MNEs, and hence on the rate of expansion of foreign investment in U.S. markets. *RND* and *MAD* both indicate the significance of investments in proprietary intangible assets; they have repeatedly proved significant predictors of the importance of foreign investment. The variable *MGT* indicates the importance in an industry of skilled and specialized management; the effective management cadre in a successful firm may possess some excess capacity that is usable for supervising the operations of foreign subsidiaries. Similarly, multiplant operation reflects scale economies in coordinating plants that outrun production scale economies in the plants themselves; if the economies of coordination do not stop at the national boundary, then we expect a positive relation of *MLTP* to foreign investment.[15] *KBE*, a variable associated in industrial-organization research with capital-cost barriers to entry, indicates that the price tag for entry into a market is high enough to deter newcomers who are not already large and profitable companies well established in other markets.[16] Tariffs and ocean transport costs dispose production to take place near the site of consumption; with other inducements controlled, these variables predict higher steady-state levels of foreign investment.[17]

Industry Sample and Statistical Results

Since 1975 the U.S. Bureau of the Census has published data annually on employment and other attributes of foreign-controlled establishments in U.S. manufacturing industries. The level of disaggregation is generally the three-digit level of the Standard Industrial Classification (SIC), with some three-digit categories aggregated in sectors subject to small amounts of foreign investment. A total of seventy-five industries were reported on a consistent basis for 1975 and 1981, and these formed the sample for our statistical analysis. The sample represents nearly all two-digit categories of SIC. The exogenous variables specified previously are available on various bases of classification and were aggregated (when necessary) to match the dependent variable using industry shipments as weights. Some of the independent variables have observations missing, even after we decided to tolerate representing a three-digit industry by four-digit observations covering as little as half of its value of shipments. As a result, differently specified equations have different numbers of observations.

The estimations of equation (2) appear in Table 14.1. We present several versions to expose the effects of varying numbers of degrees of freedom and including or excluding the long-run share variables. In our model the coefficient of *TSCG* is predicted to be one, and the constant term indicates the estimated share of the market's growth that is claimed by foreign MNEs. The coefficient of *TSCG* differs from zero at a high level of statistical significance, but it never differs significantly from one. The constant term is estimated quite imprecisely (significant only in equation 1.5), but its antilog indicates plausible

Table 14.1 Determinants of Planned Increase in Shipments by Foreign-Controlled Establishments in 75 U.S. Manufacturing Industries, 1975–81

Independent variable	Equation				
	1.1	1.2	1.3	1.4	1.5
Constant	−0.968 (0.61)	−0.848 (0.46)	−1.052 (0.61)	−0.626 (0.34)	−3.216[b] (1.75)
TSCG	1.147[a] (4.23)	1.265[a] (3.94)	1.321[a] (4.41)	0.885[a] (3.38)	1.061[a] (4.23)
DMSH		−0.657[c] (1.34)			
IMGRO		−0.200 (0.27)	−0.189 (0.47)		0.247 (0.64)
EXCAP	−0.340 (1.28)	−0.492[c] (1.63)		−0.205 (0.82)	−0.215 (0.86)
USFI			−0.459 (0.35)		
RND				0.190[a] (2.50)	0.105 (1.21)
MAD				−0.017 (0.27)	−0.093[c] (1.38)
MGT				14.144[b] (1.80)	19.845[b] (2.09)
MLTP				0.783[b] (1.84)	0.492 (1.16)
KBE				0.146 (1.23)	0.104 (0.87)
NTFHR					0.496[c] (1.58)
NTFLR					0.091 (0.51)
NTRHR					0.430[c] (1.38)
NTRLR					0.269[b] (1.71)
$\bar{R}^2$	0.380	0.381	0.385	0.483	0.582
D.f.	66	45	54	61	47

NOTE: Tests of significance (one-tailed): a = 1 percent; b = 5 percent; c = 10 percent.

values for MNEs' marginal market share of 0.35 to 0.43 in equations 1.1 to 1.3.[18]

The variables that adjust keeping-up investment for changing trade patterns do not perform strongly in Table 14.1. *IMGRO*'s coefficient is negative in equations containing only the investment-flow variables, but it is not statistically significant. The same holds for its alternative form, *MSCG* (not shown in Table 14.1).[19] *DMSH* takes the expected negative sign, indicating that the MNEs' market share increases more, the greater exports' share of market growth is. In equation 1.2 (and similar specifications), it is correctly signed but significant only at the 10 percent level. We also experimented with fitting our model in nonlogarithmic form, which is theoretically less desirable in general but does allow a direct test of the hypothesis that the expected change in exports has a significant effect on investment decisions of MNEs after the expected growth of the total market (domestic plus exports) is controlled.[20] When this is done, the export component is significant at the 1 percent level, and its coefficient indicates that foreign investors are more than twice as sensitive to expected export growth as to domestic-market growth. Therefore, we are inclined to accept the hypothesis despite the weak result shown in equation 1.2. The trade-related variables offer substantial evidence that MNEs do pursue global strategies.

EXCAP always exhibits the predicted negative influence of excess capacity on investment decisions of MNEs. With only the keeping-up variables in the equation, its significance ranges between 6 and 11 percent (equations 1.1 and 1.2). But it becomes insignificant when the long-run share variables are added.

The final keeping-up variable proposed above, AVEMB, does not appear in Table 14.1. When included in these equations, it takes not its expected negative coefficient, but a positive coefficient that is significant at 5 percent. The reason is not hard to find. Market-to-book ratios of companies themselves depend on the growth rates of their industries and some of the stock-adjustment variables, so that AVEMB can in fact be predicted rather well by other independent variables in the model. As we suggested previously, gross arbitrage opportunities do not lie open to MNEs entering the U.S. market. The decision to enter by acquisition (investigated in the next section) therefore should depend on organizational and product-market variables and not on general conditions in the market for corporate equities. We conclude that AVEMB does not belong in the model.

We turn to the long-run share variables (equations 1.3 to 1.5). USFI, the difference between the share of assets held abroad by U.S. companies and the 1975 share of U.S. employment held by foreign MNEs, is never significant, and the sign of its coefficient is erratic (see equation 1.3).

The alternative approach (equations 1.4 and 1.5), which employs the predictors of MNEs' long-run equilibrium shares, turns out to increase the model's explanatory power appreciably. All signs of these variables are positive as expected except for advertising (MAD),[21] and RND, MGT, and MLTP are significant. In equation 1.5 the tariff and transport-cost variables are added. They increase the multicollinearity in the model, which probably accounts for IMGRO's sign reversal and the reduced significance of other variables. We expected that the significance of tariffs and transport costs would depend on the values taken by other long-run share variables, and they are indeed insignificant if entered additively (not shown). In equations 1.4 and 1.5, they are allowed to take different slopes depending on whether *RND* is above (*HR*) or below (*LR*) its mean value for the sample.[22] Tariff protection exerts a positive influence significant at about 7 percent in the research-intensive industries. The influence of transport costs is at least somewhat apparent in both high- and low-research industries. It should be stressed, though, that these significance levels deteriorate when *IMGRO* is not included in the model. This deterioration is not a plain case of simultaneous-equations bias, because *IMGRO* indicates the growth of imports, while the trade-barrier variables are expressed as levels. Nonetheless, the significance of the trade-barrier variables cannot be proclaimed confidently without further investigation.

CHOICE OF METHOD OF ENTRY: ACQUISITION VS. GREEN-FIELD

Although we could not confirm that bargains in corporate control influence the interindustry distribution of foreign investment, acquisition of existing assets is an increasingly important method of market entry by MNEs (Curhan, Davidson, and Suri 1977, p. 21). During 1979–82, no less than 77 percent of U.S. investment outlays by foreign direct investors were for the acquisition of existing assets (Belli 1983). In 1980–82, the proportion of investments made via acquisition averaged 84 percent in manufacturing, varying narrowly between 71 and 86 percent in subsectors of manufacturing. The choice of method of entry affords insight into several aspects of business behavior and market operation:

1. The firm is a bureaucratic coalition that incurs costs of information and adjustment—costs that increase with the size of changes that it makes in the scope and character of its activities. This organizational model implies testable relationships between the initial scale and pattern of activities of a firm and its chosen method of entering a new market.

2. The market for corporate control provides to the firm the option of entering via acquisition. The better it functions, the better the matching of buyers and sellers, and the more attractive the acquisition method becomes—another testable implication.

3. The firm bringing new capacity to a market expands total supply, while the entrant making an acquisition need not. Competitive conditions in the entered market determine incumbents' reactions to new capacity and may thereby affect the relative attraction of entry by acquisition.

We develop a model to explain the choice between green-field investment and acquisition on the basis of these theoretical considerations. It is tested on a sample of entries by foreign MNEs into the United States during the years 1974 through 1980. Although the factors predicting the method of entry are not specific to the MNE, it provides a strategic subject for testing the model. By confining the sample, as we do, to first-time investors in the U.S. market, we observe a class of entrants who are likely to face high information costs and considerable uncertainty. Furthermore, they differ in national as well as industrial origins, thereby providing us with an additional source of statistical leverage.[23]

We first set forth the hypotheses and the variables that we use to embody them, then describe the data set and report the statistical results.

Hypotheses and Explanatory Variables

The choice of an entry method can be studied in isolation only if it is independent of other decisions that the MNE must reach about its entry into the U.S. market. One of these decisions is clearly not independent: the initial scale at which to enter. The larger the initial scale, the more likely entry is to occur through acquisition (for reasons explained later). The entry method depends on various characteristics of the parent MNE, but these traits also influence the preferred scale of entry. Therefore, we cannot fully evaluate the determinants of the method of entry without exploring the influence of these same factors on the initial scale of entry. We explore the determinants of the entry method first, then consider the complications that result from its interdependence with entry scale. The determining influences arise from the three general factors listed previously: the organizational and structural characteristics of the parent MNE, the market for corporate control, and competitive conditions in the entered market.

Hypotheses Related to the Parent Firm

The first variable expected to affect the entry method is simply the relative size of the subsidiary:

$SIZPAR$ = employment in the subsidiary at initial operating scale divided by total (global) employment of the foreign parent.

We expect the probability of acquisition to increase with $SIZPAR$, because acquisition helps the firm to avoid some constraints that otherwise may limit its ability to make large additions to its asset holdings. The going firm comes with its own management cadre, which reduces the force of Penrose constraints (Penrose 1959) on the growth rate of the parent MNE. It may possess unutilized borrowing capacity or marketable assets that can serve to reduce the parent's financial constraints. Acquiring an established firm generally entails a less uncertain stream of returns than does a green-field venture, and a risk-averse parent may apply a higher discount rate when a proportionally larger sum is at stake.[24] Notice that we observe only the initial scale of the new subsidiary and not whatever equilibrium size the parent may plan for it. That fact will affect our interpretation of the statistical results.

With *SIZPAR* controlled, several other traits of the parent enterprise are expected to influence the form of its subsidiary. One is the extent of the parent's previous foreign experience:

MULT = number of countries in which parent firm has subsidiaries.

Although our sampled firms are first-time investors in the United States, their previous experience with foreign investment elsewhere varies considerably. That variance affects the parent's stock of experience relevant to founding and managing foreign subsidiaries, if the experience bears on foreign activities generally and is not entirely country-specific. A great deal of evidence indicates that expansion processes of MNEs entail taking the easy steps first, thereby gaining knowledge useful for more remote ventures.[25] If the going-concern value of an acquired subsidiary substitutes for the parent's experience, the mature MNE should be more inclined toward green-field entry, and the probability of entry by acquisition should be negatively related to *MULT*.

If the acquisition probability depends on the parent's stock of prior experience, it should be affected by experience with the product line of the subsidiary. Because the parent's product-market diversification will be controlled by another variable, we utilize:

SPEC = dummy variable set equal to one if the subsidiary's principal product is one made abroad by its parent, and the parent's production is confined to the three-digit industry that includes this product (zero otherwise).

That is, *SPEC* designates a "horizontal" foreign investment by a relatively undiversified parent. The parent then possesses various skills and intangible assets usable in its new subsidiary, as well as tangible capacities that can be coordinated with the new subsidiary's, reducing the incentive to seek these in the asset bundle of a going firm. The probability of entry by acquisition should be negatively related to *SPEC*.[26]

SPEC equals zero if either the U.S. subsidiary represents a diversification for its parent, or the parent is itself a diversified enterprise. Parental diversification should increase the probability of entry by acquisition. Diversification itself is often accomplished by means of acquisitions (see Markham 1973, pp. 129–32, on large U.S. enterprises). The diversifying firm sets up an apparatus to make acquisitions, reducing the incremental cost of merger transactions, and it is likely to adopt a corporate organization congenial to managing large numbers of relatively independent subsidiaries. Stopford and Wells (1972) showed that firms generally diversify some in home-country markets and move toward multidivisional organizations before they become major foreign investors. Therefore, we expect the probability of acquisition to be positively related to:

DIV = number of two-digit industries in which the parent operates worldwide.

This hypothesis was confirmed by Wilson (1980) for both U.S. and foreign multinationals.

A final hypothesis related to the parent's experience flows from the possibility that information about conditions in a U.S. industry becomes in part a public good shared among potential parent firms in a given foreign country. In that case, the first entrant faces greater informational disadvantages than do those that follow it and learn from its mistakes and successes. If entry by acquisition economizes on information costs and reduces uncertainty, then the probability of entry by acquisition should be positively related to:

$FSTINV$ = dummy variable set equal to one if the parent firm was the first from its country to invest in the subsidiary's four-digit industry (zero otherwise).

A complementary implication is that the more compatriots have preceded a given parent to the U.S. market, the larger is the information stock on which it can draw, and the less likely entry by acquisition is. But that hypothesis immediately reminds us of another that runs counter to it, stemming from the work of Knickerbocker (1973). He found that entries by U.S. MNEs into a given foreign country and industry tend to be bunched in time. This bunching, which could result from disturbances in the entered market, is significantly more extreme in moderately concentrated U.S. industries that we can characterize as loose-knit oligopolies. Knickerbocker proposed that the bunching results from imitative behavior designed to avert destabilizing of the partial oligopoly bargain. Information externalities may also be involved, as one firm's entry spills information to its rivals about opportunities in the remote market. If Knickerbocker effects are indeed widespread, then the follower firms feel some temporal urgency about completing their investments, and acquisition becomes more attractive because it is quicker than green-field entry. We define the variable:

OLIGOP = percentage increase 1974–78 in the number of MNEs based in the parent's home country and two-digit industry who have invested in the United States.[27]

The sign of OLIGOP's influence on the probability of entry by acquisition is indeterminate, because of the conflicting predictions stemming from the shared-experience (negative) and Knickerbocker (positive) hypotheses.

A final variable specific to the parent firm and its subsidiary is:

JV = dummy variable set equal to one if the subsidiary is organized as a joint venture between the parent and another firm (U.S. domestic or foreign), zero otherwise.

Joint ventures are themselves selected for a number of specific reasons related to the traits of the parent firm and the activities that it undertakes.[28] These reasons can in turn be related to the probability that the parent will prefer to start with a going business and therefore enter by acquisition. They are complex, however, and point in diverse directions, so we simply include JV without seeking to establish a definite sign prediction.

Hypotheses Relating to the U.S. Industry Entered

The remaining hypotheses about the determinants of the probability of entry by acquisition address conditions in the U.S. four-digit industry that the foreign parent enters. They bear on the availability of going firms to be acquired and the consequences of expanding the industry's capacity through a green-field investment. They also extend the preceding hypotheses about the specialized assets that the parent firm may bring or, alternatively, wish to acquire through the purchase of a going concern.

The entrant's ability to make an acquisition depends on the supply of potential acquirees that fit its general specifications. The more numerous they are, the better the entrant's chances of finding one with the desired attributes and an acceptable reservation price. We employ the variable:

TARG = number of companies classified to the subsidiary's size-class within its four-digit industry.

Survey evidence from intermediaries in the corporate-control market indicates that potential acquirers typically supply guidelines delineated by size, geographic location, and other attributes.[29] In introducing the variable SIZPAR, we argued that entrants' growth processes will cause them to have preferences about the size of the subsidiary that they found or acquire. Therefore, TARG is constrained to a specific size-class of firms. The probability of entry through acquisition should be positively related to *TARG*.

The parent's preferred method of entry may depend on competitive conditions in the entered market. Suppose that the minimum efficient scale of production (MES) in the target industry is large relative to the market, and that industry demand is inelastic. Entry through the construction of an efficient-scale plant expands output appreciably and drives down the market price. Acquisition of a going firm mitigates this problem, in that industry capacity may be left unchanged after the acquisition or may be expanded by increments smaller than the output of the MES plant. Other things equal, this consideration points to acquisition when the desired scale of entry is large. The variable used is:

> *SIZIND* = size of the subsidiary (employees) divided by total production workers in the four-digit industry.

In principle, the variable should be interacted with the elasticity of industry demand, but that variable is unavailable and must be relegated to the error term. *SIZIND* should be positively related to the probability of entry by acquisition.

The variable *SIZIND* can be derived on the assumption that competitors hold their outputs constant, so that the entrant drives down the market price in proportion to the extra quantity he supplies (the Cournot assumption). However, the rivals' possible reactions inject an additional influence on the preferred method of entry. When incumbent firms are few enough to recognize their interdependence, entry entails various consequences that are difficult for the entrant to predict (Will the incumbents "make room" for him? Will they retaliate?). *SIZIND* therefore may matter only in industries displaying moderate or high seller concentration—both because *SIZIND* should generally be high only in such industries, and because high concentration itself signals the possibility that incumbents may respond aggressively to the enlargement of capacity via green-field entry. We employ the variable:

> *CONC* = share of shipments in the U.S. market controlled by the largest four sellers, corrected for errors in market definition and the presence of import competition.[30]

CONC does not enter as a regressor: rather, we use its estimated threshold value of 45 percent[31] to distinguish those markets in which concentration presumably is (*SIZHIC*) and is not (*SIZLOC*) high enough for *SIZIND* to influence the entrant's preferred method of acquisition.

A final variable related to competitive conditions is the growth rate of shipments in the U.S. industry. On the one hand, slow growth in an industry reduces the return expected from adding new capacity (by increasing initial underutilization, or lengthening the period in which market price is depressed by the expanded output). That consideration suggests a negative influence on the probability of entry by acquisition for:

GROWTH = rate of growth of price-deflated industry shipments.[32]

However, an alternative consideration suggests a premium for speedy entry into rapidly growing industries. If entry can be accomplished more quickly through acquisition, rapid growth may be positively associated with that method of entry. In the statistical analysis, we allow for the possibility that these influences are mutually compatible, because each works only in one tail of the observed growth rates.

Several variables describe structural traits of the entered industry that may affect the method of entry, although the predicted directions of influence are not particularly clear. One is:

RND = research and development expenditures as a fraction of industry sales.

Acquisition can prove an attractive entry route in a high-research industry if the going firm's research capacity helps to adapt the parent's technological assets to the local market, or if the parent lacks appropriate technology and hopes to make system-wide use of the acquiree's stock.[33] On the other hand, MNEs in high-research industries often bring their technologies with them and need not seek those assets from a local going firm. The same considerations apply to:

MAD = media advertising expenditures as a fraction of industry sales.

Acquisition in an industry marked by high sales-promotion outlays may bring the advantages of an established distribution system and local market knowledge, or it may hold little attraction when the MNE brings its own product-differentiating skills. Finally, we employ:

DRBL = dummy variable set equal to one if the subsidiary's industry manufactures a durable good.

Differentiated goods tend to require adaptation to local market conditions, although perhaps less in the case of durable goods with complex configurations, which involve fixed specifications and leave less room for local adaptation. We offer no sign prediction for RND or MAD but do propose a negative influence for DRBL on the probability of entry by acquisition.

To summarize, we expect the probability of entry by acquisition to be positively related to SIZPAR, DIV, FSTINV, OLIGOP, TARG, and SIZHIC. It should be negatively related to MULT, SPEC, and DRBL. GROWTH is subject to a nonlinear hypothesis; RND, JV, and

	Equation							
			2.3		2.4		2.5	
Independent variable	2.1	2.2	High RND	Low RND	High ADS	Low ADS	Durable	Non-durable
Constant	-0.613	-1.020[c]	-0.658		-0.441		-0.665	
	(1.37)	(1.71)	(1.03)		(0.58)		(0.70)	
SIZPAR	0.026[a]	0.029[a]	0.058[b]	0.013	-0.040	0.031[a]	0.036[a]	-0.053
	(3.01)	(3.09)	(1.97)	(0.97)	(0.73)	(3.14)	(3.28)	(1.33)
MULT	0.051[aa]	0.048[bb]	0.037	0.063[bb]	0.061	0.038	0.053[bb]	0.082
	(2.92)	(2.43)	(1.01)	(2.41)	(1.21)	(1.73)	(2.48)	(0.91)
SPEC	-0.323	-0.391	-1.329[c]	-0.172	-0.639	-0.203	-0.251	-0.555
	(1.02)	(1.05)	(1.53)	(0.34)	(0.78)	(0.43)	(0.59)	(0.49)
DIV	0.272[a]	0.295[a]	0.742[a]	0.135	0.291[c]	0.375[b]	0.269[b]	0.359
	(2.54)	(2.55)	(2.48)	(0.87)	(1.54)	(2.17)	(2.24)	(0.90)
FSTINV	0.309	0.384	0.804	0.427	1.131[c]	-0.079	0.450	1.490[c]
	(0.99)	(1.03)	(0.36)	(1.02)	(1.65)	(0.16)	(1.05)	(1.35)

Table 14.2 Determinants of Probability That Foreign MNE Enters U.S. Market by Acquiring a Going Firm (Probit Estimation)

(cont.)

Variable			RDD	ADD		
OLIGOP	0.015 (0.87)	0.042[c] (1.48)	0.015 (0.68)	0.008 (0.41)	0.013 (0.60)	
JV	−1.295[a] (2.42)	−1.711[b] (2.10)	−2.532[b] (2.27)	−2.144[a] (2.37)	−2.287[b] (2.15)	
TARG	0.278 (0.26)	—	0.872 (0.47)	1.368 (0.71)	2.474 (1.01)	2.238 (0.38)
SIZHIC	0.340[b] (1.82)	0.641[b] (1.86)	0.688[b] (1.88)	0.928[a] (2.41)	0.915[a] (2.39)	
SIZLOC	0.061 (0.12)	0.017 (0.20)	0.031 (0.39)	0.054 (0.30)	0.096 (0.63)	
GROWDEV	0.331[b] (1.77)	0.445[b] (2.07)	0.314[c] (1.40)	0.403[b] (1.97)	0.479[b] (2.34)	
DRBL	−0.993[a] (3.19)	−0.869[b] (2.14)	−0.999[a] (2.37)	−1.462[a] (2.88)	−1.571[c] (1.50)	
Other		−0.079 RND (0.69) −4.397 TARGHI (1.00) 2.696[c] TARGLO (1.31)	0.368 RDD (0.44)	0.201 ADD (0.19)		

NOTE: Tests of significance (one-tailed): a = 1 percent; b = 5 percent; c = 10 percent. Double superscripts indicate these significance levels where two-tailed tests are appropriate.

Table 14.2 (cont.)

MAD lack sign predictions, and *SIZLOC* is expected to be insignificant.

Statistical Procedures and Results

The preceding hypotheses were tested on a sample of 138 entries by foreign multinationals into the United States during the period 1974–80. The sample was built up by starting from the Conference Board's quarterly publication *Announcements of Foreign Investments in U.S. Manufacturing Industry,* which lists entries of foreign MNEs by company name, giving some information on the acquired firm or new plant site, including its initial employment level, principal product line, and joint-venture status. From entries for which sufficient information was given, we then proceeded to foreign directory sources for the necessary information on the entering MNEs. The sample that resulted consists of those first-time entrants to the U.S. market during this period for which sufficient information was available.[34] The sample has no more than the usual claim for pure randomness, but it entails no obvious bias except that sufficient information was more likely to be available on large foreign parents.

The dependent variable is a dummy set equal to one if the entry occurred through acquisition (80 cases of 138). The dichotomized dependent variable violates the assumptions required for ordinary least squares regression, and so the probit method of estimation was employed instead. We can now turn to the statistical results, which appear in Table 14.2.

The results reported in equation 2.1 convey our basic findings. All signs are as predicted except for *MULT,* which is robustly significant but with an unexpected positive sign. *SIZPAR, DIV, JV, SIZHIC,* and *DRBL* are significant (1 percent, except for *SIZHIC*), while the coefficients of the remaining variables are insignificant but robust with respect to sign. *RND* and *MAD,* omitted from this equation, are never remotely significant; because of their ambiguous sign predictions, their aptness in the model is dubious (including them leaves other coefficients essentially unaffected). In equation 2.1 *GROWTH* has been transformed into *GROWDEV,* which is the absolute value of *GROWTH*'s deviation from its sample mean, expressed in standard-deviation units. The positive sign (significant at 5 percent, one-tail test), confirms our expectation that entry by acquisition is encouraged when growth is especially fast or slow.[35] *SIZLOC* is insignificant, confirming that entry with a large market share disposes the MNE toward acquisition only if the entered market is significantly concentrated.[36]

Overall, the only puzzle offered by equation 2.1 is *MULT*'s significant positive coefficient, and on reflection that seems unsurprising. Although previous research indicates a negative sign, *MULT* and *DIV* both indicate positively the extent of the parent's multicountry and multinational operations prior to entering the U.S. market. A parent with high values for either or both variables may have routinized the process of expanding through searching out and making acquisitions. It may also be a late entrant to the U.S. market, therefore placing a premium on speed.[37]

Equation 2.2 provides an example of a number of interactive specifications that we explored. TARG, the size of the target-firm population, is always insignificant as an additive variable (whether in natural units or logarithms). Clearly this failure could occur because TARG measures inaccurately the number of plausible acquirees that the entering MNE actually can identify. Nonetheless, we wondered if the abundance of potential acquirees may be overridden in some cases by other influences. Knickerbocker's hypothesis, underlying OLIGOP, suggests that a situation of strong imitative rivalry among entering MNEs may dampen the relevance of the varying abundance of potential acquirees. In equation 2.2, we allow TARG to take a different slope depending on whether OLIGOP is above (TARGHI) or below (TARGLO) its mean value in the population. TARGLO's coefficient is indeed positive and just significant at the 10 percent confidence level—a modest showing but worthy of note. OLIGOP's positive coefficient in the process becomes significant at 10 percent (one-tail test).

The remaining three equations in Table 14.2 pursue the possibility that the structural traits of the entered U.S. market, while not directly determining the probability of entry by acquisition, do affect the influence of the parent MNE's attributes on its method of entry. In equation 2.3, we allowed each of the company variables to take a different slope depending on whether or not research and development (RND) exceeds its mean value in the sample.[38] Separate columns of coefficients indicate the effects of the company variables on the probability of acquisition in high-research and low-research industries respectively. Equation 2.4 applies the same treatment to the advertising–sales ratio (MAD), using its sample mean value to split the observations into two groups. And equation 2.5 repeats the procedure for durable and nondurable goods.[39] We find that parent-company attributes affect the method of entry quite differently depending on the structure of the entered market. Although the coefficients on a given variable in the split subsamples often differ greatly in magnitude, more noteworthy are their differences in statistical significance. More consensus appears among companies about how their overseas structures affect their preferred method of entry in some market structures than others. Roughly speaking, the entry method is more tightly linked to the parent's global structure in durable-goods industries and those employing low advertising and high research and development.[40] It proves convenient to postpone interpreting this pattern until we have considered the determinants of the scale of entry.

Determinants of Initial Market Share

We mentioned previously that the firm's method of entry into the U.S. market should not be independent of the scale by which it chooses to enter. We did confirm in Table 14.2 that the probability of entry by acquisition increases with the new subsidiary's size relative to the market (in concentrated industries), and also with its size relative to the parent's global size. These results imply that the MNE's plan for entering the U.S. market should reflect its preferred initial scale of U.S. operations as well as its method of entry. Therefore, we investigate the determinants of *SIZIND*, defined above as employment in the subsidiary divided by employment in the four-digit industry entered. One likely determinant of *SIZIND* is surely the following variable:

PARIND = total (global) employment of the foreign parent divided by employment in the entered U.S. industry.

The more ample the parent's resources—financial, managerial, intangibles—the larger is its preferred initial size likely to be relative to the U.S. market. A positive coefficient is expected for *PARIND*.[41]

Although we lack much theoretical guidance about other determinants of *SIZIND*, it does seem clear that most or all of the determinants of the method of entry should also influence the preferred initial scale. A diversified parent can include secondary products among its subsidiary's outputs and therefore opts for a larger scale relative to the U.S. base industry (positive coefficient for *DIV*). The first investor arriving from a foreign national market has the opportunity to make a pre-emptive strike against its compatriots with a large initial scale (positive coefficient for *FSTINV*). The foreign investor replicating its base activity in the United States should prefer a larger scale (positive coefficient for *SPEC*). *MULT* and *JV* will be included in the analysis, although no obvious sign predictions pertain to them.

One industry variable not previously used should influence *SIZIND:*

MESGF = minimum efficient scale of production (proxied by median plant size) expressed as a fraction of market size, in those cases where green-field entry occurs.[42]

This consideration should not influence preferred initial scale for the parent entering by acquisition, because any disadvantage of suboptimal scale is capitalized in the purchase price. However, rather than forcing this assumption on the model, we can test it directly by also including *MESAC*, which is the same variable but for cases of entry by acquisition. We expect a positive coefficient for *MESGF*, while *MESAC* should be insignificant. Several industry variables introduced previously are again employed, although we lack really strong bases for predicting their signs. *MAD* (advertising–sales ratio) should wield a positive influence. *RND* should exert a negative influence to the extent that subsidiaries in research-intensive industries perform listening-post functions, for which large-scale production is not necessary. MNEs in durable-goods industries can source any components subject to large-scale economies in efficient-scale units abroad, and so (with *MES* controlled) prefer a smaller production scale in the U.S. market.

These hypotheses are tested in Table 14.3.[43] As equation 3.1 indicates, the hypotheses about *PARIND, DIV,* and *FSTINV* are strongly confirmed, and these variables account for most of *SIZIND*'s variance that we can explain. The market-structure variables prove insignificant as additive influences, as they did with the method of entry. We expected that the effects of the company variables on *SIZIND* might again depend on market structure, even if the market-structure elements exert no additive influence. That conjecture is tested by estimating equations constructed exactly like equations 2.3 to 2.5. Once more, the influence of company variables proves more predictable (higher level of statistical significance) in some market structures than others. In Table 14.3, the results for advertising and the durable/nondurable goods distinction appear as equations 3.2 and 3.3 (the equation for the interaction with research and development resembles the one for advertising so closely that it was omitted).[44] Clearly the three variables that exert an influence on *SIZIND*— *PARIND, DIV,* and *FSTINV*—do so only in durable goods industries and those with low rates of spending on advertising and research. In equation 3.4, the same treatment is applied to the method of entry, with the company variables' influences apparent only where entry occurs by acquisition.[45]

An interpretation of the interaction of company and industry variables now seems to be within reach. Equation 3.4 conforms to the commonplace that companies entering a market by acquisition pick a target sector and size of acquiree, then search for a candidate. No influence that we could identify controls the initial scale of green-field entries. Where company variables are unrelated to initial size (nondurable goods; high advertising and research), *initial* size of the subsidiary is least tied to whatever size it ultimately attains. Where intangible assets (research, brand reputations) are important, the subsidiary's ultimate market-share potential is more uncertain, and the "quality" of the parent's assets becomes an important variable not directly captured in the regressors.[46] That suggestion leads us back to Table 14.2, in which the interaction between market-structure and company variables emerged quite similar to that in Table 14.3, at least for advertising and durability as market-structure variables. If initial scale and method of entry are jointly determined, and initial scale in

		Equation						
			3.2		3.3		3.4	
Independent variable	3.1	High ADS	Low ADS	Durable	Non-durable	Acqui-sition	Green-field
Constant	-1.065 (0.66)		-0.502 (0.31)	0.776 (0.37)			-0.195 (0.09)
PARIND	1.662[a] (3.63)	0.281 (0.57)	4.734[a] (6.19)	4.482[a] (6.14)	0.291 (0.48)	1.651[a] (3.53)	2.643 (0.80)
MULT	-0.059 (1.03)	0.049 (0.40)	-0.177[aa] (2.91)	-0.167[aa] (2.82)	0.074 (0.55)	-0.081 (1.16)	-0.006 (0.05)
SPEC	0.128 (0.11)	-1.230 (0.57)	0.965 (0.75)	1.184 (0.95)	-1.873 (0.82)	0.585 (0.31)	-0.274 (0.16)
DIV	0.954[a] (3.44)	0.375 (0.73)	0.893[a] (2.99)	0.842[a] (2.93)	0.396 (0.67)	1.047[a] (3.44)	0.114 (0.15)
FSTINV	3.383[a] (2.85)	1.434 (0.78)	2.679[b] (1.94)	3.193[a] (2.38)	1.687 (0.93)	4.982[a] (3.33)	0.410 (0.22)
JV	1.551 (0.85)	1.091 (0.64)		1.525 (0.91)		1.826 (0.97)	
MESGF	-0.058 (0.34)	0.012 (0.05)		0.067 (0.32)		0.019 (0.06)	
MESAC	-0.059 (1.03)	-0.257 (1.54)		-0.210 (1.30)		-0.077 (0.43)	
DRBL	0.294 (0.24)	-0.649 (0.54)		-0.680 (0.76)		0.530 (0.42)	
R&D	0.063 (0.18)	0.076 (0.23)		-0.025 (0.08)		-0.003 (0.01)	
MAD	-0.212 (0.69)	—		-0.055 (0.19)		-0.205 (0.66)	
Other		1.766 ADD (0.74)					-1.216 AC (0.55)
R̄²	0.219	0.358		0.355		0.214	

NOTE: Tests of significance (one-tailed): a = 1 percent; b = 5 percent; c = 10 percent. Double superscripts indicate these significance levels where two-tailed tests are appropriate.

Table 14.3 Determinants of Ratio of Initial Size of Subsidiary to Size of U.S. Four-Digit Industry (Ordinary Least Squares Estimation)

some market structures bears little relationship to the parent's planned ultimate scale, then the method of entry will be poorly predicted in those same market structures.

SUMMARY AND CONCLUSIONS

The foreign-investment decision represents a critical strategic move for the company operating in a global industry—a move that the company determines jointly with the use and development of its production and distribution facilities worldwide. We have presented two statistical investigations to expose the links between this decision and the investor's organizational structure and the structures of its markets. The rapidly expanding presence of foreign MNEs in U.S. markets was investigated by relating the increase in shipments planned by foreign-controlled establishments in U.S. manufacturing industries to two classes of determinants—those that should influence the flow of MNEs' resources into these industries, and those that should govern the steady-state market shares toward which these investment decisions proceed. The results confirm the aptness of this analytical framework. The growth of MNEs' activities is closely related to the growth of the U.S. domestic market. They expand their shares with the proportion of U.S. production exported, but we did not confirm that their shares of domestic production decline with the share of the U.S. market held by imports. The short-run changes in MNEs' shares are also propelled by the factors that, according to previous research on various national markets, determine the long-run steady-state shares that MNEs hold of national production activities. This finding confirms the conjecture that the large inflow of foreign investment to the United States in the 1970s was partly a catch-up game, as fast-maturing foreign multinationals moved to claim shares in U.S. manufacturing activities commensurate with those held by U.S. (and other) MNEs in overseas markets. We confirmed the affinity of MNEs for industries intensive in research and skilled management, including those where multiplant coordination is important. We did not find evidence that marketing skills or capital supplies are assets that significantly influence foreign MNEs' expansion in the United States. Some intriguing although nonrobust evidence shows that both high tariffs and transport costs exert upward pulls on the equilibrium shares held by foreign investors.

We found no evidence that the chance to pick up U.S. corporate assets at bargain stock-market prices enlarges the foreign presence. Therefore, when we proceeded to explore the determinants of MNEs' method of entering the U.S. market (acquisition vs. green-field), we expected the driving forces to lie in the entrant's corporate organization and the structural traits of its product market. We also expected that the entrant would simultaneously decide on its method of entry and the scale of its initial presence in the U.S. market. We tested this model on a sample of 138 foreign enterprises that entered the U.S. market for the first time during 1974–80.

We discovered that an entrant is more likely to choose acquisition, the larger its chosen initial operating scale in the U.S. market is relative to its size overseas. Acquisition is also favored by the MNE that is diversified among countries and product markets, but is avoided when the new subsidiary is a joint venture. Acquisition grows more probable when the entrant is claiming a large share in a concentrated market, because it avoids the depression of market price when industry capacity expands and reduces the threat of reactions by oligopolistic rivals. Acquisition is also favored when the entered market is growing very rapidly (probably because entry by acquisition is quicker) or very slowly (probably because the prices of in-place assets are depressed). The entry method otherwise shows little dependence on the structure of the entered market, but we did discover that the effects of the parent's existing organization are much more predictable when the market structure dictates a close link between the initial scale of the subsidiary and its ultimate market share.[47] That same interplay between market structure and parental organization appeared strongly when we investigated the other dimension of the entry decision—initial size relative to the U.S. market. We found only weak evidence that acquisition is favored where the entrant has many potential target firms to choose from. In general, neither of our statistical investigations succeeded in exposing any effects on foreign investment of conditions in the market for corporate control.

These results can be related to the distinction between global industries and industries in which MNEs need little integration of their multicountry activities. Our results confirm, first of all, the development sequence by which successful companies go multinational and extend their international configurations of activities. This expansion process is driven by the pursuit of investment opportunities—as for any company—but also by the prospect of utilizing the parent's special assets and abilities and achieving gains from the international coordination of activities. Special sensitivity of MNEs to export opportunities is consistent with high planned levels of interaffiliate trade, although our data do not specifically distinguish between the pulls of interaffiliate and arm's-length export transactions.

The choice between acquisition and green-field entry tells much about the coordination process in MNEs. Product-specialized parents choose green-field entry to extend their product lines into the United States, presumably because they plan a fairly high level of coordination with their overseas activities and hence prefer installing their own company culture and procedures at the outset. Conversely, MNEs already holding far-flung networks of subsidiaries and offering diverse products are prone to enter by acquisition: they operate in the multicountry mode with low coordination; or their coordination skills have been honed to the point where they can easily ingest the newcomer management team of the acquired subsidiary; or they are simply late-comers catching up with rivals in the U.S. market. However this may be, the evidence clearly shows that the parent selects its method of entering the U.S. market consonant with its general practices for co-ordinating its expanding configuration of international activities.

APPENDIX
DATA SOURCES

Data on employment in foreign-controlled establishments are taken from U.S. Bureau of the Census, *Selected Characteristics of Foreign-Owned Firms,* 1975 and 1981. Industry categories used in this publication are generally three-digit Standard Industrial Classification, and other variables were aggregated (when necessary) to this level. Industry shipments and employment data come from Bureau of the Census, *Annual Survey of Manufactures,* various years; rates of growth of productivity and real output from Bureau of Labor Statistics, *Time-Series Data for Input-Output Industries,* BLS Bulletin No. 2018. Import and export data come from Bureau of the Census, *U.S. Commodity Exports and Imports as Related to Output.* These sources together sufficed to construct *FCSCG, TSCG, XSCG, DMSH,* and *IMGRO.* Capacity-utilization data to construct *EXCAP* come from Bureau of the Census, *Survey of Plant Capacity,* various years. *AVEMB* was calculated from Compustat tapes, using that source's classification of companies to industries. U.S. foreign investment (used to construct *USFI*) is reported in Bureau of the Census, *Enterprise Statistics,* 1972. Rates of spending on research (*RND*) and media advertising (*MAD*) come from Federal Trade Commission, *Annual Line of Business Report,* 1974–76. Managerial personnel (*MGT*) are reported in Bureau of the Census, *Census of Population, 1970, Occupation by Industry,* PC(2)-7C. Multiplant operation (*MLTP*) and capital-cost entry barriers (*KBE*) are calculated from data in Bureau of the Census, *1977 Census of Manufactures,* various volumes. Clark (1981) is the source of estimated rates of tariff and transport-cost protection.

For the analysis of entry by acquisition or green-field, we secured the basic sample of entries from Conference Board, *Announcements of Foreign Investments in U.S. Manufacturing Industry,* 1978–80, and from unpublished tabulations by the Conference Board for 1974–77, years when this publication reported less explicit detail on individual MNE entries. Data on the foreign parent's size (employment) and diversification (*SIZPAR* and *DIV*) was obtained from *Dun & Bradstreet Key International Business Directory, Kompass Country-Company Directory,* and other overseas company directories. Extent of multinational operations of these parents was estimated from international editions of *Who Owns Whom.* The parent's status as a first-time investor in the United States was ascertained from David A. Ricks and Jeffrey S. Arpan, *Directory of Foreign Manufacturers in the United States,* 1974 and 1978 editions. *OLIGOP* was also obtained from this source. *TARG* was taken from Internal Revenue Service, *Sourcebook of Statistics of Income, Corporations,* 1977. Adjusted concentration ratios for 1972 (*CONC*) are from unpublished tabulations prepared by Leonard Weiss and George Pascoe for the Federal Trade Commission.

Most variables were secured in machine-readable form from the PICA data base, Harvard Business School, and that program's facilities were used to perform aggregations and match industries in combining variables taken from diverse statistical sources.

NOTES

1. For a survey of earlier research, see Arpan, Flowers, and Ricks (1981).
2. No attempt is made here to quote exact figures, because differences in the vintages and collection methods of the data make precision impossible.
3. These unweighted means are calculated from the dataset employed in this chapter and exclude those industries that are not comparably defined in data published for the two years. See Belli (1982, 1983) for information on recent patterns of foreign investment in the United States.
4. The concept of a steady-state foreign share has dominated previous research on the prevalence of foreign multinationals. For studies taking this approach to the extent of U.S. investment abroad, see Lall (1980) and Pugel (1981). The numerous studies of MNEs' shares in other countries' markets were summarized by Caves (1982, chap. 1). Lall and Siddarthan (1982) applied the approach to foreign investment in the United States. This model shares with the one developed later in this section the property of addressing mainly the "horizontal" type of foreign investment in which the MNE extends to a new geographic market the manufacture of product lines that are already in its repertoire. However, our model will be developed so as to recognize that subsidiaries may supply components to their corporate affiliates or serve as processing or marketing arms for imports from affiliates (both are forms of vertical integration). In our analysis of the method of entry, we shall allow explicitly for the degree to which a particular foreign investment represents a diversification for the foreign MNE.
5. This same assumption warrants examining changes in employment as a proxy for changes in investment and sales. If we suppose that firms' preferred capital-labor ratios are independent of their scales of operation, then the proportional increases observed for their assets and employment levels should be the same. Assuming away capital-cost differences is not ideal, because firms with different national origins and overseas configurations may well face different opportunity costs of funds. We considered getting at these differences through the variations from industry to industry of the national-origin mix of foreign multinationals operating in the United States, but found the data inadequate to support this approach.
6. Other methods of developing the respective influence of flow and stock factors on foreign investment were considered (see note 13). Goldsbrough (1979) developed an interesting time-series model to integrate these considerations.
7. An advantage of this formulation is its consistency with the many surveys of reasons behind foreign-investment decisions, which invariably rank "market growth" at or near the top. On foreign MNEs entering the United States, see Ajami and Ricks (1981).
8. The annual rate of productivity growth observed 1972–77 is expanded to a six-year growth rate, which we assume was the MNEs' best guess about the 1975–81 outcome at the (various) times when they made their deci-

sions. Sources of this and other variables are described in the statistical appendix.

9. We would have preferred to use 1972–78 uniformly as the base period on which we assume MNEs form their expectations for 1975–81. However, for most variables 1977 was the latest year available. Exports is the exception.

10. Notice that this prediction weakens to the extent that the existing domestic producers are themselves MNEs, either U.S. or foreign.

11. Little (1981) found some evidence that the targets of foreign takeovers in U.S. industry had price-earnings ratios below their industry averages.

12. The year 1972 is dictated by the availability of these data in the Enterprise Statistics, 1972 Census of Manufactures. However, the recent stability or decline of MNEs' shares in the typical non-U.S. market warrants this choice. Two observations of highly aggregated or "miscellaneous" industries were dropped because of noncredibly high values reported for foreign assets.

13. We considered other approaches to combining the keeping-up and long-run share factors that influence the inflow of foreign investment. One alternative was to estimate a model that relates shares held by foreign MNEs in 1981 to putative determinants of equilibrium shares, then use the residuals from this equation to test whether the 1975–81 inflow to an industry was related to its 1981 shortfall from its estimated value. We also examined the correlation of residuals from such steady-state share equations for 1975 and 1981. Neither approach proved revealing because, we believe, both impose the assumption that foreign MNEs' shares in U.S. markets are converging on long-run equilibrium at the same rate. The approach embodied in equation (1) imposes less formal structure on industries' rates of convergence on steady-state shares, and also is consistent with the possibility that the steady-state share is itself a moving target.

14. The construction of the variables NTR and ETR is explained in the source (Clark 1981).

15. In exploratory research we included a variable indicating the prevalence in the United States of highly localized markets. However, it turned out to be, plausibly enough, highly collinear with $MLTP$. The presence of multiplant operation in an industry, thus, is a proxy for a variety of underlying structural characteristics (Scherer et al. 1975).

16. In general, MNE's possess advantages in surmounting entry barriers that may deter new and single-nation enterprises. Therefore, the theory of entry barriers predicts that an industry surrounded by high barriers will have a large proportion of multinational firms.

17. This hypothesis implies that the influence of tariffs and transport costs is conditional upon other factors (RND, MAD, $MLTP$, MGT, etc.) that provide some margin of advantage to MNEs over other entrants. Appropriate interactions are discussed later. One can also predict that the flow of foreign investment into an industry should be related to the *change* in tariffs—indeed, to the change in any X_i variable. We lack suitable industry-level data on changes in tariff rates, properly measured, and the other X_j variables are sufficiently stable for most industries to make the influence of their changes unmeasurable.

18. In equations 1.4 and 1.5 it picks up intercept influences due to the long-run share terms and can no longer be given a direct interpretation.

19. Recall that the expansion of imports and a local subsidiary's output can be complementary for an ongoing MNE but substitutes for the MNE

contemplating the start-up of local production. The best studies of this question of complements versus substitutes in U.S. foreign investment came down largely on the side of complementarity, but with various complicating factors that imply no clear sign prediction for *IMGRO* or *MSCG* (Caves 1982, 137–47, summarized this discussion).

20. That is, *FCSCG* is regressed on *TSCG* and *XSCG* without taking logarithms. The inferior performance of *DMSH* reported in equation 1.2 may be due to the reduced variance that survives after *XSCG*'s transformation into *DMSH*, but of course it also may result from the shift to a logarithmic function form.

21. One might argue, as did Lall and Siddarthan (1982), that U.S. marketing skills still suffice to repel most invaders. However, the conventional results obtained for the other predictors of long-run shares weaken this argument.

22. *RND* was picked as the strongest predictor appearing in equation 1.4. *MGT* was also tried and gives about the same results. More elaborate procedures could be employed, such as a factor analysis of the other long-run share variables.

23. Some of these hypotheses have been tested in previous studies (Dubin 1976; Wilson 1980), but their research designs are rather incomplete. Furthermore, they analyzed the entry behavior of a fixed panel of multinationals, rather than a fixed set of markets entered, and hence concentrated on the characteristics of the entering MNEs with little control for those of the entered markets.

24. Dubin (1976, chap. 5) found that during 1948–67 large U.S. MNEs established greater proportions of their subsidiaries via new ventures than did small MNEs, especially after 1958 and in developing host countries. This conclusion, like most cited from Dubin, rests on a simple bivariate relationship without controls for other influences.

25. Newbould, Buckley, and Thurwell (1978) found that small British MNEs are more successful if they preface their foreign investments by other activities that give them familiarity with foreign markets. Davidson (1980) observed that U.S. MNEs proceed abroad by sequences that take them from familiar and nearby foreign markets to far-flung and unfamiliar ones. Wilson (1980) confirmed the influence of previous experience, measured by the number of years the firm had been multinational.

26. Some evidence indicates that acquisition is more common when the foreign subsidiary represents a product-market diversification for its parent (Dubin 1976, chap. 6).

27. We maintain Knickerbocker's implicit assumption that oligopolists who exhibit imitative behavior recognize their dependence within their national home bases but not across national boundaries. The two-digit classification is undesirably broad (Knickerbocker used three-digit industries); it is forced upon us by the available data, and so we assume that bunching reflected in the data for two-digit industries is correlated with bunching in the appropriately defined subindustries. A given parent observed in our database might have been the one that started a Knickerbocker race to the U.S. market inadvertently and hence had no *ex ante* incentive to acquire in order to hasten its entry. However, if Knickerbocker's hypothesis is correct, the *average* parent entering the U.S. market during the 1974–78 period is more prone to enter by acquisition, and so the hypothesis continues to apply.

28. Stopford and Wells (1972, chap. 7) and Hladik (1985) have studied international joint ventures. Ferguson (1981) provided an extensive statistical test of the motives for joint ventures among U.S. domestic firms.

29. Daniel (1971, p. 63) indicated that European firms entering through acquisition typically find fewer than twelve potential target firms in the desired industry or product segment.

30. Gort (1969) found that during 1951–59 merger rates were significantly higher in more concentrated industries. His "disturbance" model of mergers, based on discrepancies in valuations between current and prospective owners, suggests the possibility that uncertainty in concentrated markets raises the variance of expectations about the future cash-flows from firms' assets and thereby raises the frequency with which outsiders' valuations substantially exceed those of a firm's current owners.

31. A number of papers have explored the question of a critical concentration ratio at which mutual dependence starts to become recognized, generally placing the threshold somewhere between 50 and 60 percent for the unadjusted four-firm concentration. Our 45 percent seems appropriate to translate this finding into a value for the adjusted ratio, which is lower because it allows for import competition (and sometimes other corrections as well).

32. Exactly what time period should be observed for this variable is an inductive question that depends on the process by which entrant MNEs predict future market growth from the available evidence of the past. We experimented with alternative periods stretching from 1975–79 back to 1967–75.

33. This latter motive for entering the U.S. market has been noted for both European (Business International 1971, 22) and Japanese (Tsurumi 1976, 116–19) firms.

34. The Conference Board publication has supplied much more explicit detail since 1978, but we were also able to secure this information for 1974–77, when it was collected but not published.

35. *GROWTH* was measured over the period 1972–79. Replacing it with other periods leaves the sign intact but reduces significance to 10 to 15 percent. Therefore, the result cannot be considered particularly robust. *GROWTH* itself is quite insignificant, no matter how it is measured.

36. We also tested the hypothesis that MNEs are more apt to enter by acquisition when the scale of a new subsidiary is smaller than the estimated minimum efficient scale in the U.S. market. Its basis is that any cost disadvantage suffered by a unit smaller than optimal scale presumably is capitalized (negatively) into its price, whereas the disadvantage cannot be avoided when a small-scale plant is built anew. No support was found for this hypothesis.

37. Interactive models reported below suggest that *MULT*'s positive influence is stronger in durable-goods industries and those without extensive R & D, where global rivalry might place a stronger premium on matching rivals' international moves.

38. Also included as a regressor is the dummy variable *RDO*, set equal to one if *RND* exceeds its mean value, to capture any intercept shift associated with the interactions.

39. Equation 2.5 also tests the possibility that *TARG*'s significance is different in durable and nondurable-goods industries. Only weak confirmation results—a conclusion that also applies when this modification is made to equations 2.3 and 2.4.

40. This pattern has its exceptions: *FSTINV* is weakly significant in the high-*ADS* observations; *MULT* is significant in low- rather than high-*RND* industries.

41. Notice that a statistical bias tends to produce a positive coefficient. *SIZIND* and *PARIND* share the same denominator, so that any errors in

measuring this magnitude tend to produce a positive correlation between them.

42. The proxy for minimum efficient plant size, conventional in research on industrial organization, is the size of the plant accounting for the 50th percentile of the industry's output when plants are ranked from the largest to the smallest.

43. The equations explaining *SIZIND* are estimated by ordinary least squares. The equations for *SIZIND* and the method for entry are "only seemingly unrelated" and for maximum efficiency should be estimated by generalized least squares. However, it is not clear how to employ this method when a probit equation is involved.

44. In equation 3.2 *MAD* is replaced by *ADD*, a dummy variable indicating high advertising, in order to allow for the possibility of an intercept shift.

45. Here the variable *AC* indicates the entry occurred by acquisition; it serves to test for an intercept shift.

46. Recall that the sampled MNEs are late entrants to the U.S. market, and hence probably not the best-endowed with these assets among global competitors in their industries.

47. These findings seem generally consistent with the limited evidence that is available on the acquisition/green-field choice for domestic entrants to U.S. markets. See Yip (1982, chap. 4).

REFERENCES

Ajami, R. A., and D. A. Ricks. "Motives of Non-American Firms Investing in the United States." *Journal of International Business Studies* 12 (Winter 1981): 25–34.

Arpan, J. S., E. B. Flowers, and D. A. Ricks. "Foreign Direct Investment in the United States: The State of Knowledge in Research." *Journal of International Business Studies* 12 (Spring–Summer 1981): 137–54.

Belli, R. D. "U.S. Business Enterprises Acquired or Established by Foreign Direct Investors in 1981." *Survey of Current Business* 62 (June 1982): 27–31.

———. "U.S. Business Enterprises Acquired or Established by Foreign Direct Investors in 1982." *Survey of Current Business* 63 (June 1983): 27–32.

Business International. *European Business Strategies in the United States*. Geneva: Business International S.A., 1971.

Caves, R. E. *Multinational Enterprise and Economic Analysis*. Cambridge, England: Cambridge University Press, 1982.

Clark, D. P. "On the Relative Importance of International Transport Charges as a Barrier to Trade." *Quarterly Review of Economics and Business* 21 (Winter 1981): 127–35.

Curhan, J. P., W. H. Davidson, and R. Suri. *Tracing the Multinationals*. Cambridge, Mass.: Ballinger, 1977.

Daniel, J. D. *Recent Foreign Direct Manufacturing Investment in the United States*. New York: Praeger, 1971.

Davidson, W. H. "The Location of Foreign Direct Investment Activity: Country Characteristics and Experience Effects." *Journal of International Business Studies* 11 (Fall 1980): 9–22.

Dubin, M. "Foreign Acquisition and the Spread of the Multinational Firm." D.B.A. thesis, Graduate School of Business Administration, Harvard University, 1976.

Erland, O. "International Take-overs and Technological Intensity," in Lars Engwall and Jan Johnson, eds., *Some Aspects of Control in International Business*. Uppsala: University of Uppsala, 1980, chap. 2.

Ferguson, R. W., Jr. "The Nature of Joint Ventures in the American Manufacturing Sector," Ph.D. diss., Harvard University, 1981.

Goldsbrough, D. J. "The Role of Foreign Direct Investment in the External Adjustment Process." *IMF Staff Papers* 26 (December 1979): 725–54.

Gort, M. "An Economic Disturbance Theory of Mergers." *Quarterly Journal of Economics* 83 (November 1969): 624–42.

Hladik, K. J. *International Joint Ventures: An Economic Analysis of U.S.-Foreign Business Partnerships*. Lexington: Lexington Books, 1985.

Knickerbocker, F. T. *Oligopolistic Reaction and Multinational Enterprise*. Boston: Division of Research, Graduate School of Business Administration, Harvard University, 1973.

Lall, S. "Monopolistic Advantages and Foreign Involvement by U.S. Manufacturing Industry." *Oxford Economic Papers* 32 (March 1980): 102–22.

Lall, S., and N. S. Siddarthan. "The Monopolistic Advantages of Multinationals: Lessons from Foreign Investment in the U.S." *Economic Journal* 92 (September 1982): 668–83.

Little, J. S. "The Financial Health of U.S. Manufacturing Firms Acquired by Foreigners." *New England Economic Review* (July–August 1981): 5–18.

Markham, J. W. *Conglomerate Enterprise and Public Policy*. Boston: Division of Research, Graduate School of Business Administration, Harvard University, 1973.

Newbould, G. D., P. J. Buckley, and J. C. Thurwell. *Going International: The Experience of Smaller Companies Overseas*. Somerset, N.J.: Halstead Press, 1978.

Penrose, E. T. *The Theory of the Growth of the Firm*. Oxford: Basil Blackwell, 1959.

Pugel, T. A. "The Determinants of Foreign Direct Investment: An Analysis of U.S. Manufacturing Industries." *Managerial and Decision Economics* 2, no. 4 (1981): 220–27.

Rowthorn, R. *International Big Business, 1957–1967: A Study of Comparative Growth*, University of Cambridge, Department of Applied Economics, Occasional Papers No. 24. Cambridge, England: Cambridge University Press, 1971.

Scherer, F. M., et al. *The Economics of Multi-Plant Operation: An International Comparisons Study*. Cambridge, Mass.: Harvard University Press, 1975.

Stopford, J. M., and L. T. Wells, Jr. *Managing the Multinational Enterprise: Organization of the Firm and Ownership of the Subsidiaries*. New York: Basic Books, 1972.

Tsurumi, Y. *The Japanese Are Coming: A Multinational Spread of Japanese Firms*. Cambridge, Mass.: Ballinger, 1976.

Wilson, B. D. "The Propensity of Multinational Companies to Expand through Acquisitions." *Journal of International Business Studies* 11 (Spring–Summer 1980): 59–65.

Yip, G. S. *Barriers to Entry: A Corporate Strategy Perspective*. Lexington: Lexington Books, 1982.

15

Case Studies in Global Competition: Patterns of Success and Failure

Marquise R. Cvar

While there is an increasingly rich body of knowledge about global competition, theoretical development has outpaced empirical testing. Relatively few studies have taken a careful look at the history of global competition in particular industries to expose the reasons for industry globalization or the causes of a firm's success or failure. This study takes an in-depth look at a sample of firms competing in a series of global industries. The objectives were threefold:

1. *Identify the causes of industry globalization.* I sought to explore the reasons why industries had adopted global patterns of competition.
2. *Describe the process of evolution of an industry to the global state.* The research sought to expose the process by which industries move from a multidomestic to a global state. This required isolating the "triggers" that initiated the process: environmental factors that encouraged global competition and strategic moves on the part of competitors that unleashed globalization.
3. *Explore the characteristics of successful global competitors.* I sought to identify the common underpinnings of successful firms' strategies for competing in global industries.

I identified twelve industries for study based on the following criteria:

1. *Product categories in the early to late maturing stage in their product life cycle,*[1] at least in the developed countries. This allowed a period of history to be studied. The peculiar conditions in emerging industries were deemed of less interest at this stage of our inquiry.

2. *A reasonable cross section of parent company nationalities, product types, and apparent strategies on the part of the firm.* This included a cross section of U.S. and European businesses; commodity, consumer package goods, and specialty items; and a set of two businesses each following a global cost leadership, global differentiation, global segmentation, and focus strategy (national responsiveness and protected niche).

3. *A mix of successful and unsuccessful business units*[2] in order to compare and contrast the patterns underlying the two sets. Eight successful business units include:

- a U.S. manufacturer of disposable syringes;
- a U.S. manufacturer of commercial fasteners who was apparently following strategies of global cost leadership;
- a U.S. manufacturer of pet food;
- a Swiss manufacturer of medical diagnostic equipment following strategies of global differentiation;
- a U.S. manufacturer of specialty fasteners for aeronautical applications employing a global segmentation strategy based on technological superiority;
- an Italian manufacturer of prestige toiletries following a global segmentation approach based on a "snob" or premium image appeal;
- a French manufacturer of radiotelephone telecommunications equipment following a government-protected market strategy;
- and a British manufacturer of newsprint following a national responsiveness approach.

The four unsuccessful firms were a U.S. manufacturer of semiconductor molding products, a Swiss manufacturer of watch components, a U.S. manufacturer of process/crushing machinery, and a U.S. marketer of baby products.

A questionnaire was employed that measured the basic characteristics of the industry; the preliminary indicators of the strategies of the top competitors (in terms of market shares, coverage, product standardization, production centralization and sharing, marketing strategy, product-line structure, government policy, organization and participation structure, and R & D strategy), as well as the business identified (which may or may not have been a top competitor) and the financial performance of the business studied.

The research was based on field interviews and a questionnaire augmented by library research. A total of 156 interviews were conducted with various members of management of the firms, including the corporate chairman and/or president, the vice president of strategic planning, the president of the division concerned, and the vice president of marketing, finance, research, and production. Sensitive data in the cases have been disguised.

In this chapter, I summarize four of the case studies of successful global competitors.[3] Each case is organized into two major sections. The first provides an overview of the industry involved, its evolution to a global state, and the position of the subject firm. The second section presents an analysis of the firm and its final strategy.

BECTON DICKINSON SUPPLIES, INC. (DISPOSABLE SYRINGES)

A disposable plastic syringe is a single-use hypodermic needle and vacuum container for the intravenous injection of drugs. It represents a major technological innovation over the glass syringe, with similar cost per usage to glass syringes, but with greater safety and convenience. A syringe was typically sold as a package, including a plastic container and a hollowed needle. Syringes were sold to hospitals, medical clinics, and distributors. In 1982, hospitals represented 65 percent of sales, clinics 10 percent, and distributors 25 percent. In 70 percent of the hospitals and clinics, the key decision maker in purchasing was a professional purchasing agent; head nurses represented the decision maker in the balance.

Syringes were made in a continuous production process involving long runs of approximately 350,000 units per batch. The important raw materials were high-grade specialty plastic and high-tension clinical steel. The plastic was cold-formed to vacuum container shapes; the steel was drawn to needle shape.

On a global basis, the medical industry was highly dependent upon government funding. Until the late 1970s, developed economies such as Europe and Japan had a higher proportion of government reimbursements compared to total health-care expenditures (over 50 percent of per capita expenditures). However, the emergence of Medicare and Medicaid programs meant that the United States had caught up in terms of public spending, and the three leading developed regions had similar levels of government involvement.

U.S. medical schools, the world's leaders in financial training, were experiencing a marked increase in their admission of European students. In the late 1960s, medical schools had been encouraged by the U.S. government to admit foreign students with a quota of at least 20 percent of the entering class. The number enrolled jumped from 6,000 to 11,882 over the decade.[4] By 1980, medical staffs of the world's leading hospitals, which represented a small but highly influential group, had increasingly similar educations. This led to the demand for similar medical products and services worldwide.

Developing (e.g., Brazil) and less developed (e.g., Indonesia) nationals also progressed rapidly in health care relative to other facets of their economies. Improvements in health care were spurred by its political visibility and funded by raw material exports (e.g., oil in Mex-

ico, agricultural products in Brazil). Young doctors returning from
U.S. and U.K. medical schools were another force for health-care
modernization. Since the 1970s, the severe economic problems of
many developing countries placed increasing cost pressures on public
health services.

These developments meant that three major aspects of hospital
operations had become much more homogeneous worldwide: purchasing practices, facilities management, and buyer needs for health-
care products and services. The disposable syringe was affected by
these developments, representing one of the products used in bulk
by hospitals and clinics. Syringes represented about 20 percent of total purchases of frequently ordered supplies, and purchases were
under constant scrutiny for cost savings opportunities—both in purchase price and inventory control.

The change that globalized the syringe industry was the shift in
product technology from glass to plastic components. Transport cost
averaged less than 3 percent of total costs for plastic, versus 15 percent
for glass. At the same time, in the early 1970s, government tariff barriers fell. Critical hospital supplies were allowed into the developing
economies at minimal tariff rates, and the establishment of the European Community (EC) in 1973 relaxed European tariff restrictions.

Worldwide demand for disposable syringes had increased steadily
since the 1960s at an average annual rate of over 20 percent, leveling
off in 1982 to 12 percent (10 percent in developed markets; 15 percent in Japan and developing countries). In 1982, the total market
amounted to $790 million; with the United States accounting for $275
million; Europe $290 million; and Japan [5] and the developing markets
$215 million. By 1987, market size was expected to reach over $1
billion.

Several small U.S. companies pioneered the technological change
from glass to disposable plastic syringes in the 1950s, namely Rorr,
Inc. and Pharmacil. In the 1960s, these firms were acquired by large
U.S. multinationals. Strong local competitors developed outside the
United States, including a Japanese and a German competitor.

Becton Dickinson, which had been founded in 1895 to produce
glass thermometers, entered the glass syringe industry in 1940. It began marketing the plastic syringe in 1960. Although a later entrant
into plastic than a number of small entrepreneurial firms, Becton
Dickinson was the first to capitalize on the emerging demands for low
cost by adopting modern injection-molding technology. In the 1970s,
Becton Dickinson established "conversion teams" to work country by
country overseas. Each team of trained technical specialists went into
hospitals to present the concept of a standardized disposable state-of-
the-art syringe to medical personnel in the use of the product. Becton
Dickinson understood that once the syringe was adopted, a hospital
would treat it as a "controlled item," subject to careful inventory trac-

Table 15.1 Market Shares in the Disposable Syringe Industry in 1981

	Universal (%)	Competitor A (%)	Competitor B (%)	Competitor C (%)	Competitor D (%)	Other (%)
Developed Country Markets						
United States	51	—	39	—	7	3
Japan	—	80	—	—	—	20
France	18	20	—	10	—	52
Germany	10	—	—	60	—	30
United Kingdom	20	—	40	—	—	40
Developing Country Markets						
Mexico	94	2	—	—	—	4
Brazil	50	50	—	—	—	—
South Africa	7	—	20	—	—	73
Australia	8	60	—	—	—	32
Underdeveloped Country Markets						
Philippines	8	43	—	—	—	49
Singapore	9	60	—	—	—	31
Balance of World	40	25	—	—	—	35
Global Market Position	31	18	16	2	—	33

ing and dispensing. As a result, once a hospital adopted one manufacturer's product, it tended to resist brand change.

On a worldwide basis, competition in the industry was quite concentrated (see Table 15.1). The top two firms had a presence in all key local markets, and the industry had become an increasingly global one. Major worldwide positions were occupied by Becton Dickinson (U.S.) with a 31 percent market share; Turumo (Japanese) with 18 percent; and Sherwood/Brunswick (U.S.) with 16 percent. In the previous five years to 1985, the industry had become more concentrated: Becton Dickinson gained five share points, Turumo two points, and Sherwood five points. Pharmacil/American Hospital Supply, once a strong contender with a 25 percent share in the United States and 16 percent worldwide, dropped to only 6 percent in the United States after reducing its marketing budget. Johnson and Johnson (Gelco), reaching only a domestic share of 5 percent in 1978 after ten years in the business, dropped out of the market in 1979.

The newest technological advances in the industry required substantial levels of investment. Fixed and working capital to sales levels averaged over 60 percent of sales. Minimum economic scale of production represented at least 60 percent of the combined sales of the two key global markets (i.e., the United States and Japan). A doubling of volume was believed to lower cost by 20 percent of production, 22 percent in marketing, 5 percent in purchasing, and 50 percent in R & D (or 25 percent of total costs on a weighted average basis).

Becton Dickinson's Strategy

Becton Dickinson became interested in disposable syringes as a global business due to a top management team with the foresight to identify key lead global markets of the future. Specifically, they wanted to transfer experience from other medical-product areas into *new globally defined units*. These units were to represent businesses and industries that held only a secondary position in the portfolio of the existing key competitors.

Becton Dickinson's strategy in disposable syringes sought to capitalize on the global forces at work in the syringe marketplace, and it had made Becton Dickinson the number-one worldwide competitor in the industry as well as in related businesses. Becton Dickinson's service strategy was to be the world's lowest-cost producer through selling a wide line of mass-produced syringes in all the important country markets worldwide, employing large-scale plants and aggressive missionary marketing efforts to convince local doctors of the merits of disposables.

Market Selection

Becton Dickinson chose geographic markets based on their size, growth, and homogeneity of product needs. A secondary requirement was to operate in markets that were leading in technology, providing a testing ground for new product derivatives.

Becton Dickinson competed in the United States, Europe, Mexico, Brazil, and Australia. Becton Dickinson's desire to establish a "blocking position" to resist further Japanese penetration led it to enter the Orient (Philippines, Singapore, Hong Kong) as well. Becton Dickinson sought to be the market leader in each market, and achieved an average national market share of 45 percent. Its global share, measured by its sales divided by worldwide sales, was 30 percent.

Product Policy, Marketing, and Distribution

Becton Dickinson's physical product was standardized worldwide. Approximately 55 percent of syringes was manufactured in the United States, 20 percent in Ireland, 5 percent in Spain, and 10 percent in Mexico and Brazil, respectively. Fifty percent of the U.S. production, 90 percent of the Irish, and 70 percent of the Mexican and Brazilian production was shared with other markets. Becton Dickinson united its disjointed regional operations in 1979. The first step was to standardize needle production, representing 63 percent of product value-added. Modern plants were built in Brazil in 1973 and in the United States in 1975. A European plant, designed for a different product standard, was gradually phased out. The next step in global coordination was to standardize the diverse packaging materials used in each market, accomplished by 1981. Becton Dickinson also began marketing syringes together with the needle. Separate marketing of the two components had been traditional, but by 1983, Becton Dickinson had educated buyers about the cost and convenience benefits of purchasing both together.

Becton Dickinson established worldwide quality standards rather than country-by-country standards. Product standards were based on those of the most advanced or "lead" markets (the United States, Japan, and France), which were markets representing advanced technology as well as substantial volume. In some countries, this standard was more stringent than was necessary for that market. Becton Dickinson realized three benefits from this approach: it led the development of the developing markets; it capitalized on economies of scale; and it maintained a consistent high-quality image worldwide with the cosmopolitan medical customer base.

Becton Dickinson's worldwide-standardized product also afforded the flexibility to export from any plant location that enjoyed advantageous exchange rates. For example, as the Mexican peso plummeted against the dollar, the Mexican plant was shifted from local to export production, giving Becton Dickinson a competitive advantage against Turumo's U.S.-based plant.

Becton Dickinson's standardized product approach differed from the practices of its key competitors. Turumo and Sherwood marketed lower-quality syringes in less developed countries. Competitor C of Germany had quality consistent with its high technology, but a low-volume home market. The product line was very uniform. Over 80 percent of the value-added was the same across items of the line. Additionally, the line had a "vertical structure." It was composed of the basic unfilled disposable syringe; the basic syringe plus disposable needle; the basic syringe plus needle with the drug in the syringe; and, finally, the special disposable syringe and needle package for specific therapeutic treatment (e.g., diabetes, heart surgery). The product-line item uniformity reaped economies of scale, while the vertical structure of the line afforded an excellent opportunity to "trade up" the customer and lead market development.

Becton Dickinson's marketing strategy was formulated centrally and standardized worldwide. Becton Dickinson's marketing approach sought to stimulate the development of the less-developed country markets, first emphasizing the basic position of the product line and then educating the market to accept more sophisticated items. Pricing was also standardized at 100 to 103 percent of the average price of global competitors, while Becton Dickinson's prices averaged 5 to 10 percent below those of local domestic competitors in each market.

Pricing below local competitors reflected the cost advantages of Becton Dickinson's global strategy and had established Becton Dickinson as the leading competitor in each region.

Becton Dickinson's distribution strategy focused on large distributors to maximize sales volumes. Its product was sold exclusively through large medical supply dealers. Many hospitals had formed buying groups that established contracts with dealers. Becton Dickinson maintained a sales force of 120 salespersons to call on hospital buying groups who, in turn, placed the order with the distributors. The faster turnover of syringes allowed Becton Dickinson to set gross margins of 10 to 12 percent instead of the 15 to 20 percent characteristic of lower-turnover items such as blood pressure bands. Top management of Becton Dickinson met with distributors quarterly to plot worldwide strategy.

It is important to note that Becton Dickinson's distribution strategy was in direct response to the globalization of the distribution channels. Distributors had begun to consolidate and integrate their activities. Although most were still regional, as opposed to global in their reach, the *characteristics* of each major distributor became more similar.

Becton Dickinson's R & D staff was located in the United States, the most technologically advanced market. Turumo had located its R & D facility on the East Coast of the United States. The U.S. market led developments in other major markets. Becton Dickinson spent 3 percent of sales on R & D, 30 percent more than the industry average.

Production and Sourcing

Becton Dickinson purchased high-tolerance, chemically neutral specialty plastics and steel. Becton Dickinson sought to maximize scale by concentrating its purchases among a few suppliers—only 2 percent of suppliers accounted for 50 percent of purchases. Chosen suppliers were large in their respective markets. Becton Dickinson represented an important part (over 40 percent) of each supplier's sales of the items it purchased.

Becton Dickinson's production system was managed with a global perspective. Two Becton Dickinson plants, located in Ireland and France, only produced syringes. Syringe production was capital-intensive and the cost of capital in Ireland was low. Two other plants, located in Brazil, only produced needles and capitalized on Brazil's low labor costs in the more labor-intensive needle production process. Becton Dickinson employed a modern logistical system to ensure the lowest-cost transport, and its transportation costs were 5 percent below the industry average. Specifically, the firm shipped to deep-water port facilities that easily handled the distribution of the product to high-volume regional marketing outlets (e.g., metropolitan areas).

The maximum amount of product could be shipped via the cheapest means to four or five major regional distribution centers (e.g., Paris, Madrid, Milan).

Coalitions Policy

To maximize control over its worldwide activities, Becton Dickinson was the sole owner of all subsidiaries. Tariffs and local content requirements were small in most countries with the exception of Mexico and Brazil, whose industrial policies mandated local production. Universal refused to participate in markets with inflexible local requirements.

Organization, Compensation, and Evaluation

Becton Dickinson formed a worldwide hypodermic division in 1979, headed by a group president. The group president had the responsibility and authority for most decisions and reported to the president and CEO. The remaining decisions, principally administrative, were delegated to local unit managers at the country level who were responsible to the global SBU president for all line-related activities and to a vice president of International for administrative support matters. The unit managers had full-line responsibilities for those SBUs that had been defined as multidomestic businesses, such as lab products and microbiology. In these businesses, the unit managers reported to the vice president of International. Local unit managers had 100 percent of the line. Some of the multidomestic SBUs were slated to become the new global local markets as a source of ideas for refining, producing, and marketing the new products developed in the United States. When country markets were identified as future growth opportunities, a regional organization was established to support all of Becton Dickinson's products in the region. As the country developed, more of the responsibility for individual product lines would shift to the appropriate global SBU president.

Compensation was based on product-line performance. Salary and bonus awards in each country market were affected by the performance of other markets. For example, if in the year-end review the European manager did not meet pricing objectives, the bonus of the manager in the unit where the product was manufactured would be affected. This was based on the rationale that pricing was tied to quality and product cost. Thus, if a portion of the European manager's product was manufactured in the United States, the U.S. bonus would be adjusted downward to reflect Europe's less-than-acceptable pricing/sales performance.

Management

Becton Dickinson's management team was selected to create a cosmopolitan corporate culture. The management team for the worldwide syringe business was drawn from many nationalities and top management included North and Latin American, English, and French. There was an extensive interchange of executives among countries in order to avoid solely a U.S. outlook.

Becton Dickinson had adopted a global approach to strategy in all its product lines. The company's global strategic business units included syringes, blood collection tubes, thermometers, surgical blades, vinyl examination gloves, and respiratory care and suction products. Top management had designated twelve of the seventeen SBUs of the company as global. Each global SBU manager typically had managed previously in more than one country.

PAN, INC. (PET FOOD)

The pet food category consisted of commercially prepared and pack-aged cat and dog food. The $4.4 billion category was segmented into dry pet food (dogs only), representing 60 percent of sales; canned food (split 75/25 percent cat versus dog, and representing 25 percent of sales); semimoist pet food (5.5 percent of sales); and pet biscuits and snacks (3 percent).[6] Pet food was sold direct to retail chains (65 percent of worldwide sales), direct to independent stores (20 percent), and through wholesalers (15 percent). Marketing costs, such as sales force, advertising, and promotion accounted for over 45 percent of the total cost.

Pet food manufacturing involved the mixing of various animal or-gans, meat, and muscle with water, breadstuff, and vegetable com-pounds. Depending upon the water content of the end product, pet food was classified as dry (10 percent moisture), canned (75 percent moisture), or semimoist (35 percent moisture). Products were formed into various shapes, such as cubes or "bones" for dry pet food, cylin-ders for canned, and patties for semimoist. Pet food production re-quired dedicated assets, but capacity could be transferred across cat-egories. The same mixing, forming, and dehydration equipment could be used for semimoist, canned, or dry forms, and for cat or dog foods.

Manufacturing represented approximately 10 percent of the total cost. Plants were highly automated, and production took place in batches of 500,000 units (8-oz. cans). The manufacturing process was capital-intensive and fixed capital to sales levels averaged 65 to 70 percent. A significant portion of costs (over 40 percent) was purchased materials. Raw material sourcing was concentrated in a few areas of the world: Thailand, South America, and the United States.[7]

Scale economies in the pet food business were estimated to be quite significant. Marketing costs per unit were believed to decline over 35 percent, with a doubling of volume. Purchasing costs were believed to decline over 50 percent, with a doubling of volume, due to the bargaining power a large manufacturer had over suppliers as well as the processing economies that suppliers realized from large orders. This unusually high scale sensitivity in purchasing was the result of the sources of supply for pet food being concentrated in two locations in Southeast Asia. The processing, shipping, and preservation costs associated with the raw materials of pet food—animal organs, brains, and sweetbreads—were greatly affected by the number of customers and the size of each customer's order. Further, there were few large customers for the suppliers to bargain with; it was optimal for the supplier to tie up as large a contract as possible with one of the "Big Two" (discussed later). Manufacturing costs were believed to decline 15 percent with a doubling of production from the minimum efficient scale.

Since 1975, there had been a major increase in the concentration and bargaining power of retail grocery chains and major pet food wholesalers. Worldwide inflation and cost pressures in the 1970–80 period were combined with limited real growth in the grocery market; less than 3 percent over the period (down from 10 to 15 percent in 1950–60). Grocery outlets had run out of ways to differentiate themselves; as consumer package goods items were typically branded (standardized), the only means of gaining competitive advantage was with pricing.[8] In order to gain scale in purchasing and operating costs to allow retail pricing flexibility while sustaining margins, grocery outlets began to consolidate. As a result, one or two retail chains (such as Loblaws in Canada and Carrefour in France and Spain) dominated each country, with the exception of the United States.[9]

At the same time, logistics systems were improving to allow lower shipping costs by sea. In pet food, significant economies were achieved by shipping semiprocessed unpackaged raw materials to refining and packing plants located near the major customers. Those costs declined 140 percent from 1955 to 1980.

The technological changes in production and logistics and the scale economies in purchasing had raised the advantages of a global strategy in pet food. Wholesale and grocery store consolidation placed an even greater premium on cost-effectiveness. The pet food industry began to evolve to a global structure similar to cola or cigarettes.[10]

Demand for wet (canned and semimoist) pet food dropped 9.6 percent in 1982, while dry pet food demand increased only 4.0 percent, resulting in overall market growth of only 3.2 percent worldwide. The worldwide pet food market was expected to grow to $5.5 billion by 1990. The United States was expected to contribute over 40 percent of the total market; Europe, 25 percent; the Far East, 20 percent; and Latin America, 15 percent.

In 1982, the world pet food industry consisted of five major firms: Pan, with a 45 percent share; Competitor A at 13 percent; and Competitors B, C, and D, each at 8 percent (see Table 15.2). A number of competitors had experienced difficulties in coping with industry

Table 15.2 Market Shares in the Pet Food Industry in 1981

	Pan (%)	Competitor A (%)	Competitor B (%)	Competitor C (%)	Competitor D (%)	All Others (Local) (%)
United States	26	22	14	18	15	14
United Kingdom	40	5	5	—	—	50
Germany	60	15	8	7	—	—
Italy	60	27	18	33	5	2
Japan	50	—	—	—	—	30
France	52	—	12	—	—	36
Australia	65	—	—	—	20	15
Spain	60	10	—	—	—	30
Hong Kong/ Far East	50	15	—	—	—	35
Balance of World	30	10	—	—	—	60
Global Market Share	45	13	8	5	5	24

changes. Competitor B sold its $120 million European operation to Competitor A in late 1982, while Competitor D was rumored to be selling its entire pet food division in 1983.

Pan's Strategy

Pan was a successful worldwide cigarette producer, and had become interested in the dog food business because it was a large and profitable category initially unoccupied by any major multinational competitors in all the key country markets. Pan acquired a French pet food company in 1935 and expanded into other national markets via a series of start-up businesses.

Each country market had a different mix regarding the pet food product forms (canned, semimoist, and dry). The United States had a higher-than-average demand for semimoist forms, for example, while the United Kingdom had a higher-than-average demand for dry. Each market appeared to have its unique needs.

Pan defined its target market as *all* means of providing for the caloric needs of pets. This consumer need existed in all countries. Pan categorized the global market according to the three stages of pet food usage: the pet as a working animal, the pet as a companion, and the "lap" pet (the pet is actually regarded as a member of the family).[11] These roles tended to correspond to the development stages of an economy—the less developed economies had more "worker" animals, while the highly developed countries had a larger proportion of lap/ luxury pets.

As an economy developed, two additional segments of pet food demand would appear: "economy maintenance" (healthy, economical food to maximize pet performance and well-being),[12] and "premium/special-family."[13] Between 1960 and 1982, the market for economy dog food (dry) increased over 15 percent and the market for premium brands over 30 percent. At the same time, the basic pet food segment (canned, semimoist) declined 13 percent.[14] The premium segment grew because of rising income and education, while the economy segment grew because of development of more powerful retail grocery networks.

Pan's long-term principal target was the global premium segment worldwide, while taste and functional appeals were appropriate for national strategies and national industries (e.g., Welch's grape juice, a taste idiosyncratic to the U.S. market); the premium image-based appeal was universal.[15] In the low price/economy segment, Pan could benefit from global scale in manufacturing and purchasing, though pricing was constrained by powerful regional distribution channels.

Product/Market Positioning

Pan followed a carefully planned schedule of strategies to lead the evolution of each market. Its product line and marketing approach for each line was standardized worldwide, but the products it emphasized differed depending on each country's stage of evolution. Pan used the lead markets for each particular item to gain knowledge that it could apply elsewhere. France, for example, was the lead market for the premium, high-image segment served by Pan's brand "Champagne." Pan gained a 60 percent market share in three years, and employed a similar strategy in other countries where the premium segment was emerging.

Pan did historical analysis of the factors that accompanied market evolution, and used "an accelerated marketing concept" to try to accelerate the normal product life cycle by which a country's demand for particular product characteristics evolved. Typically, a market evolved from the use of scraps as pet food to fresh forms of food to prepared/processed products. Entry to the developing market was done via an economy product, because demand was price-sensitive. Gradually, the market demand could be shifted to more premium brands for pets viewed as "companions." By migrating countries toward the premium segment, Pan achieved a worldwide share of 80 percent in this segment, which was far superior to any competitor.[16]

Production, Distribution, and Research

Pan's distribution strategy focused on establishing close relationships with large chains, and capitalizing on the evolution of the retail grocery industry. Packaging plants were located close to these customers to facilitate responsive service and minimize logistics costs. Purchasing was managed on a worldwide basis to maximize scale and bargaining leverage. R & D was centralized at headquarters in the most technologically advanced market (the United States) in order to tap into this market's development.

Organization

Pan was international and cosmopolitan in its management structure. Each member of management had traveled extensively and lived in various parts of the world. The president of the cigarette business unit was Danish, while the head of pet food was Italian. The unit managers and regional presidents were all nationals of their respective areas.

Pan's organizational structure was a matrix. The global divisions' unit presidents were responsible for the key cost components of the business: marketing, purchasing, and strategy. The regional management was responsible for local performance (which essentially translated as cost center control). While regional managers and global business unit presidents had overlapping responsibility, there was a high level of interaction among members of management. In geographic regions where the company's business was well developed, the global product organization played the dominant role. In regions where business was developmental, the product organization deferred to the regional organization. To ensure a high level of control, Pan had no joint ventures or other coalition agreements.

REXNORD (SPECIALTY FASTENERS)

A specialty fastener was a mechanical item designed to bind two materials under high-tolerance, heat-resistant, or air-tight conditions. Demand was relatively small, specialized, and technically sophisticated. The largest buyer of specialty fasteners was the aerospace industry, representing 75 percent of the total industry sales. Boeing, Rockwell, General Dynamics, Grumman, Lockheed, McDonnell Douglas, and NASA were important customers. Top engineers in these companies typically made the purchasing decision. The remaining 25 percent of the market for specialty fasteners was commercial, primarily sales to the electronics industry.

Specialty fasteners were typically developed through close contact engineers of aerospace firms. The product was sold first to aerospace firms, and then to industrial OEMs. As a product's application became more generalized and it became widely accepted, the item was stocked by the key distributors.[17] Given limited product size, individual items were produced in a batch process involving small runs from specialized high-tolerance materials, among them stainless steels and carbon-content metals.

Production costs for specialty fastener production were high, and the selling price was set accordingly. However, users were price-insensitive due to extremely high failure risks. The price of a rivet was a small proportion of the total cost of the end product, but the risk of nonperformance in an airplane, fighter, or space shuttle was astronomical.

Industry Changes

Two major global developments occurred in the decade prior to 1982 that transformed specialty fasteners from a multidomestic to a global industry.

1. *The most technologically advanced products became critical to the national security of the world powers:* The U.S. and Soviet space programs of the 1950s accelerated the pace of technological change. Rapid change also required a global information network and presence to tap into technological advances in any part of the world. Only the large multinational aerospace and aerospace component firms could compete. This consolidated the aerospace industry to a few global competitors. Suppliers to the industry consolidated in response to the aerospace manufacturers' concentration.

2. *Every major nation wanted the same product technology:* In the 1970s, state-of-the-art defense systems became an important part of every major country's budget. Product needs began to become more standard as countries desired the best hardware available in the world. Aerospace manufacturers and their component suppliers were increasingly able to amortize the heavy R & D needed to command state-of-the-art technology across global markets.

The worldwide market for specialty fasteners increased steadily since the 1970s at a rate of 40 percent per year, leveling off in 1982 at a growth rate of 15 percent. The world fastener market was $70 million, broken down at United States $30 million; Japan $20 million; Europe $10 million; and Israel, South Africa, and Latin America another $10 million. By 1990, global market demand is expected to reach $110 million.

R & D represented over 15 percent of sales in 1982, and R & D expenditures were often capitalized.[18] Production scale economies were also significant, as a doubling of volume had a major effect on cost given the typically small unit volume in the industry.

Industry structure was characterized by the presence of several small companies who pursued particular segments: Microdot (U.S.) in solid bushing inserts for high-tech industrial applications; Dzeues (German) in quarter-turn fasteners, 60 percent of which were used in aerospace; and Voishan (since 1980 a part of Fairchild, a U.S. firm) in stressed panel fasteners for military and commercial aircraft.

While a specific segment was emerging, the market was highly concentrated—only a few large multinational firms could afford the R & D, marketing, and support necessary to introduce new products. Once the product/segment became familiar, small local competitors often imitated and successfully undercut the larger ones. In 1982, solid bushing inserts and stressed panel fasteners were still in the growth stage, while quarter-turn fasteners were mature. While the former businesses and industries were becoming more concentrated, local competitors had gained some share in the latter.[19]

In mid-1983, the industry was very concentrated. In each segment, the top two contenders had a presence in all important markets. The top global positions were occupied by Rexnord (80 percent) and Microdot (15 percent) in solid bushing inserts; Rexnord (60 percent) and Dzeues (20 percent) in quarter-turn fasteners; and Rexnord (90 percent) and Voishan (Fairchild, 5 percent) in stressed panel fasteners.

Microdot was a focused global competitor, dedicated to several markets and the integration of its facilities across those markets. Microdot was a unit of Northwest Industries, Inc., where it represented only 8 percent of total corporate sales, but 54 percent of profits. Dzeues, a German, family-owned firm, appeared to be highly competitive in Europe, but had limited penetration outside the Continent. Dzeues held 20 percent of the European market in 1982, a drop from 25 percent in 1978. Dzeues succumbed to local competition and dropped out of the U.S. market in 1980.

Rexnord's Strategy

Rexnord originally became interested in specialty fasteners as a result of its involvement with standard commercial fasteners in the Nordburg group. The firm acquired Camlock, Inc. and the quarter-turn fasteners business in 1970; Tridair in 1977 in stressed panel fasteners; and Vosan in 1982 in solid bushing inserts. Specialty fasteners were considered to be a natural extension of the distribution leverage gained by the basic business. However, as the customers of commercial versus specialty fasteners were entirely different (commercial was sold to the construction as well as to the aerospace industry and to cost-conscious purchasing agents in both; specialty was sold largely to the aerospace markets performance-conscious engineers), and the appropriate distribution strategies were unrelated (commercial fasteners were sold through large distributors; specialty fasteners directly to OEMs), Rexnord apparently made the right acquisition for the wrong reasons.

In 1981, a new general manager assumed responsibility for Vidair and Hemlock. He integrated the two firms, later adding Tosan to the global business unit. Rexnord emerged in 1983 as the only global competitor in all of its product lines. Rexnord actively promoted an image as a technologically superior, high-quality supplier, expanding its technological base from commercial and aerospace fasteners (quarter-turn) to advanced aerospace fasteners (stressed panel) and high-tech commercial fasteners (solid bushing inserts). Given low buyer price sensitivity, Rexnord sought to differentiate based on technology, brand name, and its "crack" teams of aerospace engineers, who worked directly with customers for extended periods on new technology and customized designs. As development time for new products typically was three to five years, Rexnord had the opportunity to establish close, personal relationships with OEMs, which led to long-term (twenty-year) contracts once final specifications were decided.

Market Selection and Positioning

Rexnord operated in every major developed and developing country: the United States, Germany, the United Kingdom, France, Mexico, Brazil, South Africa, and Israel. Less developed countries had no aerospace industries. Rexnord's share of each country market's total fastener business was small, but it dominated the specialized aerospace fasteners segment. Its average country share was 69 percent, while its global share was 61 percent. Rexnord targeted the quality-sensitive, price-insensitive, multinational buyers of specialty fasteners. It charged a premium price (115 percent) relative to competitors. Rexnord managed its fastener business to transfer products across countries and customer groups. Technological advances in aerospace were moved into the commercial market. Rexnord sought to participate in all markets with future volume potential. For example, Japan had just begun to develop its defense industry. It represented a low-volume market, but one of the most advanced technologically.

Rexnord managed its fastener business as a portfolio of global products in different stages of their product life cycle, demanding different tactical maneuvers. The firm capitalized on their technological advancement in aerospace by carrying it on in commercial. Notwithstanding, Rexnord knew when to phase out of a particular item, as local competitors imitated the technology and undercut Rexnord's "umbrella" prices.

Specifically, Rexnord regarded its new technology business of Tridair solid bushing inserts as having an entirely different strategy than its older technology operation of Camlock quarter-turn fasteners. Tridair focused on *manufacturing and design*, as the products were targeted for the defense and aerospace industries, with high engineering and product development costs (20 to 25 percent of sales). Product life cycles were very long (20 years), as they represented the life cycle of the unit for which the fastener was designed (e.g., the Boeing L1011, Concorde aircraft). The major strategic focus was a leading technological posture. Sales expenditures were low (< 2 percent sales). Only seven or eight actual salespersons were used for the business. Eighty percent of the sales were to OEMs. Distributors handled 20 percent of sales that represented "after market" orders to OEMs.

In contrast, Camlock's strategy focused on *marketing and design modification*. The products were targeted for specialty commercial applications such as electronics. Product life cycles were short, only one to three years. Sales were price-sensitive and sales costs high (> 13 percent of sales). R & D was low (< 3 percent sales) and devoted to process, not product. Hence, the major strategic thrust was the leading marketing prowess. Seventy percent of sales were to OEMs; however, as any one product matured, sales shifted to distributors.

Finally, Rexnord continually dropped items at the lower end of the aerospace or commercial lines. The firm gave this type of business to local price-cutting firms, thereby avoiding commodity competition. In 1981, Rexnord phased out the mature technology of spring pins. In 1982, the firm phased out of sandwich panel inserts, a technology of cumbersome hardware that has now been totally displaced.

In 1983, Rexnord began to phase out of quarter-turn fasteners and placed additional emphasis on solid bushing inserts. Specifically, marketing support was increased from 40 to 60 percent of the total specialty fastener budget; $1.2 million of fixed investment was added to the business to increase plant capacity from $28.2 million.

Production and Research

Rexnord did not centralize production nor attempt to integrate the production facilities of its string of local acquisitions. This strategy was in response to the moderately low economies of scale in production (< 15 percent); the local sourcing requirements of fasteners, as a defense-related, politically sensitive product; and Rexnord's desire to encourage a sensitivity to the technological developments which occur on a local basis.

On the other hand, marketing and purchasing were highly centralized to capitalize on the buyer and supplier market structures. The buyers were all multinationals, and their purchasing was centralized. The suppliers were also multinational suppliers of specialty steels (e.g., titanium) and Rexnord gained some purchasing economies (25 percent) by concentrating procurement.

Rexnord centralized and focused R & D efforts on the newest in fastener developments. The R & D effort was targeted to the most technologically advanced markets in order to capitalize globally on a new development. Rexnord worked closely with the major aerospace customers in the markets where they focused their efforts.

Although Rexnord's *process* R & D was highly centralized, its *start-up product* R & D was not. Rexnord's expansion strategy via acquisition (versus internal development) capitalized on the high-technology nature of the business. Rexnord's growth strategy allowed it to capitalize on the R & D dynamics of the industry, without having to spend the tremendous capital and time to develop new products internally. The firm added small companies to its portfolio on an ongoing basis. These companies tended to be privately held family firms that had developed a technological advancement in the field. Rexnord monitored them closely and typically purchased them upon the family founder's retirement.

The product line afforded key customers the opportunity to "price up:" a strategy to lead the development of the entire global market, as any change in one country's products of defense demanded a change in everyone else's.

Organization

Rexnord's top management maintained an intricate balance between global strategic direction and local autonomy. The top management maintained control over R & D, acquisitions, and marketing to the key OEMs. Local management had only the responsibility for production. By treating each national operation as a cost center, each local unit was encouraged to minimize its costs; however, by tying local units' compensation to the global sales performance, regional management was encouraged to cooperate with others and adhere to the global quality standards set by the group. R & D was centralized worldwide. Rexnord focused in R & D efforts on the newest in fastener developments and sought to work closely with the major aerospace customers.

ARIEL (RADIOTELEPHONES)

A radiotelephone was a cordless and wireless telephone that could be transported over a specified radius for communication with a like unit. Radiotelephones employed a central transmitter to transmit signals from any mobile point to another. In 1983, the typical use for such a system was private, as in repair services (30 percent of the market); taxis, hospitals/ambulances, and police (40 percent); and intercompany communication (10 percent). About 20 percent of the market represented public transmission, e.g., passenger car telephones able to communicate with any public telephone point. Private uses of radiotelephones accounted for sales of $1.5 billion worldwide, which was expected to grow at a real rate of 7 percent. The potential market for public radiotelephones was much larger. Radiotelephones were slated by 1988 to become a common item in any automobile, and in other locations.

Production of the radiotelephone unit involved a relatively simple assembly operation, employing 250–300 component parts, most of small individual value and all of which were typically purchased from outside vendors like Texas Instruments and Israel. Over 80 percent of the value was in semiconductors.

Since 1975, competition in the telecommunications industry demanded a larger and larger portfolio in overlapping technologies: commercial videotex and teletex services, personal computers, fiber optics, direct broadcast satellites, cellular mobile-telephone services, video-conferencing, and digital private automated branch exchange equipment. Telecommunications equipment was used in both defense and commercial applications. The initial customers for telecommunications products tended to be governments.

The key suppliers of defense communication equipment had to have state-of-the-art products. In addition, the need for low-cost production and amortizing R & D expenditures (averaging 12 to 15 percent of sales per firm) encouraged the major firms to compete not only in government markets, but also in the consumer mass market. The consumer market raised even stronger demands for low-cost production, as well as access to mass distribution channels.

The worldwide pressure for standardization and state-of-the-art products in telecommunications equipment had fallen upon the radiotelephone industry as well. In 1980, a major change in radiotelephone technology allowed this industry to respond, specifically in the production and operation of the switching systems needed for transmissions of signals from unit to unit. A large reduction in manpower with a significant increase in distance and output capabilities allowed for tremendous scale economies in the operation of the unit and its mobile transmitters—a 25 percent cost reduction with a doubling of volume from a minimum efficient scale that represented approximately 20 percent of the global volume.

Additionally, government barriers to foreign communications networks relaxed in the late 1970s. The U.S., European, and South American nations allowed satellite transmissions into their national boundaries and lowered the tariff rates to imported components and finished parts. Further, various countries began to establish standardized switching technology to allow cross-border communications from the same cellular phone base: Switzerland and Germany did so in 1979; Germany and France in 1982; the United Kingdom and France in 1983.

In 1981, the development of the cellular radio system opened the potential of radiotelephones to the consumer market. Rather than having to rely on a single powerful transmitter to connect callers with regular phone lines, a cellular radio system employed low-power transmitters, each of which served a limited area, or cell. The limited range of each transmitter allowed the same frequency to be used simultaneously in different cells, increasing the amount of open "lines" from an average of 21 to 666. The cellular system allowed call transfer from one cell to the next as a mobile vehicle traveled across cells. This was handled by a central computer and switching system with its own transmitter/receiver and controller.

By 1983, worldwide demand had homogenized for radiotelephones. The newest research advances in the industry required substantial levels of investment in production and R & D. The ratio R & D to sales averaged 12 percent. The production of the radiotelephone unit and switching system (the production of which represented 20 percent of value-added); the raw materials (20 percent of the value-added); the marketing and service package (planning, delivery, technical expertise, or 30 percent of value-added); and the new product technology (or R & D, at 22 percent of the value-added).

The major competitors in radiotelephones were Motorola (U.S.); General Electric (U.S.); Phillips (Dutch); L. M. Ericsson (Swedish); and Matsushita (Japanese). Motorola was the largest competitor in the private radiotelephone market sector with 35 percent of the business in France, 60 percent in the United States, and 45 percent worldwide. General Electric had 19 percent of the public and 20 percent of the private market in France; 30 percent in the United States, and 20 percent worldwide. Phillips had 20 percent of the private market in France, 5 percent in the United States, and 20 percent globally. The balance of the worldwide private market went to L. M. Ericsson (10 percent) and Matsushita (5 percent), neither of which competed on the public side. Ariel (French) had 25 percent of the private market in France and a negligible global share. (See Table 15.3.)

The strategies of the competitors in the industry were mixed. Motorola and the Japanese competed head to head in the basic mobile-unit business. Both shared significant experience with related telecommunications businesses and managed the radiotelephone business as a globally integrated operation.

Ariel's Strategy

Ariel was known in France as the "Defense Company," specializing in all forms of weaponry, communications, and transport related to defense. The company became interested in the telecommunications business as a part of its diversification strategy out of military-related areas. In 1979, Ariel moved into telecommunications radiotelephone equipment as a result of pressure by the French government to acquire a failing firm.[20]

Ariel followed a focused "government niche" strategy in the telecommunications industry. It used a base of French government demand to establish a leading position in the high-end, private radiotelephone market of Europe. In 1978, Ariel agreed to cooperate with the government in the design of the radio switching systems and transmitting towers. Ariel convinced the government to fund 100 percent of the development and construction of the 600 units in France, so by

	Ariel		Motorola		G.E.		Philips		L. M. Ericsson		Matsushita		Thompson	
	Private %	Public	Private (%)	Public	Private (%)	Public	Private (%)	Public	Private (%)	Public	Private (%)	Public	Private (%)	Public
United States	—	—	60	—	30	30	5	—	10	—	30	30	—	5
Germany	25	—	35	—	20	20	20	—	3	—	—	—	—	80
France	25	—	35	—	20	20	20	—	5	—	80	—	—	—
Japan	—	—	10	—	10	10	1	—	10	—	—	40	—	—
South America	—	—	30	—	20	20	5	—	10	—	—	60	—	—
Global	4	—	45	—	20	20	20	—	10	—	30	30	—	—

Table 15.3 1981 Telecommunication's Industry Competitive Positions

1983, the French government represented 50 percent of Ariel's R & D expenditure and 100 percent of the production capacity.

Ariel was not prepared to compete on a global segmentation or efficiency basis. In the midst of what was a global game played by giants like ITT, Motorola, and Siemens, Ariel was a secondary contender. It did not have the financial means, management expertise, operational flexibility, or corporate culture to support a global strategy. The firm's top management realized that the French government rendered it incapable of a global approach as well.[20]

Ariel sought to build a strong position in the high end of radiotelephones in Europe under the government's protection and support, with the long-term objective of joint venturing with a global concern. The firm would represent an attractive joint-venture partner for a strong global competitor when the low-cost public line of products began to overlap with the privately based high-end.

Market Selection and Positioning

Ariel competed only in France and Germany, with 20 percent of the private radiotelephone system. Plans were to expand across Europe to achieve major penetration in what Ariel termed the "cream"—the high-priced specialty system market.

Ariel tailored its product in order to meet local government demands. However, the product line was quite uniform, with over 80 percent of the value-added activities the same across the items of the line. Ariel's line ranged from a basic radiotelephone unit to one with extensive capabilities and ultramodern design. Pricing was typically at a premium of 10 to 20 percent over competitors.

Production and Sourcing

Ariel sourced from low-cost multinational competitors, but only those with long-standing French subsidiaries. This was a strategy to minimize costs, while responding to the nationalistic bent of the government. Ariel bought 40 percent of its electronic and plastic components from Northern Telecom; 30 percent from a sister unit, Ariel-Harris; and 10 percent from Intel. Although Ariel represented a minor customer of the suppliers' total sales, it was a significant factor (over 75 percent) in the suppliers' specialty components sales.

Affiliate and Local Relationships

Relationships with the other markets were joint-venture arrangements in cooperation with the local governments. Ariel agreed to cooperate with other markets in joint-venture arrangements to develop special applications of the cellular technology. Specifically, the German government wanted a European-manufactured product to fit the German-designed communications system.

Organization, Compensation, and Evaluation

In 1981, Ariel formed a worldwide telecommunications division with a group president over five key related businesses: radiotelephones, switching systems, telephone hand sets, video terminals, and satellites. The president, a newly appointed French national from the National Broadcasting System (fired by the Socialists and replaced by a confirmed left-wing representative), had the responsibility for 30 percent of the decision making and a line-reporting relationship back to the president of Ariel. The remaining 70 percent was delegated to local "unit" managers organized by country area, each responsible to the president for all activities of the business.

The Ariel telecommunications worldwide division was formed with the objective of establishing a short-term, strategic focus for long-term objectives.[21] Importantly, a French national, well-versed in international relations with political experience in the broadcasting field, was placed in charge. A unit manager for France and one for Germany reported to him. Compensation was tied to national performance in order for each unit manager to be motivated to appeal to local demands.

As of 1982, the firm had no international presence in any of its businesses. It grew from the defense industry, a nationally oriented business. Ariel diversified into a myriad of global industry businesses: automobiles, computers, satellites, telephones, data processing, and horology. However, the firm maintained a focused national or regional approach in each segment.

The compensation system was aligned with the organizational structure. All bonuses were paid according to local performance.

COMMON CHARACTERISTICS OF GLOBAL COMPETITION

Our case studies provide a setting in which some of the characteristics of a global industry can be identified, and the forces that lead to globalization exposed. We summarize some of the most important findings here, drawing from the four cases described as well as selectively from our broader sample.

Our case studies illustrated that a significant level of cross-border trade in semifinished or finished products is a necessary, but not sufficient, indication of integrated worldwide competition. The pattern of trade in an industry is the outcome of the forms of coordination that lead to competitive advantage. The evidence from this study suggests that the actual levels of cross-border, semifinished, or finished product

Table 15.4 International Cross-Border Product Flows and Strategy of the Leading Competitor by Industry

Industry	Estimated Cross-Border Trade Flows as a Percentage of Total Industry Production[a]	Leading Competitor's Average Percent of Value-Added across Countries
Disposable Syringes	50	80
Commercial Fasteners	45	60
Diagnostic Equipment	55	60–70
Pet Food	25	60–70
Specialty Fasteners	90	80
Prestige Toiletries	60	70
Radiotelephone Telecommunications	40	80
Newsprint	60	70–80
Crushing Machinery	80	70–80
Watch Components	70	80
Semiconductor Molding Powder	50	60
Baby Products	40	40

[a]SOURCE: United Nations Yearbook of International Trade Statistics, 1981, New York, 1982; and company data.

flow as a percentage of total production were significant. The total imports and exports of product in each major market area of the world[22] were approximately 55 percent of total industry production.[23] In the industries with significant cross-border flows of products, the top competitors implemented the same strategy in each major market of the world. They standardized over 70 percent of their value-added across the globe,[24] as shown in Table 15.4.

The Factors Leading to Globalization

Homogeneous Demand

The global industries examined were all characterized by significant levels of demand for standardized products. All the leading global firms marketed a standardized product in many countries.[25] Over 70 percent of the worldwide market for syringes was for a product with standardized characteristics: a state-of-the-art, disposable, general-purpose hygienic syringe at a cost-efficient price. Fully 90 percent of the specialty fastener market was in state-of-the-art, high-tolerance, energy-efficient specialty fasteners. Over 70 percent of the market demanded a high-quality, nutritious, cost-effective pet food product (while a much smaller, but homogeneous segment, wanted a high-quality, high-image, price-insensitive product). Over 70 percent of the radiotelephone market of the telecommunications industry demanded a standardized, state-of-the-art, cost-effective unit.

Susceptibility to Scale Economies

The value chain in each global industry had activities that were highly susceptible to scale economies, allowing a cost advantage to global configuration. Components of the value chain representing important costs were most susceptible to scale. For example, the major cost component of syringes was the physical product (63 percent of costs). Over 80 percent of product cost was standardized worldwide. The same held true for radiotelephones, where the physical product represented 58 percent of costs. In specialty fasteners, R & D expenditures were amortized globally. In premium pet food, the major cost of the product was marketing (over 50 percent of costs). This reflected the component of the item appealing to the global demand in the premium segment: a high-image, prestige, quality, "world-class" brand.

Scale effects were realized in different ways, dependent upon the industry. In syringes, scale was realized by the concentrating production facilities employing an international logistics system. In syringes and other industries, the centralization of purchasing was a significant source of scale economies.

Evolution to a Global Structure

Two major categories of factors can be responsible for triggering the globalization of an industry as described in chapter 1: environmental and strategic. Among environmental triggers, some raise the payoff to a global strategy, while others reduce the impediments.

Environmental Triggers

The industries examined in this study revealed a number of environmental triggers to globalization:

1. *Narrowed economic and social circumstances:* The homogenization of demand in each global industry resulted from two broad factors: (1) economic circumstances converged, for example, as developing markets become developed in terms of technological sophistication, economic planning, and consumer demand; and (2) economic conditions caused one attribute of the product to assume prime importance.

2. *Rationalized distribution channels:* Aspects of the distribution infrastructure became concentrated, placing pressure on the manufacturers to become scale-efficient and offer lower prices. The distribution channels consolidated, in some cases, in response to pressures from the end-user market for low-cost product (such as the retail channels of pet food). In the cases of disposable syringes, medical diagnos-

tics, commercial fasteners, and molding powders, the manufacturers educated, led, and forced the channels to realize greater efficiencies through consolidation.

3. *Technological change:* A primary development that allowed the products to standardize globally was technological change. Technology allowed new product varieties to be developed, which shifted the sources of competitive advantage to the economical production, manufacture, marketing, and transport of global volumes.

4. *Government changes:* A reduction in government resistance to cross-border flows was a feature of many of the industries examined. Reduced government restraints (lower quotas and tariffs) helped promote transnational exports and imports. Some governments actively promoted global competition, realizing that the global firm could substantially augment exports.

Strategic Triggers

In every industry studied, a competitor initiated the globalization of the industry. A number of strategic changes were prominent as the means of doing so:

1. *The identification of global market segments:* One of the most prevalent strategic triggers was the identification and appeal to market segments common to many nations but poorly served in any of them. In different industries, these global segments were latent or even nonexistent until discovered by a competitor. Global segments sometimes represent a large percentage of industry volume or small global niches. Becton Dickinson, for example, identified the latent demand for a global product that could be developed through the education of doctors, nurses, and technicians, and was first to capitalize on this emerging demand by working country by country to present the concept and its economic justification.

2. *Product redefinition:* Evidence in this study suggests that firms frequently precipitated global competition by redefining the product from a nationally defined one to one that appealed to a worldwide market need. Rexnord followed this approach in marketing a new aerospace fastener product from its home country to global defense markets.

3. *Consolidated sources of supply:* In each of the industries, firms consolidated their sources of supply to gain efficiency and greater bargaining power.

Successful Strategies in Global Industries

A number of factors were common to all the successful global competitors studied:

1. *Pre-emptive Strategy:* The cases revealed that the successful firms pre-empted competition in the global industry. Some firms ap-

peared to seize the opportunity to move an industry ripe for globalization *to* a global state and to concurrently establish their strategic position in a segment of the industry. Where the industry had already been another competitor, other successful firms established themselves by being first in a *particular segment* that had not been preempted.

2. *Global versus national performance standards:* In each of the successful cases, firms measured their strategic positions according to a global as opposed to national position. They measured market share on a worldwide basis, and tested their cost and quality against global competitors.

3. *Substantial investment in R & D:* The successful firms had higher R & D investment versus competition; 40 percent higher than the industry average. The location of R & D facilities tended to be in the lead technological markets of the world (such as Israel for defense systems and specialty fasteners, or Japan in telecommunications).

4. *Explicit global configuration/coordination in important value activities:* Each successful firm managed its value chain with a global perspective. While the nature of configuration/coordination varied based on industry conditions, each firm concentrated some activities and engaged in active worldwide coordination.

5. *Active efforts to overcome impediments to globalization:* Institutional barriers to global strategies existed in all the industries studied, particularly those considered affecting important government objectives. For example, preferential procurement by government entities existed in the telecommunications industry, and government insistence on locally produced product components was present in the specialty fastener industry. The disposable syringe industry had to contend with established distribution channels and local sales forces. The channels were needed to stock a product that was purchased in small quantities.

The research revealed that the successful firms contended with global impediments in several ways:

a. *Subsystems of global coordination:* Several of the successful firms chose "subsystems" of countries within which to coordinate their efforts (such as in diagnostics) instead of attempting a full global coordination scheme. The boundaries of these subsystems were defined according to the sophistication of the needs of end-user groups. Ariel set the boundaries of its (short-term) focus strategy in telecommunications according to special technically defined French specifications. In specialty fasteners, Rexnord coordinated production within subsystems defined by political inclinations. This resulted in one plant serving the United States, one in Europe, one in Israel, and one in the Far East.

b. *Reconfiguration of country infrastructure:* Firms made efforts to reconfigure the infrastructure within which it had to operate. To offset the costs of dealing with idiosyncratic distribution channels and local sales forces and detail persons in various parts of the world, for example, Becton Dickinson went directly to the end users to educate them in the use of the Becton Dickinson product and to encourage them to demand it.[26]

c. *An organizational setup that put global considerations first:* Each successful firm had a worldwide product organization with control over key strategic choices. Managers were cosmopolitan, and incentives were provided for cross-country cooperation.

Strategic Approaches for Competing Globally

The case studies exposed a number of different types of global strategies that were discussed in chapter 1, and made it clear that there is no single global strategy. Global cost leadership and differentiation strategies called for deep market penetration. Average national shares were 50 percent, while global shares averaged 35 to 40 percent. Markets were chosen on the basis of the size and growth of the market's demand for a universal product as well as the presence of advanced buyers to develop and test products. These criteria identified a common set of desirable geographic areas in all the cases; namely, the United States, Europe, and the Orient. Mexico and Brazil were frequently part of global strategies based on volume criteria, as these markets represented large emerging countries demanding a universal product. They offered firms the chance for pre-emptive investment in tipping worldwide system balance in their favor.

Product standardization across countries was high. The development of product policy was highly centralized in each of the cases studied. Eighty percent of the decision making was conducted at headquarters by senior management. Management attempted to identify the common denominators across national markets in order to formulate a product that could best meet homogeneous global demand. A relatively broad product line was marketed across the world, with the variety sold linked to market conditions. Items in the product line were sold according to the stage of a market's development. For example, Becton Dickinson promoted the basic syringe in the developing markets (e.g., Brazil) and the most advanced items in the developed areas (e.g., the United States). As a country developed, firms attempted to trade up demand. This tactic apparently allowed firms to lead the marketplace.

Firms with global cost leadership or differentiation strategies concentrated on capital-intensive production of the major product cost components. Production took place in only one to three plant sites, *not* in each country-market location. Each production facility tended to specialize in one component or product for use worldwide. Procurement of inputs was highly concentrated. Shifts in production occurred to capitalize on international currency fluctuations.

The location of the plant sites appeared to be determined by the proximity to high-volume markets, relative factors cost, and the role of local governments and unions. A production site was typically located in Europe to capitalize on large markets, advantageous tariff agreements with the EC, and tax and labor concessions of the local government. Similar reasons led to plants in the United States (particularly for U.S.-based firms), Mexico, and Brazil. Countries such as India (with substantial local content requirements), Venezuela (with large government demands), and Canada (with high local tariff barriers) were avoided. Japan was the common production location, but typically through some type of joint-venture arrangement.

The firms successfully implementing global cost leadership or differentiation strategies preferred wholly owned subsidiary arrangements to coalitions.

Global segmentation strategies were also successful. They sought to capitalize on a standardized product sold to a limited, but worldwide market. Rexnord specialty fasteners illustrates this type of segmentation strategy with technology-intensive industry. The global segmentation strategy called for broad but shallow market penetration. Shares averaged less than 15 percent in each country and 6 to 8 percent globally. Markets were evaluated on a region-by-region basis (e.g., Europe, the Orient) in terms of the presence of advanced buyers. For example, Rexnord chose its specialty markets on the basis of the existence of price-insensitive buyers attracted to premium state-of-the-art products.

The global segmentation strategy involved a high degree of product standardization (over 80 percent) across country boundaries. A high-quality product was marketed in the cases studied at a premium price (+110 percent). In contrast to the global cost leadership or differentiation strategy, the product line was not made to encourage trading up. However, each component of the marketing mix in global segmentation strategies was highly standardized across country boundaries.

In the national responsiveness strategies, firms focused on one or two national markets. The strategy was typically in equilibrium with a global competitor in the same national market. The nationally focused firm dominated a segment of the market with idiosyncratic demands outside of the standardized product line of the global competitors, and therefore was uneconomical for the global player to serve. These demands represented special needs of the end-user and/or distribution market.

Production was evaluated on a national (or domestic) basis. The primary objectives were apparently to (1) source the most suitable goods to appeal to a national/domestic demand; (2) enhance relationships with the local government, business, and export; and, (3) give local management clear goals and objectives, as well as control, because there was no transshipment of goods.

In the national responsiveness and protected niche strategies, R & D was conducted in the home country and the national market (in a 50/50 split); however, new products were evaluated only according to local market needs. Ideas for new products came from the local markets, while the basic up-front technological investment was done at headquarters. Joint ventures were common in such strategies.

Unsuccessful Global Competitors: The "Losers"

Four firms were examined in the study that were not successful in their attempts to compete in the global environment. They dealt separately in process machinery, watch components, semiconductors, and baby products.

A common problem faced by all these firms was that their worldwide subsidiaries were managed with national organization structures and compensation systems. This led to distinct national product lines and a generally uncooperative spirit among country managers, who were all competing with each other for resources. Firms suffered from an inconsistent product offering and pricing strategy to a cosmopolitan customer base.

The baby products firm was simply pre-empted by a smart global competitor, who capitalized on the new developments in the medical services industry (see the Becton Dickinson case earlier in this chapter) by standardizing its product worldwide and marketing the item to the consumer at the start of brand loyalty—in the hospital, right after delivery. The competitor marketed "First Moments" kits that included its entire line of baby care items. In addition, the global winner marketed baby products to adults, thereby increasing primary demand and providing a base for improved scale economies.

In contrast, the loser in this case managed its baby products as a portfolio of national businesses in a global competitive arena. Each market had a product and strategy unique to the others. The company's image was not the same from one market to the next; the key cost component, marketing, was decentralized. Finally, the foreign markets were evaluated as profit centers for the short run; not as a portfolio of growth and cash opportunities.

A second common problem was not aggressively investing in new technology. By failing to see the new developments drawing country markets together, unsuccessful firms allowed themselves to be pre-empted in important markets. They got so far behind in cost and quality that it became nearly impossible to catch up. For example, changes in the watch industry forcing it toward globalization came largely from technological advancements. The quartz crystal watch was invented, which meant that a watch could be made in a cost-effective manner, with low labor inputs, scale economies, and quality control. The other change that occurred was that watches became a true "branded" item—highly susceptible to advertising and distributed through a new outlet—the retail supermarket or discount store.

The unsuccessful firm missed the new developments in its industry and failed to adapt an end-game strategy. With the mechanical watch market disappearing, this loser continued to sell a high-priced product to a price-sensitive market.

A final common difficulty was a uniform hurdle rate applied across all of a firm's business units. A growth opportunity would not receive extra funds to nurture its development. Investments in R & D and marketing were limited as a result. Firms invested too little to compete in a cost-driven global game and began to lose their market positions rapidly.

NOTES

1. The early to late maturity stage of the product life cycle, where customers in developed markets have become reasonably familiar with the product and the product's real growth rate has stabilized at 8 to 15 percent.
2. A "successful" business was defined as one with financial performance above the industry average; "unsuccessful" was defined at least 30 percent as "negative financial operating returns for a minimum of three years."
3. The cases are presented in full form in M. R. Cvar's "Competitive Strategies in Global Industries," Ph.D. diss., Harvard Graduate School of Business Administration, Harvard University, 1984.
4. National Board of Medical Examiners, "Statistics in Foreign Medical Students," and cross-references with Institute of International Education, New York, N.Y.
5. Japan, although a highly "developed" economy in 1982, was considered a developing market in terms of its growth of health-care facilities and service.
6. Bird and fish food were typically not included in the pet food consumer package goods category. There were two reasons for this: (1) the market was very small, representing 5 percent of the total dog and cat food market; and (2) it was dominated by one firm, Hartz Mountain, with a 95 percent market share.
7. These areas represented major ranching, fishing, or wild game lands.
8. This assumed equal location, parking space, hours of operation, and so on.
9. Antitrust laws largely prevented horizontal mergers of this type in the United States. Large regional chains, however, were the result of the merger/acquisition phenomenon: Stop & Shop in the East; Jewel in the Midwest; Winn Dixie in the South; Safeway in the West.
10. The industries that serviced the globalized manufacturers, such as the advertising agencies and PR firms, began to develop global integrated units as well. They managed the packaged goods manufacturers account

out of headquarters, standardized advertising across boundaries, and realized huge scale economies. Indeed, the cost/benefit of standardization caused some of the agencies to globalize *before* their clients. They, in turn, encouraged their clients to do the same, using this argument to differentiate their work from other agencies (e.g., Young & Rubicam, Ted Bates). Next, the packaged goods firms were being *pulled* by their immediate customers (the retailers), and *pushed* by their suppliers (agencies, transport companies) to globalize their operations.

11. "The market" was still primarily the United States, which represented 45 percent of sales.
12. e.g., Purina Dog Chow.
13. In the United States, the Science Diet brand.
14. This segment experienced a temporary increase in volume during the introduction of Gainesburgers and several "me-too" brands. By 1981, this segment began to experience rather severe declines (−18 to −30 percent).
15. By this reasoning, Procter & Gamble could not succeed as a true global competitor in its nonproprietary brands (e.g., Charmin toilet paper, Crest dentifrice), as its primary brand appeal has been functional. Indeed, as of 1983, P & G's international presence was limited. Colgate-Palmolive outpaced P & G in dentifrice by a 25 share-point advantage (C-P had a 35 percent global share versus 10 percent for P & G).
16. As a poignant example of this phenomenon, in 1978 this practice forced the number-one tomato soup brand—at the time, Heinz—out of its own brand franchise, and into the private label business.
17. The highly profitable replacement market, where the originally specified manufacturer has a monopoly position.
18. The capitalization of approximately 50 percent of R & D expense was common in the strategic analysis of several industries, particularly pharmaceuticals and software. This afforded a more realistic evaluation of the key factors operating in the business and more accurately represented highly trained people as the assets of competitive advantage in these industries.
19. In the case of solid bushing inserts, the local firms lost 30 points of share to the new entry, Microdot.
20. As in the United States, government contracts in France were often awarded based on political ties and favoritism. With Mitterrand's regime, this practice became much more prevalent. Indeed, it was said that top management of the nationalized firms had to spend 85 percent of its time "politicking" with the ministers to insure government contracts.
21. If the Socialists remained in power during the next decade, according to many industry experts, France's entire future was questionable. If they were ousted, Ariel could expect an upswing when the markets and company autonomy remained.
22. Includes the United States/Canada, Latin America, Europe, South Africa, and the Orient.
23. Internal company data and United Nations International Trade Statistics.
24. Measured according to percentage of product costs that reflect a standardized component promoted across major regions of the world.
25. The percentage of the product's total cost that was standardized across country boundaries.
26. "Distribution channels" is used broadly here to cover all aspects of the distribution infrastructure: distributors, wholesalers, jobbers, brokers, and warehouse agents. Becton Dickinson made the sale and let the *distributor* "take the order."

16

Global Competition in a Salient Industry: The Case of Civil Aircraft

M. Y. Yoshino

Commercial airframes represent the epitome of a global industry. R & D is critical and extremely expensive: today, it is estimated to cost over $1 billion to design a new generation of airframes. To recoup this investment, firms seek sales worldwide. Economies of scale in manufacturing are significant, and there is a steep learning curve in assembly. The market is worldwide and homogeneous in character, and the customers are highly sophisticated. The choice of a particular type of aircraft represents a critical decision for an airline; once made, the decision commits the airline to a particular type of equipment over a long period of time, often several decades. The buying decision is complex and time consuming. The potential buyer carefully studies the various options, weighing evidence gathered from other airlines. The world airline industry, though geographically scattered throughout the globe, is a small community. There are ready channels of communication among its members, so the performance of an aircraft quickly becomes known. Therefore, effective marketing of aircraft requires a highly sophisticated and well-coordinated marketing force. Also essential is the manufacturer's ability to provide service anywhere in the world, at any time and with a minimum of delay, which requires a highly efficient worldwide service organization. These economic motivations for a global strategy have narrowed the major airframe competitors worldwide to three: Boeing and McDonnell Douglas in the United States and Airbus Industrie in Europe.

Against these powerful economic forces favoring a global strategy, there are equally compelling forces often impeding the pursuit of such a strategy. These forces are political in nature. Governments have a major stake in the industry for a variety of reasons. Aircraft production is an embodiment of high technology with large spill-over effects in a variety of industries; it has a close linkage to national defense. Moreover, it can provide substantial exports. For example, the aerospace industry accounts for about 8 percent of the total exports of the United States and 6 percent of the United Kingdom. Moreover, in most countries, airlines are owned by the government, which can and does exert considerable power in equipment decisions.

Against such a background, the airframe manufacturers must manage economic and political forces that are often in conflict. This chapter will examine global competition in commercial aircraft during the postwar period. I will describe how a small number of competitors rose to global leadership, and how they have sought to reconcile the tension between the economic imperative for a global strategy and the political realities of national government's interest. I will also show how competitors have increasingly turned to coalitions as a strategic option, and I will illustrate the complexities involved in choosing and managing coalition partners. By examining global competition in a highly salient industry, this chapter seeks to examine issues that will be faced to greater or lesser degrees by many global firms.

THE AMERICAN ERA

Though the airframe industry began in the early part of this century, it experienced tremendous growth in the post–World War II era. In the postwar decades, through the mid-1970s, three U.S. firms, namely, Boeing, McDonnell Douglas, and Lockheed had a virtual monopoly in the world market. The advanced technology and extensive manufacturing experience gained from the war were unleashed in the commercial field in the late 1940s, and the United States was by far the most important market in the world, accounting at its height for as much as 80 percent of the total passenger miles traveled. The large, booming home market provided fertile soil for product innovation and rapid diffusion of advanced technology. Lockheed was the first to come up with a new commercial aircraft based on the Constellation, a highly successful bomber developed during the war. McDonnell Douglas and Boeing sought to leapfrog Lockheed by betting on jet technology—a new technology imported from Great Britain during the war. Two widely acclaimed airliners, the Boeing 707 and the McDonnell Douglas DC-8 ushered in the jet age. The advent of jet technology, which made air travel faster and more comfortable, provided a further impetus to the growth of air travel. Meanwhile, Pan American Airways, a leading U.S. airline, quickly expanded its own global network, literally reaching the four corners of the earth.

With the postwar recovery of Europe and Japan and the emergence of the former colonies as independent nations, a large number of new airlines came into being, almost always with the support of their own governments. Almost invariably they turned to the U.S. airframe manufacturers because of their state-of-the-art technology and their wide product offerings. In addition to the large domestic market and the rapidly growing demand abroad, the U.S. airframe manufacturers had another advantage. They were the direct beneficiaries of the largest defense market in the world. Until recently civil aircraft programs, almost without exception, had their origins in the military field. The military promoted the development of new technologies and their applications. Military contracts also helped enable the companies to come down the learning curve, thus providing direct benefits for the derivative civilian programs.

The active military demand and the booming civilian market in the United States encouraged the U.S. manufacturers to introduce new generations of aircraft. After the 707s and DC-8s, designed for long distance, came the Boeing 727s and DC-9s to satisfy the requirements for short- to medium-distance travel. The airlines and airframe manufacturers then took on the next challenge—to meet the growing demand for fast, economical intercontinental flights. Boeing was the first to rise to this challenge. With the persistent encouragement of Pan American, then the world's leading airline, it committed itself to the task of developing such an aircraft. Boeing almost went bankrupt in the process, but after considerable agony and delay, the 747, a much-touted aircraft with many innovative features, was launched. Both McDonnell Douglas and Lockheed entered this market with smaller aircraft—the DC-10 and L-1011. As it turned out, the latter two models were too similar, with disastrous consequences.

Through the 1960s, Boeing faced little resistance from the national governments of the key nations. Great Britain and France, two European nations historically strong in aerospace, fell behind the United States in the early postwar years. Their airframe manufacturers were weak and so limited in the range of product offerings that they were not able to satisfy the demands of their own flag carriers. After all, their airlines had to be competitive in the world market, which meant that the British or the French governments could hardly insist on their airlines buying only their respective national products. The Germans were concentrating on military programs, and the Japanese were concentrating their interest on other industries and the commercial aerospace industry did not rank high in their national priorities.

For the purpose of the present analysis, the most significant development during the 1960s was the emergence of Boeing as the global leader. The company was the first to recognize the advantages of pursuing global strategy. Boeing owed a part of its early lead to the spectacular success of the 727 and subsequently of the 747 and 737 series. The Boeing management deserves much credit for daring to take on the huge risks associated with the development of new generations of aircraft. The company persistently pursued the goal of dominating every segment of commercial aviation.

The company's strategy for achieving this overriding goal consisted of several elements. The first part was to become a technological leader; the second was to develop a basic model for every market segment, from which derivatives could be developed to expand the market and extend the model's life cycle. This strategy offered a real potential of locking up a customer for many years because of the high switching cost for the airlines. Anxious to increase their operating efficiency and improve their services, airlines have a strong preference for commonality of equipment. Boeing's conscious pursuit of this strategy, evident in the case of the 727, helped generate a stream of cash flow to fund the development of the next generation of aircraft, thus providing a powerful entry barrier. Boeing also understood the importance of developing close relationships with key airlines throughout the world.

Another element in Boeing's strategy has been to build a strong, well-coordinated marketing team on a global basis. This not only enabled the company to identify potential sales early, thereby preempting its competitors, but also to respond to rivals' moves quickly and effectively. The final element in the company's strategy was to become a low-cost producer by pursuing manufacturing efficiency through building a tightly controlled and centrally coordinated R & D and manufacturing system. Indeed, Boeing was the first to reap the benefits associated with being a first-mover in developing a global strategy, described in chapter 1. The pursuit of a global strategy enabled the company to capture the benefits of the economies of scale in R & D, manufacturing, and marketing. It was able to roll out their new models quickly throughout the world. Having recognized the basic homogeneity in the market, the company was able to standardize the basic product designs, marketing, and services. Moreover, global marketing and service network have served as a valuable antenna for collecting up-to-date market and marketing information. These advantages enabled Boeing to establish the industry standard of excellence in technology, manufacturing, marketing, and product service. This was particularly important in the early stages of development of a new aircraft. To design a commercially successful program, it is vital for a manufacturer to work closely with a few major airlines from the very inception. It is an interactive process, and these airlines often become the launch customers, thus guaranteeing a certain minimum volume. The reputation of the launch customers is vitally important in subsequent sales. The spectacular success of the 727 enabled Boeing to generate a stream of cash flow to fund the implementation of its global strategy, providing significant entry barriers for would-be rivals.

THE EUROPEAN CHALLENGE

In the postwar period, Great Britain, an early leader in the industry, had a difficult time reestablishing itself in the civil aircraft industry. There were a variety of reasons. The domestic market was small, the industry was fragmented among several companies, and the government's policy toward aviation lacked consistency. In contrast, the French government pursued a consistent policy of rebuilding and nurturing the aerospace industry. But the French also faced a decisive disadvantage—the limited size of the home market and their inability to gain access to the U.S. market, dominated by three major U.S. companies. Moreover, the French were also preoccupied with achieving technical brilliance. Unlike their U.S. rivals, Boeing in particular, the French manufacturers were not always responsive to the needs of the airlines.

By 1970, the total annual sales of commercial aircraft by the three U.S. firms exceeded $25 billion, while that of the European firms was only $3.8 billion. In the same year, nearly 90 percent of all the world's commercial airplanes in service were produced in the United States. Particularly disturbing to the European manufacturers was the definite preference shown by their own flag carriers toward U.S. aircraft. Anxious to overcome the U.S. dominance in this critical industry and to improve their own past disappointing national efforts, several major European companies, such as British Aircraft Corporation, Hawker Siddeley, Aerospatiale, and Fokker, began to consider European-wide collaboration as a way to launch a viable commercial program. Because there had been several successful multinational collaborative programs in the military field, they considered a similar success to be replicable in the commercial field as well. They realized that collaboration was the only way to overcome the enormous entry barriers erected by the U.S. rivals, particularly Boeing.

The first major European collaboration was the ill-fated Concorde project, jointly sponsored by the French and British governments. There were some discussions in Europe in the mid-1960s, particularly in Great Britain and France, about developing a high-capacity, short- to medium-range airliner suited for the European market. The Germans, with their once advanced aerospace industry totally demolished at the end of World War II, had been watching these developments with keen interest. They too had become increasingly interested in entering civil aviation. The Germans organized a small committee to study their industry's vision of an aircraft to serve the same market niche and to signal their interest in a European consortium. Both

France and Britain welcomed Germany's growing interest in civil aviation and hoped it would join them in a unified effort in what by this time had become generally known as Airbus. Germany could bring considerable technical and financial resources, including government subsidies, as well as a preferred access to the home market.

In the ensuing two years, rounds of discussion among the key manufacturers in the three countries took place, and the manufacturers individually and collectively talked with the major European airlines. The initial negotiations were slow and painful, as each company was jockeying for position. Two issues were particularly controversial. One had to do with a rather fundamental disagreement among the flag carriers of the three countries over the design of the proposed aircraft. British Airways and Air France disagreed on the size of the proposed aircraft. Lufthansa, a loyal customer of Boeing's, was lukewarm at best to the notion of the European Airbus.

Another controversy centered around the choice of an engine. The British insisted on the adoption of the RB207, a Rolls Royce engine, while the French and Germans preferred Pratt & Whitney's JT9D. The latter engine, having been selected to power the 747, was further along in the development cycle. Moreover, both the French and Germans by this time had become aware that an access to the U.S. market was important if not essential to the success of the proposed program and that the choice of a U.S. engine would enhance that possibility. These negotiations were further complicated by a broader political development—de Gaulle's rejection of Great Britain's entry into the Common Market. These considerations eventually led to a British withdrawal from further negotiation; the French and Germans decided to proceed on their own and formed Airbus Industrie.

In setting up the consortium, the founders of Airbus Industrie were anxious to create an efficient organization that would enable them to pursue a global strategy. As an organization model, Airbus leadership used the French concept of *groupement d'intérêt économique* (GIE), a grouping of economic interests. GIE enabled Airbus to have clearly defined corporate objectives and exercise total management control over the operations. Airbus consisted of one management group headed by a managing director instead of two parallel national organizations, as in the case of the Concorde. The central organization was empowered to coordinate activities ranging from R & D, to manufacturing and marketing, to product support. Moreover, the GIE concept made each member totally responsible for the commitments made by the consortium to suppliers and customers. In other words, Airbus products had the guarantee of the two powerful European nations—France and Germany—not an insignificant factor in establishing its much-needed credibility. With the formation of Airbus Industrie, the consortium announced the launching of the A-300, a wide-body twin jet designed for local and regional routes.

THE EARLY BATTLES

Airbus got off to a rocky start. The first sales were made to Air France (six airplanes), but no sales were made in 1972 and 1973. Airlines, including Europe's major flag carriers excepting Air France, were not willing to commit themselves to a new aircraft designed and manufactured by a fledgling consortium. The oil crisis and subsequent recession dealt a severe blow to the entire aviation industry, particularly Airbus Industrie. The losses mounted, and by early 1977 the Germans began to complain about the large financial burden and threatened to leave the consortium. The French persuaded them to stay.

In 1977, Airbus succeeded in cracking the Middle East, a Boeing stronghold, by selling to Egypt. A major break came in 1978, when Eastern Airlines bought twenty-three A-300s, a much-desired foothold in the U.S. market. The A-300 won wide acclaim for its technical excellence and operating efficiency. By the early 1980s, the Airbus market extended considerably beyond the flag carriers of the sponsoring nations and even well beyond Europe. For the first time ever, a European aerospace manufacturer had established a position in the global market. Until the late 1970s, the U.S. manufacturers had dismissed Airbus as just another feeble and disappointing effort of the postwar European commercial aerospace industry.

There is no question that the support of powerful European governments played and continues to play an essential role in the success of Airbus Industrie; but history has proved repeatedly that public funding is no guarantee of success. A number of other factors contributed to its success, but for the purpose of present analysis one factor merits special attention. From the beginning, the management of Airbus Industrie recognized the need to be a global player if it was to succeed at all. The previous European efforts were designed primarily to serve the national or Europe's regional needs. The management felt that such a view would be fatal given the nature of the industry, particularly with Boeing firmly committed to a global strategy.

Airbus management sought to fill a particular niche in the global market—fuel efficient mass transport aircraft suited for short to medium distances, with frequent landings and takeoffs. This was one of the very few market segments left unfilled by Boeing, and it also happened to have strong appeal to European carriers. To reach beyond Europe, the Airbus consortium first concentrated their marketing efforts on certain rapidly growing markets. The Middle East and Southeast Asia presented a special target of opportunities, and to cultivate these markets they exploited every resource they had at their command. They also recognized the importance of the U.S. market, by far the largest single national market in the world and the home of their global rivals.

Recognizing the importance of Airbus's being a global player, the company made a large investment to build a centrally coordinated marketing and service organization. From the beginning, in spite of Airbus's identity as a multinational consortium, it was decided to present a single face to the customer and to have all marketing and service activities centralized at Toulouse. The consortium also sought to exploit the technical strengths of each of the partner countries. Each country was assigned to manufacture certain components; but, in order to gain efficiency, assembly was centralized at Toulouse, paying careful attention to logistics. Airbus Industrie is a national champion, or more accurately, a national champion of three powerful European nations. But unlike most national champions who are eager to exploit the national advantages within their own boundaries, Airbus Industrie pursued a global strategy from its very inception.

It is indeed remarkable that Airbus was able to overcome the high entry barriers and become a major player in the industry in slightly over a decade with only one product, the A-300. Of course, it is important to recognize that the consortium had yet to become profitable in a commercial sense; furthermore, the particular form of the Airbus organization made it difficult to estimate the total scope of the investment. One must recognize, however, that the principal goal was political rather than economic. Its mission was to keep Europe in the technological forefront in commercial aviation and related industries to bolster export and provide employment in a key sector. Each participating nation considered it an important national project. The foregoing is not meant to suggest that economic considerations were ignored. Indeed, as mentioned earlier, Airbus management was keenly aware of the importance of being responsive to market needs and of efficient operation, and it exerted strong discipline over its operations.

As the consortium became a significant global player, it confronted the U.S. companies with an unfamiliar set of challenges. Prior to the emergence of Airbus, the participants in the industry understood each other well. The industry had been characterized by an extremely small and tightly knit web of relationships; it was an intensely personal business. According to one senior executive at Boeing, as late as the mid-1970s there were no more than two dozen individuals in the industry throughout the world—among the customers, the engine suppliers, and the airframe manufacturers—who made key decisions. All the participants shared similar basic goals, particularly a profit orientation, and had to live under the same economic discipline.

The emergence of Airbus introduced a new element into competition and changed the rules of the game in important ways. For the first time, the U.S. companies had to compete against a rival rooted in a different political and social system, supported by public funds and committed to a fundamental goal that was different from their own. The rise of the new rival was also accompanied by other important changes in the industry, including the rapid escalation of fuel prices, a new set of noise control regulations, and deregulation of the airline industry in the United States. Another significant development was a shift in the pattern of demand. The U.S. market continued to dominate the rest of the world throughout the 1970s, but by the early 1970s it had begun to show signs of maturity. Between 1971 and 1976, five major U.S. airlines, which accounted for 30 percent of the world's passenger traffic, placed only 4 percent of the orders for new aircraft.[1] About 70 percent of Boeing's orders came from foreign airlines.[2] Against this background, competition between the U.S. manufacturers and Airbus intensified around the introduction of a new generation of aircraft.

COMPETING FOR NATIONAL PARTNERS

In the mid-1970s, the major airframe manufacturers began to discuss the next generation of aircraft. The 747s had all but locked up the large capacity and long-range market. The successful entry of the A-300 had filled a distinct niche in the short- to medium-range mass transport market. As the key participants looked ahead, two segments of the market seemed increasingly appealing. One was short- to medium-range aircraft with 180 to 200 seats. The other was the replacement for the highly successful but aging 727s and DC-9s. All three U.S. manufacturers initiated discussions with the major airlines to explore their expected needs. Boeing began to test a new model that eventually became known as the 757.

Airbus watched these developments with keen interest. Recognizing that it would not be able to survive with only one product, Airbus was anxious to broaden its product line. Airbus was also interested in the short- to medium-range airliner with 200 to 250 seats, a configuration particularly well suited to the densely populated European market. It estimated in 1976 that they could sell as many as 1,300 such airliners over its lifetime.

The aircraft market improved considerably in 1977, and the market prospects for 1978 appeared to be excellent. To launch a new program however, the manufacturers faced a common problem—rapid escalation of R & D costs. There was also a growing interest by this time in several countries, including Japan, Italy, and Australia, in playing some role in the commercial aerospace industry. These countries also began to insist on an offset arrangement as a condition for the purchase of new aircraft; that is, the governments insisted that when the national carrier purchases new equipment, a certain percentage of the aircraft must be produced or procured in its country.

Though a number of countries wanted to become active players in the world aerospace industry, they were painfully aware that it would not be feasible to do so alone. Practical considerations forced them to consider partnership arrangements with one or more of the existing players. The combination of rapidly escalating R & D expenditures, higher risk, and the growing desire of several nations to participate in the commercial aerospace industry enhanced the possibility of international collaboration. The success of Airbus Industrie, the first multinational consortium, provided a further impetus. By the late 1970s, a jockeying for partnerships began around the introduction of a new generation of aircraft. Great Britain became the first battleground.[3]

The renewed British interest in the commercial aerospace industry in the mid-1970s culminated in the creation of the national champion, British Aerospace, engineered by the government through the merger of three major companies, British Aircraft, Hawker Siddeley, and Scottish Aviation. It was hoped that the combined organization could become a force in the world aviation industry. By this time, however, the British too had recognized that it would be nearly impossible to launch a new commercial program on their own.

Thus, the setting and timing were ripe for both Great Britain and foreign manufacturers to begin discussions about possible collaboration. Airbus was anxious to secure British participation to broaden its resource base. The Germans were particularly concerned about the magnitude of the additional investment required to launch the proposed A-310 and about the risks associated with it. At this very time, British Airways was considering the purchase of a fleet of new medium-size and medium-range airplanes and were examining both the A-310 and the 757. Naturally, Airbus was anxious to attract British Airways, a strong customer of Boeing's, and to gain an immediate and important customer base for the A-310 while weakening Boeing's position.

McDonnell Douglas, seeing in a model the possibility of recovering from the disastrous DC-10 program, had talked to a number of continental companies about possible collaboration but none bore fruit. Britain offered a special attraction. For one thing, McDonnell Douglas had had a long and harmonious collaborative relationship with British Aerospace in the field of military aircraft. Its proposal to British Aerospace was to collaborate in launching an entirely new medium-range aircraft, seating 180 to 200 passengers, and incorporating the latest technology available. As a minimum launch condition, it proposed seventy orders with three major airlines, one or two of them in the United States. McDonnell Douglas management believed it could provide only one-third of the funding and looked to the partners for the rest, about $800 million. Recognizing that British Aerospace would not be able to provide this alone, the company proposed a three-way equal partnership among McDonnell Douglas, British

Aerospace, and a third partner from the Continent. McDonnell Douglas stressed that the partnership would be an equal one and that it could provide access to the much-coveted U.S. market.

Boeing's British strategy was built around the 757. The company offered the British 40 percent participation in the development and production of the 757 as a risk-sharing subcontractor. The British would work primarily on the wings. Boeing sought to take advantage of traditionally superior British wing technology, the most difficult part of the airframe design. At the same time the collaboration would be likely to cripple Airbus, because it depended on the British for the wings for both the A-300 and the proposed A-310. In Boeing's offer, Rolls Royce would be the launch supplier of the engines for the 757. With the airframes and the engines, the British content on the 757 would reach 55 percent of the total value of the aircraft. Boeing's main appeal to the British was that the alliance would stand the greatest chance of commercial success, given Boeing's strengths, which meant more jobs and greater British exports. Boeing's proposal merited serious consideration. It was not unrealistic to think that the 757 would sell 1,000 or more aircraft within the first few years after the launch.

In early 1978, just as the market for new airplanes began to pick up briskly, Great Britain faced a tough decision. McDonnell Douglas's offer had a distinct advantage over Boeing's—a full partnership—but it had several shortcomings. One was uncertainty regarding the third partner to be found on the Continent. Moreover, British Aerospace was far from certain as to McDonnell Douglas's commitment to commercial business because of the disastrous performance of the DC-10.

A major appeal of the Airbus proposal was that it would represent European-wide efforts and also offered full partnership. There was a concern in Great Britain, particularly at the Foreign Office, that Europe was leaning toward the Paris–Bonn axis and that Britain's future would be enhanced by seeking a closer identity with the Continent. Moreover, Airbus had begun to show early, albeit tentative, signs of success and the door might not long be open on such attractive terms. There were two problems associated with the Airbus proposal, however. The first was the economic viability of Airbus. The second was the effect of joining Airbus on the future relationship with U.S. manufacturers regarding airframes and engines. There was also a concern within the government over the terms of entry. One of the demands made by Airbus was the purchase of the A-310 by British Airways.

The decision turned on the two basic considerations. One was the choice between the United States and Europe. The other was the nature of the alliance, namely, full partnership with a weaker organization on one hand versus subcontracting relationships with the global leader on the other. A flurry of high-level activities followed, including a series of meetings with the heads of the major players and senior officials of the governments involved. Given the importance of the whole matter, Prime Minister James Callaghan took charge for Britain. Gradually, Callaghan began to lean toward Airbus. Negotiations with Boeing broke down over the partnership issue. The British insisted on full partnership, including R & D, marketing, and service.

There was one serious flaw, Callaghan concluded, in the McDonnell Douglas proposal: the lack of concreteness. This reinforced his suspicion about the company's real commitment to the commercial field. Callaghan, a skilled politician, saw that Britain was in an excellent bargaining position with Airbus. The consortium needed substantial financial support to launch the A-310. Moreover, Airbus wanted to assure itself of continuing access to the British wing technology. Callaghan at the same time wished to engineer a tie-up between Boeing and Rolls Royce. He took a calculated risk by refusing to intervene in British Airways's decision to purchase a fleet of Boeing 757s. Callaghan told Airbus that he could not force British Airways to buy Airbus, which the French found difficult to believe. After a series of clever political moves, the British clearly came out the winners. British Airways was able to buy the 757s that it wanted, and British Aerospace gained a full partnership with Airbus, albeit at 20 percent. Rolls Royce became the launch supplier of engines for the 757.

ENTRY OF JAPAN

The "Battle of Britain" is suggestive of the change in the pattern of competition in the commercial aerospace industry in the late 1970s. For the first time, the principal players competed over national partners to launch a new airliner. Boeing and Airbus were attracted by British technological capabilities and financial resources. Airbus was in dire need of cash and of access to British technology. Even mighty Boeing felt that it could benefit from British government subsidies as well. The 747 and 737, which had required enormous investment, had not reached the break-even point. Sales of the 727 were tapering off, and the company was considering launching two new airliners, the 757 and the 767. The latter with 216 to 280 seats was positioned to compete directly against the A-310. Airbus had also turned out to be a much more serious competitor than anticipated. Both Boeing and Airbus, of course, were anxious to deny each other the resources the British could bring to the enterprise. Despite these considerations, it is important to note that Boeing rejected the British request for full partnership for fear that it might compromise its ability to implement its global strategy.

Soon after, another battle began to unfold. This time the battleground was shifted to Japan. Aerospace had been one of the few industries missing in postwar Japan. Japan had built up a substantial military aerospace industry, but it was totally destroyed at the end of the war. In the early 1950s, Japan began to re-arm on a small scale and turned to the United States to equip a new air force. Later the Japanese began to build a military aerospace industry, though a very small one. The key participants were three major diversified companies: Mitsubishi, Fuji, and Kawasaki Heavy Industries. By the mid-1950s, MITI and the industry had begun to turn their attention to manufacturing their first commercial aircraft: a short-haul, medium-sized, turbo prop aircraft called YX-11.

The YX-11 was introduced in 1962 but sold only 182 units over its entire life. It was a commercial disaster, with a total estimated loss of over $10 million. The Japanese learned expensive but important lessons from the experience, which were carefully documented in a subsequent government study. The report indicated that the failure was attributable to the lack of basic knowledge and experience in design, production, and marketing of aircraft and that there was not even a launch customer. The program was ineptly managed; poor coordination among the participating companies caused serious delays. Furthermore, the program suffered from bad timing because the YX-11 was introduced at a time when jets were gaining in popularity. Significantly, the report noted that the most fundamental problem was the absence of discipline and profit orientation, a rare phenomenon in Japanese corporations. This was mainly because the private sector lacked enthusiasm.

Against such a background, the government and industry participants began to recognize that the only realistic option for Japan was to join an international consortium, but little happened during the following several years because of the oil crisis and the serious recession that followed. MITI finally instructed the aerospace subcommittee of the Council on Industrial Structure, one of MITI's important advisory boards, to undertake a study in 1976. The purpose was to recommend a viable long-term strategy in the commercial aircraft industry for Japan. The subcommittee's report reaffirmed that Japan had no choice but to be a part of the consortium, but should work toward increasing the country's influence in such a collaboration over time. Further, Japan's role in the consortium had to be significant; the project had to have technical as well as economic viability; and the private sector had to have a strong commitment, willingness, and capability to implement the project. In sum, the report served as a formal invitation to the key players in the world to consider Japan as a potential partner.

Simultaneously, the Japanese began extensive negotiations with Boeing concerning their participation in a new program that eventually became the 767. After having decided to go it alone with the 757, Boeing needed a partner to launch the 767. Initially, the Japanese companies had hoped that the collaborative relationship on the new airliner would be on equal terms, a manifestation of a certain naïveté on their part. The actual agreement was a risk-sharing, subcontracting relationship in which Japan would manufacture a major portion of the fuselage, about 15 percent of the total value of the aircraft. With this agreement, Japan made her debut in the global commercial aerospace industry as a subcontractor in a new program that incorporated the most up-to-date technology, an important condition insisted on by MITI. In doing so, the Japanese would use the time-tested formula of learning from the leader. For its part, Boeing was able to take advantage of the Japanese government's subsidies to the industry and 'of Japan's strong manufacturing capabilities without compromising its global strategy. Boeing specified what was to be made, negotiated the terms and the time of delivery. Moreover, Boeing maintained total control over R & D, product design, marketing, and service. This relationship, though limited, reinforced an already strong tie with Japan Airlines, the nation's publicly owned airline. It also denied Airbus, which had been courting Japan as a potential partner for some time, access to these benefits.

The introduction of the two new generations of airliners, Airbus's A-310 and Boeing's 767, triggered another important change in commercial aircraft cooperation. For the first time, the two manufacturers collided head-on in a number of markets, ranging from Thailand to Australia, Japan, and the United States. As a part of its strategy to counteract Airbus's growing influence, Boeing sought to underscore that it was a private company pitted against a rival heavily subsidized by powerful governments. This message was intended for the U.S. government and the financial community. Boeing also tried hard to persuade U.S. airlines that they should think twice before they considered buying Airbus because such an act might be detrimental to the long-term viability of the U.S. commercial aerospace industry. Boeing executives argued that Airbus could offer much more liberal discounts and incentives to potential customers than Boeing, which was a private company whose performance was judged by the bottom line; this economic advantage, coupled with Airbus's ability to mobilize political influences and pressures were awesome competitive threats. Boeing noted Airbus's eagerness to escalate sales negotiations to the political level whenever possible, and claimed that a number of the Middle Eastern countries had bought Airbus because of France's pro-Arab policy. The Boeing executives were quick to cite what they considered blatant use of brute political muscle by Airbus, including the granting of landing rights to Korean Airlines in Paris, preferred routes for Iberia, and a special traffic agreement with France for Swissair. Other examples included military assistance by France to South Africa, an atomic power plant for Iran, petrochemical facilities to Kuwait, and favorable import quotas for Australian lamb. These allegations were hotly denied by Airbus; but there is little doubt that competition had begun to take on a political dimension.

BATTLES OVER THE "150-SEAT AIRCRAFT"

In 1981, Lockheed announced that it would stop manufacturing the L-1011, its only commercial product. Almost at the same time, a new phase of competition began for the three remaining manufacturers (Boeing, Airbus, and McDonnell Douglas) over the next generation of aircraft, which was likely be the last new program in this century. The emerging market segment was for a small, short-range aircraft of around 150 seats. It was estimated about 2,000 such airplanes would be needed during the remainder of this century.[4] While the need for this particular size of aircraft had become increasingly apparent by the early 1980s, the economic climate could hardly have been worse. The recession of the early 1980s dealt the industry a severe blow, and, furthermore, deregulation created havoc among the U.S. trunk carriers. The IATA carriers, responsible for some 75 percent of the passenger traffic in the noncommunist world, lost $2 billion from 1981 through 1983. For many of the leading U.S. airlines, debt/equity ratios deteriorated, and most of the flag carriers elsewhere experienced a similar crunch.[5] The industry was also plagued by considerable excess capacity. In 1983, for example, there were some 600 secondhand airplanes for sale. In 1982, total orders of new airliners fell to 223 ($5.3 billion), from 332 in 1981, representing less than one-third of the number of units sold in late 1978.[6]

Against this background, launching of a new airliner presented to each of the three players a serious strategic dilemma. It was becoming clear to the remaining manufacturers that, if they all decided to enter the same market with competing models, the consequent process of jockeying for position would be disastrous for the industry. Airbus was the first to move, by starting a round of informal discussions among the major airlines on the new 150-seat aircraft, designated the A-320. Airbus described the future long-term prospect of the 150-seat aircraft in rosy terms. Its management estimated that there would be a demand for some 6,700 of this aircraft from 1983 through the remainder of this century, with the total sales approaching $27.5 billion. Airbus hoped that it could capture one-third of the market.

Convinced that not even Boeing, with the 767 and 757 under way and facing a depressed market, was in a position to embark on another new program, Airbus was anxious to pre-empt McDonnell Douglas. But Airbus management also faced a major problem, with disagreements among the partners. The French were the first to make a commitment. As early as 1981, Air France gave them a firm order for twenty-five and an option for the same number. The Germans and the British questioned the wisdom of an early commitment. They were concerned about the commercial viability of the A-320 program, whose total development cost was estimated to be around $1.7 billion and with sales of 600 airplanes required to break even.

As Airbus intensified its search for customers for the proposed A-320, McDonnell Douglas suddenly began to promote its DC-9-80 (called the MD-80), a fuel-efficient, narrow-body twin jet with roughly 150 seats. Because it was a derivative of the old but highly popular DC-8 series, they were able to offer it for less than if it were a totally new airliner. Moreover, the MD-80s were immediately available. Responding to the poor financial condition of the airlines, McDonnell Douglas devised an ingenious leasing plan at extremely attractive terms, which appealed to a number of airlines including American Airlines and TWA. By September 1983, the company had delivered 135 MD-80s and had 85 more on order, including 20 for short-term lease. The success of the MD-80s surprised both Airbus and Boeing. Airbus felt particularly threatened, because the market niche for the proposed A-320 was being filled by an aircraft using old technology and selling for a considerably lower price. Seeing an opportunity to exploit the momentum, McDonnell Douglas began to explore the possibility of developing its own new 150-seat airplane in collaboration with B. V. Fokker. The companies soon exchanged a memorandum of understanding but recognized the need for more partners, and this time they turned to Japan. They stressed that the partnership would, unlike the relationship with Boeing, be on an equal basis, and, furthermore, that Japan's interests would be better served by having multiple relationships with foreign companies.

These developments began to put increasing pressure on Airbus. Against popular expectation, 1982 and a good part of 1983 passed without a formal announcement of the A-320. The poor economic climate was a factor, but even more basic was German and British reluctance. This did not stop Airbus's efforts to secure an order from a non-French airline, however. It persuaded British Caledonia to be another launch customer. The commitment from British Caledonia, hardly a leading airline, was hailed by Airbus management as a major victory because it was a private airline.

Until the very end, the German and British governments pushed hard for economic discipline in the consortium. When approving the program, the German Cabinet went on record to stress the point. Prime Minister Thatcher held up the British share of the initial funding of roughly $365 million to hammer home this point. It was publicly acknowledged by British officials that Britain's delay in approving the deal was in part related to its insistence that Airbus Industrie become profitable. In early March 1984, the project received a formal go-ahead from the member states.

Boeing found itself in a serious dilemma. The company had just launched two new programs that required a huge amount of cash in the foreseeable future. Moreover, the premature introduction of a new aircraft could certainly cannibalize the sales of existing lines. Even though production of the 727 would soon end, the company had two models bracketing the 150-seat capacity range, the 737 series at the lower end and the new 757 at the high end. The 737, with a capacity of roughly 130 seats, had won a broad customer base and offered promising possibilities for a series of major derivatives. But given the move being contemplated by Airbus, however, could Boeing afford to wait indefinitely?

Boeing's strategy to counter Airbus's offensive evolved over a period of time and consisted of several major elements. First, Boeing attempted to "persuade" Airbus to delay the launch of the A-320. Convinced that the French were determined to go ahead with the new airliner, Boeing concentrated its efforts on the Germans and British. Boeing used industry conferences and conventions as a forum. There are several important, regularly scheduled conferences, and the speakers include high-ranking government officials and key executives from airframe and engine manufacturers as well as airlines. In these forums, Boeing management stressed the magnitude of the investment required for launching a new generation of airliners and the risks associated with such an effort. They urged caution. Such warnings uttered by the top management of the world's leading manufacturer carried considerable weight. Boeing executives also added that although the company had no immediate plans to launch a new aircraft, it would be prepared to match the move by Airbus if the consortium were to proceed. Boeing thus sent an unambiguous message to its principal rival.

Another move in Boeing's defensive strategy was to remind its customers of the presence of significant market and technological uncertainties and of the danger of premature commitment to the wrong aircraft. Boeing management urged the airlines to think creatively about different configurations, stressing that there is nothing magical about the 150-seat airliner. They suggested that the optimum size might vary from 100 to 160 seats. Boeing executives pointed out further that the current technology did not justify a completely new generation of aircraft and that there were a number of exciting new technological developments in materials, electronics, and aerodynamics that could be incorporated into future generations of aircraft, though these developments were not yet ready for practical application. Particularly important in this regard were engines. The Boeing executives argued that a truly new aircraft generation would have to be fitted with a new engine. Recognizing that a new engine would require a year or two longer to develop than a new airframe, Boeing urged the airlines to wait until the new engine being proposed by the consortium of Pratt & Whitney, Rolls Royce, MTU, Fiat, and the three Japanese companies became available. The fact that there were some uncertainties associated with the formation of the engine consortium itself was a further point in Boeing's favor.

The company encouraged its customers in the interim to buy or lease existing airplanes with proven technology. Boeing had just introduced the 130-seat 737-300, which incorporated considerable improvements and more efficient engines. It had also been discussing additional derivatives such as the 737-400, 737-500, and the 737-Lite (100 passengers). Because Boeing could introduce a major derivative for $300 to $400 million instead of the $1.7 billion required to launch the A-320, it could sell the 737-300 at a considerably lower price. It assured the airlines that they would continue discussions with them to define the optimum design of its version of the new airliner so that once its design was finalized it would be superior to the A-320. Boeing management stressed that the new airliner will make the A-320 prematurely obsolete.

Into this picture entered Japan. Having become a risk-sharing subcontractor to Boeing on the 767, it was anxious to play a greater role in the next program, and the 150-seat aircraft would present a significant opportunity. Japan had already held brief discussions with McDonnell Douglas and Airbus, without any tangible results. MITI officials and industrial leaders felt that strengthening ties with Boeing, the world leader, would be the best way to enhance the Japanese presence in the industry. The negotiations took many months, due to market uncertainties and Boeing's reluctance. Boeing, however, had to make certain that Japan would not join one of its rivals. In early 1984, Boeing and Japan finally agreed to collaborate on the proposed 7J7, Boeing's version of the 150-seat plane.

The Japanese would provide roughly one-quarter of the total funding; in return, this time they would be allowed to participate not only in manufacturing, but in design, marketing, and product support. The Japanese hailed the arrangement as a full partnership. Boeing noted in its announcement that the action should not be construed as a countermove to match the A-320, indicating that the 7J7 would be likely to appear a few years after the introduction of the A-320 and with more advanced technology, thus quickly making the latter obsolete. Boeing management stressed that the partnership would continue to explore with the airlines the optimum design, and indeed the company's announcement was deliberately vague regarding the specifications of the design and the timing of 7J7's introduction.

Amidst these developments, McDonnell Douglas abruptly canceled all its new commercial aircraft programs. The company had three programs under development, including its own version of the 150-seat aircraft. The McDonnell Douglas board cited as its reason the poor market conditions, but the decision merely confirmed a long-held suspicion in the industry about the company's lack of total commitment to the commercial field. Airbus's determination to launch the A-320 might have also weighed heavily, and McDonnell Douglas had incurred substantial losses in the commercial field and had become only a marginal player with limited and aging product lines.

Now, in the mid-1980s, Boeing faces only Airbus. Boeing recognizes the need to match the advantages of the government-funded rival by allying itself with Japan for the 7J7. Although this alliance is fundamentally different from that of Airbus, it still requires considerable adjustment in Boeing's traditional way of operating. Moreover, the goals of Boeing and those of Japan may be at odds in the long run. Japan may some day aspire to be an independent force in commercial aerospace. Boeing's strategic challenge in this regard is to pre-empt Japan's potential entry by convincing the Japanese that their future lies with Boeing.

Airbus management faces quite different challenges. They still have a long way to go to catch up with Boeing. Though it succeeded in selling a fleet of A-320s to Pan American in 1985, the U.S. market largely remains the domain of Boeing. It must also broaden its product coverage even further to match the economies of Boeing's broad-line strategy. The recent push by the Germans and British to insure the economic viability of the consortium may constrain management's discretion to market the A-320. As a result, Boeing may well find Airbus becoming a more "reasonable" competitor than it has been in the past.

Another significant issue facing both Airbus and Boeing is the effectiveness of their efforts to be nationally responsive. A presumed benefit of being "nationally responsive" is preferred access to the home market. Although Air France has been consistently loyal to Airbus, the national carriers of Germany and the United Kingdom acted quite independently. Many national airlines have also been under pressure to show satisfactory economic performance, which figures heavily in their equipment decision. Moreover, at times, the presumed benefits of nationally responsive strategy are submerged in broader considerations. For example, Boeing almost lost its Japanese order on the 767 to Airbus, despite its partnership arrangement with powerful Japanese interests. This was because Airbus almost succeeded in persuading the Japanese that the purchase of a fleet of A-310s would go a long way toward improvement of the deteriorating European/Japanese economic relationship of the presence of huge trade imbalances. Though far from conclusive, these incidents do raise questions about the benefits that are presumably associated with a strategy built around national responsiveness.

SUMMARY

An examination of the evolution of the commercial airframe industry over the past four decades presents a fascinating model of strategic accommodations made by the three major players—Boeing, Mc-

Donnell Douglas, and Lockheed—to the changing market and competitive environment and how new firms backed by powerful national governments were able to achieve successful entries. Boeing was the first to recognize the value of a global strategy. The other two U.S. rivals lacked strong commitment to the commercial aerospace industry and failed to keep up with Boeing's persistent and consistent effort to become a truly global player. The strategy proved highly successful for Boeing through the mid-1970s, enabling the company to establish an uncontested leadership in the world market.

The challenge to Boeing's dominance came from Europe, when the three powerful European nations formed an alliance. Given the presence of high entry barriers, the Europeans understood the cold reality that a coalition was the only answer. Much to its credit, Airbus management brought to the enterprise a strong sense of discipline and an acute recognition of the need to be a global player. Airbus Industrie has demonstrated with considerable success how a multinational consortium with inherent risk of fragmentation can pursue global strategy. Boeing faced in Airbus a competitor different from those it had faced earlier. For one thing, it was backed by the national treasuries of the three most powerful European governments. It was equally significant that profit was not their dominant concern.

Almost at the same time, Boeing faced another new development—the growing interest of several major nations, particularly Japan, in having a place in the industry. These nations, recognizing the futility of going it alone in such a difficult arena, began to search for partners. Boeing faced a considerable dilemma. First it had to prevent these nations from joining Airbus. Airbus offered two advantages. Being a coalition itself, it had an infrastructure designed to bring in additional partners with more accommodating terms. Boeing, on the other hand, had based its global strategy on the notion of total control over every aspect of the value chain. It feared that the participation of a foreign partner, particularly across the entire value chain, would risk the integrity of its global strategy, a strategy that had proved so successful. Boeing, however, was anxious to match the strength of Airbus—its access to the coffers of powerful nations as well as to the particular strengths such nations can offer—the advanced wing technology available in Great Britain, or the overall manufacturing efficiencies of Japan. With Airbus's ability and willingness to make significant price concessions, Boeing was under increasing pressure to improve its efficiency and productivity even further.

These considerations called for a change in its traditional strategy. Boeing moved cautiously. Initially, it offered the British and the Japanese a risk-sharing subcontracting relationship on a new program. The relationship was unambiguous—it was subcontracting, not a partnership. The British rejected Boeing and joined Airbus; Japan accepted the arrangement, hoping that in future programs its role would be expanded. Airbus's continued challenge further reinforced Boeing's need to capitalize on the resources of foreign partners.

Boeing again turned to Japan. This time Japan insisted on a partnership in every phase of the value chain from R & D to services. This would create a dramatic change in Boeing's traditional strategy. Boeing's coalition strategy in the production of the 767 with Japan had been an X-type coalition as described by Porter and Fuller in chapter 10 of this book. Simply put, Boeing purchased low cost and efficient manufacturing capabilities in the form of specific components. Recall that such low cost was partially achieved through the Japanese government's subsidies to the industry. Boeing maintained tight control over manufacturing activities and Japanese suppliers agreed to work within the framework. In the subsequent 7J7 coalition, however, the relationship broadened to include joint performance of all the activities in the value chain, increasingly taking on the characteristics of what Porter and Fuller call the Y-type coalition.

An examination of the commercial airframe industry demonstrates a number of important points. First, it highlights the importance of a global strategy in such an industry. All the winners pursued global strategies and all the losers failed to do so. Boeing was the first to develop such a strategy and successfully implement it. Ultimately Lockheed exited from the commercial market, and McDonnell Douglas has become a marginal player. The success of Airbus Industrie is to a large extent attributable to the founders' fundamental, initial commitment to a global strategy.

Secondly, the study provides us with a fascinating glimpse into the benefits and problems of coalition. For Airbus, coalition was the only feasible answer for challenging the global pre-eminence of Boeing. Boeing had discovered the benefits of coalition—the pooling of financial and technical resources, sharing of risks, and a preferred access to the market of the participating countries. Yet coalition presents a set of distinct management challenges. The management of Airbus Industrie has found it necessary to devote considerable energy, attention, and time to reconciling the different interests of its national partners. Boeing, because of its market dominance, has so far been able to structure its coalition in such a way to maintain its control over the partners; but, as we have seen, conflicts in the long-term goals of the partners is ever present. Moreover, partnerships do not always guarantee access to the relevant national markets. Another key strategic challenge facing the major players that we have noted is the importance of pre-empting attractive potential partners.

Finally, the commercial airframe industry illustrates the importance of political influence in competition in global industries. The national government in most countries has a tremendous influence on purchasing decisions. In addition, governments have become the key participants in the industry, either directly or indirectly. Airbus Industrie draws its capital from three powerful European governments. MITI has provided a major impetus to Japanese participation in the industry. In the United States too, the government has played and continues to play a central role, albeit different from that of the European and Japanese governments. The presence of a huge military market helped propel Boeing to its dominant position in the first place and has helped to sustain it.

There is hardly another industry where the economic and political stakes are so high, not only for the key players, but also for the governments. The commercial airframe industry has evolved into two hegemonies, each with its own set of partners and the strong backing of its respective governments. The battle for global dominance has just begun.

NOTES

1. "The Next Commercial Jet . . . If," *Business Week*, April 12, 1976, 62–68.
2. John Newhouse, *The Sporty Game* (New York: Alfred A. Knopf, 1982), 195.
3. The section on the British role draws heavily from Newhouse, *The Sporty Game*, 185–213.
4. *The Economist*, May 28, 1983, 10.
5. *Aviation Week and Space Technology*, November 14, 1983, 87.
6. *The Economist*, May 28, 1983, 7.

17

Changing Global Industry Leadership: The Case of Shipbuilding

Dong Sung Cho
and
Michael E. Porter

INTRODUCTION

Until the first half of the nineteenth century, at a time when 90 percent of the world's merchant vessels were still made of wood, the United States was an undisputed leader in the shipbuilding industry with its abundant supply of cheap timber. With the advent of the steam-powered steel ship, however, the supremacy of the U.S. shipwright was quickly eroded by the British shipbuilders, who by 1882 captured 80 percent of the world's shipbuilding market. In the post–World War II period, the British shipbuilders succumbed to the other Western European shipbuilders who by then commanded the most sophisticated technologies.[1] Before long, however, these Western European shipbuilders lost their market share leadership to the Japanese. By 1965, Japan firmly established its leadership and held on to it with about 50 percent of the world market. Today a potent challenge to the indomitable Japanese shipbuilders is coming from Korea, and its prospect for overtaking the Japanese seems to be within reach. Toward the end of the twentieth century, however, China may well emerge as the industry leader.

Surveying the history of shipbuilding one can immediately raise a number of questions: Why has one country emerged as the clear leader in the shipbuilding industry at each point in time, unlike multidomestic industries in which a number of firms can enjoy leadership positions in different regional markets? What caused the shift of leadership in shipbuilding over time? What happened to the firms who lost their previous leadership position? How can firms position themselves to survive and prosper as nonleaders? These questions are not only relevant to the shipbuilding industry, but apply also to aircraft, color televisions, automobiles, and many other industries that are global in nature.

This chapter attempts to answer these questions. It focuses on the country factors and firm characteristics that determine leadership in a global industry, as well as the strategic alternatives faced by firms competing in such an environment. In order to provide evidence of the actual workings of global competition, we chose the shipbuilding industry as an example of a global industry in which a firm's competitive position in one country is strongly impacted by its position in other countries (see chapter 1). The major shipbuilding companies in the world compete with one another in many countries. In significant shipbuilding projects, prospective buyers invite from twenty to thirty shipbuilders from all over the world to submit tenders. For example, the United Arab Shipping Company invited bids from twenty-three major shipbuilders when it was ordering nine container vessels in 1981. This same group of world-class shipbuilders compete with one another repeatedly for most of the major contracts.

The global configuration/coordination of a shipbuilding firm's activities is best characterized by an upper right-hand position (concentrated configuration and high coordination) in Porter's matrix shown in Figure 1.4 of chapter 1. Major shipbuilders operate yards in only one country because of economies of scale in infrastructure, fabrication facilities, procurement, and inbound logistics. Product needs are quite standardized for a given vessel type worldwide, and transport costs for completed vessels are low. Sales forces of shipbuilders are centralized at headquarters. Such a concentration of marketing is effective because major ship buyers are few, the size of orders is typically large, and sales opportunities are infrequent. Coordinated marketing activities in various regions are critical because major competitors are well informed and react quickly to competitive moves anywhere in the world. For example, when Japanese shipbuilders monopolized the historic order of 125 handy-size bulk carriers from Sanko Steamship Company in 1983, Korean shipbuilders replicated it by bidding aggressively for orders for the same kind of ship in Iran.

The shipbuilding industry is thus an extreme case of a global industry in which most activities are geographically concentrated and regional marketing activities are highly coordinated from a global perspective. Moreover, the industry has always been global, at least since the nineteenth century when steam-powered iron and steel ships were introduced. History illustrates the failure of shipbuilders who perceived the industry as regional in character and based their sources of competitive advantage on protected raw material supplies or access to local markets. As described at the outset of this chapter, industry leadership has shifted repeatedly.

Despite the global character of shipbuilding competition, there

Figure 17.1 Competitive Forces in the Shipbuilding Industry

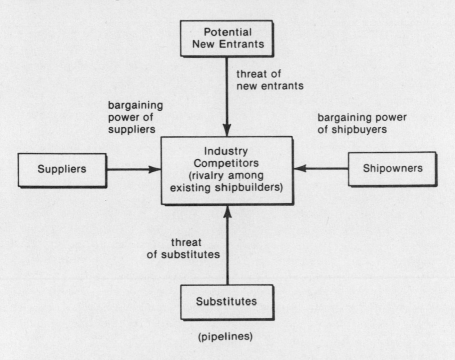

(pipelines)

exist numerous impediments to global coordination that must be overcome by successful players. The most important relate to nationalistic
purchasing and government intrusion into the market.[2] Currently,
about 40 percent of global demand is consummated by domestic shipbuilders, indicating a preference of ship buyers for local sources. Government often reinforces the tendency to purchase locally while at the
same time providing many forms of assistance to local firms. As a result, inefficient firms tend to hang on in the industry, albeit grimly
and unprofitably.

THE STRUCTURE OF THE SHIPBUILDING INDUSTRY

The preceding section showed that the shipbuilding industry has been
and continues to be global in competitive character. As a prelude to
describing the changing leadership in the industry, we outline here its
industry structure. The state of competition in the shipbuilding industry is a function of five basic competitive forces as shown in Figure
17.1.[3] In shipbuilding, rivalry and buyers (shipowners) affect the competitive position of participants most strongly. Government affects a
number of the forces in one way or another.

Industry Competitors

Competitors in shipbuilding can be categorized by country or by firm. In shipbuilding, the competitive advantage of a participant in the industry tends to be more location-specific than firm-specific. Shipbuilding is highly labor-intensive, depending mostly on semiskilled workers. The domestic availability of steel and ship component industries influences the competitiveness of the shipbuilding firms in that country. A shipbuilding contract invariably involves a substantial amount of financing to a ship buyer. A well-established local financial market (often influenced by government) is a key to the competitive position of a shipbuilding firm. Given the importance of country factors, we will use the shipbuilding country as a unit of analysis frequently throughout this chapter.

Currently, shipbuilding firms are present in about thirty countries. From a global perspective, however, the relevant players fall into three major groups: Japan, Western European countries (including the United Kingdom), and developing countries (including Korea). There are other free world countries (including the United States) as well as communist countries who participate, but they do not affect the world shipbuilding market significantly. The market shares of the three major groups have changed substantially during the past decades. Figure 17.2 shows that in 1984 the Japanese held 57.6 percent of the market; Western Europeans 13.2 percent; and the developing countries 26.5 percent. These groups have different sources of competitive advantage in terms of cost structure, financing capability, level of shipbuilding technology, quality standards, and delivery time.

Rivalry among shipbuilding firms is intense, mostly in the form of price competition. The following structural factors have led to vigorous price competition over time.

1. *High fixed costs and excess capacity.* High fixed cost of facilities leads to rapid escalation of price cutting whenever excess capacity is present.
2. *Diverse competitors*. Diverse strategies, countries of origin, and management styles among different shipbuilders increase the volatility of rivalry. For example, state-run shipbuilders of certain communist countries are satisfied with a rate of return that is not acceptable to the leading shipbuilders of the free world.
3. *High exit barriers*. Shipbuilding facilities are highly specialized and costly to liquidate or convert to other uses. Furthermore, in most countries the industry is strongly influenced by government policy for reasons of employment, economic development, and national defense. These barriers lead unsuccessful shipbuilders to continue op-

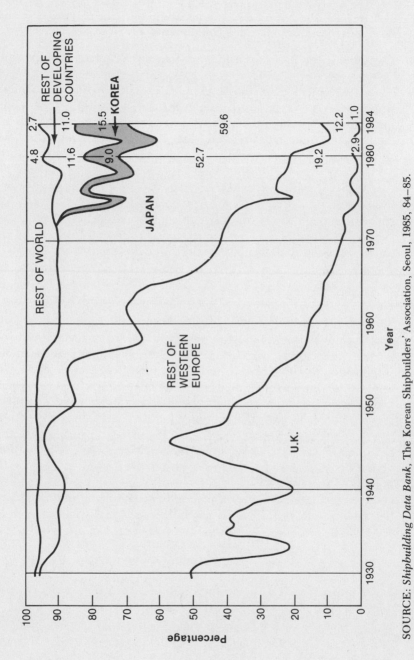

SOURCE: *Shipbuilding Data Bank*, The Korean Shipbuilders' Association, Seoul, 1985, 84–85.

Figure 17.2 Share of New Orders by Major Shipbuilding Countries

erating, often with government subsidies, and to persistently wage price wars at the expense of industry profitability.

Potential Entrants

Throughout the past century, potential new entrants to shipbuilding have always been in the wings. Japan and then Korea rose to prominence. A number of developing countries, such as Brazil and Taiwan, also entered on a significant scale in the 1970s but did not succeed. In spite of relatively high entry barriers to the industry, such as extensive capital requirements and a need to accumulate substantial experience, governments have repeatedly helped finance entry. China, with its abundant pool of inexpensive labor, is expected by many to emerge as the latest successful entrant. China has already begun to develop its shipbuilding industry as a foreign currency earner. CSSC, China's government-controlled shipping and shipbuilding corporation, was formed in May 1982 as a vehicle for coordinating twenty-five shipyards with eighty-eight new building docks and twenty-four repair docks.

Ship Buyers

The prospects of the shipbuilding industry are heavily influenced by those of the shipping industry, and the business cycles of the two industries are closely correlated.[4] The buyers' bargaining position in shipbuilding is generally strong for a number of reasons. First, there tend to be a number of potential suppliers of ships of a given quality and technology, though industry participants differ widely in technological ability. Second, the shipping industry is itself highly competitive, making buyers very sensitive to the price of ships. Third, major ship buyers purchase new ships in large volumes relative to shipbuilders' sales volumes. This creates leverage over builders because their high fixed costs raise the incentive to utilize capacity. Buyers are also knowledgeable and expend substantial resources in ship purchasing because the cost of ships is by far their largest investment.

Ship buyers consider various factors when selecting a builder. For any type of ship, the four major considerations are price, delivery, quality, and government policy. The relative weight placed on each factor varies by type of vessel. As a general rule, price is more important when buying less-sophisticated vessels, such as oil tankers, bulk carriers, and general cargo ships. Quality is more important when buying high-technology vessels, such as container ships, liquified natural gas (LNG) tankers, and passenger ships. Delivery date is moderately important for most vessel categories, but very important for those vessels used by merchant shipping companies that want to reduce the risks associated with fluctuating freight rates. Government policy exerts a considerable influence over the building of some vessel

Table 17.1 Buyers' Major Buyer Purchase Criteria by Ship Type

Vessel Category[a]	Vessel Sophistication	Purchase Criteria			
		Price	Delivery	Quality	Government
Oil Tankers	low	8	2	0	0
Bulk Carriers	↑	7	3	0	0
General Cargo Ships		6	3	1	0
Container Ships		4	3	3	0
LNG Carriers		2	2	6	0
Passenger Ships	↓	1	2	7	0
Oil Rigs		1	3	3	3
Navy Ships	high	0	1	4	5

[a]In each vessel category, the total of 10 points is assigned to the four purchase criteria according to their relative importance. The assigned numbers reflect the opinions of four shipbuilding experts: one British, two Japanese, and one Korean.

types, such as oil rigs and navy ships. Numerically ranking the relative importance of these factors is hard to accomplish precisely, but Table 17.1 summarizes the opinions of industry experts.[5]

Suppliers

There are two categories of suppliers to the shipbuilding industry: labor; and manufacturers of steel, engines, other machinery, and components. The shipbuilding industry requires numerous skilled and unskilled workers at every stage of construction. Labor costs account for a large portion of the total production cost. Where shipbuilders encounter a tightly unionized labor force, as in most Western European countries, the industry's potential profits can be bargained away in the form of high labor costs or restrictive labor practices. In the United Kingdom, for example, unions' restrictive rules often require four tradesmen for a job done by a single worker in shipyards of other countries. In Japan and Korea, workers have tended to cooperate with the management, especially in difficult times. They may even volunteer to cut their wages in order to keep the companies alive and their co-workers on the payroll.

Japanese industry has a larger market share in ship engines and other machinery than Japanese shipbuilders have in their industry. For example, the Japanese ship machinery industry represented 57 percent of the world total production in 1981, while the Japanese shipbuilding industry had 49 percent in the same year. Japanese suppliers play an important role in determining the competitiveness of shipbuilders elsewhere in the world. Because of long-established relations, Japanese suppliers are believed by many observers to supply products to their own nation's shipbuilders at lower prices than those offered to foreign shipbuilders. European materials, engines, and other components tend to be more expensive than Japanese products.

Most shipbuilding components are manufactured by many vendors. The ship's engine, which accounts for about 15 percent of the total production cost of a ship, is a major exception; its supply is dominated by a few licensor/manufacturers, such as Sulzer Brothers of Switzerland, Burmeister & Wein of Denmark, MAN of West Germany, and Mitsubishi Heavy Industries of Japan.[6] However, the recently depressed market, together with ship buyers' increased willingness to forego brand names in order to get lower prices, has improved shipbuilders' positions against engine manufacturers.

Government

Government plays an important role in shipbuilding, influencing each of the five forces. For shipbuilding companies, home governments play the role of a partner. A number of host governments have also raised import barriers against foreign shipbuilding companies. It was not until the 1950s that home governments became export promoters of their shipbuilders. In the period immediately after World War II, the shipbuilding industry was perceived by many nations as a strategically important basis for enhancing both their military and commercial strength. Japan and most Western European countries provided local shipping and shipbuilding companies with subsidies and other incentives to build up domestic fleets.

For example, the Japanese government introduced a program called Keikaku Zosen (Planned Shipbuilding) in 1947.[7] It was a system to encourage construction of ships in which the government determined the tonnage of each type of vessel to be built in each fiscal year in accordance with its marine transport policy, selected qualified shipowners out of those who wished to participate in the program, and accommodated them with public funds to cover up to 92 percent of the vessel price at little or no interest. This system of planned shipbuilding played a particularly important role in facilitating technical improvements as well as providing a base load of demand for Japanese shipyards until 1954, when they began regularly winning export orders for ships. The tonnage of ships constructed under the program between 1947 and 1953 amounted to approximately 70 percent of the total Japanese output.[8]

As worldwide shipbuilding capacity increased dramatically in the 1960s, competition became more intense. Governments moved to protect their domestic shipbuilders from losses and sometimes from failing. Although there was much debate in Western European countries over the extent of supportive measures that could be justified from the standpoint of sensible allocation of resources, most countries implemented supportive measures to protect their shipbuilders. West German shipbuilders, for example, receive up to 20 percent of the ship price in direct subsidy for building high value-added vessels such as containerships and LNG carriers. The German government spent 240 million Deutschemarks in subsidies in 1979 and another 240 million in 1980.

Government support to shipbuilding has been provided in various direct and indirect ways, including government ownership of shipyards (the United Kingdom, Sweden, Italy, Spain, Netherlands, and member countries of COMECON); provision of building subsidies (West Germany, the United Kingdom, the United States, Brazil); provision of operating subsidies for locally built ships (the United States); establishment of favorable tax systems permitting special depreciation (Japan, West Germany, France); and planned shipbuilding for domestic shipping companies (Japan, Korea). The home government, in essence, has sometimes been a partner to domestic shipbuilders.

Governments also increased their role as protectors of declining domestic shipbuilding companies. For example, in 1980 the government of the United Kingdom under the pressure of public opinion intervened in the contract between Sedco, an oil-drilling contractor for Royal Dutch Shell, and a Korean shipbuilding firm. Sedco was originally planning to award the Korean firm a contract to build two oil-drilling rigs at about $70 million each, but had to split the project by awarding a British shipbuilder one of the rigs at a much higher price and later delivery date. In 1982, the Japanese government, concerned about the low operating rates of its domestic shipbuilding companies, pressured Esso Production Japan, which had already awarded the contract to build an offshore gas production platform at about $100 million to the same Korean shipbuilder, to cancel the contract and award it to Nippon Steel Company.

GLOBAL CONFIGURATION/COORDINATION IN THE SHIPBUILDING INDUSTRY

We described earlier how shipbuilders have adopted a highly concentrated and coordinated configuration of activities for competing globally.[9] Shipbuilding can be considered an extreme case of global configuration/coordination, which makes it a good example. In this section, we explore the economics of shipbuilding in more detail to expose the reasons underlying this choice.

The Shipbuilding Value Chain

The value chain can be a useful concept in helping a firm identify those parts of the business to concentrate geographically and to coordinate on a global basis (see chapter 1). In the case of shipbuilding, the value chain divides into a number of important primary activities: operations (steel cutting, keel laying, launching), outbound logistics (delivery), marketing and sales (initial contact, contract signing), and after-service. Figure 17.3 shows that each of these value activities consists of labor costs, general and administrative expenses, and commissions. These activities are supported by the procurement of inputs, technology development (including ship design), and firm infrastructure in the form of corporate overhead.

The numbers in Figure 17.3 illustrate the range of cost of each value activity as a percentage of a representative vessel's market price.[10] The range is rather wide because the costs of shipbuilding vary by type of vessel, by country, and by time of construction. A VLCC,[11] for example, would cost about $240 per dwt (deadweight ton),[12] while a sophisticated 25,000 dwt chemical tanker would cost as much as $1,200 per dwt. In the Western European countries, construction of a 40,000 dwt class bulk carrier would cost $20 million; in Korea, the same type of vessel would cost only $13 million. The prices of a vessel fluctuate widely according to the market situation. The price of a VLCC in 1983 was about $60 million, down from over $75 million three years before.

As shown in Figure 17.3 the major portion (63 to 70 percent) of the total cost of a ship consists of inputs such as steel, engines, and other components. The second biggest item is cumulative labor costs (12 to 30 percent), which vary by the country of shipbuilding and the type of vessel. Then come infrastructure costs (1 to 11 percent), which include interest expense and depreciation. Marketing activities account for 2 to 3 percent, indicating the relative insignificance of these costs in the shipbuilding industry.

The shipbuilding value chain shows why three production-related factors (procurement of input materials, labor efficiency, and economies of scale in operations) are the major determinants of cost position. This is why major shipbuilding companies have invariably concentrated their production activities in a single site.

Generic Strategies of Shipbuilding Firms

Porter has illustrated five strategic alternatives present in any global industry: global cost leadership, global differentiation, global segmentation, national responsiveness, and protected markets.

The *global cost leadership* strategy aims to capture the buyers who are not sensitive to differentiation across product categories and national boundaries, based on the firm's global cost advantage. The shipbuilding industry has been dominated by large-scale firms that compete with this strategy.

The *global differentiation* strategy seeks to serve a wide range of products and countries but to differentiate in ship technology, quality, and other areas to command premium prices. In shipbuilding, a firm can differentiate on the basis of extended and low-cost financing, and punctual delivery as well as product characteristics.

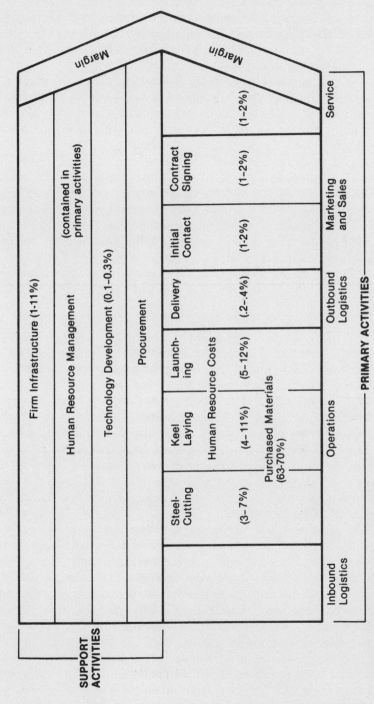

Figure 17.3 The Shipbuilding Value Chain

The *global segmentation* strategy focuses on a particular category of vessel(s) that is sold worldwide. In shipbuilding, a firm can aim at certain specific products, such as specialty vessels or passenger cruisers, that require sophisticated engineering know-how or a high standard of workmanship.

The *national responsiveness* strategy focuses on a certain regional market and capitalizes on differences in buyer needs or channels in that particular country. Ships are a mobile product, and buyer needs across countries are quite homogeneous. Therefore, this strategy is not employed in shipbuilding.

The *protected market* strategy focuses on a certain country, as does the national responsiveness strategy. In this strategy, however, a firm's unique position in the market is not based on its economic advantages but on the willingness of the local government to protect it. In the shipbuilding industry, a number of countries have employed this practice. The U.S. government, for example, has retained the Jones Act, which mandates that domestic liners be built by domestic shipbuilders. Japan's Keikaku Zosen provides another example of the protected market strategy. A substantial number of ships are bought locally.

HISTORICAL CHANGES IN GLOBAL LEADERSHIP

The first major actor in the modern shipbuilding industry was the United States. Before the 1830s, when steam-powered steel ships were introduced, wooden sailing ships were the industry norm. Industry competitiveness during this time was influenced by the availability and cost of raw materials, and the United States had abundant sources of cheap timber along the Atlantic coastline. Another factor contributing to U.S. leadership was a compelling need to develop faster, speedier, and more reliable merchant and naval fleets in order to carry goods and immigrants across the Atlantic and Pacific. The flow of traffic with Europe took off with the end of the Napoleonic era in 1815 and the end of the war between the United States and England in 1818. The Chinese market was freed from the British and Dutch monopolies around this time, and U.S. trade with China began. The Australian continent also started to attract U.S. adventurers, while the gold rush led to settlement in the West. As a result of all of these developments, the United States built a most extensive fleet of merchant vessels, which included the fastest and the largest in the world. The fastest merchant ship at the time was a California clipper called the Flying Cloud, which was built in 1851 and set a speed record by making a voyage from New York via Cape Horn to San Francisco in eighty-nine days. The clipper was the most widely used merchant vessel during this era, and was often called the Yankee clipper because it was originally developed in the United States.

A strong naval fleet was also in great demand because of the need to protect the merchant ships from pirates and to control smuggling. The U.S. navy developed the world's most advanced fleet of frigates, which played an important role in defeating the British navy during the 1812–18 war.

Mid-Nineteenth Century to World War II: British Leadership

The early nineteenth century saw two technological breakthroughs in the shipbuilding industry: the introduction of the steam engine and the use of iron and steel as shipbuilding materials. The steam engine, which had been invented by James Watt and which triggered the industrial revolution in England in the late eighteenth century, became widely used in ships by the 1830s. Its adoption was pioneered by British, French, and Americans, but most notably by Robert Fulton, an American who successfully built the first steamship called the Clermont in 1807.

The use of iron in shipbuilding started in the late eighteenth century with an introduction of a low-cost iron-making technology called the puddle-rolling method in 1784 by an Englishman named Henry Cort. Industrywide application awaited the time when an iron ship could be equipped with a steam engine. The first such ship, called the Great Britain, was built in 1843, and made a successful voyage across the Atlantic two years later. British shipbuilders quickly developed the new concept by building a series of iron steamships for merchant shippers and the navy in the 1850s. During this time, the United States was caught up in internal strife that resulted in the Civil War.

In 1862, the British also pioneered in steel shipbuilding, taking advantage of the new steel-making technology developed by Bessemer in 1858. The steel ship proved to be particularly effective as a naval vessel. In the 1860s, England began to transform its wooden and iron ships to steel ships and subsequently claimed supremacy as a naval power.

In large part, as a result of these technological breakthroughs in shipbuilding, world vessel tonnage increased dramatically from 7 million gross tons (gt) in 1850 to 45 million gt in 1914. The composition of the fleet changed dramatically: 96.5 percent of the total tonnage was sailing ships in 1850; by 1914, this had dropped to 8 percent while the steamship share increased to 92 percent. During the same era, steel ships increased from zero to 90 percent of the vessels produced.

The period between the two world wars was not a good one for the world shipping and shipbuilding industries, as the total vessel tonnage stayed more or less flat at the 60 to 68 million gt level throughout the 1920s and 1930s. This was a direct result of the Great Depression. England was able to sustain world leadership in shipbuilding technology and capacity through World War II, in part because it pioneered the use of diesel engines in the early 1900s.

World War II to Late 1950s: Western European Leadership

During the 1950s, the global economy was recovering from the devastation of World War II. Most Western European countries other than the United Kingdom made a conscious effort to expand merchant fleets. Although wage rates were already high (20 to 30 percent higher than in Japan), highly advanced ship component industries, especially in the production of engines and on-deck machinery, enabled European builders to set the total price of vessels as much as 10 percent lower than Japanese builders. As a result, Western European builders had low costs together with excellent product quality, capturing 70 to 80 percent of world market share as shown in Figure 17.2. Labor unionization was not yet a major handicap to most European countries, except for the United Kingdom.

The wage level in the United Kingdom was higher than in the rest of Western Europe, but its substantial scale economies in production, superiority in components (especially in electric components), and its credibility established over a long period of time enabled it to command 41 to 57 percent of the world market in the late 1940s. English shipbuilders competed with the "global differentiation" strategy.

Japan's shipyards, being partly under water, survived World War II without much damage, but virtually all of Japan's ships had been destroyed by the end of the war. Japan began the war with over 6 million gt of commercial vessels and ended it with less than 0.6 million gt of serviceable ships.[13] In order to rebuild the domestic merchant fleet, the government implemented the Keikaku Zosen program described earlier.

Late 1950s to the Energy Crisis: Japanese Leadership

Toward the latter half of the 1950s, Japanese shipbuilders began to penetrate the world shipbuilding market. Several factors contributed to the rise of Japan as the major shipbuilding nation during this period. First, the government-sponsored Keikaku Zosen provided minimum orders for the shipbuilders to maintain a steady level of operations, so they could compete in the international market with prices based on marginal costs.

Second, the so-called Korean war boom during 1950–51 was succeeded soon after by another boom when Egypt declared the nationalization of the Suez Canal in June 1956. The demand for new ships initially went to Western European shipyards. However, their order backlogs accumulated during the Korean war boom, and delivery times rose from three to five years. As a result, Japan became the only place where oil companies and commercial shippers could obtain oil tankers and cargo ships quickly in order to meet the much greater shipping needs caused by having to go around the southern tip of Africa instead of passing through the Canal.

Third, with a series of financial subsidies by the government, such as the practice that was then called the "temporary measures pertaining to the reduction of cost in shipbuilding" (effective August 1953 to March 1954) and the system to link ship exports with imports of crude sugar (January 1953 to November 1954), Japanese shipbuilders began innovating in construction techniques and renovating their production facilities throughout the 1950s. By the early 1960s, Japanese shipbuilders boasted the biggest and most modern shipyards in the world and successfully built the world's largest tankers: Nissho Maru in 1962, Tokyo Maru in 1965, and Idemitsu Maru in 1966.

Fourth, with the modernization of production equipment, Japanese yards started to utilize the block construction method, greatly reducing building time. The ability to deliver quickly enabled the Japanese shipbuilders to monopolize the market requiring urgent delivery. To make the situation even more favorable, the Export-Import Bank of Japan, together with city banks, cooperated with shipbuilders in financing exports. Interest rates on loans to ship buyers became quite attractive.

Based on these factors, Japanese shipbuilders became firmly established as low-cost producers and captured most of the incremental share of the market. Their market share reached 15.6 percent in 1955, behind the United Kingdom's 27.7 percent and West Germany's 17.5 percent. In 1956, Japan surged to the lead with 26.2 percent of the market, a lead it has never given up.

As described in chapter 1, the decade of the 1960s and the early 1970s was the period in which low-priced and abundant energy accelerated the industrialization of the world economy, and competition globalized. World seaborne trade grew threefold from 1.0 billion tons to 3.1 billion tons during this period, while vessel tonnage increased 2.2 times, from 129.8 million gt to 289.9 million gt. Crude oil, iron ore, coal, and grain were the four major commodities in world trade, and the demand for crude tankers and bulk carriers accounted for 70 percent of total ship volume. Based on an estimated 5 to 20 percent cost advantage over their Western European competitors, Japanese shipbuilders served much of the demand in these standardized vessel categories. Japan exceeded Western Europe's total output in 1965 with a market share of 41.4 percent. Since then, Japan's share of the world market has remained at about 50 percent. Table 17.2 shows Japan's dominance in most vessel categories, especially in price-sensitive categories such as oil tankers and bulk carriers, in 1967—the first year *Lloyd's Register of Shipping* tabulated shipbuilding statistics by vessel categories.

Western European shipbuilders slowly recognized that they could

Table 17.2 Country Market Shares of Ships Launched during 1967 by Principal
Categories (in 1,000 gross tons)

	United Kingdom		Western Europe[a]		Japan		Total	
		(%)		(%)		(%)		(%)
Oil Tankers	260	5	1,905	38	2,777	54	4,990	100
Bulk Carriers	657	10	1,958	30	3,628	55	6,564	100
General Cargo Ships	236	9	1,062	38	801	29	2,768	100
All Fishing Types	6	1	100	21	121	25	481	100
Total	1,298	8	5,444	34	7,497	48	15,780	100

[a]Excluding the United Kingdom.
SOURCE: *Lloyd's Register of Shipping*, London, 1968.

not compete with Japanese shipbuilders on a cost basis and began to
seek alternative strategies. West German, French, and Scandinavian
shipbuilders chose various kinds of "global segmentation" strategies
by developing sophisticated vessels, such as containerships and chemical carriers, using their advanced technology in vessel design and
manufacturing. Based on its expertise in the fishing industry, Norway
specialized in trawlers and other fishing ships. Italy, Sweden, and England developed hydrofoil boats, hovercraft, and luxury cruisers to
meet the needs for passenger transportation within and across the
Mediterranean, North Sea, and the Atlantic Ocean. Finland developed a strong position in icebreakers. European yards also imported
low-wage foreign laborers into their shipyards in order to cope with
rising wage rates.

The result of their "global segmentation" strategies is illustrated
in Table 17.3, which shows Western European shipbuilders' leadership in high value-added vessel categories in 1973. Their combined
market share was 51 percent in container ships and 78 percent in LNG
and chemical carriers, compared to an overall market share of 35 percent.

In the United Kingdom, however, shipbuilders were handicapped
by the diverging demands of as many as twenty different unions as
well as considerable labor unrest. It was not price or quality, but inability to promise rapid delivery and meet deadlines that turned prospective ship buyers away from English shipbuilders.[14] Table 17.3
shows that the United Kingdom was not competitive even in high
value-added vessel categories.

Energy Crisis to the Present: The Emergence of Developing
Countries

In the 1970s and early 1980s, the shipbuilding industry experienced
severe price competition, rising capital intensity, a higher proportion

Table 17.3 Market Shares of Ships Launched during 1973 by Principal Categories (in 1,000 gross tons)

	United Kingdom		Western Europe[a]		Japan		Total	
		(%)		(%)		(%)		(%)
Oil Tankers	354	2	6,397	38	9,251	55	16,683	100
Bulk Carriers	404	4	3,107	31	5,001	51	9,902	100
General Cargo Ships	193,	8	549	23	644	27	2,352	100
Container Ships	11	2	372	51	236	32	728	100
Liquefied Gas and Chemical Carriers	2	0.4	438	78	115	20	32,520	100
All Fishing Types	13	3	124	25	119	24	500	100
Total	1,018	3	11,085	35	15,673	50	32,520	100

[a]Excluding the United Kingdom.
SOURCE: *Lloyd's Register of Shipping*, London, 1974.

of demand for homogeneous vessels, and fewer marketing channels. Price competition in the early 1980s was the worst in the industry's history. As shown in Figure 17.2, 1983 prices for tankers and bulk carriers were 20 to 30 percent below those prevailing in 1980 due to severe recession in the ocean transport industry.[15] Shipbuilders scrambled for orders to fill their empty docks and to provide steady work for their labor forces. In the case of Sanko Steamship Company,[16] which in 1983 placed the largest order in history for construction of 125 handy-size bulk carriers,[17] for example, Japanese shipbuilders accepted a price of $330–340 per dwt, which was considered by industry experts to barely meet variable costs.

The need for capital investment also intensified as new product and process technologies such as robotics were introduced. Until the 1960s, shipbuilding had been one of the most conservative industries in introducing new technologies. Since the 1830s, when the substitution of iron steamships for wooden sailing vessels marked the beginning of modern shipping and shipbuilding, basic technology in the industry had remained virtually unchanged.[18] Shipbuilding was a labor-intensive industry in which productivity depended in large part on the dexterity of skilled laborers with many years of experience. The energy crises of 1973 and 1979 altered the cost structure of vessel operations, which in turn prompted builders and owners to shift their emphasis from maximizing the capacity and speed of ships to minimizing the costs of vessel operation. Fuel consumption by traditional vessels was reduced by as much as 60 percent with the introduction of more efficient engines. At the same time, robotics automated most of the welding processes. The new technology was more capital-intensive and had greater economies of scale.

A parallel trend was a shift in demand toward more homogeneous vessels. In order to lower ship prices and maintenance costs, buyers began increasingly to sacrifice their traditional desire to satisfy personal taste. Instead, they began to order series of vessels with the same design and configuration. Medium- and small-size vessels that used to be built locally were now built by large shipbuilders who employed advanced technologies and low-cost production facilities. In order to make maximum use of their existing facilities, large shipbuilders introduced the "parallel shipbuilding" technique, which enabled them to build a number of medium- and small-size vessels simultaneously in their gigantic docks.

The consolidation of marketing channels in the shipbuilding industry was expedited by the drastic shrinkage of demand. Instead of depending on shipbrokers and general trading companies that traditionally acted as intermediaries, aggressive shipbuilders began to search for prospective buyers themselves. Eliminating brokerage commissions, which could amount to a few percentage points, also became a significant way to improve squeezed margins.

As a result of these changes, market shares in the shipbuilding industry experienced yet another major shakeup in the form of the emergence of developing countries at the expense of Western European countries. As shown in Figure 17.2, Japan and Western European countries accounted for 93.3 percent of the world output of new ships in 1970, while the production of eighteen developing countries amounted to only 1.1 percent.[19] By 1982, the market share of developing countries had risen to 30.7 percent of the total orders received.

Among the developing countries, Brazil was the first major force, moving into fifth position among world shipbuilding nations with 5.4 percent of the market in 1974 and to second position with 7.0 percent in 1975. The rise of Brazilian shipbuilders was mainly attributable to cheap labor and the export promotion policy of the government, which provided generous export subsidies (up to 30 percent of the ship price). These subsidies were used effectively by Hong Kong shipowners, as they ordered new ships at Brazilian shipyards that were immediately leased back to major Brazilian shipowners (mainly Petrobras, which had a virtual monopoly of carrying crude oil to Brazil). However, the Brazilian government sought to exploit the widening trade surplus in ships too prematurely, and mandated that a high proportion of components be made in Brazil. Also, the government applied a tight monetary policy to the industry and eliminated the generous terms it had offered to foreign customers, badly eroding the Brazilian shipyards' competitiveness in the world market.

Poland succeeded Brazil by moving into third place with 5.8 percent of the market in 1975 and to second place with 7.0 percent in 1976. Like all other COMECON countries, Polish shipyards benefited from their isolated currencies and low labor costs. As a result, the Polish could quote substantially discounted vessel prices and captured a large market share in low-technology vessel categories, such as tankers. For example, it was reported in 1979 that Poland was taking orders for 800,000 dwt tankers at prices around $18 million, when Japan was offering similar vessels at around $25 to 26 million and U.K. yards at about $50 million.[20]

Korea followed Brazil and Poland by capturing 5.7 percent of the market in 1977 and reached second position with 9.0 percent in 1980. Korea's shipbuilding industry was dominated by a single firm called Hyundai. This firm started in 1973 with a single dock capable of building two VLCCs, but rapidly added two super docks, each with a capacity to build 1 million dwt tankers. Its total capacity to build 3.4 million dwt of ships simultaneously in a single site made the company the world's largest and one of the most efficient in production. Using an abundant supply of moderately efficient and inexpensive labor, Hyundai aggressively competed on price with Japanese shipbuilders. Although the company did not have advanced technologies at the time, Western European companies such as Scott Lithgow and Govan Shipbuilders of the United Kingdom provided Hyundai with sophisticated technologies as a way of gaining incremental revenues in a depressed market. The company's use of the "parallel shipbuilding" technique allowed Hyundai to be more efficient than its Japanese competitors, who were not permitted to use the same techniques by the Japanese government in an effort to limit competition among the Japanese shipbuilders by effectively reducing their capacity. By the end of the decade, Hyundai completed over 4 million tons of ships and emerged as the world's low-cost producer.

By this time, Japanese shipbuilders faced two problems: a depressed market compared to their huge capacities; and increased price competition from shipbuilders of Korea and other developing nations. They reacted to these challenges with two strategies: differentiation and diversification. They could not compete with Korean shipbuilders on a pure cost basis. Thus, with government support, shipbuilding companies as a group invested in developing technologies for the construction of ships with higher technology and designed to meet new demands, such as fuel-efficient ships and super-automated ships, which would reduce fuel and crew costs substantially.[21] In the case of Sanko Steamship's order, for example, the newly built handy-size bulk carriers were expected to consume 40 percent less fuel than existing vessels. This strategy put the Japanese shipbuilders in a "globally differentiated" position.

At the same time, large Japanese firms diversified by moving into the construction of steel structures and plants (all of the seven major shipbuilders), and the manufacturing of aircraft engines and bodies (Mitsubishi Heavy Industries, Ishikawajima-Harima Heavy Industries, and Kawasaki Heavy Industries). In the process, shipbuilding capacity was reduced by 38 percent from its peak. By 1980, all of the seven major shipbuilders had transformed themselves to varying degrees and with varying levels of success into integrated heavy machinery companies in which vessel construction accounted for only 6 to 49 percent of their total revenues.[22]

Wide fluctuations in exchange rates between the yen and other major currencies compelled Japanese shipbuilders to accept only yen-based contracts, decreasing their competitiveness vis-à-vis Korean shipbuilders who accepted U.S. dollars or any other major currency. As a result, the ten largest shipbuilding companies in Japan, whose profit had averaged 0.7 percent of their revenues in 1977, incurred an average loss of 2.1 percent in 1978. In 1979 and 1980, these companies posted 0.4 percent and 0.8 percent returns on average.[23]

Western European shipbuilders were the most seriously hurt by the rise of shipbuilding in developing nations. Their combined share fell to 20 to 25 percent during the years 1975 to 1980, from 25 to 39 percent during the previous five years. Such a decline can be attributed to the loss of price competitiveness due to older and highly paid work forces and run-down facilities compared with the modern, efficient facilities and equipment of the new entrants. As a result, Western European shipbuilders had to resort to "protected market" strategies, appealing to their home governments for direct subsidies and for protected domestic markets. To many of the governments, nationalization of the industry was the only choice. The United Kingdom established the British Shipbuilders Corporation in 1977, which was used as a vehicle for nationalizing 90 percent of British shipyards. In Spain, the government nationalized the three largest shipbuilders in 1978—Astillero Espanole, Astano, and Bazan—which accounted for 92 percent of the nation's shipbuilding capacity. Sweden, Italy, and the Netherlands also nationalized many of their shipyards.

STRATEGY OF GLOBAL COMPETITORS TODAY

A review of the history shows that a number of shipbuilding countries took turns as industry leaders. The current market shares of participants, and especially the trends in these shares, reveal the differences in competitive position of the countries in the 1980s. Figure 17.4 shows that Western European shipbuilders cannot cover even the variable costs of materials (70 percent) and labor (36 percent) if the current depressed prices of vessels continue. The negligible profit (0.9 percent) of Japanese shipbuilders implies that they are the price setters in the industry. Korean shipbuilders are the price takers. They have relatively high material costs (70 percent) and corporate overhead (11 percent), but their low overall labor cost (12 percent) is only one-third of their European and two-fifths of their Japanese counterparts. Koreans are realizing moderate profits (2.8 percent) even at the depressed level of new vessel prices.

e 17.4 Cost Structures of the Shipbuilding Industries in Western Eu-
Japan, and Korea[a]

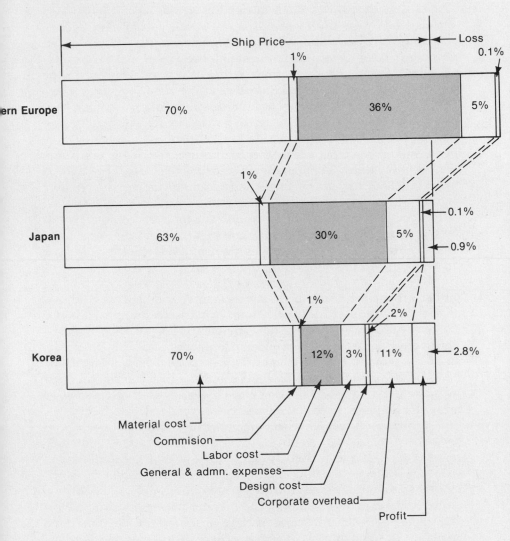

struction of handy-size bulk carriers is used as an example.
RCE: Authors' estimates based on industry interviews.

Today, shipbuilders in the major nations are pursuing very different strategies. Western European shipbuilders are pursuing global
segmentation strategies, and are noted for their superior quality and
workmanship on particular vessel types. The world's most sophisticated ships, such as icebreakers used in the Arctic or luxurious passenger cruisers, are invariably built in the shipyards of Sweden, West
Germany, Finland, or other Western European countries.

Japanese shipbuilders are competing based on overall differentiation. Japanese shipbuilders can be counted on to keep delivery dates. Their technology allows them to build even the most sophisticated vessels while their quality standard, especially in finishing, is high enough to satisfy any ship buyer. Japanese shipbuilders' critical weakness lies in labor costs and in their adherence to yen-based contracts.

Korean shipbuilders are acclaimed as the most efficient in the world. Their labor force is disciplined and works twelve hours per day. Night shifts are available if needed. Yards seldom miss delivery schedules and in many cases significantly shorten the normal building period of twenty-four to thirty months by as much as ten to fifteen months. Korean shipbuilders offer financing through Korea's Ex-Im Bank, but the loan conditions are not as favorable as OECD guidelines that Western European countries and Japan are supposed to enforce on their shipbuilders.[24] The bank allows financing of up to 70 percent of the contracted price, but at 10 percent interest (compared with OECD's 8 percent). Often, the bank is not able to finance large shipbuilding loans when the Korean government limits the extent of bank financing in order to reduce the money supply and curb inflation.

Korea has emerged as the most appropriate location for building oil tankers, bulk carriers, general cargo ships, and container ships— all of which are sensitive to price, and to a lesser extent, to delivery. Western European countries show strength in LNG carriers and passenger ships, both of which require high-quality standards. In oil rigs and navy ships, the home country is pre-eminent in building solely based on government protection. Japan positions itself in second place in every single category of commercial vessels, based on its broader array of advantages in cost, delivery, and quality.

From the evaluation of each shipbuilding country's sources of competitive advantage, we can suggest the following set of hypotheses regarding the strategies likely to be chosen by the major shipbuilding countries. Korean shipbuilders can employ a low-cost leadership strategy, based on their cost advantage. Japanese shipbuilders can utilize a "global differentiation" strategy. They do not possess an absolute advantage in any of the criteria considered in ship purchasing, but their combined position appeals to certain differentiated customer groups. In the low-sophistication vessel categories, they can focus on quality-sensitive customers to edge out Korean shipbuilders; in high-technology categories, they can focus on price-sensitive customers to beat the Western Europeans.

Successful Western European shipbuilders are employing a "global segmentation" strategy in complex vessel categories such as LNG carriers and passenger cruisers, based on their superior quality and workmanship. Shipbuilders in significant buyers' home countries can adopt a "protected market" strategy by appealing to their governments on the grounds of strategic need and employment advantages.

FUTURE GLOBAL COMPETITION
IN SHIPBUILDING

The year 1985 was another hard year for the major shipbuilders around the world. Total orders plummeted to a meager 15.4 million gt in 1984 from the previous year's 19.6 million gt.[25] By the middle of 1985, there was no sign that the market would turn around. In Korea, the near monopoly of the industry by Hyundai was broken in 1981 with the entry of Daewoo Shipbuilding and Heavy Machinery Company. Hyundai had accumulated substantial experience and had depreciated most of its investment in facilities and equipment. Daewoo chose to adopt a "global segmentation" strategy, concentrating on high-sophistication vessels, such as stainless steel chemical tankers and semisubmersible oil-drilling rigs. The technologies needed for building these sophisticated products were licensed by such companies as Friede & Goldman of the United States and B & W of Denmark. Daewoo successfully completed four chemical tankers that subsequently received "The Most Distinctive Ship" award from the prestigious *Marine Engineering/Log* in 1982. By building seven semisubmersibles, Daewoo became the most experienced company in the world in this product category.

While Korea charged ahead and Japan held on to its market share, Western European shipbuilders' market share fell to 12 percent in 1983 and 13 percent in 1984. They could not compete with Korean and Japanese shipbuilders on either price or delivery, while generous licensing of advanced technologies weakened their superiority in high-technology ships. A number of companies, such as AKER Group of Norway, decided to collaborate in major shipbuilding projects with shipbuilders in developing countries who had cost competitiveness. AG Weser[26] of West Germany and Scott Lithgow[27] of the United Kingdom closed their yards during this period, resulting in the loss of 2,000 and 4,250 jobs respectively. To avoid further embarrassment of having to close down shipyards, governments have poured in a substantial amount of direct subsidies: 840 million pounds by the United Kingdom during 1979–83;[28] 2.5 billion guilders by the Netherlands during 1977–83;[29] 4.6 billion kroner by Sweden during 1981–82;[30] 980 billion lire by Italy in 1982;[31] and 650 million francs by France in 1983.[32] West Germany was planning to spend 650 million Deutschemarks during 1984–86.[33]

Table 17.4 shows the market shares of major shipbuilding countries in 1984 by vessel category. The figures used in the table are based on vessel tonnage completed, so they differ slightly from previously quoted market shares, which are based on the amount of orders. According to this table, Japan's aggregate market share and the shares by vessel category are nearly the same, although the market share in the general cargo ship category is slightly smaller than the

Table 17.4 Shares of All Ships Completed by Principal Categories, 1984 (in 1,000 gross tons)

	Western Europe[a]	(%)	Japan	(%)	Korea	(%)	Total	(%)
Oil Tankers	634	11	2,191	39	1,198	21	5,621	100
Bulk Carriers	1,038	6	8,070	49	3,631	22	16,391	100
General Cargo Ships	1,078	22	1,582	32	612	12	4,999	100
Liquefied Gas and Chemical Carriers	233	23	463	45	215	21	1,033	100
Total	4,642	15	13,072	43	5,798	19	30,688	100

[a]Including the United Kingdom.
SOURCE: *Shipbuilding Data Bank,* The Korea Shipbuilders' Association, Seoul, 1985, 106.

others. The same is true with Korea's market shares. Price levels quoted by Japanese shipbuilders are in general higher than those by Koreans.

Western European countries show an aggregate market share of 15 percent but much higher shares in high-technology categories of general cargo ships and liquefied gas and chemical carriers with 22 percent and 23 percent respectively, and much lower shares in the low-technology categories of oil tankers and bulk carriers with 11 percent and 6 percent. At the same time, however, their small but noticeable position in the low-technology segment indicates the implementation of a "protected market" strategy in certain countries.

Some experts projected that the worldwide market in the next fifteen years would belong to Korean shipbuilders. The projection of Mr. Hong In-Kie, former president of Daewoo Shipbuilding and Heavy Machinery Company, went further into the future. According to him: "In Korea, we expect to assume a leadership role in the world's shipbuilding industry. However, we are realistic enough to know that no one lasts at the top forever. Some developing countries such as China will become competitive sooner or later and will eventually supplant Korea. In the meantime, we must work hard to realize our potential."[34]

These projections by the industry experts are based on three key assumptions. The first is that Korea, and then China, will gradually backward integrate into areas such as steel and ship components so that they can compete with other advanced nations in the area of procurement, the single most important category of cost in the industry. The Korean government has already established a steel industry through the state-run POSCO, which intends to double its current capacity of 8 million tons within a few years. The ship component industry has also been encouraged to grow under the umbrella of the major Korean shipbuilders. The Chinese government, employing another approach, has actively promoted joint ventures and technology transfer with ship component suppliers from England, Switzerland, France, Hong Kong, and Japan.

The second assumption is that Korea and China will continue to maintain cost advantages in semiskilled labor. The labor force in Korean shipyards is still young, with an average age of twenty-four, and wage levels have been kept low through the stringent policy of the government in this respect. On the other hand, the Chinese are more concerned about developing a skilled labor force than suppressing wage levels, which are at a negligible level. The Chinese government has designated six universities to graduate a total of 3,000 shipbuilding engineers every year.

The third assumption is that the shipbuilding market will continue to be depressed. This assumption does not preclude a possibility of sudden interruption of the world economy, such as the start of a major war or another round of energy crises.

SUMMARY

Through the example of the shipbuilding industry, we have examined the process of global competition over time. By identifying the sources of competitive advantage of each participant, we were able to identify appropriate strategies for firms based in different countries and test these with the strategies employed in practice.

Figure 17.5 summarizes the preceding review of the changing strategies of Western European, Japanese, and Korean shipbuilders. From our analysis we can draw the following observations.

First, a clear pattern emerges in terms of changes in national strategies over time. Both Western European countries and Japan show a succession of strategies from low-cost leadership to global segmentation or global differentiation and then to protected market. This change of strategies does not necessarily coincide with a shrinkage of market share; it did in Western Europe, but not in Japan, which held a constant market share of about 50 percent throughout the period.

Second, the locus of low-cost leadership has moved from the United States to the United Kingdom, to Western Europe, to Japan, and then to Korea. In the post–World War II era, each move from one country to another required approximately fifteen years. This pattern suggests that simple factor-based comparative advantage has been shifting over time and that strategies predicated purely on factor cost advantage are difficult to sustain.

Third, certain strategies are most appropriate to a country at a particular time. This does not imply, however, that every firm in a

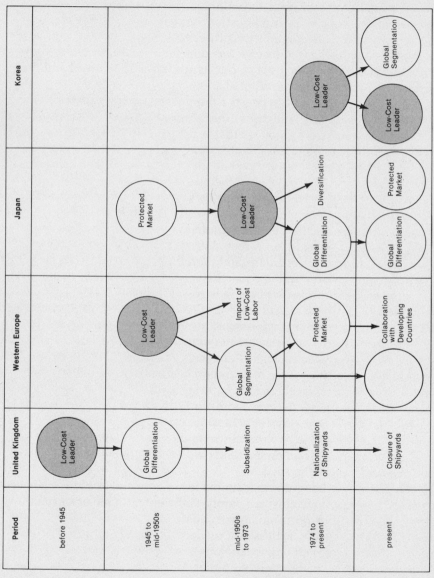

Figure 17.5 Changes in Strategy by Major Shipbuilding Nations

particular country should choose only the strategy dominant in that country at the time to be successful. For example, two Korean firms today have chosen different strategies, low-cost leadership and global segmentation, both to their advantage.

Fourth, protected market strategies tend to be chosen at the declining phase of the industry and seem to be sustainable for only a short period. This appears to be due to the limited size of local markets, none of which provide the minimum scale necessary to be efficient in the industry. The implication is clear for a national government compelled to implement protective measures to save the domestic shipbuilding industry: the domestic industry can survive with a protected market strategy, but its success is short-lived and the cost of such a strategy is substantial.

The shipbuilding case suggests a number of broad implications for competition in global industries. First, global competition must be viewed in a dynamic fashion so that a firm in a global industry can reshape and refocus its global strategy periodically in accordance with the changes in environment. No one global strategy succeeds indefinitely, and firms must reposition themselves to sustain their position as the Japanese have done. Second, cost leadership is often the preferred entry strategy for new nations, while global differentiation and global segmentation strategies are limited to existing participants with accumulated capabilities. A protected market strategy, however, is not based on competitive advantage and therefore can last only temporarily. Its high cost raises serious questions about its appropriateness.

Finally, the shipbuilding case illustrates the insufficiency of simple factor-based comparative advantage in explaining the international success of a nation. Drawing on the ideas in chapter 1, in shipbuilding we see the role of the country's local needs and the importance of first-mover effects and technological change. The United States rose to prominence in part because of a strong need for fast and efficient vessels to solve its pressing needs in transport and defense. Britain gained first-mover advantages from innovations, while the postwar growth in demand in Western Europe helped those nations' shipbuilders as did their technological strength in allied industries. Japan's innovations in construction methods were as important as its labor costs in determining its success.

Shipbuilding illustrates that simple factor advantages such as labor costs or low-cost financing are rarely sufficient to gain or sustain a strong international position. Brazil, Spain, and Poland did not succeed despite them. Firms that succeeded combined initial factor advantages with rapidly rising technology. This case also shows that creating advantages through pure subsidies or cheap financing is also not sustainable. If governments are to intervene successfully in international competition, they must do so in more subtle ways.

NOTES

1. For the purposes of this chapter, Western Europe is defined as twelve member countries of the Association of Western European Shipbuilders. They are: Belgium, Denmark, Finland, France, West Germany, Italy, the Netherlands, Norway, Portugal, Spain, Sweden, and the United Kingdom.
2. For a more detailed discussion of the impediments, see M. E. Porter, *Competitive Strategy: Techniques for Analyzing Industries and Competitors* (New York: Free Press, 1980), 281–87.
3. For a description of the competitive forces and their determinants see Porter, *Competitive Strategy*. In the shipbuilding industry, government plays an important role in affecting each of the competitive forces.
4. For a detailed description of the relation between shipping and ship-building industries, see D. S. Cho, "Shipbuilding Industry: Trends, Characteristics, and Global Competition," Graduate School of Business Administration, Harvard University, Working Paper Series 9-784-060, February 1984.
5. This matrix was produced based on the opinions expressed by managers of major British, Japanese, and Korean shipbuilding companies.
6. Sulzer Brothers Limited (A), Case 0-384-127. Boston: Harvard Business School, 1984, 1.
7. See E. F. Vogel, "Shipbuilding: High Priority Basic Industry," Working Paper, Harvard University, Spring 1984, 20–21.
8. *Shipping and Trade News*, October 25, 1974, 29–32, 66–71.
9. Coordination is not always beneficial to a firm in a global industry, because it involves cost in the form of conflicts among the personnel involved and substantial management time and effort. For a firm to justify the coordination of international activities, the benefits accrued from coordination must outweigh its cost. For a more detailed discussion of the organizational issues see chapter 12.
10. The costs of handy-size bulk carriers built in Japan and Korea in 1983 were taken as representative of all ships. Drewry Shipping Consultants, Ltd., also used this vessel category as one of the two vessel categories in its price analysis of the shipbuilding industry, in addition to oil tankers. See "The Outlook for World Shipping," Economic Study, Number 114, July 1983, 13. Handy-size bulk carriers are relatively simple ships and thus may overstate the advantages of lower-technology builders on an average ship.
11. Very large crude carrier. It indicates a crude carrier in size between 200,000 and 300,000 dwt.
12. Dwt expresses the weight of all cargoes a ship can load, including fuel, crewmen, and their baggage. Therefore, the actual shipping tonnage of commercial cargoes is less than dwt.
13. See Vogel, "Shipbuilding," 3–5.
14. Ibid., 43.
15. Cho, "Shipbuilding Industry," 4–10.
16. For a detailed description of this case, see D. S. Cho, "Sanko Steamship Company," Case 0-684-260. Boston: Harvard Business School, 1984.
17. A term traditionally used to describe a bulk carrier of roughly 20,000 to 40,000 dwt.
18. The only noticeable advancement in shipbuilding technologies in the past century is the increase in vessel size to an infinite degree, as epitomized by the appearance of ultra large crude carriers (ULCCs). These

vessels, however, did not prove to be economically feasible. Conventionally, it refers to a crude carrier in excess of 300,000 dwt capacity.

19. A. J. Cornford and R. B. Glasgow, "The Process of Structural Change in the World Economy: Some Aspects of the Rise of the Shipbuilding Industry in Developing Countries," in *Trade and Development, an UNCTAD Review*, no. 3 (Winter 1981): 103.

20. "Prospects for the World Shipbuilding Industry," HPD Shipping Publications, Survey No. 20, August 1979, 89.

21. *Zosen*, January 1983, 14.

22. See D. Anderson, "Managing Retreat," in Thomas McCraw, ed., *America Versus Japan* (Boston: Harvard Business School Press, 1986), for an interesting description of the capacity reduction process in the shipbuilding industry.

23. *Yearbook of Shipbuilding Statistics*, The Ministry of Transportation, Tokyo, 1983, 118–19.

24. According to the OECD guideline, member countries can provide ship buyers finance of up to 70 percent of the ship price at 8 percent annual interest and eight-year maturity. This guideline, however, does not have a binding force.

25. *Shipbuilding Data Bank*, Seoul, The Korea Shipbuilders' Association, 1985, 84–5.

26. *Seatrade*, November 1983, 65.

27. *The Wall Street Journal* (Europe), January 1, 1984, 5.

28. Ibid.

29. *Nachrichten für Aushandel*, July 4, 1983, 3.

30. *Journal Pour le Transport International*, April 29, 1983, 1944.

31. *Economic News from Italy*, May 30, 1983, 5.

32. *Financial Times* (London), October 26, 1983, 26.

33. *Seatrade*, November 1983, 65.

34. D. S. Cho, "Daewoo Group," Case 9-385-014. Boston: Harvard Business School, 1984, 24.

Contributors

MICHAEL E. PORTER is professor at the Harvard Business School and a leading authority in the field of competitive strategy. He received a BSE from Princeton University and an M.B.A. and Ph.D. in Business Economics from Harvard. Professor Porter is the author of eight books and numerous articles. His book *Competitive Strategy: Techniques for Analyzing Industries and Competitors*, published in 1980, is in its twenty-second printing. A companion book, *Competitive Advantage: Creating and Sustaining Superior Performance*, received the George F. Terry Award of the Academy of Management as the most outstanding contribution to the advancement of management knowledge in 1985. Professor Porter serves as a director or strategic consultant to many U.S. and international companies as well as counselor to government. Appointed by President Ronald Reagan to the President's Commission on Industrial Competitiveness in 1983, he chaired the strategy committee charged with formulating a strategic blueprint for America.

CARLISS Y. BALDWIN is associate professor of finance at the Harvard Business School. Her research has focused on the impact of illiquidity and irreversibility on real capital decisions. Recent work considers the forms of financial incentives and contractual guarantees necessary to induce firms to commit resources to long-lived investments. Her publications include: "Productivity and Labor Unions: An Application of the Theory of Self Enforcing Contracts," *Journal of Business*, 1983, and "Inflation, Uncertainty and Investment," *Journal of Finance*, 1986.

CHRISTOPHER A. BARTLETT is associate professor of business administration at the Harvard Business School. His major interest is the organization of multinational firms. Currently, he is engaged on a major project examining the strategic implications of organizational differences among American, European, and Japanese multinational corporations. Professor Bartlett has written extensively on international management issues. Among his recent articles on multinational organizations are: "How Multinational Organizations

Evolve," *Journal of Business Strategy*, Summer 1982, "MNC's: Get Off the Reorganization Merry-Go-Round," *Harvard Business Review*, March–April 1983. Professor Bartlett also consults on strategic and organizational issues with a variety of large multinational corporations.

RICHARD E. CAVES is professor of economics at Harvard University and a leading authority in the field of industrial organization with special reference to its international aspects. He has also done research in the past on international capital movements and on air transportation and its regulation. He has done comparative work on the industrial organization of Great Britain, Japan, Canada, Australia, as well as the United States. He has written dozens of articles and numerous books including, *Multinational Enterprise and Economic Analysis*, 1982, and *Competition in the Open Economy: A Model Applied to Canada*, (with M. E. Porter and A. M. Spence), 1980.

ALFRED D. CHANDLER, JR., is Straus Professor of Business History at the Harvard Business School and a leading authority on the evolution of the modern corporation. He has written extensively and his major works include *Strategy and Structure—Chapters in the History of the Industrial Enterprise*, 1962 and *The Visible Hand: The Managerial Revolution in American Business*, 1979. The latter book was awarded the Pulitzer and Bancroft prizes and the Newcomen Award. In addition to his articles and books on business and economic history, he was assistant editor for four volumes of the *Letters of Theodore Roosevelt* (1950–1952) and editor of five volumes of the *Papers of Dwight D. Eisenhower* (1970).

DONG SUNG CHO is associate professor of international business and business policy at Seoul National University. He received a B.B.A. in 1971 from Seoul National University and a D.B.A. in 1976 from Harvard Business School, and spent two years at Gulf Oil Corporation as a senior planner before joining the faculty of Seoul National University in 1978. He has written eight books and more than thirty articles, which include *International Resources Management*, 1981, (chosen as the best book of the year in economics/business) and *General Trading Company: Concept and Strategy*, 1983. He has researched and lectured extensively overseas, serving as a senior research fellow at the Institute of Developing Economy of Tokyo in 1983, visiting associate professor of general management at the Harvard Business School in 1983–1984, and as a visiting professor at INSEAD in France in 1985.

MARQUISE R. CVAR is the CEO of her own New York-based management consulting, financial valuation, and investment firm; the Cvar-Von Habsburg Group, a joint venture with Shearson Lehman Brothers/American Express. Ms. Cvar has a D.B.A. from the Harvard Business School. Her thesis, *Competitive Strategies in Global Industries*, was based on research on a group of Fortune 500 and foreign multinational firms. She has consulted with the top management of firms in France, Switzerland, England, Brazil, and Mexico, and is the author of a number of articles on international strategy. Before her doctoral work, Ms. Cvar worked in Brand Management at Procter & Gamble.

YVES L. DOZ is associate professor of business policy at INSEAD, The European Institute of Business Administration. Professor Doz conducts research on the strategies, structures, management processes, and administrative systems in multinational corporations, and has a particular interest in government impact on multinationals. He has authored a number of articles, including "Strategic Management in Multinational Companies," *Sloan Man-*

agement Review, 1980, and is the author of *Government Control and Multinational Strategic Management*, 1979, and of *Strategic Management in Multinational Companies*, 1986. His research on the management of multinationals in the telecommunication equipment and electrical power system industries won the A. T. Kearney Academy of Management Award in 1977. He is currently leading a research program on the management of technology and innovation in large complex multinational firms.

DENNIS J. ENCARNATION is an assistant professor at the Harvard Business School, where he specializes in the management of international business. He currently teaches an M.B.A. elective on this topic. Before joining the Harvard faculty in 1982, Professor Encarnation undertook postdoctoral research at Stanford University, worked in the U.S. Office of Management and Budget, and completed the joint Ph.D. program in political science and public policy at Duke University. Aided by ongoing work for the World Bank and the Harvard Institute for International Development, Professor Encarnation has written several articles that examine the process and outcome of bargaining among multinationals, agencies of the state, and local enterprises in developing countries. The most recent of these articles—"Evaluating Foreign Investment" coauthored with Professor Louis T. Wells, Jr.,—will appear in a 1986 volume edited by the Overseas Development Council. As the culmination of this work, Professor Encarnation is writing a book, *Bargaining in the Uneasy Triangle*, that analyzes the evolution of business-government relations in India over the last forty years, and compares this to trends in other countries. Bargaining relations also figure prominently in his new research on American-Japanese cross-investment, the subject of an article that will appear in a 1986 volume edited by Professor Thomas K. McCraw and entitled *America Versus Japan*.

M. THERESE FLAHERTY is associate professor at the Harvard Business School in the production and operations management area. Her research is concerned with the management of technology and multiple operating sites. She has published several papers on competition in technologically intensive industries such as, "Marketshare, Technology Leadership and Competition in International Semiconductor Markets," *Research on Technological Innovation Management and Policy*, 1983, "Global Resource Deployment in High Technology Competition," (working paper with Ruth S. Raubitschek), October 1985. Professor Flaherty has worked as a management consultant and served on several U.S. government-sponsored advisory committees studying high-technology industries and international trade.

MARK B. FULLER is managing director of Monitor Company, a firm specializing in counseling corporations on competitive strategy. Mr. Fuller graduated from Harvard College and holds an M.B.A. from Harvard Business School and a J.D. from Harvard Law School. He was formerly assistant professor at the Harvard Business School, where he taught Business Policy and Industry and Competitive Analysis. His research has been concerned with competitive strategy in the world automotive industry, corporate strategy, and the processes by which strategy is developed in large corporations.

PANKAJ GHEMAWAT is assistant professor at the Harvard Business School, where he is head of the second-year Industry and Competitive Analysis course. His research focuses on the use of strategic investments to build and sustain competitive advantage. Recent publications include "Building Strategy on the Experience Curve," *Harvard Business Review*, March–April 1985,

"Exit," (with Barry Nalebuff), *Rand Journal of Economics*, 1985, and "Learning Curve Spillovers and Market Performance," (with A. Michael Spence), *Quarterly Journal of Economics, 1985.* Professor Ghemawat also consults with several large corporations on strategy formulation.

DONALD R. LESSARD is professor of management at the Sloan School of Management, Massachusetts Institute of Technology. A specialist in international aspects of corporate finance, competitive strategy, and finance for developing countries, his recent research includes the development of methods for measuring and managing the exposure of firms' operating profits to shifts in exchange rates and for restructuring the interface between finance and operations in an international setting. He has written over two dozen articles on international aspects of financial management and is a frequent speaker on the subject. Recent publications include *International Financial Management: Theory and Application,* 1985, *Financial Intermediation Beyond the Debt Crisis,* (with J. Williamson), 1985, "Volatile Exchange Rates Can Put Operations at Risk," (with J. Lightstone), *Harvard Business Review,* July–August 1986.

AMIR MAHINI is Director of International Business Research for McKinsey & Company based in New York. He works extensively with multinational companies on corporate strategy, business unit strategy, and organizational problems, with a particular emphasis on those involving global markets and international competitors. Recent work has focused on the competitive structure of worldwide industries, the impact of industrial policy on comparative advantage, and strategic partnerships between foreign competitors. He is a frequent speaker and writer on these subjects.

SANJEEV K. MEHRA is presently completing the M.B.A. program at the Harvard Business School and is a graduate of Harvard College. His interests include the role of direct foreign investment in global markets and international corporate strategies; he is currently conducting research on entry strategies of international computer manufacturers in India. He previously worked as an analyst at McKinsey & Company, where he specialized in advising electronics and related industries on business unit strategies.

RICHARD A. RAWLINSON is a senior consultant in the London office of Monitor Company. He was previously Associates Fellow at the Harvard Business School, where he worked on research and course material with Professor Michael E. Porter. Mr. Rawlinson is a graduate of Oxford University and holds an M.B.A. with High Distinction from the Harvard Business School.

A. MICHAEL SPENCE has been dean of the Faculty of Arts and Sciences at Harvard since 1984. As dean, he oversees the finances, organization, and educational policies of Harvard and Radcliffe Colleges, the Graduate School of Arts and Sciences, and the Office of Continuing Education. Spence earned his undergraduate degree in philosophy *summa cum laude* at Princeton and was selected for a Rhodes Scholarship. He was awarded a B.A.-M.A. from Oxford and earned his Ph.D. in economics at Harvard. Prior to becoming dean, he was a professor of economics, chairman of the economics department and George Gund Professor of Economics and Business Administration. Dean Spence has written numerous books and papers, including *Competition in the Open Economy,* (with R. E. Caves and M. E. Porter), and "Competition, Entry, and Antitrust Policy," (in S. Salop, ed.), *Strategy, Predation, and*

Antitrust Analysis, 1981. Spence was awarded the John Kenneth Galbraith Prize for excellence in teaching and the John Bates Clark medal for a "significant contribution to economic thought and knowledge."

HIROTAKA TAKEUCHI is associate professor at Hitotsubashi University in Japan, having recently returned to Japan after more than seven years on the Harvard Business School faculty. His research centers on international marketing strategy and innovation within organizations. Professor Takeuchi has written numerous articles and papers, including four *Harvard Business Review* articles. He is also consultant to international companies in marketing and a frequent speaker at top management conferences of various companies and national associations. His co-authored book, *Self-Innovation Within Japanese Firms* (in Japanese), was published in May 1986.

LOUIS T. WELLS, JR., is the Herbert F. Johnson Professor of International Management at Harvard Business School. His research is on the relations between developing country governments and multinational enterprises and foreign investment by firms from developing countries. He is author or co-author of a number of books including *Manager in the International Economy*, 1986, *Managing the Multinational Enterprise*, 1972, *Negotiating Third World Mineral Agreements*, 1976, and *Third World Multinationals*, 1983. Professor Wells has been a consultant to the governments of Bolivia, Peru, Egypt, Haiti, Canada, and New Guinea as well as other government organizations and private firms.

M. Y. YOSHINO is professor of business administration at the Harvard Business School and has taught International Business and Business Policy in the M.B.A. and executive programs of the school, and in company-sponsored programs in the United States, Europe, and Japan. He is a member of the editorial boards of the *Harvard Business Review* and the *Strategic Management Journal*. He is the author of numerous articles and books, the most recent of which is *The Invisible Link: Japan's SogoShoSha and the Organization of Trade*, co-authored with Thomas Lifson, 1986.

Index

Stihl chain saws, production configuration in, 50
Stopford, John, 367
Stopford and Wells, 462
Strong dollar, impact of, 168
Subsidization, 185
Suez Canal, nationalization of, 552
Suntory, Japanese liquor manufacturer, 113

Taiwan, Foreign Investment Board, 267
"Taking companies private," 199
Tanaka riots of 1974, 378
Tandy Corporation, 113, 114
Tariff barriers, 372, 373, 433, 439
Tax havens, 197
Technology transfer
  to Japan, 241, 252
  limitations of, 241
  "Technopolis" program, 274
Teleconferencing, 132
Television set industry, United States versus Japan, 41
Teradyne's Semiconductor Test Division, 131
Texas Instruments, 131, 213
Throughput, 412, 414, 417, 438
  as measure of capacity utilization, 412
Toyota
  and coordination, 27
  and global networks, 6
  as low-cost producer, 29, 47
  process of globalization, 37
Transnational coalitions, 255–258
"Transnational organization," 377–392
Transnational strategy, definition of, 372
Treaty of Rome, 440

Uniform product line, 96
Unilever, 126
United Auto Workers (UAW), 211
United Nations Center on Transnational Corporations, 56n(2)
United States–Japan accords of November 1983, 215n(9)
Universal Segment across countries, 138

Value activities, 19, 162
Value chain, 19–22, 172, 210, 262, 370, 374, 510
Value chain theory, 22
van der Klugt, C.J., 376
Vernon, Raymond, 442
Vertical merger, 336
Volkswagen, 441
  and Pennsylvania incentive package, 211, 272
Volvo, 171

The Wall Street Journal, 346, 348, 355
Western Electric, 42
Westinghouse Corporation, 206
World capital market, 202
World Cup soccer, 124
World GNP, 15
"World" product, 133
Worldwide "teleconferences," 123
Worldwide Warranty (WWW), 132

Xerox, 28, 51, 294, 296

Zaibatsu, 374, 431, 432, 440
Zaire, 138
Zero-based organization, 375